DOS Programmer's Reference

4th Edition

Terry Dettmann

Revised for 4th Edition by
Allen L. Wyatt, Sr.

PROGRAMMING
S E R I E S

que

This book was written for DOS versions through DOS 6.0. The examples in this book should work with the following versions of MASM, Microsoft C, Turbo C and Borland C++; QuickBASIC, QBasic; and Borland (Turbo) Pascal (unless noted otherwise):

Borland C++ through version 2.0
MASM versions through 6.1
Microsoft C/C++ versions through 7.0
QBasic version 1.0
QuickBASIC versions through 4.5
Turbo C and Turbo C++ versions through 2.0
Borland (Turbo) Pascal versions through 7.0

Publisher: *David P. Ewing*

Associate Publisher: *Rick Ranucci*

Operations Manager: *Sheila Cunningham*

Publishing Plan Manager: *Thomas H. Bennett*

Marketing Manager: *Ray Robinson*

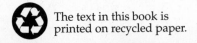

Dedication

This book is dedicated to friends who were hackers before it became a dirty word; without them, much of the information in this book would not be as freely available as it is.

Terry Dettmann

Credits

Publishing Manager
Joseph Wikert

Acquisitions Editor
Sarah Browning

Production Editor
Jodi Jensen

Editor
Rebecca Whitney

Technical Editor
Greg Guntle

Book Designer
Amy Peppler-Adams

Production Team
Jeff Baker
Claudia Bell
Danielle Bird
Julie Brown
Laurie Casey
Brook Farling
Carla Hall-Batton
Heather Kaufman
Bob LaRoche
Caroline Roop
Linda Seifert
Sandra Shay
Tina Trettin
Michelle Worthington

Indexers
Joy Dean Lee
Caroline Roop

Composed in *ITC Century Light* and *MCPdigital* by Que Corporation

About the Authors

Terry Dettmann

Terry Dettmann's love affair with computers began in the 1960s and has continued sporadically ever since. He has written numerous articles about computers, has taught computer courses, and has been a consultant, programmer, and editor. Mr. Dettmann has done doctoral work in electrical engineering and computer science. Currently he is the chief scientist for Digital Systems International, Inc., in Redmond, Washington, where he designs computer-based solutions to productivity problems in the telecommunications and banking industries.

Allen L. Wyatt, Sr.

Allen Wyatt has been working with small computers for more than a dozen years and has worked in virtually all facets of programming and computer publishing. He has written more than 15 books related to computing, programming, and programming languages. He is the president of Discovery Computing Inc., a microcomputer consulting and services corporation. Allen likes to spend his spare time doing "family stuff" with his wife, Debra, and his three children.

Trademarks

DOS
PROGRAMMING

Overview

Table of Contents

Table of Tables

Introduction

Welcome to *DOS Programmer's Reference*, 4th Edition. This book was written for two reasons. First, we want to demonstrate to people who program at the DOS level how the use of DOS, BIOS, and related functions can help their programming. Second, we want to encourage high-level language programmers to use DOS functions to extend their control of the PC system.

Most books about DOS or BIOS programming seem to focus on assembly language. A few books discuss the use of DOS functions from high-level languages, but most are spotty in their coverage and are virtually useless as references. *DOS Programmer's Reference*, 4th Edition, exemplifies a range of techniques that serve as a starting point for greater use of the DOS or BIOS functions in your programs. As you are programming, you will want to keep it next to your computer — not on a dusty bookshelf.

To make this book as useful as possible, we have tried to strike a balance between breadth and depth of coverage to give you a start into any single programming topic. Entire books could be written about many programming topics and techniques. This book does not provide exhaustive coverage of any particular technique. Rather, it shows you a starting point and gives you enough information to get you "down the path." It provides you with the building blocks you need to make your programs strong and vibrant.

DOS Programmer's Reference, 4th Edition, discusses each major area in which BIOS and DOS functions can be applied. The discussion and examples in this book should help beginners learn how to use these functions and give more advanced programmers a way to organize what they have learned. We emphasize the *why* wherever possible.

A book like this one is truly useful only if it provides programmers with pertinent reference information. The last part of this book is devoted to a detailed function-by-function listing of all DOS and BIOS functions (including many that are otherwise undocumented). For each function, the available information is summarized and details of register requirements are provided. The function listings alone should make this reference useful for any DOS programmer, whether you work in assembly language, BASIC, C, or Pascal.

This type of book is useful only if it is up-to-date too. This edition covers MS-DOS 6, including information about extended memory drivers, expanded memory drivers, and mouse drivers. The sections on hardware describe how to identify which CPU chip is in use, which coprocessor is available, and which video board your system is using.

This edition adds several features not available in the earlier editions of *DOS Programmer's Reference*. In addition to updated "how-to" code, the reference sections have been revamped to make them more complete and to help you find information faster. We are sure that you will benefit from the enhanced information available only in this edition.

In some cases, information about undocumented features might seem incomplete or sketchy. It is presented because programmers need the widest variety of information about DOS and the BIOS and because only by distribution of the known data can the full set of undocumented features be uncovered. The use of these features is risky; because they are not documented, there is no guarantee that they will operate in the same way in all DOS implementations or that they will even be present in any specific implementation.

Purpose of This Book

A principal aim of this book is to show you how to work at appropriate levels to program the DOS system. Available functions are discussed, but you do not *always* have to resort to assembly language to use them. Some programming tasks can be performed efficiently only in assembly language. (Some, in fact, can be performed only by going "right down to the bare metal"—even BIOS and DOS services sometimes get in your way.) Working at the highest possible level, however, has definite benefits. This book provides the information you need to decide which level to use in your own programming.

The examples are oriented toward high-level interfaces to the DOS and BIOS routines. Although the use of assembly language is minimized, it is not neglected. By emphasizing that you can access and use routines effectively from C/C++, BASIC, or Pascal, we hope to make these techniques more widely usable.

Who Should Use This Book?

If you are a programmer interested in working with DOS to make the most effective programs possible, *DOS Programmer's Reference* is for you. It deals with DOS at many levels, from high-level programming-language services down to the BIOS interrupts.

This book is intended for programmers who have some experience in C/C++, BASIC, or Pascal and are comfortable with assembly language. It is assumed that you are familiar with at least one programming language, curious about others, and familiar also with MS-DOS or its cousin, IBM's version of DOS.

A fundamental assumption is that you want to speed up your programs or access facilities unavailable in your language. We will go after these facilities through DOS and BIOS functions. This book deals with advanced program design and freely uses elements from high-level languages in addition to assembly language.

Although a certain technique might be illustrated in a particular programming language, the *technique* — not the *language* — is of primary interest. After you learn how to use a technique, it is equally applicable whether you use it in C/C++, Pascal, BASIC, or assembly language. It applies, in fact, in any language that provides access to DOS and BIOS interrupts.

What You Should Know to Use This Book

This book is written for C/C++, BASIC, or Pascal programmers. It includes little or no explanatory information about how to program in assembly language. If you want to learn more about this topic, see *Using Assembly Language,* 3rd Edition, also published by Que Corporation, or some of the other books listed in Appendix E.

The examples in *DOS Programmer's Reference* are drawn from assembly language, BASIC, C/C++, and Pascal, with a tendency toward C/C++. We have tried to make the examples clear, regardless of your programming background. The listings help demonstrate the actual use of the DOS and BIOS functions.

How to Use This Book

This book is divided into five parts. Readers interested in learning the fundamentals of DOS programming will want to start with Part I. Those who want specific information about various aspects of programming at the system level can find useful information in Parts II, III, and IV. More advanced programmers who simply want a quick reference should concentrate on Part V.

The four chapters in Part I, "An Overview of DOS," lay the groundwork. Part I looks first at some of the history of the system and at how DOS works, both statically and dynamically. Then it introduces you to the general principles of programming at the DOS level and to the language resources available for this type of work. Finally, it explores the "nitty-gritty" of programming at the DOS level.

In Part II, "Character Devices and Serial Devices," Chapters 5 and 6 discuss output devices (the video display and printer) and input devices (the keyboard and mouse). Chapter 7 describes serial input and output devices; the 8250 UART is discussed also.

Part III, "Disks, Directories, and Files," contains two chapters. Chapter 8 describes the partition table, boot record, and file allocation table (the FAT) and discusses disk functions. Chapter 9 covers the root directory, directory entries, subdirectories, and volume labels. Chapter 9 also explains how files are handled through DOS by discussing file control blocks (FCBs) and handle functions and when to use them.

Part IV, "Memory Management and Miscellaneous Topics," covers program and memory management (Chapter 10), interrupt handlers (Chapter 11), and device drivers (Chapter 12). Chapter 13, "Miscellaneous Functions," provides information about such topics as equipment information and extended error processing.

The chapters in Parts II, III, and IV introduce you to the subject and illustrate it with practical examples you can use as the basis for your own library of functions.

All the sample programs illustrate basic techniques only. If you learn a basic technique from one of these simple programs, you then can extend it to your own programming.

Part V is a reference section. Typography, icons, and other design elements were carefully planned to make this section easy to use. The BIOS and DOS services are presented in numerical order. Every function is listed in a standard reference format, with cautions or restrictions for the various functions included in the comments. In addition to the BIOS and standard DOS functions, Part V includes sections on the functions of the mouse (DOS Int 33h), expanded memory (DOS Int 67h), XMS, DPMI, the task switcher, and the DoubleSpace specification.

Five appendixes are filled with additional information. Appendix A contains the ASCII character set; Appendix B is a table of selected memory locations; Appendix C describes a proposed standard for TSR interfacing; Appendix D discusses the use of undocumented features of DOS, including two sample programs for exploring them; and Appendix E is a resource list of other titles.

Why Type Code?

If you have been programming for any length of time, you know that a considerable amount of time is consumed by simply entering your code and making sure that it is error free. The same can be said for the code in this book. Although you can choose to type all the programs contained in this book, doing so could easily consume several days. Correcting typing errors could take even longer. If you have the time, fine. If not, you might consider purchasing the companion disk offered in this book. Send the coupon in the back of this book, or order it directly by contacting Discovery Computing Inc. at the address and phone number provided in the following section.

Talk to Us

Many people have worked on this book to make it the best possible programmer's reference available. As with any book of this magnitude, errors can occur. Let us know of any errors or omissions you find so that the next edition can be even more complete. You can either write directly to Que Corporation or contact the author at the following:

Allen L. Wyatt
Discovery Computing Inc.
2323 State Route 585
P.O. Box 738
Sundance, WY 82729
800-628-8280
307-283-2714 (fax)
72561,2207 (CompuServe)

Part I
An Overview of DOS

1

An Introduction to DOS

You should have a clear idea about what DOS is before you read further. This chapter provides an overview of DOS, in addition to a short history of the operating system; original sources were used for details of how DOS came to be. This chapter also touches on DOS structure and interfacing. Because this examination is a cursory one, do not be concerned if some terms are unclear. Each one is explained in detail in later chapters.

What Is DOS?

DOS consists of four basic modules:

- *The boot record.* This record begins on track 0, sector 1, side 1 on every disk formatted by the DOS FORMAT command. On fixed disks, the boot record is on the first sector of the DOS partition. This record, which requires one sector of space, identifies the disk and contains the initial boot program for the disk.

- *The BIOS.* The basic input/output system (BIOS) is located in ROM. This low-level interface to the physical machine is responsible for hiding the vagaries of the hardware from all other software. It is augmented, for DOS, by the I/O system loaded from disk.

- *The DOS programs.* Two programs implement DOS. One, the I/O system, is an interface module loaded from disk that augments the ROM BIOS functions and usually contains a set of standard device drivers. The other, the disk operating system (DOS), is the high-level interface for all programs that run on the computer, whether or not they make use of the disk.

- *The command processor.* Most people think of this module as DOS. The command processor, the normal interface to DOS services for people working with the system, generates the command prompt (c>), accepts commands, and executes programs requested by users of the system.

Each module is described in detail in Chapter 2, "The Structure of a DOS System," and Chapter 3, "The Dynamics of DOS." At this point, however, some basic explanations are in order.

The BIOS provides a series of functions that programmers can use to perform operations without having to concern themselves with the details of the underlying hardware. Throughout this book, BIOS functions are used to perform necessary operations in programming examples. Part V of this book, "Reference," contains a function-by-function reference to the capabilities of the BIOS.

Even though the BIOS is powerful, it is far from comprehensive. DOS, built on the platform provided by the BIOS, provides many services essential to programming. In the early days of computers, before general-purpose operating systems (such as DOS) became available, programmers wrote programs that included the functional equivalent of DOS. The process of debugging applications, therefore, was terribly complex.

With the DOS functions already programmed by Microsoft (and other vendors), the authors of DOS become your partner in program development. Although you should not assume that *everything* in DOS works without error, you can assume that DOS is solid (unless proven otherwise). Part V contains a function-by-function breakdown of the DOS functions.

The History of DOS

Over the years, DOS has emerged as the primary operating system for microcomputers. DOS has more users today than any other operating system. It has become a sophisticated environment with tools and applications to meet a wide spectrum of needs.

DOS's foreseeable growth involves expansion to handle more of the features of sophisticated microprocessors such as the 80386 and 80486. Future releases of DOS may even handle multitasking and multiuser operations, although Microsoft certainly is not providing any information about this possibility. Some people may question this statement, in light of the emergence of Windows and Windows NT.

DOS was first marketed by Seattle Computer Products as 86-DOS for that company's line of computers. The original DOS was written by Tim Paterson, beginning in April 1980, and first shipments were made in August of that year. At that time, the Digital Research CP/M was the most widely used microcomputer operating system. 86-DOS was designed specifically to make porting applications from CP/M easy: It kept the same structure for file control blocks and functions so that a mechanical translator could convert a program directly to 86-DOS.

Because 86-DOS worked only with 8086/8088 CPU chips, which were just coming into the marketplace in 1980, few people even knew that it existed. Those who did use the 8086 CPU on their S-100 systems as an upgrade from the 8-bit 8080/Z80 standard and CP/M found 86-DOS useful, and Seattle Computer Products established a base of several dozen customers, including at least one other hardware manufacturer. Then Microsoft approached SCP about writing a customized version for an anonymous customer. Although at the time no one (except Microsoft) knew it, IBM was looking for an operating system. By January 1981, Paterson knew who the customer was, and Microsoft had taken out a license to distribute 86-DOS under its own name. In April of that year, Paterson left Seattle Computer Products and joined Microsoft, where he spent the next several months tailoring the system to IBM's needs.

In July 1981, Microsoft bought from Seattle Computer Products all rights to 86-DOS for a relatively small price (less than $100,000). Later lawsuits SCP brought against Microsoft challenged that purchase, and Microsoft eventually settled out of court for several million dollars. The result was that Microsoft owned, undisputed, all rights to the most popular operating system ever.

When IBM released the PC on August 10, 1981, Microsoft was ready with MS-DOS 1.0 (Personal Computer DOS, *not* PC DOS, for IBM machines; IBM never accepted the popular term *PC DOS* in reference to the system, and the latest IBM versions are identified simply as *DOS*.)

Paterson's direct involvement with DOS ended during 1982, but he remains active on the PC scene, most recently as a consultant to Phoenix Technologies Inc., the clone BIOS experts.

After the PC's original release, DOS still was not prominently displayed in some stores. IBM had selected CP/M-86 and Softech's p-system as alternative PC operating systems. Vendors were slow to deliver both products, however, and few languages were available for development under those operating systems. Microsoft already had earned a reputation for programming languages. IBM released its own software using DOS, and developers rapidly picked up the ball, which has never stopped rolling. CP/M-86 and the p-system never got off the ground as serious contenders in the PC marketplace.

DOS has been changed officially many times (and several versions exist that were not available for general use). Although both improvements and bug fixes have figured in this evolution, each release usually has involved a response to some hardware change—particularly, a change in disk-drive format or capability.

Table 1.1 lists every major official DOS release (to date) and the primary change involved. (Some minor releases have been omitted from this list.)

11

Table 1.1 DOS Versions

Version	Date	Hardware or Operating-System Change
86-DOS	August 1980	Seattle Computer Products' version (begun in April 1980, by Tim Paterson)
1.0	August 1981	Original PC, single-sided disk
1.1	March 1982	Double-sided disk, date-time stamping
1.25	March 1982	First OEM version (ZDOS), VERIFY added
2.0	March 1983	PC XT, including hard disk
2.1	October 1983	IBM PC*jr* and Portable PC
3.0	August 1984	Personal Computer AT, including high-capacity disk
3.1	March 1985	Networking
3.2	December 1985	Enhanced support for new media
3.3	April 1987	Support for PS/2
4.0	June 1988	Support for disk drives larger than 32M; integration of EMS memory capability
5.0	June 1991	Support for XMS, upper memory blocks, and the HMA
6.0	March 1993	Support for disk doubling, defragmentation, an improved CONFIG.SYS structure, and virus production

As you look at Table 1.1, consider the trade-off between memory and features that each new version of DOS has required. DOS V1.0 could exist in 16K of memory, and the original IBM PC was available with only 64K. Version 2 needed at least 24K of memory (more, if device drivers were installed). Any useful programming required a minimum of 128K of memory. As of V3, DOS needed 36K of memory (and could require much more for file sharing and installed device drivers). Machines with less than 512K were almost impractical. With V4, 512K became essentially a requirement and more than 640K (expanded and extended memory, see Chapter 2) was definitely desirable. Because of the memory squeeze, DOS 5.0 provided methods to load DOS into upper memory areas. It took less conventional memory than DOS 4, but it took more overall memory. Finally, DOS 6 is the largest DOS version, but it provides improved memory management so that you can make the most of the memory you have installed.

Let's look at each version of DOS to see what was involved in each change. Throughout this book, *V1*, for example, refers to a generic subversion of V1, and *V1.n* means a specific subversion *n*.

Version 1.0

DOS V1.0 was the original support for the PC system. It supported the basic single-sided, 8-sector disk format and provided all the basic disk services. Changes (from CP/M) included a much improved disk directory structure that managed file attributes and exact file size. Version 1.0 also added to the original 86-DOS improved disk allocation and management, better operating-system services, and an AUTOEXEC batch file for start-up initialization. IBM was the only vendor to ship this version. Interestingly, this version of DOS did not include the date-time stamping of files that later became known as one of the major distinguishing features of DOS.

Version 1.1

In V1.1 (the last IBM-only edition), the date-time stamp and support for double-sided disk drives were added, as were some bug fixes. It was released in March 1982.

Version 1.25

V1.25 was the first version to be distributed by original equipment manufacturers (*OEMs*) other than IBM. (The jump in version numbers from 1.1 to 1.25 reflects the difference between IBM's version count and Tim Paterson's private revision control system, in which IBM V1.1 was known as V1.24.) The VERIFY capability was added in this version, as was the 00h end-of-directory flag byte (which did not appear in IBM versions until V2.0).

V1 was far from a uniform standard; Microsoft did not distribute it directly to end users, but rather licensed it to OEMs, who were free to modify it or even to rename it (as Heath-Zenith did in March 1982, by naming it ZDOS, which was the first non-IBM use of DOS).

Version 2.0

In DOS V2.0, support was added for double- and single-sided 9-sector floppy disks, fixed disks, and cartridges that would be used on the PC*jr*. DOS services were enhanced significantly. This version also added hierarchical file systems similar to those in UNIX. The following list shows some of the significant changes incorporated into DOS V2.0:

- File handles
- I/O redirection
- Pipes
- Filters
- Print spooling

13

- Volume labels

- Expanded file attributes

- System-configuration file

- Program-environment block maintenance

- ANSI display driver

- Dynamic control of memory by programs

- Support of user-customized command processors

- International support

As with V1, V2 was licensed to OEMs, who made changes. By this time, though, most OEMs were aware that the marketplace was demanding near-total compatibility with the IBM machines; the changes, therefore, were much less wide-ranging. Some, such as Tandy with the Model 2000 (its first MS-DOS machine, which used DOS V2), went so far as to provide dual vectors in its BIOS interfaces for IBM BIOS compatibility.

Some variations between editions bearing the same version number but coming from different OEMs can still be found. This is true of all V2 editions.

Version 2.1

In V2.1, only timing changes were made to allow better handling of IBM's PC*jr* and Portable PC. The MS-DOS version, known as 2.11, is still sold in some machines; one Toshiba laptop unit has V2.11 burned into ROM.

Version 3.0

DOS V3.0 was the earliest version offered for the Personal Computer AT. This version added support for high-capacity (1.2M) floppy disks and additional hard disk formats, in addition to the foundation for support of networked disks. Some major new features included the following:

- Control of the print spooler by applications

- Extended error reporting

- Suggested error-recovery codes

- Support for file and record locking

The release of V3 marked the end of near-total freedom on the part of the OEMs to change the structure of DOS, although some variations between Microsoft and IBM editions continue today. IBM, for example, provides most of the support utilities as COM files, and Microsoft supplies them in EXE format. Other less obvious changes abound in the code.

Support for network operations, however, made it necessary to enforce stricter standards on the structure of DOS and especially on its internal data formats, and the OEM contracts were changed to reflect this requirement. Life for independent developers became simpler because the key parts of DOS became essentially stable at this time.

Version 3.1

DOS V3.1 added networked disks, including support for file sharing, in addition to some bug fixes. This version has been standard with many vendors for some time.

Version 3.2

V3.2 added support for 3 1/2-inch floppy disks. It also integrated formatting control into the peripheral device drivers. Version 3.2 was the first version to be sold to the end-user market by Microsoft under its own name.

Version 3.3

In DOS V3.3, two new user commands (NLSFUNC and FASTOPEN) and two new functions were added, many other services upgraded, and device support expanded to cover IBM's PS/2 line. Effective with this version, the maintenance and development responsibility for DOS was transferred from Microsoft to IBM, which freed Microsoft to devote its resources to OS/2. (As part of the trade, IBM relinquished its own OS/2 development responsibilities to Microsoft.) Both firms continued to release and support their own unique versions of both products, however.

Version 4.0

In DOS V4.0, many user commands were enhanced, several more functions were added, and a graphic user shell program was introduced. The most significant changes, however, were the addition of support for hard disk drives of more than 32-megabyte capacity and the inclusion of expanded-memory drivers as a standard part of DOS. (Both features had been available for some time as add-on options.)

Two months after IBM released Version 4.0, an update—identified *only* on the disk labels as V4.01—was released to correct several problems. The VER command still identifies the version as 4.00, though; the only way to distinguish the versions is by the file dates on the two hidden files and on SHARE.EXE. V4.01 bears dates of 08/03/88 or later, and V4.00's date is 06/17/88. Microsoft delayed its own release of V4, and its V4.00 is the equivalent of IBM's 4.01. Microsoft has also released V4.01, however, which has additional corrections.

Version 5.0

In DOS V5.0, support for extended memory was added, many user commands were enhanced, and new user commands were added, notably UNDELETE, UNFORMAT, MIRROR, and a mouse-aware, full-screen text editor. A task switcher API (applications program interface), which is supported in the shell program, was added. The kernel was restructured, which resulted in DOS taking up less space for the first time. In addition, DOS can now be run from ROM. SHARE is no longer necessary to safely support DOS partitions in excess of 32M.

DOS V5.0 is the first real update of DOS from Microsoft since V3.3; Microsoft's support of V4.0 was a result of reverse-engineering IBM's DOS V4.0.

Version 6.0

DOS V6.0 was released in March, 1993. The changes primarily involved additional utilities added to the operating system. For instance, utilities were added for the following:

- *Anti-virus protection.* Provides utilities to run under both DOS and Windows, protects your system against known viruses. The anti-virus utility can be updated with information on new viruses also.

- *Deleted file recovery.* A utility that will recover your deleted files. Unlike third-party products, UNDELETE provides three levels of security you can employ.

- *Disk doubling.* A utility called DBLSPACE compresses and decompresses disk files on the fly.

- *File backup.* An improved, menu-driven backup utility for backing up your hard drive to floppy disks. Will work under both DOS and Windows.

- *Improved memory management.* MEMMAKER is a utility that will modify your CONFIG.SYS and AUTOEXEC.BAT files for the optimal use of memory.

In addition, other DOS utilities have been improved and the CONFIG.SYS file structure was changed so that you can have multiple boot scenarios. You can have one configuration if you want to use your CD-ROM, for instance, and another if you want to use a tape drive. DOS can ask which scenario you want to use every time you boot.

The Future

As DOS continues to evolve, new services and options become available to programmers. The advent of windowed environments such as Microsoft Windows and DESQview has made sophisticated new services available for DOS-level programmers. Each new service hides more of the machine from your programs and allows you to do more without having to reinvent the proverbial wheel. The cost of any high-level service, however, tends to be a compromise in the maximum amount of speed and responsiveness that can be achieved. As processors get faster, however, the need for lower-level tricks diminishes. Applications programs will use the services of DOS and its cousins. Only systems-level programmers working inside DOS, Windows, or DESQview will have to worry about direct access to the machine or its services. Such is progress.

The Structure of DOS

As this book examines DOS and the PC system, you will notice a layering of functions. Figure 1.1 should help you visualize this layering.

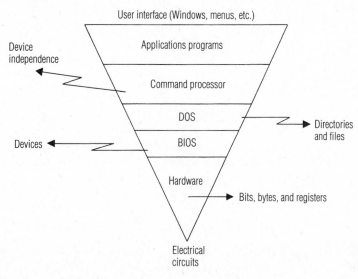

Figure 1.1 System layering.

Fundamental to the design of the entire DOS/PC system is a kind of "system within a system" approach to design. Starting with the electrical circuits at the bottom of the system, for example, notice that the circuits implement a device (called a computer) with definite capabilities and features.

The BIOS integrates this circuitry level into a new "computer system" with well-defined features and functions. The BIOS level is characterized by the presence of devices that have standard features. No matter which kind of display you use or whose keyboard you bought, the BIOS makes them all respond similarly. Taken together, all the BIOS's features make it capable of supporting a programming environment. Within this environment, DOS was developed. To standardize the interface between DOS and the various BIOS conventions used by different manufacturers, the DOS designers introduced a cushioning layer you can call the I/O system. It is often considered to be part of BIOS. Because the I/O system comes on disk, however, as part of the DOS package (and changes when necessary to meet DOS requirements), technically it should be thought of as an entity unto itself, associated more with DOS than with the BIOS.

The DOS environment defines yet another computer system—but at a much higher level. A computer language that can manage files and file systems is introduced at this level, as are the devices on which the language is based. At this level, DOS integrates the features you need in order to operate in a standardized environment. Whether you use a Toshiba or Maxtor disk drive, for example, the operating system treats them the same way. To programs working with DOS, the lower-level details are unimportant.

On the next level (the command processor) is yet another computer: an interactive one characterized by device independence. At this level, you can deal with devices and files as though they were the same. Although DOS has to keep things straight, at the command-processor level you can direct output (that was supposed to go to the screen) to a file. You do not have to worry about the implications of speed or differences between the devices.

Up one more level is a computer system defined by your applications programs. The system is even simpler when it interfaces with users rather than with programmers. Now the "computer language" consists of menu selections and windows. This layer, like all the others, is built on what precedes it.

As you read this book and work your way down through these levels (or layers), keep in mind what you gain (and lose) by skipping parts of the system hierarchy. Because DOS is built on the BIOS routines, programs that skip around DOS to the BIOS *can* affect the way DOS works. You could use the disk read and write functions, for example, to write your own file handling at the BIOS level. You probably would need to work for years, however, to make it work as well as DOS does. Conversely, you can stay at the highest level, but all the lower levels will eat away at your program speed. There are trade-offs up and down the hierarchy. The choice is yours.

The Programmer's Interface to DOS

Programmers who work in high-level languages are accustomed to working with predefined functions. In BASIC, all the functions (such as PRINT and INPUT) are defined in the language. Pascal also defines the standard functions you can access. C and C++ compilers come with a standard set of library functions. For many people, these functions represent the limits of the language.

The functions provided with BASIC, C/C++, and Pascal, in fact, are based on a much lower level of interaction with DOS and the BIOS functions. The language functions are written to handle requests for services in standard ways. In some cases, language functions are defined to be compatible with national or international standards. To be implemented, however, the functions must refer directly to DOS, the BIOS, or the hardware.

Ordinarily, you are protected from the world of functionality beneath the level of language functions. Because language functions are written for general use by many people who could not "program their way out of a paper bag," these functions must provide error checking and control for generalized cases. Generalizing slows things, but you do not have to give up on speed. DOS and BIOS services are directly available from any language, if you take the time to learn how to work with that language.

The software interrupt is the mechanism for using DOS and BIOS services. (Chapter 11, "Interrupt Handlers," discusses interrupts.) In the present context, think of a software interrupt as a high-level language's subroutine call. You have to set entry parameters and you get a result. But you can run into trouble if you do not have the language functions to smooth the way.

By going beyond the language functions, you give up not only their error-checking, control capabilities, and the reliability of standard libraries, but also a considerable amount of portability. C programs written in standard Microsoft or Turbo C functions often can be taken, with few changes, directly to a UNIX system. DOS and BIOS functions cannot, but you can build in your own error checking and control based on what you need, not what a Microsoft or Borland programmer thought would be suitable for the mass market.

By slipping down to the DOS and BIOS level, you regain a degree of control and speed your programs. The cost (some extra programming effort) is minimal. For the highest speed possible, you need to access the hardware directly. Doing so makes sense for some devices such as screen displays and serial ports, but makes little or no sense for other devices such as disks.

Ordinarily, a slow program that works correctly can be made faster by recoding critical modules at a lower level or by changing the programming algorithm. Throughout this book, the pros and cons of working at the various programming levels are presented. *You* decide what is appropriate for your application. As a general rule, however, you should always work at the highest possible level. When software works for you, errors are easier to find. The lower you go, the more subtle the errors—and the harder they are to locate.

Summary

The IBM-compatible line of computers has been built on a firm foundation of BIOS and DOS. BIOS provides the low-level interface to the outside world; DOS provides the functionality of higher-level services that augment the development of computer programs. As the most popular operating system in the world, every successive version of DOS has provided a solid footing on which to build.

How you develop your programs—which language you use, whether you use BIOS or DOS services, and so on—depends largely on your programming needs. There are trade-offs to any programming decision you make. As you think through options and formulate strategies, you will begin to find ways to make your computer system work for you (not against you). *DOS Programmer's Reference* is designed with that end in mind: to make your programming experience the best it can be by making full use of your computer environment.

Chapter 2, which covers the structure of DOS, looks more closely at the conceptual foundation on which DOS is built and how it relates to your programs. It also examines the tools, resources, and building blocks available to you as a programmer in a DOS environment.

2

The Structure of a DOS System

The structure of DOS involves the entire machine—not just the operating system but also the entire computer, from the hardware up. You must understand the structure of DOS if you want to make the best decisions about which functions to use and how to use them.

The "Virtual Machine" Concept

A useful way to think about a DOS system is to view it as a hierarchical structure in which functions are distributed among subsystems. Each level in the hierarchy provides a well-defined set of services on which the next higher level can build. Every level therefore becomes a virtual machine; it is the computer to the next higher level. Figure 2.1 illustrates this concept in relation to a DOS system.

The physical machine, or hardware, is the lowest level of the hierarchy. Many differences between systems exist at this level.

The common threads among the machines include the ones in the following list:

- A processor from the Intel 8086 family: the 8086, 8088, 80186, 80286, 80386, or 80486

- A similar mapping of physical equipment within the system (in other words, similarly assigned interrupts and addresses)

- One of a limited number of bus designs

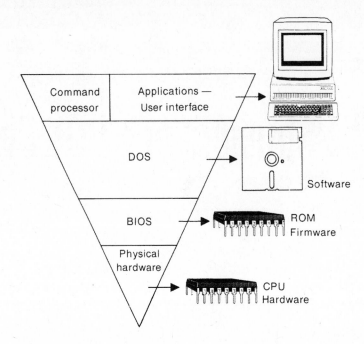

Figure 2.1 The virtual machine hierarchy.

One of the major purposes of DOS is to hide physical differences between machines so that a standard method of accessing the computer's capabilities exists at both the programming and user levels. DOS successfully provides a uniformity that has made it the operating system of choice on a variety of IBM-compatible computers.

The Physical Machine

The greatest differences between machines occur at the hardware level—the level at which you generally discover whether "compatibles" are truly compatible. Programs that operate at this level do not work on machines with major hardware differences.

The physical computer system (see Fig. 2.2) can be broken down into several major components:

- *The central processing unit* (CPU) performs the operations of the computer system.

- *ROM and RAM* hold programs and data.

- The *input channel (or channels)* feed information to the computer.

- The *output channel (or channels)* feeds information to users.

- The storage devices (floppy disks and hard disks) hold information temporarily or permanently.

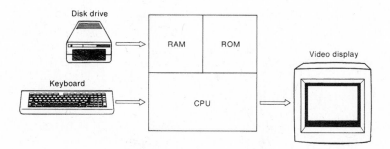

Figure 2.2 A block diagram of the basic computer.

An understanding of all these elements of the computer system is integral to the successful development of quality software—particularly when you use DOS and BIOS functions. Let's look at these elements.

The Processor

The *central processing unit (CPU)* used in a PC or compatible is a member of Intel Corporation's 8086 series of processor chips. You are likely to see an 8086, 8088, 80186, 80286, 80386, or 80486 chip in the computers you program. Intel has come out, in the instances of the later chips, with minor versions of each chip, such as the 80386SX, 80386DX, 80486SX, 80486DX, or 80486DX2. Every chip in the Intel family not only implements unique qualities that set it apart from its predecessors, but also retains compatibility with their earlier versions. An 80386 (SX or DX), for example, can therefore do all that an 80286 or 8088 can, in addition to its own unique operations.

This book does not explore specific differences between the chips, but you should be aware that the majority of DOS is based on the capabilities of the 8086 or 8088 chip. In discussions of DOS, the BIOS, and programming, the examples run on the 8086 or 8088 (without taking advantage of the unique capabilities of the newer chips). Throughout this book, all references to the 8086 imply the entire family of Intel processors. Some of the newer additions and enhancements to DOS require knowledge of the differences between the CPU chips; examples that require this type of knowledge are clearly identified.

CPUs are basic processing engines that perform only the simplest operations. Because you have to know something about this basic processor engine, this section provides an overview of microprocessors in the 8086 series. If you are already familiar with the subject, you can skip this section. If you want details about programming the 8086 family, see the bibliography at the end of this book.

Later in this section, the CPU registers that are accessible to you as a programmer are discussed. First, however, because memory addressing is fundamental to many of the programming operations you perform at a DOS level, you must understand how the 8086 addresses memory. Let's look at this area.

8086 Memory Addressing

Some programmers criticize the 8086's segmented memory-addressing scheme. Memory segmentation limits the size of data items and complicates pointer arithmetic. For DOS programmers, however, segmented memory is here to stay. It represents a reasonable solution to a problem inherent in the 8086's design: finding the best way to represent 20-bit address values by using the 16-bit registers of the 8086. The 8086 has 20 address pins, which allow the addressing of 2^{20} (1,048,576, or 1M) unique memory locations, yet its registers are only 16 bits wide (register use is discussed later in this chapter, in the section "The 8086 Register Set").

The solution to this problem is to divide an absolute memory address into "pieces" that can be stored individually in the 16-bit registers. Two registers, therefore, are used to represent a single address; one of these registers stores a base (or segment) address, and the other stores an offset from that base. Such a method theoretically can generate 2^{32} (more than 4 billion) unique addresses. Even though such an address range would require 32 address lines for the microprocessor, and therefore is beyond the capabilities of the 8086, an example that uses this address range is helpful.

Figure 2.3 shows the four corners of a memory space that contains 100000000h (4,294,967,296, or 2^{32}) locations. Every row is a portion, or *segment*, containing 10000h (65,536, or 2^{16}) locations. The address of every location in a segment can be expressed as an offset from where the segment begins, with the first location at offset 0. The convention for writing addresses in this segment-offset form is *segment:offset*, and is always expressed in hexadecimal notation.

The last byte of the first segment (at 0000:FFFFh) is followed immediately by the first byte of the next segment (at 0001:0000h). The absolute address of every memory location—its ordinal position, counted from the first memory location—therefore can be calculated from this formula:

```
actual_address = ( segment_number * segment_interval ) + offset
```

Figure 2.3 shows that, when the segment interval is 10000h, the segment number forms the four most significant digits of the 8-digit absolute address. Similarly, the offset address can be regarded as the four least significant digits of the absolute address.

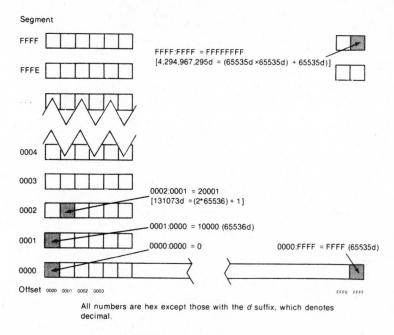

All numbers are hex except those with the *d* suffix, which denotes decimal.

Figure 2.3   Memory segments with 10000h-byte intervals.

In practice, the relationship between the base address and the absolute address does not have to be as simple as that shown in Figure 2.3. Sophisticated hardware can rapidly perform address translations equivalent to those that we humans use to calculate absolute addresses from segments and offsets.

Even though an understanding of this example is helpful, it still leaves you in a quandary: The 8086 uses 20 (not 32) bits for addresses. This example therefore must be adapted to the reality of the situation. The addressing scheme Intel developed regards the contents of the segment register (the segment portion of the absolute address) as the 16 most significant bits of the absolute address; the 4 least significant bits are assumed to be zero. In other words, the segment register contains the four most significant hex digits of the address, and the least significant (rightmost) digit is zero. The addition of the contents of the offset register to this calculated address results in the absolute address you want. Figure 2.4 shows how an absolute address is determined from a segment-offset pair under the Intel addressing scheme.

Now that you have a conceptual basis of how the 8086 addresses memory, let's look at the register set of the 8086.

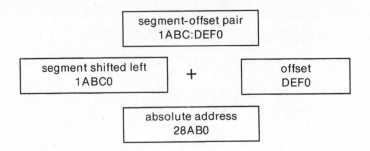

Figure 2.4 Calculating an absolute-memory address.

8086 Memory Addressing

The 8086's use of segment-offset pairs for addressing memory results in an interesting anomaly: Virtually every absolute memory address can be addressed in a multitude of ways. All of the following valid segment-offset pairs, for instance, reference the same absolute memory address:

```
0101:FFF0      1000:1000
03F1:D0F0      1001:0FF0
0900:8000      1002:0FE0
0CB7:4490      1003:0FD0
0FFF:1010      1100:0000
```

All these segmented addresses refer to the same absolute address: 011000h. Notice that every increment or decrement of the segment portion of the address has a corresponding increase or decrease of 10h in the offset portion. As you can see, memory segments can overlap in many different ways.

The 8086 Register Set

The 8086 family uses 14 separate 16-bit registers that can be grouped, by purpose, in the following four categories:

- General-purpose registers
- Segment registers
- Offset registers
- The flags register

Table 2.1 shows the registers and their categorization.

Table 2.1   The 8086 Register Set

Register	Category	Use
AX	General purpose	
BX	General purpose	
CX	General purpose	
DX	General purpose	
CS	Segment	Code segment
DS	Segment	Data segment
ES	Segment	Extra segment
SS	Segment	Stack segment
SP	Offset	Stack pointer
BP	Offset	Base pointer
SI	Offset	Source index
DI	Offset	Destination index
IP	Offset	Instruction pointer
Flags	Flags	Status flags

When you deal with individual registers, you clearly work directly with the CPU at a hardware level. Note that, although this usually is accomplished through assembly language, high-level languages such as BASIC, C, and Pascal have ways to access the registers. (Some techniques that are used to do this are discussed in Chapter 4, "The DOS and BIOS Interface.")

As mentioned, the 8086 register set can be divided, according to purpose, into four categories. Let's examine each category and its registers.

General-Purpose Registers

The general-purpose registers, as their name implies, are used for such general purposes as the storage of immediate results or other temporary needs. When you use a DOS or BIOS function, you load these registers with values necessary for the completion of the function. You always include a value that represents the specific function, in addition to other parameters that might be necessary. On return from a DOS or BIOS function, values that your program can use can be returned in the registers.

The general-purpose registers are AX, BX, CX, and DX. To facilitate the use of 8- and 16-bit values, each 16-bit register can be addressed also as a pair of 8-bit registers. The register names AL, AH, BL, BH, and so on are used to address the lower or higher 8 bits (*L* and *H* signify low and high, respectively). Figure 2.5 shows this relationship.

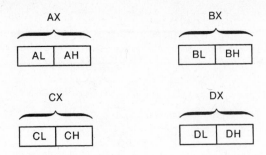

Figure 2.5   The 16-bit registers can be addressed as a pair of 8-bit registers.

These registers are used extensively in programming, whether you are working in assembly language or using high-level language calls to access the DOS or BIOS routines.

Segment Registers

The segment registers play an important role in the 8086's memory-addressing scheme. They store 16-bit values that represent the base addresses of 64K memory segments. As you might recall, these values represent the upper 16 bits of a 20-bit base address; the lower 4 bits are assumed to be zero. The 8086's memory-addressing hardware combines these base addresses with offset values stored in one of the CPU's offset registers, which are discussed in the following section.

The segment registers are shown in this list:

- The CS (code segment) register

- The DS (data segment) register

- The ES (extra segment) register

- The SS (stack segment) register

Every segment register specifies a distinct segment. As a programmer, you can use these segment registers in any way you choose, within certain limits. In Chapter 3, "The Dynamics of DOS," you see how programs are developed and how the segment registers are put to use. The segment registers are designed to be used in the following manner:

- CS holds the base address of the segment containing the code that is executing.

- DS holds the base address of the segment containing the program's data.

- ES supplements the DS register, holding the base address of an "extra" segment often used for data.

- SS holds the base address of the program's stack, which is used for temporary storage of data.

The previously mentioned limits on the use of segment registers include restrictions on the use of the CS and SS registers. To operate properly, the 8086 expects that the CS register will *always* point to the segment of the program that is executing and that the SS register will *always* point to the current stack (which is necessary for 8086 operations).

The Stack

Processors in the 8086 family use a structure called a *stack* to keep track of information during function calls and other operations. The processor puts registers on the stack whenever a subroutine is called (a PUSH operation) and takes them off (a POP operation) on return from the subroutine. Every PUSH causes the stack pointer to point to a lower address than before; every POP reverses this "movement" of the pointer. These effects on SP are built into the '86 chips and cannot be changed. The practical effect is that SP initially must be set to point to the top of the stack memory space rather than to the bottom, as you might expect.

Programmers use the stack to store intermediate values in calculations or to pass values to subroutines. Programming languages make extensive use of the stack for the same purpose.

The stack works like a stack of dishes in a cafeteria: As items are added (PUSHed on) to the stack, the stack gets larger. When something is removed (POPped off), the first item to come off is the last item added to the stack. This type of structure is called a *last-in first-out* (LIFO) structure.

Offset Registers

The offset registers, as their name implies, generally are used as the offset portion of memory addresses. The segment portions of the addresses usually are stored in the segment registers.

Because the addresses are split between a segment register and an offset register, every offset register is paired (by default) with a specific segment register that contains the "other" part of the address. These pairings are automatic, unless they are overridden by specific commands.

The five offset registers and the associated default segment register for each are shown in this list:

- The SP (stack pointer) register (paired with SS)

- The BP (base pointer) register (paired with SS)

- The SI (source index) register (paired with DS)

- The DI (destination index) register (paired with ES)

- The IP (instruction pointer) register (paired with CS)

Because the registers in this group differ in their common uses, they frequently are subdivided into two separate classes: pointer registers and index registers.

Pointer Registers

The pointer registers provide a convenient way to access values within a segment. SP always points to the current top of the stack and is updated automatically by various assembly language instructions. The other pointer register, BP, typically is used as a base (or reference) pointer for indexed operations. Some programmers use BP, for instance, to point to a fixed position in the stack. This position then is used as a reference point for retrieving variables that were placed on the stack before the subroutine was called. With high-level language compilers, this use of the BP register is a standard means of accessing parameters.

The instruction pointer (IP) holds the offset address of the next instruction to be executed by the CPU. When the IP and code segment (CS) registers combine, they point to the absolute address of the instruction. (The CS:IP register pair is always used in this manner.) The value of IP is incremented automatically by the CPU after each instruction is fetched from the current code segment.

Index Registers

The index registers, SI and DI, are specialized offset registers. Typically, SI and DI are used with the DS and ES segment registers. In string operations, for example, you would use DS:SI to point to the address of the source string and ES:DI to point to the destination string. In non-string operations, programmers generally use SI and DI for what their name implies—an index (offset) to the source or destination data.

The Flags Register

The flags register in the 8086 uses 9 of its 16 bits as flags that reflect the processor's status or control its operations. These flags are divided into two categories: status flags and control flags.

The status flags are shown in this list:

- The CF (carry flag)
- The PF (parity flag)
- The AF (auxiliary carry flag)
- The ZF (zero flag)
- The OF (overflow flag)
- The SF (sign flag)

These flags report on the status of the last instruction that was executed. If the last instruction generated a value of zero, for example, the zero flag is set. The status flags are set and cleared automatically, but programs also can set and clear the flags. Many DOS and BIOS routines use the carry flag to signal errors.

The control flags are

- The DF (direction flag)

- The TF (trap flag)

- The IF (interrupt flag)

The direction flag controls certain aspects of the 8086's instructions for copying ranges of memory. The trap flag puts the CPU in "single-step" mode (which debuggers use to control program execution). The interrupt flag enables or disables hardware interrupt response.

The 80286 and Beyond

Beginning with the 80286, it became possible to break out of the 1M memory limitation imposed by the 8088/8086 segmented architecture. The CPU could be programmed in real mode, which has the same programmer's model and the same limitations as the 8086 and 8088, or in protected mode.

In protected mode, *descriptor tables* are constructed. These tables contain the information previously found in segment registers—the base addresses of the segments—plus information about the segments, such as whether they can be written to. Segment registers are now *segment selectors*, indices to descriptor tables.

In protected mode on the 80286, a descriptor table entry contains a 24-bit base address. When the 80286 is running in protected mode, it can therefore access as much as 16M of memory.

The 80386 and 80486 continued the expansion of memory-addressing capabilities. Like the 80286, they can be programmed in protected mode; however, now the descriptor table entries have 32-bit base addresses, which allows access to more than 4 billion bytes (4 gigabytes) of memory. In addition to this addressing leap, the general-purpose, offset, and flags registers now have 32-bit versions: EAX, EBX, ECX, EDX, ESP, EBP, ESI, EDI, EIP, and EFLAGS. The old 16-bit registers (AX and BX, for example) still exist as the least significant words of their 32-bit counterparts.

Not only can the CPU access 4G of memory, a single segment can span the full 4G of memory. That, and the fact that 32-bit arithmetic now can be performed as easily as 16-bit arithmetic, has created a market for 80386-/80486-specific software in the DOS environment, including two competing protected mode environments: the DOS protected mode interface (DPMI) and the virtual control program interface (VCPI).

In addition, there are DOS extenders, which are programs that allow 80386-/80486-aware software to operate in protected mode while allowing access to the real mode DOS and BIOS functions. DOS extenders allow programs to be created that use DOS and BIOS facilities while taking advantage of the 32-bit power of the CPU. These types of programs tend to run faster than do their 16-bit equivalents and are not restricted by DOS memory constraints.

Identifying the CPU Chip

To use the advanced capabilities of the 80286, 80386, and 80486 CPUs, the software must know that it is running on one of the chips, and it must know on which one it is running. There are three solutions to the problem of determining which chip is present. The first solution is based on the fact that the 80386 and 80486 tell you who they are at power-up with an ID byte (3 or 4) in the DH register. The second is to ask users which chip they are using. The third is to deduce which chip is present from known differences between the chips.

The first method involves reprogramming the BIOS chips, which is beyond the scope of most programmers and intrusive for users. It also cannot be used to tell an 80286 from an 8086. The second method assumes that the user knows what CPU is under the hood; in too many cases, this assumption is not a valid one. The third method requires more work than the second but far less than the first, and is reliable.

The code in Listing 2.1 demonstrates how to determine which CPU is present. The first test differentiates the 8088, 8086, 80188, and 80186 from the 80286 and above. When a value is pushed on the stack on the 8088, the stack pointer is decremented before the value is written to the stack. Beginning with the 80286, the value is written first, and then the stack pointer is decremented. By pushing the stack pointer, you can check the value written to the stack to see whether the stack pointer was decremented before or after the value was written. If it is determined that an 80286, 80386, or 80486 is present, you can attempt to set bits in the flags register that the 80286 does not use. The 80286 does not let you meddle with those bits, but the 80386 and 80486 do. If you can change the bit values, the chip is either an 80386 or an 80486. A similar trick is used to differentiate an 80386 from an 80486. Notice that you use the 66h-size override prefix to force the 32-bit flags register to be pushed and popped. This trick is perfectly safe; at that point, you know that it is at least an 80386.

Listing 2.1

```
        page 60,132

; checkcpu.asm
; Determines whether the CPU in use is an 8088/8086, an 80286, an
; 80386, or an 80486. Print the CPU and return an errorlevel of 0,
; 2, 3, or 4 for 8088/8086, 80286, 80386, or 80486, respectively.

        .model   small
        .stack

        .data
say86   db       "8088 or 8086$"
say286  db       "80286$"
say386  db       "80386$"
say486  db       "80486$"

        .code
        .startup
checkcpu proc
```

```
; The first step is to determine whether the chip is an 8088/8086.
; The key difference is based on what the CPU does when it executes
; the PUSH instruction.  The 8088/8086 decrements the stack
; pointer first and then writes the saved value to the stack. The
; 80286, 80386, and 80486 write the value to the stack and then
; decrement the stack pointer. Thus, when SP is pushed and the
; pushed value is popped off, the value popped off equals the
; current stack pointer, unless the chip is an 8088 or 8086.

        push    sp
        pop     ax
        cmp     ax,sp           ; if values are not the same,
        jne     is_86           ;   it is 8088/8086

; The second step is to determine whether the chip is an 80286.
; The key difference is the IOPL bits in the flags register;
; the 80386 and 80486 have them, and the 80286 does not. The
; 80286 does not let them be set; the 80386 and 80486 do.

        pushf
        pop     ax              ; get flags in ax
        or      ax,03000h       ; set IOPL bits
        push    ax              ; stuff them back
        popf                    ; pop flags--this is where the 80286
                                ;   will put them back the way they were
        pushf
        pop     ax              ; get flags in ax
        test    ax,03000h       ; if the IOPL bits are reset, the chip
        jz      is_286          ;   is an 80286

; The third step is to determine whether the chip is an 80386.
; The key difference is the alignment check bit in the flags
; register; the 80486 has one, and the 80386 does not. The 80386
; does not let you set that bit, but the 80486 does.

        db      66h             ; (32 bit instruction)
        pushf
        pop     ax              ; read low word of flags
        and     ax,00FFFh       ; clear IOPL bits--level zero
        pop     dx              ; read high word
        or      dx,00004h       ; set alignment check bit
        push    dx              ; push flags back
        push    ax
        db      66h             ; (32-bit instruction)
        popf                    ; pop flags register--this is where
                                ;   the 80386 undoes your work
        db      66h             ; (32-bit instruction)
        pushf                   ; push flags back
        pop     ax              ; read what you did
        pop     dx              ; find out if the CPU reset the
        test    dx,4            ;   alignment check bit
        jz      is_386          ; if it did, the chip is an 80386

is_486:
        mov     dx,offset say486
        mov     al,4            ; errorlevel 4
```

continues

Listing 2.1 Continued

```
          jmp      sayso

is_386:
          mov      dx,offset say386
          mov      al,3              ; errorlevel 3
          jmp      sayso

is_286:
          mov      dx,offset say286
          mov      al,2              ; errorlevel 2
          jmp      sayso

is_86:
          mov      dx,offset say86
          mov      al,0              ; errorlevel 0

sayso:
          push     ax               ; save errorlevel
          mov      ah,9             ; call DOS write string function
          int      21h
          pop      ax               ; retrieve errorlevel
          mov      ah,04Ch          ; terminate process with return code
          int      21h

checkcpu endp
          end
```

Math Coprocessors

The Intel 80×86 family of processor chips, from the 8088 to the 80386, can perform only integer arithmetic. For many applications, integer arithmetic is all that is necessary. For applications that require floating-point arithmetic, the math must be performed by specially written procedures. For most applications, users do not notice the overhead of performing the calculations in software. For math-intensive applications, however, the overhead becomes a problem, and a math coprocessor becomes essential; some applications do not even run unless the system has a math coprocessor.

The math coprocessor can handle floating-point math with the same ease with which the processor handles integer arithmetic. Furthermore, it performs its math in parallel with the processor. Except for loading data to and from the coprocessor and directing the coprocessor's activities, the processor is free to go about its business while the math coprocessor performs its functions.

Identifying the Math Coprocessor

Three math coprocessors designed by Intel work with its processor chips: the 8087, the 80287, and the 80387. There is no 80187; the 8087 works with the 80186 and 80188. There is no 80487 either; the 80486 has the equivalent of an 80387 coprocessor built in.

Identifying the math coprocessor is not simple. Seemingly disparate pairings of processor and coprocessor can occur, particularly the combination of an 80386 CPU and an 80287.

As in the method for differentiating one CPU from another, the technique for identifying the math coprocessor exploits the subtle differences between one chip and its successor. Complicating the task of discerning which math chip is in the system is the possibility that there is no chip. (The math chips have never been so inexpensive—and applications requiring them have never been so common—that vendors automatically put them in the system. On the other hand, few vendors want to put their products in a position of losing 100 percent compatibility by locking out applications that require a math chip. As a compromise, they place a socket for a math chip on the motherboard, and the user has the option to install a math coprocessor.)

To determine whether a math chip is present, a bit pattern is written to memory, and an attempt is made to initialize the math chip. The math chip then is instructed to write the coprocessor status word to that memory location. If the chip is present, a new value is written to memory. If the chip is not present, you can tell from the bit pattern that is written—it will not be valid for the coprocessor status word.

After you know that a math chip is present, you can differentiate an 8087 from the 80287 and 80387 by disabling interrupts on the math chip and reading the control word. This procedure has an effect on the 8087, but not on the 80287 or the 80387. An 80287 can be differentiated from an 80387 by creating a positive infinity value (dividing positive 1 by 0), creating a negative infinity value, and then comparing the two values with the math coprocessor. The 80387 differentiates between the two; the 80287 does not.

The procedure in Listing 2.2 can be called to determine which math coprocessor, if any, is present.

Listing 2.2

```
        page 60,132

; checkfpu.asm
; Determine the type of math coprocessor (fpu) installed.

        .model  small
        .stack

        .data
scratch dw      (?)                 ; have the math chip store data here
```

continues

Listing 2.2 Continued

```
saynone  db      "No math coprocessor$"
say87    db      "8087$"
say287   db      "80287$"
say387   db      "80387$"

         .code
         .startup
checkfpu proc
         fninit                      ; initialize the fpu
         mov     scratch,055AAh      ; the fpu will not write this
         fnstsw  scratch             ; have the fpu write its status word
         cmp     byte ptr scratch,0  ; check lsb--it should be 0
         jne     no_math             ; if not, return
         fnstcw  scratch             ; now have the fpu write its control word
         mov     ax,scratch          ; read the value
         and     ax,0103Fh           ; mask expected bits
         cmp     ax,0003Fh           ; this is what you should see
         jne     no_math             ; if different, no math chip

; Now that you know that you have an fpu, which one is it?

         and     scratch,0FF7Fh      ; clear interrupt bit
         fldcw   scratch             ; load the control word
         fdisi                       ; disable interrupts
         fstcw   scratch             ; write the control word back
         test    scratch,00080h      ; any effect on the word?
         jnz     found_8087          ; if so, it is an 8087

; The chip is not an 8087, so it is an 80287 or 80387.

         finit                       ; reinitialize the chip
         fld1                        ; push +1.0 onto the chip's stack
         fldz                        ; push 0.0 onto the chip's stack
         fdiv                        ; produce positive infinity
         fld     st                  ; produce negative infinity
         fcompp                      ; compare
         fstsw   scratch             ; write the status word
         mov     ax,scratch
         sahf                        ; copy AH into the flags register
         je      found_80287         ; if Z bit set (equal), the
                                     ;   coprocessor found positive and
                                     ;   negative infinity to be equal

; The chip is an 80387
         mov     dx,offset say387
         mov     al,3                ; errorlevel 3
         jmp     sayso

no_math:
         mov     dx,offset saynone
         mov     al,0                ; errorlevel 0
         jmp     sayso
```

```
found_8087:
        mov     dx,offset say87
        mov     al,1            ; errorlevel 1
        jmp     sayso

found_80287:
        mov     dx,offset say287
        mov     al,2            ; errorlevel 2

sayso:
        push    ax              ; save errorlevel
        mov     ah,9            ; call DOS write string function
        int     21h
        pop     ax              ; retrieve errorlevel
        mov     ah,04Ch         ; terminate process with return code
        int     21h

checkfpu endp
        end
```

Memory

PCs and compatible computers have four classes of memory:

- *ROM (read-only memory)* is permanent memory installed in the computer. It usually holds a portion of BIOS specific to the physical machine.

- *RAM (random-access memory)* holds nonpermanent program code and data.

- *Extended memory* (memory above one megabyte) can be accessed by an 80286 processor running in protected mode.

- *Expanded memory* is added to the system and is not part of the memory mapped directly by the processor. This memory is accessed through a special expanded memory driver system.

You might have heard about variations on the ROM, such as PROM (programmable read-only memory) or EPROM (erasable programmable read-only memory); all such memory is covered under the ROM heading. Although purists might object to this move, from the standpoint of those who program the DOS system, PROM and other such variations represent permanent memory.

The memory map in Figure 2.6 shows how the basic system memory is allocated.

In Chapter 10, "Program and Memory Management," which discusses in greater detail the allocation and uses of memory, you learn how to control memory and how to use it for your programs.

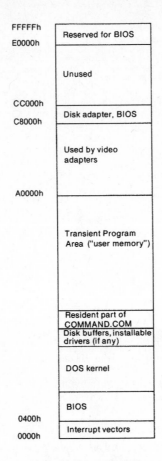

Figure 2.6 A memory map for a machine with 1 megabyte of memory.

I/O Channels

The standard input/output (I/O) devices on the PC and compatibles are the keyboard, the video monitor, and the printer (see Chapter 5, "Output Devices," and Chapter 6, "Input Devices"). In addition to these standard devices, you frequently see a mouse and one or more serial ports (see Chapter 6 and Chapter 7, "Serial Devices").

You can add custom devices, such as touch-sensitive screens and sensors of all types, to a PC system. Although a discussion of these types of specialized devices is beyond the scope of this book, Chapter 12, "Device Drivers," shows you how to write your own drivers for specialized devices.

The Keyboard

The PC keyboard knows nothing about *what* you type. The keyboard does not interpret your keystrokes—it simply tells the computer that a specific key has been pressed or released. The keyboard does not assign meaning to the keys, but it does assign a unique number (a *scan code*) to every key. This scan code is passed to the PC for interpretation by the BIOS. Figure 2.7 shows the scan codes of the original 84-key version; later keyboards added more keys and codes, which are described in Chapter 6.

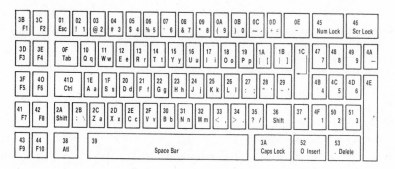

Figure 2.7   The keyboard scan codes.

As you type, the keyboard notifies the computer (through Int 09h) that a key has been pressed or released. When the processor executes Int 09h, the BIOS takes momentary control of the computer and reads the key's scan code, checking first for toggle keys such as Shift and Num Lock. If a toggle key has been pressed or released, the BIOS updates the keyboard status bits kept in memory addresses 0417h–0418h. Next, the BIOS checks for special key combinations (such as Ctrl-Alt-Del) and, if necessary, executes their special handlers.

If the scan code still has not been "weeded out" as a special-purpose character (such as Num-Lock, Ctrl-Alt-Del, Shift, or Ctrl), BIOS translates it into its ASCII equivalent. If no corresponding ASCII character is available for the key, it is given an ASCII value of zero. Then the ASCII character, in addition to its original scan code, is stored in the keyboard buffer. This buffer is large enough to hold 15 characters and their scan codes. If the buffer is full, BIOS issues a "beep" (signaling that the keyboard buffer is full) and then discards the character.

After the character is in the keyboard buffer, it is available for use by any program (including DOS) that is running. Because the computer usually responds in a fraction of a second, the chances of filling the keyboard buffer are slim, *unless the computer is busy performing another task.*

This overview of the keyboard should suffice for now. Programming the keyboard is discussed in greater detail in Chapter 6, "Input Devices."

The Display Screen

The PC supports several types of video adapters, and most adapters work in more than one text or graphics mode. Writing programs to accommodate the various kinds of adapters is not as difficult as you might think, however, because DOS provides facilities for determining the kind of adapter and the current mode.

Chapter 6 discusses these matters in detail. This section is an introduction to typical kinds of adapters.

Types of Display Adapters

For most PC programming, you should be familiar with six types of display adapters. Other types of display adapters exist, but they usually are used for special applications.

The original "standard" display was the Monochrome Display Adapter (MDA). This system, with its crisp, clear characters and a nice professional appearance, was expected to be the standard for business use of the computer. Other video adapters (the CGA, EGA, HGA, MCGA, and VGA) became available as users began to demand different display enhancements. Table 2.2 lists these display adapters and the year that each became available.

Table 2.2   Display Adapters and the Year They Became Available

Adapter	Year Introduced
MDA	1981
CGA	1982
HGA	1982
EGA	1984
MCGA	1987
VGA	1987

In addition to the monochrome adapter, the Color Graphics Adapter (CGA) was available for those to whom color was important. The CGA display shows color and graphics, but the characters are not as sharp as those displayed by the MDA. This difference in sharpness is due to the number of dots, or pixels, used to create each character. The MDA uses a 9×14 character box to create characters, and the CGA uses an 8×8 box. Because of this difference in resolution, the characters on the CGA tend to look "fuzzy" compared to the MDA.

The Hercules Graphics Adapter (HGA) display, which combines the monochrome screen's clear characters with the graphics capabilities of the color graphics display, produces high-resolution monochrome displays that rapidly became the standard of comparison for text and graphics. HGAs cannot produce color, but this lack was not a big drawback.

With the introduction of the Enhanced Graphics Adapter (EGA) color graphics system, people (and businesses) began to discover that color added a rich, new dimension to their work. Highlighting alone is never adequate for showing a wide range of things on-screen; you can call attention to many more things with color.

The standards for displays have been revised again, albeit only slightly, by the introduction of the MultiColor Graphics Array (MCGA) for IBM Personal System/2 Models 25 and 30 and the Video Graphics Array (VGA) for IBM PS/2 Models 50, 60, and 80. The MCGA is similar to the CGA but has higher resolution. (The MCGA's resolution is 320 × 400; the CGA's resolution is 320 × 200.) The VGA's resolution (640 × 480) is a modest extension of the EGA (640 × 350). The major improvement in both displays is that they use analog rather than digital monitors. By working with analog signals, these new video systems can display palettes of 256 colors (of the possible 262,144 colors available).

Memory Mapping and Display Adapters

The video displays in the IBM family all use *memory mapping*. In other words, what you see on the screen is a direct reflection of what resides in the memory area controlled by the display adapter. To put it simply, characters are written to the display memory, and then the display adapter reads the characters from the display memory and shows them on the video screen. In graphics modes, the display adapter treats the data in the video memory as an array of individual bits that control the dots on the screen. The memory areas used by the different display adapters vary according to the type of display. Table 2.3 details the starting memory locations and length of video buffers for every display adapter.

Table 2.3   Memory Configurations for Display Adapters

Display Type	Video Mode	Buffer Segment Address	Buffer Length	Display Pages
MDA	Text	B000h	4K	1
CGA	Text	B800h	16K	4/8
	Graphics	B800h	16K	1
HGA	Graphics	B800h	64K	1
EGA	Mono	B000h	Varies	Varies
	Text	B800h	Varies	Varies
	Graphics	A000h	Varies	Varies
MCGA	Text	B800h	32K	8
	Graphics	A000h	64K	1
VGA	Mono	B000h	Varies	Varies
	Text	B800h	Varies	Varies
	Graphics	A000h	Varies	Varies

DOS
PROGRAMMING

Although this section provides an overview of the way display adapters function, you should refer to Chapter 5, "Output Devices," for more detailed information. That chapter provides specific information about how the display adapters interpret the video memory and how to use the BIOS and DOS functions to display information.

The Printer

In this book, the term *printer* generally refers to a printer attached to the parallel printer port, not to the serial port. (Serial ports are discussed briefly in the following section; Chapter 7, "Serial Devices," discusses them in more detail.) With a parallel printer interface, you can send the printer an initialization message and read the printer's status to determine, for example, whether it is out of paper. This is typically what you will do at the DOS level with a printer. Printer gymnastics are beyond the scope of this book.

In Chapter 5, "Output Devices," you learn how to write programs that access the printer directly, by using the BIOS and DOS functions. You can access several printers (LPT1 and LPT2, for example) and interpret the return codes to determine the printer's status.

The Serial Port

With a parallel printer connection, you have limited control of the parallel printer port. The hardware has been designed to handle almost every task. You can buy a printer off the shelf and be confident that it will run correctly as soon as you plug it in. Serial ports are different, however.

Most of today's computers are equipped with at least one serial port. Used predominantly to drive serial printers, mice, or modems, serial ports pose special problems. Their parameters must be set identically on both sides of the connection; if the parameters are not set correctly, nothing gets through. These parameters include baud rate, parity, stop and start bits, and data length. Although standards govern the way wires are physically connected for most (but not all) devices, the parameters have not been completely standardized. Even if you make the correct physical connections, you still must make the correct *logical* connections.

There is no quick-and-easy way to make these connections. Serial port parameters specify the number of bits per second at which information is transferred; the number of bits that make up a character; whether there is parity checking and, if there is, the type of parity; and the number of stop bits used to indicate the end of a character. You might have to specify flow control over the line with software, such as XON/XOFF or ETX/ACK; or, you might have to use a special line protocol, such as Xmodem or Kermit. It is no wonder that beginners rarely succeed in getting their computers connected to the telephone line the first time they try.

Chapter 7, devoted to the intricacies of serial channels and how to program them, discusses the meaning of all the serial port parameters and how to determine how best to incorporate this information into the programs you write.

The Mouse

When the original PC was designed, the mouse was not considered an important device. Routines inside the BIOS enabled programmers to access the more popular joysticks and light pens. But times (and users) change—today, the mouse has a sizeable following.

Generally, a mouse is connected to a PC either through a custom hardware board that plugs into the PC's internal system bus or through a serial port. The mouse driver software determines the location of the mouse and handles the interface to the board.

The Mouse

In its simplest form, a mouse is a device with a small ball fitted on the bottom. When you roll the mouse across a flat surface, sensors measure the device's movement in both X and Y directions. The mouse sends to the computer system signals that indicate changes in position. An *optical mouse* does not use a ball. Rather, it tracks the movement of the device across a reflective grid. No matter which type of mouse you use, the computer responds to the changes in position by moving a visible pointer on the screen. All this activity is handled at the driver level.

In addition to movement sensors, the mouse usually is fitted with one, two, or three switches (called *buttons*) that can be tested and used to control program actions.

DOS Int 33h accesses the mouse when you use the standard mouse driver software. The interrupt provides information about the mouse and its movement, and permits control of this data. Even though the mouse is an add-on to the DOS system, you can learn more about it in Chapter 6, "Input Devices."

Storage Devices

As DOS has evolved, so have its capabilities for greater disk storage capacity. Table 2.4 shows the increases in floppy disk capacity and in the number of drive formats supported.

Table 2.4 Floppy Disk Capacities

DOS Version	Floppy Disk	Capacity
1.0	5 1/4-inch SSDD	160K
	5 1/4-inch DSDD	320K
2.0	5 1/4-inch SSDD	180K
	5 1/4-inch DSDD	360K

continues

43

Table 2.4   Continued

DOS Version	Floppy Disk	Capacity
2.1	5 1/4-inch DSHD	1.2M
3.2	3 1/2-inch DSDD	720K
3.3	3 1/2-inch DSHD	1.44M
6.0	3 1/2-inch DSHD	2.88M

Physical Disk Structure

The recording surface of a disk is divided into concentric tracks, and every track is divided into sectors. The number of tracks and sectors varies according to the type of disk (floppy disk or hard disk; single sided or double sided; double density or high density; 3 1/2-inch or 5 1/4-inch). Figure 2.8 shows the arrangement of tracks and sectors on the disk.

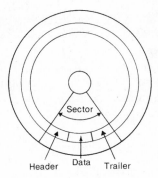

Figure 2.8   Disk track formatting.

Because hard disk drives (also known as "fixed disk" drives, as opposed to drives with removable media) contain more than one platter, hard disk space is divided into cylinders. Every cylinder includes one track on each side of every platter in the drive. Figure 2.9 shows how tracks combine to make cylinders.

Chapter 8, which discusses disk structure, has a more detailed discussion of the disk's physical format. Chapter 8 also explains how to access the internal formatting routines that control the lowest level of the track-formatting operation.

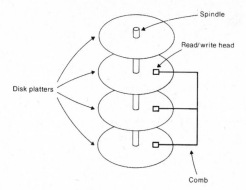

Figure 2.9 A fixed disk.

Logical Disk Structure

The FORMAT program establishes not only the disk's sector structure but also a logical structure, unique to DOS, that controls the way data is stored on the disk. Figure 2.10 shows this logical structure.

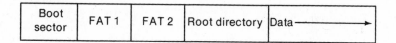

Figure 2.10 The disk's logical structure.

FORMAT's largest, most time-consuming task is to format the disk—it divides the physical disk into logical tracks and sectors and fills them with an initial value.

After formatting the disk, the FORMAT program creates three areas on the disk: the boot record, the file allocation table (FAT), and the root directory. The remainder of the disk (the portion not included in any of these areas) is the file storage area.

The Boot Record

The *boot record* is the first sector on every logical disk. Beginning with DOS V2, the boot record contains the disk boot program (only a few hundred bytes long) and a table of the disk characteristics. When the system is started, the boot program is loaded into memory and the boot program loads the operating system files from the disk. If those files are not found, the boot program displays an error message. The booting process is covered in greater detail in Chapter 3, "The Dynamics of DOS."

The File Allocation Table

The *file allocation table* (*FAT*) is a map of the disk. It tracks which portions of the disk are assigned, unassigned, and not assignable (because of formatting errors, for example). Areas of the disk are assigned to files in clusters, with every cluster represented by an entry in the FAT. Depending on the disk's size, clusters can vary in size from one to eight or more sectors. To accommodate the increased storage capacity of hard disks, FAT entries (originally 12 bits per entry) now can be as large as 16 bits per entry. The FAT-entry size is one of the most significant differences between DOS V2, V3, and V4.

It should be stressed that the FAT is essential to the proper functioning of DOS in relation to a disk. The FAT makes it possible to have files larger than 512 bytes, and any damage to the FAT can chop off files and programs. A detailed description and discussion of the FAT would be premature here; for more detailed information about the FAT, see Chapter 8, "Disks."

The Root Directory

The last part of the system information on the disk, the *root directory*, is located immediately after the FAT. It contains the following information about each file accessible through the root directory:

- An 8-byte file name

- A 3-byte file extension

- The file size (in bytes)

- A date and time stamp for the file

- The starting cluster number for the file

- The file attribute codes

Every entry is 32 bytes long, with extra space reserved for future expansion. The root directory for a given disk is a fixed size. On 160K, single-sided disks, the root directory can accommodate 64 entries; on a 20M hard disk, it can hold 512 entries. Directory size is limited so that DOS can tell where the disk's data area begins. In DOS V2 and later versions, this limitation is not a problem; you can bypass the limit on the number of files by creating subdirectories, which have no size limit.

For a more detailed discussion about the structure of disks and directories, see Chapter 8, "Disks," and Chapter 9, "Directories and Files."

The Software

The software provided with a PC or compatible system builds, above the physical machine, another layer on the virtual machine. This software begins with the BIOS, which builds a standard view of the machine that attempts to hide the specifics of the installed hardware. DOS builds, above the BIOS, the machine you are familiar with (in terms of files and directories).

The BIOS

The first software level in the virtual machine is the BIOS (basic input/output system). This software forms the lowest-level machine you normally deal with.

The true BIOS consists of firmware contained in a ROM that implements the most basic machine functions. Many descriptions also include the I/O system software as part of the BIOS. This software, loaded from disk, extends the BIOS functions so that they can handle all system input and output requests. The purpose of the BIOS is to insulate higher levels of software from possible hardware changes in the computer; the purpose of the I/O system is to cushion the interface between the BIOS and DOS. Together, the BIOS and the I/O system provide a uniformly defined set of services as a base for higher software levels.

Every computer manufacturer (including IBM) provides the BIOS, and customizes the I/O system, for its machines. Microsoft Corporation provides a module called SYSINIT (see Chapter 3), which manages system initialization and the loading of DOS. The BIOS and the I/O system combination must meet certain specifications for the higher-level software to function properly. Microsoft's DOS kernel, for example, uses BIOS services to implement many of its own operations.

PC-compatible computers often come with versions of the BIOS ROM provided by the manufacturer. None of them can duplicate the code in an IBM BIOS ROM, but they can provide BIOS services by handling the same interrupt structure and using the same data table areas the IBM BIOS uses. Although the code is different, they provide the BIOS services necessary to run DOS.

If third-party BIOS ROMs are accessed through the defined BIOS interrupts, you can expect them to work the way the IBM PC services work. If you write a program that depends on knowledge of the undocumented BIOS ROM functions to get something done, all bets are off. A common example of this type of code is a program that toggles the speed switch on multi-speed compatibles; because the IBM PC never had this type of feature, no standard exists for interfacing to it and you must work by trial and error.

The "BIOS Reference" section at the back of this book describes the BIOS interrupt functions in detail. All these functions work with the BIOS ROMs provided by all manufacturers of IBM-compatible computers.

The DOS Kernel

Microsoft provides the DOS kernel as a proprietary program based on the standard BIOS services. The DOS kernel provides hardware-independent services that can be used by

47

DOS
PROGRAMMING

application programs on a variety of systems. You will spend a great deal of time working with these DOS services. (*Note:* "DOS" refers to IBM's version of DOS *or* to MS-DOS, unless specifically mentioned otherwise.)

DOS services can be divided arbitrarily into the following categories:

- Character I/O

- Directory operations

- Disk control

- Dynamic memory allocation

- Error handling

- File operations

- Miscellaneous system functions

- Network functions

- Program initiation and termination

You can access the DOS services in two ways. Some services are accessed directly through software interrupts. Most DOS services, however, are accessed through DOS function calls by placing a function number in register AH and then executing Int 21h. The "DOS Reference" section at the back of this book describes the DOS interrupt functions in detail. These interrupts are available on all PCs and compatibles. This section points out known differences between systems.

The Command Processor

To most people who work with a PC, the command processor (or shell) *is* the operating system. These people are used to thinking of the c> prompt as coming from the operating system and not from a program. Only a few years ago, interactive operating systems *were* built this way.

Today, however, shell interfaces are the standard. The shell makes the process of changing and adding new features easy because only one part of the operating system has to be changed. Although the shell interface was not invented by the designers of UNIX, this type of program (COMMAND.COM, for example) was popularized by the UNIX operating system. UNIX systems have several standard shells (csh, ksh, and sh, to name a few).

The structure of COMMAND.COM is important to its operation. The program has three parts: an initialization section, a resident section, and a transient section.

When COMMAND.COM starts, the initialization and resident sections are loaded from disk. The initialization section sets up the system, runs the AUTOEXEC.BAT file, then loads and turns control over to the transient section. As its name implies, the transient section comes and goes (according to the demands of memory); the resident section, which "is always there," is responsible for reloading the transient section, in addition to other things.

If all the capabilities of COMMAND.COM were coded in a single program, the program would take up a substantial amount of memory (more than 20K). Although this amount of memory is a drop in the bucket compared to the amount most applications require, if you are trying to fit the last few paragraphs into a document or the last few cells into a spreadsheet, the amount can be considerable. To minimize the program's memory consumption, the COMMAND.COM code for normal operations and the code for the program's built-in commands are kept in the transient section. Because this section is sometimes overwritten by another program, COMMAND.COM's resident section checks to see whether the transient section has to be reloaded and, if it does, reloads it.

COMMAND.COM executes programs from three categories of commands:

- *Internal commands* (built into COMMAND.COM)

- *External commands* (stored on the disk)

- *Batch files* (stored on the disk)

The transient section of COMMAND.COM includes the code for the internal commands. When the user types a command name, COMMAND.COM first searches to see whether the command is an internal command. If COMMAND.COM does not find the named command among the internal commands, the program searches for it first in the current directory and then along the search path. COMMAND.COM searches for an external command with the .COM extension, and then for one with the .EXE extension. If it finds neither of these in a given directory, COMMAND.COM looks for a batch file (extension .BAT) with the appropriate name.

Batch files are a special type of "program" allowed by a command processor. These files consist of scripts of commands to execute in a given sequence, with a small control language that allows for parameter substitution, decisions, and branching within the batch file. Batch files are executed by COMMAND.COM on a line-by-line basis. Every line consists of a command to be executed: either an executable command or an internal control command allowed only in batch files. Actual operation is simple. The transient portion of COMMAND.COM takes one line of the batch file, performs any parameter replacements, and then uses the DOS EXEC function to execute the command. As each line is finished, COMMAND.COM gets the next line and executes it.

Device Drivers

Most advances in the art of software have involved ways to make the underlying hardware disappear. High-level languages, for example, are an advance because they do not require the programmer to know about registers, bits, and bytes (not everyone agrees with this statement). Similarly, operating systems are a major improvement over the days when we all had to write our own drivers for every device we wanted to use.

CP/M used standard devices for handling the console and printer. DOS has gone a step further by making the devices more interchangeable and making it possible to install your own devices without having to recompile the entire operating system. Think about it! Previously, if you wanted to add new devices to a system, you had to get down to the internals of the operating system to make your devices work. Today, DOS includes a more flexible driver model that enables you to write a driver for a device and to choose whether to add it when the system starts. To understand how this works, you have to understand a little about device drivers.

The operating system software includes a set of device drivers (the resident drivers) that run the hardware. Every driver meets certain specifications for its calling interface so that DOS can operate the hardware *without having to know how the hardware works*.

When you boot the computer, DOS initializes all the drivers through standard initialization entry points (see Chapter 3, "The Dynamics of DOS"). For now, all you need to know is that you operate a device through a series of functions defined by standard entry points. The type of device you are trying to control determines which entry points are meaningful. In Chapter 12, "Device Drivers," you learn a great deal about device drivers—in fact, you create a simple one.

DOS divides devices into character devices and block devices. *Character devices* operate on a character-by-character basis (the keyboard and video display, for example); *block devices* (disks and RAM disks) operate on a block-transfer basis. Every type of driver has entry points appropriate for handling specific functions.

You can write your own device drivers and then add them to your CONFIG.SYS file. These device drivers are added to the system the next time you boot the system. Your drivers operate on an equal footing with the resident drivers. You can even replace an existing character driver with completely new code, as ANSI.SYS and other drivers do for the video display.

Installable drivers let you add to the system some new equipment not envisioned in the original design. (MOUSE.SYS does this for the mouse; EMM.SYS, for expanded memory). In short, DOS has created an environment you can expand to meet your needs as new equipment becomes available.

Summary

You learned in this chapter that DOS systems exist as a hierarchy of "virtual computers." Beginning with the hardware at the lowest level and continuing up through the BIOS and DOS systems, every level provides a consistent, logical computer with special functions necessary to implement the next level of the computer system.

The lowest level, hardware (the combination of components that comprise a system) can vary widely between systems. At the next level, the BIOS provides a "computer" with defined services that you can depend on to work in the same way from one system to another. These basic input/output services allow raw access to the devices on the system. DOS provides a higher level of services (and therefore a higher level of abstraction) than does the BIOS. The DOS services create what is commonly thought of as "the system"—files and directories, for example. At the highest level, COMMAND.COM provides a user interface that gives you control of the different services.

Now that you understand something about the structure of DOS, let's move on to DOS in a dynamic environment and learn how it all works.

3

The Dynamics of DOS

Chapter 2, "The Structure of a DOS System," described the layout of DOS, its hardware support, and its basic software modules. This chapter shows you what happens when these elements operate in a dynamic environment. You see what happens as the system starts up, how it processes commands, and how programs are executed.

Then, having gained an overview of system and program operation, you get a more detailed look at interrupts and memory management under DOS. This chapter and Chapter 4 lay the groundwork for the practical programming in Chapters 5 through 13.

The DOS Boot Sequence

When you power up or reset a system based on the 8086 family of microprocessors, the microprocessor automatically starts program execution at address FFFF:0000h. This happens because of processor design and has nothing to do with DOS. The ROM BIOS at FFFF:0000h provides a jump instruction to the beginning of the hardware test routines and the ROM bootstrap code. (In the following discussion, *ROM BIOS* applies to PCs and compatibles.)

When a system is turned on (a cold start), a series of hardware tests called the *Power-On Self Test* (POST) check the amount of installed memory and test which peripheral devices are available and operable. At this point during start-up, most machines show rapidly changing memory-size figures and report on serial ports, parallel ports, and so on.

If the system is being warm-booted (typically through the use of the Ctrl-Alt-Del key combination), the POST is skipped. The computer knows whether a cold or warm boot is in effect by the value stored at memory location 0040:0072h. If the value is 1234h, a warm boot is assumed. Any other value causes a cold boot. This special value is placed there by the interrupt handler for Ctrl-Alt-Del.

Regardless of whether a warm or cold boot is occurring, control is transferred next to the ROM bootstrap initialization procedure.

The bootstrap initialization routine sets up important parts of the interrupt vector table in low memory (especially vectors for hardware located by the POST). The routine also initializes the ROM BIOS tables at memory location 0400:0000h, and may do some hardware setup, such as starting dynamic memory refresh. The routine then searches the memory area from A000:0000h through F000:0000h to locate other ROM extensions; these extensions are marked with a unique byte sequence that identifies them as ROM. (Typical ROM extensions are the EGA or VGA graphics ROM, a SCSI controller, and other plug-in controllers that use ROM space.) The bootstrap routine initializes any ROM extensions it finds. After initialization is complete, the ROM bootstrap code starts the system itself.

The ROM bootstrap routines now read the disk bootstrap code from the first sector (the *boot sector*) of the boot disk. The bootstrap code is a minimal-services routine responsible for getting the system up and running. The ROM bootstrap routines check all bootable disk drives, starting with drive A, for the presence of a boot sector on the disk. The first such disk that is found is used; this feature makes it possible to regain control by booting from a backup floppy, if the hard disk becomes damaged. If no boot sector is found, an IBM PC transfers control to ROM BASIC and starts up as a diskless system; PC compatibles prompt you to insert a system disk and then wait for you to press a key. The exact procedure varies from one manufacturer's ROM to another.

When a boot sector is located, the ROM bootstrap loads it into high memory (at address 007C:0000h), away from where DOS will be loaded. Control is then transferred to the disk bootstrap routine.

After the disk bootstrap code has been loaded and has control, it looks back to the disk to locate the IO.SYS and MSDOS.SYS files.

 Note: On an IBM PC and many compatibles, these files are named IBMBIO.COM and IBMDOS.COM. In this discussion, *MSDOS.SYS* refers to two modules (MSDOS.SYS and IBMDOS.COM), and *IO.SYS* refers to two others (IO.SYS and IBMBIO.COM). Unless a specific difference is pointed out, all operations are performed alike in either set of modules.

The disk bootstrap does not know about file systems or disk structures—indeed, it can't. All details of the disk's file layout are built into the MSDOS.SYS file and, because that file has not yet been loaded and initialized, that data is not available. The following requirements are therefore imposed on a boot disk:

1. IO.SYS must be the *first* entry in the root directory.

2. MSDOS.SYS must be the *second* entry in the root directory.

3. The IO.SYS file itself *must* be the first file on the disk and must be stored in contiguous clusters in the correct order. Originally, the second file was required to follow the first and also be in contiguous clusters; beginning with Version 3, however, it may be located anywhere on the disk and may be fragmented. This made it possible to upgrade easily from Version 2 to the significantly larger Version 3 (the differences between Version 1 and Version 2 were so great that ease of upgrading was not a consideration).

Now you know why the SYS.COM program "complains" when it tries to make bootable a disk that already has had something stored on it. A bootable disk must be built when the disk is empty (or appears to be empty; that is, the first directory entry begins with a byte containing 00h, indicating that it has never been used). Otherwise, SYS.COM will not work.

If the disk bootstrap does not know about the file system, how does it know about the directory entries and where the files are located? It learns this information from the *BIOS parameter block* (*BPB*)—the area of the boot sector from byte 0Bh through 17h (see Fig. 3.1).

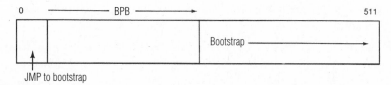

Figure 3.1   The boot sector.

The BPB tells the boot program enough about the disk layout that the boot program can locate the beginning of the directory and the file space. After locating the files, the boot program copies IO.SYS (IBMBIO.COM) into low memory above the BIOS tables. Then, depending on which system you are using, either the boot program or the IO.SYS initialization routine copies MSDOS.SYS to memory in an area above IO.SYS.

 Note: Before Version 3, no use was made of the BPB, even though it was introduced with Version 2. Because of this, many non-IBM manufacturers failed to include the BPB in their boot sectors. Disks formatted under such versions of DOS may not be readable by Version 3 and later, but can be made so by copying the boot sector from a Version 3 disk with the same characteristics over the original one to provide a BPB. This incompatibility has given rise to legends about Version 3 not being fully compatible, but it was the offending Version 2 variant that was incompatible with DOS standards.

There are two parts to IO.SYS. The system manufacturer (IBM or some other firm) supplies the first part—the BIOS. The BIOS contains resident device drivers with hardware-specific initialization code that is run only when the BIOS is loaded. Microsoft supplies the second part: a module called SYSINIT.

When IO.SYS takes control of the computer, it runs any hardware-specific initialization the system may need. During initialization, IO.SYS checks the BIOS-table area of low memory (set up earlier by the ROM BIOS initialization) to see what hardware is being used. Unneeded drivers can be deleted automatically at this point; most versions of DOS, however, provide only bare-bones drivers in IO.SYS and make no changes. Control is then transferred to the SYSINIT module.

SYSINIT checks the available memory and relocates itself in high memory. No permanent memory space is allocated for SYSINIT, because it is a temporary module whose services are needed for only a short time. The relocation of SYSINIT to high memory allows the module to serve its purpose, but gets it out of the way so that all low memory is available for DOS.

The high-memory copy of SYSINIT copies MSDOS.SYS over the IO.SYS initialization code (which means that the original copy of SYSINIT is also copied over). This operation makes available to DOS all the memory used for system initialization. Next, using the DOS Int 21h file services (which became available when MSDOS.SYS was copied into RAM), SYSINIT opens the CONFIG.SYS file (if it exists). The entire file is loaded into memory, all characters are converted to uppercase, and CONFIG.SYS is interpreted (one line at a time) for system configuration information.

Memory is allocated for file tables, disk buffers, and file control blocks. Default values are assigned if CONFIG.SYS does not exist or does not specify explicit values through the FILES, BUFFERS, and FCBS directives. If CONFIG.SYS specifies that DOS is to be loaded high, portions of the DOS kernel are relocated in high memory and the memory is marked as in-use. Additionally, any drivers referenced in CONFIG.SYS are loaded, initialized, and linked into the list of drivers maintained by the system, at the front of the list. (If new character drivers and resident drivers have the same name, the new character drivers are always found first when access to a driver is needed, thereby effectively replacing the existing driver.) The initialization function for each device driver checks the driver's status, initializes the hardware, sets up any interrupts serviced by that driver, and then releases any excess memory that was used when the driver loaded.

When configuration is complete, SYSINIT calls the MSDOS.SYS initialization code. This initialization code sets up internal tables and the interrupt vectors and then initializes the original drivers resident in IO.SYS.

MSDOS.SYS also determines how many disk drives are attached to the system and examines the BIOS parameter block for each one to determine the largest disk-sector size for all these disk drives. MSDOS.SYS uses this value to set up a disk-sector buffer for use by the system. Finally, MSDOS.SYS displays the DOS copyright message and returns control to SYSINIT.

After completing the initialization process, SYSINIT closes all file handles and opens the console device (CON) as standard input, standard output, and standard error; the printer device (PRN) as standard list; and the auxiliary device (AUX) as standard auxiliary. Finally, SYSINIT calls the DOS EXEC function to load and execute COMMAND.COM or the shell specified by CONFIG.SYS. (The EXEC function is described later in this chapter, in the section "Command Processing.")

After control transfers to the shell, SYSINIT is no longer necessary. It is therefore overwritten when COMMAND.COM initializes itself.

When COMMAND.COM is loaded, it immediately relocates part of itself in high memory. The low-memory section of COMMAND.COM (the resident section of the code) contains code essential for restarting COMMAND.COM when it regains control, as well as handlers for three interrupts: Int 22h (Terminate Address), Int 23h (Ctrl-C), and Int 24h (Critical Error). The high-memory section of COMMAND.COM (the transient portion) holds the code necessary for the internal commands and for batch-file processing. By splitting itself in two, COMMAND.COM tries to use the smallest possible amount of memory for functions that *must* remain in memory at all times.

When COMMAND.COM is first loaded by SYSINIT, it sets up the vectors for Interrupts 22h through 24h. COMMAND.COM then executes the AUTOEXEC.BAT file (if one exists). When that step is complete, control is transferred to the transient portion of COMMAND.COM, the DOS prompt is displayed, and the system is ready to go.

Now that all the software necessary for running the computer has been loaded and initialized, let's see how COMMAND.COM processes commands.

Command Processing

COMMAND.COM is a shell program that controls access to system resources and provides a working environment for users. This working environment consists of defined ways in which users can locate and execute functions on the system. When you ask COMMAND.COM to execute a command, the program tries to locate the command in the following manner:

1. By searching for the requested operation in the list of internal commands (such as DIR, COPY, and DEL).

2. By searching for an executable file (with the extension .COM, .EXE, or .BAT) in the current directory, as external commands.

3. By searching for a program in the directories listed in the PATH environment variable.

When COMMAND.COM searches a directory, it looks first for the command file with the .COM extension, then with the .EXE extension, and then with the .BAT extension, thereby setting up a precedence of program types for execution. If two programs in the same directory have the same root name but different extensions (FORMAT.COM and FORMAT.EXE, for example), DOS always executes the COM file. The extension is disregarded. Even if you enter FORMAT.EXE, DOS executes the COM file. (A common misconception, repeated in some other books, is that by entering the extension you can "force" DOS to run the executable file of your choice. You cannot! You *can* force the EXE file to be run first, however, by renaming the COM file to have some other extension, and by renaming the EXE file to COM; the loader ignores the extension when it is determining the file type and relies instead on information contained in the file.)

DOS
PROGRAMMING

When a program is identified as either a COM or an EXE file, COMMAND.COM calls the DOS EXEC function to execute that program. The EXEC function performs the following tasks:

1. Checks whether enough memory is available to load the program. If sufficient memory is available, the required memory is allocated. If the memory is not available, EXEC issues an error message and does not execute the program.

2. Builds a program segment prefix (PSP) at the bottom of the allocated memory area (see Fig. 3.2). (For a more detailed discussion of the PSP, see Chapter 10, "Program and Memory Management.")

3. Loads the program into the memory space above the PSP and determines whether the program is COM or EXE by examining the first two bytes of the program. COM programs are simply copied as a memory image; EXE programs are loaded according to the loading information in the header.

4. Transfers control to the program's entry point. COM files *always* have an entry point at 100h (just after the PSP), whereas the entry points for an EXE file are specified in the EXE program header.

5. Returns control, when the program terminates, to the resident portion of COMMAND.COM. The resident portion of COMMAND.COM does a checksum of the area occupied by the transient portion. If the checksum is OK, control of the computer is transferred back to the transient portion and the system prompt reappears; otherwise, the transient portion is reloaded from disk and regains control. If, for any reason, a reload of the transient portion of COMMAND.COM is required and cannot be performed, the system displays an error message to the effect that COMMAND.COM is "bad or missing" and halts operation. Rebooting is necessary to restart the system in this case.

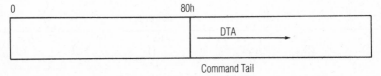

Figure 3.2 Program segment prefix (PSP).

A shell program intended to replace COMMAND.COM *must* provide handlers for Interrupts 22h through 24h; the shell can provide other features as necessary. On many systems, COMMAND.COM has been replaced by either a simplified shell that is friendlier to novice users or by a shell that offers more features than COMMAND.COM (4DOS, a shareware command processor, is an example of this type of replacement).

Programs under DOS

Applications programs under DOS take two basic and significantly different forms: COM files (COM programs) and EXE files (EXE programs). You must have a thorough understanding of the differences to do useful work on the system.

COM Programs

COM programs are the smallest and simplest of programs. On disk, they exist as memory images; in memory, they are loaded into a single 64K memory segment. Even though COM programs are supposed to exist entirely within a single segment, they frequently stray outside. COM programs that access video memory directly, for example, *must* access memory outside their assigned 64K memory area.

Early programs for the PC and compatibles often did much more than simply access video memory. Frequently, because the rest of memory was assumed to be available for its use, a program would set up tables, load program overlays, or control the extra memory in any way needed for its function. Some relatively nice programs acted this way (under Version 1, some programs even did their own assignment of temporary files by going directly to the disk and bypassing the entire DOS file structure).

If DOS assumed that a COM program used only its assigned segment of memory, another program executed by DOS could easily mess up a program that was already there. To eliminate the problem, DOS gives all free memory to a COM program that is being executed. Later in this chapter (and again in Chapter 10), you learn in greater detail about the way this memory is assigned.

A COM program easily can exceed the assumed bounds of the data area. It simply modifies the processor's segment registers to point to memory areas the program needs to access. By modifying the data segment (DS) register, for example, a COM program can manipulate data in any portion of memory. This capability is absolutely necessary if the program is going to modify the screen memory directly rather than use DOS services for video output, because the screen memory cannot be in the program's data segment.

Although you may consider access to all of the system's memory a great capability, it leaves DOS with the possibility that a program can modify anything—therefore, nothing is "safe." To obviate this problem, DOS takes the safe way out by assigning all available memory to the program. (Technically, this statement is only partly correct; for a more detailed explanation, see the section "Memory Allocation and Management" at the end of this chapter.)

If you write a COM program that uses DOS's EXEC function (the program and overlay loader) to execute another program, your COM program should release any memory it is not using. DOS provides memory-management functions that can be used to allocate, deallocate, and change the size of memory blocks your programs use. These functions are detailed in the last part of this chapter and in the "DOS Reference" section at the end of this book (see DOS

Functions 48h through 4Ah). Because high-level languages handle memory-management automatically, you do not have to worry about memory management unless you are programming in assembly language or writing memory-critical applications such as TSR programs (discussed more fully in Chapter 11).

Listing 3.1, a sample COM program written in assembly language, is the simplest of programs. It uses a standard DOS function (09h) to write a string to the screen.

Listing 3.1

```
; Sample COM Program
        name    dosbook

; DEMOCM.ASM - .COM file version of simple print
; Prints "DOS Programmer's Reference"

;------ Procedure Book ------
; PURPOSE:        To illustrate programming for a .COM
;                 file. Displays a string on the screen
; USES:           DX, AX
; RETURNS:        Nothing

        .model  tiny
        .code
        .startup
book    proc
        mov     dx,offset msg       ; Get message location
        mov     ah,9                ; Output character string
        int     21h
        mov     al,0                ; Exit code
        .exit
book    endp

;------ End of Procedure Book ------
msg     db      'DOS Programmer',027h,'s Reference',0dh,0ah,'$'
        end
```

Let's go through the program, line by line, to see what it does.

After the initial comment section, the simplified segment directives of MASM (.model, .code, and .startup) instruct the assembler to configure this program as a COM file. This is primarily accomplished by the .model tiny directive, although the .startup directive establishes the program start at location 100h. Starting at 100h is mandatory for COM files and allows space in the segment for the program's PSP. (See Chapter 10 for a discussion of the PSP's layout and use.)

With the program established, the next step is creating the program's only procedure (book). By default, MASM assumes that this will be a NEAR procedure (all references will be within a single segment) because you are creating a COM file. The body of the program, which is simplicity itself, consists of these steps:

1. Put the offset address of the message in the DX register.

2. Set the AH register to 9 (the code for the DOS function that writes a string to the screen).

3. Execute Int 21h to invoke the DOS interrupt processor.

4. Set the AL register to 0 (the exit code for the program) in preparation for program termination.

5. Use the simplified MASM `.exit` directive to exit the program through DOS function 4Ch (the function number for a DOS program-termination call).

At the end of the procedure, the data string for printing is defined in memory with special ASCII characters 27h (the apostrophe), 0Dh (carriage return), and 0Ah (line feed). The DOS function requires that the string be terminated with a dollar sign.

Use the ML command when you assemble the program. This step creates an object file from the assembly language source code and links it to create the COM file. The object file is nothing but a direct translation of the source file into machine code acceptable to the CPU chip. The COM file is created by the linker.

As you can see from figure 3.3, which shows a COM program dump as it exists on disk, only the program code is kept in the file. The program uses minimal disk space (the file size is only 42 bytes).

```
0000   BA 0D 01 B4 09 CD 21 B0-00 B4 4C CD 21 44 4F 53    ......!...L.!DOS
0010   20 50 72 6F 67 72 61 6D-6D 65 72 27 73 20 52 65    Programmer's Re
0020   66 65 72 65 6E 63 65 0D-0A 24 00 00 00 00 00 00    ference..$......
```

Figure 3.3 A COM program dump.

EXE Programs

EXE programs are much more complex and versatile than COM programs. Instead of being limited to a single memory segment, EXE programs frequently occupy several segments and may include more than one segment of code and data. EXE program files have a special header area, which is used by the DOS EXEC function to load the program. This header block contains information DOS uses to relocate the file and determine memory requirements. The program header is essential for program operation because, unlike a COM program, which is stored as an absolute memory image, an EXE program is stored as a relocatable memory image. The system can adjust such an image to conform to overall space and memory-use needs as determined by DOS.

EXE programs are more flexible than COM programs and sometimes are much larger (reaching the limits of memory). They also coexist better in memory because they can be broken into discrete segments and assigned to available free space. This coexistence is of little use on PC systems in a single-user, single-task environment. Coexistence becomes more and more of a problem, however, as you move into multitasking (using systems such as Windows or DESQview) or to OS/2. Programs that ignore the possibility of coexistence may not run.

The sample COM program (in Listing 3.1) can be rewritten as an EXE program, as shown in listing 3.2.

Listing 3.2

```
; Sample EXE Program
        name    dosbook

; DEMOEX.ASM - .EXE file version of simple print
; Prints "DOS Programmer's Reference"

;------ Procedure Book ------
; PURPOSE:      To illustrate programming for an .EXE
;               file. Displays a string on the screen
; USES:         DX, AX
; RETURNS:      Nothing

        .model  small

        .stack
        .data
msg     db      'DOS Programmer',027h,'s Reference',0dh,0ah,'$'

        .code
        .startup
book    proc
        mov     dx,offset msg      ; Get message location
        mov     ah,9               ; Output character string
        int     21h
        mov     al,0               ; Exit code
        .exit
book    endp
        end
```

You can see immediately that the EXE version of the program in Listing 3.2 is structured differently than the COM version in Listing 3.1. To some programmers, this difference may make the program more complex. The program code does the same job in both versions but, in the EXE version, more program lines are needed to do that job. If you compare the COM and EXE versions, you find that many portions are identical but that significant differences also are apparent. The biggest differences are in the MASM directives that are used and the way the data area has to be defined.

In EXE programs, you must declare the data segment as a separate part of the program. This is done with the .data directive. (In this program, the data segment contains one string—the same constant string used in the COM version.) You also have to declare the stack segment; this is done with the .stack directive. This directive instructs MASM to create a default 1K stack for the program. (Stacks are discussed briefly in a sidebar in Chapter 2.)

Figure 3.4 shows a complete dump of the disk image of the EXE program. Because it includes the EXE header and the relocation table, this program is much larger than the COM version. The EXE version needs considerably more disk space (577 bytes) and is therefore slower to load than its COM counterpart.

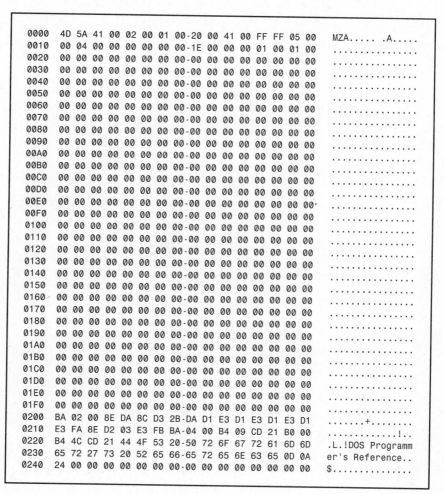

```
0000   4D 5A 41 00 02 00 01 00-20 00 41 00 FF FF 05 00   MZA..... .A.....
0010   00 04 00 00 00 00 00 00-1E 00 00 00 01 00 01 00   ................
0020   00 00 00 00 00 00 00 00-00 00 00 00 00 00 00 00   ................
0030   00 00 00 00 00 00 00 00-00 00 00 00 00 00 00 00   ................
0040   00 00 00 00 00 00 00 00-00 00 00 00 00 00 00 00   ................
0050   00 00 00 00 00 00 00 00-00 00 00 00 00 00 00 00   ................
0060   00 00 00 00 00 00 00 00-00 00 00 00 00 00 00 00   ................
0070   00 00 00 00 00 00 00 00-00 00 00 00 00 00 00 00   ................
0080   00 00 00 00 00 00 00 00-00 00 00 00 00 00 00 00   ................
0090   00 00 00 00 00 00 00 00-00 00 00 00 00 00 00 00   ................
00A0   00 00 00 00 00 00 00 00-00 00 00 00 00 00 00 00   ................
00B0   00 00 00 00 00 00 00 00-00 00 00 00 00 00 00 00   ................
00C0   00 00 00 00 00 00 00 00-00 00 00 00 00 00 00 00   ................
00D0   00 00 00 00 00 00 00 00-00 00 00 00 00 00 00 00   ................
00E0   00 00 00 00 00 00 00 00-00 00 00 00 00 00 00 00·  ................
00F0   00 00 00 00 00 00 00 00-00 00 00 00 00 00 00 00   ................
0100   00 00 00 00 00 00 00 00-00 00 00 00 00 00 00 00   ................
0110   00 00 00 00 00 00 00 00-00 00 00 00 00 00 00 00   ................
0120   00 00 00 00 00 00 00 00-00 20 00 00 00 00 00 00   ................
0130   00 00 00 00 00 00 00 00-00 00 00 00 00 00 00 00   ................
0140   00 00 00 00 00 00 00 00-00 00 00 00 00 00 00 00   ................
0150   00 00 00 00 00 00 00 00-00 00 00 00 00 00 00 00   ................
0160   00 00 00 00 00 00 00 00-00 00 00 00 00 00 00 00   ................
0170   00 00 00 00 00 00 00 00-00 00 00 00 00 00 00 00   ................
0180   00 00 00 00 00 00 00 00-00 00 00 00 00 00 00 00   ................
0190   00 00 00 00 00 00 00 00-00 00 00 00 00 00 00 00   ................
01A0   00 00 00 00 00 00 00 00-00 00 00 00 00 00 00 00   ................
01B0   00 00 00 00 00 00 00 00-00 00 00 00 00 00 00 00   ................
01C0   00 00 00 00 00 00 00 00-00 00 00 00 00 00 00 00   ................
01D0   00 00 00 00 00 00 00 00-00 00 00 00 00 00 00 00   ................
01E0   00 00 00 00 00 00 00 00-00 00 00 00 00 00 00 00   ................
01F0   00 00 00 00 00 00 00 00-00 00 00 00 00 00 00 00   ................
0200   BA 02 00 8E DA 8C D3 2B-DA D1 E3 D1 E3 D1 E3 D1   .......+........
0210   E3 FA 8E D2 03 E3 FB BA-04 00 B4 09 CD 21 B0 00   .............!..
0220   B4 4C CD 21 44 4F 53 20-50 72 6F 67 72 61 6D 6D   .L.!DOS Programm
0230   65 72 27 73 20 52 65 66-65 72 65 6E 63 65 0D 0A   er's Reference..
0240   24 00 00 00 00 00 00 00-00 00 00 00 00 00 00 00   $...............
```

Figure 3.4   An EXE program dump.

Table 3.1 decodes the EXE header shown in this dump. (All entries in the table are 2-byte words.) *Note:* Programs intended to run only with Windows are EXE files also, but use a significantly different header scheme. Such programs are beyond the scope of this book.

Table 3.1   Decoding an EXE Program Header

Offset	Typical Values	Meaning
00h	4Dh	
	5Ah	Link program EXE file signature
02h	E0h	
	00h	Length of image
04h	02h	
	00h	Size of file in 512-byte pages (2)
06h	01h	
	00h	Number of relocation-table items (1)
08h	20h	
	00h	Size of header in paragraphs (32)
0Ah	00h	
	00h	Minimum number of paragraphs necessary (MINALLOC)
0Ch	FFh	
	FFh	Maximum number of paragraphs desired (65,535) (MAXALLOC)
0Eh	04h	
	00h	Displacement of stack segment in paragraphs
10h	A0h	
	00h	Offset in SP register
12h	9Ah	
	CFh	Word checksum
14h	00h	
	00h	IP register offset
16h	00h	
	00h	Code segment displacement
18h	1Eh	
	00h	Displacement of first relocation item
1Ah	00h	
	00h	Overlay number (resident code = 0)

The EXE program header provides the information the EXEC module needs in order to control the loading of the program and to assign its segments correctly. Each entry consists of a 2-byte data word stored low-order-byte first. Table 3.1 shows the meaning of each entry.

1. At offset 00h, a unique pair of bytes (4Dh 5Ah—ASCII codes MZ, which may stand for Mark Zbikowski, a principal designer of DOS) identify the file as an EXE file. Whenever the DOS EXEC function sees a file that starts with this byte sequence, the function automatically handles it as an EXE file. This is true no matter *what* extension (if any) the file name carries. Only the MZ signature is used to determine the file type; any file not containing this signature is treated as a COM file.

2. At offset 02h, the length of the file (modulo 512) is stored. This value, in addition to the values at offsets 04h and 08h, is used to determine the size of the program.

3. At offset 04h, the length of the file (including the header) in 512-byte pages is stored. This value may be zero if the file occupies less than 512 bytes; Microsoft utilities never create EXE files shorter than 512 bytes, but those from some other vendors do.

4. Offset 06h has the number of items in the relocation table (the location of the relocation table is stored at offset 18h).

5. Offset 08h is the size, in paragraphs (16 bytes per paragraph), of the EXE program header.

6. Offset 0Ah is the minimum number of paragraphs necessary to run the program (MINALLOC). If this much memory is not available, the program does not run. The linker sets this to zero unless it is overridden by a LINK command-line switch.

7. Offset 0Ch is the maximum number of paragraphs the program wants to get. The linker sets this to FFFFh (1M) unless it is overridden by a LINK command-line switch. If less than the amount specified here is available, the program gets all that can be assigned.

8. Offset 0Eh is the offset of the stack segment, in paragraphs, from the beginning of the program.

9. Offset 10h is the initial value of the SP register when the program is started.

10. Offset 12h is a checksum of the program for use by the EXEC function at run-time. (In most versions of DOS, it appears that no use is made of this checksum.)

11. Offset 14h is the initial value of the IP register when the program starts (the program's entry point).

12. Offset 16h is the segment displacement of the program's code segment.

13. Offset 18h is the offset (in the EXE file) of the relocation table's first entry.

14. Offset 1Ah is the overlay number. For a program, this value is zero.

Immediately after the header, a small amount of reserved space is followed by the program's relocation table. Items in the relocation table are read, one at a time, into a work area. Each item's segment value is added to the program's start segment value, which the EXE loader calculates from the values at offsets 04h, 08h, and 02h in the EXE header. The resulting segment value and the item's offset value point to a word in the program; the calculated segment value is written to that location.

The relocation table is followed by another small amount of reserved space. (Either of the reserved spaces can vary in size.) Then comes the program itself, followed by the stack segment.

Some High-Level Language Examples

Now that you have looked at assembly language programs as examples of COM and EXE programs, let's look at some examples that use high-level languages to do the same simple function. In a high-level language, the program source is *much* simpler to write. This advantage is significant. As programs grow in complexity, program maintenance is easier if the source code is less complex.

Frequently, the high-level language version of the executable program is longer than the assembly language version for the same program. This happens because high-level languages must provide for many variations of use. For example, `printf` in C is loaded with special features not used in our simple example.

To provide a basis for comparison, several language compilers (in various high-level languages) were used to compile programs with the same function as the assembly language examples in the preceding section. As you will see, the high-level language versions have much larger executable files loaded and stored on disk.

Although it is difficult to detect differences in execution speed in programs this small, you can easily set up experiments to test their speed. This section focuses on the simplicity of the programs, not on their speed or size.

 Note: To keep this book to a reasonable size, comments have been omitted from sample listings when they duplicate text discussions. Obviously, this practice is not encouraged in your own programs.

A Turbo Pascal Program

Many people prefer working in BASIC to working in Turbo Pascal. To print just one line in Turbo Pascal, for example, you must deal with overhead on a program-language level. You must identify your program code as a program module and use a Begin-End pair to set off the program's executable code (see Listing 3.3). Although this organizational detail may seem ridiculous at such a trivial level, you will see that, as the program expands, your work also expands. The overhead then becomes more of a device for guarding against mistakes.

Listing 3.3

```
{ DEMOTP.PAS                                    }
{ Listing 3.3 in DOS Programmer's Reference    }
{ ============================================= }
Program Demo;
Begin
     writeln('DOS Programmer's Reference');
End.
```

You will see that Pascal compilers to a large extent control the computer's memory. Because determinations about memory use are made at compile-time, the use of functions such as program execution and memory management requires a considerable amount of forethought.

A Compiled C Program

The C programming language was designed with systems-level programming in mind. Because access to system resources was originally much easier in C than in Pascal or BASIC, C generally is the language chosen for programs that have to make extensive use of DOS or BIOS functions. Later versions of Pascal have blurred the differences, but the trend has already been set.

The C version is shown in Listing 3.4. As in the Pascal version, the overhead in C is minor in large, complex programs and is a major help in keeping the program understandable.

Listing 3.4

```
/* demo.c
   listing 3.4 of DOS Programmer's Reference */

#include <stdio.h>

main()
{
        printf("DOS Programmer's Reference\n");
}
```

C compilers produce code that gives programmers the most direct control of the underlying machine. This capability is intentional: The C programming language was designed to be used for writing operating systems.

The capability of providing tight control of a machine while still providing high-level language functions and control structures similar to those provided in Pascal make C the language of choice for most serious applications.

Most applications in this book are written in C. The examples in BASIC and Pascal are included to illustrate how you can use the same techniques in other languages. (Limited space precludes duplication of all examples in all languages.)

Comparing Different Versions of a Program

The results of a comparison of the compiled modules from each version of the program are shown in Table 3.2. This table reflects neither an exhaustive test of one compiler versus another nor a performance test—it simply shows the comparative sizes (in bytes) of the compiled modules. If you compare these sizes to your sizes for the same files, you may notice some differences. The language version you have, the options you use, and the way you compile all can affect final program size.

Table 3.2   Size (in Bytes) of Compiled Modules

Language	Source File	Object File	Executable
Assembly (COM)	741	162	42 (COM file)
Assembly (EXE)	738	215	577 (EXE file)
Turbo Pascal 6.0	222	N/A	1936 (EXE file)
Turbo Pascal 7.0	222	N/A	2208 (EXE file)
Borland C++ 2.0	148	443	5584 (COM file)
Microsoft C/C++ 7.0	148	329	6695 (EXE file)

Keep in mind that any comparison of compilers depends on your perspective and your needs. Speed, the most frequently cited yardstick, is important in some programs but not in others. For example, if a program that transfers characters to a printer is already faster than the printer and has to wait, what difference does speed make?

This exercise *is* useful if you understand that your choice of a language influences the size and operation of your program and makes your conceptual work easier or more difficult. And remember—no matter what the benefits of a high-level language may be, nothing beats assembly language and hand coding if you need to squeeze the most from the available memory space and processor speed.

COM versus EXE Programs

Should you or shouldn't you? Is it worthwhile to write a program you can convert to COM format, or should you leave it in EXE format? To decide, you should consider the following factors:

- A COM program is faster to load and start because it is a direct memory image.

- A COM program is limited to a maximum of 64K, including data and program code. (You can increase these limits, however, by manipulating the segment registers.)

- A COM program hogs all memory and has to release memory in order to EXEC other programs. (This item is important only if you are using concurrent programs. It is unimportant if the program will run on a single-user, single-task system.)

- A COM program uses less space on disk because it does not include the EXE program header or relocation table. In some cases, the difference is considerable because the relocation table may be the largest part of the program.

- COM programs run faster because they cannot use FAR calls, which are a little slower than NEAR calls. In most programs, the difference is imperceptible unless many such calls are executed per second.

COM programs are most useful when you need to squeeze into a limited space as many programs as possible. For example, if you want to take with you a floppy disk filled with simple utilities, COM files are the answer. For most programming, however, building a COM program makes no sense. An EXE program does as good a job and is likely to remain compatible with extensions to the DOS system well into the future. A well-designed EXE program can limit FAR calls to those needed for crossing segment boundaries. And, by using NEAR calls for most of the repetitive work, an EXE program can eliminate much of the overall speed advantage of a COM program.

If you work with a high-level language, you may not have a choice. Most compilers produce either COM or EXE programs; others produce both. Basically, the decision to convert an EXE program to a COM program is determined largely by your particular circumstances.

Now, having laid the groundwork, let's look at interrupts. Interrupts affect the way DOS, the BIOS—the entire system—work.

Interrupts

Old-style computer systems, which ran one program at a time to completion, were simple in theory, simple in design, and simple to operate. An early system I worked on had punch-card input and a line printer for output. Large data sets were stored on one of five magnetic-tape drives (disks did not exist), and memory was 32K of magnetic core. When you programmed that system, you *knew* you had total control of your computer. When your program needed some data from a tape drive, the program simply waited. When it needed some input from the console (not even a keyboard—just switches!), it waited again. Working with that computer was extremely uncomplicated—but you waited much of the time.

Interrupts are a way to eliminate the waiting. When a computer requests a hardware service, such as a disk read, it waits for the results in one of three ways:

- It waits until the operation is completed.

- It continues with other tasks and checks periodically to see whether the operation is completed.

- It continues with other tasks and is notified by the operating system when the operation is completed.

Every method has its advantages and disadvantages. Consider serial communications, for example.

When your computer communicates with another computer over the telephone line, characters arrive at your serial port at random intervals. If all you had to do was read the characters from the line and dump them in a buffer, you could simply wait for a character to arrive, read it and write it to the buffer, and then wait again. This type of tightly looping process is frequently called a *busy wait*.

This method would be acceptable if your computer were handling only communications between computers—nothing else. But you want your computer to pay attention to *you*. If you want the computer to pay attention to you *and* the serial line, you have to use a different method.

You can write a program, for example, that checks repeatedly for something to do and, if it finds something to do, does it. You might write a simple program that performs the following steps:

1. If a character is at the keyboard, write it to the serial port.

2. If a character is at the serial port, write it to the screen.

3. Go to Step 1.

(In Chapter 7, you build a program just like this one to demonstrate basic serial communications.)

With communications at 1200 baud (1200 bits per second), however, about 120 characters arrive every second. A new character reaches the serial port every 8.33 milliseconds; if you are not ready to receive an incoming character, you lose it. How much can *you* do in 8.33 milliseconds? In computer terms, 8.33 milliseconds is a relatively long time, but not if you want to do one of the following:

- Place a character on the screen.

- Scroll the screen up and blank the bottom line if the character was at the end of your screen.

70

- Carry out a sequence if the character is part of a screen-control sequence.

- Decide how to handle a nonprintable character.

In addition to all this activity, you want to be ready to handle every character the moment it is typed on the keyboard. As you discover, even if you work through the DOS and BIOS functions or read directly from the serial port, there is simply not enough time for you to do everything. In practice, this simple approach can lose as many as three incoming characters (at 1200 bps) every time the CRT has to scroll up one line!

Your only option is to use the interrupt system. Some people are afraid of interrupts, which have a reputation as an arcane technique known only to gurus and hackers. Nothing could be further from the truth. As soon as you understand basic interrupt operation, you can write an interrupt handler. (You write several in Chapter 11.)

Think of an interrupt as a doorbell. If you did not have a doorbell on your home, you would have to check periodically to see whether someone was at your door. This repeated checking, or *polling*, tends to be inefficient and wastes your time—as it would waste the computer's time in a computer environment. Going to the door only when the doorbell rings is much more efficient. An interrupt works like a doorbell for your computer.

When a program is running, events such as a character's arrival on the serial line cause an interrupt to occur. When an interrupt occurs, the system stops your program, saves the program's *state* (the CS, IP, and flags registers) on the stack, and branches to a handler for that interrupt. Basically, an interrupt handler is just another program, although (as you discover in Chapter 11) interrupt handlers are somewhat restricted in what they can do.

Whether you realize it or not, the system you work with interrupts your work regularly. For example, the timer interrupt occurs about 18.2 times per second. Some programs tie in to this interrupt in order to display an on-screen clock.

Another important interrupt is generated whenever you press a key. This keyboard interrupt handles the keystroke. All you see is the character appearing on-screen. Interrupt control makes everything happen, however.

A PC has 256 interrupt routines. It accesses them through an interrupt vector table located at 0000:0000h through 0000:03FFh. (The addresses used are built into the CPU chip and cannot be changed by software.) Each 4-byte entry in this table corresponds to an interrupt routine; the four bytes are the address of that routine's *entry point*. To understand the interrupts, you need to know how they are classified.

The 8086 processor family has four basic types of interrupts:

- Internal interrupts

- The non-maskable interrupt

- Hardware interrupts (also called *maskable* interrupts)

- Software interrupts

Let's look briefly at each type.

Internal Interrupts

The 8086 microprocessor family generates many interrupts that are sensed directly by the CPU. In the divide-by-zero interrupt, for example, the processor automatically issues the appropriate interrupt request when it detects a divide-by-zero error.

The Non-Maskable Interrupt

The non-maskable interrupt (NMI) is tied directly to a special NMI pin on the processor chip. The non-maskable interrupt forces the processor to deal immediately with some kind of catastrophic system failure. (You can think of the NMI as the "now move immediately" interrupt.)

On the PC and compatibles, this interrupt is activated by a memory-parity error—an error indicating a major problem in the system's memory. The standard handler for this interrupt writes the message Memory Parity Error to the screen and then locks up the computer because there is no safe way to recover on a PC when a memory-parity error occurs.

Hardware (Maskable) Interrupts

Interrupts generated by external devices are called *maskable* interrupts. They come through a pin on the CPU that you can tell the processor to ignore temporarily. On a PC, interrupts come through the 8259 Programmable Interrupt Controller chip and can be masked individually. (You learn more about the 8259 in Chapter 11.) The state of the interrupt flag in the flags register determines whether the processor pays attention to a maskable interrupt. To mask an interrupt, you use the clear interrupt instruction (CLI) to clear the flag. (See Chapter 2 for a detailed discussion of flags and the flags register.)

Maskable interrupts tend to be frequent and unpredictable. Because they come from external hardware, a program cannot predict when such interrupts will occur. Maskable interrupts must be handled quickly so that the program can continue. Interrupt handlers should be optimized to perform only necessary operations.

Software Interrupts

Software interrupts are generated by programs, not by hardware. All DOS and BIOS functions are accessed through software interrupts. These interrupts do not have to "know" anything about the system to create a flexible method for programs to access system resources.

Ordinarily, software interrupts are synchronized to your program's operations. Handlers for these interrupts frequently provide special functions, such as mouse control and file handling. Although software interrupts are not as critical as hardware interrupts, they are called frequently and must be efficient.

As you will discover from the discussion of TSRs (terminate-and-stay-resident programs) in Chapter 11, some software interrupts trigger special programs that may take complete control of the computer. (Borland's SideKick is a good example of this type of program.) Efficiency becomes more a matter of packing features into as little space as possible than of operating speed, although speed remains important. To keep the entire system from bogging down, other services (such as a handler for keyboard characters or a clock handler that updates a screen display) must be extremely speed-efficient.

Interrupt service routines, or *handlers,* must be designed to minimize interaction with other programs, unless such interaction is a requirement for the specific handler. An example of a case in which such interaction *is* a requirement is Int 24h, the Critical Error handler. It is called only when DOS runs into an unpredictable problem while trying to perform input or output, and therefore *must* interact with the running program.

To understand how Int 24h affects the stack, you need to examine how DOS uses the stack. When an Int 21h function is invoked, the Int 21h handler pushes all CPU registers on the stack. DOS then uses an internal stack for its own purposes. If a critical error occurs, the user stack is selected again, but the register values pushed by Int 21h are left on the user stack. Then Int 24h is invoked and the resulting stack appears (see Fig. 3.5).

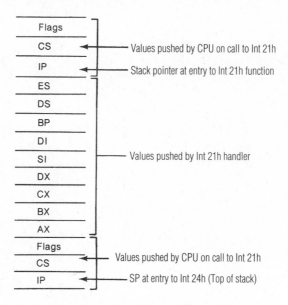

Figure 3.5 A stack on entry to Int 24h (the critical-error handler).

With all these registers available, you can easily determine where you were before the error occurred. The critical-error handler is extremely important. We all are familiar with its characteristic message:

```
Abort, Retry, Ignore?
```

(Note that in Version 3.3 it became the `Abort, Retry, Fail?` message.)

The error message usually tells you that a floppy disk drive is not ready. The default handler handles the situation in a straightforward, simple way. If you press *I* to ignore the error, control returns to the program and processing continues. If you press *R* (for Retry), the handler tries the function again to see whether the problem has been fixed. When you press *A* (for Abort), the handler aborts the process and returns to DOS. Beginning with Version 3.3, the Fail option, which forces DOS to return an error condition to the calling program, replaced the Ignore option.

You must be wary of DOS critical errors. If a critical error occurs during execution of a program that creates its own general interrupt handlers (such as a terminal program that creates an interrupt handler for the serial port), the program may be terminated *without* restoring its interrupt handlers to their previous state. Chaos can result. If an interrupt for one of the affected handlers occurs after such a happening, the system probably will lock up because no interrupt handler is available to deal with the data. The newer Fail option makes it possible to prevent such occurrences, but it cannot guarantee that they won't happen.

When you understand interrupts well enough to be able to add interrupt handlers for various conditions, you probably will want to write some of your own.

Interrupt handlers are not limited to dealing with an external event or processing a hardware function; they can do straight software work such as sorting and searching. There are several advantages to building a software package with standard utilities needed by a system. You might be writing a system that needs, for example, standard menu displays, command input controls, or search procedures. If the system involves several independent programs, you might include all the standard functions in a package accessed through a system interrupt. All the programs then have access to the same routines.

This approach has specific advantages. First, because the common routines are tied to an interrupt and are not compiled into each program, the programs are smaller. Second, because the functions are accessed through a common interrupt, you do not have to relink the individual programs when you change functions in the library.

A number of commercial programs, including Novell NetWare and the Btrieve file-management system, use exactly this approach. Many of them tie into the standard DOS function interrupt

(Int 21h) and add additional codes. A discussion of their codes is beyond the scope of this book; if you run into any strange high-numbered functions for Int 21h while browsing through software, however, they are probably parts of such systems.

The DOS function interrupt (Int 21h) is a collection of standard functions available to all programs that need them. Mouse functions (Int 33h) and expanded memory functions (Int 67h) are other examples of such collections. With the functions provided in this form, people do not have to change their programs when newer versions of the functions become available—they can continue using the same programs.

With a standard run-time package loaded in memory, you can share its resources with all your programs. When you change the package, all programs receive the change without your having to relink them. You can include interrupt handlers in a resident package and not have to worry about critical errors crashing the program. A handler always will be in the correct place. And, because memory-resident run-time routines do not have to be added to a compiled module, your compiled programs will be smaller and simpler to work with. One drawback to this type of package is that your library must be bug-free because bugs in an interrupt library are hard to find.

Most programs do not use this technique. Rather, they build programs with overlays; the common routines are in the master overlay, which is always resident (even for programs that do not use it). If you have a mouse, you already have some experience with this. You cannot UNLOAD the mouse driver after it has been loaded—the memory has already been used.

All these techniques are options. You can use them when appropriate, but you must be aware of the trade-offs.

Finally, let's look at another important topic: memory management.

Memory Allocation and Management

After the operating system is loaded and you are running programs, memory allocation becomes extremely important. Unless enough memory is available, you cannot even load your program. You must understand how to manage memory before you can understand how memory management affects your programs.

DOS organizes available memory as a pool of blocks that are chained together from bottom to top. This chain, or *memory arena*, includes all available memory. Every *memory block* (or *arena entry*) is made up of a 16-byte (one paragraph) *memory control block* and the memory controlled by that block. Table 3.3 shows how the control block is organized.

Table 3.3   The Memory Control Block

Byte	Meaning
00h	90h (Z) if last block
	77h (M) otherwise (Mark Zbikowski again?)
01h–02h	0 if the block is not allocated
	Process ID of owning process otherwise
03h–04h	Size of the block in paragraphs
05h–07h	Not used (DOS V4; 05h–15h not used previously)
08h–0Fh	File name (no extension) of owning program (DOS V4, only for programs run through EXEC; otherwise, unused)

Memory blocks are organized as a chain (or *linked list*) in which every memory control block represents a contiguous area of memory directly above the control block. Each control block points to the next control block in the chain (bytes 3–4 serve as this pointer). Figure 3.6 shows a conceptual picture of this memory-allocation chain. Starting from a DOS pointer to the first memory control block, each block gives the offset to the next block when it records the size of its own block. If two free blocks come together, DOS combines them in a single memory block. When they are separated by a block in use for some other reason (see Fig. 3.6), no attempt is made to relocate the information and reassign the block locations.

A block can be as small as a single paragraph (16 bytes) or as large as all available memory. DOS uses the blocks to assign memory to programs, as necessary.

When DOS receives a request for memory, it looks through the chain of memory blocks to find a block large enough to fill the request. If DOS finds a break in the chain or some other anomaly, it returns an error. If the calling program is COMMAND.COM trying to execute a program, for example, DOS displays the message Memory allocation error and then halts the system. You must reboot to recover.

When a request for memory can be filled, DOS uses one of the following memory-allocation strategies to return a block:

- *First fit.* DOS allocates the first memory block on the chain that is large enough to fill the request.

- *Best fit.* DOS allocates the smallest memory block that is large enough to fill the request.

- *Last fit.* DOS allocates the highest memory block large enough to fill the request.

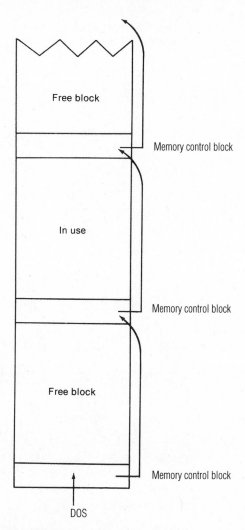

Figure 3.6 A chain of memory blocks.

The first-fit strategy, which minimizes the time spent searching for a block of memory, is the fastest—but it may fragment memory. When a block is assigned, it is divided into two blocks: one that exactly matches the request, and the remainder (which is returned to the chain for later use).

No matter which allocation strategy is used, if more than one block is in use at any given time, memory is fragmented into smaller and smaller blocks. A program that alternately grabs and frees blocks of memory can create free blocks surrounded by blocks in use. Requests for memory may fail when a program has created a large number of small blocks that cannot be recombined into a single block large enough to handle the request.

DOS
PROGRAMMING

Suppose that a program grabs all available memory in 16K blocks and then releases to the operating system ten of those blocks, none of which is next to another. Even though 160K of memory is available, a request for 32K of memory fails because no single block is large enough to handle the request.

This type of memory fragmentation can be a serious problem in some systems. DOS does not do any special clean-up (often called *garbage collection*) to move allocated blocks around to recover space. If this sort of problem is important for one of your programs, look in any good book on algorithms or data structures for information about garbage-collection techniques.

DOS provides access to the following three basic memory-allocation functions:

- *Allocate a memory block:* a function that requests assignment of a memory block to meet program requirements

- *Free memory block:* a function that returns a previously allocated memory block to the pool after the program has finished using it

- *Resize memory block:* a function that lets you make a previously allocated memory block larger or smaller, as needed; this function normally is called to shrink a program's memory block needed for a program to the smallest size possible

Beginning with DOS V3.2, you can use an additional function to determine the memory-allocation strategy. DOS defaults to the first-fit strategy, but the new function lets you override the default.

The most obvious use of the allocation functions is during program execution. When a program starts up, it receives memory for its operation. As you may recall from the discussion earlier in this chapter, a COM program gets all of the memory and an EXE program gets the amount requested. Let's see how that arrangement works in terms of the memory-allocation scheme.

When a COM program is executed, it is allocated all of the available memory in the first block large enough to hold the program, the PSP, and the stack (at least two bytes). Although all of the memory is not allocated directly to the COM program, it might as well be. Ordinarily, only one block is in the chain at program execution time, and that block holds all of the memory.

EXE programs, on the other hand, are allocated the amount of memory requested in the EXE program header's MAXALLOC field (maximum memory to allocate to the program), if that amount of memory is available. If the amount of memory specified in the MINALLOC field (minimum memory needed for the program to run) is not available, the program is not executed.

When a program is linked, the linker automatically sets the MAXALLOC field to FFFFh (1M), unless it is overridden by command-line switches to request a smaller amount of memory. Therefore, an EXE program (like a COM program) is allocated all of the memory on entry. You can override this allocation, however, and use command-line switches to request less than 1M of memory—you cannot do that with a COM program. Although most programmers do not bother with it, they should.

When you program in C, the program's start-up code (supplied with the compiler) ordinarily releases unused memory without your having to worry about it. Pascal and BASIC use all available memory for their data structures, but, beginning with Version 4.0, Turbo Pascal offered an option that lets you specify how much memory to use.

When you work in Pascal, a portion of memory set aside by the compiler is used for an area called the *heap*. This area of memory is used by the compiler for allocation of dynamic variables (those created in specific program blocks) and for memory allocated with the standard Pascal routines. If you want memory available for running other programs when you are using Pascal or BASIC, you have to tell the compiler to leave the space available.

This overall management scheme works well. Because programs usually occupy the highest available memory (parents usually are at a lower memory address, although TSRs do not have to be), the allocation scheme ordinarily results in all of the available memory being held in a single block—the largest (and usually the only) block. Inherent in this scheme, however, is the capability of allocating memory to multiple tasks that run concurrently.

Summary

This chapter has introduced the dynamics of DOS and has shown how the hardware and software elements of the system interact dynamically in operations such as the boot sequence, command processing, and program execution. You have learned that the ROM bootstrap code is executed automatically when the PC's CPU is powered up. That code, in turn, loads and transfers control to the bootstrap record, which then loads IO.SYS and MSDOS.SYS (or their PC DOS analogs, IBMBIO.COM and IBMDOS.COM). Those programs perform other work necessary to get the system up and running.

Command processing is a function of COMMAND.COM, the DOS shell. COMMAND.COM interprets user commands by searching its internal table for a command matching the user's command; if no match is found, COMMAND.COM then searches for an executable file with a name matching that of the user's command.

This chapter also discussed the differences between COM and EXE programs. Each has its advantages and disadvantages: COM programs are easier to code and faster to load but are limited in the code and data they can contain. EXE programs, on the other hand, are more complex and somewhat slower in loading but offer the programmer greater control over memory allocation and other parameters.

Interrupts, an important feature of the DOS landscape, were covered here also. Interrupt-driven control of the computer was compared with other methods, and its advantages were made clear. Interrupts are of four major types: internal interrupts, the non-maskable interrupt, hardware (or maskable interrupts), and software interrupts. Software interrupts are the principal programming interface to DOS.

Finally, you learned about DOS's memory-management functions. DOS manages memory as a series of blocks. Every memory block includes a memory-control block, which tells whether the memory block is allocated to a program and tells the location of the next block. DOS makes available three memory-allocation strategies, provides services for allocating, deallocating, and resizing memory blocks, and (in Version 3.2 and above) provides a function for determining the memory-allocation strategy.

Now you have learned the fundamentals of DOS as a system of dynamically interacting parts. In the next chapter, you learn about using DOS's capabilities in your own programs.

4

The DOS and BIOS Interface

This chapter shows how your programs can access the services available from the DOS kernel and the BIOS. To access these services, you can invoke software interrupts from any language, discussed in this book. You won't learn everything about accessing system resources, but you'll learn enough to get started.

This book focuses on four languages: assembly language, C (and C++), Pascal, and BASIC. The implementations described are Microsoft Macro Assembler, Microsoft C/C++, Borland C/C++, Turbo Pascal Version 7.1 (with a few notes about earlier versions), and Microsoft QuickBASIC. All four languages have features that let you directly access DOS and BIOS functions. But because not every necessary operation is provided by a built-in language feature, you have to code some operations yourself. In this chapter, you learn what is ready-made in the language you use, in addition to what you need to do for yourself and how to do it.

Accessing DOS and BIOS from Your Programs

To access DOS and BIOS resources, you follow these simple steps:

1. Load the CPU's registers with appropriate values.

2. Generate a software interrupt to invoke the desired system resource.

3. Interpret the results (if any) returned in the CPU's registers.

Ordinarily, the values loaded in the registers are either 8- or 16-bit numeric parameters or the addresses of larger data structures. All the languages discussed in this book provide a convenient means for loading the CPU's registers, generating interrupts, and reading the returned results. For a quick overview of the CPU's registers and their uses, refer to Chapter 2, "The Structure of a DOS System."

Figure 4.1 is a diagram of the contents of the CPU's registers immediately before and after a system call.

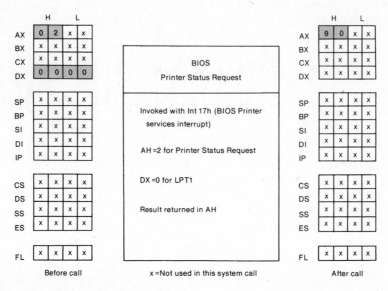

Figure 4.1　The contents of registers before and after a typical system call.

Depending on which resource you want to invoke, you may need to do some additional work before you load the registers and generate the interrupt. Many file-oriented services, for example, require your program to load registers with the segment:offset address of a string or other data structure before the interrupt is generated. (If you are not familiar with the segment:offset form of address representation, refer to the section "Memory Segmentation and the 8086" in Chapter 2.)

First, your program must get the data item's address. Getting an item's address is a relatively simple procedure; any complexity is partly a function of the language you use. For each language covered in this book, a section later in this chapter demonstrates techniques for getting addresses of data items.

The string or other item must be in the appropriate form. Many DOS functions that take string arguments require strings in *ASCIIZ* (ASCII plus zero) format: Characters are represented in their ASCII format, and the final character in the string is ASCII character zero (\0 in C, CHR$(0) in BASIC, and Chr(0) in Pascal). Figure 4.2 shows the structure of an ASCIIZ string.

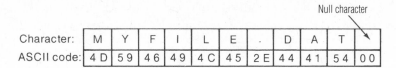

Figure 4.2 The structure of an ASCIIZ string.

If you program in C, you probably know that ASCIIZ is precisely the format in which the C language stores strings internally. In BASIC or Pascal, you have an extra step to perform to create an ASCIIZ string. The examples later in this chapter show how it is done.

Because assembly language provides the most direct access to the CPU and to system resources, the introductory examples in the following sections are in assembly language. For an introduction to the general principles of accessing DOS and BIOS resources, be sure to read the following subsections; the examples are clear, even if you are not fluent in assembly language.

Higher-level language resources for talking to the operating system are described later in this chapter. First, let's look at some simple assembly language examples that explore the DOS and BIOS interface.

A Simple Call to DOS

Each of the programming languages in this book has several services that provide access to the basic DOS and BIOS interrupts. The simplest of these languages is assembly language, which enables you to access the Int (interrupt) instruction directly to generate calls to BIOS or DOS functions.

The following code fragment, which uses Int 21h, Function 02h to output the character *X* to the console, is a typical call to DOS:

```
mov     ah,2        ; Character output function
mov     dl,'X'      ; Character X
int     21h         ; Execute DOS function interrupt
```

Int 21h, Function 02h is easy to use:

1. *Load the necessary registers with the appropriate values:* The value 2 is loaded in AH to select DOS Function 2 (Console Character Output). The character *X* is loaded in DL.

2. *Generate the interrupt:* The assembly language mnemonic Int is followed by the value 21h, the generic DOS interrupt number. Because Microsoft's Macro Assembler (MASM) is the standard by which assembler compatibility is measured, the Int instruction should be available with any assembler you choose.

Because Function 2 of Int 21h returns nothing, the third part of this DOS-call prototype is missing. The following example demonstrates the third step and illustrates basic techniques for obtaining and passing to DOS the addresses of data items "wider" than 16 bits.

Passing String Addresses to DOS

As mentioned, the CPU's registers often must be loaded with the segment and offset of data items larger than 16 bits. The following code fragment demonstrates one method for passing the address of a character string:

```
; Path_Name contains name of file to be opened
mov     ax,seg Path_Name         ; Segment address of path
mov     ds,ax                    ;    in DS
mov     dx,offset Path_Name      ; Offset address of path
mov     al,c2h                   ; Mode for opening file
mov     ah,3dh                   ; Open the file
int     21h                      ; DOS interrupt
jc      Error                    ; Carry set; there's an error
mov     File_Handle,ax           ; Save file handle
```

This code fragment uses Int 21h, Function 3Dh to open a file. This function requires that DS and DX contain the segment and offset, respectively, of the file's path name. The first three lines of the code fragment load the registers accordingly. The next line puts C2h into AL; the value in AL specifies the mode in which the file is to be opened. (The encoding of modes in this value is explained in the "DOS Reference" section of this book.) With registers properly loaded, the DOS interrupt is then generated.

Like many DOS services, this one sets the carry flag if the service fails (if the file could not be opened); the code therefore jumps to an error-handling routine if the carry flag is set (jc Error). If the carry flag is clear, however, indicating success in opening the file, the file handle (returned in AX) is stored to a memory location allocated for that purpose.

Note that the original DOS services (those that were provided in Version 1.0) do *not* use the carry flag to indicate an error. Like services in CP/M (the ancestor of DOS), they return their information in the AL register. Consistency has not always improved since Version 1.0, either; not all the services subsequently added use the carry flag to indicate an error. Some services (such as the Get PID service available in Version 3) are incapable of error because they merely return to the caller the content of a storage location used by DOS. These services sometimes clear the carry flag, but some DOS versions just return from the service with the flag in whatever state it had before DOS was called.

The point is that the carry flag should be relied on to indicate an error *only* if the called function is documented as using it to do so. If the function is not officially documented, see the reference section of this book to learn whether it returns error indications and, if so, how.

High-Level Language Resources

High-level languages offer many different ways to call DOS and BIOS routines. Each language has a unique method that does not resemble that of any other language. Even within the same language, different implementations and releases utilize differing methods. Turbo Pascal 3.0 provided no built-in means for accessing all files that match a wild-card file specification (such as C:\QTRLY\QTR?1993.DAT). To access such a group of files, you had to write two procedures: one that called DOS Int 21h, Function 4Eh to find the first file matching the specification and another that called Function 4Fh to find any remaining matching files. When Turbo Pascal 4.0 was introduced, it not only enabled the user to create such routines and store them in a run-time library but also provided the procedures FindFirst and FindNext for those purposes (in addition to many others in a run-time library "unit"). With the advent of Turbo Pascal 5.0, even the source code to these routines was made available (although at extra cost).

Each of the following sections presents two sample programs. For each language, the first sample program (a simple one that illustrates the basic operations required for accessing operating system resources) uses BIOS Int 17h, Function 2 to check the printer's status. The second example is a slightly more complex program that illustrates the interpretation of results returned from a system call.

The more complex example differs according to the language. In accordance with the philosophy that you should not do unnecessary work, the programming examples that have been chosen provide services you cannot get from the language. The BASIC examples show how to use DOS Int 21h, Functions 4Eh and 4Fh to retrieve file names that match a wild-card file specification, and assign those file names to BASIC variables. Because analogous functions are built into Turbo Pascal and C, the sample programs in those languages perform different actions. The Pascal example uses DOS Int 21h, Function 57h to get the date and time of a specified file. The C example uses DOS Int 21h, Function 43h to get and set file attributes (archive, hidden, system, and read-only). The examples use other functions as needed to perform necessary setup and cleanup work. Those ancillary function calls are described in the text and documented in the code.

Avoiding Unnecessary Work

Many high-level languages have predefined functions, procedures, or variables that provide ready-made access to system resources. In most cases, these language elements access the same DOS and BIOS functions you would work with directly if you had to implement the system call yourself; the people who implemented the languages already have built the code for you. If you are considering the use of system resources in a language that is new to you—or in a new implementation of a familiar language—make sure that you are not reinventing the wheel. A principle repeated in this book is that you should go to the system only when necessary. You should, therefore, use the built-in language resources unless your program has special needs the language resources do not answer.

continues

> *continued*
>
> Always read your manual carefully. This basic advice is worth repeating: *Read your manual!* Many programmers, particularly those who are new to a language or operating system, have spent hours or days on unnecessary work. If they had read their language manuals more carefully, they would not have wasted their time in programming resources that are already available.

The C Programming Language

For talking to an operating system, C is a programmer's delight. If you read the sections about other languages, you see that the high-level character of Pascal and BASIC often gets in your way when you want to get down to nuts and bolts. The languages obscure or limit your access to system-level data structures and other information you have to get your hands on when you access DOS and BIOS resources.

The C programming language, with its handy blend of high-level and low-level resources, has been described as "high-level assembly language." C lets you "think like a microprocessor" while sparing you the drudgery of a detailed setup for operations at the level of bits and bytes.

C has a similar relationship to the operating system: Many C functions are "DOS in C clothing." Those functions often take the same arguments as their DOS equivalents, and the same results are returned; indeed, the data structures accepted as input and returned as output often are identical to those used by their DOS equivalents.

Consequently, the more complex sample program in this section is presented in two versions: chmd.c calls DOS directly and chmc.c uses the equivalent C function. Only one version of the simpler example, called _pronok.c, is presented; the program provides a capability not directly available from the Borland C++ library.

The C programs in this section were developed with the Borland C/C++ compiler. For information concerning the differences between Borland C++ and Microsoft C, be sure to read the comments in the listings and code fragments.

Accessing Registers and Generating Interrupts

The principal data structures for the interface between C and DOS are defined by the REGS union and the SREGS and REGPACK structures. These objects are declared in the header file DOS.H. Their declarations are shown in the following code fragment:

```
struct WORDREGS {
    unsigned int  ax, bx, cx, dx, si, di, cflag, flags;
};

/*Microsoft C lacks flags element */
```

```
struct BYTEREGS {
    unsigned char al, ah, bl, bh, cl, ch, dl, dh;
};
union REGS {
    struct WORDREGS x;
    struct BYTEREGS h;
};

struct SREGS {
    unsigned int es;
    unsigned int cs;
    unsigned int ss;
    unsigned int ds;
};

struct REGPACK {        /* Not defined in Microsoft C */
    unsigned r_ax, r_bx, r_cx, r_dx;
    unsigned r_bp, r_si, r_di, r_ds,  r_es,  r_flags;
};
```

In addition, the contents of the CPU registers are available in Borland C++ through the pseudovariables _AX, _AL, _AH, and so on. Each of the 8086's general-purpose, offset, and segment registers (except IP) has a corresponding pseudovariable. Variables corresponding to the 16-bit and 8-bit registers are used (but not declared) as though they were of type `unsigned int` and `unsigned char`, respectively:

```
unsigned int _AX;
unsigned char _AL;
```

These declarations should *not* be included in your programs.

The pseudovariables described in the preceding paragraph are not available in Microsoft C. Because their absence necessitates small changes in the programs at some points, be sure to read the comments in the listings if you want to adapt the code for Microsoft's C compiler.

The DOS.H header file contains the following prototypes of the C functions for generating software interrupts:

```
int int86 (int intno, union REGS *inregs,
                       union REGS *outregs);
int int86x (int intno, union REGS *inregs,
                        union REGS *outregs,
                             struct SREGS *segregs);
int intdos (union REGS *inregs,
            union REGS *outregs);
int intdosx (union REGS *inregs,
             union REGS *outregs,
             struct SREGS *segregs);

void intr (int int_type, struct REGPACK *preg);
```

The `intdos()` function generates Int 21h, the principal DOS interrupt; `int86()` and `intr()` generate the interrupt specified by the function's first argument (`intno` or `int_type`). Each `intdos` and `int86` has an *x* version that uses the segment registers in addition to the general-purpose and offset registers. The `intr()` function is not available in Microsoft C.

PRNOK.C, shown in Listing 4.1, demonstrates the use of the `int86()` function to verify that LPT1 is on-line.

Listing 4.1

```
/* prnok.c
   Listing 4.1 of DOS Programmer's Reference */

#include <conio.h>
#include <dos.h>

#define PRN_INT 0x17  /* Printer-services interrupt    */
#define STAT_RQ 0x02  /* Status-request service number */

int prnok(void)
{
    union REGS regs;

    regs.h.ah = STAT_RQ;   /* AH = 02 for printer status */
    regs.x.dx = 0;         /* DX = 00 for LPT1 */

    int86(PRN_INT, &regs, &regs);

    return( ((regs.h.ah & 0x80) == 0x80 ) ? 1 : 0 );
}

main()
{
    if (prnok())
        cputs("Ready to print!\n");
    else
        cputs("Please check the printer!\n");
}
```

A Note About the BIOS Printer-Status Request

The first sample program for each language uses BIOS Int 17h, Function 2 to verify that LPT1 is on-line. For this function, put 2 in AH and the printer number (0 for LPT1, 1 for LPT2, and so on) in DX. The function returns the printer's status, encoded in the bits of AH as follows:

Bit	Meaning (if set)
0	Time-out
1	Unused
2	Unused
3	I/O error
4	Printer is selected
5	Out of paper
6	Acknowledge
7	Printer not busy

The meanings of bit 0 and bits 3 through 7 are well defined, but the two hardware configurations that were tested do not return the same result for the same condition. In every test case, the high bit of AH was set when the printer was powered up and on-line. On a Toshiba P351 printer connected to an IBM Personal System/2 Model 50, however, the program reports `Ready to print` when the printer is connected but not powered up. On an Epson RX-80 printer connected to a COMPAQ Portable Computer, the program responds with the message `Please check the printer!` if the printer is connected but powered down. This is just a demo routine; a program with truly powerful status-checking capabilities needs more sophisticated logic.

Getting and Setting File Attributes

This section presents two sample C programs for changing the attributes of a specified file. These programs resemble the useful FA (file attribute) program included in the Norton Utilities; they differ from FA in that they accept only a literal file name, not a file specification containing wild-card characters. To keep the code as simple as possible, options are not included for simply inquiring about the file's attributes or for changing more than one attribute at a time. The programs, which expect a command-line argument specifying an attribute to be set or cleared, terminate with an error message if an invalid argument is given.

If you are proficient in C programming, you should have no difficulty adding further options (such as "inquire") to the capabilities of this program. The information provided throughout this book makes it easy to add a capability for processing files specified by a wild card.

The two sample programs differ in that one calls the DOS interrupt directly, whereas the other uses a corresponding C library function to call the interrupt. The first example, shown in Listing 4.2, makes a direct call to DOS Int 21h, Function 43h.

Listing 4.2

```
/* chmod.c
   Listing 4.2 of DOS Programmer's Reference */

#include <conio.h>
#include <stdio.h>
#include <ctype.h>
#include <process.h>
#include <dos.h>
#include "attrmask.h"                    /* Omit for Turbo C 2.0 */

#define GS_FATTR    0x43
#define GET_FATTR   0x00
#define SET_FATTR   0x01
/* For Turbo C 2.0, add these #define statements:
        define ARCHIVE_BIT  FA_ARCH
        define HIDDEN_BIT   FA_HIDDEN
        define RDONLY_BIT   FA_RDONLY
        define SYSTEM_BIT   FA_SYSTEM
*/

typedef enum { clr, set } clrorset;

void showattr(int attr);
int parsearg(char *thearg, clrorset *action, char *selection);

main( int argc, char *argv[] )
{
    extern char *sys_errlist[];    /* Provided by Turbo C */
    extern int errno;              /* Ditto              */

    union REGS regs;
    struct SREGS sregs;

    clrorset action;
    char selection;

    unsigned attrib, setting;
    int goahead;

    if (argc == 3) goahead = parsearg(argv[2], &action, &selection);
    else goahead = 0;

    if (!goahead)
        {
        if (argc == 3)
                {
                cputs("Can't parse ");
                cputs(argv[2]);
                }
```

```
        else
                cputs("No input");
        exit(1);
    }

    switch(selection) {
        case 'A': setting = ARCHIVE_BIT; break;
        case 'H': setting = HIDDEN_BIT;  break;
        case 'R': setting = RDONLY_BIT;  break;
        case 'S': setting = SYSTEM_BIT;  break;
        default:
            cputs("Bad input: "); cputs(argv[2]); cputs("\n\r");
            exit(1);
    }

    regs.h.ah = GS_FATTR;
    regs.h.al = GET_FATTR;
    regs.x.dx = (unsigned) argv[1];      /* Offset of first argument */
    sregs.ds  = _DS;
/* --------------------
   For Microsoft C, use the following in place of the preceding line:
        segread(&sregs);
*/

    intdosx(&regs,&regs,&sregs);  /* Get the current attribute word */

    if (!regs.x.cflag) {          /* If carry is clear, success    */
        attrib = regs.x.cx;
        cputs("------------ Initial -----------\n\r");
        showattr(attrib);

        if (action == clr) {
            setting = ( (~setting)&attrib );
        } else {
            setting = (setting | attrib);
        }

        regs.h.ah = GS_FATTR;
        regs.h.al = SET_FATTR;
        regs.x.cx = setting;
        regs.x.dx = (unsigned) argv[1];
        sregs.ds  = _DS;
/* --------------------
   For Microsoft C, use the following in place of the preceding line:
        segread(&sregs);
*/

        intdosx(&regs,&regs,&sregs);  /* Set the attribute */

        attrib = regs.x.cx;
        cputs("------------ Final -----------\n\r");
```

continues

91

Listing 4.2 Continued

```
        showattr(attrib);

    } else {          /* That is, if carry is not set */
        char *msg;
        cputs("function 0x43 failed: ");
        switch (regs.x.ax) {
            case 1:  msg = "Bad function code\n"; break;
            case 2:  msg = "Bad file name\n"; break;
            case 3:  msg = "Bad path\n"; break;
            case 5:  msg = "Can't change attribute\n"; break;
            default: msg = "Unknown cause\n";
        }
        cputs(msg);
    }
} /* End main */
```

Int 21h, Function 43h takes the following input:

Register	Value
AH	43h
AL	0 to get file attribute, 1 to set file attribute
DS:DX	Segment:offset address of the file path name

The program uses `#define` preprocessor directives to "name" the DOS function and the desired action (get or set). The file path name is provided as a command-line argument.

For a program compiled under the small memory model in Turbo C, you use the following statements to put the path name's segment and offset into DS and DX:

```
regs.x.dx = (unsigned) argv[1];
sregs.ds  = _DS;
```

Other methods of assignment may be necessary in other memory models. Because Microsoft C lacks register pseudovariables, the following statement:

```
segread(&sregs);
```

should be used instead.

If the operation is successful, the carry flag is clear and CX contains the file's attribute word. Bits of the attribute word and their corresponding attributes are shown in this table:

Bit	Meaning (If Set)
0	Read only
1	Hidden
2	System
5	Archive

If the bit is set, the file has the corresponding attribute. (A set archive bit means that the file has not been backed up since the file was created or last modified.)

For convenience and legibility, #define directives are used also to create bit masks for the meaningful bits of the attribute word. (These definitions are in the ATTRMASK.H file; see the following code fragment.) The bit masks are used for changing and reading the file-attribute word.

```
/* attrmask.h - from Chapter 4 of DOS Programmer's Reference   */

#define ARCHIVE_BIT 0x20  /* Bit 5 of CX is the archive bit   */
#define SYSTEM_BIT  0x04  /* Bit 2 of CX is the system bit    */
#define HIDDEN_BIT  0x02  /* Bit 1 of CX is the hidden bit    */
#define RDONLY_BIT  0x01  /* Bit 0 of CX is the read-only bit */
```

Listings 4.3 and 4.4 show miscellaneous functions used by the two versions of the second sample program.

Listing 4.3

```
/* parsarg.c
   Listing 4.3 of DOS Programmer's Reference */

#include <conio.h>
#include <ctype.h>

typedef enum { clr, set } clrorset;

int parsearg(char *thearg, clrorset *action, char *selection)
{
    if (*(thearg) == '/') {
        switch( *(thearg+2) ) {
            case '+':
                *action = set; break;
            case '-':
                *action = clr; break;
```

continues

93

Listing 4.3   Continued

```
                default:
                    cputs("Use '+' to set or '-' to clear\n\r");
                    return(0);
            }
            *selection = toupper(*(thearg+1));
            return(1);
    } else {
        cputs("Usage: chmd filename /xy\n\r"
                "where x = A (archive) or H (hidden) or\n\r"
                "          R (read-only) or S (system),\n\r"
                " and y = + (set) or - (clear)\n\r");
        return(0);
    }
}
```

Listing 4.4

```
/* showatr1.c
   Listing 4.4 of DOS Programmer's Reference */

#include <conio.h>
#include "attrmask.h"

#define CLEAR 0
#define isclear(x,y) ((x&y)==CLEAR)      /* Parens around x, y ? */
#define putstat(x,y) cputs( isclear(x,y) ? "clear   " : "set     " )

void showattr(int attr)
{
    cputs("Archive System  Hidden  Read-only\n\r");

    putstat(attr,ARCHIVE_BIT);
    putstat(attr,SYSTEM_BIT);
    putstat(attr,HIDDEN_BIT);
    putstat(attr,RDONLY_BIT);
    cputs("\n\r");
}
```

If you compare Listing 4.2 (the first version of this program) to Listing 4.5 (the second version), you can see that error checking is slightly more sophisticated in a program that uses the interrupt rather than the C library function. Because of differences in the libraries, this program compiles under Turbo C only. Modifications are necessary for Microsoft C, which lacks the _chmod function.

Listing 4.5

```
/* chmod2.c
   Listing 4.5 of DOS Programmer's Reference */

#include <conio.h>
#include <stdio.h>
#include <io.h>
#include <ctype.h>
#include <process.h>
#include "attrmask.h"

#define GET_FATTR   0x00
#define SET_FATTR   0x01

typedef enum { clr, set } clrorset;

void showattr(int attr);         /* Show file attribute       */
int parsearg(char *thearg,       /* Parse command-line argument */
             clrorset *action,   /* Clear or set attribute    */
             char *selection);   /* Selected attribute        */

main( int argc, char *argv[] )
{
    extern char *sys_errlist[];  /* Provided by Turbo C  */
    extern int errno;            /* Ditto                */

    clrorset action;
    char selection;

    unsigned attrib, setting;
    int goahead;

    if (argc == 3) goahead = parsearg(argv[2], &action, &selection);

    if (!goahead)
        {
        if (argc == 3)
            {
            cputs("Can't parse ");
            cputs(argv[2]);
            }
        else
            cputs("No input");
        exit(1);
    }

    switch(selection) {
        case 'A': setting = ARCHIVE_BIT; break;
        case 'H': setting = HIDDEN_BIT;  break;
        case 'R': setting = RDONLY_BIT;  break;
        case 'S': setting = SYSTEM_BIT;  break;
        default:
            cputs("Bad input: "); cputs(argv[2]); cputs("\n\r");
            exit(1);
    }
```

continues

Listing 4.5 Continued

```
        attrib = chmod(argv[1], GET_FATTR );

    if (attrib != 0xFFFF) {
        cputs("----------- Initial -----------\n\r");
        showattr(attrib);
        if (action == clr) {
            setting = ( (~setting)&attrib );
        } else {
            setting = (setting ¦ attrib);
        }
        attrib = chmod(argv[1], SET_FATTR, setting );
        cputs("------------ Final ------------\n\r");

        showattr(attrib);
    } else {
        cputs("function _chmod failed:\n\r");
        cputs(sys_errlist[errno]); cputs("\n\r");
    }
} /* end main */
```

Notice that the chmod() C library function returns the file-attribute word as a functional return value (with −1 signaling an error), whereas Int 21h, Function 43h returns the attribute word in register CX and signals an error (as do most DOS functions) by setting the carry flag. Because the results returned by the C library function are the same as those returned in CX by the DOS function, you can use the showattr() function to decode the attribute word for both programs.

Turbo Pascal

Version 4.0 of Turbo Pascal improved on Version 3.0, which provided excellent support for calling DOS and BIOS functions. The subsequent step to Version 5.0 restored several useful features lost during the step from Version 3 to Version 4 and added for the first time a built-in debugger, which is a great help in complex programs. Version 5.5 added object-oriented programming capabilities to Turbo Pascal and support for math coprocessors. Version 6.0 added TurboVision, an object-oriented application framework for DOS programs, and an enhanced development environment. Version 7.0 continued adding functionality in addition to support for Windows.

The language has an extensive set of built-in facilities that provide access to system resources and minimize the need for programmers to write their own system-level code.

The file and console input/output functions meet almost any programming need; most common file and directory operations (get file size, get current directory, change directory, make directory, and so on) are fully supported. As mentioned earlier in this chapter, Versions 4.0 and 5.0 simplify the writing of programs that process a group of files selected by a wild-card file specification.

So complete is this collection of resources that you would have difficulty finding a DOS or BIOS service you would want to call directly from your program. Why call DOS or the BIOS for console input and output when Turbo Pascal has a full complement of functions and procedures for those operations?

The time may come, however—if it hasn't already—when your program needs something the language does not provide. This section therefore presents two sample programs that make direct calls to DOS and the BIOS. For tutorial purposes, the programs duplicate operations available on a higher level, in Turbo Pascal itself.

The first of these programs uses BIOS Int 17h, Function 2 to verify that the printer is on-line. (Similar results—with equally sophisticated error checking—are available through the language's built-in procedures and functions.) The second sample program, which also duplicates a function built into Turbo Pascal 4.0, gets a file's date and time of creation or most recent modification.

Accessing Registers and Generating Interrupts

Turbo Pascal's main data structure for accessing registers is the Registers record. The structure of this record, which is defined in the Dos unit of Turbo Pascal 4.0, is shown in the following lines of code; in Version 3.0, the record must be user-defined:

```
Type
{ Registers record used by Intr and MsDos }
    Registers = Record
        Case Integer of
            0: (AX,BX,CX,DX,BP,SI,DI,DS,ES,Flags : Word);
            1: (AL,AH,BL,BH,CL,CH,DL,DH : Byte)
        End;<RS>
```

Turbo Pascal has the following two procedures for generating interrupts:

```
MsDos(vars Regs :  Registers)
Intr(IntNo : Byte; vars Regs : Registers)
```

MsDos generates Int 21h, the "generic" DOS interrupt. Intr can generate *any* software interrupt, including 21h. (In Version 3.0, the first argument of Intr is an integer.)

The first sample Turbo Pascal program, in Listing 4.6, demonstrates a simple call to the BIOS. The PrinterOnline function invokes BIOS Int 17h, Function 2 (Printer Status Request) to verify that the printer is on-line. Function 2 returns in AH a byte that indicates whether the printer is busy, selected, out of paper, and so on. (Be sure to see the note about this BIOS interrupt in the section "High-Level Language Resources," earlier in this chapter.) This program, however, checks only bit 7 of AH; if the bit is set, the printer is selected.

DOS
PROGRAMMING

Listing 4.6

```
{ PRTRDEMO.PAS                                   }
{ Listing 4.6 in DOS Programmer's Reference   }
{ =========================================== }
Program PrinterDemo;
Uses Dos;

    Function PrinterOnline : Boolean;
        Const
            PrnStatusInt : Byte = $17;
            StatusRequest : Byte = $02;
            PrinterNum : Word = 0; { 0 for LPT1, 1 for LPT2, etc. }
        Var
            Regs : Registers;        { Type is defined in Dos unit. }
    Begin
    Regs.AH := StatusRequest;
    Regs.DX := PrinterNum;
    Intr(PrnStatusInt, Regs);
    PrinterOnline := (Regs.AH and $80) = $80
    End;

Begin                  { Program }
If PrinterOnline Then
    WriteLn('Ready to print!')
Else
    WriteLn('Please check the printer!')
End.
```

Reading a File's Date and Time Stamp

The date and time that you created or last modified a file are available through DOS Int 21h, Function 57h. The GetDateAndTime Pascal procedure demonstrates that DOS function's use (see Listing 4.7).

Listing 4.7

```
{ GETDTTM.PAS                                     }
{ Listing 4.7 in DOS Programmer's Reference    }
{ Designed to be called from FILEDTTM.PAS      }
{ =========================================== }
Procedure GetDateAndTime(Pathname : PathStr;
                     Var DateWord, TimeWord : Word);
    Const
        GetDateAndTime : Byte = $57;
        CloseFile : Byte = $3E;
    Var
        Regs : Registers;
        Handle : Word;

    Function CarryClear(Regs : Registers) : Boolean;
```

```
    Begin CarryClear := ((Regs.Flags and 1) = 0) End;

    { ============================================ }
    Function GetFileHandle(Pathname : PathStr) : Word;
        Const GetHandle : Byte = $3D; ReadAccess : Byte = 0;
        Var PathSeg, PathOfs : Word;
    Begin
    Pathname := Pathname + Chr(0);
    PathSeg := Seg(Pathname[1]);  PathOfs := Ofs(Pathname[1]);

    Regs.AH := GetHandle; Regs.AL := ReadAccess;
    Regs.DS := PathSeg;   Regs.DX := PathOfs;
    MsDos(Regs);
    If CarryClear(Regs) Then
        GetFileHandle := Regs.AX   { No semicolon before Else! }
    Else
        Begin
        WriteLn('Handle function failed!');
        Exit
        End; { If carry is clear }
    End;                   { Function GetFileHandle }


{ ==================================================== }
Begin                          { Procedure GetDateAndTime }

Handle := GetFileHandle(Pathname);

Regs.AH := GetDateAndTime; Regs.AL := 0;  Regs.BX := Handle;
MsDos(Regs);
If CarryClear(Regs) Then
    Begin  DateWord := Regs.DX;  TimeWord := Regs.CX  End
Else
    Begin
    DateWord := 0; TimeWord := 0; { Error flag for caller }
    End;
Regs.AH := CloseFile;    Regs.BX := Handle;
MsDos(Regs);
If NOT CarryClear(Regs) Then
    WriteLn(
        'Warning: Procedure GetDateAndTime did not close ',
        pathname)
End;          { Procedure GetDateAndTime }
```

The principal input item for Function 57h is a file handle. Turbo Pascal has a full complement of file-oriented procedures and functions, but the system-level details of Turbo's file management are concealed from the programmer. To use Function 57h, the GetDateAndTime procedure must "go around" Turbo's normal file-management routines. Therefore, rather than use Pascal's procedures for opening a file (Assign and either Reset or Rewrite), the function calls DOS Int 21h, Function 3Dh. This system call is performed by the GetFileHandle function, which is nested in the GetDateAndTime procedure.

Function 3Dh requires the address of an ASCIIZ string that contains the file's path name. Because Turbo Pascal strings are not terminated by a zero byte, the function appends Chr(0) to the string Pathname. Because the length byte at the first position in the Turbo Pascal string

99

must not be included in the string argument passed to Function 3Dh, the address of `Pathname[1]` is passed to the function. The `Seg` and `Ofs` functions give straightforward access to the components of the string's address.

Having obtained the file handle, the `GetDateAndTime` procedure passes it to DOS Function 57h. The AL register is set to 0, signaling that the DOS function should get (not set) the file's date and time. If Function 57h succeeds (as indicated by a clear carry flag), it returns the file's encoded time and date in CX and DX, respectively.

FILEDTTM.PAS, the program shown in Listing 4.8, demonstrates the use of the Turbo Pascal `GetDateAndTime` function.

Listing 4.8

```
{ FILEDTTM.PAS                                 }
{ Listing 4.8 in DOS Programmer's Reference    }
{ ============================================ }
Program FileDateAndTime;

    Uses Dos;
    Type
        PathNameType = String[64];
        String5 = String[5];
        { Max DOS path is 63; add 1 for the null. }

    Var
        Pathname : PathNameType;
        DateWord, TimeWord : Word;    { Use Integer in 3.0 }
        Hours, Mins, Secs, Year, Month, Day : Integer;

        Ch : Char;

{$i GETDTTM.PAS}
{ ============================================ }
Begin                             { Program }

Write('Pathname? >');  ReadLn(Pathname);
GetDateAndTime(Pathname, DateWord, TimeWord);
If (DateWord <> 0) Then
    Begin
    { Decode date }
    Year  := ((DateWord AND $FE00) SHR  9) + 1980;
    Month := (DateWord AND $01E0) SHR  5;
    Day   := (DateWord AND $001F);

    { Decode time }
    Hours := (TimeWord AND $F800) SHR 11;
    Mins  := (TimeWord AND $07E0) SHR  5;
    Secs  := (TimeWord AND $001F) SHL  1; { Shift left to double }

    WriteLn('File Time: ', Hours:2,':', Mins:02,  ':', Secs:2);
```

```
    WriteLn('File Date: ', Year:4, '/', Month:02, '/', Day:2);

    End                     { No semicolon before Else }
Else
    WriteLn('GetDateAndTime has failed!');

End.
```

QuickBASIC

QuickBASIC includes the familiar file-oriented statements of its forerunners, BASICA and GW-BASIC. The KILL FileName$ statement deletes files, CHDIR changes the current directory, and so on. Input and output routines are flexible.

BASIC's file-handling capabilities are lacking in some respects, however. For instance, the procedure for processing file names that match a wild-card file specification (with * or ?) is convoluted. You have to monkey around with passing a DOS command to the SHELL, directing the command's output to a file, and reading the output file into your program one line at a time, parsing file names (and skipping superfluous lines) as you go. Empty disk drives, write-protect tabs, and full disks can bring your program to an abrupt halt. And, how do you *know* that the name you are using for SHELL's output is not the same as that of an existing file?

By programming at the DOS level, you can avoid all that hassle. The second sample program in this section shows how to call DOS Int 21h, Functions 4Eh and 4Fh to find the names of all files that match a file specification, which may contain one or more wild-card characters. (Some of the best uses of programming at the DOS level not only make programming convenient but also make running your programs more convenient for the user.)

First, let's look at a simple program that introduces the fundamentals of calling DOS from BASIC. This first QuickBASIC example (like those in the other languages) uses BIOS Int 17h, Function 2 to verify that the printer is on-line.

Accessing Registers and Generating Interrupts

QuickBASIC's principal data structure for the DOS and BIOS interface is the Registers record:

```
TYPE Registers
    AX AS INTEGER
    BX AS INTEGER
    CX AS INTEGER
    DX AS INTEGER
    BP AS INTEGER
    SI AS INTEGER
    DI AS INTEGER
    SI AS INTEGER
    FLAGS AS INTEGER
    DS AS INTEGER
    ES AS INTEGER
END TYPE
```

101

Register-type variables are declared by means of the DIM statement:

```
DIM InRegs AS Registers, OutRegs AS Registers
```

Because these variables obey the normal rules regarding scope, they can be declared as local to procedures.

QuickBASIC has the following two built-in procedures for generating interrupts:

```
CALL INTERRUPT(IntNumber, InRegs, OutRegs)

CALL INTERRUPTX(IntNumber, InRegs, OutRegs)
```

CALL INTERRUPT ignores the DS and ES registers (or the DS and ES fields of the Registers arguments), whereas CALL INTERRUPTX uses these registers or fields. If you want to leave DS and ES unchanged in a call to INTERRUPTX, assign the value –1 to the record's DS and ES fields.

Listing 4.9 demonstrates the use of the BIOS Printer Status Request function. Because the results of this function are not entirely consistent across hardware configurations, be sure to read "A Note about the BIOS Printer-Status Request" (in this chapter's section on C) if you want to use the function in a program.

Listing 4.9

```
'PRNOK.BAS - Listing 4.9 in DOS Programmer's Reference

CONST PRN.Status.rq% = &H200         '2 in AH
CONST BIOS.PRN.INT% = &H17

TYPE Registers
     AX AS INTEGER
     BX AS INTEGER
     CX AS INTEGER
     DX AS INTEGER
     BP AS INTEGER
     SI AS INTEGER
     DI AS INTEGER
     FLAGS AS INTEGER
     DS AS INTEGER
     ES AS INTEGER
END TYPE

DIM InRegs AS Registers, OutRegs AS Registers

InRegs.AX = PRN.Status.rq%

CALL INTERRUPT(BIOS.PRN.INT%, InRegs, OutRegs)

IF ((OutRegs.AX AND &H8000) = &H8000) THEN
    PRINT "Printer OK"
ELSE
    PRINT "Please check the printer"
END IF

END        'PROGRAM
```

Finding Files That Match a File Specification

Frequently, sophisticated programs must process groups of files described by wild-card file specifications. QuickBASIC does not provide a built-in facility for finding the file names that match a user-supplied file specification; by building such a facility, you can make the language much more useful.

The DOS resources for using file specifications are Functions 4Eh (Find First) and 4Fh (Find Next) of Int 21h. These functions find, respectively, the first matching file name and any remaining matching names. Both place their output—the file names and other information—in the DTA (disk transfer area). By default, the DTA is a 128-byte buffer at offset 80h in the program segment prefix. The sample program presented in this section, however, uses DOS Function 1Ah to set a different DTA address, to avoid any possibility of interference with other DOS functions.

Most BASIC implementations, QuickBASIC included, do not store strings at a fixed location. A 4-byte string descriptor keeps track of each string's location. The descriptor contains a 16-bit pointer to the string; this pointer contains the string's offset into the default data area. You do not have to bother with locating this descriptor and retrieving the address because the following QuickBASIC function:

```
SADD(TheString$)
```

returns the offset of the string supplied as an argument. (If you need to access the string descriptor, you can retrieve its segment and offset with the VARSEG and VARPTR functions.) SADD should be called immediately before your program accesses the string because a string can be "moved around" in memory during program execution, especially if your program changes the string's length.

The program in Listing 4.10 demonstrates the use of Functions 4Eh and 4Fh to retrieve file names that match a file specification.

Listing 4.10

```
'FILEDEMO.BAS - Listing 4.10 from DOS Programmer's Reference

DECLARE SUB SetDTA (TheDTA$)
DECLARE SUB FindFirst (FileSpec$, FileName$)
DECLARE SUB FindNext (FileName$)
DECLARE SUB BuildName (TheName$)

TYPE Registers
    AX AS INTEGER
    BX AS INTEGER
    CX AS INTEGER
    DX AS INTEGER
    BP AS INTEGER
    SI AS INTEGER
```

continues

Listing 4.10   Continued

```
            DI AS INTEGER
            FLAGS AS INTEGER
            DS AS INTEGER
            ES AS INTEGER
     END TYPE

     DTA$ = SPACE$(43)

     LINE INPUT "Filespec? >", FileSpec$

     CALL SetDTA(DTA$)

     ' Get the first matching file name
     CALL FindFirst((FileSpec$), FileName$)

     IF FileName$ <> "" THEN
        PRINT "First match: "; FileName$
        DO
          CALL FindNext(FileName$)
          IF FileName$ <> "" THEN
             PRINT " Next match: "; FileName$
          END IF
        LOOP UNTIL FileName$ = ""
     ELSE
        PRINT "No files match "; FileSpec$
     END IF

     END             ' PROGRAM

     ' ===== Subroutines =====

     SUB BuildName (TheName$)
         SHARED DTA$
         EndOfStr% = INSTR(31, DTA$, CHR$(0))
         TheName$ = MID$(DTA$, 31, EndOfStr% - 31)
     END SUB

     SUB FindFirst (FileSpec$, FileName$)
         FileSpec$ = FileSpec$ + CHR$(0)     'make ASCIIZ
         DIM InRegs AS Registers, OutRegs AS Registers
         InRegs.AX = &H4E00              'find first matching file
         InRegs.DX = SADD(FileSpec$)     'offset of FileSpec$
         InRegs.DS = VARSEG(FileSpec$)   'seg of FileSpec$
         InRegs.CX = 0                   'normal files only--no dirs, etc.
         CALL INTERRUPT(&H21, InRegs, OutRegs)
```

```
                ' Got a match? Yes, if CARRY FLAG (bit 0 of FLAGS) is clear.
                IF (OutRegs.FLAGS AND 1) = 0 THEN
                   CALL BuildName(FileName$):
                ELSE
                   FileName$ = ""
                END IF
        END SUB

        SUB FindNext (FileName$)
            DIM InRegs AS Registers, OutRegs AS Registers
            InRegs.AX = &H4F00                'find next matching file
            CALL INTERRUPT(&H21, InRegs, OutRegs)
            IF (OutRegs.FLAGS AND 1) = 0 THEN
               CALL BuildName(FileName$):
            ELSE
               FileName$ = ""
            END IF
        END SUB

        SUB SetDTA (DTA$)
            DIM InRegs AS Registers, OutRegs AS Registers
            ' Set the Disk Transfer Area address
            InRegs.DX = SADD(DTA$)            'offset of DTA
            InRegs.DS = VARSEG(DTA$)          'segment of DTA
            InRegs.AX = &H1A00                'DOS function for setting DTA addr
            CALL INTERRUPT(&H21, InRegs, OutRegs)
            ' no return value for function &H1A
        END SUB
```

The following procedure:

```
    SetDTA(TheDTA$)
```

sets the disk transfer area address to the address of its string argument.

The following procedures:

```
    FindFirst(FileSpec$, FileName$)
```

and

```
    FindNext(FileName$)
```

locate the matching file names. If matching file names are found, both procedures assign the matching name to `FileName$`; if matching names are not found, they assign the empty string (" "). Although the sample program simply displays the file names, you can have your program do whatever you want with the returned values.

Summary

This chapter introduced the fundamentals of system-level programming in assembly language, C, Pascal, and BASIC. The procedure for accessing DOS and BIOS resources has three major components:

- Loading registers with appropriate values

- Generating a software interrupt

- Interpreting the results returned in registers

Sometimes additional work is needed, such as when your program must pass to the system the address of a string or other data item. Each language offers resources for getting the addresses of items; the simplicity of using addresses varies according to the language.

If you have read the sections about each language (not just about your language of choice), you probably have noticed that the languages differ greatly in the convenience and the amount of support they provide for accessing DOS and BIOS resources. You may want to consider these differences when you choose a language for your next programming project.

Part II

Character Devices and Serial Devices

5

Output Devices

This chapter discusses the video display and the printer, the two fundamental output devices. They are perhaps the most important devices in computer programming because they serve as the interaction points between the program and the programmer.

Most computer books treat the auxiliary devices (the RS-232 ports) as character-output devices and describe them in chapters similar to this one. In this book, however, RS-232 ports are treated separately because of their unique nature and diverse capabilities (see Chapter 7, "Serial Devices").

Like other chapters, this one emphasizes the utility of working with the highest available coding level to complete a task. Generally, you should use a service available directly from a high-level language; in many situations, however, you must go lower, to either the DOS or BIOS level, to perform specific tasks. This chapter describes the DOS and BIOS services that control the video display and printer.

Basic Character Devices

Programming the video display and the printer can be a simple procedure or an extremely sophisticated one. Beyond the level of simple character I/O, programming can quickly become a complex process, particularly when you work with graphics.

Although this book is not a comprehensive manual about graphics, it provides the basic principles for working with graphics. In this chapter, useful routines for system programming are developed and, most important, useful tools for working with output are constructed.

In C, services already available for working with the display and printer are adequate for typical programming chores. When you build a program, these services generally are the best ones to use, for two reasons:

- By using standard library functions, you reduce your program's sensitivity to changes in DOS design.

- If standard calls are used properly, they can make your program compatible with UNIX or XENIX systems.

If you need to move beyond the level of standard library functions, you must balance carefully what might be lost against what might be gained. By moving from standard library functions to DOS services, you gain great control over output operations and preserve a fair amount of insensitivity to system design. You lose the convenience of the standard library functions, and you lose compatibility with UNIX or XENIX.

When are insensitivity and compatibility important considerations for programmers? Obviously, if you work with both DOS and UNIX or XENIX, having program code that compiles successfully without modification under the various operating systems can simplify program development and maintenance. These programs typically are simple utilities or simple interactive programs.

This dual-world approach does not work well with real-time interactive programs. Programs such as 1-2-3 and Microsoft Word would suffer from this approach. These types of programs are not acceptable unless they are written to utilize the fastest possible routines. In many instances, because the hardware is programmed directly, compatibility is eliminated but speed (and therefore productivity) is maximized.

Looking at How the Display System Works

The PC display system has evolved from simple beginnings to encompass the following variety of standards in use today:

- Monochrome Display Adapter (MDA)

- Color Graphics Adapter (CGA)

- Hercules Graphics Adapter (HGA)

- Enhanced Graphics Adapter (EGA)

- MultiColor Graphics Array (MCGA)

- Virtual Graphics Array (VGA)

All the standards except the Hercules Graphics Adapter are endorsed and supported by IBM through standard BIOS and DOS services. The MDA, CGA, and EGA are used in the PC line of computers, and the MCGA and VGA are used in the Personal System/2 line. The HGA's popularity makes it the de facto standard for high-resolution monochrome graphics on the PC line, but a special driver is required in order to take advantage of its graphics capabilities. Neither the BIOS nor DOS has built-in services to take full advantage of the HGA. The HGA's unique nature and lack of support directly through BIOS or DOS services make an explanation of its programming beyond the scope of this book.

You might wonder why super VGA (SVGA) is not mentioned as a graphics standard on the PC. The reason is that no clear standard has developed. Rather, several competing approaches to this higher-resolution screen definition have surfaced. It might be some time (if ever) before a clear standard emerges.

Types of Display Monitors

Many types of display monitors are available, and more are becoming available all the time. Not all types of display monitors can be mentioned in this chapter, but some of them are described in the following list:

Direct monochrome monitors display high-resolution text and character-level graphics. They can be driven by a monochrome display adapter (MDA), the Hercules adapter (HGA), or an EGA card set to emulate a monochrome adapter.

Composite monochrome monitors are inexpensive monochrome (often amber or green) monitors that can be driven from a CGA output. They can display CGA graphics but not color. Some of these monitors implement shading to indicate color differences.

Composite color monitors produce color and graphics output, but their resolution typically is poor on 80-column text displays. Television sets are at the low end of this range, but their poor resolution produces unsatisfactory results in text-display modes, except when you use 40-column lines.

RGB monitors produce clear, crisp color output in both text and graphics modes by using separate electrical lines for each primary color (red, green, and blue).

Enhanced RGB monitors provide color text and graphics that are superior to those provided by normal RGB monitors. These monitors use the same technology (separate RGB lines) but use advanced display circuitry to provide a higher-quality image.

Multisync monitors currently provide the highest-quality text and graphics plus added flexibility. By using RGB connections, multisync monitors go beyond the capabilities of normal or enhanced RGB monitors. Multisync monitors can imitate any other type of monitor and provide enhanced display capabilities.

The video display can be accessed in one of these three ways:

- *Through DOS function calls.* This method is the most compatible, but slowest, form of access. With DOS V2.0 and higher, the ANSI.SYS driver lets programs using this method of access have control of the screen through control-code sequences.

- *Through BIOS function calls.* This fairly compatible method of accessing the display is faster than DOS. Most, but not all, systems are compatible with this screen-access method. Through BIOS function calls, you can use graphics and other screen effects not available from the DOS level.

- *Directly at the hardware level.* This method is incompatible because wide hardware differences can exist among systems. Programs that use this method are generally not compatible with all systems considered PC-compatible. This method is not compatible in multiuser or multitasking systems. Both its advantage and the reason for its frequent use stem from the snappy displays and fast operations that occur at this level.

Programmers who decide to build sophisticated displays do not have to begin at the hardware level (which should be, in fact, the "level of last resort"). Most good programs begin at the other end of the spectrum, with a high-level language. BASIC prototypes of major commercial programs frequently are a starting point for development. (VisiCalc, the original spreadsheet program, which was developed for the Apple II, was first coded in BASIC.) After a program is working correctly, you can increase its speed and sophistication to make it as fast and tight as possible. You can make a correct program fast more easily than you can make a fast program correct.

You *can* write sophisticated, useful programs by using DOS and BIOS screen access. Programs that do sophisticated processing can work without direct access to the screen display. As you begin to work with multitasking environments such as Windows or DESQview, you begin to appreciate this access level.

Storing and Displaying Video Data

The PC display system originally was based on the Motorola 6845 cathode ray tube controller (CRTC) chip. This chip was used in the MDA, CGA, and HGA video cards. The EGA, VGA, and later systems use custom chips, which perform all the basic functions the 6845 provides and enhance its capacity significantly. The video controller chips manage many important display tasks so that programmers do not have to manage them:

- Detect light-pen signals

- Increment the video-buffer address counter

- Synchronize the display and timing

- Select the video buffer

- Determine the size and location of the hardware cursor

The PC display system's design is conceptually simple. A PC display is a *memory-mapped* device, in which everything that appears on-screen reflects what is in the computer's memory (see Fig. 5.1). A memory buffer stores information that appears on the display. The memory buffer's starting address and length vary, depending on the type of video display in use, the current display mode, and the amount of memory allocated to the display.

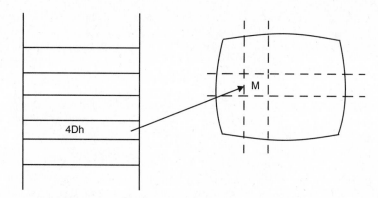

Figure 5.1   A display system that shows memory mapping.

Display adapters generally contain from 4K to 256K of memory, and VGA adapters commonly provide 512K or 1M of memory. Because the data needed to define a display screen can occupy significantly less space than this amount, some display adapters can control more than one display screen. That's display *screen*, not display *monitor*. Display screens, or *pages*, are the memory representation of what appears on your screen. Table 5.1 shows the beginning memory-buffer locations, the buffer lengths, and the number of display pages for the different display types.

Table 5.1   Memory Configurations for Display Adapters

Display Type	Video Mode	Buffer Segment Address	Buffer Length	Display Pages
MDA	Text	B000h	4K	1
CGA	Text	B800h	16K	4/8
	Graphics	B800h	16K	1
HGA	Graphics	B800h	64K	1
EGA	Mono	B000h	Varies	Varies
	Text	B800h	Varies	Varies
	Graphics	A000h	Varies	Varies
MCGA	Text	B800h	32K	8
	Graphics	A000h	64K	1
VGA	Mono	B000h	Varies	Varies
	Text	B800h	Varies	Varies
	Graphics	A000h	Varies	Varies

For all display adapters, the number of display pages available for text modes is the result of two bytes per screen position. With 80 text characters per line, the result is 2×80×25, which equals 4,000 bytes, or approximately 4K. If you use the adapter for 40 text characters per line (2×40×25), every screen occupies 2,000 bytes, or about 2K of space. Using these calculations, you can easily see why the CGA can get eight display pages from 16K of buffer space.

The buffer sizes for the EGA and VGA cards vary because they can have anywhere from 64K to 1M of memory. This RAM is a video buffer for the screen images and also holds patterns (fonts) for as many as 1,024 display characters. The calculations from the preceding paragraph can help you determine the number of display pages available.

Table 5.1 shows that the EGA, MCGA, and VGA have two different graphics-buffer beginning addresses. These adapters can emulate the CGA (segment address B800h) and their native beginning segment address of A000h.

The CRTC chip, independently from a computer system's operation, scans the display memory area and, based on the information stored there, updates the video display. The actual screen display is produced by an electron beam that turns small screen dots (called picture elements, or *pixels*) on or off as each line of the screen is scanned. The beam traces a path from left to right and from top to bottom over the entire screen.

To provide a steady image, the screen is refreshed (the electron beam makes one complete cycle of the entire screen) at a rate of 60 times per second. At the end of every line, the beam has to move from the right side of the screen back to the left side. This time period is called the *horizontal retrace interval* (HRI). Similarly, after the beam completes one cycle, it must move from the lower right to the upper left corner of the screen to begin a new cycle. This movement is called the *vertical retrace interval* (VRI). During both the HRI and the VRI, the beam is turned off and nothing is written to the screen.

Programmers whose programs write directly to display memory should be aware of the HRI or VRI for some types of display adapters because of the way the adapters use the display memory. The memory used in some display adapters is a special *dual-ported* memory, in which the computer can write values in memory at the same time the CRTC reads them. Because this type of memory is more costly than "ordinary" RAM, other display adapters omit the frill. If your computer happens to address a video memory location in a non-dual-ported adapter while the CRTC is reading the value at that same location, you might see a display-screen distortion called *snow*.

This snow problem is particularly important when you work with a genuine IBM CGA or with any clone that duplicates the CGA circuit. In these types of systems, snow has been so bad that users coined a special word to describe it: *chromablizzard*. To avoid snow on this type of system, access the screen memory only during the HRI or VRI.

You can tell whether an HRI or VRI condition exists by polling the CRTC status register at I/O port 3DAh. Bit 0 indicates whether an HRI exists; bit 3 reflects the same information about the

VRI. The respective bit is on when the retrace interval begins, and is off when it is complete. Because HRIs happen much more often than VRIs and are easier to detect when you are programming, most direct screen-memory routines test only for the HRI condition. When the bit goes on, you have time to put only one character in display memory (assuming the standard 4.77 MHz system speed) without screen interference. To get even this much time, you must disable all interrupts while polling; otherwise, some other action can steal the interval for which you were waiting.

This guideline about screen interference applies both when you write to screen memory and when you read from screen memory. (Although it is not obvious why reading should interfere, experience shows that it does on many CGA boards.)

Video Display Formats

The display adapter's interpretation of video data depends on the display *mode*, which controls the way data appears on-screen. Table 5.2 details the display modes available with the different display adapters.

Table 5.2 Video Modes

| | | | | | | Adapters | | | |
Mode	Type	Colors	Resolution	MDA	CGA	EGA	MCGA	VGA	PCjr
00h	Text	16	40×25		X	X	X	X	
01h	Text	16	40×25		X	X	X	X	
02h	Text	16	80×25		X	X	X	X	
03h	Text	16	80×25		X	X	X	X	
04h	Graphics	4	320×200		X	X	X	X	X
05h	Graphics	4	320×200		X	X	X	X	X
06h	Graphics	2	640×200		X	X	X	X	X
07h	Text	Mono	80×25	X		X		X	
08h	Graphics	16	160×200						X
09h	Graphics	16	320×200						X
0Ah	Graphics	4	640×200						X
0Bh	——RESERVED——								
0Ch	——RESERVED——								
0Dh	Graphics	16	320×200			X		X	
0Eh	Graphics	16	640×200			X		X	

continues

Table 5.2 Continued

| | | | | Adapters | | | | | |
Mode	Type	Colors	Resolution	MDA	CGA	EGA	MCGA	VGA	PCjr
0Fh	Graphics	Mono	640×350			X		X	
10h	Graphics	16	640×350			X		X	
11h	Graphics	2	640×480				X	X	
12h	Graphics	16	640×480					X	
13h	Graphics	256	320×200			X		X	

The numbers in the resolution column represent rows and columns for text modes and represent pixels for graphics modes.

The MDA supports only 1 screen-display mode (mode 7), the CGA supports 7, and the EGA supports 12. The most sophisticated adapter is the VGA system, which supports 15 display modes. The VGA also supports graphics on a monochrome display, a display of 43 lines per screen, and a color palette of as many as 256 colors.

The BIOS keeps track of the current display mode and stores the number at memory address 0040:0049. The number of columns per line is stored at 0040:004A. Although you can change these values directly, doing so is not wise because the BIOS not only changes the numbers at these memory locations but also performs other operations necessary for setting a video mode correctly.

Now let's look at the two major display-mode categories: text and graphics.

Text Mode Display

Text mode is also called alphanumeric mode, as most IBM documentation refers to it. In text modes, two bytes of memory are assigned to every character position displayed on-screen: one byte to hold the character and one to hold its attribute. The character is in the byte at the even address, and the attribute is in the odd byte. *Character attributes* indicate to the display adapter how the character should be displayed. Table 5.3 shows the meaning of the character-attribute bits for monochrome text mode; Table 5.4 shows the bit meanings for color text mode.

Table 5.3 Monochrome Character Attributes

Bits *76543210*	*Meaning*
0.......	Normal character
1.......	Blinking character
.000....	Black background (normal)
.111....	White background (inverse)
....0...	Normal intensity
....1...	High intensity
.....000	White foreground (normal)
.....001	Underlined white foreground
.....111	Black foreground (inverse)

Table 5.4 Color Character Attributes

Bits *76543210*	*Meaning*
0.......	Normal character
1.......	Blinking character
.xxx....	Background (see Table 5.5)
....xxxx	Foreground (see Table 5.5)

Notice in Table 5.4 that only three bits are allowed for the background color and that four bits are allowed for the foreground. The reason is that the standard video display circuits provide the capability to make each character blink on and off by setting the high bit of the background field to 1. By modifying the value sent to the video adapter's mode display register, however, you can obtain the full range of brightness values for the background (at the expense of losing the blink capability).

To disable the blink feature and add intensity control to the background for a CGA, you must read the value stored by the BIOS at location 0040h:0065h, AND that byte with 0DFh to clear the blink bit, and OUT the result to port 03D8h (the CGA's MDR address). To do so for the HGA or MDA, you perform the same operation but send the result to port 03B8h.

117

The following sample assembly language code permits bright CGA backgrounds:

```
push   es              ;save the register
mov    ax,40h          ;address BIOS work area
mov    es,ax
mov    al,es:65h       ;get last value sent to mode control
and    al,0DFh         ;clear blink control bit
mov    es:65h,al       ;save value for future reference
mov    dx,03D8h        ;get CGA mode control port address
out    dx,al           ;send to CGA mode control port
pop    es              ;restore saved segment register
```

This modification remains in effect *only* until the video mode is changed again by the BIOS; making it effective for all video modes requires alteration of the video tables pointed to by the Int 1Dh vector. Because the video tables normally reside in ROM, it is not a trivial task to copy them to RAM and be sure that they remain unchanged at all times; it is easier to just change the register as required.

For the EGA and later adapters, toggling the blink bit is much simpler. You use the BIOS interface at Int 10h, with AX set to 1303h:

```
mov    ax,1303h
int    10h
```

Table 5.5 lists the possible bit settings for each color. Be aware, however, that because the *normal* background is determined by three bits, only values up to 7 can be stored in the background unless the blink-enable bit has been toggled as just described.

Table 5.5   Possible Bit Settings for Color Text Mode

——— *Bit Value* ———		
Binary	*Decimal*	*Color*
0000	0	Black
0001	1	Blue
0010	2	Green
0011	3	Cyan
0100	4	Red
0101	5	Magenta
0110	6	Brown
0111	7	White
1000	8	Gray

_____ **Bit Value** _____

Binary	Decimal	Color
1001	9	Light blue
1010	10	Light green
1011	11	Light cyan
1100	12	Light red
1101	13	Light magenta
1110	14	Yellow
1111	15	High-intensity white

After the character's ASCII value is stored in the character's memory location and the attribute is set in the attribute byte, the adapter card's display circuitry creates the physical display of the character. Every character is converted on-screen to a dot pattern that corresponds to the character the display adapter generates. The characters are converted from data contained in a ROM character generator on the adapter. The EGA and VGA cards also enable programmers to specify additional user-defined character sets for character display.

In addition to monochrome and color text displays, two other types of text displays exist. The distinction between these displays lies in the number of characters displayed per line.

Some display adapters can display either 40 or 80 characters per line. The basic video-display format is the 80-by-25 display screen. Because the 40-column format generally is useful only when your video display is a composite television set, in which 40 characters per line is about right for readability, the major emphasis in this book is on the 80-column format, which closely matches the standard 80-by-24 computer-terminal display.

Graphics Mode Display

IBM refers to the graphics display modes as the APA, or *all-points addressable*, modes. In graphics modes, every screen pixel is specified by a set number of memory bits. Each bit indicates whether the pixel is on or off and which color it is. The number of bits used for each pixel depends on the type of display adapter and the graphics mode being used. The EGA system, for example, can display 16 colors from a palette of 64 available colors. To indicate which of the 16 colors a specific pixel should be, you need four bits. The number of bits required for each pixel can be represented by the following equation:

$$\text{BITS} = \frac{\log (\text{COLORS})}{\log (2)}$$

119

COLORS is the number of colors to be represented, and BITS is the number of bits required. With 16 colors available at any time for each EGA-screen pixel, the equation looks like this:

$$\text{BITS} = \frac{\log(16)}{\log(2)} = \frac{1.20412}{0.30103} = 4 \text{ bits}$$

The resolution of a graphics display screen (refer to Table 5.2) is expressed by pixels, with a horizontal and vertical resolution. Table 5.2 lists the resolution for mode 0Eh, for example, as 640-by-200, or 640 pixels wide by 200 scan lines (pixels) deep. This number represents a total of 128,000 pixels for the display screen. When you work with graphics, keep in mind the relationship between resolution, available colors, and memory requirements.

Identifying the Video Display Adapter

Although it is generally agreed that a well-behaved DOS application should use BIOS or, preferably, DOS functions to handle video, sometimes you must throw out the rule book and program "down to the bare metal." You can write a paintbrush program, for example, by using the BIOS video functions to read and write pixels to the screen. If you know which video adapter you are using, however, you can program the video controller directly, which results in dramatic improvements in speed. Although the detailed programming of the individual video adapters is beyond the scope of this book, determining which video adapter is present is not.

The listing in this section is a set of procedures that identify the following display adapter types:

    Monochrome Display Adaptor (MDA)

    Hercules Graphics Adapter (HGA)

    Hercules Graphics Card Plus (HGA+)

    Hercules InColor Card

    Color Graphics Adaptor (CGA)

    Enhanced Graphics Adaptor (EGA)

    MultiColor Graphics Array (MCGA)

    Video Graphics Array (VGA)

    SuperVGA

Within the SuperVGA adapters, the manufacturer and chip type are further identified.

120

The following display types also are identified:

MDA compatible (monochrome)

CGA compatible

EGA compatible

PS/2 compatible monochrome

PS/2 compatible color

Finally, the procedures detect as many as two video hardware systems and differentiate between which is active and which is not.

Identification of the video adapter begins by attempting VGA- and EGA-specific video BIOS calls. If these calls succeed, two tasks remain: Identify a CGA or MDA card the EGA or VGA BIOS is unaware of and identify (in the case of a VGA adapter) a potential SuperVGA adapter.

You identify a CGA or MDA adapter by detecting the CRT controller (CTRC). The MDA's CRTC status port is usually found at I/O address 3B4h, and the CGA's is usually found at 3D4h. The program assumes that the address is correct, and an attempt is made to write to the cursor location low register. If, after a short delay, the value can be read back, you can assume that the CTRC status port has been found and that the CGA or MDA has been located.

If an MDA adapter is detected, it can be further identified as a plain MDA or a Hercules Graphics Adapter (HGA). You do this by exploiting a difference between the MDA and HGA: The vertical sync bit never changes on the MDA, but it does on the HGA. The HGA can be further separated into a Hercules Graphics Card Plus, a Hercules InColor Card, or a regular Hercules Graphics Adapter by observing certain bits of the status port.

Detecting and identifying a SuperVGA adapter is an interesting problem. When vendors began cloning IBM's EGA and VGA, they produced adapters virtually indistinguishable from the original IBM adapters. Vendors went their own way, however, in developing the SuperVGA. Every adapter supports an 800×600 video mode (which is the usual criterion for deciding whether an adapter is VGA or SuperVGA), but each one achieves it in a different, proprietary manner. Each one also supports resolutions or provides features that the others do not. Similarly, the method of identifying each SuperVGA adapter varies from vendor to vendor. The technique for identifying a particular vendor's adapter is described in the procedure for each one. The technique of differentiating a SuperVGA from a VGA is a matter of trying every SuperVGA identification technique; if they all fail, it is a simple VGA adapter.

Listing 5.1 identifies the video adapter (note that it is not a stand-alone program).

Listing 5.1

```
        page 55,132
        name video_id

;   video_id.asm
;   Procedure for identifying the video system(s)

;        ----- Equates -----

; Adapter types
UNKNOWN_ADAPTER      equ   000h
CGA                  equ   001h
MDA                  equ   002h
EGA                  equ   003h
MCGA                 equ   004h
VGA                  equ   005h
SVGA                 equ   006h
VESA_SVGA            equ   007h


ADAPTER_SYSTEM_MASK equ   007h


; Monitor types
UNKNOWN_MONITOR      equ   000h SHL 3
MDA_MONITOR          equ   001h SHL 3
CGA_MONITOR          equ   002h SHL 3
EGA_MONITOR          equ   003h SHL 3
VGA_MONO             equ   004h SHL 3
VGA_COLOR            equ   005h SHL 3


MONITOR_MASK         equ   007h SHL 3


; SVGA BIOS types
UNKNOWN_BIOS         equ   000h SHL 6
AHEAD                equ   001h SHL 6
ATI                  equ   002h SHL 6
CIRRUS               equ   003h SHL 6
CTI_BASED            equ   004h SHL 6
GENOA                equ   005h SHL 6
HEADLAND             equ   006h SHL 6
EVEREX               equ   007h SHL 6
PARADISE             equ   008h SHL 6
TSENG_BASED          equ   009h SHL 6


; Video chip types
UNKNOWN_CHIP         equ   000h SHL 10


HGC                  equ   001h SHL 10
HGCPLUS              equ   002h SHL 10
HERCULESINCOLOR      equ   003h SHL 10


AHEAD_VERSION_A      equ   001h SHL 10
AHEAD_VERSION_B      equ   002h SHL 10


ATI18800REV1         equ   001h SHL 10
ATI18800REV2         equ   002h SHL 10
```

```
ATI18800W18810       equ   003h SHL 10

CIRRUS_510_520       equ   001h SHL 10
CIRRUS_610_620       equ   002h SHL 10
CIRRUS_VSEVEN        equ   003h SHL 10

CTI82C451            equ   001h SHL 10
CTI82C452            equ   002h SHL 10
CTI82C453            equ   003h SHL 10

TRIDENT_8800BR       equ   001h SHL 10
TRIDENT_8800CS       equ   002h SHL 10

; Start of simplified directives
; Change the model size to match the program in which
; these will be used

                     .model small
                     .data

PrimarySystem        dw    0000       ; Primary video system
SecondarySystem      dw    0000       ; Secondary video system
adapter_table        db    UNKNOWN_ADAPTER OR UNKNOWN_MONITOR
                     db    MDA OR MDA_MONITOR
                     db    CGA OR CGA_MONITOR
                     db    UNKNOWN_ADAPTER OR UNKNOWN_MONITOR
                     db    EGA OR EGA_MONITOR
                     db    EGA OR MDA_MONITOR
                     db    UNKNOWN_ADAPTER OR UNKNOWN_MONITOR
                     db    VGA OR VGA_MONO
                     db    VGA OR VGA_COLOR
                     db    UNKNOWN_ADAPTER OR UNKNOWN_MONITOR
                     db    MCGA OR EGA_MONITOR
                     db    MCGA OR VGA_MONO
                     db    MCGA OR VGA_COLOR
                     db    (16 - 13) dup (0)
ega_table            db    EGA OR CGA_MONITOR
                     db    EGA OR EGA_MONITOR
                     db    EGA OR MDA_MONITOR
                     db    EGA OR CGA_MONITOR
                     db    EGA OR EGA_MONITOR
                     db    EGA OR MDA_MONITOR
                     db    (8 - 6) dup (EGA OR UNKNOWN_MONITOR)
AHEAD_BIOS_Sig       db    "AHEAD"
ATI_BIOS_Sig         db    "761295520"
ATI_BIOS_Sig2        db    "31"
CIRRUS_BIOS_Sig      db    "CL"
GENOA_BIOS_Sig       db    77h,11h,99h,66h
PARADISE_BIOS_Sig    db    "VGA="
VESA_BIOS_Sig        db    "VESA"
scratch_pad          db    256 dup (?)

; ----- Program Code -----
                .code
```

continues

Listing 5.1 Continued

```
; Main procedure for identifying the video systems
video_ident    proc
        push bx
        push cx
        push ds              ;save caller's DS
        mov  ax,seg video_ident
        mov  ds,ax           ;get new DS

;       Initialize structures
        mov  PrimarySystem,0
        mov  SecondarySystem,0

;       Test for VGA presence
        mov  ax,01A00h       ; Read display code's function
        int  10h             ; Call video BIOS
        cmp  al,01Ah         ; Successful call?
        jne  no_vga_present

;       we have VGA at least
        or   bh,bh           ; Secondary system detected?
        jz   no_secondary

;       We have a secondary system present
        push bx              ; Preserve bx
        mov  al,bh           ; Put secondary type in AL
        and  al,00Fh
        mov  bx,offset adapter_table  ; Get lookup table
        xlat
        xor  ah,ah           ; Clear byte
        or   SecondarySystem,ax       ; Set flags
        pop  bx              ; Restore bx

;       What is the primary system?
no_secondary:
        mov  al,bl                   ; Put primary type in AL
        and  al,00Fh
        mov  bx,offset adapter_table ; Get lookup byte
        xlat
        xor  ah,ah                   ; Clear byte
        or   PrimarySystem,ax        ; Set flags
        and  ax,ADAPTER_SYSTEM_MASK  ; What adapter?
        cmp  ax,VGA                  ; Did we detect a VGA?
        je   pVGA_detected
        mov  ax,SecondarySystem      ; How about the secondary?
        and  ax,ADAPTER_SYSTEM_MASK
        cmp  ax,VGA
        jne  noVGA_detected
        mov  bx,offset SecondarySystem
        jmp  short detect_SVGA
pVGA_detected:
        mov  bx,offset PrimarySystem

;    Attempt to detect SVGA systems
detect_SVGA:   call SVGA_detect
```

```
;     Although enhanced video BIOS call succeeded, no VGA was found
noVGA_detected:
        mov  ax,SecondarySystem       ; Is secondary system MDA?
        and  ax,ADAPTER_SYSTEM_MASK
        cmp  ax,MDA                    ; Is secondary system MDA?
        je   clarify_MDA               ; If it is, identify further
        mov  ax,PrimarySystem          ; How about the primary?
        and  ax,ADAPTER_SYSTEM_MASK
        cmp  ax,MDA                    ; Is secondary system MDA?
        jne  swap_systems
clarify_MDA:
        call Hercules_detect           ; Identify the specific MDA system
        jmp  short swap_systems

;     The enhanced video BIOS call failed

no_vga_present:
        mov  bl,010h          ; Attempt to find EGA
        mov  ah,012h
        int  10h
        cmp  bl,010h          ; Call failed?
        je   no_ega_present
        mov  bx,offset ega_table
        mov  al,cl            ; Get switch settings
        shr  al,1
        and  ax,7
        xlat
        or   PrimarySystem,ax         ; Set values
        and  ax,ADAPTER_SYSTEM_MASK   ; What did we find?
        cmp  ax,MDA          ; MDA?
        je   seek_CGA        ; Then look for a CGA
        call MDA_detect      ; Else look for MDA
        jmp  short swap_systems
seek_CGA:
        call CGA_detect
        jmp  short swap_systems

;     Efforts to find EGA failed too
no_ega_present:
        call CGA_detect      ; Seek CGA
        call MDA_detect      ; and MDA

;     May need to swap primary/secondary systems
swap_systems:
        mov  ax,SecondarySystem   ; Get current mode
        and  ax,ADAPTER_SYSTEM_MASK
        cmp  ax,UNKNOWN_ADAPTER
        je   vid_exit
        cmp  ax,MCGA
        jae  vid_exit
        mov  ax,PrimarySystem
        and  ax,ADAPTER_SYSTEM_MASK
        cmp  ax,MCGA
        jae  vid_exit
        mov  ah,00Fh          ; Get current video mode
```

continues

125

Listing 5.1   Continued

```
                int   10h
                and   al,7
                cmp   al,7            ; Current mode is mono?
                jne   current_color
                mov   ax,PrimarySystem
                and   ax,MONITOR_MASK
                cmp   ax,MDA_MONITOR
                je    vid_exit
do_swap:
                mov   ax,PrimarySystem
                xchg  ax,SecondarySystem
                mov   PrimarySystem,ax
                jmp short vid_exit
current_color:
                mov   ax,PrimarySystem
                and   ax,MONITOR_MASK
                cmp   ax,MDA_MONITOR
                je    do_swap

;       Return to caller
vid_exit:
                mov   ax,PrimarySystem    ; Set return values
                mov   dx,SecondarySystem
                pop   ds                  ; Restore caller's DS
                pop   cx
                pop   bx
                ret                       ; Return

video_ident    endp

; Routine to detect SVGA cards
; On entry, BX is a pointer to the VGA system word

SVGA_detect    proc
                push  ax              ; Save registers
                push  cx
                push  di
                push  dx
                push  si
                push  es
                mov   ax,0C000h       ; Point to ROM
                mov   es,ax
                mov   di,00025h       ; Signature is at C000:0025
                mov   si,offset AHEAD_BIOS_Sig
                mov   cx,5            ; Length of signature
                cld
                repe  cmpsb
                jne   not_ahead_bios

;       It's an AHEAD BIOS—now identify which chip version

                and   word ptr [bx],NOT ADAPTER_SYSTEM_MASK
                or    word ptr [bx],SVGA OR AHEAD
                mov   dx,003CEh       ; Get i/o address
                mov   al,00Fh         ; Get index of enable register
```

```
                out   dx,al
                inc   dx                ; Get I/O address of data
                mov   al,020h           ; Get enable value
                out   dx,al
                jmp   $+2
                in    al,dx             ; Get value
                cmp   al,020h           ; Version A?
                je    ahead_a
                cmp   al,021h           ; Version B?
                jne   test_vesa_isle
                or    word ptr [bx],AHEAD_VERSION_B
                jmp   short test_vesa_isle
ahead_a:
                or    word ptr [bx],AHEAD_VERSION_A
test_vesa_isle:
                jmp   test_vesa

;     Wasn't AHEAD. Test for ATI
not_ahead_bios:
                mov   di,00031h         ; ATI signature at C000:0031
                mov   si,offset ATI_BIOS_Sig
                mov   cx,9
                repe  cmpsb
                jne   not_ati_bios

;     So far, so good...
                mov   di,00040h         ; "31" at C000:0040
                mov   si,offset ATI_BIOS_Sig2
                mov   cx,2
                repe  cmpsb
                jne   not_ati_bios

;     It's an ATI BIOS--now identify the chipset
                and   word ptr [bx],NOT ADAPTER_SYSTEM_MASK
                or    word ptr [bx],SVGA OR ATI
                mov   al,es:043h
                cmp   al,'1'            ; Which chipset?
                je    ati_1
                cmp   al,'2'
                je    ati_2
                cmp   al,'3'
                jne   test_vesa_isle
                or    word ptr [bx],ATI18800W18810
                jmp   test_vesa
ati_1:
                or    word ptr [bx],ATI18800REV1
                jmp   test_vesa
ati_2:
                or    word ptr [bx],ATI18800REV2
                jmp   test_vesa

;     Now check for Cirrus

not_ati_bios:
                mov   di,6
                mov   si,offset CIRRUS_BIOS_Sig
```

continues

Listing 5.1   Continued

```
                mov   cx,2
                repe  cmpsb
                jne   not_cirrus_bios

;       It's a Cirrus BIOS--now identify the chip

                and   word ptr [bx],NOT ADAPTER_SYSTEM_MASK
                or    word ptr [bx],SVGA OR CIRRUS
                xor   ax,ax          ; Find CRTC
                mov   es,ax
                mov   dx,es:00463h
                push  dx
                mov   al,00Ch        ; Get start address
                out   dx,al
                inc   dx
                in    al,dx          ; Read register
                mov   ah,al          ; Save what we read
                mov   al,00Ch
                push  ax
                xor   al,al          ; Clear register
                out   dx,al
                dec   dx
                mov   al,01Fh        ; Get ID register
                out   dx,al
                inc   dx
                in    al,dx          ; Read unlock password
                mov   ch,al          ; Save it--it's the key to the chip ID
                mov   dx,003C4h      ; Address of sequencer
                mov   al,006h        ; Extension control reg
                out   dx,al
                inc   dx
                mov   al,ch          ; Get unlock password
                out   dx,al
                in    al,dx          ; Read it back
                cmp   al,1           ; Unlocked?
                jne   not_cirrus_chip
                mov   al,ch
                mov   cl,4
                ror   al,cl
                out   dx,al
                in    al,dx
                or    al,al          ; Locked?
                jnz   not_cirrus_chip
                cmp   ch,0ECh        ; 510/520?
                jne   not_cirrus_510
                or    word ptr [bx],CIRRUS_510_520
                jmp   short not_cirrus_chip
not_cirrus_510:
                cmp   ch,0CAh        ; 610/620?
                jne   not_cirrus_610
                or    word ptr [bx],CIRRUS_610_620
                jmp   short not_cirrus_chip
not_cirrus_610:
                cmp   ch,0EAh        ; Video seven?
                jne   not_cirrus_chip
```

```
            or    word ptr [bx],CIRRUS_VSEVEN
not_cirrus_chip:
            pop   ax                ; Restore CRTC
            pop   dx
            out   dx,ax
            jmp   test_vesa

;     Check for CTI
not_cirrus_bios:
            cli                     ; Disable interrupts
            mov   dx,046E8h         ; Put chip in setup mode
            in    al,dx
            or    al,010h
            out   dx,al
            mov   dx,00103h         ; Read extended enable register
            in    al,dx
            or    al,080h           ; Turn enable on
            out   dx,al
            inc   dx                ; Read global ID
            in    al,dx
            mov   ah,al             ; Save it
            mov   dx,046E8h         ; Turn setup back off
            in    al,dx
            and   al,0EFh
            out   dx,al
            sti                     ; Reenable interrupts
            mov   dx,003D6h         ; Read version
            xor   al,al
            out   dx,al
            inc   dx
            in    al,dx
            cmp   ah,0A5h           ; Right global ID?
            jne   not_cti_bios

;     Seems to be a CTI chip. Which version?
            and   al,0F0h           ; Check version
            cmp   al,000h
            jne   not_cti82C451
            and   word ptr [bx],NOT ADAPTER_SYSTEM_MASK
            or    word ptr [bx],CTI82C451 OR SVGA OR CTI_BASED
            jmp   test_vesa
not_cti82C451:
            cmp   al,010h
            jne   not_cti82C452
            and   word ptr [bx],NOT ADAPTER_SYSTEM_MASK
            or    word ptr [bx],CTI82C452 OR SVGA OR CTI_BASED
            jmp   test_vesa
not_cti82C452:
            cmp   al,030h
            jne   not_cti_bios
            and   word ptr [bx],NOT ADAPTER_SYSTEM_MASK
            or    word ptr [bx],CTI82C453 OR SVGA OR CTI_BASED
            jmp   test_vesa

;     Check for Genoa
```

continues

129

Listing 5.1 Continued

```
not_cti_bios:
        mov  di,0037h        ; Read pointer
        les  di,es:[di]      ; Dereference it
        mov  si,offset GENOA_BIOS_Sig
        mov  cx,4
        repe cmpsb
        jne  not_genoa_bios
        and  word ptr [bx],NOT ADAPTER_SYSTEM_MASK
        or   word ptr [bx],GENOA OR SVGA
        jmp  test_vesa

;     Try Headland
not_genoa_bios:
        push bx
        xor bx,bx            ; Special Headland BIOS call
        mov  ax,06F00h
        int  10h
        cmp  bx,'V7'
        jne  not_headland
        mov  ax,06F07h
        int  10h
        cmp  bl,070h
        jb   not_headland
        cmp  bl,07Fh
        ja   not_headland
        pop  bx
        and  word ptr [bx],NOT ADAPTER_SYSTEM_MASK
        or   word ptr [bx],HEADLAND OR SVGA
        jmp  short test_vesa
not_headland:
        pop  bx              ; Restore pointer

;     Try Trident/Everex
        push bx              ; Save pointer
        mov  ax,07000h       ; Extended BIOS call
        xor  bx,bx
        int  10h
        cmp  al,070h         ; OK?
        jne  not_everex_bios
        and  dx,0FFF0h       ; Get board number
        cmp  dx,06780h
        jne  not_everex_bios
        pop  bx
        and  word ptr [bx],NOT ADAPTER_SYSTEM_MASK
        or   word ptr [bx],EVEREX OR SVGA
        jmp  short test_trident
not_everex_bios:
        pop  bx
test_trident:

;     Identify the chip itself
        mov  dx,003C4h
        mov  al,00Bh
        out  dx,al
        inc  dx
```

```
                in    al,dx
                and   al,00Fh
                cmp   al,1
                je    found_8800BR
                cmp   al,2
                jne   not_trident
                and   word ptr [bx],NOT ADAPTER_SYSTEM_MASK
                or    word ptr [bx],TRIDENT_8800CS OR SVGA
                jmp   short test_vesa
found_8800BR:
                and   word ptr [bx],NOT ADAPTER_SYSTEM_MASK
                or    word ptr [bx],TRIDENT_8800BR OR SVGA
                jmp   short test_vesa

;       Try Paradise
not_trident:
                mov   ax,0C000h
                mov   es,ax
                mov   di,0007Dh
                mov   si,offset PARADISE_BIOS_Sig
                mov   cx,4
        repe cmpsb
                jne   not_paradise
                and   word ptr [bx],NOT ADAPTER_SYSTEM_MASK
                or    word ptr [bx],SVGA OR PARADISE
                jmp   short test_vesa

;       Try Tseng
not_paradise:
                mov   dx,003CDh
                in    al,dx
                mov   ah,al
                and   al,0C0h
                or    al,055h
                out   dx,al
                in    al,dx
                cmp   al,055h
                jne   test_vesa
                mov   al,0AAh
                out   dx,al
                in    al,dx
                cmp   al,0AAh
                jne   test_vesa
                and   word ptr [bx],NOT ADAPTER_SYSTEM_MASK
                or    word ptr [bx],SVGA OR TSENG_BASED

;       Test for VESA BIOS
test_vesa:      mov   ax,04F00h
                mov   di,offset scratch_pad
                push  ds
                pop   es
                int   10h
                cmp   ax,0004Fh
                jne   svga_exit
                cld
```

continues

Listing 5.1 Continued

```
                mov   si,offset VESA_BIOS_Sig
                mov   cx,4
          repe cmpsb
                jne   svga_exit
                and   word ptr [bx],NOT ADAPTER_SYSTEM_MASK
                or    word ptr [bx],VESA_SVGA
svga_exit:
                pop   es
                pop   si
                pop   dx
                pop   di
                pop   cx
                pop   ax
                ret
SVGA_detect     endp

; Routine to detect Hercules MDA card

Hercules_detect  proc
                push si
                push dx
                push cx
                push bx
                push ax
                mov   si,offset PrimarySystem
                mov   ax,[si]
                and   ax,ADAPTER_SYSTEM_MASK
                cmp   ax,MDA
                je    test_Hercules
                mov si,offset SecondarySystem
test_Hercules:
                mov   dx,003BAh        ; Get status port
                in    al,dx
                and   al,080h          ; Save VSYNC bit
                mov   bl,al            ; Save it
                xor   cx,cx
VSYNC:
                in    al,dx            ; Read port
                mov   ah,al
                and   ah,080h          ; Isolate VSYNC
                cmp   ah,bl
                jne   found_Hercules
                loop VSYNC
                jmp   short Herc_exit
found_Hercules:

;      Now that we found it, try to identify which board

                and   al,070h
                cmp   al,010h          ; HGCPlus?
                jne   not_HGCPlus
                or    word ptr [si],HGCPLUS
                jmp   short Herc_exit
not_HGCPlus:
                cmp   al,050h
```

```
                jne    is_HGC
                or     word ptr [si],HERCULESINCOLOR
                jmp    short Herc_exit
        is_HGC:
                or     word ptr [si],HGC
        Herc_exit:
                pop    ax
                pop    bx
                pop    cx
                pop    dx
                pop    si
                ret
        Hercules_detect        endp

        ; Attempt to detect MDA card

        MDA_detect  proc
                mov    dx,003B4h        ; If MDA, CRTC is 3B4h
                call   CRTC_detect
                jne    no_MDA
                mov    ax,PrimarySystem      ; Found MDA; primary or secondary?
                and    ax,ADAPTER_SYSTEM_MASK
                cmp    ax,UNKNOWN_ADAPTER
                je     MDA_primary
                or     SecondarySystem,MDA OR MDA_MONITOR
                jmp    short found_MDA
        MDA_primary:
                or     PrimarySystem,MDA OR MDA_MONITOR
        found_MDA:
                call   Hercules_detect    ; See if it's a Hercules board
        no_MDA:
                ret
        MDA_detect     endp

        ; Attempt to detect CGA card

        CGA_detect  proc
                mov    dx,003D4h        ; If CGA, CRTC is 3D4h
                call   CRTC_detect
                jne    CGA_exit
                mov    ax,PrimarySystem      ; Found CGA; primary or secondary?
                and    ax,ADAPTER_SYSTEM_MASK
                cmp    ax,UNKNOWN_ADAPTER
                je     CGA_primary
                or     SecondarySystem,CGA OR CGA_MONITOR
                jmp    short CGA_exit
        CGA_primary:
                or     PrimarySystem,CGA OR CGA_MONITOR
        CGA_exit:
                ret
        CGA_detect  endp

        ; Attempt to detect the CRT controller
        ; On entry, DX is the alleged CRTC port
        ; If detected, returns Z set; else Z reset
```

continues

133

Listing 5.1 Continued

```
CRTC_detect  proc
             push dx              ; Save registers
             push cx
             push bx
             push ax
             mov  al,00Fh         ; Select (alleged) cursor low
             out  dx,al           ;   register
             inc  dx              ; Select register
             in   al,dx           ; Read old value
             mov  bl,al           ; Save it in BL
             mov  al,066h         ; Write new value
             out  dx,al
             xor  cx,cx           ; Loop a while
CRTC_Delay:
             nop
             loop CRTC_Delay
             in   al,dx           ; Get new value
             mov  bh,al           ; Save it
             mov  al,bl           ; Get old value
             out  dx,al           ; Write it out
             cmp  bh,066h         ; Is new value correct?
             pop  ax              ; Restore registers
             pop  bx
             pop  cx
             pop  dx
             ret
CRTC_detect  endp

             end
```

Video Functions

Now that you know how screen displays work, you can try some simple functions to see how the functions work. Like most of the topics discussed in this book, the video functions are available in two categories: DOS and BIOS. Unlike other programming areas, however, the preponderance of video functions is relegated to BIOS. No DOS services are available for controlling the screen; only a few DOS services are available for displaying information on-screen.

The DOS services are the simpler to use. Every DOS service provides a simple output mechanism that is redirectable and compatible with all system operations.

The BIOS services generally are the functions of choice for serious programming in which you do not directly access video memory. These services not only provide extensive control of a video system but also are faster and much more flexible than the DOS services are. The BIOS services provide access to the cursor, to attributes for display, and to other controls.

An undocumented function of DOS—Int 29h—may prove handy when you want the fastest possible output to the CRT and want to avoid using BIOS in order to maintain as much compatibility as possible with generic MS-DOS systems. Int 29h is fast because, unlike the documented DOS output functions, it does not check for Ctrl-C every time it puts a character on-screen.

To use Int 29h, put in the AL register the character to be displayed and then invoke the interrupt:

```
mov    al,'A'
int    29h
```

Unlike other services, Int 29h uses whichever screen attributes are already in place and recognizes only the bell (ASCII 07), CR (ASCII 13), and LF (ASCII 10) characters as control actions; all other "control" characters are displayed on-screen. When a character is put on the last column of the last row, or when an LF is sent while the cursor is anywhere on the last row, the screen automatically scrolls up one line.

Because Int 29h is not documented, it can be taken away in a future version of DOS; this is unlikely, however, because Int 29h is the method DOS uses most (beginning with version 2.0) and because it is an integral part of the ANSI.SYS alternate display driver system. You should evaluate the risks involved in its use, however (like the use of any other undocumented feature), before you reach a decision.

Remember that DOS and BIOS simply provide the building blocks for creating screens. A programmer's imagination and skill provide much of the "glitz" that makes a program perform well or look snappy. If your abilities in creating displays are not on par with your programming techniques, your displays might look shoddy.

Programming with DOS and BIOS Video Functions

In this section, you build some simple window functions to see how easy the use of the BIOS and DOS functions can be. The purpose of this chapter is not to build a complete windowing system—this type of endeavor is beyond the scope of this book. Screen operations are investigated in terms of some simple window display functions that illustrate the use of the BIOS and DOS functions.

The `testscn.c` program is a simple test that fills the screen with data and then clears a window in the middle of the screen (see Listing 5.2). You will write more data to the screen and then put the original window data back in place and scroll it.

Listing 5.2

```
/* Testscn.c
   Listing 5.2 in DOS Programmer's Reference */

#include <stdio.h>
#include <dos.h>

/* Prototypes */
    void savewin(int lr, int lc, int rr, int rc);
    void clearwin(int lr, int lc, int rr, int rc);
    void putwin(int lr, int lc, int rr, int rc);
    void border(int lr, int lc, int rr, int rc);
    void upwin(int n, int lr, int lc, int rr, int rc);
    void gotoxy(int r, int c);
    void cls(void);

void main()
{
    int i;

    /* Display a screen full of lines */
    cls();
    for (i=0; i<50; i++)
        printf("DOS Programmer's Reference          ");

    /*  Save the data in the rectangle (5,5) to (12,40), and
        then clear that area and put a border around it. */
    savewin(5,5,12,40);
    clearwin(5,5,12,40);
    border(5,5,12,40);

    /*  Wait 5 seconds and then scroll the screen again.
        (Note: Everything scrolls, including the window.) */
    sleep(5);
    gotoxy(24,0);
    for (i=0; i<50; i++)
        printf("This is the Second Screen of the Demo    ");

    /* Wait 5 seconds and then clear the window and fill it. */
    sleep(5);
    clearwin(5,5,12,40);
    putwin(5,5,12,40);

    /*  Scroll the inside of the window up one line every
        2 seconds for 10 steps. */
    for (i=0; i<10; i++) {
        sleep(2);
        upwin(1,6,6,11,39);
    }

    /*  Finally, clear the screen again and then end the
        program. */
    cls();
}
```

Testscn.c is built on three simple function collections contained in the files window.c, screen.c, and chario.c. Window.c, in Listing 5.3, handles the window functions called by testscn.c. With the functions in window.c, you can do the following:

savewin()	Save the current data in the window
clearwin()	Clear the window
putwin()	Put data in a window
border()	Put a border around a window
upwin()	Scroll the window up

This small collection of functions makes no attempt to be super-sophisticated. It just handles single, nonoverlapping windows such as those you might use to display help information. Because it uses nothing lower than the BIOS functions, it is compatible with other environments, such as DESQview.

Listing 5.3

```c
/* Window.c
   Listing 5.3 of DOS Programmer's Reference */

#include <stdio.h>
#include <dos.h>

#define VIDEO 0x10

/*   Basic screen-size definitions */
#define     LINES    24
#define     COLS     80

/* Prototypes */
    void gotoxy(int i, int j);
    void rch(char *ch, char *attr);
    void wch(char ch, char attr);
    void border(int lr, int lc, int rr, int rc);

/* Structure for each character position--character and
   attribute. */
struct   charpos {
    char ch;
    char att;
};

/* The screen is made up of LINES*COLS character positions */
struct charpos screen[LINES][COLS];

/* Function: savewin() */
void savewin(lr,lc,rr,rc)
```

continues

137

Listing 5.3   Continued

```
    int lr, lc, rr, rc;
{
    int i, j;
    for (i=lr; i<=rr; i++)
        for (j=lc; j<=rc; j++) {
            gotoxy(i,j);
            rch(&screen[i][j].ch,&screen[i][j].att);
        }
}

/* Function: clearwin() */
void clearwin(lr,lc,rr,rc)
    int lr, lc, rr, rc;
{
    union REGS regs;

    regs.h.ah = 0x06;
    regs.h.al = 0;
    regs.h.bh = 7;
    regs.h.ch = lr;
    regs.h.cl = lc;
    regs.h.dh = rr;
    regs.h.dl = rc;
    int86(VIDEO,&regs,&regs);
}

/* Function: putwin() */
void putwin(lr,lc,rr,rc)
    int lr, lc, rr, rc;
{
    int  i, j;

    for (i=lr; i<=rr; i++)
        for (j=lc; j<=rc; j++) {
            gotoxy(i,j);
            wch(screen[i][j].ch,screen[i][j].att);
        }
    border(lr,lc,rr,rc);
}

#define VERTLINE    186
#define UPPERRIGHT  187
#define LOWERRIGHT  188
#define LOWERLEFT   200
#define UPPERLEFT   201
#define HORIZLINE   205

/* Function: border() */
void border(lr,lc,rr,rc)
    int lr, lc, rr, rc;
{
    int  i, j;

    for (i=lr; i<=rr; i++) {
        gotoxy(i,lc); wch(VERTLINE,7);
```

```
        gotoxy(i,rc); wch(VERTLINE,7);
        if (i==lr ¦¦ i==rr) {
            for (j=lc; j<=rc; j++) {
                gotoxy(i,j);
                wch(HORIZLINE,7);
            }
            if (i==lr) {
                gotoxy(lr,lc); wch(UPPERLEFT,7);
                gotoxy(lr,rc); wch(UPPERRIGHT,7);
            }
            if (i==rr) {
                gotoxy(rr,lc); wch(LOWERLEFT,7);
                gotoxy(rr,rc); wch(LOWERRIGHT,7);
            }
        }
    }
}

/* Function: upwin() */
void upwin(n,lr,lc,rr,rc)
    int n, lr, lc, rr, rc;
{
    union REGS regs;

    regs.h.ah = 0x06;
    regs.h.al = n;
    regs.h.bh = 7;
    regs.h.ch = lr;
    regs.h.cl = lc;
    regs.h.dh = rr;
    regs.h.dl = rc;
    int86(VIDEO,&regs,&regs);
}
```

The functions in the screen.c file handle screen-related functions, such as positioning the cursor and clearing the screen (the gotoxy() and cls() functions, respectively). Note that cls() is just clearwin() with set values for the upper left and lower right corners corresponding to the entire screen.

The screen.c functions are global to the entire screen display (see Listing 5.4). They act on a screenwide basis. Window.c functions work within a single window. Additional functions can be added to handle working within a window.

Listing 5.4

```
/* Screen.c
   Listing 5.4 of DOS Programmer's Reference */

#include <stdio.h>
#include <dos.h>

#define    VIDEO  0x10
```

continues

Listing 5.4 Continued

```
/* Function: gotoxy() */
void gotoxy(r,c)
    int r, c;
{
    union REGS regs;

    regs.h.ah = 0x02;
    regs.h.bh = 0;
    regs.h.dh = r;
    regs.h.dl = c;
    int86(VIDEO,&regs,&regs);
}

/* Function: cls() */
void cls()
{
    union REGS regs;

    regs.h.ah = 0x06;
    regs.h.al = 0;
    regs.h.bh = 7;
    regs.h.ch = 0;
    regs.h.cl = 0;
    regs.h.dh = 25;
    regs.h.dl = 80;
    int86(VIDEO,&regs,&regs);
}
```

At the lowest level of the program, screen-character functions enable you to look at a single screen position or to change it by using the BIOS screen-display functions (see Listing 5.5).

Listing 5.5

```
/* Chario.c
    Listing 5.5 of DOS Programmer's Reference */

#include <stdio.h>
#include <dos.h>

#define VIDEO 0x10

union REGS regs;

/* Function: wch() */
void wch(ch, attr)
    char ch,  attr;
{
    regs.h.ah = 0x09;
    regs.h.bh = 0;
    regs.h.bl = attr;
    regs.h.al = ch;
```

```
        regs.x.cx = 1;
        int86(VIDEO,&regs,&regs);
}

/* Function: rch() */
void rch(ch, attr)
        char *ch, *attr;
{
        regs.h.ah = 0x08;
        regs.h.bh = 0;
        int86(VIDEO,&regs,&regs);
        *ch = regs.h.al;
        *attr = regs.h.ah;
}
```

If you are using Microsoft C/C++, you do not have a `sleep()` function as of Version 4.0. The function shown in Listing 5.6 implements the same sort of routine for Microsoft C/C++. It waits until a specified number of seconds have passed before proceeding.

Listing 5.6

```
/* Sleep.c
   Listing 5.6 of DOS Programmer's Reference */

#include <stdio.h>

; For use with Microsoft C/C++
void sleep(n)
        int n;
{
        long timeval, time();
        timeval = time(NULL);
        while(time(NUL) < timeval + n);
}
```

Using Multiple Display Pages

Because all the display functions used for this simple windowing system deal specifically with only one screen page (page 0), they are independent of the type of monitor system you are using. You can add screen-page control, but not all functions allow it. The scrolling functions, for example, have no page assignment among their arguments. You therefore cannot use these facilities for paging the display. (If you write your own window functions to access display memory directly, you are not bound by this limitation.) Also, Function 0Eh does not work with all pages on all BIOS ROMs. In all non-IBM ROMs that were tested, this function worked only on the currently displayed page and not on a nondisplayed page.

One way to add screen-page control is to change the routines to include a current screen-page number and a way to set it. You can change screen.c, for example, to include a setpage command (see Listing 5.7).

Listing 5.7

```
/* Screen2.c
   Listing 5.7 of DOS Programmer's Reference */

#include <stdio.h>
#include <dos.h>

#define     BOOL    int
#define     VIDEO   0x10

/* Prototypes */
    void cls(void);

static int cpage = 0;           /* Current display page */

/* Function: gotoxy() */
void gotoxy(r,c)
    int  r, c;
{
    union REGS regs;

    regs.h.ah = 0x02;
    regs.h.bh = cpage;
    regs.h.dh = r;
    regs.h.dl = c;
    int86(VIDEO,&regs,&regs);
}

/* Function: cls() */
void cls()
{
    union REGS regs;

    regs.h.ah = 0x06;
    regs.h.al = 0;
    regs.h.bh = 7;
    regs.h.ch = 0;
    regs.h.cl = 0;
    regs.h.dh = 25;
    regs.h.dl = 80;
    int86(VIDEO,&regs,&regs);
}

/* Function: setpage() */
void setpage(n,clrflg)
    int  n;
    BOOL clrflg;
{
    union REGS regs;
```

```
        cpage = n;
        regs.h.ah = 0x05;
        regs.h.al = n;
        int86(VIDEO,&regs,&regs);
        if(clrflg) cls();
    }

    /* Function: pgprint() */
    void pgprint(str)
        char *str;
    {
        union REGS regs;

        regs.h.ah = 0x0e;
        regs.h.bh = cpage;
        while (*str) {
            regs.h.al = *str;
            int86(VIDEO,&regs,&regs);
            str++;
        }
    }
```

In Listing 5.7, the pgprint() function has been added to let you print strings to the current page. By adding page control to your screen functions, you can build programs in which you use the window and page functions together to preserve displays that can be recovered rapidly by simply shifting the display page. The testpage.c sample program lets you try the new setpage() and pgprint() functions (see Listing 5.8).

Listing 5.8

```
    /* Testpage.c
       Listing 5.8 of DOS Programmer's Reference */

    #include <stdio.h>
    #include <dos.h>

    #define FALSE 0
    #define TRUE  !FALSE

    /* Prototypes */
        void setpage(int n, int clrflg);
        void pgprint(char *str);

    void main()
    {
        int i;

        setpage(1,TRUE);
        for (i=0; i<50; i++)
            pgprint("DOS Programmer's Reference          ");
        sleep(5);
        setpage(0,FALSE);
    }
```

If you have a monochrome monitor system, you cannot see anything. When the `setpage()` function is executed, in fact, your screen does not change; you simply see everything remain static for a few seconds and then return to the next action. If you have a CGA or EGA monitor or better, however, the screen changes and displays the test line and then returns to the same display you had on the screen when you executed the program.

The use of a current display page for all functions is not as impressive as is working with undisplayed pages. By including the display page in the function arguments, you can apply a function such as `gotoxy()` to pages that are not yet displayed. You then can build a complete display and, when you make it the current display, users see it displayed instantaneously.

Printer Functions

The printer is the only other major output device over which you have direct control. Printer functions are much simpler than screen functions because they deal only with character output and minimally with input from the printer.

The simplest way to write to the printer is to use the DOS-level printer-output function (Int 21h, Function 05h), as shown in Listing 5.9. This function enables you to send characters to the printer device. DOS handles error conditions by invoking the critical-error handler if a problem occurs in using the function.

Listing 5.9

```
/* Prtout.c
   Listing 5.9 of DOS Programmer's Reference */

#include <stdio.h>
#include <dos.h>

/* Prototypes */
    void outprt(char *str);

void main()
{
    outprt("This is a line to the printer\012\015");
}

void outprt(str)
    char *str;
{
    union REGS regs;

    regs.h.ah = 0x05;
    while (*str) {
```

144

```
                regs.h.dl = *str;
                intdos(&regs,&regs);
                str++;
        }
    }
```

You can invoke the BIOS print functions (Int 17h) at a lower level to get greater control over the print function. At this level, you can check the printer's status directly and respond to printer errors in your program as necessary. Listing 5.10 shows an example of how you might use the BIOS functions to handle printer interfacing.

Listing 5.10

```
/* Prtchk.c
   Listing 5.10 of DOS Programmer's Reference */

#include <stdio.h>
#include <dos.h>
#include <stdlib.h>

/* Prototypes */
    void outprt(char *str);
    int prtrdy(void);

void main()
{
    int i;

    for (i=0; i<10; i++) {
        if(!prtrdy()) exit(1);
        outprt("This is a line to the printer\012\015");
    }
}

#define PRINTER 0x17

void outprt(str)
    char *str;
{
    union REGS regs;

    regs.x.dx = 0;
    while (*str) {
        regs.h.ah = 0x00;
        regs.h.al = *str;
        int86(PRINTER,&regs,&regs);
        putchar(*str);
        str++;
    }
}
```

continues

Listing 5.10 Continued

```
int prtrdy()
{
    union REGS regs;

    regs.h.ah = 2;
    regs.x.dx = 0;
    int86(PRINTER,&regs,&regs);
    printf("Printer Status: %x\n",regs.h.ah);
    if (regs.h.ah & 0x20)
        printf("Printer out of paper\n");
    if (regs.h.ah & 0x08)
        printf("Printer I/O error\n");
    return((regs.h.ah&0x20)==0 && (regs.h.ah&0x08)==0);
}
```

As these examples show, you can perform printer output directly from your programs and at the same time recognize what is happening with the printer.

Sophisticated printer-control functions such as graphics and font control are specific to the printer you are using. Neither the BIOS nor DOS has any built-in functions for handling printers other than simply sending characters to them. A discussion of specialized printer-control functions is beyond the scope of this book.

Summary

This chapter has discussed a wide range of functions for output, related primarily to the video display. You have learned about the screen modes available and the different screen displays you can use.

In DOS, screen control is limited to a few simple functions that allow basic output to the screen and little else. More sophisticated control requires access to the BIOS functions to allow, for example, cursor positioning and character-attribute control. At the BIOS level, you can do graphical displays, screen positioning, and even window functions. Programs that create sophisticated screens almost always must work at the BIOS level or below, by using direct access to the screen-display memory.

Printer functions are even more limited than are screen functions. There are no primitive functions for anything other than outputting characters to the printer and checking the printer's status. You cannot call BIOS or DOS functions to do printer graphics or special printer functions such as font changing. Any special control must be performed by your programs.

Chapter 6 moves on to input functions, which complement the output functions discussed in this chapter.

6

Input Devices

Input and output are so tied together in most people's minds that we normally think in terms of "I/O" or "input/output" and rarely deal with only one or the other. In this chapter, which complements the discussion of output devices in Chapter 5, you learn about input devices.

This chapter focuses on the two most popular input devices: the keyboard and the mouse. The keyboard is handled by DOS and BIOS functions included in the system, whereas a driver must be added to the system to make the mouse's functions available.

Keyboards are much more sophisticated than most people realize. An intricate piece of engineering, the keyboard works with low-level functions in the BIOS and makes keyboard operations almost invisible to programs by buffering character input and providing interrupts to enable the BIOS to handle keyboard characters as they are typed.

Because interrupts are not discussed until Chapter 11, "Interrupt Handlers," this chapter deals with the mouse in a simplistic manner. But even that makes for an interesting program. By using the mouse functions (when they are present), you can build mouse-control functions into a variety of programs.

Both keyboard and mouse functions can be made much more interesting by combining them with interrupt-handling functions. Terminate-and-stay-resident programs that use hotkeys to start, or mouse-driven programs that interrupt on mouse input, provide for immediate response to users' needs. Chapter 11 discusses interrupts in greater detail. For now, however, you need to learn about the basic input functions.

Keyboards

You can always count on the PC to have a keyboard as an input device—every PC has one, and most programs use them. Although alternative input devices such as the mouse have gained popularity for some types of programs, few programs can operate without some keyboard input.

This section looks at the use of BIOS and DOS functions for keyboard input. These functions, when used instead of the normal input functions of a high-level language, result in the following advantages:

- Maximum control over your input. You can add user-oriented editing features and special help functions, for example.

- Smaller programs than those that are possible when you are using the keyboard input routines provided with high-level languages. These routines, written to provide for virtually every possible input situation and condition, carry a great deal of "overhead code."

- Snappier, more responsive input because you can make the program react however you choose.

Before we discuss programming, let's look at how the keyboard works.

Learning How the Keyboard Works

To programmers, the keyboard probably is the most familiar but least understood device on a computer. Most of us understand file systems and disk operations because we have read books about them. But the lowly keyboard is discussed minimally and is well known to only a few specialists.

Rather than try to describe the hardware that makes keyboards work, this book concentrates on the sequence of events you must understand if you want to use the keyboard-related DOS and BIOS services.

First, imagine that you are looking from your computer through the cable that connects your computer and the keyboard. As you press keys, you can see numbers (the keyboard "scan codes") coming from the keyboard through the cable to the computer.

Every time a key is pressed, it generates a unique 8-bit number (the most significant bit is always 0, to tell the difference between a keypress and its later release), with even the left and right Shift keys represented by different numbers. These scan codes indicate exactly which keys are pressed.

Whenever a key is released, another scan code is generated. This code is the same as that for the keystroke, except that the high-order bit is set (which adds 128 to the scan code). In this way, the scan code signals to the ROM BIOS that the key has been released.

Although many different types of keyboard configurations are available, the majority of keyboards follow one of three basic designs. These designs are patterned after the three different keyboard designs IBM developed for its different computers. These three designs are the PC (83-key) keyboard, the Personal Computer AT (84-key) keyboard, and the enhanced (101-key) keyboard. Although most of the scan codes remain the same for all three designs, there are differences. Figures 6.1, 6.2, and 6.3 show the scan codes (hexadecimal) on the PC, Personal Computer AT, and enhanced keyboards, respectively. Note that the enhanced keyboard uses multiple scan codes to identify some of its additional keys.

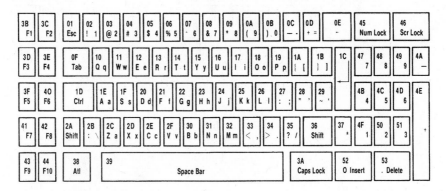

Figure 6.1   Hexadecimal scan codes for a PC keyboard.

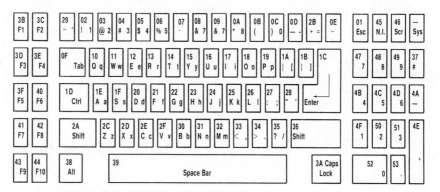

Figure 6.2   Hexadecimal scan codes for an AT keyboard.

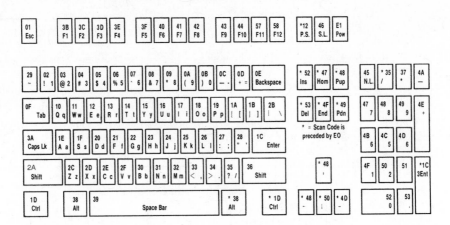

Figure 6.3 Hexadecimal scan codes for an enhanced keyboard.

When you hold down a key for more than half a second, the keyboard generates a sequence of scan codes that corresponds to the keystroke, repeated at a specified rate. The BIOS can tell that a key is being held down (not pressed repeatedly) because the keyboard does not generate any key-release codes in this sequence.

The keyboard recognizes only the *key* (not the character) you press, and supplies only the scan code that corresponds to the key. (The scan code simply indicates that a specific key has been pressed.) The BIOS interprets the scan code to determine which ASCII character corresponds to the keystroke. BIOS ROMs designed for the older 83-key and 84-key designs ignore the extra keys on the 101-key board; for this reason, many programs make no use of these additional keys.

Whenever you press a key, the keyboard generates not only the scan code but also Int 09h, which tells the ROM BIOS that a key has been pressed. Control of the system is transferred momentarily to the interrupt handler for Int 09h, which reads port 96 (60h) to determine which key was pressed. The service routine reads the scan code and converts it to a 16-bit code that represents the keystroke. The code's lower byte is the keystroke's ASCII value; its upper byte is the scan code. See Table 6.1 for a list of these codes.

Table 6.1 ASCII and Scan Codes

	Scan Code		
Key	PC	AT	Enhanced
Esc	01	01	01
! 1	02	02	02
@ 2	03	03	03
# 3	04	04	04

| Key | Scan Code | | |
	PC	AT	Enhanced
$ 4	05	05	05
% 5	06	06	06
^ 6	07	07	07
& 7	08	08	08
* 8	09	09	09
(9	0A	0A	0A
) 0	0B	0B	0B
_ -	0C	0C	0C
+ =	0D	0D	0D
Backspace	0E	0E	0E
Tab	0F	0F	0F
Q q	10	10	10
W w	11	11	11
E e	12	12	12
R r	13	13	13
T t	14	14	14
Y y	15	15	15
U u	16	16	16
I i	17	17	17
O o	18	18	18
P p	19	19	19
{ [	1A	1A	1A
}]	1B	1B	1B
Enter	1C	1C	1C
Left Ctrl	1D	1D	1D
A a	1E	1E	1E
S s	1F	1F	1F
D d	20	20	20
F f	21	21	21
G g	22	22	22
H h	23	23	23

continues

151

Table 6.1 Continued

Key	Scan Code		
	PC	AT	Enhanced
J j	24	24	24
K k	25	25	25
L l	26	26	26
: ;	27	27	27
" '	28	28	28
~ `	29	29	29
Left Shift	2A	2A	2A
| \	2B	2B	2B
Z z	2C	2C	2C
X x	2D	2D	2D
C c	2E	2E	2E
V v	2F	2F	2F
B b	30	30	30
N n	31	31	31
M m	32	32	32
< ,	33	33	33
> .	34	34	34
? /	35	35	35
Right Shift	36	36	36
PrtSc *	37	37	E0 12
Left Alt	38	38	38
Spacebar	39	39	39
Caps Lock	3A	3A	3A
F1	3B	3B	3B
F2	3C	3C	3C
F3	3D	3D	3D
F4	3E	3E	3E
F5	3F	3F	3F
F6	40	40	40
F7	41	41	41
F8	42	42	42

		Scan Code	
Key	PC	AT	Enhanced
F9	43	43	43
F10	44	44	44
Num Lock	45	45	45
Scroll Lock	46	46	46
7 Home	47	47	47
8 Cursor up	48	48	48
9 PgUp	49	49	49
Gray -	4A	4A	4A
4 Cursor left	4B	4B	4B
5	4C	4C	4C
6 Cursor right	4D	4D	4D
Gray +	4E	4E	4E
1 End	4F	4F	4F
2 Cursor down	50	50	50
3 PgDn	51	51	51
0 Ins	52	52	52
. Del	53	53	53

Personal Computer AT keyboard only

SysRq	N/A	54	N/A

Enhanced keyboard only

Gray Enter	N/A	N/A	E0 1C
Right Ctrl	N/A	N/A	E0 1D
Gray /	N/A	N/A	E0 35
Gray *	N/A	N/A	37
Right Alt	N/A	N/A	E0 38
Gray Home	N/A	N/A	E0 47
Gray C Up	N/A	N/A	E0 48
Gray PgUp	N/A	N/A	E0 49
Gray C Left	N/A	N/A	E0 4B
Gray C Right	N/A	N/A	E0 4D
Gray End	N/A	N/A	E0 4F

continues

DOS
PROGRAMMING

Table 6.1 Continued

	Scan Code		
Key	PC	AT	Enhanced
Gray C Down	N/A	N/A	E0 50
Gray PgDn	N/A	N/A	E0 51
Gray Ins	N/A	N/A	E0 52
Gray Del	N/A	N/A	E0 53
F11	N/A	N/A	57
F12	N/A	N/A	58
Pause/Break	N/A	N/A	E1

Special keys, such as the function keys and numeric keypad keys, have a zero in their lower byte to indicate that the keystroke is not a standard ASCII character and must be specially processed.

When the BIOS keyboard interrupt handler finishes processing a keystroke, it places the code in the keyboard buffer, where it remains until a program requests it. Two very special keystrokes, Ctrl-Break and Shift-PrintScreen, are *not* processed in this manner; rather, they generate interrupt requests that are processed immediately by other portions of the BIOS. Ctrl-Break invokes Int 1Bh, which DOS sets up to force a Ctrl-C into the buffer for later "normal" processing. Shift-PrintScreen invokes Int 05h, which performs the screen-printing actions.

You will not write any programs that access keyboard data at this level. Rather, the code in this chapter relies on the BIOS or DOS to preprocess all keyboard input data so that you have to deal with only the ASCII codes for normal keys and the scan codes for special keys.

Reading the Keyboard from BASIC

Before you start using DOS and BIOS calls to read the keyboard, let's look at a BASIC program that uses standard BASIC functions for keyboard input. The KEYBD.BAS program uses functions available in the BASIC interpreter (see Listing 6.1).

Listing 6.1

```
10 REM --- KEYBD.BAS     Basic keyboard demonstration
20 C$=INKEY$:IF C$="" THEN 20
30 GOSUB 100:GOTO 20
100 REM --- Display keyboard input
110 IF LEN(C$)>1 THEN GOSUB 200 ELSE GOSUB 300
```

```
120 PRINT USING "Character: ! ### ###";CH$;C;SC
130 RETURN
200 REM --- Keystroke has scan code included
210 CH$=".":C=ASC(MID$(C$,1,1)):SC=ASC(MID$(C$,2,1))
220 RETURN
300 REM --- Keystroke is character only
310 CH$=C$:C=ASC(C$):SC=0
320 RETURN
```

For compatibility with the BASIC interpreter, this program is written with line numbers. The simple structure of this program is shown in these steps:

1. Wait for a keystroke.

2. Print the keystroke character, ASCII code, and scan code.

3. Repeat from step 1.

INKEY$ (which is put in a tight loop in line 20 of Listing 6.1) provides a way to read the keyboard and not have to wait for a keystroke. The subroutine at line 100 translates the return from INKEY$ according to whether the string is more than one character long. In BASIC, if the string returned by INKEY$ is more than one character long, the first character is the character's ASCII value, and the second one is the scan code. (The subroutine beginning at line 200 deals with such a case.) Usually, the string is one character long. The subroutine at line 300 is used to decode the string.

If you run the program in Listing 6.1, you notice that the scan codes correspond only to a limited extent to individual keys (refer to Figures 6.1 and 6.2). The KEYBD.BAS program has the following limitations:

- INKEY$ returns only "meaningful" characters (in this case, characters that are "meaningful" only to the BASIC interpreter).

- Scan codes are returned only for completed keystrokes that are *not* ASCII characters. (You do not see the Shift keys, the Ctrl key, or the Alt key.)

From now on, rather than continue with an interpreter-compatible BASIC program, this book will work with the QuickBASIC compiler. Listing 6.2 shows the program modified for QuickBASIC to take advantage of the features of the compiler.

Listing 6.2

```
' KEYBD2.BAS

'QuickBASIC Keyboard Demonstration

Start:
    C$ = INKEY$: IF C$ = "" THEN GOTO Start
    GOSUB Display: GOTO Start
```

continues

Listing 6.2   Continued

```
Display:
    'Display Keyboard Input
    IF LEN(C$) > 1 THEN GOSUB Scan ELSE GOSUB Char
    PRINT USING "Character: ! ### ###"; CH$; C; SC
    RETURN

Scan:
    'Keystroke includes scan code
    CH$ = ".": C = ASC(MID$(C$, 1, 1)): SC = ASC(MID$(C$, 2, 1))
    RETURN

Char:
    'Keystroke is character only
    CH$ = C$: C = ASC(C$): SC = 0
    RETURN
```

Starting from the sample program in Listing 6.2, BIOS function calls will be substituted to perform input. Then you can see more of the keystrokes on the keyboard.

Using Int 16h to Access the Keyboard

When you get ready to use the BIOS functions, the first thing you notice is that Int 16h, Function 0 (the BIOS keyboard input function) waits for a keystroke (see Listing 6.3).

Listing 6.3

```c
/* Waitkey.c
   Listing 6.3 of DOS Programmer's Reference */

#include  <stdio.h>
#include  <dos.h>

void main()
{
    unsigned char  scancode;
    unsigned char  charcode;
    union REGS     regs;

    printf("Test of Int 16 keyboard services\n");
    printf("Press Esc to exit program\n");
    while (charcode != 27) {
        regs.h.ah = 0;
        int86(0x16, &regs, &regs);
        scancode = regs.h.ah;
        charcode = regs.h.al;
        printf("Scan: %.3d   ASCII: %.3d  [%c]\n",
            scancode, charcode, charcode);
    }
}
```

Rather than wait for a keystroke, you can read a keystroke only when one is available. Int 16h, Function 1 indicates whether a keystroke is waiting. If no key is waiting, the zero flag is set in the processor's flags register. You can test that register as shown in Listing 6.4.

Listing 6.4

```
/* Waitkey2.c
   Listing 6.4 of DOS Programmer's Reference */

#include  <stdio.h>
#include  <dos.h>

void main()
{
    unsigned char  scancode;
    unsigned char  charcode;
    union REGS     regs;

    printf("Test of Int 16 keyboard services\n");
    printf("Press Esc to exit program\n");
    while (charcode != 27) {
        while (1) {
            putchar('.');
            regs.h.ah = 1;
            int86(0x16, &regs, &regs);
            if ((regs.x.flags & 0x40) == 0)
                break;
        }
        regs.h.ah = 0;
        int86(0x16, &regs, &regs);
        scancode = regs.h.ah;
        charcode = regs.h.al;
        printf("\nScan: %.3d   ASCII: %.3d  [%c]\n",
            scancode, charcode, charcode);
    }
}
```

Before getting the key from the keyboard, the program first looks to see whether a key is ready. If no key is ready, it simply prints a dot on the screen. Whenever a key is pressed, the program stops printing dots and displays information that tells you which key was pressed. Then the program resumes printing dots.

Rather than "idle" while they wait for a keystroke, programs that have a way to check for keyboard input can do other tasks. You might use this type of routine, for example, to move data on-screen and terminate the operation when a key is pressed.

Int 16h, Function 2 lets you determine the state of keys you cannot "see": the Ins, Caps Lock, Num Lock, Scroll Lock, Alt, Ctrl, and left and right Shift keys. The next version of the keyboard input program lets you check the status of these keys (see Listing 6.5).

157

Listing 6.5

```
/* Keystat.c
   Listing 6.5 of DOS Programmer's Reference */

#include  <stdio.h>
#include  <dos.h>

#define VIDEO   0x10

/* Prototypes */
    void gotoxy(int r, int c);
    void cls(void);

void main()
{
    unsigned char  scancode;
    unsigned char  charcode;
    union REGS     regs;
    int  ins, caps, num, scroll;
    int  alt, ctrl, left, right;

    cls();
    gotoxy(0,0);
    printf("Test of Int 16 keyboard services\n");
    printf("Press Esc to exit program\n");
    gotoxy(10, 12);
    puts(" INS CAPS  NUM SCRL  ALT CTRL LEFT RGHT");

    while (charcode != 27) {
        while (1) {
            regs.h.ah = 2;
            int86(0x16, &regs, &regs);
            ins = regs.h.al & 0x80;
            caps = regs.h.al & 0x40;
            num = regs.h.al & 0x20;
            scroll = regs.h.al & 0x10;
            alt = regs.h.al & 0x08;
            ctrl = regs.h.al & 0x04;
            left = regs.h.al & 0x02;
            right = regs.h.al & 0x01;
            gotoxy(11, 12);
            printf("%s %s %s %s %s %s %s %s\n",
                ins ? " ON " : " OFF",
                caps ? " ON " : " OFF",
                num ? " ON " : " OFF",
                scroll ? " ON " : " OFF",
                alt ? " ON " : " OFF",
                ctrl ? " ON " : " OFF",
                left ? " ON " : " OFF",
                right ? " ON " : " OFF");
            regs.h.ah = 1;
            int86(0x16, &regs, &regs);
            if ((regs.x.flags & 0x40) == 0) break;
        }
```

```
                regs.h.ah = 0;
                int86(0x16, &regs, &regs);
                scancode = regs.h.ah;
                charcode = regs.h.al;
                printf("Scan: %.3d   ASCII: %.3d  [%c]\n",
                    scancode, charcode, charcode);
            }
        cls();
        gotoxy(0,0);
    }

    void gotoxy(row,col)
        int row, col;
    {
        union REGS regs;

        if (row<0 || row > 24) return;
        if (col<0 || col > 79) return;

        regs.h.ah = 2;
        regs.h.bh = 0;
        regs.h.dh = row;
        regs.h.dl = col;
        int86(VIDEO,&regs,&regs);
    }

    void cls()
    {
        union REGS regs;

        regs.h.ah = 0x06;
        regs.h.al = 0;
        regs.h.bh = 7;
        regs.h.ch = 0;
        regs.h.cl = 0;
        regs.h.dh = 25;
        regs.h.dl = 80;
        int86(VIDEO,&regs,&regs);
    }
```

In the program in Listing 6.5, `putchar('.')` has been replaced by code that checks the status of the special keys and prints their status in the center of the screen. This status information gives you a complete picture of what is happening on the keyboard. If you want your program to check for a trigger event such as both the left and right Shift keys being pressed, Int 16h, Function 2 can tell when that event occurs.

Int 16h, Function 2 returns a single byte in the AL register. Every bit corresponds to a specific keystroke. Table 6.2 shows the bit assignments for this function.

Table 6.2 Keyboard Flag Byte

Bit 76543210	Meaning
.......0	Right Shift key not pressed
.......1	Right Shift key pressed
......0.	Left Shift key not pressed
......1.	Left Shift key pressed
.....0..	Ctrl key not pressed
.....1..	Ctrl key pressed
....0...	Alt key not pressed
....1...	Alt key pressed
...0....	Scroll Lock off
...1....	Scroll Lock on
..0.....	Num Lock off
..1.....	Num Lock on
.0......	Caps Lock off
.1......	Caps Lock on
0.......	Insert off
1.......	Insert on

BIOS functions for keyboard input represent the most primitive level of access short of going to the machine. The BIOS level is the lowest level you can use and still be guaranteed that a program is portable to compatible PCs.

Using Int 21h to Access the Keyboard

When you go to the DOS level to get keyboard input in the conventional way, you lose immediate access to every possible keystroke. DOS input functions indicate whether special keys have been pressed (if the first byte returned is a zero, the next byte is the scan code). But DOS functions do not give you the scan code for any key that has an ASCII code, nor does DOS report on the status of Alt, Shift, and so on. In addition, the most often used DOS input functions wait for a keystroke, which can force use of the BIOS interface in some programs. Later, this chapter looks at one DOS input function that overcomes this limitation.

Int 21h, Function 1 (Character Input with Echo) is the most basic DOS character input function you might want to use (see Listing 6.6).

Listing 6.6

```c
/* Keyin.c
   Listing 6.6 of DOS Programmer's Reference */

#include <stdio.h>
#include <dos.h>

#define CTRL_D    0x04
#define LF        0x0a
#define ENTER     0x0d

/* Prototypes */
    unsigned int keyin(void);

void main()
{
    int c;

    printf("Testing Int 21h input functions\n");
    printf("Press Ctrl-D to exit program\n");
    while ((c = keyin())!=CTRL_D)
        if (c >= 256)
            printf("SPECIAL: %d\n",c - 256);
        else if (c==ENTER)
            putchar(LF);
}

unsigned int keyin()
{
    union REGS regs;
    int offset;

    offset = 0;
    regs.h.ah = 0x01;
    intdos(&regs,&regs);
    if (regs.h.al == 0) {
        offset = 256;
        regs.h.ah = 0x01;
        intdos(&regs,&regs);
    }
    return(regs.h.al + offset);
}
```

The keyin.c program takes the following approach:

1. Wait for a character from the keyboard.

2. If the character is a special character (a function key or a cursor key, for example), print SPECIAL and the key's scan code.

3. If the character is the Enter key, the character input function outputs a Return without a line feed; you must output a line feed to the screen.

4. Repeat from Step 1.

161

If you try to run the program without the special portion that prints the line-feed character to the screen, you will see the characters echoed by the DOS function as you type them; when you press Enter, however, the cursor does not move to the next line. Remember that the function echoes the *characters you type* and that the Enter key represents only the carriage return—not the line-feed character.

One of the program's interesting features is its special coding that differentiates function keys from regular keys. Because ASCII characters are always less than or equal to 255, this feature creates an extended character set by adding 256 to the scan value of a key that returns a 0 ASCII code. In practice, this method often simplifies the process of decoding the keystrokes and causes no problems. Many programmers do not use this method because they associate the keystrokes with character variables. By associating the returned characters with integers, you have a larger range of special codes for representing special keystrokes.

A problem with this approach to reading in characters when you expect special keys (function keys and arrows, for example) is that when you make the second call to get the special key's scan code, the DOS function prints the scan code's ASCII equivalent as though you were retrieving the ASCII code rather than the scan code. To prevent this situation from occurring, you can use Int 21h, Function 8 and echo the characters yourself (see Listing 6.7).

Listing 6.7

```
/* Keyin2.c
   Listing 6.7 of DOS Programmer's Reference */

#include <stdio.h>
#include <dos.h>

#define CTRL_D  0x04
#define LF      0x0a
#define ENTER   0x0d

/* Prototypes */
    unsigned int keyin(void);

void main()
{
    int c;
    printf("Testing Int 21h input functions\n");
    printf("Press Ctrl-D to exit program\n");
    while ((c = keyin())!=CTRL_D)
        if (c >= 256) {
            printf("SPECIAL: %d\n",c - 256);
        } else {
            putchar(c);
            if (c == ENTER)
                putchar(LF);
        }
}

unsigned int keyin()
```

```
    {
        union REGS regs;
        int offset;

        offset = 0;
        regs.h.ah = 0x08;
        intdos(&regs,&regs);
        if (regs.h.al == 0) {
            offset = 256;
            regs.h.ah = 0x08;
            intdos(&regs,&regs);
        }
        return(regs.h.al + offset);
    }
```

The differences between this program and the one in Listing 6.6 are so subtle that you can miss them if you do not look closely. First, in the `keyin()` function, you set up to call Int 21h, Function 8 rather than Function 1. Your main routine must echo every character to the screen as it is typed (because the DOS kernel is not echoing characters for you). Because the special keys are handled separately, you are not plagued by the echo of bogus function-key codes—only the keys you type are echoed.

Every DOS function used so far in this chapter waits for a keystroke, but, as with the BIOS functions, you can check periodically to see whether a character is waiting (this process is called *polling*). Interrupt 21h, Function 0Bh indicates whether a character is waiting to be read. Listing 6.8 shows how to use this function to perform a task while you wait for a keystroke.

Listing 6.8

```
/* Keyin3.c
   Listing 6.8 of DOS Programmer's Reference */

#include <stdio.h>
#include <dos.h>

#define CTRL_D 0x04
#define LF     0x0a
#define ENTER  0x0d

/* Prototypes */
    unsigned int keyin(void);
    unsigned int charwait(void);

void main()
{
    int c;

    printf("Testing Int 21h input functions\n");
    printf("Press Ctrl-D to exit program\n");
    while ((c = keyin())!=CTRL_D)
```

continues

Listing 6.8 Continued

```
            if (c >= 256) {
                printf("SPECIAL: %d\n",c - 256);
            } else {
                putchar(c);
                if (c == ENTER)
                    putchar(LF);
            }
    }

unsigned int keyin()
{
    union REGS regs;
    int offset;

    while (!charwait())
        putchar('.');
    offset = 0;
    regs.h.ah = 0x08;
    intdos(&regs,&regs);
    if (regs.h.al == 0) {
        offset = 256;
        regs.h.ah = 0x08;
        intdos(&regs,&regs);
    }
    return(regs.h.al + offset);
}

unsigned int charwait()
{
    union REGS regs;

    regs.h.ah = 0x0b;
    intdos(&regs,&regs);
    return(regs.h.al);
}
```

This program introduces a new function, charwait(), which watches for a character at the keyboard. If a character is waiting, charwait() returns TRUE; otherwise, it returns FALSE.

The charwait() function is based on Int 21h, Function 0Bh, which sets the AL register to FFh (255) if a character is waiting, and to 0 otherwise. By returning the value of the AL register, the charwait() function indicates whether a character is waiting (FALSE is a zero value, and TRUE is a nonzero value).

To gauge how quickly the program checks for characters, run it and watch the periods march across the screen while the program waits for you to type a character. This program is fairly responsive to input. You can make it extremely sluggish by substituting a long, complicated operation for the simple putchar('.').

Earlier, this chapter mentioned a special DOS input function that overcomes many of the limitations of conventional DOS input: the general I/O function Int 21h, Function 06h.

If the DL register contains 0FFh when Int 21h, Function 06h is invoked, the function obtains input from the keyboard buffer (and returns with the zero flag set if no character is available). If anything else is in the DL register, it is output to the CRT and no checks are performed. This single function, therefore, provides most of the capability you would get by using direct BIOS input and output, and it retains full DOS compatibility. Because it is one of the original "CP/M legacy" functions, it unfortunately is not as popular as it might be.

Listing 6.9 is a translation of Listing 6.8 from C to Turbo Pascal, modified to use Int 21h, Function 06h for both input and output. Function and procedure names remain the same, and the action is identical. Rather than use Int 21h, Function 0Bh to check for key-ready status, however, this program simply tests the zero flag by using the ZFlag constant provided by the DOS unit of Turbo Pascal, and therefore eliminating the charwait function; rather than use putchar for single-byte output, this program adds the putch function to perform output through Function 06h.

Listing 6.9

```
{ keyin4.pas }

program keyin4;
uses DOS;                   { run-time DOS library  }

const
  CTRL_D  = $04;
  LF      = $0a;
  ENTER   = $0d;

var
  c   : integer;
  reg : registers;          { declared in DOS unit }

procedure putch( i : integer );
  begin
    reg.ah := $06;          { general I/O function }
    reg.dl := byte(i);      { OUTPUT the character }
    MsDos(reg);
  end;

function keyin : integer;
  var
    i      : integer;
    offset : integer;

  begin
    repeat                  { wait for keystroke   }
      putch( $2E );         { put '.' on CRT       }
      reg.ah := $06;        { general I/O function }
      reg.dl := $FF;        { flag for INPUT use   }
      MsDos(reg);
      i := reg.flags AND FZero;
```

continues

Listing 6.9 Continued

```
        until i <> FZero;       { declared in DOS unit }

      if (reg.al = 0) then   { flag as extended key }
        begin
          offset := 256;
          reg.ah := $06;      { and go get scan code }
          reg.dl := $FF;
          MsDos(reg);
        end
      else                    { set as normal key    }
        offset := 0;

      keyin := reg.al + offset;
    end;

begin
  writeln('Testing Int 21h input functions');
  writeln('Press Ctrl-D to exit program');
  c := keyin;
  while (keyin <> CTRL_D) do
    begin
      if (c >= 256) then
        begin
          writeln('SPECIAL: ',c - 256);
        end
      else
        begin
          putch(c);
            if (c = ENTER) then
              putch(LF);
        end;
      c := keyin;
    end;
end.
```

If you are willing to relinquish control over the input until Enter is pressed, you can call the buffered input function (Int 21h, Function 0Ah) and let it get your input, echo it, and allow line editing. Some books about DOS programming indicate that the function will return function keys, arrows, and other special keys by returning a 2-byte sequence (including a zero byte and the scan code). The keyin5.c program (see Listing 6.10) was written to show these special keys if they are returned—but they aren't. The *IBM Technical Reference* manual states that the 2-byte key codes are not included.

Listing 6.10

```
/* Keyin5.c
   Listing 6.10 of DOS Programmer's Reference */

#include <stdio.h>
#include <dos.h>
```

```
#define CTRL_D  0x04
#define LF      0x0a
#define ENTER   0x0d

/* Prototypes */
    char getline(char *b, int n);

void main()
{
    char buffer[11];
    printf("Testing Int 21h Input Functions\n");
    printf("Press Enter with no input to exit program\n");
    while (getline(buffer,10) > 0) {
        printf("<<%s>>\n",buffer);
    }
}

char getline(buffer,n)
    char *buffer;
    int n;
{
    union REGS regs;
    char locbuf[514];
    int i, j;

    locbuf[0] = n;
    locbuf[1] = 0;
    regs.h.ah = 0x0a;
    regs.x.dx = (int)&locbuf;
    intdos(&regs,&regs);
    for(i=0, j=0; i<locbuf[1]; i++, j++)
        if (locbuf[i+2]==0) {
            i++;
            buffer[j] = 'X';
        } else {
            buffer[j] = locbuf[i+2];
        }
    buffer[j] = NULL;
    return(locbuf[1]);
}
```

The requirements of the buffered input function make it special. Because of its layout, the buffer does not fit naturally with the way strings are handled in BASIC, C, or Pascal. When the function is invoked, you must pass it a buffer large enough to handle the input characters plus two extra characters. The first character in the buffer is the *maximum* number of characters to be entered; the second, which is filled in by DOS, represents the number of characters read.

Identifying the Level of Keyboard Support

If the BIOS supports the enhanced keyboard, two sets of BIOS functions access the keyboard: Functions 00h, 01h, and 02h support the older keyboards, and Functions 10h, 11h, and 12h support the newer keyboards. How can a program tell whether it can use the enhanced keyboard functions?

You can use Function 05h, Write to Keyboard Buffer, to test for the presence of enhanced keyboard functions. When you write a value of FFFFh to the buffer, you should find AL set to either 00h or 01h. If this is the case, use Function 10h, Get Keystroke, to read the buffer. If the enhanced keyboard functions are present, you will read the FFFFh value in a maximum of 16 calls (because there are 16 words in the keyboard buffer).

With DOS 5.0, detection of the enhanced keyboard is automatic; Functions 01h, 06h, 07h, 08h, 0Ah, 0Bh, and 0Ch all use the enhanced keyboard functions if they are present (see Listing 6.11).

Listing 6.11

```
        page 55,132

; kbdtype.asm
; Determine whether the BIOS enhanced keyboard functions are
; present. Prints the level supported and returns an errorlevel
; of 0 (no enhanced keyboard) or 1 (enhanced keyboard).

        .model  tiny
        .code
        .startup
check   proc

        ;   clear keyboard buffer
clear:  mov     ah,1            ; check for keystroke present
        int     16h
        jz      buffer_clear    ; if none, proceed...
        mov     ah,0            ; read the keystroke and discard it
        int     16h
        jmp     clear           ; check again

        ;   stuff 0FFFFh into buffer
buffer_clear:
        mov     ax,5FFh         ; stuff FFFF in
        mov     cx,0FFFFh
        int     16h
        cmp     al,1            ; success?
        ja      no_enhanced     ; no, BIOS plainly doesn't support it

        ;   try to read 0FFFFh
        mov     cx,1            ; 16 entries in the standard buffer
tryit:  mov     ah,11h          ; use enhanced check for keystroke present
        int     16h
        jz      no_enhanced     ; nothing there, it didn't work
        mov     ah,10h          ; use enhanced function to read keystroke
        int     16h
        cmp     ax,0FFFFh       ; our keystroke?
        je      enhanced
        loop    tryit
```

```
        ;    no enhanced keyboard
no_enhanced:
        mov    dx,offset no   ; print negative message
        mov    al,1           ; set error code to 1
printit:
        push   ax             ; save error code
        mov    ah,9           ; print string
        int    21h
        pop    ax             ; restore error code
        mov    ah,04CH        ; exit with error code
        int    21h            ; exit

        ;    enhanced keyboard
enhanced:
        mov    dx,offset yes  ; print positive message
        xor    al,al          ; zero error code
        jmp    printit
check   endp

no      db     "NO "
yes     db     "ENHANCED KEYBOARD FUNCTIONS SUPPORTED$"
        end
```

The Mouse

The use of a mouse (or an equivalent device, such as a trackball) as part of computer systems is increasing. Furthermore, software products that depend on a mouse for their effective use are increasing. Microsoft Windows can be used with only the keyboard, but the full convenience of the graphics interface can be obtained only with a mouse. Although programs such as Microsoft Paint (which runs under Windows) can be used with a keyboard, doing so easily is impossible. Guide (Owl International's Hypertext system) cannot be used without a mouse.

DOS does not include a mouse driver. As you probably are already aware, DOS does not include drivers for many different types of peripherals you might want to use. When DOS was developed, the decision was made to make it extensible by enabling users to add device drivers to control additional devices. One of these drivers, Microsoft's MOUSE.SYS, is added to the operating system when you boot the system. (Microsoft provides MOUSE.SYS if you purchase one of its mice.) This section describes how the mouse software works.

Learning How the Mouse Works

The mouse is one of the truly simple pieces of equipment you can attach to a computer. It consists of nothing more than a little ball inside a "mouse" that rolls on a flat surface. As the ball rotates, circuitry in the mouse reports the movement to the computer, which interprets and translates that movement into mouse-cursor movement on-screen. In addition to the ball, the mouse contains two or three buttons (pressure switches) you can use to signal the computer.

169

Initializing the Mouse Driver

Depending on which software you have, you may have one of several ways to set up the mouse driver. Some packages create a TSR to handle the mouse; others have a driver. If you have a driver, you install it on the system by including in your CONFIG.SYS file a line that tells the system to load the driver when it boots. If you have Microsoft's mouse driver stored in the root directory on drive C, you use the following line:

```
DEVICE=C:\MOUSE.SYS
```

Where Is the Mouse?

First, your program must determine whether a mouse is installed. Int 33h, Function 0 tells you that a mouse is available if AX is nonzero on return. (With DOS versions earlier than 3.0, the vector for Int 33h is not initialized to point to an IRET; before using the Function 0 test, you should verify that the vector does not point to location 0000:0000.)

If you know that a mouse is available, you can use it by either periodically polling it for changes in position and key clicks or by setting up an interrupt service routine to act whenever the mouse moves or a button is clicked. For simplicity, only the polling technique is discussed here.

Because the mouse driver takes care of the mouse cursor's on-screen position, your program does not have to do so. You simply need to know that the mouse is positioned where users want something done. The sample program Mouse.c, which is based on Keyin3.c, shows how you can the check the mouse while you wait for other input (see Listing 6.12).

Listing 6.12

```c
/* Mouse.c
   Listing 6.12 of DOS Programmer's Reference */

#include <stdio.h>
#include <stdlib.h>
#include <dos.h>
#include <string.h>

#define CTRL_D   0x04
#define LF       0x0a
#define ENTER    0x0d
#define MOUSE    0x33
#define VIDEO    0x10

static int Buttons = 0;

/* Prototypes */
    unsigned int keyin(void);
    unsigned int charwait(void);
    void gotoxy(int r, int c);
```

```
        void cls(void);
        void mousepos(void);
        void chk_mouse(void);
        void mouseon(void);
        void mouseoff(void);
void main()
{
    int c;

    cls();
    gotoxy(0,0);
    printf("Testing Mouse Input\n");
    printf("Press Ctrl-D to exit program\n");
    chk_mouse();
    while ((c = keyin())!=CTRL_D)
        if (c >= 256) {
            printf("SPECIAL: %d\n",c - 256);
        } else {
            putchar(c);
            if (c == ENTER)
                putchar(LF);
        }
    mouseoff();
    cls();
    gotoxy(0,0);
}

unsigned int keyin()
{
    union REGS regs;
    int offset;

    while (!charwait())
        mousepos();
    offset = 0;
    regs.h.ah = 0x08;
    intdos(&regs,&regs);
    if (regs.h.al == 0) {
        offset = 256;
        regs.h.ah = 0x08;
        intdos(&regs,&regs);
    }
    return(regs.h.al + offset);
}

unsigned int charwait()
{
    union REGS regs;

    regs.h.ah = 0x0b;
    intdos(&regs,&regs);
    return(regs.h.al);
}

void chk_mouse()
```

continues

Listing 6.12 Continued

```c
{
    union REGS regs;

    struct SREGS sregs;
    regs.x.ax = 0x3533;
    intdosx(&regs,&regs,&sregs);
    if ((regs.x.bx | sregs.es) == 0) {
        printf("No mouse driver present\n");
        exit(255);
    }
    regs.x.ax = 0;
    int86(MOUSE,&regs,&regs);
    if (regs.x.ax != 0) {
        Buttons = regs.x.bx;
        mouseon();
    }
}

void mouseon()
{
    union REGS regs;
    struct SREGS sregs;
    if (Buttons) {
        regs.x.ax = 0x01;
        int86(MOUSE,&regs,&regs);
    }
}

void mouseoff()
{
    union REGS regs;
    struct SREGS sregs;
    if (Buttons) {
        regs.x.ax = 0x02;
        int86(MOUSE,&regs,&regs);
    }
}

void mousepos()
{
    union REGS regs;
    char status[6];

    gotoxy(12,10);
    if (Buttons) {
        regs.x.ax = 0x03;
        int86(MOUSE,&regs,&regs);
        switch(regs.x.bx & 0x03) {
            case 0:     /* no buttons */
                strcpy(status,"NONE ");
                break;
            case 1:     /* left button */
                strcpy(status,"LEFT ");
                break;
```

```
                    case 2:    /* right button */
                        strcpy(status,"RIGHT");
                        break;
                    case 3:    /* both buttons */
                        strcpy(status,"BOTH ");
                        break;
                }
                printf("X = %4.4d  Y = %4.4d %s",
                    regs.x.cx,regs.x.dx, status);
            } else {
                printf(" No mouse");
            }
        }

        void gotoxy(row,col)
            int row, col;
        {
            union REGS regs;

            if (row<0 || row > 24) return;
            if (col<0 || col > 79) return;

            regs.h.ah = 2;
            regs.h.bh = 0;
            regs.h.dh = row;
            regs.h.dl = col;
            int86(VIDEO,&regs,&regs);
        }

        void cls()
        {
            union REGS regs;

            regs.h.ah = 0x06;
            regs.h.al = 0;
            regs.h.bh = 7;
            regs.h.ch = 0;
            regs.h.cl = 0;
            regs.h.dh = 25;
            regs.h.dl = 80;
            int86(VIDEO,&regs,&regs);
        }
```

Mouse.c includes the chk_mouse() function, which checks for the existence of a mouse driver and, if the driver is present, for the mouse. Rather than print periods as it waits for input, the program moves the cursor to the center of the screen and displays information about the mouse's position and buttons.

If you have a mouse installed, move it around and watch the mouse status change to reflect the mouse's movement. Within these basic functions is a minimum level of operability for mouse functions. The gotoxy() function, which uses the BIOS screen-addressing routines to position the cursor on-screen, also has been added to the Mouse.c program. (Chapter 5, "Output Devices," explains how this function operates.)

The sample program includes only three basic mouse functions. The first, which determines whether a mouse is installed and how many buttons it has, sets the number of buttons in a global variable. When other mouse functions are called, they can check this variable to determine whether they have anything to do.

If a mouse *is* installed, you call the second function (Int 33h, Function 1) to display the mouse cursor on-screen. With the mouse available, you call Int 33h, Function 3 to check for the mouse status (position and button status) whenever you check for (but do not find) a character. This function returns the status of the buttons coded into the bottom two bits of the BX register. If bit 0 is set, the left button has been pressed; if bit 1 is set, the right button has been pressed.

The mouse's position on-screen is always given in the range from 0 to 639 across the screen (x-coordinate) and from 0 to 199 down the screen (y-coordinate). Depending on the current display mode, you can determine from Table 6.3 the mouse's position in terms of columns or coordinates.

Table 6.3   Mouse Coordinates

Screen Mode	Coordinates
0 or 1	row = DX/8, column = CX/16
2 or 3	row = DX/8, column = DX/8
4 or 5	x = CX/2, y = DX
6	x = CX, y = DX
7	row = DX/8, column = CX/8
14 to 16	x = CX, y = DX

Additional mouse functions (described in the section "Interrupt 33h: Mouse Functions" near the end of this book) help you control the size, shape, and on-screen boundaries of the mouse cursor, and the speed of on-screen movement in response to that of the mouse. You also can set a function to be called whenever a mouse event (such as a keypress or key release) occurs. You learn about this type of routine, called an interrupt handler, in Chapter 11.

Summary

This chapter looked at keyboard and mouse functions and described some basic operations you can use to implement input functions. By using the keyboard functions available through the BIOS, you can tell which keys are pressed on the keyboard and keep track of operations. You can see not only the ASCII codes for character input (like those returned from high-level language input functions) but also the scan codes, which are returned for only some keys. You can monitor the position of the Shift, Alt, Ctrl, Scroll Lock, Num Lock, and Caps Lock keys.

Using the mouse functions on DOS Int 33h, you can monitor the position of the buttons on the mouse and the position of the mouse on-screen. You can even set interrupts for mouse functions that execute special handlers whenever mouse events (such as a key click) occur.

7

Serial Devices

The modern computing world's serial devices are fascinating. Thanks to serial devices, we can communicate with different people around the world through such services as CompuServe or MCI Mail. Why serial devices work the way they do and how you can exploit their properties are the subjects of this chapter.

Throughout this chapter, you will work with serial devices in terms of communications with other computers—the most visible use of such communications today. Serial communications can be used also with printers, sensors, and many other devices, and the communications do not have to be two-way. Communications with printers, for example, are predominantly one-way: from computer to printer. Or you might build a program to read the Associated Press news wire, which is a 1200 bps (bits per second) one-way data feed, or the NOAA weather wire, which is a 50 bps, one-way data feed.

This chapter concentrates on a simple two-way terminal communications program, which embodies all aspects of serial communications. Before you write a terminal program, however, you should understand how the serial interface works. After defining some basic terminology, specifics are provided about the way the IBM PC's serial interface chip (the UART) works. Then the discussion progresses to the hardware level so that you learn how to control the chip directly.

With the groundwork laid, you will write two terminal programs. The first one uses the BIOS functions to access the serial port. You will see that this type of program is too slow for serious communications. You can gain some speed and control by working directly with the UART chip. Although the second terminal program illustrates this technique, even this program is too slow for practical communications at 1200 bps. For a truly practical communications program, you have to combine the skills learned in this chapter with those you learn in Chapter 11, "Interrupt Handlers." Writing an interrupt-driven communications program, a subject not covered in this book, tests the mettle and understanding of any PC programmer. For a practical example of writing an interrupt-driven communications routine, refer to the book *Advanced Assembly Language,* by Allen L. Wyatt (Que Corporation).

Serial Interfaces

Fundamentally, a serial interface transforms the computer's internal, parallel format of data (an 8-bit byte) into a serial format (1 bit) that can be transmitted over a single data line. This transformation can be performed by software; in a PC, however, it is performed more effectively by hardware.

Figure 7.1 illustrates the basic purpose of a serial interface: to convert information from parallel to serial format or from serial to parallel format. Data enters one side of the interface and emerges, translated, from the other side. The interface converts data to a serial format by converting each character into a "packet" of information that can be transmitted in a way that is agreed on by both the sender and the receiver. (The subject of serial formats is discussed in greater detail later in this chapter.) Computers can communicate successfully with one another only if each end of the *serial link* (the serial connection between two computers or between a computer and another device) uses the same format for the data and the same transmission speed.

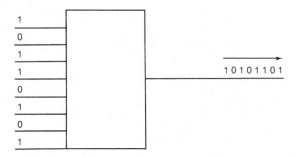

Figure 7.1 A serial interface converts the format of data from parallel (in) to serial (out).

Two methods of transmitting serial information are generally accepted. Both are named for the timing method that paces the information transmitted and received over the serial link. The first method, called *synchronous communication*, maintains rigid control of transmission and reception of data through the link. In this process, data is transmitted at precisely timed intervals. The clocking information is transmitted with the data so that the receiving computer can be synchronized with the information received. A discussion of this type of communications, generally used in minicomputer or mainframe applications, is beyond the scope of this book.

In the second method, called *asynchronous communication*, individual information packets are placed on the communications line with no precisely defined timing between them. These data packets can be transmitted quickly, one after another, or with varying time delays between each transmission. The asynchronous method is native to most microcomputers, including the IBM family.

Although you can buy hardware interfaces for other types of serial communication (such as the previously mentioned synchronous method), asynchronous communication should suffice for most general-purpose needs.

Figure 7.2 shows a serial information packet (as a function of time for asynchronous communications) on a communications line. The line usually is kept in a *mark state* (high voltage). The start of a character (the start bit) is signaled by a drop to the *space state* (low voltage). To determine whether the next bit is high or low, the line is sampled at precisely timed intervals based on the bit rate. The data bits are followed by one or more stop bits, in the mark state, which allow sufficient time for the character to be processed and for the system to get ready for the next character.

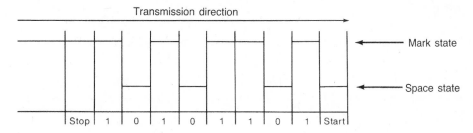

Figure 7.2   Serial transmission.

In preparation for a more detailed discussion of asynchronous communications, you should understand basic communications terminology. As you will recall, a serial interface converts parallel data into packets of information that can be transmitted easily through a serial communications link. These packets are made up of a specific number of bits of information, each with a specific purpose: start bits, data bits, stop bits, and parity. The following list defines these and a few other critical terms:

- *Start bit.* A bit sent before the actual character data, to alert the receiving computer that a character is coming. Start bits are sent automatically by the serial device.

- *Data bits.* The bits representing the individual character being transmitted. (The number of data bits is often referred to as the *word length.*) Normal communications to serial devices use a word length of either seven bits if parity is computed (see the following definition) or eight bits if no parity is computed. The serial communications chip on an IBM PC can handle from five to eight data bits.

- *Parity.* A simple character-level "goodness" check the receiver can use to see whether the character was received correctly. Parity is computed by counting the number of bits set to 1 in the data portion of the information packet being transmitted and then appending a parity bit representative of the type of parity you want. For EVEN parity, the total number of data bits set to 1 plus the parity bit must result in an even number. Conversely, for ODD parity, the number of data bits set to 1 plus the parity bit must result in an odd number. Other possible settings for the parity bit include MARK (always set to 1), SPACE (always set to 0), or NONE (always ignored).

- *Stop bits*. The bits sent at the end of the information packet to give the receiver time to process a character before the next one arrives. One stop bit is normal for all communications you are likely to handle. (Two stop bits are necessary only when communications occur at extremely slow speeds, such as 110 bps.)

- *Baud rate*. An electrical term that represents the signaling (or transfer) rate of a communications line. This term is frequently (albeit incorrectly) used to refer to the bit rate.

- *Bit rate*. The transmission speed, expressed as bits per second, and frequently (albeit incorrectly) referred to as the baud rate. Bit rate, the more accurate term, is used in this book.

- *Full duplex*. A means of communication in which the information displayed on your screen is an echo of the character you have transmitted to a remote computer.

- *Half duplex*. A means of communication in which the information sent to a remote computer is not echoed back to your computer.

When one computer communicates with another, both machines must operate by a set of predefined parameters that define the format in which information is transferred. If both computers are not set to the same values, communication between them is not reliable. One reason communication between computers is less widespread than it might be is that programmers have been unable to agree on a standard for communication that doesn't require users to understand a specialized, frustrating terminology.

Several configurations, however, are fairly standard. Generally, either eight data bits, no parity, and one stop bit or seven data bits, EVEN or ODD parity, and one stop bit will work. The bit rate for most on-line computer systems is fairly well-established at 1200, 2400, or 9600 bps. If you try one of these configurations, you almost always can match one of the on-line computer systems.

After an information packet has been transmitted, timing is critical. The communications line is idle until the start bit is received. After the start bit arrives, the line has to be sampled at precise intervals to receive the individual bits that make up the character. The parity bit, used to calculate the correctness of the transmitted character, follows the data. Finally, the stop bits are received and discarded, and the receiver again waits for a start bit.

If this background information has confused you, relax. IBM microcomputers are equipped with hardware that manages the low-level details of serial communication. After you have determined which communications parameters to use and have entered that information, the serial-conversion hardware ensures that you get what you want.

Serial Conversion: The UART

IBM microcomputers (and most compatibles) use a hardware chip originally based on the 8250 Universal Asynchronous Receiver/Transmitter, manufactured by National Semiconductor. Other models of this chip have been used since the early days of the PC and PC/XT. The latest are the PC16450 and PC16550. Both chips are functionally equivalent to the 8250 but offer more efficiency and greater speed. The PC16550, in addition to being compatible with the 8250, also has an operation mode that uses a FIFO (first-in, first-out) data buffer that greatly increases throughput. Throughout this chapter, all three of these chips are referred to simply as the UART (Universal Asynchronous Receiver/Transmitter).

Compared to some systems that rely on software to manage their communications properly, the UART is a wonder. By attending to the details of receiving and transmitting bits of information, the UART frees the programmer for other tasks.

Suppose that you want to send data across a series of wires while the voltage level on the line changes. If you were to write a program to manage the line, you could control the line directly and signal anything you wanted. Sound difficult? In concept, it isn't. But the process is tedious and subject to subtle errors. Some systems (the original TRS-80 Color Computer, for example) can handle serial communications in only this way.

With the UART, you do not have to go to the trouble of programming a software controller to get data on and off a communications line. For much less effort than you would spend writing and testing a software UART, the UART chip gives you an enormous amount of control and allows rapid, standard communications with other devices.

The 8250 and 16450 UARTs each have 10 programmable 1-byte registers; the 16550 has 11. These registers control and monitor the serial port. Most of the registers are used for initialization, and only a few are used regularly. All the registers are accessed through seven I/O port addresses. These addresses are calculated as an offset from a base address that varies according to which communications port is used. The base addresses for COM1: through COM4: are shown in Table 7.1; the offsets from these addresses, which control each UART register, are listed in Table 7.2.

Table 7.1   Base Addresses for the IBM Communications Ports

Communications Port	Base Address
COM1:	03F8h
COM2:	02F8h
COM3:	03E8h
COM4:	02E8h

Table 7.2   UART Registers: Offset from Base Address

Offset	LSR Bit 7	Meaning
0	0	Transmitter holding register (THR) and receiver data register (RDR)
0	1	Baud rate divisor, low byte (BRDL)
1	0	Interrupt enable register (IER)
1	1	Baud rate divisor, high byte (BRDH)
2	x	Interrupt identification register (IIR) and FIFO control register (FCR—16550 UART only)
3	x	Line control register (LCR)
4	x	Modem control register (MCR)
5	x	Line status register (LSR)
6	x	Modem status register (MSR)

You may have noticed that, even though the UART has 10 or 11 registers to control its operation, there are only seven port addresses. Several of these seven addresses serve more than one register. At offset 0, the THR is accessed whenever you *write* to the port, and the RDR is accessed whenever you *read* from the port. Because neither register requires both read and write access, this combination makes sense. This arrangement is the same one used on the 16550 UART; the IIR and the FCR share the same register. The IIR is a read-only register, and the FCR is a write-only register.

Register offsets 0 and 1 serve another function when bit 7 of the LSR is set to 1. When this happens, these two ports access the BRD registers. (Because the BRD registers are accessed only during initialization of the chip, they can be kept safely out of the way during normal operations.)

Let's look at what each UART register does.

The Transmitter Holding Register (THR)

The transmitter holding register (THR) holds the byte of data that is about to be sent. You write data to this register when bit 5 of the line status register (LSR) indicates that the register is empty.

The Receiver Data Register (RDR)

The receiver data register (RDR) holds the byte of data most recently received from the communications line. You read this register when LSR bit 0 indicates that a byte has been received.

The Baud Rate Divisor (BRD)

The baud rate divisor (BRD) is a 16-bit number that specifies the bit transfer rate (*not* the baud rate, despite the official name given by the UART designers) used by the UART. It is divided between two 8-bit ports (BRDL and BRDH). To determine the bit transfer rate, you divide the UART's internal clock rate (1.8432 MHz) by the BRD, as shown in the following formula:

$$BRD = \frac{clock\ speed}{16\ x\ desired\ bps}$$

If you use this formula, determining the settings for different bit speeds is easy. You can calculate the BRD for 9,600 bps, for example, as follows:

$$BRD = \frac{1843200}{16\ x\ 1200} = \frac{1843200}{19200} = 96 = 0060h$$

BRDH, therefore, must be set to 0, and BRDL must be set to 0Ch.

You can use the equation to construct the BRD for the typical bit rates listed in Table 7.3.

Table 7.3   Baud Rate Divisors

Bit Rate	BRDH	BRDL
50	09h	00h
110	04h	17h
300	01h	80h
1200	00h	60h
2400	00h	30h
4800	00h	18h
9600	00h	0Ch
19200	00h	06h

Note: *IBM cautions users of its early versions of BIOS not to set the rate higher than 9600 bps. You can safely drive the UART, however, at rates of 19,200 bps (or even higher).*

183

To set the BRD, you first must set bit 7 of the line control register (LCR) to 1. Then you can safely output the required divisors to their I/O locations (refer to Table 7.2). After you have set the BRD, good practice dictates that you immediately clear bit 7 of the LCR.

The Interrupt Enable Register (IER)

The interrupt enable register (IER) controls the type of interrupts generated by the UART. You can enable one or more interrupts at a time, depending on how you have written your interrupt handler. Whenever an interrupt is enabled, note that a specific action must be taken to clear it. Table 7.4 shows the assignments of interrupts to bits in the register and the appropriate action necessary to clear each interrupt.

Table 7.4 Interrupt Enable Register

Bit	Activates	Action
0	Data received	Read RDR
1	THR empty	Output to THR
2	Data error or break	Read LSR
3	MSR change	Read MSR
4–7	Unused; always set to zero	

Interrupts are generated when one of the activating conditions shown in Table 7.4 occurs and the corresponding IER bit is set to 1.

The Interrupt Identification Register (IIR)

When an interrupt occurs, a communications program can identify it from the bit settings of the interrupt identification register (IIR). Table 7.5 lists the meanings of these bits.

Table 7.5 Interrupt Identification Register

Bit	Meaning
0	More than one interrupt has occurred
1–2	Interrupt ID
3	Interrupt ID (MSB—16550 UART only; always set to 0 on other UARTs)

Bit	Meaning
4–5	Unused; always set to zero
6–7	FIFO buffer enabled flag (16550 UART only; always set to 0 on other UARTs)

If your software is interrupt driven, you first must specify the type of interrupts you want to generate (refer to Table 7.4). Then, after an interrupt request is received, you must examine the IIR to see which type of interrupt occurred. Table 7.6 indicates the possible settings for the three bits (only bits 1 and 2 on the 8250 and 16450 UARTs) that are used to identify an interrupt.

Table 7.6   Interrupt ID Bit Settings

Bit 3	Bit 2	Bit 1	Meaning
0	0	0	Change in modem status register (MSR)
0	0	1	Transmitter holding register (THR) empty
1	1	0	Receiving FIFO character time-out
0	1	0	Data received
0	1	1	Data reception error or break

The FIFO Control Register (FCR)

The 16550 UART added the capability to buffer data being sent or received. This buffer is known as the FIFO—first in, first out. This buffer is not available on the earlier UART models. Table 7.7 shows the bit meanings for this register.

Table 7.7   FIFO Control Register

Bit	Meaning
0	Enable and clear the FIFO buffers
1	Receiving FIFO buffer reset
2	Transmitting FIFO buffer reset
3	DMA mode select
4–5	Reserved
6	Receiver trigger (LSB)
7	Receiver trigger (MSB)

185

Bits 6 and 7 of the FCR are used to indicate which trigger level should be used for generating an interrupt. This level indicates how full the receiving buffer should be before an interrupt is generated. If you have a quick interrupt service routine, you can set the trigger level high and therefore have fewer interruptions of your main program. The possible trigger levels are shown in Table 7.8.

Table 7.8 FCR Interrupt Trigger Levels

Bit 6/7	Level
00	1 byte
10	4 bytes
01	8 bytes
11	14 bytes

The Line Control Register (LCR)

The line control register (LCR) is the primary control register for the serial line. Table 7.9 details the bit assignments for this register.

Table 7.9 Line Control Register

Bit	Meaning	Settings	Notes
0–1	Character Length		
	5 bits	00	
	6 bits	01	
	7 bits	10	
	8 bits	11	
2	Stop Bits		
	1 bit	0	
	1.5 bits		If using 5-bit characters
	2 bits	1	If using 6-, 7-, or 8-bit characters

Bit	Meaning	Settings	Notes
3–5	Parity		
	IGNORE	000	
	ODD	100	
	EVEN	110	
	MARK	101	
	SPACE	111	
6	Break Condition		
	Disabled	0	
	Enabled	1	
7	Port Toggle		
	Normal	0	Use THR/RDR and IER registers
	Alternate	1	Use BRDL and BRDH registers

The Modem Control Register (MCR)

The modem control register (MCR) sets control lines to the modem and, through these lines, tells the modem that the computer is ready to send characters, receive characters, or both. Table 7.10 shows the bit assignments for this register.

Table 7.10   Modem Control Register

Bit	Meaning
0	Set DTR line active
1	Set RTS line active
2	User output #1 (Hayes Reset)
3	User output #2 (Enable Ints)
4	UART loopback
5–7	Unused; set to zero

The data terminal ready (DTR) line tells the modem that the computer is powered on and ready to receive information from the modem. The request to send (RTS) line tells the modem that the computer is ready to send something to the line. Ordinarily, you can safely set both DTR and RTS to 1 to turn on these lines. Some modems ignore (or can be set to ignore) these signals, but older modems cannot be set to ignore them. Bit 2 (user output #1) is used only by specialized hardware (such as the Hayes SmartModem internal board, which uses bit 2 to reset the modem) and should be initialized to 0. Bit 3 (user output #2), which is tied to the interrupt servicing for the UART, blocks interrupt handling if *not* set to 1. Bit 4 allows testing of a communications program with no over-the-line communications. In this *loopback* state, data you send out the port reappears as input.

The Line Status Register (LSR)

The line status register (LSR) gives you the status of the communications line (see Table 7.11). From this register, you can diagnose common line problems.

Table 7.11   Line Status Register

Bit	Meaning
0	Data received; byte in RDR
1	Overrun error occurred because the previous byte was not read before the next byte arrived
2	Parity error
3	Framing error occurred because the transmission was not in sync (no stop bit was found after the character had been read)
4	Break detect
5	THR is empty; OK to output a character to the line
6	Transmitter shift register (TSR) is empty; the TSR places the character from the THR on the line, one bit at a time
7	Time out (permanently set to 0 in the 16450 and 16550 UARTs)

The Modem Status Register (MSR)

The modem's status depends on whether a certain status line is high or low and whether the status on a specified line has changed since the last register read. Table 7.12 shows how the bits are assigned in the modem status register.

Table 7.12 Modem Status Register

Bit	Meaning
0	Change in clear to send (CTS)
1	Change in data set ready (DSR)
2	Change in ring indicator (RI)
3	Change in data carrier detect (DCD)
4	Clear to send (CTS) set high
5	Data set ready (DSR) set high
6	Ring indicator (RI) set high
7	Data carrier detect (DCD) set high

The modem signals correspond to changes in the status of an electrical signal line connecting the computer and the serial device. Depending on the device, these hardware signals may or may not be used. Some modems make no use of them and rely solely on the Hayes command set to handle communications. Because your modem (or other serial device) may use modem signals, their meaning is described in Table 7.13.

Table 7.13 Modem Signals

Signal	Meaning
CTS	Clear to send: The modem is ready to receive characters from the computer.
DSR	Data set ready: The modem is powered on and ready to operate.
RI	Ring indicator: The telephone line is ringing. As the line rings, RI is held high (electrically) so that your computer can detect the rings.
DCD	Data carrier detect: The modem is connected to another modem.

Initializing the Communications Port

Working directly with the UART is not as easy as it might seem. Even initialization can become a complex operation that depends on sequencing registers in the correct order to produce a specific effect. For many programs (even those that intend to access the UART directly), you do not have to initialize the chip directly. You can control initialization through a BIOS function designed to simplify the task. In this area of programming (as elsewhere), never make more work for yourself than necessary.

To access the BIOS function that initializes a serial port, load the AH register with 0 and the DX register with a zero-based number that represents the communications port to be initialized (therefore, 0=COM1:, 1=COM2:, 2=COM3:, and 3=COM4:). Because some versions of the IBM BIOS do not intrinsically support four communications ports, you may be limited to a DX setting of either 0 or 1. All the PS/2 series of computers support four communications ports.

Finally, you load AL with the initialization parameters you want; each bit is significant. Table 7.14 lists the possible AL settings.

Table 7.14 BIOS Communications Port Initialization Settings for AL

Bit	Meaning	Settings
0–1	Word length	
	Not used	00
	Not used	01
	7 bits	10
	8 bits	11
2	Stop bits	
	1 bit	0
	2 bits	1
3–4	Parity	
	NONE	00
	ODD	01
	NONE	10
	EVEN	11
5–7	Bit rate	
	110 bps	000
	150 bps	001
	300 bps	010
	600 bps	011
	1200 bps	100
	2400 bps	101
	4800 bps	110
	9600 bps	111

After you have loaded AH, AL, and DX with the necessary values, issue an Int 14h; the communications port will be set according to your specifications. (For a summary of the register settings necessary for this BIOS function, see Table 7.17. Further information about this function is available in the "BIOS Function Reference" section in Part V.)

As you can see from Table 7.14, you cannot set a data length of 5 or 6 bits, nor can you set a bit rate below 110 bps or above 9600 bps. Your initialization options are limited for certain applications. When you try to tie in to a specialized application, for example, such as the NOAA weather wire, which is 50 bps with a 5-bit word length, your only option is to initialize the communications port through direct manipulation of the UART registers.

The IBM PS/2 series computers have another BIOS function that provides an additional degree of control over your communications interface. You access this function by loading the AH register with 4 and, as in the normal BIOS function, by loading the DX register with a zero-based number that represents the communications port to be initialized. Next, AL is set to either 0 or 1, depending on whether you want a break condition on the line. Ordinarily, AL is set to 0 (no break). BH must be set to the desired parity, as outlined in Table 7.15.

Table 7.15   Parity Settings for BH (Function 14/4)

Setting	Parity Meaning
0	NONE
1	ODD
2	EVEN
3	MARK
4	SPACE

BL must be set to the number of stop bits you want: 0 represents 1 stop bit, and 1 represents either 1.5 (for a 5-bit data length) or 2 (for 6-, 7-, and 8-bit data lengths) stop bits.

The data length is specified in CH, with the value in CH equaling five less than the number of data bits required. A value of 0, therefore, represents five data bits, and a value of 3 equals eight data bits.

Finally, CL is loaded with the bit rate you want. This value is determined by the settings detailed in Table 7.16.

191

Table 7.16   Bit Rate Settings for CL (Function 14/4)

Setting	Bit Rate
0	110 bps
1	150 bps
2	300 bps
3	600 bps
4	1200 bps
5	2400 bps
6	4800 bps
7	9600 bps
8	19200 bps

After you have loaded all the registers (AH, AL, BH, BL, CH, CL, and DX), issue an Int 14h to set the communications port as specified. Table 7.17 summarizes the register settings necessary for the two BIOS functions presented in this section. Further information about these functions is available in the "BIOS Function Reference" section in Part V.

Table 7.17   Summary of BIOS Communications Port Initialization Functions

Function	Parameter	Notes and Possible Settings
AH=0	AL	Set according to information in Table 7.14.
	DX	Communications port desired:
		0 (COM1:) through 3 (COM4:)
AH=4		(Works only on PS/2 series)
	AL	Break condition setting
	BH	Parity
	BL	Stop bits
	CH	Word length
	CL	Bit rate
	DX	Communications port desired:
		0 (COM1:) through 3 (COM4:)

Despite the BIOS's capabilities for initializing communications ports, you may have to access the UART directly if you cannot set a certain register (through the BIOS function) to a value you need. Before you make the assumption that "BIOS can't do it," try to work with the BIOS initialization functions—you may find them more than adequate.

If the thought of doing all the setup for the UART seems frightening, remember that you can change any part of the setup at any time. This statement means that you can use the BIOS routine to set all the parameters in its range and then go directly to the UART hardware to modify the speed, word size, or parity.

By using direct UART initialization, you can set any speed up to 115.2K bps. The secret to achieving this speed is implied in the speed equations shown earlier in this chapter; they are a little simpler, though, when you reduce the format to the following:

$$\text{Divisor} = \frac{115,200}{\text{desired bps rate}}$$

The major difference here is that the clock speed and 16-time multiplier have been combined into the single numeric constant. You can see that the 115.2K bps rate achieved by some laptop computer data-transfer programs is the maximum possible from the serial interface (a divisor of 0001).

Tables 7.1 through 7.10 provide all the information you need to do this; the only caution is to avoid attempting to *IN*put from a port immediately after doing an *OUT* to it because the UART is significantly slower in reacting than many modern CPUs. The BIOS code includes the `JMP $+2` command after every OUT command, specifically to introduce enough delay to be certain that no problems result at high clock speeds; this is a good rule to copy if you add your own initialization procedures.

Modems

Modem is a contraction of the term *modulator-demodulator*. Although detailed instructions about using a specific modem are beyond the scope of this book, this chapter makes some general observations.

First, most modems are advertised as Hayes-compatible, which means that all modem control is in the command sequences (character strings) sent to the modem rather than in the modem control lines. Many sophisticated terminal programs use these Hayes command sequences to communicate with the modem; these programs can control the modem's many functions directly. All you have to do is tell the program what you want.

If your modem uses the modem control lines rather than a string command set, you can control the modem only by manipulating the modem control lines directly at the BIOS or hardware level. The BIOS and DOS functions generally do a good job of hiding these control lines from your program, which means that you have to go directly to the UART to control them.

193

You do not need a modem for all serial communications. In most offices with serial connections to a central computer, for example, the connections can be wired directly to a PC if the central computer and the PC are relatively close to each other. Technically, they should be no more than 150 feet apart, although runs of as much as 400 feet can work if there is no outside interference. You also can run printers and serial devices without a modem if they meet the cable-length requirements.

To communicate through a telephone line, you *must* use a modem. The bandwidth of most telephone systems is relatively limited (from 300 to 3,000 Hz). The output from the UART is a series of square waves that will be distorted beyond recognition if you try to send them, unaltered, through a telephone line. The result would be no communication. A modem translates the square wave output from a UART into a series of tones that fall within the telephone line's bandwidth.

Older, slower modems translated the output simply: one tone corresponded to 0, another to 1. Newer, faster modems use not only tones but also multiplexing, phasing, and other electrical-signal components to pass a greater volume of information through a line.

Writing a Terminal Program

Now that you have seen how the UART functions and how modems work, you are almost ready to design a simple terminal program. Before you begin, however, you should be aware of several other considerations, which are discussed in this section.

A communications program can be implemented in two ways. The first uses a polling method: Your program periodically checks the serial port to determine whether an incoming character is available. If a character is available, you can process it and continue. The second method, which is more efficient in terms of computer time, is based on interrupts: You and the computer work until you are interrupted by the UART when an incoming character is available. You process the character and then return to the task on which you were working before the interruption.

Only the polling method of serial interfacing is described in this chapter. The method has problems, however. Although your computer can communicate with other computers, you may lose some incoming characters at speeds greater than 300 bps, especially when the screen fills and has to scroll up a line. These polling-based programs are for learning rather than for general use. As mentioned at the beginning of this chapter, you have to combine the knowledge you learn here with the information in Chapter 11, "Interrupt Handlers," to create your own interrupt-driven communications routines.

Duplex Considerations

Before you can use the polling method of serial control, you must decide whether you want your communications to be full duplex or half duplex. You may recall from the terms introduced earlier in this chapter that, in full-duplex communications, every character sent over the communications link is echoed back from the remote computer. A character you see on-screen is the character received by the other computer, echoed back (or retransmitted) by the other computer. These characters travel in both directions simultaneously—you can send characters to the remote computer while it sends others back. The outline, therefore, for a full-duplex implementation of a simple terminal program is as follows:

1. If a character is at the keyboard, send it.

2. If a character is at the serial port, display it.

3. Go to Step 1.

Although most computers use full-duplex communications, some use half duplex (characters travel in only one direction at a time). Because the remote computer does not echo back (retransmit) the characters it receives, the concept of a half-duplex terminal program differs from that of the full-duplex version in only one minor point:

1. If a character is at the keyboard, send *and* display it.

2. If a character is at the serial port, display it.

3. Go to Step 1.

The differences in implementation rest in the coding section that handles getting a character from the keyboard. The following section shows how your coding is affected.

The Controlling Program: Term.c

At the highest conceptual level, the communications program is simple. The program in Listing 7.1, written in C, implements the basic concepts discussed so far in this chapter.

Listing 7.1

```
/* Term.c
   Listing 7.1 of DOS Programmer's Reference */

#include <stdio.h>
#include <conio.h>
#include <stdlib.h>

#define FALSE 0
#define TRUE !FALSE
```

continues

195

Listing 7.1 Continued

```
main()
{
    void setup(void);
    int  keybd(void);
    void serial(void);

    clrscr();
    printf("Simple Terminal Program\n\n\n");
    setup();
    while(TRUE){
        if(!keybd())
            exit(0);
        serial();
    }
}
```

Except for clearing the terminal screen (accomplished by the cls() function) and setting up the port (through the setup() function), this is a simple application of the terminal procedure. It repeats forever, retrieving characters alternately from the keyboard (with the keybd() function) or from the serial port (with the serial() function).

Notice that this program provides a way to end the program, as all reasonable programs should: if the keyboard-handling routine ever returns FALSE, the program ends. (As shown in Listing 7.4, the keyboard function has been programmed to return FALSE whenever the Shift-F1 key combination is pressed.)

Supporting Functions

Let's look at each supporting function. Two versions of the keybd() function are provided: One handles full-duplex operation and the other handles half-duplex operation. Use whichever fits your needs.

Initialization: Setup() Function

Setup(), the first user-developed function, initializes the serial port. As presented here, the function uses a simplified, hard-coded setup for 1200 bps, 8 bits, no parity, and 1 stop bit. Listing 7.2 shows how this setup is implemented.

Listing 7.2

```
/* Setup.c
   Listing 7.2 of DOS Programmer's Reference */

#include <stdio.h>
#include <dos.h>
```

```
#define    COM1       0
#define    RS232      0x14
#define    SETUP      0x83   /* 1200 baud, 8 bits, no parity, */
                            /*   1 stop bit */

void setup()
{
    union REGS regs;
    printf("Setup the serial port\n");
    regs.h.ah = 0;
    regs.x.dx = COM1;
    regs.h.al = SETUP;
    int86(RS232, &regs, &regs);
}
```

As stated in the program comments, `setup()` initializes COM1: to 1200 bps, an 8-bit word length, no parity, and 1 stop bit. `Setup()` uses the basic BIOS communications-port initialization function presented earlier in this chapter.

`Setup()` initializes COM1 by using the basic BIOS communications-port initialization function presented earlier in this chapter.

An Initialization Alternative

The `setup()` function in Listing 7.2 is not flexible—it can be used only to set the serial port to one specific bit rate and data format. As an alternative, you can create a more flexible `setup()` function to handle multiple initialization parameters (see Listing 7.3).

Listing 7.3

```
/* Setup2.c
   Listing 7.3 of DOS Programmer's Reference */

#include <stdio.h>
#include <dos.h>

#define    RS232        0x14

#define    B300         0x40
#define    B1200        0x80
#define    B2400        0xa0

#define    NOPARITY     0x00
#define    EVEN         0x18
#define    ODD          0x08

#define    WORD7        0x02
#define    WORD8        0x03

#define    STOP1        0x00
#define    STOP2        0x40
```

continues

Listing 7.3 Continued

```c
int setup(port,bps,word,parity,stop)

int  port,              /* COM port, 0=COM1, 1=COM2, etc.*/
     bps,               /* bps rate */
     word,              /* word length */
     parity,            /* 0 = off, 1 = EVEN, 2 = ODD */
     stop;              /* number of stop bits */

{
     union REGS regs;
     unsigned char setup;

     setup = 0;
     printf("Set up the serial port\n");

     if(port!=0 && port!=1)
          return(-1);          /* bad COM port */

     switch(bps){
          case 300:
               setup |= B300;
               break;
          case 1200:
               setup |= B1200;
               break;
          case 2400:
               setup |= B2400;
               break;
          default:
               return(-2);          /* not 300/1200/2400 bps */
     }

     if(word==7)
          setup |= WORD7;
     else if(word==8)
          setup |= WORD8;
     else
          return(-3);          /* not 7 or 8 bits */

     if(parity==0)
          setup |= NOPARITY;
     else if(parity==1)
          setup |= EVEN;
     else if(parity==2)
          setup |= ODD;
     else
          return(-4);          /* bad parity code */

     if(stop==1)
          setup |= STOP1;
     else if(stop==2)
          setup |= STOP2;
     else
          return(-5);          /* not 1 or 2 bits */
```

```
        regs.h.ah = 0;
        regs.x.dx = port;
        regs.h.al = setup;
        int86(RS232, &regs, &regs);    /* set up the port */
        return(0);
    }
```

This longer version of setup() enables you to error-check each parameter and gives you greater flexibility in setting parameters. The version of term.c in Listing 7.1 cannot use this alternate setup() function. It is written on the assumption that the setup values are built into the program. You can add it if you want, but then you also must provide a means of setting the proper initialization parameters, either from the command line or as inputs to the program.

If you initialize a port other than COM1, you must change also the other supporting functions— xmit(), chrdy(), rch(), and loopback()—to support other communications ports. For testing, and until you feel comfortable with basic serial-port programming, you may want to use the limited version of setup() shown in Listing 7.2 and then experiment later with the version in Listing 7.3.

Keyboard Control: Keybd() Function

Through the keybd() function, which manages the keyboard, you can determine whether a character has been entered at the keyboard and then, if it has, transmit the character (see Listing 7.4).

Listing 7.4

```
/* Keybd.c
   Listing 7.4 of DOS Programmer's Reference */

#include <stdio.h>
#include <dos.h>

#define    FALSE    0
#define    TRUE     !FALSE
#define    SF1      84

int keybd()
{
    char c;

    int get_ch(void);
    void xmit(int ch);

    if((c=get_ch())>=0){
        /* There has been a keystroke */
        if(c == 0){
        /* The first character was zero */
            if((c = get_ch())==SF1)
                return(FALSE);
```

continues

Listing 7.4 Continued

```
                return(TRUE);
        }
        xmit(c);
    }
    return(TRUE);
}
```

Operation of the `get_ch()` function, which is integral to `keybd()` operation, is discussed in the following section. You need to understand now that, if `get_ch()` returns a 0, a special character or key combination has been entered from the keyboard. In this case, `get_ch()` must be called again to retrieve the keyboard scan code of the key pressed.

`Keybd()` specifically looks for this special character value (a zero); if `keybd()` finds the value, it looks for a second character. If the second character is Shift-F1, that character returns FALSE to the calling routine; if it is not Shift-F1 (if you pressed another special key combination or non-ASCII character, for example), the value TRUE is returned and the character entry is ignored.

If you enter a normal ASCII value from the keyboard, the `get_ch()` function does not return a 0; the character is transmitted (as entered, without alteration) through the `xmit()` function.

Keybd() for Half-Duplex Communications

Only one additional line is necessary to make the `keybd()` function compatible with half-duplex operations. You insert the following line immediately after the line containing the `xmit()` function:

```
    putscrn(c);
```

Basically, this function displays a character to the screen. (You learn about the exact development and use of `putscrn(c)` later in this chapter.)

I/O Control: Get_ch() and Xmit() Functions

Two functions support the basic `keybd()` function: `get_ch()`, shown in Listing 7.5, retrieves a character from the keyboard (if a character is available), and `xmit()` transmits a character through the serial port.

Listing 7.5

```
/* Get_ch.c
   Listing 7.5 of DOS Programmer's Reference */

#include <stdio.h>
#include <dos.h>

#define   MASK     0x7f
#define   ZFLAG    0x40
```

```
int get_ch()
{
    union REGS regs;
    regs.h.ah = 6;
    regs.h.dl = 0xff;
    intdos(&regs,&regs);
    if(regs.x.flags & ZFLAG)
        return(-1);
    return(regs.h.al & MASK);
}
```

Get_ch() uses the DOS direct console I/O function (see Chapter 6) to input characters. You may recall that this DOS function sets the zero flag (ZFLAG) to indicate whether a character is available. Get_ch() tests the ZFLAG to see whether a character is available. If a character is available, it is in AL; the function returns it to the calling routine with the high-order bit set to 0. (The high-order bit is stripped by ANDing it with the MASK value. This masking process eliminates any possible problems with transmitting 8-bit characters.)

Xmit.c(), the other routine necessary for the successful completion of keybd(), is shown in Listing 7.6.

Listing 7.6

```
/* Xmit.c
   Listing 7.6 of DOS Programmer's Reference */

#include <dos.h>

#define    RS232      0x14
#define    WRITECH    1
#define    COM1       0

void xmit(ch)
    char ch;
{
    union REGS regs;

    regs.h.ah = WRITECH;
    regs.x.dx = COM1;
    regs.h.al = ch;
    int86(RS232, &regs, &regs);
}
```

The xmit() function simply writes the character to the serial port handler in the BIOS. As you can see from Listing 7.6, this BIOS function requires the use of only three registers: AH contains the desired function number (1), AL is the character value to transmit (passed to xmit() by the calling routine), and DX is the communications port to use for the transmission (0, designating COM1). For additional information about this BIOS function, see the "BIOS Function Reference" section in Part V.

201

Receiving Characters: Serial() Function

Now that you understand keybd(), get_ch(), and xmit(), you are ready to examine the other major part of your terminal program—the part that receives and displays any incoming characters. Listing 7.7 shows this function, called serial().

Listing 7.7

```
/* Serial.c
   Listing 7.7 of DOS Programmer's Reference */

#include <stdio.h>
#include <dos.h>

void serial()
{
    char c;

    int  chrdy(void);
    int  rch(void);
    void putscrn(int c);

    if(chrdy()){
        c = rch();
        putscrn;
    }
}
```

Let's examine each of the three functions necessary for the successful completion of serial(): chrdy(), rch(), and putscrn().

Serial Port Status: Chrdy() Function

The chrdy() function checks whether an incoming character is available at the serial port. It uses BIOS Int 14h, Function 03h, which returns the communications port status. (For details about this BIOS function, see the "BIOS Function Reference" section in Part V.) Listing 7.8 shows how chrdy() is implemented.

Listing 7.8

```
/* Chrdy.c
   Listing 7.8 of DOS Programmer's Reference */

#include <stdio.h>
#include <dos.h>

#define   RS232     0x14
#define   STATUS    3
#define   COM1      0
#define   DTARDY    0x100
```

```
int chrdy()
{
    union REGS regs;

    regs.h.ah = STATUS;
    regs.x.dx = COM1;
    int86(RS232, &regs, &regs);
    return(regs.x.ax & DTARDY);
}
```

Accessing Received Characters: Rch() Function

When chrdy() returns TRUE, informing you that a character is waiting, the rch() function is used to retrieve the character (see Listing 7.9).

Listing 7.9

```
/* Rch.c
   Listing 7.9 of DOS Programmer's Reference */

#include <stdio.h>
#include <dos.h>

#define   COM1      0
#define   RS232     0x14
#define   READCH    2
#define   MASK      0x7f

int rch()
{
    union REGS regs;

    regs.h.ah = READCH;
    regs.x.dx = COM1;
    int86(RS232, &regs, &regs);
    return(regs.h.al & MASK);              /* strip parity bit */
}
```

The high-order bit of the incoming character is stripped here, as it was in get_ch(), by ANDing the value in AL with the MASK value.

Screen Display: Putscrn() and Put_ch() Functions

The final portion of serial() is the routine for displaying a character on-screen. Because only printable characters can be displayed, putscrn(), shown in Listing 7.10, is designed to ignore all control characters except a carriage return and a line feed.

Listing 7.10

```
/* Putscrn.c
   Listing 7.10 of DOS Programmer's Reference */

#include <stdio.h>
#include <dos.h>

#define   CR    0x0d
#define   LF    0x0a

void putscrn(c)
     char c;
{
     void put_ch(int);

     if(c>=' ' || c==CR || c==LF)
          put_ch(c);
}
```

Putscrn() calls put_ch() to write the character to the display, by using the basic character-out DOS function. (For a detailed description of this function, see the "DOS Reference" section in Part V.) Listing 7.11 shows how put_ch() works.

Listing 7.11

```
/* Put_ch.c
   Listing 7.11 of DOS Programmer's Reference */

#include <stdio.h>
#include <dos.h>

#define   CHAROUT   2

void put_ch(c)
     char c;
{
     union REGS regs;

     regs.h.ah = CHAROUT;
     regs.h.dl = c;
     intdos(&regs,&regs);
}
```

Using Term.c

Now that you have learned about each function necessary for term.c, enter them and try using term.c. You will discover that, although your computer can communicate with other computers, you may lose some of the incoming characters if more than a few arrive in quick succession. A short message of only one or two lines probably will overload the program. What's wrong?

Several problems exist:

- Because the terminal program has not been programmed for efficiency, it includes many subroutine calls—each of which uses time. You could speed up the program by coding it with fewer individual functions.

- DOS function calls were used to handle the keyboard and screen. Although you are not likely to type faster than the characters can be read, the time spent on DOS function calls is time taken away from the needs of the serial channel.

- The BIOS function calls used are not spectacularly efficient.

Despite these problems, we will not change the program's basic design—its primary purpose is to show *how* to use the BIOS and DOS functions in the program. But you *can* speed up the program by changing it so that it can work directly with the UART chip. This process may reduce, but does not eliminate, the loss of incoming characters at speeds greater than 300 bps; the loss is due largely to the time the BIOS routines require to scroll the screen, and nothing can be done in a polling program to get around that problem.

Directly Accessing the UART

Direct UART access is one way to make the program tighter and faster, but you need to know when direct access is suitable and justifiable. You should be aware of some important trade-offs when you go directly to the UART.

Working directly at the hardware level does the following:

- Results in the largest speed increases you can get from the computer

- Provides the greatest programming flexibility

- Is the most machine-dependent type of programming and is most susceptible to compatibility problems when you transfer the program to another type of computer

IBM's promise to maintain serial-interface compatibility with the UART may be a great comfort if you work with computers produced by IBM. This promise is not a guarantee, however. Nor is it a safe bet when you work with other computers that use DOS. Although most of these computers currently use the UARTs that are compatible with the 8250, be on the lookout for subtle differences in some models that use different UARTs.

As mentioned in the preceding section, the version of term.c in Listing 7.1 causes loss of incoming characters because that version cannot keep up with a steady stream of characters. Many programmers cannot get the required performance from the DOS or BIOS serial-interface functions; they have solved this dilemma by always working directly with the UART. To do this, you must access it through I/O ports. Although some languages do not provide ways to access the I/O ports, every language used in this book does.

205

Assembly

In assembly language, you access the ports with the IN and OUT instructions: IN reads a word or byte into the AL or AX register; OUT writes a word or byte from the AL or AX register to the port. Variations of the OUT instruction include OUTS (BL or CX registers), OUTSB (byte from DS:[SI]), and OUTSW (word from DS:[SI]).

C

In Microsoft and Borland C++, the inport and outport functions input or output words to a port. Inportb and outportb do the same for bytes.

BASIC

Basic functions INP and OUT read bytes from or write bytes to a port.

Pascal

Unlike the other languages, Pascal has no function for accessing the ports. Rather, Turbo Pascal treats the ports as an array (Port for bytes, Portw for words). Input and output to the port are accomplished by reading and writing to the array.

Modifying Term.c

To modify the terminal program, you simply change the three serial-port routines: chrdy(), xmit(), and rch(). You can (and will) safely leave control of the setup to the BIOS function.

When you access the UART directly, chrdy() is simplified considerably (see Listing 7.12).

Listing 7.12

```
/* Chrdy2.c
   Listing 7.12 of DOS Programmer's Reference */

#include <dos.h>

#define   COM1      0x3f8
#define   LSR       5
#define   DTARDY    0x01

int chrdy()
```

```
    {
        return(inportb(COM1+LSR) & DTARDY);
    }
```

The rch() function for reading a character is also simplified considerably (see Listing 7.13).

Listing 7.13

```
/* Rch2.c
   Listing 7.13 of DOS Programmer's Reference */

#include <dos.h>

#define    COM1       0x3f8
#define    RDR        0
#define    MASK       0x7f

int rch()
{
    return(inportb(COM1+RDR) & MASK);
}
```

The modified xmit() function takes the form shown in Listing 7.14.

Listing 7.14

```
/* Xmit2.c
   Listing 7.14 of DOS Programmer's Reference */

#include <dos.h>

#define    COM1       0x3f8
#define    LSR        5
#define    THR        0
#define    THRRDY     0x20

int  xmit(ch)
     char ch;
{
    register int cnt;

    cnt = 0;
    while(!(inportb(COM1+LSR) & THRRDY) && cnt < 10000)
        cnt++;
    if(cnt>=10000)
        return(-1);
    outportb(COM1+THR,ch);
    return(0);
}
```

The modified version of xmit() is slightly more complicated than the earlier version because you must be sure that the transmitter holding register (THR) is ready for a character before you write one to it. A maximum-retry counter is set to prevent the system from locking into an infinite loop.

The other term.c functions do not need to be modified to make the program work. My comments about the BIOS version of term.c and why it is slow still apply here. Even when you access the UART directly, you will not have enough speed to handle 1200 bps without problems.

In this instance, the problems are caused by the method used for handling the incoming serial characters. As you may recall, a polling method is used in the examples in this chapter. In other words, the program sequentially checks the keyboard and then the serial interface, *ad infinitum*. If more than one character arrives at the serial port while the program's attention is focused on the keyboard or, usually, on the screen, those incoming characters may be lost before the program has a chance to record them.

Loopback Testing

When you use the modified version of term.c, you can also add a function that allows loopback testing. In other words, the UART "thinks" that it is talking to a remote computer; what really happens is a local echo (in the UART) of what is being sent to the serial interface. The process is implemented as shown in Listing 7.15.

Listing 7.15

```
/* Loopback.c
   Listing 7.15 of DOS Programmer's Reference */

#include <stdio.h>
#include <dos.h>

#define    MCR        0x3fc
#define    LOOPBACK   0x10

void loopback()
{
    int   mcr_value;
    printf("Toggling Loopback\n");
    mcr_value = inportb(MCR);
    mcr_value = mcr_value ^ LOOPBACK;
    outportb(MCR,mcr_value);
    mcr_value = mcr_value & LOOPBACK;
    printf("Loopback ");
    if(mcr_value == 0)
        printf("cleared");
    else
        printf("set");
    printf(" ... continuing\n");
}
```

Invoking `loopback()` from `term.c` (immediately after the `setup()` function is called) causes all characters you type to be echoed back rather than transmitted over the serial communications link. Why use `loopback()`? It is helpful for testing to make sure that communications software functions properly before you test the software on-line with another computer.

Note also that this routine accesses directly the modem control register (MCR) for COM1. After your computer has been set in loopback mode with this function, the only way to turn off loopback is to turn off your computer and then turn it on again or to invoke `loopback()` a second time. (The best place to add this second `loopback()` to the `term.c` program is immediately preceding the final closing brace.)

Evaluation of the Serial I/O Services

The basic serial I/O services are wholly inadequate for the job of high-performance communications applications. In high-speed (greater than 1200 bps), error-free file transfers or multihost, real-time terminal operations, speed is essential and should not be sacrificed (not lightly, at any rate) to achieve compatibility. To achieve throughput and responsiveness, direct access to hardware is often more justifiable in communications than in other applications.

The basic `term.c` terminal program is adequate but cannot handle high speeds. Before you can improve its capability, you need to learn about interrupts and interrupt handlers. Chapter 11 discusses the basics of handling interrupts. If you want a more thorough discussion and a practical example of how to write an interrupt-driven communications routine, see *Advanced Assembly Language,* by Allen L. Wyatt (Que Corporation).

This section is not saying that a non-interrupt-driven program is useless. If you can put together a program in which the PC's undivided attention is devoted to the communications link, you can manage safely without interrupts. A package created on exactly this basis is used nationwide as a master control system; it provides control of a PC from a UNIX-based system. All communications to the PC are in packets and are either file transfers or commands to be executed. This program, built in a few hours by programmers using only the simplest techniques, has been in use for several years. It runs at speeds as high as 19,200 bps. Simple, direct programming can sometimes be the best solution to problems. This package, however, does not display received data on the screen and does not process packets too large to fit entirely in RAM.

Summary

This chapter has focused on the use and control of the IBM microcomputer family's serial interface. This interface, based on the original 8250 UART (and its successors), offers programmers a good deal of hands-off control over a serial communications link.

Despite the capabilities and freedom presented by the UART, the task of programming serial-communications software can be tedious and frustrating. Although BIOS and DOS services can be used to simplify the task somewhat, their value is diminished because they offer only limited access to the UART's power. Furthermore, they introduce overhead that can seriously degrade the performance of time-critical software.

Part III
Disks, Directories, and Files

8

Disks

When you learn a programming language, you usually start by learning about basic input and output (as you did by reading Chapters 5, 6, and 7). You learn how to get data into and out of a computer, and you play with it.

Before you can begin to write serious programs, you need to learn about files (and you will, in Chapter 9, "Directories and Files") because most programs work with different types of files. Some programs work directly with the disk and directory structure. To lay the groundwork for Chapter 9, let's examine disks.

First you will learn how basic magnetic-disk technology works. Floppy disks and hard disks differ in capacity but are alike in the way they can be accessed through the DOS functions. The function calls used to open or close files, read or write files, or access directories are the same on any disk. As you work through this chapter, you will learn about tracks, sectors, and clusters and the role they play when you build a program.

Then, by applying your newfound knowledge about how disks work, you will produce a basic track-formatting function with which to reformat disks. Using this function requires special caution, however; you can easily make a mistake that may destroy critical disks.

Disk Internals

Anyone who uses a PC works with disks. No matter what kind of system you have, you most likely store information on disks. Given the importance of disks in the operation of personal computers, you would expect people to know how disks work—but they don't. If you plan to work on the disks themselves (even if only to examine their structure or the data stored on them), you should understand how they work.

You can think of a disk as a collection of files—not unlike a drawer in a file cabinet. Each disk holds many files, and you can access any file "folder" directly.

During the formatting process, the operating system imposes the familiar file structure on your disks. DOS creates an index to the files (the directory) in addition to a way to determine the files' location on the disk (the file allocation table, or FAT). DOS records information about the disk's layout (the boot record), which—even on disks without the system files—includes a start-up program.

Basically, each side of a disk is a magnetically coated surface. This surface is magnetized by a read/write head that passes over the rotating disk. Double-sided disks have two recording surfaces; single-sided disks have only one (although both sides are coated, only one side is certified to meet quality standards). Hard disks typically have two to four platters, or disks, with recording surfaces on both sides.

On any disk drive, the read/write head or heads are moved across the disk surface by a special *stepper motor*. This motor has precisely defined stops (called *steps*) at which the head comes to rest. Each of these resting points defines a *track* on which data can be recorded. Most hard disks have a multiple-platter system in which the heads move together on all platters. The tracks (on all platters) corresponding to one step of the stepper motor are referred to as a *cylinder*.

The FORMAT program divides the tracks into 512-byte sectors to create more manageable disk segments: 8 or 9 sectors per track on a floppy disk and 17 sectors per track on a hard disk.

DOS allocates space to a file in units called *clusters*. Each cluster consists of two to eight sectors, depending on the type of disk. When a file needs additional disk space, the operating system allocates one or more additional clusters to that file. Figure 8.1 shows a typical disk platter layout.

The disk is divided into the following five important areas:

- Partition table
- Boot record
- File allocation table (FAT)
- Directory
- Data space

All of these items are discussed in the following sections.

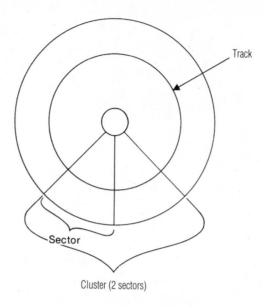

Figure 8.1 A disk platter (showing a track, sector, and cluster).

The Partition Table

Almost every hard disk has a master record that resides at cylinder (track) 0, head (side) 0, sector 1. (The few that do not are eligible for museum status; you are unlikely to run into one in use.) This master record is responsible for reading and deciphering the disk partition table contained at the end of the master record. Control then passes to the boot record of the currently bootable hard disk partition, as indicated in the partition table. If a disk has no such master record, its place is taken by the *boot record*, which is discussed in the next section.

The partition table describes how the hard disk is divided. To be recognizable by programs such as FDISK, this partition table must conform to a standard layout. As many as four partitions can be on a hard disk, each with a corresponding entry in the partition table. Figure 8.2 shows a memory dump of the master boot record from a COMPAQ Deskpro 286. Notice the partition table information stored at the end of the sector. Entries begin at offset 01BEh for partition 1, 01CEh for partition 2, 01DEh for partition 3, and 01EEh for partition 4. The last two bytes of the sector (those immediately following the partition table at offset 01FEh) are a signature word for the sector—AA55h, in this case.

DOS
PROGRAMMING

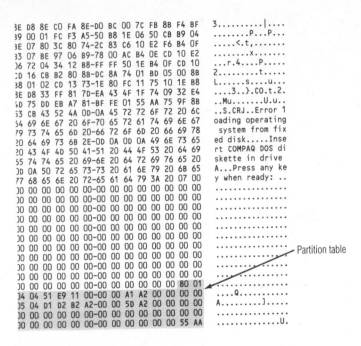

Figure 8.2 Hard disk master boot record, disk partition table.

Notice that the partition table information shown in Figure 8.2 has only two entries filled in—there are only two partitions on this hard disk. Each entry in the partition table is 16 bytes long. Table 8.1 details the layout for each partition table entry, using sample values taken from the partition table shown in Figure 8.2.

Table 8.1 Hard Disk Partition Table Entry Layout

Byte Offset	Field Length	Sample Value	Meaning
00h	Byte	80h	Boot indicator
			00h = Nonbootable
			80h = Bootable
01h	Byte	01h	Starting head
02h	Byte	01h	Starting sector (bits 0–5; bits 6–7 are bits "8 and 9" for cylinder)
03h	Byte	00h	Starting cylinder (low 8)
04h	Byte	04h	System ID
			00h = Unknown
			01h = DOS, 12-bit FAT

Byte Offset	Field Length	Sample Value	Meaning
			04h = DOS, 16-bit FAT
			05h = DOS, extended disk, 16-bit FAT
05h	Byte	04h	Ending head
06h 6–7	Byte	51h (11)	Ending sector (bits 0–5; bits are bits "8 and 9" for cylinder)
07h	Byte	E9h (1E9)	Ending cylinder (low 8)
08h	Double word	00000011	First partition sector
0Ch	Double word	0000A2A1	Sectors in partition

Notice the information stored in the partition table. Most of this information describes boundaries for each partition, but two fields, the boot indicator and the system ID, are of particular interest. The boot indicator signals whether the partition is bootable. Only one of the four possible partitions can be labeled as bootable. The system ID is used to designate the partition type. Table 8.1 indicates several possible system ID values, but various other operating systems (such as XENIX, UNIX, and Pick) necessarily expand the possible system ID list.

Because this table must be recognized not only by DOS but also by other operating systems, its format is not subject to change from one DOS version to another (or from one operating system to another); any tampering with the partition table format would destroy all chance of selling the software commercially.

During the system boot, the BIOS consults the first sector on the disk to continue with the booting process. With a floppy disk, this is the boot sector (see the following section). With a hard disk, this first sector is the master record described earlier. Within this master record, the partition table is located and the BIOS determines (by the boot-indicator fields) which partition is bootable. After the bootable partition has been located, control is passed to the boot sector of that partition and booting continues as it would for a floppy disk.

Disk partitioning establishes a set of logical disks on the hard disk. Each logical disk acts like a smaller disk drive (and is assigned a drive letter by the disk driver). A single hard disk can use all logical drives for one operating system, or each logical drive can hold a different one. Systems often have MS-DOS in one partition and XENIX in another—not unlike having two computers for the price of one.

Partitioning is often necessary when you use hard disks with a capacity greater than 32M. Most versions of DOS before 4.x are limited to 32M or less in a single partition. By using multiple partitions, you can make use of disks as large as 160M. Commercial utilities are available to eliminate the 32M limit with special disk drivers. Because the disks frequently cannot be used without the drivers, however, this limitation can lead to problems if you try to run other operating systems or boot from floppy disks.

217

One of the major features of DOS Version 4 is that it removes the 32M limit on the size of a hard disk. By permitting sector numbers to be as large as 32 bits and permitting the file allocation table to grow to 64K sectors, the disk capacity limit was pushed into the gigabyte region.

Because of this, you are not *required* to do partitioning when you use a large hard disk and DOS Version 4. But you can do so if you prefer to organize your system in the traditional manner or if you maintain multiple operating systems.

The Boot Record

When the system has determined where to locate the boot record for the bootable disk partition, the BIOS loads the boot record into memory. Typical boot sectors for a floppy disk are shown in Figure 8.3; note how they differ from one DOS version to another.

Figure 8.3   Boot sector for a floppy disk

```
                Jump instruction        System name          BPB
                      /                      /                 /

        0000  E9 8D 00 00 00 00 00 00-00 00 00 00 02 02 01 00   ...............
        0010  02 70 00 00 02 FB 02 00-09 00 02 00 00 00 00 00   .p.............
        0020  00 0F 02 25 02 0F 2A FF-50 F5 00 00 02 0D 0A 4E 6F   ...%..*.P.....No
        0030  6E 2D 53 79 73 74 65 6D-20 64 69 73 6B 20 6F 72   n-System disk or
        0040  20 64 69 73 6B 20 65 72-72 6F 72 2E 0D 0A 52 65    disk error...Re
        0050  70 6C 61 63 65 20 61 6E-64 20 70 72 65 73 73 20   place and press
        0060  61 6E 79 20 6B 65 79 20-77 68 65 6E 20 72 65 61   any key when rea
        0070  64 79 0D 0A 07 00 49 4F-20 20 20 20 20 20 53 59   dy....IO      SY
        0080  53 4D 53 44 4F 53 20 20-20 53 59 53 00 00 00 00   SMSDOS   SYS....
        0090  FC 33 C0 8E D8 8E C0 FA-8E D0 BC 00 7C FB A1 78   .3..........|..x
        00A0  00 A3 8C 7C A1 7A 00 A3-8E 7C 8D 06 21 7C A3 78   ...|.z...|..!|.x
        00B0  00 8C 1E 7A 00 E8 38 00-A1 8E 7C A3 7A 00 A1 8C   ...z..8...|.z...
        00C0  7C A3 78 00 8A 16 20 7C-EA 00 00 70 00 A1 8E 7C   |.x... |...p...|
        00D0  A3 7A 00 A1 8C 7C A3 78-00 BE 2C 7C AC 0A C0 74   .z...|.x...|...t
        00E0  09 B4 0E BB 07 00 CD 10-EB F2 B4 00 CD 16 CD 19   ................
        00F0  33 C0 CD 13 72 D7 8B 36-0E 7C A0 10 7C B4 00 F7   3...r..6.|..|...
        0100  26 16 7C 03 F0 8B EE BB-20 00 A1 11 7C F7 E3 B1   &.|...... ...|...
        0110  09 05 FF 01 D3 E8 03 E8-8D 1E 00 05 B8 01 00 E8   ................
        0120  3B 00 BE 76 7C BF 00 05-B9 0B 00 F3 A6 74 02 EB   ;..v|........t..
        0130  9C BF 20 05 B9 0B 00 F3-A6 74 02 EB 90 BB 00 07   .. ......t.....
        0140  8B F5 A1 1C 05 B1 09 05-FF 01 D3 E8 E8 0E 00 8B   ................
        0150  1E 1C 7C 03 DD 8B 0E 1E-7C 83 D1 00 C3 96 03 06   ..|.....|.......
        0160  1C 7C 8B 16 1E 7C 83 D2-00 F7 36 18 7C 8B CA 41   .|...|....6.|..A
        0170  BA 00 00 F7 36 1A 7C 8A-E8 B0 00 D1 E8 D1 E8 8A   ....6.|.........
        0180  E1 0A C8 8A F2 8A 16 20-7C A0 18 7C 2A C4 FE C0   ....... |..|*...
        0190  B4 00 3B F0 73 02 8B C6-BF 03 00 50 B4 02 CD 13   ..;.s......P....
        01A0  58 73 06 4F 75 F5 E9 24-FF 2B F0 74 26 8A E0 B0   Xs.Ou..$.+.t&...
        01B0  00 D1 E0 03 D8 80 E1 C0-80 C9 01 80 C6 01 3A 36   ..............:6
        01C0  1A 7C 75 0A B6 00 80 C5-01 73 03 80 C1 40 A1 18   .|u....s...@..
        01D0  7C EB BF C3 00 00 00 00-00 00 00 00 00 00 00 00   |...............
        01E0  00 00 00 00 00 00 00 00-00 00 00 00 00 00 00 00   ................
        01F0  00 00 00 00 00 00 00 00-00 00 00 00 00 00 55 AA   ..............U.

                        ───── Loader routine ─────
```

A) Boot sector layout for V2 disk

218

Jump instruction   System name   BPB

```
0000 EB 34 90 4D 53 44 4F 53-33 2E 32 00 02 04 01 00  k4.MSDOS 3.2.....
0010 02 00 02 BC CB C8 33 00-11 20 41 80 80 00         ...<Kx3. ........
0020 00 00 00 00 00 00 00 00-03 00 00 00 00 00 0F      ....... ........
0030 00 00 00 00 00 00 FA 33-C0 8E D0 BC 00 7C 16 07  ......z3 @.P<.|..
0040 BB 78 00 36 C5 37 1E 56-16 53 BF 2B 7C B9 0B 00  ;x.6E7.V .S?+|9..
0050 FC AC 26 80 3D 00 74 03-26 8A 05 AA 8A C4 E2 F1  |,&.=.t. &..*.Dbq
0060 06 1F 89 47 02 C7 07 2B-7C FB 8A 16 FD 7D CD 13  ...G.G.+ |{..}}M.
0070 72 66 A0 10 7C 98 F7 26-16 7C 03 06 1C 7C 03 06  rf .|.w& .|...|..
0080 0E 7C A3 3F 7C A3 37 7C-B8 20 00 F7 26 11 7C 8B  .|#?|#7| 8 .w&.|.
0090 1E 0B 7C 03 C3 48 F7 F3-01 06 37 7C BB 00 05 A1  ..|.CHws ..7|;..!
00A0 3F 7C E8 94 00 B0 01 E8-A9 00 72 19 8B FB B9 00  ?|h..Oh ).r..{9.
00B0 00 BE D5 7D F3 A6 75 0D-8D 7F 20 BE E0 7D B9 00  .>U}s&u. .: >'}9.
00C0 00 F3 A6 74 18 BE 76 7D-E8 61 00 32 E4 CD 16 5E  .s&t.>v} ha.2dM.^
00D0 1F 8F 04 8F 44 02 CD 19-BE BF 7D EB EB A1 1C 05  ....D.M. >?}kk!..
00E0 33 D2 F7 36 0B 7C FE C0-A2 3C 7C A1 37 7C A3 3D  3Rw6.|.. .<|.7|.=
00F0 7C BB 00 07 A1 37 7C E8-3F 00 A1 18 7C 2A 06 3B  |;...7|h ?.!.|*.;
0100 7C 40 50 E8 4D 00 58 72-CF 28 06 3C 7C 76 0C 01  |@PhM.Xr O(.<|v..
0110 06 37 7C F7 26 0B 7C 03-D8 EB D9 8A 2E 15 7C 8A  .7|w&.|. XkY...|.
0120 16 FD 7D 8B 1E 3D 7C EA-00 00 70 00 AC 0A C0 74  .}}..=|j ..p,.@t
0130 21 B4 0E B3 FF CD 10 EB-F3 33 D2 F7 36 18 7C FE  !4.3.M.k s3Rw6.|.
0140 C2 88 16 3B 7C 33 D2 F7-F3 36 1A 7C 88 16 2A 7C A3 B..;|3Rw 6.|..*|
0150 39 7C C3 B4 02 8B 16 39-7C 8A EA DO CE DO CE 80  9|C4..9 |.jPNPN.
0160 E6 C0 8A 0E 3B 7C 80 E1-3F 0A CE 8A 36 2A 7C 8A  f@..;|.a ?.N.6*|.
0170 16 FD 7D CD 13 C3 0D 0A-4E 6F 6E 2D 53 79 73 74  .}}M.C.. Non-Syst
0180 65 6D 20 64 69 73 6B 20-6F 72 20 64 69 73 6B 20  em disk  or disk
0190 65 72 72 6F 72 20 0D 0A-52 65 70 6C 61 63 65 20 61  error..R eplace a
01A0 6E 64 20 73 74 72 69 6B-65 20 61 6E 79 20 6B 65  nd strik e any ke
01B0 79 20 77 68 65 6E 20 72-20 72 65 61 64 79 00 0D  y when r eady....
01C0 0A 44 69 73 6B 20 42 6F-6F 74 20 66 61 69 6C 75  .Disk Bo ot failu
01D0 72 65 0D 0A 00 49 4F 20-20 20 20 20 53 59 53  re...IO     SYS
01E0 4D 53 44 4F 53 20 20 20-53 59 53 00 00 00 00 00  MSDOS    SYS.....
01F0 00 00 00 00 00 00 00 00-00 00 00 00 00 80 55 AA  ........ ......U*
```

L——————————— Loader routine ———————————J

B) Boot sector layout for MS-DOS 3.2

Jump instruction   System name   BPB

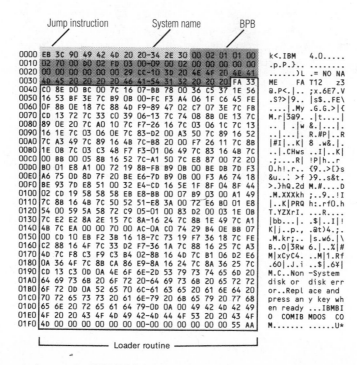

```
0000 EB 3C 90 49 42 4D 20 20-34 2E 30 00 02 01 01 00  k<.IBM   4.0.....
0010 02 70 00 D0 02 FD 03 00-09 00 02 00 00 00 00 00  .p.P.}.. ........
0020 00 00 00 00 00 00 29 C0-10 33 20 4E 4F 20 4E 41  ......)L .= NO NA
0030 4D 45 20 20 20 20 46 41-54 31 32 20 20 20 FA 33  ME    FA T12   z3
0040 C0 8E D0 BC 00 7C 16 07-BB 78 00 36 C5 37 1E 56  @.P<.|.. ;x.6E7.V
0050 16 53 BF 3E 7C B9 0B 00-FC AC 26 80 3D 00 74 03  .S?>|9.. |s$..FE\
0060 0F 8B 0E 18 7C 88 4D F9-89 47 02 C7 07 3E 7C FB  ....|.My .G.G.>|{
0070 CD 13 72 33 C0 39 06-13 7C 74 08 8B 0E 13 7C  M.r|3a9. .|t....|
0080 89 0E 20 7C A0 10 7C F7-26 16 7C 03 06 1C 7C 13  .. | .|w &.|...|.
0090 16 1E 7C 03 06 0E 7C 83-D2 00 A3 50 7C 89 16 52  ..|...|. R.#P|..R
00A0 7C A3 49 7C 89 16 4B 7C-B8 20 00 F7 26 11 7C 8B  |#I|..K| 8 .w&.|.
00B0 1E 0B 7C 03 C3 48 F7 F3-01 06 49 7C 83 16 4B 7C  ..|.CHws ..I|..K|
00C0 00 BB 00 05 8B 16 52 7C-A1 50 7C E8 87 00 72 20  .;....R| !P|h..r
00D0 B0 01 E8 A1 00 72 19 8B-FB FB B9 0B 00 BE DB 7D F3  0.h!.r.. {9..>[}s
00E0 A6 75 0D 8D 7F 20 BE E6-7D B9 0B 00 F3 A6 74 18  &u..: >f }9..s&t.
00F0 BE 93 7D E8 51 00 32 E4-CD 16 5E 1F 8F 04 8F 44  >.}hQ.2d M.#....D
0100 02 CD 19 58 58 58 EB E8-BB 00 07 B9 03 00 A1 49  .M.XXXh ;..9..!I
0110 7C 8B 16 4B 7C 50 52 51-E8 3A 00 72 E6 B0 01 E8  |..K|PRQ h:.rf0.h
0120 54 00 59 5A 58 72 C9 05-01 00 83 D2 00 03 1E 0B  T.YZXrI. ...R...
0130 7C E2 E2 8A 2E 15 7C 8A-16 24 7C 8B 1E 49 7C A1  |bb...|. .$|..I|!
0140 4B 7C EA 00 00 70 00 AC-0A C0 74 29 B4 0E BB 07  K|j..p., .@t)4.;.
0150 00 CD 10 EB F2 3B 16 18-7C 73 19 F7 36 18 7C FE  .M.kr;.. |s.w6.|.
0160 C2 88 16 4F 7C 33 D2 F7-36 1A 7C 88 16 25 7C A3  B..O|3Rw 6.|..%|#
0170 4D 7C F8 C3 F9 C3 B4 02-8B 16 4D 7C B1 06 D2 E6  M|xCyC4. ..M|1.Rf
0180 0A 36 4F 7C 8B CA 86 E9-8A 16 24 7C 8A 36 25 7C  .60|.J.i ..$|.6¥|
0190 CD 13 C3 0D 0A 4E 6F 6E-2D 53 79 73 74 65 6D 20  M.C..Non -System
01A0 64 69 73 6B 20 6F 72 20-64 69 73 6B 20 65 72 72  disk or  disk err
01B0 6F 72 20 0D 0A 52 65 70-6C 61 63 65 20 61 6E 64  or..Repl ace and
01C0 20 70 72 65 73 73 20 61-6E 79 20 6B 65 79 20 77 68  press an y key wh
01D0 65 6E 20 72 65 61 64 79-20 0D 0A 00 49 42 4D 42 49  en ready ...IBMBI
01E0 4F 20 20 43 4F 4D 49 42-4D 44 4F 53 20 20 43 4F  O  COMIB MDOS  CO
01F0 4D 00 00 00 00 00 00 00-00 00 00 00 00 00 55 AA  M....... ......U*
```

L——————————— Loader routine ———————————J

C) Boot sector layout for IBM DOS 4.01

DOS
PROGRAMMING

Jump instruction   System name   BPB

```
0000  EB 3C 90 4D 53 44 4F 53 35 2E 30 00 02 04 01 00    k<.MSDOS5.0.....
0010  02 00 02 77 FF F8 40 00 11 00 08 00 11 00 00 00    ...w.x@.........
0020  00 00 00 00 80 00 29 E0 7D EF 16 20 20 20 20 20    ......)'}o.
0030  20 20 20 20 20 20 46 41 54 31 36 20 20 20 FA 33         FAT16   z3
0040  C0 8E D0 BC 00 7C 16 07 BB 78 00 36 C5 37 1E 56    @.P<.|..;x.6E7.V
0050  16 53 BF 3E 7C B9 0B 00 FC F3 A4 06 1F C6 45 FE    .S?>|9..|s$..FE~
0060  0F 8B 0E 18 7C 88 4D F9 89 47 02 C7 07 3E 7C FB    ....|.My.G.G.>|{
0070  CD 13 72 79 33 C0 39 06 13 7C 74 08 8B 0E 13 7C    M.ry3@9..|t....|
0080  89 0E 20 7C A0 10 7C F7 26 16 7C 03 06 1C 7C 13    .. | .|w&.|...|.
0090  16 1E 7C 03 06 0E 7C 83 D2 00 A3 50 7C 89 16 52    ..|...|.R.#P|..R
00A0  7C A3 49 7C 89 16 4B 7C B8 20 00 F7 26 11 7C 8B    |#I|..K|8 .w&.|.
00B0  1E 0B 7C 03 C3 48 F7 F3 01 06 49 7C 83 16 4B 7C    ..|.CHws..I|..K|
00C0  00 BB 00 05 8B 16 52 7C A1 50 7C E8 92 00 72 1D    .;....R||P|h..r.
00D0  B0 01 E8 AC 00 72 16 8B FB B9 0B 00 BE E6 7D F3    0.h,.r..{9..>f}s
00E0  A6 75 0A 8D 7F 20 B9 0B 00 F3 A6 74 18 BE 9E 7D    &u... 9..s&t.>.}
00F0  E8 5F 00 33 C0 CD 16 5E 1F 8F 04 8F 44 02 CD 19    h_.3@M.^....D.M.
0100  58 58 58 EB E8 8B 47 1A 48 48 8A 1E 0D 7C 32 FF    XXXkh.G.HH...|2.
0110  F7 E3 03 06 49 7C 13 16 4B 7C BB 00 07 B9 03 00    wc..I|..K|;..9..
0120  50 52 51 E8 3A 00 72 D8 B0 01 E8 54 00 59 5A 58    PRQh:.rX0.hT.YZX
0130  72 BB 05 01 00 83 D2 00 03 1E 0B 7C E2 E2 8A 2E    r;....R....|bb..
0140  15 7C 8A 16 24 7C 8B 1E 49 7C A1 4B 7C EA 00 00    .|..$|..I||K|j..
0150  70 00 AC 0A C0 74 29 B4 0E BB 07 00 CD 10 1B F2    p.,.@t)4.;..M..r
0160  3B 16 18 7C 73 19 F7 36 18 7C FE C2 88 16 4F 7C    ;..|s.w6.|~B..O|
0170  33 D2 F7 36 1A 7C 88 16 25 7C A3 4D 7C F8 C3 F9    3Rw6.|..%|#M|xCy
0180  C3 B4 02 8B 16 4D 7C B1 06 D2 E6 0A 36 4F 7C 8B    C4...M|1.Rf.6O|.
0190  CA 86 E9 8A 16 24 7C 8A 36 25 7C CD 13 C3 0D 0A    J.i..$|.6%|M.C..
01A0  4E 6F 6E 2D 53 79 73 74 65 6D 20 64 69 73 6B 20    Non-System disk
01B0  6F 72 20 64 69 73 6B 20 65 72 72 6F 72 00 0D 0A 52    or disk error..R
01C0  65 70 6C 61 63 65 20 61 6E 64 20 70 72 65 73 73    eplace and press
01D0  20 61 6E 79 20 6B 65 79 20 77 68 65 6E 20 72 65     any key when re
01E0  61 64 79 0D 0A 00 49 4F 20 20 20 20 20 20 53 59    ady...IO      SY
01F0  53 4D 53 44 4F 53 20 20 20 53 59 53 00 00 55 AA    SMSDOS   SYS U*
```

— Loader routine —

D) Boot sector layout for MS-DOS 5.0

In all four versions, the boot sector begins with a jump to the start of the bootstrap loader routine, which "bootstraps" the system into operation. The small bootstrap program is loaded and, in turn, loads the larger operating system. (See Chapter 3, "The Dynamics of DOS," for a more detailed discussion of DOS loading procedures.)

The 3-byte jump instruction is followed by an 8-byte system-name field that identifies the manufacturer whose system formatted the disk (some manufacturers do not put a name here). This is followed by the BIOS parameter block (BPB), which provides the information listed in Table 8.2. The format and content of the BPB account for most of the differences between the different boot sectors; at each major step, more data was added to it. The sample values shown in Table 8.2 are taken from the boot sectors in Figure 8.3. (All these values are from 360K DSDD floppy disks.)

Table 8.2   BIOS Parameter Block (BPB) Layout

Byte Offset	Field Length	Sample Value	Meaning
00h	Word	0200	Number of bytes per sector
02h	Byte	02	Number of sectors per cluster
03h	Word	0001	Number of reserved sectors starting at sector 0
05h	Byte	02	Number of FATs
06h	Word	0070	Maximum number of root directory entries
08h	Word	02D0	Total number of sectors (or 0 in V3 if > 65,535)
0Ah	Byte	FD	Media descriptor
0Bh	Word	0002	Number of sectors per FAT
0Dh	Word	0009	Number of sectors per track
0Fh	Word	0002	Number of heads
11h	Double word	00000000	Number of hidden sectors
15h	11 bytes	——	Reserved (before V3)
V3 BPB Extension			
15h	Double word	00000000	Total number of sectors if word at 08h = 0
19h	7 bytes	——	Reserved (BPB outside boot record area)
V4 Boot Record Extensions			
19h	Byte	00	Physical drive number
1Ah	Byte	00	Reserved
1Bh	Byte	29	Signature byte for extended boot record
1Ch	Double word	203D10CC	Volume serial number (made from date/time)
20h	11 bytes	NO NAME	Volume label
2Bh	8 bytes	FAT12	Reserved

DOS
PROGRAMMING

Note particularly in Table 8.2 how the spec has, at each change, attempted to maintain compatibility with older versions, even going to the extreme of providing two different fields for the Total Number of Sectors data when it became possible to have more than 65,535 sectors on a single disk. Unfortunately, not all manufacturers left the reserved areas alone in older versions, which may cause disks formatted with those versions to be unreadable when one of the newer versions is installed.

In all versions of DOS after V2, the BPB is critical to the operation of the bootstrap program because the program must know these parameters to find and load the operating system BIOS and kernel.

Before V3, the loaders assumed that the ROM BIOS version of the BPB was applicable at boot time and that the media code would apply after DOS had been loaded; they made no use, therefore, of the data in the boot sector. As a result, some firms (notably Tandy and Heath-Zenith) omitted the BPB data from floppy disks formatted by using DOS 2.

These disks worked well until Version 3, and they turned out to be unreadable because the new DOS was reading the bootstrap program's code as being the actual disk parameters. Because IBM's V2 produced disks that *did* follow the published rules for the BPB, those could be read satisfactorily, which created a widespread belief that the new version looked for the "magic initials" *IBM* in bytes 3, 4, and 5 of the boot sector; what it looked for was the data following that 8-byte OEM name region.

A similar situation occurred with the step from Version 3 to Version 4. In this case, however, the IBM version of DOS does look for the magic initials at the start of the BPB; if anything other than the letters *IBM* are in that location (even if it finds MSDOS), it reports an unknown media error. No reason is known for this action; changing bytes 3 through 10 to "IBM V2.0" or "IBM V3.0" makes the disk acceptable to the system.

The File Allocation Table (FAT)

DOS uses the file allocation table (or FAT) to manage the disk's data area. The FAT indicates to DOS which portions of the disk belong to each file. Because of the FAT's critical nature, DOS usually maintains two copies that reside, one after the other, on the disk. As changes are made to the original FAT, DOS meticulously updates the second copy.

The FAT follows the boot record on the disk. Because the boot record is only one sector long (sector 0), the FAT starts with sector 1. The length of the FAT (in sectors) is specified in the boot record BPB, as is the number of FAT copies.

It is interesting to note that no native DOS commands use the second FAT copy. If the original FAT is somehow damaged, a separate utility program (not supplied with DOS or even available from Microsoft or IBM) must be used with the second FAT copy to recover disk files. In practice, however, virtually every disaster that can affect one copy also destroys the other at the same time or immediately thereafter, which makes the usefulness of the second FAT copy questionable at best.

Each FAT consists of a series of entries, either 12 or 16 bits long, which record the status of each *cluster* on the disk drive. If 12-bit entries are used, two of them are packed into three consecutive bytes of the table (24 bits). This minimizes the amount of space required for each FAT.

The *cluster* is the smallest unit of disk space that can be allocated for use; it always consists of one or more consecutive logical sectors (which do not necessarily have to be on the same surface or track; the first sector of the first surface of the first track is logical sector 0, and numbering then proceeds sector by sector, surface by surface, track by track, in ever increasing sequence).

The number of sectors in a cluster is always a power of 2, to simplify conversion between cluster number and logical sector number. Floppy disks usually use a cluster size of two sectors (1,024 bytes); the first hard disks used 8-sector clusters, but users found the minimum allocation of 4,096 bytes wasteful when many small files were stored. With the introduction of V3, the cluster size for large hard disks was reduced to 4 sectors. For each disk, the cluster size is one of the key items found in the BPB (see Table 8.2).

Within the FAT, each entry corresponds exactly to one cluster on the disk. The entry corresponding to cluster 0 holds the disk media code, and that for cluster 1 is always filled with 1 bit (hex FFF or FFFF). The first cluster usable for data is numbered as cluster 2.

When any cluster is available for allocation, the value of its corresponding entry in the FAT is 0. When the first cluster is allocated to a file, its entry in the FAT is changed to FFFh or FFFFh to indicate that this cluster is the *last* one in the file. The cluster number also is recorded in the file's directory entry, which is examined in Chapter 9, "Directories and Files." As each new cluster is allocated, the FFFh/FFFFh entry moves to the new cluster's entry in the FAT, and the cluster number of the new entry replaces the FFFh/FFFFh value in the preceding one.

In this manner, the FAT links all the clusters assigned to each file, regardless of where on the disk the clusters happen to be with respect to each other.

Special codes indicate whether the cluster is damaged, and if so, in what way. The values FF7h through FFEh (FFF7 through FFFEh for 16-bit tables) are used for this purpose.

The "32M barrier" has long been a notorious feature of DOS; it vanished in V4. Before looking at the impact of these changes on FAT coding and other disk parameters, let's see where the barrier was created.

Although one of the first barriers was established by the size originally chosen for FAT entries, the real barrier was a result of the 512-byte sector size and the limit of 16-bit values for sector numbers used in all I/O routines. Because a 16-bit number cannot exceed 65,535, that became the maximum possible sector number in a volume. And with 512-byte sectors, the resulting maximum volume size became 33,553,920 bytes, or 32M.

Versions of DOS before V3 were limited to 12-bit FAT entries; the largest number of clusters a disk could contain was 2^{12} (or 4,096). Because 9 of the 4,096 possible FAT entry values are used to represent cluster status, only 4,087 clusters can be represented. That maximum-sized FAT occupies 6,144 bytes, or 12, 512-byte sectors.

Note that the actual maximum disk size these 4,087 clusters can represent depends entirely on the cluster size chosen. For a single-sector cluster size, the limit is 2,092,544 (4087 * 512) bytes. This number suffices for all popular floppy disks. (There is no explanation for how the 2-sector cluster became standard.) It is unusable, though, for even the smallest hard disk.

Increasing the cluster size to 8 sectors brings the size limit up to 16,740,352 bytes, adequate for the 10-megabyte drive of the original XT model. Doubling the cluster size to 16 sectors, with its resulting 8,192-byte minimum allocation size (for even a 1-byte file) brought the FAT capacity up to the 32M limit. This waste of space irritated users.

Additional increases in cluster size could have extended the limit in the FAT, but not in the volume. Only an increase in sector size (or an apparent increase, which is how third-party drivers did it) could break the volume size limit. The sector size was limited also by the available controller hardware.

The waste problem was circumvented in Version 3 by allowing DOS to use a FAT that is encoded differently. If the disk drive was large enough to produce more than 4,087 clusters with an 8-sector cluster size (larger than 17 megabytes), DOS V3 switches to a 4-sector cluster size and uses a 16-bit FAT entry. The 16-bit FAT allows a maximum of 65,527 clusters. With that many clusters available in the FAT, 2-sector clusters could be used and not exceed 32M.

A FAT that large, however, would require 131,072 bytes for each copy, or 512 sectors at the 512-byte standard sector size for the usual pair of FATs. To keep overhead as low as possible, the DOS designers chose to limit the number of FAT entries to 16,384, therefore keeping the 32-megabyte limit and 4-sector clusters and cutting the FAT space down to 128 sectors.

Times change, and many disks now run headlong into the 32M barrier. (This text is being written on a system with an 80M hard disk, partitioned into three 26M logical drives.) With Version 4, therefore, the sector number can be either 16 or 32 bits, and the number of bytes in the FATs can grow to its maximum value with 16-bit entries, which raise the disk capacity limit to 128M with 4-sector clusters or 256M with the old 8-sector cluster size. But drives with more than 300M are already advertised; who knows what the future will bring?

When a disk is formatted, the FORMAT program determines which coding scheme to use. If the size of the disk indicates that it can be represented adequately with a 12-bit FAT, that scheme is used; otherwise, a 16-bit FAT is used. If the volume's size exceeds 32M, 32-bit sector numbers are used also. (If not, the older 16-bit sector number size is retained.) Let's look at each type of FAT.

The 12-bit FAT

The 12-bit FAT results in a table 25 percent smaller than the 16-bit FAT. This fact was probably responsible for the adoption of the 12-bit FAT. Two 12-bit numbers are held in three bytes. Figure 8.4 shows a sample sector from a 12-bit FAT.

```
2D14:0100   FD FF FF 03 40 00 05 60-00 07 80 00 09 A0 00 0B   ....@..:........
2D14:0110   C0 00 0D E0 00 0F 00 01-11 20 01 13 40 01 15 60   ......... ..@..:
2D14:0120   01 17 F0 FF 19 A0 01 1B-C0 01 1D E0 01 1F 00 02   .............
2D14:0130   21 20 02 23 40 02 25 60-02 27 80 02 29 A0 02 2B   ! .#@.%:.'..)..+
2D14:0140   C0 02 2D E0 02 2F 00 03-31 20 03 33 40 03 35 F0   ..-../..1 .3@.5.
2D14:0150   FF 37 80 03 39 A0 03 3B-C0 03 3D E0 03 3F 00 04   .7..9..;..=..?..
2D14:0160   41 20 04 43 40 04 45 60-04 47 80 04 49 A0 04 4B   A .C@.E:.G..I..K
2D14:0170   C0 04 4D E0 04 FF 0F 00-00 00 00 00 00 00 00 00   ..M.............
2D14:0180   00 00 00 00 00 00 00 00-00 00 00 00 00 00 00 00   ................
2D14:0190   00 00 00 00 00 00 00 00-00 00 00 00 00 00 00 00   ................
2D14:01A0   00 00 00 00 00 00 00 00-00 00 00 00 00 00 00 00   ................
2D14:01B0   00 00 00 00 00 00 00 00-00 00 00 00 00 00 00 00   ................
2D14:01C0   00 00 00 00 00 00 00 00-00 00 00 00 00 00 00 00   ................
2D14:01D0   00 00 00 00 00 00 00 00-00 00 00 00 00 00 00 00   ................
2D14:01E0   00 00 00 00 00 00 00 00-00 00 00 00 00 00 00 00   ................
2D14:01F0   00 00 00 00 00 00 00 00-00 00 00 00 00 00 00 00   ................
2D14:0200   00 00 00 00 00 00 00 00-00 00 00 00 00 00 00 00   ................
2D14:0210   00 00 00 00 00 00 00 00-00 00 00 00 00 00 00 00   ................
2D14:0220   00 00 00 00 00 00 00 00-00 00 00 00 00 00 00 00   ................
2D14:0230   00 00 00 00 00 00 00 00-00 00 00 00 00 00 00 00   ................
2D14:0240   00 00 00 00 00 00 00 00-00 00 00 00 00 00 00 00   ................
2D14:0250   00 00 00 00 00 00 00 00-00 00 00 00 00 00 00 00   ................
2D14:0260   00 00 00 00 00 00 00 00-00 00 00 00 00 00 00 00   ................
2D14:0270   00 00 00 00 00 00 00 00-00 00 00 00 00 00 00 00   ................
2D14:0280   00 00 00 00 00 00 00 00-00 00 00 00 00 00 00 00   ................
2D14:0290   00 00 00 00 00 00 00 00-00 00 00 00 00 00 00 00   ................
2D14:02A0   00 00 00 00 00 00 00 00-00 00 00 00 00 00 00 00   ................
2D14:02B0   00 00 00 00 00 00 00 00-00 00 00 00 00 00 00 00   ................
2D14:02C0   00 00 00 00 00 00 00 00-00 00 00 00 00 00 00 00   ................
2D14:02D0   00 00 00 00 00 00 00 00-00 00 00 00 00 00 00 00   ................
2D14:02E0   00 00 00 00 00 00 00 00-00 00 00 00 00 00 00 00   ................
2D14:02F0   00 00 00 00 00 00 00 00-00 00 00 00 00 00 00 00   ................
```

Figure 8.4 A sample 12-bit FAT.

Notice the composition of the file allocation table. In this example, the first two FAT entries (the first three bytes) contain system information. Clusters 0 and 1 of the data area, therefore, are inaccessible by the FAT. The following 1 1/2 bytes (12 bits, the FAT entry for cluster 2) are followed by the entry for cluster 3, and so on. Notice the three bytes at offset 0103h, which are the FAT entries for clusters 2 and 3. You can divide **03 40 00** into two separate FAT entries by using the following formulas (all values are hexadecimal):

Entry 1	= ((Byte2 AND 0F) * 1000) + Byte1
Entry 2	= (Byte3 * 10) + ((Byte2 AND F0) / 10)

The FAT entry for cluster 2, therefore, is as follows:

FAT Entry 2	= ((40 AND 0F) * 1000) + 03
	= ((0) * 1000) + 03
	= 03
FAT Entry 2	= ((40 AND 0F) * 1000) + 03

The FAT entry for cluster 3 is as follows:

FAT Entry 3	= 00 * 10 + ((40 AND F0) / 10)
	= 0 + (40 / 10)
	= 04

225

Each FAT entry points to the next cluster occupied by the file. The FAT entries form a chain, therefore; when all the "links" in this chain are put together, the chain signifies the clusters occupied by a specific file.

Some values for FAT entries, however, do not represent a subsequent cluster number; rather, these values represent a status of the cluster. Table 8.3 summarizes the possible codes for a FAT entry.

Table 8.3 12-Bit FAT Assignment Bytes

Category	Codes
Free for assignment	0
Part of a file (pointer to next cluster)	2–FF6
Bad cluster	FF7
End of cluster chain	FF8–FFF

Using the 12-bit FAT shown in Figure 8.3, let's follow a cluster chain. A file's directory entry points to the first cluster occupied by a file (directory entries are discussed in Chapter 9). In this illustration, the directory entry for IBMBIO.COM (22,100 bytes long) points to a beginning cluster number of 2. If you look at the entry for cluster 2, you see a pointer to cluster 3—and cluster 3 points to cluster 4 (remember that you just worked out the math). Cluster 4 then points to 5, which points to 6, and so on until cluster 18h is reached. Here, the FAT entry is FFFh, which indicates that the end of the cluster chain has been reached.

Using cluster 2 as the starting cluster, you can find the next cluster as follows:

1. Multiply the cluster number by 2 and round down the result.

2. Get the word at the resulting offset.

3. If the original cluster number (2, in this case) was even, take the low 12 bits of the word; otherwise, take the high 12 bits.

The 16-bit FAT

The release of DOS V3 brought support for larger hard disks and a FAT that uses 16 bits (2 bytes) per entry. Figure 8.5 shows a sample sector from a 16-bit FAT.

```
2D14:0100  F8 FF FF FF 03 00 04 00-05 00 06 00 07 00 08 00    ................
2D14:0110  09 00 0A 00 0B 00 0C 00-FF FF 0E 00 0F 00 10 00    ................
2D14:0120  11 00 12 00 13 00 14 00-15 00 16 00 17 00 18 00    ................
2D14:0130  19 00 1A 00 1B 00 FF FF-78 0A FF FF 20 00 FF FF    ........x... ...
2D14:0140  FF FF FF FF FF FF 6D 04-26 00 FF FF 27 00 28 00    ......m.&...'.(.
2D14:0150  29 00 2A 00 2B 00 2C 00-2D 00 2F 00 FF FF 32 00    ).*.+.,.-./...2.
2D14:0160  FF FF 00 00 33 00 51 00-42 00 36 00 37 00 38 00    ....3.Q.B.6.7.8.
2D14:0170  FF FF 3A 00 3B 00 3C 00-3D 00 3E 00 3F 00 41 00    ..:.;.<.=.>.?.A.
2D14:0180  FF FF FF FF 43 00 44 00-45 00 48 00 FF FF FF FF    ....C.D.E.H.....
2D14:0190  49 00 4A 00 4B 00 4C 00-4F 00 FF FF FF FF 50 00    I.J.K.L.O.....P.
2D14:01A0  FF FF 52 00 53 00 54 00-55 00 57 00 FF FF 81 00    ..R.S.T.U.W.....
2D14:01B0  59 00 5A 00 5B 00 5C 00-61 00 72 00 FF FF 60 00    Y.Z.[.\.a.r...`.
2D14:01C0  FF FF 62 00 6B 00 FF FF-FF FF 66 00 FF FF FF FF    ..b.k.....f.....
2D14:01D0  FF FF 6A 00 FF FF 6C 00-6D 00 78 00 6F 00 FF FF    ..j...l.m.x.o...
2D14:01E0  71 00 FF FF 83 00 FF FF-FF FF 76 00 77 00 FF FF    q.........v.w...
2D14:01F0  7B 00 FF FF FF FF 7C 00-7D 00 7E 00 7F 00 80 00    {.....|.}.~.....
2D14:0200  FF FF 82 00 D0 00 84 00-85 00 86 00 87 00 88 00    ................
2D14:0210  8C 00 8A 00 8B 00 FF FF-8D 00 8E 00 FF FF 00 00    ................
2D14:0220  00 00 00 00 93 00 94 00-95 00 96 00 97 00 98 00    ................
2D14:0230  99 00 9A 00 9B 00 9C 00-9D 00 C3 00 FF FF A0 00    ................
2D14:0240  A1 00 A2 00 A3 00 A4 00-A5 00 A6 00 A7 00 A8 00    ................
2D14:0250  A9 00 AA 00 AB 00 AC 00-AD 00 AE 00 AF 00 B0 00    ................
2D14:0260  B1 00 B2 00 B3 00 B4 00-C2 00 B6 00 B7 00 B8 00    ................
2D14:0270  B9 00 BA 00 BB 00 BC 00-BD 00 BE 00 BF 00 C0 00    ................
2D14:0280  C1 00 FF FF FF FF C4 00-C5 00 C7 00 FF FF C8 00    ................
2D14:0290  CF 00 CA 00 CB 00 CC 00-CD 00 CE 00 FF FF FC 01    ................
2D14:02A0  D1 00 D2 00 D3 00 D9 00-D5 00 D6 00 D7 00 D8 00    ................
2D14:02B0  FF FF DA 00 DB 00 DC 00-DD 00 DE 00 DF 00 E0 00    ................
2D14:02C0  E1 00 E2 00 E3 00 E4 00-E5 00 E6 00 E7 00 E8 00    ................
2D14:02D0  E9 00 EA 00 EB 00 EC 00-ED 00 EE 00 EF 00 F0 00    ................
2D14:02E0  F1 00 F2 00 F3 00 F4 00-F5 00 F6 00 F7 00 F8 00    ................
2D14:02F0  F9 00 FA 00 FB 00 FC 00-FD 00 FE 00 FF 00 00 01    ................
```

Fig. 8.5 A sample 16-bit FAT.

Translation is much more straightforward with this file allocation table than with the 12-bit FAT. The first two entries (four bytes) are used for system information; each subsequent entry occupies two bytes. Notice the two bytes at offset 0104h (the FAT entry for cluster 2). The value here (0003h) points to the entry for cluster 3.

Just as with the 12-bit version, each FAT entry points to the next cluster occupied by the file. The FAT entries, therefore, form a chain that signifies, when all its "links" are put together, the clusters occupied by a specific file. As with the 12-bit FAT, other values for FAT entries do not represent a subsequent cluster number; rather, these values represent the status of the cluster. Table 8.4 summarizes the possible codes for a FAT entry.

Table 8.4 16-Bit FAT Assignment Bytes

Category	Codes
Free for assignment	0
Part of a file (pointer to next cluster)	2–FFF6
Bad cluster	FFF7
End of cluster chain	FFF8–FFFF

Let's follow a cluster chain, using the 16-bit FAT shown in Figure 8.5. A file's directory entry points to the first cluster occupied by a file; in Figure 8.5, the directory entry for IBMBIO.COM (22,100 bytes in length) points to a beginning cluster number of 2. The entry for cluster 2 points to cluster 3. Cluster 3 points to cluster 4, which points to 5, which points to 6, and so on until cluster 0Ch is reached. The FAT entry at cluster 0Ch is FFFFh, which indicates that the end of the cluster chain has been reached.

The larger disk capacity made available in V4 was obtained by permitting the FAT to grow to full size rather than cutting it short. This is the only difference in the FAT strategies of V3 and V4, although the sector-number size may vary.

More FAT Information

When DOS requests space for a file, that space is assigned to the file in units of one or more clusters. As you have seen from the discussions of the 12- and 16-bit FATs, the clusters in a file are chained, with each FAT entry giving the cluster number of the next entry (see Fig. 8.6).

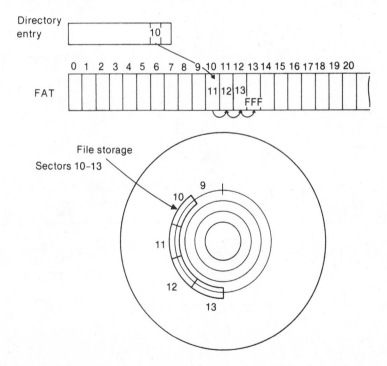

Figure 8.6 FAT cluster chaining.

The FAT reserves, but does not use, the space for entries 0 and 1. The first byte of the FAT is used for a disk identification (ID) byte that helps identify the disk format (see Table 8.5).

Because clusters 0 and 1 are reserved for the system, cluster 2 is the first cluster that can be assigned.

Table 8.5　Some Possible FAT ID Byte Values

Value	Disk Characteristics
F0	Not identifiable
F8	Fixed disk
F9	Double-sided, 15 sectors/track
F9	Double-sided, 9 sectors/track (720K)
FC	Single-sided, 9 sectors/track
FD	Double-sided, 9 sectors/track (360K)
FE	Single-sided, 8 sectors/track
FF	Double-sided, 8 sectors/track

Remember from the FAT discussion that DOS allocates the space for files by complete clusters. Regardless of the actual size of the file, therefore, the minimum disk use for a file is one cluster. A 1-byte file may occupy 512; 1,024; 2,048; 4,096; or more bytes of disk space, depending on the number of sectors per cluster.

As you learned from decoding the floppy disk BPB, the sample disk had two FAT tables. Whenever disk operations allocate or de-allocate space on the disk, both FATs are updated automatically. When a disk is first accessed, DOS compares the FATs to see whether they are consistent. Although there can be more than two FATs, in which case they are stored sequentially on the disk, most disks have two.

After the last FAT comes the root directory, with 32 bytes for each entry. The BPB gives the size of the directory so that you can determine where the file area begins (immediately after the root directory).

Now that you know where to find things on the disk, let's see what functions DOS provides to manipulate them.

Using Disk Functions

There are no BIOS functions for dealing with a DOS file system because the file system (including all the tables just discussed) is a construction of DOS. To the BIOS, the disk is just a series of sectors, beginning at sector number 0 and proceeding sequentially to the highest-numbered sector. The BIOS knows about tracks, sectors, and disk heads, but not about files, FATs, or directories. All the functions you will use are DOS-oriented functions.

Drive Information

You can use DOS function calls to get information about the disk drive. The `drvinfo.c` program illustrates how you can get and display this information (see Listing 8.1). Note that this program does not take the new 32-bit sector number possibility of V4 into account; the V4 *Technical Reference Manual* does not indicate that the drive information functions are even aware of the change.

Listing 8.1

```
/* drvinfo.c
   Listing 8.1 of DOS Programmer's Reference */

#include <stdio.h>
#include <dos.h>
#include <ctype.h>
#include "drvinfo.h"

/* Prototypes */
void get_drvinfo(char drv, struct drvinfo *info);
unsigned int get_drive(void);
void get_drvspace(char drv, struct drvinfo *info);

void main()
{
    int  drive;

    drive = get_drive();
    printf("\n\n");
    printf("Current Drive Code = %u (%c:)\n", drive, 'A'+drive);
    printf("\n");

    get_drvinfo('A'+drive, &info);
    printf("Drive %c: information from function 1Ch\n",'A'+drive);
    printf("   Number of clusters =       %lu\n",info.clusters);
    printf("   Sectors per cluster =      %lu\n",info.spc);
    printf("   Physical sector size =     %lu\n",info.secsize);
    printf("   Drive size =               %lu Kb\n",
        (info.clusters * info.spc * info.secsize)/1024);
    printf("\n");

    get_drvspace('A'+drive,&info);
    printf("Drive %c: information from function 36h\n", 'A'+drive);
    printf("   Number of clusters =       %lu\n",info.clusters);
    printf("   Sectors per cluster =      %lu\n",info.spc);
    printf("   Physical sector size =     %lu\n",info.secsize);
    printf("   Drive size =               %lu Kb\n",
        (info.clusters * info.spc * info.secsize)/1024);
```

```
        printf("   Available clusters =        %lu\n",info.avail);
        printf("   Available space =           %lu Kb\n",
            (info.avail * info.spc * info.secsize)/1024);
        printf("\n");
}

/* Fetch the current drive code */

unsigned int get_drive()
{
    union REGS regs;
    regs.h.ah = 0x19;
    intdos(&regs, &regs);
    return(regs.h.al);
}

/* Fetch drive information using function 1Ch */

void get_drvinfo(drv,info)

char drv;
struct drvinfo *info;
{
    union REGS regs;
    struct SREGS segs;
    int dn;

    /* Converts drive letter to internal representation */
    drv = toupper(drv);
    dn = drv - 'A' + 1;

    /* Set up and call DOS */
    regs.h.ah = 0x1c;
    regs.h.dl = dn;
    intdosx(&regs,&regs,&segs);
    info->spc = regs.h.al;
    info->fatseg = segs.ds;
    info->fatoff = regs.x.bx;
    info->secsize = regs.x.cx;
    info->clusters = regs.x.dx;
}

/* Fetch drive information using function 36h */

void get_drvspace(drv,info)

char drv;
struct drvinfo *info;
{
```

continues

231

Listing 8.1 Continued

```
        union REGS regs;
        struct SREGS segs;
        int  dn;

        /* Converts drive letter to internal representation */
        drv = toupper(drv);
        dn = drv - 'A' + 1;

        /* Set up and make the DOS call */
        regs.h.ah = 0x36;
        regs.h.dl = dn;
        intdosx(&regs,&regs,&segs);
        info->spc = regs.x.ax;
        info->avail = regs.x.bx;
        info->secsize = regs.x.cx;
        info->clusters = regs.x.dx;
    }
```

To get information about the drive, `drvinfo.c` calls the following three subroutines:

`get_drive()`, to get the current drive number

`get_drvinfo()`, to get general information about the drive

`get_drvspace()`, to get other information

All this information is entered into the `drvinfo` structure, as defined in `drvinfo.h`, as shown in Listing 8.2.

Listing 8.2

```
/* drvinfo.h
   Listing 8.2 of DOS Programmer's Reference */

struct drvinfo {
    unsigned long  spc;         /* Sectors per cluster */
    unsigned long  avail;       /* Available clusters  */
    unsigned long  fatseg;      /* FAT segment of ID byte */
    unsigned long  fatoff;      /* FAT offset of ID byte  */
    unsigned long  secsize;     /* Physical sector size */
    unsigned long  clusters;    /* Number of clusters   */
    char fatid;                 /* FAT ID byte */
} info;
```

By defining a structure to hold related information about the disk, you can keep the information organized logically as you work with it.

Notice that the `drvinfo.c` program shown in Listing 8.1 includes two subroutine calls; these calls illustrate that the same information can be obtained in more than one way.

Getting the drive information is a simple procedure—you call the DOS services interrupt (Int 21h). This call is performed in C by the intdos function and in Pascal by the Msdos function. The DOS service returns the drive code in the AL register.

The get_drive() function does not interpret the drive code; it simply returns the code to drvinfo.c. The process of requesting specific drive information, however, is more complex than a simple request for the drive number. Information is returned in segment registers as well as in the general-purpose registers. To access the segment registers, you must use the intdosx function, as is done in the get_drvinfo() and get_drvspace() functions.

After the functions call DOS (the intdosx function call), they save the returned information from the registers in the info structure that was passed by the function call. Handling the information in a structure such as this one enables someone with no knowledge of registers or DOS calls to access it from the program that calls the function. With a little more work, the functions can be included in a library for programmers who do not know how to deal with DOS.

Both get_drvinfo() and get_drvspace() are examples of a good programming practice—that of hiding implementation details inside the functions. In this case, the functions determine the correct drive code from the standard user-oriented designation for the drives (A, B, C, and so forth). Allowing the drive name to be passed as a letter is a way to hide the fact that the drive designations in DOS and BIOS routines are not always consistent. Some routines use 0 to designate drive A, whereas some use 0 to designate the default drive.

The information returned by get_drvspace() is probably of more use in programs than the information returned by get_drvinfo(). With get_drvspace(), for instance, you can determine how much free space is available on the disk by using the following information returned by DOS function 36h:

Register	Contains
AX	Number of sectors per cluster
BX	Number of available sectors
CX	Bytes per sector
DX	Clusters per drive

To calculate the free space on the drive, use the following formula:

BX * AX * CX

The total drive capacity is calculated by the following formula:

DX * AX * CX

To determine only how much free space is on the disk, you can write a function (get_free()) to return only this information. The free.c program in Listing 8.3 gets this information by calling get_free() with the drive name and pointers to integers for both the available and total disk space.

233

Listing 8.3

```
/* free.c
   Listing 8.3 of DOS Programmer's Reference */

#include <stdio.h>

/* Prototypes */
void get_free(char drv, unsigned long *avail, unsigned long *total);

void main(argc,argv)

int  argc;
char *argv[];

{
    unsigned long avail, total;

    get_free(*argv[1],&avail,&total);
    if(*argv[1])
        printf("Free disk space on drive %c: is %lu Kb of %lu Kb\n",
            *argv[1], avail, total);
    else
        printf("Free disk space on default drive is %lu Kb of %lu Kb\n",
            avail, total);
}
```

The program is written to check the first command-line argument for the drive name. If *no* first argument is supplied, the program assumes that it should find the information for the default drive.

The get_free() function determines which drive it should check and then sets up and makes the call to DOS (see Listing 8.4). Function 36h is used again to determine the free space, but most of the disk information is thrown away because it is not needed for the limited purpose of the function.

Listing 8.4

```
/* get_free.c
   Listing 8.4 of DOS Programmer's Reference */

#include <stdio.h>
#include <ctype.h>
#include <dos.h>

void get_free(drv, avail, total)

char drv;
unsigned long *avail, *total;
```

234

```
{
    union REGS regs;
    struct SREGS segs;
    int  dn;
    unsigned long SectCluster;
    unsigned long AvailCluster;
    unsigned long BytesSector;
    unsigned long Clusters;

    /* Determines the drive and sets the drive number */
    if(drv){
        drv = toupper(drv);
        dn = drv - 'A' + 1;
    } else {
        dn = 0;
    }

    /* Sets up and makes the DOS function call */
    regs.h.ah = 0x36;
    regs.h.dl = dn;
    intdosx(&regs, &regs, &segs);
    SectCluster = regs.x.ax;
    AvailCluster = regs.x.bx;
    BytesSector = regs.x.cx;
    Clusters = regs.x.dx;

    *avail = (SectCluster * BytesSector / 1024) * AvailCluster;
    *total = (SectCluster * BytesSector / 1024) * Clusters;
}
```

The same operations can be performed in BASIC, as you can see from the free.bas program in
Listing 8.5.

Listing 8.5

```
'free.bas

$include "REGNAMES.INC"

def fnchkspc(drv)
'determine the free space from Int 21h, Function 36
    reg %ax, &h3600
    reg %dx, drv
    call interrupt &h21

    fnchkspc = reg(%bx) * (reg(%ax) * reg(%cx)/1024)
end def

def fnsize(drv)
'determine the space from Int 21h, Function 36h
```

continues

235

Listing 8.5 Continued

```
        reg %ax, &h3600
        reg %dx, drv
        call interrupt &h21
        fnsize = reg(%dx) * (reg(%ax) * reg(%cx)/1024)
end def

'MAIN PROGRAM

        input "Drive: ",dv$
        dv$ = left$(dv$,1)
        drive = int((instr("AaBbCcDdEeFfGg",dv$)+1)/2)
        print "Free Space on Drive ";dv$;" Is " ;fnchkspc(drive);"K"
        print "Drive Capacity Is ";fnsize(drive);"K"
end
```

If you want to build a truly useful utility for yourself, why not build one that copies a group of files to a floppy disk or to a series of floppies? This type of utility checks the size of the next file you want to copy. If sufficient space is available on the disk, the utility copies the file; if not, the utility prompts for another floppy. This type of program might look like this:

```
FOR i=1 TO number_of_arguments
    TOP:
    size = size of file i
    space = get space on target drive
    IF size>space THEN
        ask for another floppy disk
        wait for user to press a key
        GOTO TOP:
    ELSE
        copy file i to floppy
    ENDIF
NEXT i
```

Although you do not yet know how to do everything needed to make this program practical, file sizes and executing other programs are discussed in Chapter 9, "Directories and Files," and in Chapter 10, "Program and Memory Management." Then you can build the program.

Formatting Disks

Disk formatting is a simple yet dangerous task most people do not need to do for themselves. The basic FORMAT program distributed with DOS is one of several adequate disk-formatting programs available. Special formatters are available (often as part of utility packages such as PC Tools) for those who want faster or more sophisticated formatting.

Beginners should plan carefully before they try to write disk-formatting programs; if handled incorrectly, these programs can wipe out critical disk systems and destroy months of work. This section describes some basic formatting techniques and shows a few examples of ways to access the formatting routines present in the system. Remember: *you put your system at risk if you make a mistake here!* When you test a formatting program, follow these simple precautions:

- Whenever possible, test a formatting program on a "floppy disk only" system (no fixed disk). Use system disks that you can afford to lose if something goes wrong.

- If you must make test runs on a system that includes a hard disk, disable the hard disk if you can (by pulling the hard disk controller, for example).

- Be sure to have a current backup of your system. (*You should always have a current backup!*)

Good programming practice dictates that you must recognize the inevitability of mistakes and that your testing must attempt to foresee and provide for all possible errors. If you are careful, nothing is likely to happen to your system when you test your programs.

BIOS provides Int 13h, Function 05h to format disk tracks. The concept is simple and the function is easy to use. Let's look at how you use this function to format a disk.

If you start with an unformatted disk (or if you want to clear an old one), you must use Int 13h, Function 05h to format the disk, track by track, as follows:

For each track from 0 to the last track
        Set up the call for the track
        Call the track-formatting routine

The disk will be formatted correctly and BIOS routines will be capable of reading it—but it is *not* a DOS disk. As you may recall from the discussion earlier in this chapter, DOS requires that a disk have certain structures: the boot sector, FAT, and root directory. The format procedure provides none of these.

To produce a disk acceptable to DOS, you must not only give a disk its basic format but also initialize the disk structure as follows:

For each track from 0 to the last track
        Set up the call for the track
        Call the track formatting routine
        Write the boot sector to the disk
        Write FAT information to the disk
        Write root directory information to the disk

You can handle the last two steps by simply writing zeros into the FAT and disk directory areas. Zero entries in the FAT table indicate that the clusters are free and ready for reassignment.

Zeros in the disk directory indicate that the directory entries have never been used. Except for the boot sector, then, the formatting process can be fairly simple: Format the tracks, write the boot sector, then zero the FAT and root directory areas.

Let's write a routine for formatting a disk track. After you know how to format one track, you can format a disk simply by "stepping through" all the tracks.

You call BIOS Int 13h, Function 05h with the register settings shown in Table 8.6.

Table 8.6   Register Settings for BIOS Int 13h, Function 05h

Register	Meaning
AH	05h (the function code)
ES:BX	Pointer to track-address field table
CH	Track number
DH	Head number
DL	Drive number

The track-address table is the heart of the formatting operation. It specifies the order of logical disk sectors on the physical disk track. Each disk sector is represented in the table by a four-byte entry that gives the label for each sector on the track. You can use the table to assign logical sector numbers in a different order than the physical sectors on the disk (a process known as *interleaving*).

The number of tracks varies according to the type of disk you use: 5 1/4-inch disks (360K, double-sided, double density) have 40 tracks per side; 3 1/2-inch disks (720K, double-sided, double density) have 80 tracks per side. The head number (for floppy disks) should be 0 or 1.

The drive number (DL) indicates which physical drive you want to work on. (Floppy drives are specified by counting from zero: drive A is number 0, drive B is 1, and so on. Hard disks, though, are identified a little differently: drive C is usually 80h.)

On an unformatted disk, a track is an unstructured blank section of the magnetic surface. The formatting procedure imposes a structure on the disk by magnetically creating "storage bins" on the track (see Fig. 8.7). Information can be stored in these bins, which are called sectors.

238

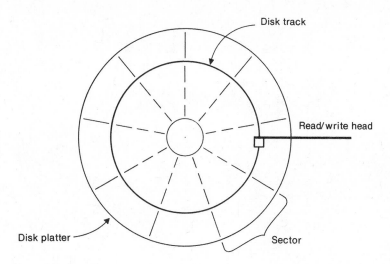

Figure 8.7 Disk track.

You can place the bins around the track in the physical order in which they occur, but this method can have drawbacks.

Think about reading from a set of disk sectors. Suppose that you copy a disk sector into memory and then come back immediately to read the next sector. This is no problem: Simply tell the disk controller which sector you want, and the controller gets the right one. If the two sectors are one after another on the disk, however, your request for the second sector will occur after the beginning of that sector has passed the read/write head. To get the sector, you must wait while the disk makes a full revolution (about a fifth of a second for a floppy at 300 RPM).

If you try to read an entire disk, one sector after another, those fifths of a second add up to more than two minutes the program spends waiting for a specific sector to rotate into position under the read/write head! In applications that do a great deal of disk I/O, the time overhead adds up quickly. By doing something to eliminate the problem, you can significantly improve these types of applications.

One way to avoid the wait for disk sectors is to interleave them so that one physical sector separates consecutive logical sectors. In other words, you alternate the sector numbers around the track. Figure 8.8 shows how nine sector-sized pieces of a file can be interleaved on a nine-sector track.

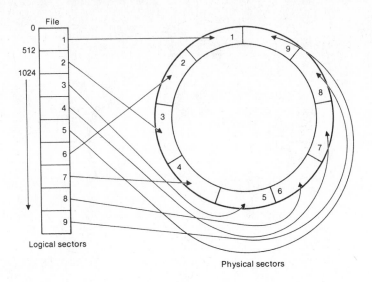

Figure 8.8 Storing file sectors.

The interleave factor has achieved considerable significance for hard disks, after IBM's default settings were reported to be inappropriate for modern equipment. For most systems, a factor of 3 or below gives the best results on a hard drive. A number of shareware programs test the factor on your system, recommend the best to use, and then, in some cases, change it for you on request.

The track-address table lets you specify (to the BIOS function) what the logical sector numbers will be for each physical sector on the track. By specifying the size of each sector, you can change the sector size around the track. The information from the track-address table is stored on the disk so that the disk controller can find a specific sector and have to consult special tables and figure out the disk's layout. When you use the track-address table to establish the layout, you create the track interleaving as a permanent part of the disk's logical structure.

The track-address table is a series of four-byte entries (one for each sector on the track) that represent the track, the head, the logical sector number, and the code size. Table 8.7 lists the allowable code sizes.

Table 8.7 Size Codes

Code	Sector Size (in Bytes)
0	128
1	256
2	512
3	1024

The information from the track-address table goes into the header written for each sector by the controller. When the controller reads the disk, it uses these sector headers to locate the desired data. Each entry in the table provides data for one header, which is written immediately before the data area for that sector. Both the beginning and end of the header are identified by special codes called *address marks*; the controller handles these automatically.

The entries in the track-address table are always arranged on the disk by physical sector number. Each physical sector can have a logical sector number (in any order you want) so that interleaving can be implemented. The track-address table sets the access order of the sectors on a track; PCs read the disk by accessing the sector header to determine which sector has been requested. To write more or less than nine sectors per track, you must change both the number of entries in the table and the size code so that the total number of bytes specified by adding all sectors together does not exceed 4,608. Larger sectors can get by with a few bytes more, and smaller sectors will permit less; the sector headers take space, too.

The track-address table for track 3 of a 360K, double-sided, double-density disk with nine sectors per track might look like the one in Figure 8.8. The logical sector numbers in Figure 8.8 correspond to the following physical sectors:

Physical Sector   1 2 3 4 5 6 7 8 9
Logical Sector   1 6 2 7 3 8 4 9 5

To indicate an error during formatting, the carry flag is set on return from the BIOS function. If the flag is set, AH contains an error code. The meanings of the individual bits of this error code are shown in Table 8.8. If an error occurs, your program should immediately call BIOS Int 13h, Function 00h (which resets the disk) and then handle the error appropriately.

Table 8.8   Disk-Error Status Bits

——————— Error Code ———————		
Hex Value	Binary Value 76543210	Meaning
01	1	Bad command
02	......1.	Bad sector address mark
03	11	Write-protect error
04	.....1..	Bad sector/sector not found
08	....1...	DMA overrun
09	....1..1	DMA error
10	...1....	Bad CRC on disk read
20	..1.....	Controller malfunction
40	.1......	Seek failure
80	1.......	Time out

241

The `fmt_trk()` function is an example of the track-formatting procedure implemented in C (see Listing 8.6). This function assumes that you are formatting a 360K, DSDD disk in a standard PC drive. The function provides only for simple error recovery; it also assumes that the calling routine handles all interaction with the user. If successful, it returns 0; any other value indicates an error.

Listing 8.6

```
/* fmt_trk.c
   Listing 8.6 of DOS Programmer's Reference */

#include <stdio.h>
#include <dos.h>

#define DISK    0x13

/* Prototypes */
int fmt_error(char code);

fmt_trk(dsk,trk,head)

int  dsk;
int  trk;
int  head;

{
     union REGS regs;
     struct SREGS sregs;
     char trktbl[36];
     int  i;

     for(i=0; i< 9; i++){
          trktbl[ i*4]   = trk;
          trktbl[ i*4+1] = head;
          trktbl[ i*4+2] = i;
          trktbl[ i*4+3] = 2;
     }
     regs.h.ah = 0x05;
     regs.h.ch = trk;
     regs.h.dh = head;
     regs.h.dl = dsk;
     regs.x.bx = FP_OFF(trktbl);
     sregs.es = FP_SEG(trktbl);
     int86x(DISK,&regs,&regs,&sregs);
     if(regs.x.cflag)
          return(fmt_error(regs.h.ah));
     return(0);
```

```
}

int fmt_error(code)

/*  This routine returns an error code of 1 to indicate that a
    write-protect error (which can be recoverable) occurred.
    All other errors are assumed to be nonrecoverable and thus
    are lumped together.
*/

char code;
{
    union REGS regs;

    regs.h.ah = 0;
    int86(DISK,&regs,&regs);
    return((code==3)?1:2);
}
```

Summary

In this chapter, you learned about the basic structure of disks and how they are formatted. You also learned that the BIOS knows only about tracks, sectors, and disk heads, not about files and directories. The BIOS knows how to locate the disk's partition table and the boot record for the disk, but its knowledge stops there.

All file-related disk operations are DOS-level functions. DOS maintains the disk's directories, files, and file allocation tables (FATs). The structure and location of these tables are given in the BIOS parameter block (BPB) stored in the boot record (the first sector of the bootable partition).

After you have the basic information about the disk, you can access information about the disk (free space, disk capacity, and so forth) from standard DOS calls. Armed with what you have learned from this chapter, you are ready to tackle Chapter 9.

9

Directories and Files

Nothing is more basic to programming than disk files. As programmers, we have to deal with disk files no matter which audience (business, development, entertainment, or scientific) we program for. Most programming languages, therefore, provide a wealth of easy ways to create, open, read, write, close, and delete files.

Dealing with files from a high-level language is so easy that you generally do not have to think about file operations on a DOS level. With the file-handling functions that C, BASIC, and Pascal provide, you can do your job safely without much fuss. If you work in assembly language, however, you need to become familiar with DOS's file-manipulation functions.

Even if you do not program in assembly language, some functions are not readily available from C, BASIC, or Pascal libraries; you cannot do certain types of operations effectively unless you use the DOS functions.

You may be wondering why this book refers only to DOS file functions—not to the BIOS. The answer is that files and directories are beyond the realm of BIOS. The BIOS "knows" nothing about files. It assigns no structure (other than tracks and sectors) to disks. Disk file structure is under the direct control of DOS, which contains all the functions necessary for accessing disk files and directories.

This chapter begins with a look at the structure of directories and proceeds by discussing disk files and file functions. Finally, you learn how you can use your newly acquired knowledge of directories and files to build a program that enables you to locate a specific file anywhere in the directory system.

Disk Directories

When directories were first introduced, they represented a major advance in the way disk operating systems handled disk files. The early operating systems (CP/M, TRSDOS, Apple

DOS, and a myriad of others) all treated files in much the same way. In these *flat file* systems, all the disk files were available through a single directory. DOS treated files this way until the advent of DOS V2.

Beginning with DOS V2, a file-ordering concept was borrowed from UNIX and XENIX. This *hierarchical directory* scheme allows easy ordering and manipulation of a large number of disk files (usually, but not always, stored on a hard disk). In a system with hierarchical directories, every disk has a predefined, fixed-size *root directory* stored at a known location on the disk. Like the flat-file concept described in the preceding paragraph, the root directory can contain a specific number of equally accessible files.

If you were to stay in the confines of the single root directory, you would be no better off than before. The root directory of a V2 disk is indistinguishable from the only directory of a V1 disk. But the hierarchical directory system lets you create special entries in the root directory (called *subdirectories*) that are similar to files except that their file space contains additional directory entries. Like the root directory, subdirectories are directories in their own right.

Unlike the root directory, subdirectories are not limited by arbitrary size restrictions. They can grow, as necessary, to accommodate additional files. Furthermore, you can create subdirectory entries within subdirectories, with each entry containing references to individual groups of files. The only limit to this nesting process is the 65-character maximum size of a pathspec (the full path from root to file that lists all directories which must be traversed), which does not permit more than 32 levels of nesting. Let's look at the way DOS keeps track of the individual files and directories on a disk.

The Root Directory

The root directory is located in a fixed position on the disk and has a fixed size, which is determined by the FORMAT program when it formats the disk. The root directory's size and disk location are recorded in the BIOS parameter block of the disk's boot sector (see Chapter 8, "Disks").

In DOS V1, the root directory was the only directory on a disk. Support for subdirectories began with DOS V2. As you now know, a subdirectory is simply a special type of file that contains other directory entries rather than ordinary data.

The first two entries in a root directory are reserved for the BIOS and DOS-kernel system file entries. The disk bootstrap program uses these entries during system start-up (see Chapter 3, "The Dynamics of DOS"). Figure 9.1 shows the first sector of a typical root directory that includes the operating system.

A) Nonbootable disk (first sector only)

```
00   53 52 43 20 20 20 20 20-20 20 20 10 00 00 00 00   SRC        .....
10   00 00 00 00 00 00 00 6E 00-9B 10 02 00 00 00 00 00   ......n.........
20   44 45 4D 4F 43 4D 20 20-41 53 4D 20 00 00 00 00   DEMOCM ASM ....
30   00 00 00 00 00 00 00 D7 83-4F 0F 09 00 79 04 00 00   .........O...y...
40   44 45 4D 4F 43 4D 20 20-4F 42 4A 20 00 00 00 00   DEMOCM OBJ ....
50   00 00 00 00 00 00 00 7B BD-9B 10 0B 00 6C 00 00 00   ......{.....l...
60   44 45 4D 4F 43 4D 20 20-45 58 45 20 00 00 00 00   DEMOCM EXE ....
70   00 00 00 00 00 00 00 81 BD-9B 10 0C 00 2B 03 00 00   ............+...
80   44 45 4D 4F 43 4D 20 20-43 4F 4D 20 00 00 00 00   DEMOCM COM ....
90   00 00 00 00 00 00 00 84 BD-9B 10 0D 00 2B 00 00 00   ............+...
A0   44 45 4D 4F 43 4D 20 20-44 4D 50 20 00 00 00 00   DEMOCM DMP ....
B0   00 00 00 00 00 00 00 2A BE-9B 10 0E 00 29 05 00 00   ......*.....)...
C0   00 00 00 00 00 00 00 00 00-00 00 00 00 00 00 00   ................
D0   00 00 00 00 00 00 00 00 00-00 00 00 00 00 00 00   ................
E0   00 00 00 00 00 00 00 00 00-00 00 00 00 00 00 00   ................
F0   00 00 00 00 00 00 00 00 00-00 00 00 00 00 00 00   ................
```

B) Bootable disk (system files included, first sector only)

```
00   49 4F 20 20 20 20 20 20-53 59 53 07 00 00 00 00   IO       SYS.....
10   00 00 00 00 00 00 00 00 66-EA 0C 02 00 3C 1F 00 00   .......f.....<...
20   4D 53 44 4F 53 20 20 20-53 59 53 07 00 00 00 00   MSDOS    SYS.....
30   00 00 00 00 00 00 00 75 6B-06 0B 0A 00 E0 6C 00 00   ......uk.....1..
40   43 4F 4D 4D 41 4E 44 20-43 4F 4D 00 00 00 00 00   COMMAND COM ....
50   00 00 00 00 00 00 00 1A 00-AF 0A 26 00 95 58 00 00   ..........&..X..
60   53 52 43 20 20 20 20 20-20 20 20 10 00 00 00 00   SRC        .....
70   00 00 00 00 00 00 00 80 01-9B 10 3D 00 00 00 00 00   ..........=.....
80   44 45 4D 4F 43 4D 20 20-41 53 4D 20 00 00 00 00   DEMOCM ASM ....
90   00 00 00 00 00 00 00 D7 83-4F 0F 44 00 79 04 00 00   ........O.D.y...
A0   44 45 4D 4F 43 4D 20 20-4F 42 4A 20 00 00 00 00   DEMOCM OBJ ....
B0   00 00 00 00 00 00 00 7B BD-9B 10 46 00 6C 00 00 00   ......{...F.1...
C0   44 45 4D 4F 43 4D 20 20-45 58 45 20 00 00 00 00   DEMOCM EXE ....
D0   00 00 00 00 00 00 00 81 BD-9B 10 47 00 2B 03 00 00   ..........G.+...
E0   44 45 4D 4F 43 4D 20 20-43 4F 4D 20 00 00 00 00   DEMOCM COM ....
F0   00 00 00 00 00 00 00 84 BD-9B 10 48 00 2B 00 00 00   ..........H.+...
```

Figure 9.1   A root-directory dump.

The root directory must start at a clearly defined point so it can be found by programs that know nothing about the file system. The kernel and BIOS files must be the very first ones stored on disk so that they can be located without having to provide a search routine during the process of booting the disk. The bootstrap loader program assumes that these files are the first ones in the root directory and that at least the BIOS file (both files in V1) is stored contiguously on the disk.

Directory Entries

An understanding of the structure of directory entries is imperative if you are to understand how DOS keeps track of files and directories. After you learn the structure of directory entries, interpreting them is easy.

Each directory entry (32 bytes of data) contains identifying information about the file: the file's name, extension, attribute, size, and starting location on the disk, in addition to the date and time of the directory entry's most recent update. Table 9.1 shows the basic structure of a 32-byte directory entry.

Table 9.1 Structure of the Directory Entry

Offset	Size	Meaning
00h	8 bytes	File name
08h	3 bytes	File extension
0Bh	Byte	File attribute
0Ch	10 bytes	Reserved (not used)
16h	Word	Time of last update
18h	Word	Date of last update
1Ah	Word	Beginning disk cluster
1Ch	Double word	File size

Every directory entry is formatted in this way; each piece of information about the file is stored at a fixed offset within the 32-byte entry. Each field in the directory entry tells you something unique about the file. With the exception of the 10 bytes reserved by DOS (offset 0Ch), this chapter takes a relatively detailed look at each field in the directory entry.

File Name (Offset 00h)

The first eight bytes of the entry are the file's root name (stored as ASCII text). Now you can see why file names in DOS are limited to eight characters—only that amount of space is available in the directory entry.

In many DOS programs, you can use file names longer than eight characters, but DOS will truncate them to fit in its 8-character limit. If the root file name is less than eight characters long, it is left-justified in the field and padded with spaces. DOS stores all file names as uppercase ASCII characters.

The first byte of the file-name field has several special meanings (see Table 9.2).

Table 9.2   Special Meanings of a File Name's First Byte

Value of First Byte	Meaning
00h	Entry has never been used; no further entries follow this one.
05h	First character of the file name is actually E5h.
2Eh	Entry is an alias for the current subdirectory. If the next byte is 2Eh, the directory entry's beginning disk cluster field contains the cluster number of the parent of the current directory.
E5h	File erased.

The 00h code saves DOS from fruitless searches of unused directory entries. When this code is encountered during a search for a file name, it is interpreted as "end of directory" and the search ends instantly.

The E5h character (displayed on an IBM as the Greek *sigma* character) can be used as the first character of a file name but is stored in the directory entry as 05h. (Why anyone would want to use it in a file name is left as a question for the reader; the automatic translation, however, makes it possible.)

An E5h as the first character marks files that have been erased; DOS ignores such entries when searching or reuses them when a new file is created. Only the first byte changes to mark an entry as deleted; the rest of the directory entry remains unaltered. Theoretically, you can resurrect an erased file by changing the first character to a valid ASCII character. If another file has already overwritten the disk space previously occupied by the erased file, however, you cannot unerase the file.

The 2Eh entry is a period. Found only in subdirectories, it marks a directory entry for the current directory. If the next byte is also a period, the entry points to the parent of the current directory. You see these dot (.) and dot-dot (..) entries at the beginning of every subdirectory whenever you use the DOS DIR command; they are created automatically when the subdirectory is brought into existence and cannot be removed.

Any attempt to ERASE . is interpreted as ERASE *.* for the subdirectory, and ERASE .. becomes ERASE *.* for the parent! The standard DOS query Are you sure (Y/N)? offers little protection because it does not indicate that mass file destruction will result. In V4, the message was expanded to tell you explicitly that the entire directory will be erased.

File Extension (Offset 08h)

The three characters that begin at offset 08h are the file type or extension (also stored as ASCII characters). If the file has no extension, or if the extension is shorter than three characters, the extension is left-justified in the field and the name is padded with spaces. Notice that the period, which generally is used as a delimiter between the root file name and the extension, is not stored with the file name in the directory entry. DOS assumes the presence of a period between the eighth and ninth bytes of the directory entry.

File Attribute (Offset 0Bh)

The file's attribute (the byte at offset 0Bh) indicates both the type of file represented by the directory entry and its accessibility. Each bit of the attribute marks one of the file's characteristics or features (see Table 9.3).

Table 9.3   An Attribute Byte

Bit 76543210	Meaning
.......x	Read only
......x.	Hidden
.....x..	System
....x...	Volume label
...x....	Subdirectory
..x.....	Archive
xx......	Reserved (unused)

The read-only characteristic means exactly what it says—the file can only be read, not written to. If this bit is set, the file cannot be deleted. Although this precaution provides some security to the file, the file can be renamed and then modified.

What about the other attributes? Hidden files are not available to DIR, COPY, or many other DOS commands. Although DOS does not provide the tools to do so, many third-party utilities permit you to set the hidden bit on a directory entry, which makes the directory entry invisible to DIR. You can use the CD command to enter it, however, and the files inside will be visible.

The term *system* refers specifically to the DOS kernel and BIOS files but can be used also for other files. (For example, you could flag COMMAND.COM and the other system utilities as both system and hidden files on systems that are used primarily by nontechnical personnel; this process saves having to restore files deleted by users during attempts to "clean house" on the disks.)

The *volume label* identifies a directory entry that contains the label (or name) for a given disk. Although each disk should have a label, until Version 4 DOS did not check for a label during most disk functions. Volume labels are discussed more fully later in this chapter.

The subdirectory bit marks the file as a special file containing other directory entries. A subdirectory is another directory subordinate to the current one. (Directories and subdirectories are discussed in more detail later in this chapter.)

The archive bit (a status bit for the file) is set whenever the file is updated. Typically, hard-disk backup programs use the archive bit to indicate which files need to be backed up.

Time of Last Update (Offset 16h)

The word (two bytes) beginning at offset 16h is the time of the file's last update. Sometimes called the file's *time stamp*, it is stored least-significant byte first.

The file's time field is set when you create the file and is updated thereafter whenever you close the file, but *only* if information has been written to the file. This field is not updated if the file is merely read, copied (with the DOS COPY command), or renamed (with the DOS REN command). When the time field is updated, the new time is retrieved from the system clock.

Table 9.4 shows the meaning of each bit in the time field. The hour is contained in five bits (24-hour clock) and the minutes in six. Because this leaves only five bits in which to store the seconds, they are divided by 2.

Table 9.4 Encoding of the Time Field

Bits		Meaning
FEDCBA98	76543210	
xxxxx...	....	Hours
.....xxx	xxx.....	Minutes
....	...xxxxx	Two-second increments

Note that, because the seconds are divided by 2, the time stamp is accurate only to an even number of seconds. (This limitation is not significant in most applications.)

A little-known fact about the file time field is that, if *all* bits in both bytes are 0, the DIR command does not show any time. If the seconds field contains a 1 and all other bits are 0, however, the file time displays as 12:00a (midnight). Some software publishers use this quirk to help identify revision levels for their distribution disks.

Date of Last Update (Offset 18h)

The word (two bytes) beginning at offset 18h is the date of the file's last update, sometimes referred to as a file's *date stamp*. It is stored least-significant byte first.

The date field is similar to the time field—it is set when you create the file and is updated whenever you close the file, but *only* if information has been written to the file. The date field is not updated if the file is read, copied (with the DOS COPY command), or renamed (with the DOS REN command). When the date field is updated, it encodes (from the system clock) the date of the file's most recent modification.

Table 9.5 shows the layout of the date field. The year is stored in seven bits, the month in four, and the day in five.

Table 9.5   Encoding of the Date Field

Bits	Meaning	
FEDCBA98	76543210	
xxxxxxx.	....	Year count (relative to 1980)
.......x	xxx.....	Month
....	...xxxxx	Day

Notice that the year entry is relative to 1980. In other words, it is an offset from 1980, not an absolute value (such as 1988). The year 1988, for example, is stored as 8. To identify the absolute year, you simply add the offset to 1980. Seven bits are allocated for the year; because 127 is the largest value that can be represented in 7 bits, the year can range from 1980 (offset 0) to 2107 (offset 127).

Beginning Disk Cluster (Offset 1Ah)

The word (two bytes) beginning at offset 1Ah is the file's beginning disk cluster. This word is stored with its least significant byte first.

This word gives only the starting point of the file. To locate the second cluster and succeeding clusters, the value of this field is also used to calculate the offset to the file allocation table (FAT). From the FAT, any additional clusters used by the file can be located. (See Chapter 8 for a detailed discussion of the FAT.)

File Size (Offset 1Ch)

The 4-byte file size field contains the exact length of the file, in bytes. The largest size DOS can handle, therefore, is 4,294,967,295 bytes. Because this number is 13 times larger than today's largest MS-DOS hard disk, we have a few years to go before reaching this limit.

Some high-level languages (early versions of BASIC, in particular) were notorious for setting this value equal to the total number of bytes in the sectors occupied by the file. If the file contained 520 bytes and occupied two 512-byte sectors, the file size would be set to a clearly misleading 1,024. Normally, however, this entry accurately reflects the file's size in bytes.

Subdirectories

It has already been mentioned that each directory entry contains an attribute byte for the file. Bit 4 of this attribute byte marks a directory entry as a pointer to a subdirectory.

A subdirectory is a file, like all the others on the system. The subdirectory entry points to the number of the directory file's beginning cluster, which can contain 16 entries; you "step through" subsequent file clusters to find subsequent entries. Figure 9.2 shows a dump of a typical subdirectory.

```
00   2E 20 20 20 20 20 20 20-20 20 20 10 00 00 00 00   .          .....
10   00 00 00 00 00 00 6E 00-9B 10 02 00 00 00 00 00   ......n.........
20   2E 2E 20 20 20 20 20 20-20 20 20 10 00 00 00 00   ..         .....
30   00 00 00 00 00 00 6E 00-9B 10 00 00 00 00 00 00   ......n.........
40   44 45 4D 4F 45 58 20 20-41 53 4D 20 00 00 00 00   DEMOEX  ASM ....
50   00 00 00 00 00 00 DC 8B-4F 0F 03 00 0D 05 00 00   ........O.......
60   44 45 4D 4F 45 58 20 20-4F 42 4A 20 00 00 00 00   DEMOEX  OBJ ....
70   00 00 00 00 00 00 91 BD-9B 10 05 00 B7 00 00 00   ...............
80   44 45 4D 4F 45 58 20 20-45 58 45 20 00 00 00 00   DEMOEX  EXE ....
90   00 00 00 00 00 00 94 BD-9B 10 06 00 E0 02 00 00   ...............
A0   44 45 4D 4F 45 58 20 20-44 4D 50 20 00 00 00 00   DEMOEX  DMP ....
B0   00 00 00 00 00 00 5A BE-9B 10 07 00 2A 05 00 00   ......Z.....*...
C0   00 00 00 00 00 00 00 00-00 00 00 00 00 00 00 00   ...............
D0   00 00 00 00 00 00 00 00-00 00 00 00 00 00 00 00   ...............
E0   00 00 00 00 00 00 00 00-00 00 00 00 00 00 00 00   ...............
F0   00 00 00 00 00 00 00 00-00 00 00 00 00 00 00 00   ...............
```

Figure 9.2   A subdirectory dump.

The structure of a subdirectory is exactly like that of the root directory, with one exception: At the beginning of each subdirectory are two special entries bearing the . and .. file names.

The first of these entries (.) points to the current directory; the beginning cluster field in this directory entry points to the first cluster of the current subdirectory. The second entry (..) does the same for the parent directory; the beginning cluster field in this file entry points to the parent directory's first cluster. If this cluster number is 0, the parent directory is the root directory. Neither of these two special directory entries can be deleted. Instead, any attempt to do so deletes *all* files in the corresponding directory!

You cannot handle subdirectories as you would handle normal files. DOS Function 43h cannot set a subdirectory's attribute bit. The subdirectory's system and hidden bits can be set to exclude the directory from normal directory listings, but its accessibility cannot be changed. CHDIR can still reach it.

Volume Labels

A volume label is a directory entry in which bit 3 of the file attribute byte is set. To interpret the entry, all you need to do is locate it—the file name is the volume label.

Although generally not used by most software before V4, volume labels can be extremely useful if software is written to take advantage of them. A program can use unique volume labels as disk identifiers. By remembering which disks are in use, a program can prompt for a specific disk by name rather than by a general title. The Macintosh, for example, does this when you use more than one disk on a single drive system. On the Macintosh desktop, the names of disks that have been identified to the system are shown and, if one of these disks is needed, it is requested by name. The system, which can tell whether you have inserted the wrong disk, continues to ask for the proper disk by name.

Although most PC programs do not handle disks in this way, they could—thanks to the volume label. The only way to create a disk label is through the extended FCB functions, described in the section "Extended File Control Blocks," later in this chapter. (For a list of DOS functions for all FCB operations, see the "DOS Reference" section at the end of this book.)

With the introduction of DOS Version 4, the volume label moved up in the world. It is now copied into the boot sector, in addition to being in the root directory, and DOS makes some use of it to determine quickly whether a disk has been changed (if the label has not changed, more detailed checks are still made).

Because there is no way to guarantee that two different disks do not bear the same label, though, something new was added to increase the likelihood that identities would be unique: the *volume serial number*. This number is created when a disk is formatted, based on the time and date stamps derived from the system clock at that time, and is stored in the boot sector with the label. The volume label and serial number together provide a highly reliable indicator of disk changes because the serial number generated changes every two seconds.

What Is a File?

We use files for all sorts of things. Simply speaking, a file is an organized place in which to store information. The term *files* is used also to refer to devices. Following the lead of UNIX, DOS V2 introduced the concept of the *file handle*. The file system can assign unique numbers, called *handles*, to devices such as the printer, the RS-232 port, the keyboard, and the video screen. Many of us were accustomed to treating these devices as special objects, but file handles have changed that.

The concept of using file handles is more powerful than many people realize. With a file handle, you can use the same techniques to access both files and devices. In a program written to deal with the keyboard and the video screen (using STDIN and STDOUT), for example, you can redirect not only the input so that it comes from a file but also the output to a file. The *same program* works in each case—you change only the handle used for input or output.

How Files Are Handled Through DOS

DOS provides two basic ways to deal with files: the FCB method or the handle-function method.

Before DOS V2 was introduced, the file control block (FCB) method (an outgrowth of the old CP/M system) was the only way to access files. FCB functions are built around the presence of a file control block the programmer controls directly.

You do not need to have all the details of the file at your fingertips for most operations, such as opening, closing, reading, writing, or maintaining a file (renaming or deleting it). For these types of file operations, you use the other method—the handle functions.

Handle functions give programmers only limited access to file information; DOS controls the files internally. Programmers request file operations either by a specific file name (to open or create files) or by using a file handle (to read, write, or close files). DOS uses the handle to look up information about the file.

Handle functions have several advantages over FCB functions:

- Because handle functions are simpler to use, it is easier to prevent or correct mistakes.

- Handle functions are likely to remain compatible with changes in DOS and, later, in OS/2.

- Handle functions can take advantage of DOS's hierarchical directory structure.

- Handle functions relieve programmers of a great deal of bookkeeping. (The bookkeeping—file location and everything stored in an FCB—is done inside the DOS kernel.)

We recommend that, whenever you can, you use the handle functions for accessing files. You have to use FCB functions to create disk volume labels but, for any other file operation, handles are a better way to work with files.

Regardless of whether you use FCB or handle functions, DOS is adept at informing you of any errors it may detect. For a comprehensive list of DOS error codes, see the "DOS Reference" section at the end of this book (see particularly Int 21h, Function 59).

Standard File Control Blocks

The standard FCB used by all FCB functions comes almost directly from the original CP/M environment. Its 36 bytes make up 11 fields, as you can see from the layout of the standard FCB shown in Table 9.6.

Table 9.6 The Standard File Control Block

Offset	Length	Meaning	Notes
00h	1	Drive specification	0=default, 1=A, 2=B, and so on
01h	8	File name	Left-justified ASCII; padded with blanks
09h	3	Extension	Left-justified ASCII; padded with blanks
0Ch	2	Current block number	
0Eh	2	Record size	Default of 80h bytes with DOS OPEN or CREATE functions
10h	4	File size	
14h	2	Date created or updated	Same format as directory entry
16h	2	Time created or updated	Same format as directory entry
18h	8	Reserved	
20h	1	Current record number	
21h	4	Random record number	Only 3 bytes used if record size is less than 64 bytes

The file control block is made up of information supplied by DOS, some of which comes directly from the values in a file's directory entry. Notice that no allowance is made for using path names with FCBs. All FCB functions operate in the confines of the current directory.

The file name, extension, file size, and date and time of last update are all reflections of the file's directory entry. The other fields are either initialized by the individual FCB functions or modified by the programmer to indicate to DOS what he or she wants.

Extended File Control Blocks

Extended FCBs allow additional file information to be included in the FCB. The extended portion of the FCB is composed of seven bytes (three fields) added to the beginning of the traditional FCB.

By examining the FCB's first byte, DOS can tell which type of FCB you are using. If the first byte is FFh, DOS assumes that you are using an extended FCB. (The first byte in a standard FCB represents the disk drive designator. FFh is an illegal value as a disk drive number.)

All DOS FCB functions can use extended FCBs. If you decide to use FCB functions, use extended FCBs so that you have to keep track of only one structured FCB area.

Most of the information in an extended FCB is identical to that in a standard FCB. If you compare Table 9.6 with Table 9.7, which details the layout of an extended FCB, you can see that (beginning with byte offset 07h) the two layouts are identical.

Table 9.7 An Extended File Control Block

Offset	Length	Meaning	Notes
00h	1	FFh	Signals DOS that this is an extended FCB
01h	5	Reserved	Used by DOS; normally 0s
06h	1	Attribute byte	Same meaning as directory entry
07h	1	Drive specification	0=default, 1=A, 2=B, and so on
08h	8	File name	Left-justified ASCII; padded with blanks
10h	3	Extension	Left-justified ASCII; padded with blanks
13h	2	Current block number	
15h	2	Record size	Default of 80h bytes with DOS OPEN or CREATE functions
17h	4	File size	
1Bh	2	Date created or updated	Same format as directory entry
1Dh	2	Time created or updated	Same format as directory entry
1Fh	8	Reserved	
27h	1	Current record number	
28h	4	Random record number	Only 3 bytes used if record size is less than 64 bytes

Basic FCB File Handling

To work successfully with FCBs, follow these basic steps:

1. Set all the bytes of the FCB to 0.

2. Get the file name information. To do so, you may need to use the DOS parse function (29h).

3. OPEN (Function 0Fh) or CREATE (Function 16h) the file.

DOS
PROGRAMMING

4. If the record-size field should not be 80h, change it.

5. Set the record-number field if you are doing random-access operations.

6. Set the DTA address (if it has not been set).

7. Execute the appropriate function.

8. After you have finished, close the file.

When to Use FCB Functions

Even in DOS V4, the use of FCB functions is justified for the following reasons:

- When you use FCBs, you can have an unlimited number of open files.

- FCBs provide the only way to create a volume label for a disk.

- FCBs ensure that methods of accessing files are compatible with DOS V1.

The first point is true because you have total control of the "housekeeping" associated with file I/O. (In the most recent versions of DOS, users can specify in the CONFIG.SYS file how many files can be open simultaneously.)

The second point is important, no matter which version of the operating system you use. If your program creates a volume label for a disk, you *must* use FCBs.

The third reason may be the most important: FCBs are the only way to verify compatibility with systems that use DOS V1. If you are sure that the software will be used on a system with DOS V2 or later, or if you can sacrifice the compatibility of earlier systems, you always should choose handle functions.

Handle Functions

As mentioned earlier in this chapter, the handle functions are an advance in programming technique. Their introduction to DOS provides file control similar to that found in UNIX. In fact, you can port UNIX applications (written in C) to DOS. These applications run just like their UNIX counterparts.

You should recognize the following two basic features of handle functions:

- Under the handle functions, no distinction is made between sequential and random-access files. All files are seen as a string of bytes, much like an array. This view of a file is standard for UNIX files.

- Handles are kept internally by DOS. The only information a program needs is the file name and handle number.

258

Not all programmers agree that these features are advantages. Some programmers object to having to give up the control provided by FCBs; others insist that, by not providing random-access record structures, the system becomes less powerful.

Which group is correct? Neither. For simple programming, nothing beats the handle functions for ease of use. Despite the objections of some programmers, programs seldom need to do their own file bookkeeping. Random file access still is available, but you must approach it differently.

A handle is simply a pointer into an internal DOS table that maintains all relevant information about an open file. Programmers do not have to maintain a detailed accounting of information, as they do when they use the FCB functions; rather, the handle functions relinquish all bookkeeping functions to DOS. For most programming applications, this feature significantly eases the programmer's burden. Because you do not have to manipulate or worry about special file control blocks, your programs, conceptually, are simpler, easier to debug, and easier to keep compatible with future DOS releases.

Basic Handle File Handling

The basic technique for using handles is much simpler than that for using the corresponding FCB functions. Because the system handles the basic details, you simply identify the file you want and let DOS do the rest. In the handle file-handling method, you follow these steps:

1. Create an ASCIIZ file name string.

2. OPEN (Int 21h, Function 3Dh) or CREATE (Int 21h, Function 3Ch) the file. (V3 and V4 provide additional OPEN/CREATE functions; see the reference section.)

3. Set the file pointer into the file (Int 21h, Function 42h).

4. Complete the required operations.

5. Close the file.

An ASCIIZ string is simply an ASCII text string that ends in a NUL character (ASCII 0). In high-level languages, such as C, strings generally are stored as ASCIIZ strings.

To set a file's size, set the file pointer where the end is to be, and then do a write of 0 bytes. Space is added or removed as required to make the file exactly that size.

When to Use Handle Functions

In certain instances, which arise because of advanced functions provided by DOS V2 and later versions, you *must* use file handles rather than FCBs. For example, use file handles in the following situations:

- Whenever you use path names

- Whenever I/O redirection and piping are important

- To support file sharing and locking

- To support networked environments

- To use enhanced error reporting

- For easy access to arbitrary locations in the file

- To set file size under program control

It is recommended that you use file handle functions whenever and wherever you can. (Be sure to use FCBs to create volume labels.) By using file handles for all your programs, you instantly gain portability for future environments in which FCBs will not exist. More important, you simplify your programming task.

Ordinarily, when you work with a high-level language such as C or BASIC, you do not want to come down to the level of detail covered in this chapter. High-level languages, after all, offer significant file-manipulation operations. But you will want to use compatible functions— handles. The latest C, BASIC, and Pascal releases all use handle functions for their file-access routines.

Directory Searching: A Practical Example

To illustrate the use of the DOS directory functions, let's develop a simple application that will tell you where a file resides in the hierarchical directory system. All you have to know is the file's name. The program described in the remainder of this chapter was developed to find a file (given its name) anywhere in the file system.

The program, called `find.c`, searches through the file structure. (C's recursive nature allows descent through the file system without making the program overly complicated.) This program illustrates how file handle functions can be used to access information quickly and naturally.

The basic technique for this simple program is

> For each argument on the command line,
> search the file system for all files that have that name.

The program is implemented as shown in Listing 9.1.

Listing 9.1

```
/* Find.c
   Listing 9.1 of DOS Programmer's Reference */

#include <stdio.h>

/* Prototypes */
void depth_search(char *dir, char *name);

void main(argc,argv)

/*   find.c
     This search program locates file names in the directory
     structure of a hard disk. It illustrates the use of the DOS
     directory functions from a high-level language.
*/

int  argc;
char *argv[];

{
    int  i;
    for(i=1; i<argc; i++)
        depth_search("", argv[i]);
}
```

Using file-search procedures that match the requirements of the file name, the search routine (depth_search) checks for files in each directory in the file system.

The basic algorithm follows:

Check the current directory for any files that match the desired file name.

Locate every subdirectory in the current directory and search all of them.

Whenever you enter this recursive routine, a new disk transfer area (DTA) is created. Whenever the function returns, the previous DTA is again made current. You do not have to work with only one DTA: you can have as many as you want, depending on what you need to solve your problem. In this case, the problem was best solved by the program in Listing 9.2.

Listing 9.2

```
/* depsrch.c
   Listing 9.2 of DOS Programmer's Reference */

#include <stdio.h>
#include <dos.h>
#include <string.h>

/* FIRST or NEXT search flags */
#define  FIRST    0
```

continues

Listing 9.2 Continued

```
#define   NEXT      1

/* File attribute for search */
#define   FILE      0
#define   DIR       16

/* Prototypes */
void depth_search(char *dir, char *name);
int search(char *fname, int flag, int type);
void set_dta(char *ptr);
int streql(char *str1, char *str2);

void depth_search(dir, name)

char *dir, *name;

{
     char filename[256];   /* File name to search for  */
     char dirname[256];    /* Directory name to search */
     char dta[43];         /* Disk transfer area       */
     int  flag;            /* Search type flag         */

     sprintf(filename,"%s\\%s",dir,name);
     /* Set the DTA to the local DTA buffer */
     set_dta(dta);

     flag = FIRST;
     while(search(filename,flag,FILE)){
          printf("DEPTH:FOUND: %s\\%s\n",dir,dta+30);
          flag = NEXT;
     }

     sprintf(filename,"%s\\*.",dir);
     flag = FIRST;
     while(search(filename,flag,DIR)){
          flag = NEXT;

          /* Specifically exclude "." and ".." from searching */
          if(!streql(".",dta+30) && !streql("..",dta+30)){
               sprintf(dirname,"%s\\%s",dir,dta+30);
               depth_search(dirname,name);
          }

          /* Return to local DTA buffer for next directory */
          set_dta(dta);
     }
}

void set_dta(ptr)
char *ptr;
{
     union REGS regs;
     regs.h.ah = 26;
     regs.x.dx = (int)ptr;
     intdos(&regs, &regs);
}
```

```
int streql(str1, str2)
char *str1, *str2;
{
    return(strcmp(str1, str2)==0);
}
```

This routine controls the search through the directory structure but uses the DOS *find first file* function (4Eh) to locate files according to the specified search criteria. Whenever a file is found, DOS updates the DTA with information about that file. This information, derived from the file's directory entry, is used in `depth_search()` to print the file name (or to access the directory).

`Search()`, the routine that interfaces with the DOS functions, is shown in Listing 9.3.

Listing 9.3

```
/* search.c
   Listing 9.3 of DOS Programmer's Reference */

#include <stdio.h>
#include <dos.h>

#define   FALSE     0
#define   TRUE ! FALSE

int search(fname,flag,type)

char *fname;
int  flag;
int  type;

{
    union REGS regs;

    regs.h.ah = 0x4e + flag;
    regs.x.cx = type;

    regs.x.dx = (int)fname;
    intdos(&regs,&regs);
    if(regs.x.cflag==1)
        return(FALSE);
    return(TRUE);
}
```

Notice in the `search()` routine that the same registers are set for each function call, whether you are looking for the first occurrence of the file or for any successive occurrences. The only difference is the setting in AH (4Eh for find first, 4Fh for find next). Although all the set information is required only for the Find First File function (4Eh), it does not deter the operation of the Find Next File function (4Fh). For more detailed information about these functions, refer to the "DOS Reference" section at the end of this book.

When a search goes to another level in the hierarchical system, you must retain the DTA from the previous level or levels to continue searching. The following routine, `set_dta()`, lets you designate a buffer area as the current DTA (this routine is included in Listing 9.2):

```
void set_dta(ptr)

char *ptr;

{
      union REGS regs;

      regs.h.ah = 26;
      regs.x.dx = (int)ptr;
      intdos(&regs,&regs);
}
```

The remaining routine, `streql()`, illustrates the convenience of programming with C functions. In this routine, `strcmp()` (the standard C library function used for comparing two strings) returns 0 if the strings are the same. Sometimes, however, especially in the early development stages of building a program, it is convenient to create functions that serve as mnemonic reminders of what you *really* want them to do. `streql()` returns either TRUE or FALSE, for example, depending on whether the two strings are equal. By using the `streql()` function, you clarify the logic a little and can concentrate more on the problems that need to be solved. You can squeeze a little speed from the routine by defining a `streql()` macro such as the following:

```
#define streql(x,y)      (strcmp(x,y)==0)
```

By using the macro, you eliminate the overhead of a function call. Why not do it then? You can—depending on your intentions. By defining `streql()` as a function, you can include it in a library and the linker will make sure it is there when you need it. If you define it as a macro, you must define the macro in the program or in an include file to make it available. One way is simpler for development; one eliminates some overhead.

For most programs, the choice of which form to use depends on the programmer. Some programmers favor functions; others favor macros. The only critical factor during program development is clarity. You want to make everything as clear as possible to minimize development problems.

The code listing for the `streql()` routine follows (this routine is included in Listing 9.2):

```
int streql(str1,str2)

char *str1,
     *str2;

{
      return(strcmp(str1,str2)==0);
}
```

Now that all the pieces of find.c have been described in detail, let's take the program for a test drive. The following test run searches for all occurrences of the autoexec.* file:

```
C>find autoexec.*
DEPTH:FOUND:  \AUTOEXEC.BAT
DEPTH:FOUND:  \AUTOEXEC.DV
DEPTH:FOUND:  \AUTOEXEC.BAK
DEPTH:FOUND:  \AUTOEXEC.WIN
DEPTH:FOUND:  \BIN\LOTUS\INSTALL\AUTOEXEC.BAT
DEPTH:FOUND:  \SYS\AUTOEXEC.DV
DEPTH:FOUND:  \SYS\AUTOEXEC.OLD
DEPTH:FOUND:  \SYS\AUTOEXEC.BAT
```

Summary

In this chapter, you learned that file access is handled through one of two methods: file control blocks (FCBs) or file handles. FCBs are the older form of file access, compatible all the way back to DOS V1. Disk volume labels can be written only with FCBs, but every other kind of file access can be done with handle functions.

Handle functions can work in and with the hierarchical directory structure introduced in DOS V2. They also make programming much simpler because they let the operating system do the bookkeeping for a file.

Building, as always, on what you have learned, you are ready to move on to the next chapter, "Program and Memory Management," which deals with program execution.

Part IV
Memory Management and Miscellaneous Topics

10

Program and Memory Management

To "get the job done," programmers have developed several dodges and devices for getting more into a program than can be contained in memory. Program chaining, overlays, and other techniques have long been staples of the programmer's art. The first system we worked on, for example, was an IBM 7040 with only 32K of memory; some programs simply could not be done without overlays (see the brief explanation of overlays at the end of this section).

Specialized techniques can turn into debugging nightmares that make programs highly nonportable. Because of the increased memory and processor speed of large systems, computer programmers have developed techniques for handling programs from within other programs. Command shells, such as COMMAND.COM, use these techniques to execute programs on demand.

On a DOS system, you can control the execution of a program from within another program by using the same functions used by COMMAND.COM. (This capability is similar to facilities provided on UNIX systems.) This method of handling program functions is relatively clean. Major modules of the system can exist as stand-alone programs. Each such program can be thoroughly tested and debugged as an independent entity. UNIX programmers have found this technique to be extremely effective for program development.

This chapter begins by describing how memory works, how you can get more memory when you need it, and how to let DOS keep the memory you do not need. When you work in a high-level language, the compiler manages this process. In assembly language, however, you should be explicit about what you want to do with memory. This chapter also looks closely at extended memory and expanded memory and examines what can be done with them.

The discussion then moves to program execution—how one process, the *parent*, executes another process, the *child*, and then regains control. A simple example is presented to show how this process works.

Finally, this chapter makes a preliminary examination of a special kind of program, the TSR (terminate and stay resident). TSRs are different in many ways from "normal" programs (applications such as word processors and spreadsheets). The most obvious difference is that, after TSRs stop, they stay in memory and are not overwritten. A TSR can get control from another program in several ways, the most important of which involves connecting to an interrupt (see Chapter 11, "Interrupt Handlers"). This chapter lays the groundwork for procedures to follow after you understand interrupts.

Let's go on, then, to memory management.

Program Overlays

A program overlay is a section of code or data that is not kept permanently in memory. The program may exist as several binary images, each of which handles some specific functions. The master segment handles overall coordination and usually has functions that are needed by all overlays.

In a typical program with overlays, the main menu and common functions are in the primary overlay, which is kept in memory at all times. Whenever the program needs a submenu, its overlay is loaded into an area in memory that holds the overlay code. The main module then transfers control to the overlay, and the submenu and its functions are operable.

When the user is finished with the submenu and returns to the program's main menu, control is transferred back to the primary overlay. Because the submenu's overlay in memory is no longer necessary, the memory space can be used by another overlay (the submenu's program code is "overlaid" by the new code).

How Memory Works

The basic PC or compatible has an address space that holds as much as 1M of memory. (Remember that a megabyte is 1,024K.) As Chapter 3, "The Dynamics of DOS," pointed out, only 640K of this memory is available for program use. The remaining 384K is assigned to the ROM BIOS, display adapters, and cartridges.

The lower 640K of memory is not for user programs only, however. In this space, 1,024 bytes of interrupt vectors are reserved by the processor. Only interrupt vectors go in these locations, which, as hardware engineers like to say, are *hard-wired* into the processor (see Chapter 11). Next come BIOS and DOS tables, the DOS kernel, system drivers, and finally the resident portion of the command processor. All this memory comes from the user area of memory.

Calculating how much memory you lose is difficult because it depends on which system you use and which drivers you have loaded. The first user programs generally loaded (in the memory map) are TSRs such as Borland's SideKick. (Figure 10.1 is a graphic representation of memory use with TSRs loaded.) You must subtract their memory use from the available space. If you add a window package similar to DESQview, only about 350K of memory may remain from a starting point of 640K—and all without really starting a program to *do* something!

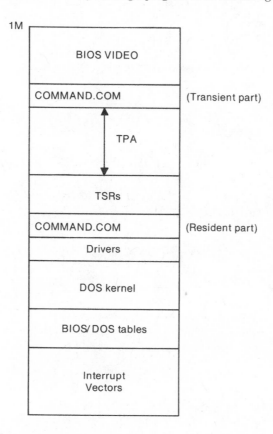

Figure 10.1 Memory use with TSRs loaded.

The space that remains after start-up (usually about 500K to 550K with SideKick loaded) is free and available for use. This space is called the transient program area (TPA), a name used also for the equivalent area on CP/M systems. The name is appropriate because user programs are transient in this area—they come and go as users working on the system need them.

The machine's 640K limit on memory for a working area seemed virtually infinite when PCs were introduced. At that time, a PC with 64K of memory was considered standard; people who had 128K and the rich few who had machines with 256K were envied, although not much software was capable of using the extra memory. As needs grew, the 640K limit became more than an interesting sidelight—it became a major system limitation. Applied to computer memory, a variation of Murphy's law, "No matter how much you have, you will need more," became more than a joke.

After the introduction of the 80286 chip, as much as 16M of memory became possible with the PC system. ("Hallelujah," some said. "Now we have a serious system," said others.) But DOS cannot utilize that memory in regular operation. The memory over the 1M limit, known as *extended memory*, is available on the 80286 processor and later models. DOS cannot use it, however; to access such memory, the 80286 chip must operate in protected mode, which DOS cannot do. Under DOS, only specially written programs capable of switching the CPU mode can use extended memory.

Protected Mode

The protected-mode feature on the 80286 and 80386 processors gives access to special processor functions that control multitasking operations. *Real mode* provides essentially the same environment as that of the 8088/8086 processors with access to only 1M of memory. When the processor is shifted to *protected mode* (generally done inside an operating system), the system can control the operation of multiple programs in memory and shift from one task to another.

This chapter does not describe the features of protected mode in great detail because DOS does not use that mode. To learn more about protected mode, consult any of the many books about 80286/80386 assembly language programming.

DOS runs everything in the processor's real mode; memory above 1M, therefore, is not accessible to programs that work through the normal DOS functions. Even when a system has the extra memory, you cannot use it effectively.

Although programs such as DESQview can tuck some of their operating code into RAM-disk drivers that use 80286 extended memory like a disk, the memory is not accessible to most programs. (Programs must shift the processor to protected mode before they access the memory and back to real mode on completion.) Even RAM disks are not necessarily fast when they operate in extended memory because the processor shifts from real mode to protected mode and back again to get to the data—a process that can be relatively slow. On an 80286 processor, going to the hard disk may be faster.

Since the introduction of the Personal Computer AT, BIOS provides two functions to help programs determine how much memory is available (Int 15h, Function 88h) and move data blocks to and from extended memory above the 1M mark (Int 15h, Function 87h). The use of these routines causes a serious problem, however, because there is no management for this extended memory space. One program can easily write over data that another program (or a RAM-disk driver) is keeping in the extended memory space; nothing senses the problem or reports the error.

Expanded memory, first introduced as a joint effort by Lotus and Intel at the 1985 spring COMDEX show (version 3.0), provides a way to allow access to as much as 8M of memory without requiring a special shift in processor mode. Expanded memory gives the processor access to extra memory through 16K *pages*, which can be mapped into an unused area in the memory space between 640K and 1M. Four 16K pages are mapped into a 64K *page frame* at a location determined by users of the system when the board is installed. (See Chapter 3, "The Dynamics of DOS," for a more extensive discussion of expanded memory.)

The expanded memory manager (EMM) causes expanded memory to act like a file with a handle. When your program asks for space in expanded memory, the EMM sets aside the space and returns a unique "handle" that can be used to get access to the space.

When you want to get to any 16K page from expanded memory, you use Int 67h to call the EMM and tell it to bring the page into the page frame. Then you can address the memory directly from your program. Figure 10.2 shows what happens.

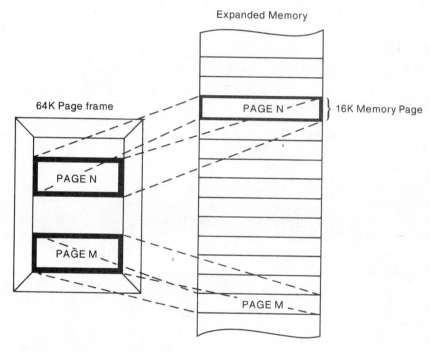

Figure 10.2 Expanded memory access.

You install EMM.SYS (the expanded memory manager driver) by adding either of the following lines to your CONFIG.SYS file:

```
DRIVER=EMM.SYS
DRIVER=EMM386.SYS
```

These expanded memory manager drivers work only partially like a true driver. (*True* drivers are described in Chapter 12, "Device Drivers"; for now, accept that the expanded memory manager drivers do not work normally.) Rather than access EMM.SYS or EMM386.SYS like a file, as you would do with any other driver, you access its functions through Int 67h. See the "DOS Reference" section for a detailed listing of the functions available through Int 67h.

The functions available through EMM.SYS include the following:

- Reporting the status of expanded memory

- Allocating pages in expanded memory

- De-allocating pages in expanded memory

- Diagnostics

- Multitasking support

- Mapping physical pages in expanded memory to logical pages assigned to programs

This paged-memory technique has been used in computers for a long time. There is no reason that your programs cannot take advantage of expanded memory when it is available.

Shortly after expanded memory was introduced, Microsoft announced its support for Version 3.2 of the standard, which included facilities useful for multitasking operating systems. Version 3.2 became known as LIM EMS (Lotus-Intel-Microsoft Expanded Memory Specification). Ashton-Tate, AST Research, and Quadram noticed a limitation in the standard: You could map only a 16K page into an unused area of memory. Why not, therefore, map a large area of memory from the TPA? These circumstances led to the development of the Enhanced Expanded Memory Specification (EEMS).

With enhanced expanded memory, you can move one entire program to the expanded memory area and substitute another program. This capability means that a PC can become multitasking in a real sense. LIM 4.0, introduced in 1988, includes EEMS in addition to the old LIM 3.2 standard in its specification. All the companies that have been involved in expanded memory technology support this new standard to at least some degree, although not all firms have implemented all the features called for in the standard.

As long as we use the basic PC machines, we have to learn to live with the 640K area of space assigned to us. Newer machines lift these 640K restrictions.

Memory Management

Memory management under DOS concerns the free area in the TPA. To maintain compatibility between programs and future releases of the operating system, DOS calls should be used for all memory allocation and de-allocation requests.

Although we currently can perform all kinds of tricks in memory, tricky programs will cease to work as we move toward multitasking. By learning to work with the limitations of DOS, you will be able to write more portable programs. Unfortunately, some of these tricks (such as direct access to video-display memory) are the staples of DOS programming. Without them, the system is not responsive enough to give users the kind of "feel" necessary for a professional program. Although these tricks make programs that use them less portable, some loss of portability is necessary at times to make good programs.

There are no tricks, however, in memory allocation. Even a tiny error causes the system to lock up. Let's look next at how DOS controls memory in the TPA.

The TPA is organized into a structure called the *memory arena*. DOS maintains a chained list of memory blocks called arena entries, each with its own special control block called an arena header (Chapter 3 examined these items, and Table 3.3 shows the header layout). Three DOS functions (Int 21h, Functions 48h, 49h, and 4Ah) request or release memory. The "DOS Reference" section of this book describes each function in detail.

The arena chain (see fig. 10.3) connects each memory block into a list of memory blocks. Whenever two free memory blocks come in contact, they are combined into a single, larger block with only one arena header in the chain.

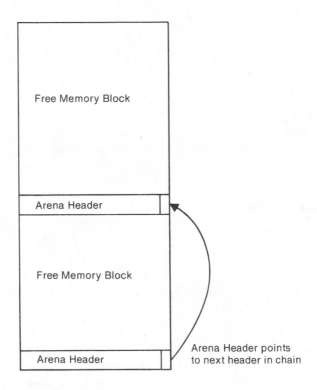

Figure 10.3 Memory-allocation chain.

When a request is made for memory, DOS searches through the arena chain to locate a block large enough to fill the request. To assign the blocks, DOS employs a *first-fit* strategy, in which it uses the first block large enough to meet the requirements. If the block contains more memory than was requested, the block is split in two and the excess memory is put back in the list as a separate memory block.

DOS uses this first-fit strategy because it is the most efficient one in general use. Beginning with DOS V3, you can change the allocation strategy to either of the following alternative methods:

- *Best fit.* In this strategy, the entire memory is searched and the memory block that most closely matches the request fills it.

- *Last fit.* The last block on the chain (the block with the highest memory address) that fits the allocation request is used.

The memory-allocation strategy does not need to be changed because the most efficient method is already in use. (Very limited testing with DOS V3 seems to indicate that DOS continues to use first fit when it is loading any program, no matter which method is set. This result is not conclusive—because of the number of variables involved, much more testing is required to provide definite answers. One problem is that the DOS loader *always* starts by attempting to get all remaining RAM.)

Whenever DOS gets an allocation request, it checks the arena list to see whether any problems exist there. If you write over arena headers and otherwise destroy the list, your program is aborted and you see this message: `Memory Allocation Error`.

Shrinking Program Memory

When a COM program starts, it is assigned all memory because DOS is inherently a single-user system that runs only one program at a time. The loader begins by asking for 65,535 paragraphs (more than possibly can be available) to find how many are available, and then it asks for exactly that number.

EXE programs also are usually assigned all memory, but in this case you can reduce the assignment if you want. The EXE program's header has two parameters: MINALLOC and MAXALLOC. MINALLOC is the minimum memory allocation the program needs to run. If a block with at least the minimum amount of memory needed is available, the program can run.

DOS always tries, however, to assign a block with MAXALLOC bytes of memory in it, if possible. The Microsoft linker always sets MINALLOC to 0 and MAXALLOC to FFFFh (1,048,560 bytes), unless you tell it other values to use. Whenever you link an EXE program without specifying these values, therefore, you guarantee that it gets all available memory.

Note that both Turbo C and Microsoft C automatically release excess memory when they start. Turbo Pascal, however, like the Microsoft linker, does not do so automatically. In Turbo Pascal Versions 4 and 5, which generate EXE files, all available memory is used by default, with the highest area managed as a heap. A compiler directive can set the size, however, if you want to control it yourself. In addition, internal variables (well documented in the manual) tell you exactly how memory is used.

With older Turbo Pascal versions, which generated COM files, the only way to limit the amount of memory used by a program was to set a maximum size for the heap during compilation. Because of the way its memory is allocated, with the stack and the heap above the program, no effective method exists for determining where a Pascal COM program will end.

BASIC also poses problems for programmers because there is no effective way to determine where the program ends in memory, nor is there a way to start a program except by accessing the EXEC function. A special MEMSET function lets the program set its upper memory limit, but this function is intended to allow a BASIC program to load assembly-language support routines rather than to provide for execution of other programs. CHAIN and RUN (BASIC statements for executing other BASIC programs) replace the existing program in memory with a new program rather than maintain the present program's status.

Among high-level languages, both C and the newer versions of Turbo Pascal are suitable for dynamic memory-allocation work. C provides good functions for memory allocation and de-allocation; you never have to access the DOS functions for this purpose. The latest Turbo Pascal versions incorporate many extensions of conventional (or "standard") Pascal and offer the same functions as C, under slightly different names.

Only programs written in assembly language must explicitly return memory to the memory pool on start-up. Listing 10.1 shows how this is done.

Listing 10.1

```
; Freemem.asm
        mov     sp,offset stack     ;Move stack to safe area
        mov     ah,4Ah              ;Set block
        mov     bx,280h             ;Retain 10K of space
        int     21h
        jc      alloc_error         ;Allocation error

;               [MORE PROGRAM CODE]

        dw      64 dup (?)
stack   equ     $
```

Getting More Memory

If a program needs additional memory, it can call for it by using the Modify Memory Allocation function (Int 21h, Function 4Ah). On return, if the memory is available, the carry flag is clear and the AX register has the segment address of the base of the memory. If not enough memory is available to fill the request, the carry flag is set, AX has an error flag (7 = memory control blocks destroyed, 8 = insufficient memory), and register BX has the size of the largest available block.

Both C and the newer versions of Turbo Pascal provide useful functions for obtaining additional memory and for de-allocating memory. The capability of older versions of Turbo Pascal (before Version 4.0) for calling for additional memory is minimal or nonexistent unless you use special compiler switches. BASIC provides no way to change allocation of memory to the BASIC program and no way to determine where to go in memory to restrict memory use.

Again, only in assembly language do you need to access the DOS allocation function directly. In C and the newer Turbo Pascal versions, the library allocation routines access the DOS functions for you. Listing 10.2 provides a way to get memory and determine how much memory is left if the first attempt is denied.

Listing 10.2

```
; Getmem.asm

getmem: mov     ah,48h              ;Allocate memory
        mov     bx,bufsize          ;16K memory
        int     21h
        jc      nomem               ;Cannot allocate
        mov     bufseg,ax           ;Save pointer
        jmp     pgm                 ;Continue program

nomem:  cmp     ax,8
        jnz     quit                ;Major alloc error
        mov     bufsize,bx          ;Save buffer size
        mov     ah,48h              ;Allocate memory
        int     21h
        jc      quit                ;Still cannot allocate

pgm:
;               [MAIN PART OF PROGRAM]

done:   mov     ah,49h              ;De-allocate memory
        mov     es,bufseg           ;Point to buffer segment
        int     21h

quit:           [EXIT CODE GOES HERE]

bufsize dw      400h
bufseg  dw      0
```

Several allocation and de-allocation functions are available to programs written in either C or the newer versions of Turbo Pascal, without access to the DOS calls for memory allocation. The use of these available functions makes sense because they significantly simplify the operation and keep it under control of the language system. Versions of Turbo Pascal before 4.0 own all available memory in the heap and, as necessary, provide for allocation and de-allocation of this space to the program. These Pascal allocation and de-allocation routines do not get or return space from the arena. BASIC requests and returns nothing.

Programmers of BASIC and Pascal (before Turbo Pascal 4.0) can limit memory artificially with compiler switches and then use DOS function calls to request or free additional memory. This exercise, however, leads to confusion and poor memory handling. Programs that must have dynamic memory handling should be written in C, the new Turbo Pascal, or assembly language.

Expanded Memory

Sooner or later (when you run out of memory on your PC and have added all the chips necessary to take your system to the 640K limit), you probably will buy an expanded memory board. Expanded memory allows quick, effective access to huge amounts of data storage (EMS) or regions for multitasking (EEMS).

Determining Expanded Memory's Availability

To determine whether expanded memory has been installed, use one of the following methods:

- Attempt to open the file EMMXXXX0 (the device driver's guaranteed name). If the open succeeds, either the driver is there or a file with the same name exists. To see whether the driver is there, use the IOCTL function to make a "get output status" request. The driver returns FFh; a file returns 00h. Close the file so that the handle can be reused.

- Inspect the address at the Int 67h vector location. This address is the interrupt entry point for the driver. If EMM.SYS (or an alternate driver) is present, the segment address given is the base of the driver; at offset 000Ah in that segment, the driver name appears as part of the driver's header. Although this process is faster than opening a file (open and close overhead is significant), the method relies on the program to access memory outside its normal memory range.

Listings 10.3 and 10.4 give two separate routines in C to check for the presence of the EMS driver.

Listing 10.3

```
/* emmtest.c
   Listing 10.3 of DOS Programmer's Reference */

#include <dos.h>

int emmtest()
{
    union REGS regs;
    struct SREGS sregs;
```

continues

Listing 10.3   Continued

```
        short int result;
        unsigned int handle;

        regs.h.ah = 0x3d;                  /* Open file */
        regs.h.al = 0;                     /* Read mode only */
        regs.x.dx = FP_OFF("EMMXXXX0"); /* File name */
        sregs.ds = FP_SEG("EMMXXXX0");  /* Set the DS register */
        intdosx(&regs,&regs,&sregs);
        handle = regs.x.ax;                /* File handle */

        /* If opened OK, then close the file */
        if(result = (regs.x.cflag == 0)){
             regs.h.ah = 0x3e;
             regs.x.bx = handle;
             intdos(&regs,&regs);
        }

        return(result);
}
```

Listing 10.3, which uses the opening-the-file method to determine whether the EMM is installed, does not bother to check the IOCTL call to see whether the open returned a file or a driver. In most cases, this is not a problem. To be safe, however, you should add a check of the IOCTL call to the function.

Note that compiling this function with Borland C++ yields a warning in the `if()` statement that sets `result`. This warning can be safely ignored because the desired effect is to set the function return value to either TRUE or FALSE, depending on the result of the test. The compiler complains but handles it.

Listing 10.4 turned out to be a real problem for some C programmers who were unaccustomed to dealing with far pointers. When you work on a PC, you must realize the difference between pointers that point within a segment (near pointers); pointers that can point anywhere in memory, given the segment and offset address (far pointers); and pointers that can point anywhere in memory as though memory were not segmented (huge pointers). Whenever pointer arguments are used, you must be precise and always match them; otherwise, unexpected results prevent your program from running.

Listing 10.4

```
/* emmchk.c
   Listing 10.4 of DOS Programmer's Reference */

#define  FALSE   0
#define  TRUE    !FALSE

#include <stdlib.h>
#include <stdio.h>
```

```
#include <dos.h>
#include <alloc.h>

int emmchk()
{
    union REGS regs;
    struct SREGS sregs;
    char far *emptr, far *nameptr, far *fmptr;
    nameptr = "EMMXXXX0";

    regs.h.ah = 0x35;              /* Get interrupt vector */
    regs.h.al = 0x67;              /* Get it for the EMM */
    intdosx(&regs,&regs,&sregs);

    /* Make a FAR pointer to access the driver */
    emptr = MK_FP(sregs.es,0);
    fmptr = farmalloc(sregs.es);
    if ((emptr = fmptr)==NULL) {
        printf("Unable to allocate far pointer.\n");
        exit(0);
    }

    /* Return TRUE if they are the same for eight characters */
    return(farcmp(emptr+10,nameptr,8));
}

int  farcmp(str1,str2,n)
    char far *str1,
        far *str2;
    int  n;
{
    while(*str2 && n>0){
        if(*str1 != *str2) return(FALSE);
        n--;
        str1++; str2++;
    }
        return(TRUE);
}
```

A more serious error stems from the way some books describe expanded memory. This error occurs because many expanded-memory discussions mistakenly explain that the pointer at Int 67h points to the beginning of the driver and that ten bytes from the memory location given in the Int 67h vector is the name EMMXXXX0. A moment's reflection tells you that this statement cannot be true; the interrupt vector points to the location at which control is transferred when the interrupt is called, but the first byte of the driver is part of the driver header and cannot be executable code. (This subject is discussed in Chapter 12, "Device Drivers.")

The vector provides the segment portion of the address, but the name is found at absolute offset 000Ah within that segment because the driver's memory is always allocated to it on paragraph boundaries (only multiples of paragraphs can be allocated). The segment address of any installed driver base is *normalized*—a fancy way of saying that the segment address is adjusted until the offset is zero.

Listing 10.5 is a small program that tests for the presence of expanded memory by both methods and shows you what each one returns.

Listing 10.5

```
/* testemm.c
   Listing 10.5 of DOS Programmer's Reference */

#include <stdio.h>

void main()
{
    int emmchk(void);
    int emmtest(void);

    if(emmchk())
        printf("MEM: Expanded memory is present\n");
    else
        printf("MEM: Expanded memory is NOT present\n");
    if(emmtest())
        printf("OPEN: Expanded memory is present\n");
    else
        printf("OPEN: Expanded memory is NOT present\n");
}
```

Using Expanded Memory

When you know that expanded memory is available, you can use the expanded memory functions tied to Int 67h to get and use memory. (The EMS reference section describes the expanded memory functions.) Listing 10.6 shows a simple example of the memory functions tied to Int 67.

Listing 10.6

```
/* emstest.c
   Listing 10.6 of DOS Programmer's Reference */

#include <stdio.h>
#include <stdlib.h>
#include <string.h>
#include <dos.h>

#define  FALSE   0
#define  TRUE    !FALSE
#define  EMM     0x67

char far *emmbase;

void main()
```

```
    {
            unsigned int emmhandle;
            char teststr[80];
            int  i;

            int emmtest(void);
            int emmok(void);
            unsigned int emmalloc(int n);
            unsigned int emmmap(unsigned int handle, int phys, int page);
            void emmmove(int page, char *str, int n);
            void emmget(int page, char *str, int n);
            unsigned int emmclose(unsigned int handle);


            /* Is there any expanded memory? */
            if(!emmtest()){
                printf("Expanded memory is NOT present\n");
                printf("   cannot run this program\n");
                exit(0);
            }

            /* Is the expanded memory manager functional? */
            if(!emmok()){
                printf("Expanded memory manager NOT available\n");
                printf("   cannot run this program\n");
                exit(0);
            }

            /* Get ten pages of expanded memory for the demo. */
            if((emmhandle = emmalloc(10)) < 0) {
                printf("There are not enough pages available\n");
                printf("   cannot run this program\n");
                exit(0);
            }

            /* Write the test string into each of the ten pages. */
            for(i=0; i<10; i++){
                sprintf(teststr,"This info is in EMS page %d\n",i);
                emmmap(emmhandle,i,0);
                emmmove(0,teststr,strlen(teststr)+1);
            }

            /* Now read them back in and recover the test string. */
            for(i=0; i<10; i++){
                emmmap(emmhandle,i,0);
                emmget(0,teststr,strlen(teststr)+1);
                printf("Reading from block %d:  %s",i,teststr);
            }

            /* Finally, release the expanded memory. */
            emmclose(emmhandle);
    }

int emmtest()
{
    union REGS regs;
    struct SREGS sregs;
```

continues

DOS
PROGRAMMING

Listing 10.6 Continued

```c
        short int result;
        unsigned int handle;

        regs.h.ah = 0x3d;               /* Open file */
        regs.h.al = 0;                  /* Read mode only */
        regs.x.dx = (int)"EMMXXXX0";    /* File name */
        sregs.ds = _DS;                 /* Set the DS register */
        intdosx(&regs,&regs,&sregs);

        handle = regs.x.ax;             /* File handle */
        if(result = (regs.x.cflag == 0)){
            regs.h.ah = 0x3e;
            regs.x.bx = handle;
            intdos(&regs,&regs);
        }
        return(result);
}

int emmok()
{
    union REGS regs;

    regs.h.ah = 0x40;               /* Get manager status */
    int86(EMM,&regs,&regs);
    if(regs.h.ah != 0) return(FALSE);

    regs.h.ah = 0x41;               /* Get page frame segment */
    int86(EMM,&regs,&regs);
    if(regs.h.ah != 0) return(FALSE);

    emmbase = MK_FP(regs.x.bx,0);
    return(TRUE);
}

unsigned int emmalloc(n)
    int  n;
{
    union REGS regs;

    regs.h.ah = 0x43;       /* Get handle and allocate memory */
    regs.x.bx = n;
    int86(EMM,&regs,&regs);
    if(regs.h.ah != 0)
        return(-1);
    return(regs.x.dx);
}

unsigned int emmmap(handle,phys,page)
    unsigned int handle;
    int  phys, page;
{
    union REGS regs;

    regs.h.ah = 0x44;               /* Map memory */
    regs.h.al = page;
    regs.x.bx = phys;
    regs.x.dx = handle;
```

```
      int86(EMM,&regs,&regs);
      return(regs.h.ah == 0);
}

void emmmove(page,str,n)
      int   page, n;
      char *str;
{
      char far *ptr;

      ptr = emmbase + page*16384;
      while(n-- > 0)
           *ptr++ = *str++;
}

void emmget(page,str,n)
      int   page, n;
      char *str;
{
      char far *ptr;

      ptr = emmbase + page*16384;
      while(n-- > 0)
           *str++ = *ptr++;
}

unsigned int emmclose(handle)
      unsigned int    handle;
{
      union REGS regs;

      regs.h.ah = 0x45;              /* Release handle */
      regs.x.dx = handle;
      int86(EMM,&regs,&regs);
      return(regs.h.ah == 0);
}
```

The program in Listing 10.6 demonstrates basic operation of expanded memory. The program does the following:

- Tests to see whether expanded memory is there

- Rests to see whether the expanded memory manager is working properly

- Attempts to allocate ten pages of expanded memory

- Maps the pages one at a time into the page frame and writes a test string into each page

- Maps the pages back into the page frame and then reads out and prints the test string

These are the most basic operations on expanded memory. They enable you to use the memory area in a variety of programs. You can use this type of technique to put a spreadsheet or database in expanded memory: to do so, you define an array of values in the page frame and fill them by their pointers. Remember to use far or huge pointers to access the page because the area certainly will be out of the current segment.

285

After the main part of the program are several small expanded memory functions the main program uses. In combination, these functions cover the expanded memory operations, although you might want to add to them by including error checking.

The functions included in the program are shown in this list:

emmtest	Tests for the presence of the expanded memory manager in memory
emmok	Tests the functionality of the expanded memory manager and determines the base address of the page frame
emmalloc	Requests a designated number of pages from the expanded memory manager
emmmap	Maps an expanded memory page into the page frame
emmmove	Moves data into a designated page in the page frame
emmget	Gets data from a designated page in the page frame
emmclose	Returns control of the expanded memory handle to the expanded memory manager

Simple applications of expanded memory can start with these basic functions and then grow as error checking and new features are added.

Extended Memory

Extended memory refers to the memory above the 8086's 1M address limitations. In the confines of the Extended Memory Specification (XMS), extended memory refers also to the high memory area (HMA) and the upper memory blocks (UMBs).

UMBs are areas of usable memory between the 640K boundary of DOS memory and the 1M boundary of the 8086. These areas are usually not contiguous to the 640K available and, until DOS 5.0, they were unavailable to the programmer except through the XMS driver. Beginning with DOS 5.0, UMBs can be accessed through DOS's memory services; the DOS memory services access the XMS driver for you.

The HMA is an oddity in which the 21st address line (line A20) is activated while the CPU is in real mode, adding 65,520 bytes to the amount of memory available for direct access by the CPU in real mode. The way this process works follows. Consider the mapping of a segment value plus an offset to physical memory. You can find the physical address accessed by multiplying the segment value by 16 and adding the offset. If this value exceeds 20 bits, the higher bits are truncated, keeping the physical address in the range 000000H through 0FFFFFH. An address of 0FFFF:0010H, therefore, describes the physical address 000000H, unless the A20 line is activated. When it is, the address 0FFFF:0010H describes the physical address 0100000H. This is where the extra 65,520 bytes of memory come from; the addresses 0FFFF:0010H through 0FFFF:FFFFH, which are normally mapped to the physical addresses 000000H through 00FFEFH, are mapped to the physical addresses 0100000H through 010FFEFH.

Five groups of services are provided by the XMS driver: driver information functions, HMA management functions, A20 management functions, extended memory management functions, and upper memory management functions. Two additional services determine whether the XMS driver is present and get the address of the XMS driver's control function.

Determining Extended Memory's Availability

To determine whether the XMS driver is present, you can execute the following code:

```
mov  AX,04300H
int  02FH
cmp  AL,080H
jne  XMS_NotPresent

; XMS is present
```

If the XMS is present, it is necessary to get the address of the XMS driver's control function. This is accomplished through the following code fragment:

```
code segment

mov  AX,04310H
int  02FH
mov  word ptr [XMS_Control],BX
mov  word ptr [XMS_Control],ES

code ends
data segment

XMS_Control    dd   (?)

data ends
```

Using Extended Memory

When you know that extended memory is available, you can use the extended memory functions to get and use memory. (The XMS reference section in Part V describes the expanded memory functions.) The two listings in this section are simple examples of the extended memory functions.

The program in Listing 10.7 demonstrates the basic operation of extended memory. The program does the following:

- Tests to see whether extended memory is present

- Gets the XMS version number, checks to see whether the HMA exists, and gets the size of the largest free block of extended memory

- Attempts to allocate an extended memory block

- Writes data to the extended memory block

- Reads data back from the extended memory block

- Frees the extended memory block

- Attempts to allocate an upper memory block

- Frees the upper memory block

These are the most basic operations on expanded memory. They enable you to use the memory area in a variety of programs. You can use this type of technique to put data in extended memory.

Listing 10.7

```
/* xmstest.c
   Listing 10.7 of DOS Programmer's Reference */

#include  <ctype.h>
#include  <dos.h>
#include  <stdio.h>
#include  <mem.h>

struct    XMS_status {
     unsigned short version;
     unsigned short revision;
     unsigned short HMA_existence;
     };

struct    XMS_memory_status {
     unsigned short largest_block;
     unsigned short total_free_memory;
     unsigned short error_status;
     };

struct    bstat {
     unsigned short lock_count;
     unsigned short free_handle_count;
     };

union     memory_address {
     unsigned long  long_offset;
     struct conventional_address {
          unsigned short conventional_offset;
          unsigned short conventional_segment;
          }         c_a;
     };
```

```
struct    XMS_move_data {
    unsigned long           transfer_size;
    unsigned short          source_handle;
    union memory_address    source_offset;
    unsigned short          destination_handle;
    union memory_address    destination_offset;
    };

struct umb_data {
    unsigned short segment_number;
    unsigned short segment_size;
    };

extern unsigned short far
    a20_stat(void);
extern unsigned short far
    alter_a20(unsigned short change_code);
extern unsigned short far
    hma_alloc(unsigned short size_in_bytes);
extern unsigned short far
    hma_free(void);
extern void far
    hma_move(unsigned short count, unsigned short direction,
             unsigned short hma_offset, void far *data);
extern unsigned short far
    umb_alloc(unsigned short size, struct umb_data far *ptr);
extern unsigned short far
    umb_free(unsigned short segment);
extern unsigned short far
    xms_alloc(unsigned short size, unsigned short far *handle);
extern void far
    xms_avail(struct XMS_memory_status far *ptr);
extern unsigned short far
    xms_bstat(unsigned short handle, struct bstat far *ptr);
extern unsigned short far
    xms_free(unsigned short handle);
extern unsigned short far
    xms_lock(unsigned short handle, unsigned long *linear_address);
extern unsigned short far
    xms_move(struct XMS_move_data far *ptr);
extern unsigned short far
    xms_realloc(unsigned short handle, unsigned short size);
extern void far
    xms_stat(struct XMS_status far *ptr);
extern unsigned short far
    xms_test(void);
extern unsigned short far
    xms_unlock(unsigned short handle);

/*   Return codes   */

#define   A20_DISABLED                  (0x0000)
#define   A20_ENABLED                   (0x0001)
#define   FAILURE                       (0x0000)
#define   SUCCESS                       (0x0001)
#define   FUNCTION_NOT_IMPLEMENTED       (0x0080)
```

continues

Listing 10.7 Continued

```
#define    VDISK_DEVICE_DETECTED              (0x0081)
#define    A20_ERROR_OCCURRED                 (0x0082)
#define    HMA_DOES_NOT_EXIST                 (0x0090)
#define    HMA_ALREADY_IN_USE                 (0x0091)
#define    NOT_ENOUGH_BYTES_TO_ALLOC_HMA      (0x0092)
#define    HMA_NOT_ALLOCATED                  (0x0093)
#define    A20_LINE_STILL_ENABLED             (0x0094)
#define    ALL_EXTENDED_MEMORY_ALLOCATED      (0x00A0)
#define    ALL_EXTENDED_MEMORY_HANDLES_USED   (0x00A1)
#define    INVALID_HANDLE                     (0x00A2)
#define    INVALID_SOURCE_HANDLE              (0x00A3)
#define    INVALID_SOURCE_OFFSET              (0x00A4)
#define    INVALID_DESTINATION_HANDLE         (0x00A5)
#define    INVALID_DESTINATION_OFFSET         (0x00A6)
#define    INVALID_LENGTH                     (0x00A7)
#define    INVALID_OVERLAP                    (0x00A8)
#define    PARITY_ERROR                       (0x00A9)
#define    BLOCK_NOT_LOCKED                   (0x00AA)
#define    HANDLE_IS_LOCKED                   (0x00AB)
#define    LOCK_COUNT_OVERFLOW                (0x00AC)
#define    LOCK_FAILED                        (0x00AD)
#define    SMALLER_UMB_AVAILABLE              (0x00B0)
#define    NO_UMBS_AVAILABLE                  (0x00B1)
#define    INVALID_UMB_SEGMENT                (0x00B2)
#define    ILLEGAL_PARAMETER                  (0xFFFF)


/*   Codes for alter_a20()    */

#define    GLOBAL_A20_LINE     (0)
#define    LOCAL_A20_LINE      (2)
#define    ENABLE_A20_LINE     (0)
#define    DISABLE_A20_LINE    (1)


/*   Codes for hma_move()     */

#define    COPY_FROM_HMA  (1)
#define    COPY_TO_HMA    (0)


#define    KILOBYTE  (1024)

unsigned char  test_buffer[ KILOBYTE ];

void test_hma(void)
    {
    int          HMA_allocated;
    int          A20_status;
    int          original_A20_status;
    unsigned short result;

    HMA_allocated = 0;
    result = hma_alloc(0xFFF0);
    switch (result)
        {
        case SUCCESS:
            printf("HMA successfully allocated to current process\n");
```

```
                HMA_allocated++;
                break;
        case FUNCTION_NOT_IMPLEMENTED:
                printf("HMA allocate not implemented by XMS\n");
                break;
        case VDISK_DEVICE_DETECTED:
                printf("VDISK device detected; couldn't allocate HMA\n");
                break;
        case HMA_DOES_NOT_EXIST:
                printf("HMA cannot be allocated; doesn't exist\n");
                return;
        case HMA_ALREADY_IN_USE:
                printf("HMA cannot be allocated; already in use\n");
                break;
        case NOT_ENOUGH_BYTES_TO_ALLOC_HMA:
                printf("Not enough bytes to allocate HMA were specified\n");
                return;
        default:
                printf("Invalid result of hma_alloc(): 0x%.4X\n", result);
                return;
        }
    if (HMA_allocated)
        {
        original_A20_status = A20_status = -1;
        result = a20_stat();
        switch (result)
            {
            case A20_DISABLED:
                original_A20_status = A20_status = 0;
                break;
            case A20_ENABLED:
                original_A20_status = A20_status = 1;
                break;
            case FUNCTION_NOT_IMPLEMENTED:
                printf("Can't get A20 line status; function not implemented\n");
                break;
            case VDISK_DEVICE_DETECTED:
                printf("Can't get A20 line status; VDISK device detected\n");
                break;
            default:
                printf("Can't get A20 line status; unexpected result 0x%.4X \n",
                    result);
                break;
            }
        if (A20_status == 0)      /* Disabled */
            {
            result = alter_a20(GLOBAL_A20_LINE | ENABLE_A20_LINE);
            switch (result)
                {
                case SUCCESS:
                    printf("A20 line globally enabled\n");
                    A20_status = 1;
                    break;
                case FUNCTION_NOT_IMPLEMENTED:
                    printf("Function not implemented; couldn't enable A20 line\n");
                    break;
```

continues

Listing 10.7 Continued

```
                case VDISK_DEVICE_DETECTED:
                        printf("VDISK device detected; couldn't enable A20 line\n");
                        break;
                case A20_ERROR_OCCURRED:
                        printf("Error occurred while attempting to enable A20 line\n");
                        break;
                case ILLEGAL_PARAMETER:
                        printf("Illegal argument to alter_a20()\n");
                        break;
                default:
                        printf("Unexpected result 0x%.4X from alter_a20()\n", result);
                        break;
                }
        }
    if (A20_status == 1)
        {
        int  k;

        memset(test_buffer, 0x55, KILOBYTE);
        hma_move(KILOBYTE, COPY_TO_HMA, 0, test_buffer);
        memset(test_buffer, 0xAA, KILOBYTE);
        hma_move(KILOBYTE, COPY_FROM_HMA, 0, test_buffer);
        result = 1;
        for (k = 0; k < KILOBYTE; k++)
                {
                if (test_buffer[ k ] != 0x55)
                        {
                        printf("Error transferring data to/from HMA\n");
                        result = 0;
                        break;
                        }
                }
        if (result)
                {
                memset(test_buffer, 0xAA, KILOBYTE);
                hma_move(KILOBYTE, COPY_TO_HMA, 0, test_buffer);
                memset(test_buffer, 0x55, KILOBYTE);
                hma_move(KILOBYTE, COPY_FROM_HMA, 0, test_buffer);
                for (k = 0; k < KILOBYTE; k++)
                        {
                        if (test_buffer[ k ] != 0xAA)
                                {
                                printf("Error transferring data to/from HMA\n");
                                result = 0;
                                break;
                                }
                        }
                }
        if (result)
                printf("Transfer of data to/from HMA test successful\n");
        if (original_A20_status == 0)
                {
```

```
        result = alter_a20(GLOBAL_A20_LINE | DISABLE_A20_LINE);
        switch (result)
            {
            case SUCCESS:
                printf("A20 line globally disabled\n");
                break;
            case FUNCTION_NOT_IMPLEMENTED:
                printf("Function not implemented; disable A20 line\n");
                break;
            case VDISK_DEVICE_DETECTED:
                printf("VDISK device detected; disable A20 line\n");
                break;
            case A20_ERROR_OCCURRED:
                printf("Error while attempting to disable A20 line\n");
                break;
            case ILLEGAL_PARAMETER:
                printf("Illegal argument to alter_a20()\n");
                break;
            case A20_LINE_STILL_ENABLED:
                printf("A20 line still enabled\n");
                break;
            default:
                printf("Unexpected result 0x%.4X from alter_a20()\n",
                    result);
                break;
            }
        }
    result = hma_free();
    switch (result)
        {
        case SUCCESS:
            printf("HMA successfully freed\n");
            break;
        case FUNCTION_NOT_IMPLEMENTED:
            printf("HMA free not implemented by XMS\n");
            break;
        case VDISK_DEVICE_DETECTED:
            printf("VDISK device detected; couldn't free HMA\n");
            break;
        case HMA_DOES_NOT_EXIST:
            printf("HMA does not exist\n");
            return;
        case HMA_NOT_ALLOCATED:
            printf("HMA was not allocated\n");
            return;
        default:
            printf("Invalid result of hma_free(): 0x%.4X\n", result);
            return;
        }
    }
else
    {
    original_A20_status = A20_status = -1;
    result = a20_stat();
    switch (result)
```

continues

Listing 10.7 Continued

```
            {
        case A20_DISABLED:
            original_A20_status = A20_status = 0;
            break;
        case A20_ENABLED:
            original_A20_status = A20_status = 1;
            break;
        case FUNCTION_NOT_IMPLEMENTED:          '
            printf("Can't get A20 line status; function not implemented\n");
            break;
        case VDISK_DEVICE_DETECTED:
            printf("Can't get A20 line status; VDISK device detected\n");
            break;
        default:
            printf("Can't get A20 line status; unexpected result 0x%.4X\n", result);
            break;
        }
    if (A20_status == 0)     /* Disabled */
        {
        result = alter_a20(GLOBAL_A20_LINE | ENABLE_A20_LINE);
        switch (result)
            {
            case SUCCESS:
                printf("A20 line globally enabled\n");
                A20_status = 1;
                break;
            case FUNCTION_NOT_IMPLEMENTED:
                printf("Function not implemented; couldn't enable A20 line\n");
                break;
            case VDISK_DEVICE_DETECTED:
                printf("VDISK device detected; couldn't enable A20 line\n");
                break;
            case A20_ERROR_OCCURRED:
                printf("Error occurred while attempting to enable A20 line\n");
                break;
            case ILLEGAL_PARAMETER:
                printf("Illegal argument to alter_a20()\n");
                break;
            default:
                printf("Unexpected result 0x%.4X from alter_a20()\n", result);
                break;
            }
        }
    if (A20_status == 1)     /* Enabled */
        {
        int  k;
        int  m;

        memset(test_buffer, 0, KILOBYTE);
        hma_move(KILOBYTE, COPY_FROM_HMA, 0, test_buffer);
```

```
            for (k = 0; k < (KILOBYTE / 16); k++)
                {
                printf("HMA:%.3X0 ", k);
                for (m = 0; m < 16; m++)
                    printf("%.2X ", test_buffer[ (k << 4) + m ]);
                for (m = 0; m < 16; m++)
                    {
                    if (isprint(test_buffer[ (k << 4) + m ]))
                        printf("%c", test_buffer[ (k << 4) + m ]);
                    else
                        printf(".");
                    }
                printf("\n");
                }
        if (original_A20_status == 0)
            {
            result = alter_a20(GLOBAL_A20_LINE | DISABLE_A20_LINE);
            switch (result)
                {
                case SUCCESS:
                    printf("A20 line globally disabled\n");
                    break;
                case FUNCTION_NOT_IMPLEMENTED:
                    printf("Function not implemented; disable A20 line\n");
                    break;
                case VDISK_DEVICE_DETECTED:
                    printf("VDISK device detected; disable A20 line\n");
                    break;
                case A20_ERROR_OCCURRED:
                    printf("Error while attempting to disable A20 line\n");
                    break;
                case ILLEGAL_PARAMETER:
                    printf("Illegal argument to alter_a20()\n");
                    break;
                case A20_LINE_STILL_ENABLED:
                    printf("A20 line still enabled\n");
                    break;
                default:
                    printf("Unexpected result 0x%.4X from alter_a20()\n",
                        result);
                    break;
                }
            }
        }
    }
}

void test_xms(void)
    {
    struct XMS_memory_status status;
    struct bstat            block_status;
    struct XMS_move_data    move_block;
    unsigned short          handle;
    unsigned short          result;
    unsigned long           address;
    int                     move_ok;
```

continues

295

Listing 10.7 Continued

```c
xms_avail(&status);
printf("Largest block of XMS memory available = %.4X Kbytes\n",
    status.largest_block);
printf("Total free memory =                 %.4X Kbytes\n",
    status.total_free_memory);
printf("Error status =                      %.4X\n", status.error_status);
if (status.error_status)
    return;
result = xms_alloc(status.largest_block, &handle);
switch (result)
    {
    case SUCCESS:
        printf("Memory allocated; handle = %.4X\n", handle);
        break;
    case FUNCTION_NOT_IMPLEMENTED:
        printf("Function not implemented: xms_alloc\n");
        return;
    case VDISK_DEVICE_DETECTED:
        printf("VDISK device detected: xms_alloc\n");
        return;
    case ALL_EXTENDED_MEMORY_ALLOCATED:
        printf("All memory allocated: xms_alloc\n");
        return;
    case ALL_EXTENDED_MEMORY_HANDLES_USED:
        printf("All memory handles in use: xms_alloc\n");
        return;
    default:
        printf("Unexpected result from xms_alloc: %.4X\n", result);
        return;
    }
result = xms_realloc(handle, status.largest_block / 2);
switch (result)
    {
    case SUCCESS:
        printf("Block successfully reallocated in half\n");
        break;
    case FUNCTION_NOT_IMPLEMENTED:
        printf("xms_realloc not implemented\n");
        break;
    case VDISK_DEVICE_DETECTED:
        printf("VDISK device detected: xms_realloc\n");
        break;
    case ALL_EXTENDED_MEMORY_ALLOCATED:
        printf("xms_realloc failed: all extended memory allocated\n");
        break;
    case ALL_EXTENDED_MEMORY_HANDLES_USED:
        printf("xms_realloc failed: all extended memory handles in use\n");
        break;
    case INVALID_HANDLE:
        printf("xms_realloc failed: invalid handle\n");
        break;
    case HANDLE_IS_LOCKED:
        printf("xms_realloc failed: handle is locked\n");
        break;
    default:
        printf("Unexpected result from xms_realloc: 0x%.4X\n", result);
        break;
```

```
            }
        memset(test_buffer, 0x55, KILOBYTE);
        move_block.transfer_size = KILOBYTE;
        move_block.source_handle = 0;
        move_block.source_offset.c_a.conventional_offset = FP_OFF((void far *)test_buffer);
        move_block.source_offset.c_a.conventional_segment = FP_SEG((void far *)test_buffer);
        move_block.destination_handle = handle;
        move_block.destination_offset.long_offset = 0L;
        result = xms_move(&move_block);
        move_ok = 0;
        switch (result)
            {
            case SUCCESS:
                printf("Data successfully written to XMS\n");
                move_ok = 1;
                break;
            case FUNCTION_NOT_IMPLEMENTED:
                printf("xms_move not implemented\n");
                break;
            case VDISK_DEVICE_DETECTED:
                printf("VDISK device detected: xms_alloc\n");
                break;
            case INVALID_SOURCE_HANDLE:
                printf("Invalid source handle\n");
                break;
            case INVALID_SOURCE_OFFSET:
                printf("Invalid source offset\n");
                break;
            case INVALID_DESTINATION_HANDLE:
                printf("Invalid destination handle\n");
                break;
            case INVALID_DESTINATION_OFFSET:
                printf("Invalid destination offset\n");
                break;
            case INVALID_LENGTH:
                printf("Invalid offset\n");
                break;
            case INVALID_OVERLAP:
                printf("Invalid overlap\n");
                break;
            case PARITY_ERROR:
                printf("Parity Error\n");
                break;
            default:
                printf("Unexpected result from xms_move(): 0x%.4X\n");
                break;
            }
    if (move_ok)
        {
        memset(test_buffer, 0xAA, KILOBYTE);
        move_block.transfer_size = KILOBYTE;
        move_block.source_handle = handle;
        move_block.source_offset.long_offset = 0L;
        move_block.destination_handle = 0;
```

continues

297

Listing 10.7 Continued

```
move_block.destination_offset.c_a.conventional_offset =
    FP_OFF((void far *)test_buffer);
move_block.destination_offset.c_a.conventional_segment =
    FP_SEG((void far *)test_buffer);
result = xms_move(&move_block);
move_ok = 0;
switch (result)
    {
    case SUCCESS:
        printf("Data successfully read from XMS\n");
        move_ok = 1;
        break;
    case FUNCTION_NOT_IMPLEMENTED:
        printf("xms_move not implemented\n");
        break;
    case VDISK_DEVICE_DETECTED:
        printf("VDISK device detected: xms_alloc\n");
        break;
    case INVALID_SOURCE_HANDLE:
        printf("Invalid source handle\n");
        break;
    case INVALID_SOURCE_OFFSET:
        printf("Invalid source offset\n");
        break;
    case INVALID_DESTINATION_HANDLE:
        printf("Invalid destination handle\n");
        break;
    case INVALID_DESTINATION_OFFSET:
        printf("Invalid destination offset\n");
        break;
    caseINVALID_LENGTH:
        printf("Invalid offset\n");
        break;
    case INVALID_OVERLAP:
        printf("Invalid overlap\n");
        break;
    case PARITY_ERROR:
        printf("Parity Error\n");
        break;
    default:
        printf("Unexpected result from xms_move(): 0x%.4X\n");
        break;
    }
if (move_ok)
    {
    int  k;

    for (k = 0; k < KILOBYTE; k++)
        {
        if (test_buffer[ k ] != 0x55)
            {
            printf("Error: corrupted data at offset 0x%.4X; data = %.2X\n",
                k, test_buffer[ k ]);
            move_ok = 0;
            }
```

```
                            }
                  if (move_ok)
                        printf("Data read from XMS verified OK\n");
                  }
            }
      result = xms_lock(handle, &address);
      switch (result)
            {
            case SUCCESS:
                  printf("Block locked; linear address = %.8lX\n", address);
                  break;
            case FUNCTION_NOT_IMPLEMENTED:
                  printf("Function not implemented: xms_lock\n");
                  break;
            case VDISK_DEVICE_DETECTED:
                  printf("VDISK device detected: xms_lock\n");
                  break;
            case INVALID_HANDLE:
                  printf("Handle is invalid\n");
                  break;
            case LOCK_COUNT_OVERFLOW:
                  printf("Lock count overflowed\n");
                  break;
            case LOCK_FAILED:
                  printf("Lock failed\n");
                  break;
            default:
printf("Unexpected result from xms_lock: %.4X\n", result);
                  break;
            }
      result = xms_free(handle);
      switch (result)
            {
            case SUCCESS:
                  printf("XMS memory freed\n");
                  break;
            case FUNCTION_NOT_IMPLEMENTED:
                  printf("Function not implemented: xms_free\n");
                  break;
            case VDISK_DEVICE_DETECTED:
                  printf("VDISK device detected: xms_free\n");
                  break;
            case INVALID_HANDLE:
                  printf("Handle is invalid\n");
                  break;
            case HANDLE_IS_LOCKED:
                  printf("Handle is locked\n");
                  break;
            default:
                  printf("Unexpected result from xms_free: %.4X\n", result);
                  break;
            }
      result = xms_bstat(handle, &block_status);
      switch (result)
            {
            case SUCCESS:
```

continues

Listing 10.7 Continued

```
                printf("Lock count =          %d\n", block_status.lock_count);
                printf("Free handle count = %d\n", block_status.free_handle_count);
                break;
        case FUNCTION_NOT_IMPLEMENTED:
                printf("Function not implemented: xms_bstat\n");
                break;
        case VDISK_DEVICE_DETECTED:
                printf("VDISK device detected: xms_bstat\n");
                break;
        case INVALID_HANDLE:
                printf("Handle is invalid\n");
                break;
        default:
                printf("Unexpected result from xms_bstat: %.4X\n", result);
                break;
        }
    result = xms_lock(handle, &address);
    switch (result)
        {
        case SUCCESS:
                printf("Block locked; linear address = %.8lX\n", address);
                break;
        case FUNCTION_NOT_IMPLEMENTED:
                printf("Function not implemented: xms_lock\n");
                break;
        case VDISK_DEVICE_DETECTED:
                printf("VDISK device detected: xms_lock\n");
                break;
        case INVALID_HANDLE:
                printf("Handle is invalid\n");
                break;
        case LOCK_COUNT_OVERFLOW:
                printf("Lock count overflowed\n");
                break;
        case LOCK_FAILED:
                printf("Lock failed\n");
                break;
        default:
                printf("Unexpected result from xms_lock: %.4X\n", result);
                break;
        }
    result = xms_bstat(handle, &block_status);
    switch (result)
        {
        case SUCCESS:
                printf("Lock count =          %d\n", block_status.lock_count);
                printf("Free handle count = %d\n", block_status.free_handle_count);
                break;
        case FUNCTION_NOT_IMPLEMENTED:
                printf("Function not implemented: xms_bstat\n");
                break;
        case VDISK_DEVICE_DETECTED:
                printf("VDISK device detected: xms_bstat\n");
                break;
```

```
        case INVALID_HANDLE:
            printf("Handle is invalid\n");
            break;
        default:
            printf("Unexpected result from xms_bstat: %.4X\n", result);
            break;
    }
result = xms_unlock(handle);
switch (result)
    {
    case SUCCESS:
        printf("Block unlocked\n");
        break;
    case FUNCTION_NOT_IMPLEMENTED:
        printf("Function not implemented: xms_unlock\n");
        break;
    case VDISK_DEVICE_DETECTED:
        printf("VDISK device detected: xms_unlock\n");
        break;
    case INVALID_HANDLE:
        printf("Handle is invalid\n");
        break;
    case BLOCK_NOT_LOCKED:
        printf("Block was not locked\n");
        break;
    default:
        printf("Unexpected result from xms_unlock: %.4X\n", result);
        break;
    }
result = xms_free(handle);
switch (result)
    {
    case SUCCESS:
        printf("XMS memory freed\n");
        break;
    case FUNCTION_NOT_IMPLEMENTED:
        printf("Function not implemented: xms_free\n");
        break;
    case VDISK_DEVICE_DETECTED:
        printf("VDISK device detected: xms_free\n");
        break;
    case INVALID_HANDLE:
        printf("Handle is invalid\n");
        break;
    case HANDLE_IS_LOCKED:
        printf("Handle is locked\n");
        break;
    default:
        printf("Unexpected result from xms_free: %.4X\n", result);
        break;
    }
result = xms_bstat(handle, &block_status);
switch (result)
    {
    case SUCCESS:
```

continues

Listing 10.7 Continued

```
                printf("Lock count =          %d\n", block_status.lock_count);
                printf("Free handle count = %d\n", block_status.free_handle_count);
                break;
        case FUNCTION_NOT_IMPLEMENTED:
                printf("Function not implemented: xms_bstat\n");
                break;
        case VDISK_DEVICE_DETECTED:
                printf("VDISK device detected: xms_bstat\n");
                break;
        case INVALID_HANDLE:
                printf("Handle is invalid\n");
                break;
        default:
                printf("Unexpected result from xms_bstat: %.4X\n", result);
                break;
        }
    result = xms_unlock(handle);
    switch (result)
        {
        case SUCCESS:
                printf("Block unlocked\n");
                break;
        case FUNCTION_NOT_IMPLEMENTED:
                printf("Function not implemented: xms_unlock\n");
                break;
        case VDISK_DEVICE_DETECTED:
                printf("VDISK device detected: xms_unlock\n");
                break;
        case INVALID_HANDLE:
                printf("Handle is invalid\n");
                break;
        case BLOCK_NOT_LOCKED:
                printf("Block was not locked\n");
                break;
        default:
                printf("Unexpected result from xms_unlock: %.4X\n", result);
                break;
        }
    result = xms_bstat(handle, &block_status);
    switch (result)
        {
        case SUCCESS:
                printf("Lock count =          %d\n", block_status.lock_count);
                printf("Free handle count = %d\n", block_status.free_handle_count);
                break;
        case FUNCTION_NOT_IMPLEMENTED:
                printf("Function not implemented: xms_bstat\n");
                break;
        case VDISK_DEVICE_DETECTED:
                printf("VDISK device detected: xms_bstat\n");
                break;
        case INVALID_HANDLE:
                printf("Handle is invalid\n");
                break;
        default:
```

```c
                printf("Unexpected result from xms_bstat: %.4X\n", result);
                break;
        }
    result = xms_free(handle);
    switch (result)
        {
        case SUCCESS:
            printf("XMS memory freed\n");
            break;
        case FUNCTION_NOT_IMPLEMENTED:
            printf("Function not implemented: xms_free\n");
            break;
        case VDISK_DEVICE_DETECTED:
            printf("VDISK device detected: xms_free\n");
            break;
        case INVALID_HANDLE:
            printf("Handle is invalid\n");
            break;
        case HANDLE_IS_LOCKED:
            printf("Handle is locked\n");
            break;
        default:
            printf("Unexpected result from xms_free: %.4X\n", result);
            break;
        }
    }

void test_umb(void)
    {
    unsigned short    status;
    unsigned short    size;
    struct umb_data   umb;

    status = umb_alloc(0xFFFF, &umb);
    switch (status)
        {
        case SUCCESS:
            printf("We somehow allocated 1Mb of UMBs!\n");
            return;
        case FUNCTION_NOT_IMPLEMENTED:
            printf("UMB alloc not implemented...\n");
            return;
        case SMALLER_UMB_AVAILABLE:
            size = umb.segment_size;
            printf("Smaller UMB available: 0x%.4X paragraphs\n", size);
            break;
        case NO_UMBS_AVAILABLE:
            printf("Sorry, no UMBs available\n");
            return;
        default:
            printf("Unexpected result from umb_alloc(): 0x%.4X\n", status);
            return;
        }
    status = umb_alloc(size, &umb);
    switch (status)
        {
```

continues

Listing 10.7 Continued

```
                case SUCCESS:
                    printf("0x%.4X paragraphs allocated at %.4X:0000\n", umb.segment_size,
                        umb.segment_number);
                    break;
                case FUNCTION_NOT_IMPLEMENTED:
                    printf("UMB alloc not implemented...\n");
                    return;
                case SMALLER_UMB_AVAILABLE:
                    size = umb.segment_size;
                    printf("Smaller UMB available: 0x%.4X paragraphs\n", size);
                    return;
                case NO_UMBS_AVAILABLE:
                    printf("Sorry, no UMBs available\n");
                    return;
                default:
                    printf("Unexpected result from umb_alloc(): 0x%.4X\n", status);
                    return;
                }
        status = umb_free(umb.segment_number);
        switch (status)
                {
                case SUCCESS:
                    printf("UMB successfully freed\n");
                    break;
                case FUNCTION_NOT_IMPLEMENTED:
                    printf("umb_free not implemented...\n");
                    break;
                case INVALID_UMB_SEGMENT:
                    printf("Invalid segment\n");
                    break;
                default:
                    printf("Unexpected result from umb_free: 0x%.4X\n", status);
                    break;
                }
        }

int main()
        {
        unsigned short      result;
        struct XMS_status   status;
        int                 k;
        int                 m;

        result = xms_test();
        switch (result)
                {
                case SUCCESS:
                printf("XMS Detected\n");
                    break;
                case FAILURE:
                    printf("XMS Not Detected\n");
                    return 1;
                default:
                    printf("Invalid result of xms_test(): 0x%.4X\n", result);
                    return 1;
                }
        xms_stat(&status);
```

304

```
printf("XMS Version:         %.2X.%.2X\n", status.version >> 8,
    status.version & 0x00FF);
printf("XMS Driver Revision: %.2X.%.2X\n", status.revision >> 8,
    status.revision & 0x00FF);
printf("HMA existence:       %.4X\n", status.HMA_existence);
if (status.HMA_existence == 1)
    test_hma();
test_xms();
test_umb();
return 0;
}
```

Listing 10.8 is a small library of the extended memory functions used in Listing 10.7. In combination, these functions cover the extended memory operations. The following functions are included in the library:

`_xms_test`	Tests for the presence of the extended memory manager
`_xms_stat`	Gets the version number of the extended memory manager and checks for the existence of the HMA
`_xms_avail`	Gets the size of the largest free block of extended memory
`_xms_alloc`	Requests an extended memory block from the extended memory manager
`_xms_realloc`	Re-allocates an extended memory block, changing its size
`xms_lock`	Locks a block of extended memory
`xms_unlock`	Unlocks a block of extended memory
`xms_bstat`	Gets the status of an extended memory block
`_xms_move`	Moves data into or out of an extended memory block
`_xms_free`	Returns an extended memory block to the extended memory manager
`hma_alloc`	Allocates the HMA
`hma_free`	Releases the HMA
`hma_move`	Moves data into or out of the HMA
`alter_a20`	Enables or disables the A20 line
`a20_stat`	Gets the status of the A20 line
`umb_alloc`	Allocates a UMB
`umb_free`	Frees a UMB

Simple applications of extended memory can start with these basic functions and then grow as error checking and new features are added.

Listing 10.8

```
        page 55,132

; XMSLib.asm
; XMS library functions

XMS_CODE   SEGMENT   'CODE'

public    _xms_test
public    _xms_stat
public    _xms_avail
public    _xms_alloc
public    _xms_realloc
public    _xms_lock
public    _xms_unlock
public    _xms_bstat
public    _xms_move
public    _xms_free
public    _hma_alloc
public    _hma_free
public    _hma_move
public    _alter_a20
public    _a20_stat
public    _umb_alloc
public    _umb_free

ASSUME    CS:XMS_CODE
ASSUME    DS:NOTHING
ASSUME    ES:NOTHING
ASSUME    SS:NOTHING


; Storage for XMS call address

XMS_Control          LABEL      DWORD
XMS_Control_Offset   dw    (?)
XMS_Control_Segment  dw    (?)

; Test for the presence of the XMS driver and, if present,
; get the address of the XMS function call
; Returns AX = 1 if XMS found; otherwise AX = 0

; Borland C++ prototype: unsigned short far xms_test(void);

        ALIGN     16

_xms_test PROC FAR

        push ES           ; Save ES
        mov  AX,04300H     ; See if XMS is present
        int  2FH
        cmp  AL,080H       ; If it is, AL = 80H
        jne  __x_t2

        ; XMS is present; get the function address

        mov  AX,04310H
```

```
        int  2FH
        mov  CS:[XMS_Control_Offset],BX
        mov  CS:[XMS_Control_Segment],ES

        ASSUME   DS:NOTHING

        mov  AX,1          ; Return 1

        ; Return...

__x_t1:
        pop  ES           ; Restore ES
        ret

        ; Return error

__x_t2:
        xor  AX,AX         ; Return 0
        jmp  __x_t1

_xms_test ENDP

; Get XMS status
; Stores the XMS version number, driver revision number,
; and HMA existence flag at the address on the stack

; Borland C++ prototype:
;     void far xms_stat(struct XMS_status far *ptr);

; Data structure:    struct   XMS_status
;                    {
;                    unsigned short version;
;                    unsigned short revision;
;                    unsigned short HMA_existence;
;                    };

        ALIGN    16

_xms_stat PROC FAR
        push SI            ; Save registers
        push DS
        push BP
        mov  BP,SP         ; Set argument pointer
        mov  AH,0          ; call XMS
        call CS:[XMS_Control]
        lds  SI,[BP + 10]  ; Get address of pointer
        mov  [SI],AX       ; Store XMS version number
        mov  [SI + 2],BX   ; Store driver revision number
        mov  [SI + 4],DX   ; Store HMA existence flag
        pop  BP            ; Restore registers
        pop  DS
        pop  SI
        ret               ; Return
_xms_stat ENDP

; Get XMS memory status
```

continues

Listing 10.8 Continued

```
; Stores the size of the largest free XMS block and the total
; amount of free XMS memory at the address on the stack

; Borland C++ prototype:
;    void far xms_avail(struct XMS_memory_status far *ptr);

; Data structure:    struct     XMS_memory_status
;                       {
;                       unsigned short largest_block;
;                       unsigned short total_free_memory;
;                       unsigned short error_status;
;                       };

; Note: the block size and the amount of free memory are in K bytes

            ALIGN    16

_xms_avail    PROC FAR
            push SI            ; Save registers
            push DS
            push BP
            mov  BP,SP         ; Set argument pointer
            xor  BX,BX
            mov  AH,8          ; Call XMS
            call CS:[XMS_Control]
            lds  SI,[BP + 10]  ; Get address of pointer
            mov  [SI],AX       ; Store largest block size
            mov  [SI + 2],DX   ; Store total memory available
            xor  BH,BH
            mov  [SI + 4],BX   ; Store error status
            pop  BP            ; Restore registers
            pop  DS
            pop  SI
            ret                ; Return
_xms_avail    ENDP

; Allocate a block of extended memory
; Returns status in AX:  0001 Success
;                        0080 Function not implemented
;                        0081 VDISK device detected
;                        00A0 All extended memory is allocated
;                        00A1 All extended memory handles are in use

; Borland C++ prototype:
;    unsigned short far xms_alloc(unsigned short size,
;    unsigned short far *handle);

            ALIGN    16

_xms_alloc    PROC FAR
            push SI            ; Save registers
            push DS
            push BP            ; Make pointer to arguments
            mov  BP,SP
            mov  DX,[BP + 10]  ; Get size in kilobytes
```

```
              mov  AH,9            ; Request memory
              call CS:[XMS_Control]
              or   AX,AX           ; Error?
              jz   __x_a2

              ; Set handle and return

    __x_a1:
              lds  SI,[BP + 12]    ; Store handle
              mov  [SI],DX
              pop  BP              ; Restore registers
              pop  DS
              pop  SI
              ret                  ; Return

              ; Return error

    __x_a2:
              mov  AL,BL           ; Get return code
              xor  DX,DX           ; Create NULL handle
              jmp  __x_a1

    _xms_alloc     ENDP

    ; Resize an XMS block
    ; Returns status in AX:    0001 Success
    ;                          0080 Function not implemented
    ;                          0081 VDISK device detected
    ;                          00A0 All extended memory is allocated
    ;                          00A1 All extended memory handles in use
    ;                          00A2 Invalid handle
    ;                          00AB Block is locked

    ; Borland C++ prototype:
    ;    unsigned short far xms_realloc(unsigned short handle,
    ;    unsigned short size);

              ALIGN    16

    _xms_realloc   PROC FAR

              push BP              ; Point to arguments
              mov  BP,SP
              mov  DX,[BP + 6]     ; Get handle
              mov  BX,[BP + 8]     ; Get size
              mov  AH,0FH
              call CS:[XMS_Control]
              or   AX,AX           ; Error?
              jz   __x_r2

              ; return

    __x_r1:
              pop  BP              ; Restore BP
              ret                  ; Return
```

continues

309

Listing 10.8 Continued

```
                ; return error

__x_r2:
        mov  AL,BL          ; Get error code
        jmp  __x_r1

_xms_realloc    ENDP

; Lock a block of XMS memory
; Returns status in AX:  0001 Success
;                        0080 Function not implemented
;                        0081 VDISK device detected
;                        00A2 Invalid handle
;                        00AC Lock count overflow
;                        00AD Lock failed

; Borland C++ prototype:
;    unsigned short far xms_lock(unsigned short handle,
;    unsigned long *linear_address);

        ALIGN   16

_xms_lock PROC FAR
        push BP              ; Save registers
        mov  BP,SP
        push DS
        push SI
        mov  DX,[BP + 6]     ; Get handle
        mov  AH,0CH
        call CS:[XMS_Control]
        or   AX,AX           ; Error?
        jz   __x_l2
        lds  SI,[BP + 8]     ; Get address of pointer
        mov  [SI],BX         ; Store linear address
        mov  [SI + 2],DX

        ; Return

__x_l1:
        pop  SI              ; Restore registers
        pop  DS
        pop  BP
        ret                  ; Return

        ; Return error

__x_l2:
        mov  AL,BL           ; Get error code
        jmp  __x_l1
_xms_lock ENDP

; Unlock a block of XMS memory
; Returns status in AX:  0001 Success
;                        0080 Function not implemented
;                        0081 VDISK device detected
```

```
;                               00A2 Invalid handle
;                               00AA Block was not locked

; Borland C++ prototype:
;     unsigned short far xms_unlock(unsigned short handle);

            ALIGN     16

_xms_unlock     PROC FAR
            push BP                ; Get pointer to argument
            mov  BP,SP
            mov  DX,[BP + 6]       ; Get handle
            mov  AH,0DH
            call CS:[XMS_Control]
            or   AX,AX             ; Error?
            jz   __x_u2

            ; Return

__x_u1:
            pop  BP                ; Restore BP
            ret                    ; Return
__x_u2:
            mov  AL,BL             ; Get error code
            jmp  __x_u1
_xms_unlock     ENDP

; Get status of an XMS block
; Returns status in AX:  0001 Success
;                        0080 Function not implemented
;                        0081 VDISK device detected
;                        00A2 Invalid handle

; Borland C++ prototype:
;     unsigned short far xms_bstat(unsigned short handle,
;     struct bstat far *ptr);

; Data structure:    struct bstat
;                    {
;                    unsigned short lock_count;
;                    unsigned short free_handle_count;
;                    };

            ALIGN     16

_xms_bstat      PROC FAR
            push BP                ; Save registers
            push DS
            push SI
            mov  BP,SP             ; Point to arguments
            mov  DX,[BP + 10]      ; Get handle
            mov  AH,0EH
            call CS:[XMS_Control]
            or   AX,AX             ; Error?
            jz   __x_b2
            lds  SI,[BP + 12]      ; Get pointer to structure
```

continues

311

Listing 10.8 Continued

```
               xor   DX,DX            ; Clear DX
               mov   DL,BH            ; Get lock count
               mov   [SI],DX          ; Store it
               mov   DL,BL            ; Get number of free handles
               mov   [SI + 2],DX      ; Store it

               ; Return

__x_b1:
               pop   SI               ; Restore registers
               pop   DS
               pop   BP
               ret                    ; Return
__x_b2:
               mov   AL,BL            ; Get error code
               jmp   __x_b1
_xms_bstat     ENDP

; Move data to or from an extended memory block
; Returns status in AX:    0001 Success
;                          0080 Function not implemented
;                          0081 VDISK device detected
;                          0082 A20 error occurred
;                          00A3 Invalid source handle
;                          00A4 Invalid source offset
;                          00A5 Invalid destination handle
;                          00A6 Invalid destination offset
;                          00A7 Invalid length
;                          00A8 Invalid overlap on move
;                          00A9 Parity error occurred

; Borland C++ prototype:
;    unsigned short far xms_move(struct XMS_move_data far *ptr);

; Data structure:     struct   XMS_move_data
;                     {
;                     unsigned long   transfer_size;
;                     unsigned short  source_handle;
;                     unsigned long   source_offset;
;                     unsigned short  destination_handle;
;                     unsigned long   destination_offset;
;                     };

               ALIGN    16

_xms_move PROC FAR
               push  BP               ; Save registers
               push  DS
               push  SI
               mov   BP,SP            ; Get argument pointer
               lds   SI,[BP + 10]     ; Get address
               mov   AH,0BH
               call  CS:[XMS_Control]
```

```
            or   AX,AX           ; Error
            jz   __x_m2

            ; Return

__x_m1:
            pop  SI              ; Restore registers
            pop  DS
            pop  BP
            ret                  ; Return

            ; Return error

__x_m2:
            mov  AL,BL           ; Get error code
            jmp  __x_m2
_xms_move ENDP

; Free a block of extended memory
; Returns status in AX:   0001 Success
;                         0080 Function not implemented
;                         0081 VDISK device detected
;                         00A2 Invalid handle
;                         00A4 Handle is locked

; Borland C++ prototype:
;    unsigned short far xms_free(unsigned short handle);

            ALIGN    16

_xms_free PROC FAR
            push BP              ; Make pointer to argument
            mov  BP,SP
            mov  DX,[BP + 6]     ; Get handle
            mov  AH,0AH          ; Free it
            call CS:[XMS_Control]
            or   AX,AX           ; Error?
            jz   __x_f2

            ; Return

__x_f1:
            pop  BP              ; Restore BP
            ret                  ; Return

            ; Return error

__x_f2:
            mov  AL,BL           ; Get error code
            jmp  __x_f1
_xms_free ENDP

; Allocate the HMA
; Returns status in AX:   0001 Success
;                         0080 Function not implemented
;                         0081 VDISK device detected
```

continues

Listing 10.8 Continued

```
;                          0090 HMA does not exist
;                          0091 HMA already in use
;                          0092 Not enough bytes requested

; Borland C++ prototype:
;    unsigned short far hma_alloc(unsigned short size_in_bytes);

             ALIGN    16

_hma_alloc      PROC FAR
             push BP                ; Get pointer to arguments
             mov  BP,SP
             mov  DX,[BP + 6]       ; Get number of bytes
             mov  AH,1              ; Request HMA
             call CS:[XMS_Control]
             or   AX,AX             ; Failure?
             jz   __h_a2            ; If so, get return code

             ; Return

__h_a1:
             pop  BP                ; Restore BP
             ret                    ; Return

             ; Set error code

__h_a2:
             mov  AL,BL             ; Return error code
             jmp  __h_a1
_hma_alloc      ENDP

; Free the HMA
; Returns status in AX:  0001 Success
;                        0080 Function not implemented
;                        0081 VDISK device detected
;                        0090 HMA does not exist
;                        0093 HMA not allocated

; Borland C++ prototype:
;    unsigned short far hma_free(void);

             ALIGN    16

_hma_free PROC FAR
             mov  AH,2              ; Release HMA
             call CS:[XMS_Control]
             or   AX,AX             ; Error?
             jz   __h_f2            ; If so, get code

             ; Return

__h_f1:
             ret                    ; Return

             ; Return error
```

```
__h_f2:
            mov   AL,BL            ; Store error code
            jmp   __h_f1
_hma_free ENDP

; Move data into or out of the HMA

; Borland C++ prototype:
;     void far hma_move(unsigned short count, unsigned short direction,
;             unsigned short hma_offset, void far *data);

; Note: If the direction is zero, data is copied to HMA; otherwise,
;       it is copied from the HMA

            ALIGN 16

_hma_move PROC FAR
            push BP                ; Get pointer to arguments
            mov  BP,SP
            push DS                ; Save registers
            push ES
            push DI
            push SI
            mov  CX,[BP + 6]       ; Get byte count
            mov  AL,[BP + 8]       ; Get direction flag
            or   AL,AL             ; If set, copy from HMA
            mov  AX,0FFFFH         ; Set HMA segment
            jz   __h_m2            ; If clear, copy to HMA

            ; Copy data from HMA

            mov  DS,AX             ; Set source = HMA
            mov  SI,[BP + 10]      ; Get offset
            add  SI,10H            ; Add 10H to offset
            les  DI,[BP + 12]      ; Get destination address

            ; Do move and return

__h_m1:
            cld                    ; Clear direction flag
            shr  CX,1              ; Convert bytes to words
      rep   movsw                 ; Copy data
            adc  CX,0              ; Add carry
      rep   movsb                 ; Copy data
            pop  SI                ; Restore data
            pop  DI
            pop  ES
            pop  DS
            pop  BP
            ret                    ; Return

            ; Copy data to HMA

__h_m2:
            mov  ES,AX             ; Set destination = HMA
            mov  DI,[BP + 10]      ; Get offset
```

continues

Listing 10.8 Continued

```
                add   DI,10H          ; Add 10H to offset
                lds   SI,[BP + 12]    ; Get source address
                jmp   __h_m1
_hma_move ENDP

; Alter the A20 line status
; Valid arguments are (GLOBAL_A20_LINE ¦ ENABLE_A20_LINE)  == 0
;                     (GLOBAL_A20_LINE ¦ DISABLE_A20_LINE) == 1
;                     (LOCAL_A20_LINE ¦ ENABLE_A20_LINE)   == 2
;                     (LOCAL_A20_LINE ¦ DISABLE_A20_LINE)  == 3

; Returns status in AX:  0001 Success
;                        0080 Function not implented
;                        0081 VDISK device detected
;                        0082 A20 error occurred
;                        0094 A20 line still enabled (args 1 and 3)
;                        FFFF Illegal argument

; Borland C++ prototype:
;    unsigned short far alter_a20(unsigned short change_code);

                ALIGN    16

_alter_a20      PROC FAR
                push BP                ; Get pointer to argument
                mov  BP,SP
                mov  AX,[BP + 6]       ; Get argument
                cmp  AX,3              ; Check range
                ja   __a_a2
                mov  AH,AL             ; Create function code
                add  AH,3
                call CS:[XMS_Control]
                or   AX,AX             ; Failure?
                jz   __a_a3
                ; Return

__a_a1:
                pop  BP                ; Restore BP
                ret                    ; Return

                ; Illegal argument

__a_a2:
                mov  AX,-1             ; Return ILLEGAL_ARGUMENT
                jmp  __a_a1

                ; Bad result

__a_a3:
                mov  AL,BL             ; Return error code
                jmp  __a_a1
_alter_a20      ENDP

; Get A20 line status
; Returns status in AX:  0000 A20 disabled
```

```
;                            0001 A20 enabled
;                            0080 Function not implemented
;                            0081 VDISK device detected

; Borland C++ prototype:
;     unsigned short far a20_stat(void);

              ALIGN    16

_a20_stat PROC FAR
          xor  BX,BX
          mov  AH,7           ; Get line status
          call CS:[XMS_Control]
          or   BL,BL          ; Error?
          jnz  __a_s2

          ; Return

__a_s1:
          ret

          ; Return error

__a_s2:
          xor  AX,AX          ; Clear AX
          mov  AL,BL          ; Get error code
          jmp  __a_s1
_a20_stat ENDP

; Allocate an upper memory block
; Returns status in AX:  0001 Success
;                        0080 Function not implemented
;                        00B0 A smaller UMB is available
;                        00B1 No UMBs are available

; Borland C++ prototype:
;     unsigned short far umb_alloc(unsigned short size,
;     struct umb_data far *ptr);

; Data structure:    struct umb_data
;                    {
;                    unsigned short segment_number;
;                    unsigned short segment_size;
;                    };

              ALIGN    16

_umb_alloc    PROC FAR
          push BP             ; Save registers
          push DS
          push SI
          mov  BP,SP          ; Point to arguments
          mov  DX,[BP + 10]   ; Get size
          mov  AH,10H
          call CS:[XMS_Control]
          or   AX,AX          ; Error
```

continues

317

Listing 10.8 Continued

```
                jz    __u_a2
                lds   SI,[BP + 12]    ; Get address of data structure
                mov   [SI],BX         ; Store segment number

                ; Return

__u_a1:
                mov   [SI + 2],DX     ; Store size in paragraphs
                pop   SI              ; Restore registers
                pop   DS
                pop   BP
                ret                   ; Return

                ; Return error

__u_a2:
                mov   AL,BL           ; Store error code
                lds   SI,[BP + 12]    ; Point to data structure
                jmp   __u_a1
_umb_alloc      ENDP

; Free UMB
; Returns status in AX:   0001 Success
;                         0080 Function not implemented
;                         00B2 Invalid segment number

; Borland C++ prototype:
;   unsigned short far umb_free(unsigned short segment);

                ALIGN    16

_umb_free PROC FAR
                push BP               ; Get pointer to argument
                mov  BP,SP            ;
                mov  DX,[BP + 6]      ; Get segment number
                mov  AH,011H
                call CS:[XMS_Control]
                or   AX,AX            ; Error?
                jz   __u_f2

                ; Return

__u_f1:
                pop  BP               ; Restore BP
                ret                   ; Return

                ; Return error

__u_f2:
                mov  AL,BL            ; Get error code
                jmp  __u_f1
_umb_free ENDP

XMS_CODE  ENDS
                END
```

Program Execution

One of DOS's most useful features is its capability to run a program, the child, from within another program, the parent, without losing the original or parent program's current state. On a UNIX system, the function can spin off parallel processes. DOS is similar, but the parent process sleeps (stops functioning) while the new one runs.

Some of the EXEC function's basic features let programs perform the following tasks:

- Spin off a child in the system's free memory

- Wait for the completion of the child's operations

- Receive from the child a return code that can be used for indicating normal completion, error terminations, or status codes

You may have heard that EXEC is difficult to use or dangerous. Nothing could be further from the truth. The V2 edition of EXEC did have a few problems with "growing pains," which are discussed later (along with how to avoid them), but all subsequent versions perform exactly as specified. The function does require that you follow all the rules, but those are made clear.

To use the EXEC function, enough memory must be available to run the new program. (See the discussion earlier in this chapter to learn how to release memory.)

The EXEC Function

When enough program memory is available, you can execute another program with the EXEC function. When you call the EXEC function (Int 21h, Function 4Bh), the registers must be set up like this:

Register	Purpose
AL=0	Load and execute program
DS:DX	Pointer to full path name
ES:BX	Pointer to parameter block

AL can be set to 03h to tell the EXEC function to load into memory an overlay that the parent process already owns. Because overlays are not a factor at this point, you can concentrate on executing programs.

The DS:DX register pair points to the path name of the executable file. The path name can be one of the following:

- The file name of the program to execute, including the .EXE or .COM extension. (In this case, the program must be in the present directory.)

- A relative path name to the file, starting with a dot (.) and giving the directories in the path from the current working directory to the program

- A full path name to the file, which starts at the root directory (\) and goes to the file, and which may include the drive letter and colon

Suppose that you want to execute the DEMO.EXE program in the \UTIL directory. If you are already in the \UTIL directory, you can refer to the program as the following:

```
DEMO.EXE
```

If you are in the \APPL directory, you can refer to the program by its relative path name:

```
.\..\UTIL\DEMO.EXE
```

In this case, you can simplify the path name by starting with the "dot-dot" directory:

```
..\UTIL\DEMO.EXE
```

Finally, from any location, you can always refer to the program as the following:

```
\UTIL\DEMO.EXE
```

A path name must include everything necessary to find the file; it cannot contain wild-card characters. The file name must be spelled out in full and must include the .EXE or .COM extension. Batch files (.BAT extension) cannot be executed directly with the EXEC function, but you can EXEC a copy of COMMAND.COM and pass both the \C option switch and the batch file's name to it as part of the parameter block, which achieves the same result.

Features you might be accustomed to using, such as wild cards in file names or path searches for the file, are functions of COMMAND.COM, not of the EXEC function. COMMAND.COM looks for files by searching the path environment variable. It also executes batch files by using internal batch-file execution procedures. None of this can be done directly with the EXEC function.

The same principle applies to COMMAND.COM internal commands. Commands such as DIR that are internal to COMMAND.COM cannot be executed separately. The trick of copying COMMAND.COM itself with the EXEC command, however, provides a way around these limitations. The one thing the trick does *not* let you do is modify the environment; as you will see, each program copied with the EXEC command gets its own copy of the environment, and changes made there cannot affect the original copy, which is the one used by any subsequent command.

The ES:BX register pair points to a parameter block that contains four additional addresses:

- Environment block (two bytes, segment address)

- Command tail (four bytes, offset then segment)

- File control block 1 (four bytes, offset then segment)

- File control block 2 (four bytes, offset then segment)

The environment block is the collection of program environment variables of the form VARIABLE=VALUE set by DOS or added by your SET instructions. The TMP variable could be set equal to \TMP, a temporary directory area, for example, so that some programs that create temporary files will create them there. The AUTOEXEC.BAT file would have the following line:

```
SET TMP=C:\TMP
```

All such variables together are what you point at with the environment block. For most circumstances, you simply want to retain the environment in which your present program works. Setting the environment block to zero causes EXEC to pass a *copy* of the parent program's environment to the child. This copy is just large enough to contain the data; it has no room for you to add more (doing so would be wasted effort because the copy is released when the child process terminates—the parent never sees it).

The command-tail pointer locates the portion of the command line that follows the command itself. For example, if you type the following command:

```
\BIN\COMMAND /C DIR
the command tail is /C DIR.
```

the command tail is stored as a count byte that gives the command-tail length, the command tail itself, and a carriage return (Function 0Dh). This command tail, fully laid out for use, would look like this:

```
1   2 3 4 5 6 7 8
06h / C   D I R C/R
```

Note that the carriage return is not included in the count.

The last two parameters are initial settings for the file control blocks (FCBs) included in the program segment prefix (PSP). Unless you use FCB functions, either to maintain compatibility with DOS V1 or to permit use of EXEC with other programs that use FCBs, you can safely let them point almost anywhere because you will ignore them. If you do intend to use FCBs, they should be set up as described in Chapter 9, "Directories and Files." These FCBs are copied into the PSP by EXEC.

The program in Listing 10.9 shows the use of the COMMAND.COM trick mentioned earlier; it executes the COMMAND.COM program with the /C DIR command tail. You should note some special features here:

- The stack pointer has not been saved explicitly, even though this function destroys it. `intdos` restores it automatically.

- The segment registers had to be retrieved in order to properly set all the pointers.

- The program simply assumes that COMMAND.COM is located in the root directory of the current drive; it is advisable, for general use, to add code that searches the environment for the COMSPEC= string and then copies all characters following the equal sign. The program then can run when the current drive does not contain COMMAND.COM.

Listing 10.9

```c
/* exectest.c
   Listing 10.9 of DOS Programmer's Reference */

#include <stdio.h>
#include <dos.h>
#include <string.h>

void main()
{
    union REGS regs;
    struct SREGS segs;
    struct {
        int     envblk;     /* Environment block */
        int     ocmd;       /* Command tail */
        int     scmd;
        int     ofcb;       /* FCB #1 */
        int     sfcb;
        int     ofcb2;      /* FCB #2 */
        int     sfcb2;
    } pblock;
    char    buffer[256];
    char    name[128];

    segread(&segs);

    strcpy(name,"\\command.com");
    printf("Executing program %s\n",name);

    /* Set up the command tail */
    buffer[0] = 6;                          /* Number of characters */
    strcpy(buffer+1,"/c dir\015");  /* Command tail */
    pblock.ocmd = (int)buffer;
    pblock.scmd = segs.ds;

    /* Use parent's environment */
    pblock.envblk = 0;

    /* Set up FCBs #1 and #2 */
    pblock.ofcb = (int)buffer;
    pblock.sfcb = segs.ds;
    pblock.ofcb2 = (int)buffer;
    pblock.sfcb2 = segs.ds;

    /* Execute the designated program using the
       EXEC function 4Bh */
    regs.h.ah = 0x4b;
    regs.h.al = 0;
    regs.x.dx = (int)name;
    segs.es = segs.ds;
    regs.x.bx = (int)&pblock;
    intdosx(&regs,&regs,&segs);
```

```
                    /* If the carry flag is set, an error code is
                       in the AX register */
                    if(regs.x.cflag==1)
                        printf("Error Code = %d\n",regs.x.ax);
        }
```

After the program knows the segment register values, it sets up each parameter for the EXEC function call, command tail, environment (the default), and FCBs. Then it executes the function and checks whether any error codes are returned.

C's perfectly good exec() function for running children is preferred in all but the most unusual cases. Turbo Pascal also provides exec(), though the usage is slightly different. As mentioned earlier, neither BASIC nor pre-4.0 versions of Turbo Pascal have such facilities.

Program Exits

One of DOS EXEC's powerful features is its capability to have a program pass back a final status to the program that spawned it. By using Int 21h, Function 4Ch (the preferred exit function), a program can pass back an exit status that can be used for further decision making. UNIX systems use this capability all the time to manage the execution of systems of programs.

One recent example is a program that sequenced a series of other programs through a succession of operations. Depending on how certain programs ended, the main program could provide branches to alternative processing. In this case, the complicated process included interfacing with an IBM mainframe and making intelligent decisions about a database. If the IBM mainframe data transfer did not take place, the "add records to database" step was skipped and the database was processed for use.

The return code from a program is available inside a batch file as the ERRORLEVEL variable, which can be used to branch the logic in the file. If you are executing the program from another program, the parent can get the return code from the child by calling Int 21h, Function 4Dh after the EXEC function returns. Register AH has one of the following exit types:

Exit Code	Meaning
00	Normal termination
01	Terminated by a Ctrl-C command
02	Critical device error
03	TSR return (Int 21h, Function 31h)

Register AL has the return code from the child process.

Possible EXEC Problems

This chapter has hinted that the DOS V2 edition of EXEC had potential problems and promised to provide you with a way to avoid them. This section presents the information.

The problem usually is apparent only when you work in assembly language; high-level languages seem to provide the solution as part of their normal DOS interfacing. The problem stems from the fact that the V2 DOS routines which perform the EXEC function begin by using block-move instructions to transfer all the blocks of data into DOS's own workspace. Block moves are controlled by a *direction* flag in the CPU chip. If this flag is set, the address passed is assumed to be the *end* of the block; therefore, the block of data ending at that address is moved. If the flag is clear, the address is taken to be the *start*, and a different block of data is moved.

The EXEC function assumed that the flag was clear but never did anything to guarantee that this was the case. Consequently, if the flag was set when EXEC was invoked, what happened next was not at all what the DOS designers intended. Most often, the system simply locked up because it was using a set of binary machine instructions as a file name and therefore was trying to load and execute a nonexistent file.

This problem was corrected in V3 by adding a CLD instruction at the beginning of the EXEC code to make sure that the flag was properly clear. The cure for V2 is to issue the CLD instruction yourself, immediately before the Int 21h that calls the EXEC function.

The only other potential pitfall, which applies to all versions and is fully documented, is that no registers except CS and IP are preserved across the call. This means that you *must* save both SS and SP in locations you can address with CS when you come back, or you will lose control of your program.

Entering a Command to DOS

When you enter a command, DOS first separates the command name from the command parameters. DOS then checks whether the command is an internal command. The code required to execute internal commands (such as CLS or DIR) is in the DOS command-line interpreter. Because these commands are checked first, you cannot write your own program named DIR and have it execute from the DOS command line. Methods exist, however, for superseding and adding to the DOS internal commands, depending on the version of DOS you are running.

Assuming that the command was not found to be an internal command, the disk system is searched for an appropriate file. The current working directory is searched for the file name, with the .COM, .EXE, and then .BAT extension, in that order. If no exact match is found in the current working directory, every directory in the PATH string of the environment variables is searched for the three names. If no file is found after exhausting the PATH, the `Bad filename or command` message is displayed and DOS returns to the prompt.

If a batch file (.BAT extension) is found, the DOS batch file interpreter is given control of the file. Otherwise, the DOS EXEC function (Function 04BH, Subfunction 000H) is invoked. If the first two bytes of the file are MZ, the file is treated as an EXE-type file, regardless of the extension. You can guarantee, therefore, that an EXE file is loaded first by renaming it with the .COM extension. A new program segment prefix (PSP) is created, the COM file is copied verbatim into memory, the segment registers are set to the paragraph in memory where the program is written, and control is passed to CS:00100H. What happens to the EXE file is a little more complex (see fig. 10.4).

As with the COM file, a PSP is created; the EXE file, less the EXE header, is loaded into memory above the PSP, at an address we will call the load address. The DS and ES registers are set to point to the PSP. The CS:IP and SS:SP registers are set from the values in the EXE header, with the load address segment added to the CS and SS registers.

Finally, the relocation table in the EXE header is used to modify segment references in the image. The relocation table consists of segment:offset pointers. These pointers are addresses of words in the image; the addresses are relative to the load address. The words pointed to, in turn, are segment values in the program. The word pointed to has the load address segment added to it. In this way, the program's segment references are modified to compensate for the address in memory where the program is loaded.

Superseding DOS's Internal Commands

There are three main techniques for superseding DOS's internal commands. The first, and the one guaranteed to work for all versions of DOS, is to modify COMMAND.COM directly with DEBUG or the third-party file editing utility of your choice and change the name of the command. This method is not difficult because the list of names in COMMAND.COM is easy to pinpoint. You can retain the utility of the original internal command's name by changing one of the letters in the name to another uppercase letter, such as changing *COPY* to *KOPY*. If you want to abolish the internal command, change one of the letters to lowercase, such as *COPY* to *cOPY*. The *cOPY* command will never be matched to the command that is typed in.

The second method, which works with DOS Version 3.0 and later, is to specify the full path for your name-alike. The example

```
C:\DOSCLONE\COPY *.*
```

invokes your version of COPY.

The third method, which works with DOS Version 3.3 and later, is to create a TSR that chains to DOS Interrupt 2F, intercepting Function 0AEH, Subfunctions 000H and 001H. These interrupt functions are called by DOS before it checks its own internal list of commands.

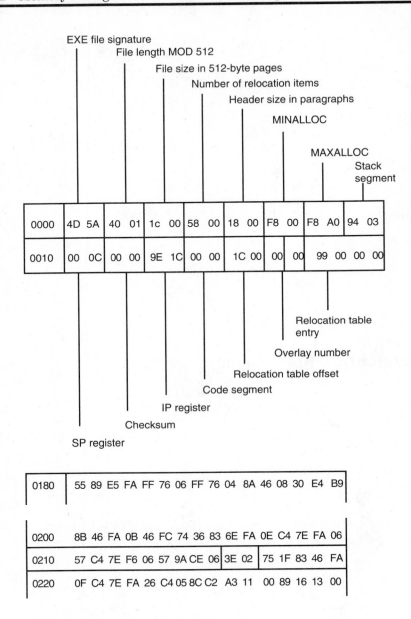

Figure 10.4 EXE file header.

The first call, to Function 0AEH, Subfunction 000H, is made with DS and ES pointing to DOS's transient area, with BX pointing to a buffer containing two count bytes and an exact copy of the DOS command line, and SI pointing to a buffer containing the command word from the command line, converted to uppercase and preceded by its character count. If your command (or one of your commands) matches the SI buffer *exactly*, it should set AL to 0FFH and return. Otherwise, it should chain to the previous interrupt handler.

In the second call, to Function 0AEH, Subfunction 001H, the registers are set as before. The data pointed to by BX, however, might have changed in the interim. It is a good idea, therefore, to copy the command-line parameters to an internal buffer while servicing the 000H Subfunction call. After executing your code, you should clear the character count in the DS:SI command buffer so that DOS knows that you executed your code.

The code you execute does not need to do anything except clear the character count. Although the code has done nothing useful, DOS is satisfied that useful work has been done. This is a convenient way to eliminate troublesome DOS internal commands, such as DEL or ERASE.

Why Some EXE Files Cannot Be Converted to COM Files

EXE2BIN does not convert an EXE file into a COM file if it fails to meet the following simple criteria:

- The EXE file must have the MZ signature in its header

- The SS:SP reference in the header must be 0000:0000

- The CS:IP reference must be either 0000:0100 or 0000:0000 (for device drivers)

- The number of items in the relocation table must be zero

The Program Segment Prefix

The program segment prefix (PSP) is a 256-byte block of data that DOS constructs for every program it runs. The PSP contains information for the program to use, in addition to information DOS needs to maintain. Table 10.1 shows the structure of the PSP.

The code at PSP:0000 and PSP:0005 are remnants of the early days of DOS when compatibility with CP/M was an issue; they function the same as CP/M CALL 0000 and CALL 0005.

Table 10.1 PSP Structure

Offset	Contents	Meaning
000H–001H	CD 20	Call to the DOS terminate routine
002H–003H	Varies	Segment address of the top of the program's allocated memory block
004H	00	Filler
005H–009H	Varies	FAR CALL to Int 21H dispatcher
00AH–00DH	Varies	Int 22H vector
00EH–011H	Varies	Int 23H vector
012H–015H	Varies	Int 24H vector
016H–017H	Varies	Segment of the parent process PSP
018H–02BH	01 01 01 00 02 FF FF FF FF FF FF FF FF FF FF FF FF FF FF FF	Indices to the system file table
02CH–02DH	Varies	Segment address of the environment copy
02EH–031H	00 00 00 00	SS:SP storage
032H–033H	14 00	Number of file handles available
034H–037H	Varies	Pointer to the file handle table
038H–03BH	Varies	SHARE's previous PSP
03CH–04FH	00 00 00 00 00 00 00 00 00 00 00 00 00 00 00 00 00 00 00 00	Unused
050H–052H	CD 21 CB	Call to Int 21H and RETF
053H–05BH	00 00 00 00 00 00 00 00 00	Unused
05CH–06BH	Varies	Default FCB 1
06CH–07FH	Varies	Default FCB 2
080H	Varies	Command tail count
081H–0FFH	Varies	Command tail

The segment address at PSP:0002 can be used by the program to determine whether enough memory is allocated to it.

The vector addresses at PSP:000A, PSP:000E, and PSP:0012 are restored by MS-DOS on exit. Programmers are warned not to amend any values below PSP:005C, but PSP:000E and PSP:0012 (the Ctrl-C and critical error handler vectors, respectively) can be modified without harm. The vector at PSP:000A is actually the return address of the parent process, immediately following the DOS EXEC call. This address can be modified to point to a user-defined procedure that can unhook any special handlers the program might have installed. The procedure then must return to the original vector at PSP:000A. When the procedure is invoked, all program memory has been freed, files have been closed, and the PSP is set to that of the parent process. No file access or other I/O should be attempted.

The parent process PSP can be used to trace the PSP chain back to the parent COMMAND.COM, whose PSP shows itself as its own parent. This COMMAND.COM may not be the master COMMAND.COM; it can be a shell.

The indices to the system file table refer to open handles for stdin, stdout, stderr, stdaux, and stdprn. The value FF refers to unopened handles. The value at PSP:0032 and the pointer at PSP:0034 can be changed to reflect a different handle table; the value at PSP:0034 is initialized as PSP:0018.

The environment segment address can be used to access the program's copy of the environment. You can trace back the parent's PSP to access and modify the parent's environment. Again, there is no guarantee that this is the master environment.

DOS uses the SS:SP storage at PSP:002E to store the program's SS:SP on entry to Int 21H. This capability enables DOS to perform multitasking, but it has not been exploited yet.

The pointer at PSP:0038H is used to store the parent PSP when SHARE is in use under DOS 3.3 and later. Before DOS 3.3, the pointer at PSP:0038H is set to FFFF:FFFF.

The code at PSP:0050H provides another mechanism to access Int 21H, this time with a far call.

The FCBs are for use by programs using FCB-style file I/O. They are loaded with the first two parameters in the command tail, under the assumption that these parameters are file names. This is another holdover from the CP/M days.

The command tail count is the length of the command tail. The command tail is the remainder of the command, from after the command name to the carriage return at the end. The command tail count does not count the carriage return. If a command has no parameters, its command tail count is 0, and the carriage return code (0DH) is found at PSP:0081.

The command tail and command tail count are also set up by DOS as the default disk transfer area (DTA). This capability, another holdover from CP/M, is of use if you use FCB file handling.

Memory-Resident Programming

The TSR utility is a hot item for programming PCs. Borland's introduction of SideKick caused a major upheaval in the PC software market. So many TSR utilities are available now that, if you used them all, you would have no room for executable programs. We always seem to want more TSRs than we can possibly accommodate.

Most people do not realize that what they consider to be a TSR is only one of two types of TSRs that can be set up and used. The TSR utility (like SideKick and others) was not the TSR function's intended purpose. TSRs originally were seen as extensions of the operating system.

The two types of TSRs are shown in this list:

- *Active TSRs.* These pop-up utilities, such as SideKick, are the most common type of TSRs. They usually are operated by responding to a specified keystroke called the hot key. When these utilities are activated, they take over the computer and perform their function before they return control to the program that originally controlled the machine.

- *Inactive TSRs.* These TSRs respond when a calling program calls a designated interrupt. When they are called, they perform a defined function, similar to a subroutine, and then return control to the calling program.

Active TSRs give users the impression of multitasking on a PC. TSRs do not actually multitask, but you get the impression that more than one operation is happening simultaneously. To give this illusion of operation, active TSRs are complex. As you know, DOS is not reentrant (you cannot break out of the middle of an internal DOS routine and restart it from somewhere else). If DOS is processing something (a disk access, for example) when a TSR activates to write something to the disk, you can cause serious problems and possibly mess up your disk.

Active TSRs have to watch what both DOS and users do. You see some of these tricks in Chapter 11's discussion of TSRs as interrupt service routines.

Inactive TSRs work in a benign environment. An inactive TSR starts nothing until it is called by a program. Because DOS is a single-tasking environment, only one operation can be in progress at a time and you know that no DOS operation can be in progress when the TSR is called. Therefore, you are safe using DOS calls from an inactive TSR.

The TSR concept has undergone some major changes since DOS was introduced. The original TSR function (Int 27h) has been superseded by Int 21h, Function 31h. This function is more convenient to use because it allows a return code to be passed and lets the TSR use more than 64K of memory. Both these factors justify the use of the preferred TSR call: Int 21h, Function 31h.

When a TSR runs, it sets up its memory tables and prepares for execution by connecting to a DOS interrupt. When everything is ready, the program determines how much memory it needs to keep; then it sets AH to 31h, AL to the return code, and DX to the number of paragraphs

(16-byte blocks) to allocate to the TSR. When the program exits, the amount of memory available for executing programs is reduced by the amount assigned to the TSR, and the exit code passes back to the parent.

Sounds simple, doesn't it? It can be—for extremely simple TSRs. If you are writing the next SideKick utility, however, you will find that much more is involved than simply executing the TSR.

First, you must have a way to trigger the TSR's action. You can attach the TSR to the timer interrupt and activate the TSR's operation every specified number of seconds. More often, you attach the TSR to the keyboard service interrupt and look for a certain keystroke. With a proliferation of TSRs, collisions will occur because most keystrokes are used somewhere.

No matter how you attach a TSR to a system, the TSR must recognize the possible presence of other TSRs in the system. To allow other operations to occur on the trigger, a TSR must call the interrupt service routine that originally handled the interrupt before the start of the TSR. Furthermore, to prevent overlap with other functions, you should be able to change the keystrokes that trigger the TSR.

When you deal with DOS functions, TSRs and interrupt service routines (ISRs) are in the same danger. The MS-DOS system was always intended to be a single-user, single-task system and therefore is not reentrant. Because an active TSR or ISR responds to events that may not be synchronized to the operation of DOS functions, it is possible for a TSR or ISR to get control of the computer while an internal DOS function is in progress. Several undocumented DOS functions help you to determine when the use of DOS functions is safe and when it is not. These undocumented functions are discussed in Chapter 11, "Interrupt Handlers."

Writing a successful TSR can be a major project, well worth a book of its own. A sophisticated TSR that includes many subfunctions, windows, and other features can take a team of sophisticated programmers a long time to implement. You build a simple TSR in Chapter 11 after you have learned enough about interrupts to make them work for you.

Summary

This chapter has discussed memory management, expanded memory, and program execution. You have learned that TPA (transient program area) memory is allocated by DOS to fill requests from programs that need memory. When programs start, they normally get all available memory in which to work and should release any memory that they will not use.

Assembly language programmers must explicitly release memory. Programmers who use C or the latest versions of Turbo Pascal have it done by the start-up code for their programs. BASIC and other Pascal programmers cannot release memory except at compile time.

Expanded memory gives you access to additional memory by paging a large amount of memory into the addressable 1M of PC memory. You can use this memory in 16K pages to store and retrieve data. To do so, you use the Int 67h function calls, which are detailed in the "EMS Reference" section at the end of this book.

Extended memory gives you access to additional memory by taking advantage of the capability of the 80286, 80386, and 80486 to address more than the conventional 1M of PC memory. You can use this memory in arbitrary units of 1K to store and retrieve data. To do so, you use the XMS function calls, which are detailed in the "XMS Reference" section at the end of this book.

When you have enough memory available, DOS lets you run programs from within other programs (just as COMMAND.COM does). You can use this memory to tie together individual programs into a software system. TSRs (terminate and stay resident programs) enable you to create programs that coexist in memory while other programs are operating. With the techniques discussed in Chapter 11, "Interrupt Handlers," you can create TSRs that can be invoked from the keyboard to give the impression of multitasking.

11

Interrupt Handlers

This chapter looks deep into the DOS system to discuss something that has a reputation for obscurity unlike anything else in computer programming: interrupt handlers. In simplest terms, interrupt handlers are nothing but programs that respond to the activation of an interrupt.

You may find that interrupt handling is really not so bad. At some levels, in fact, it is easily managed. There are still a few "black holes," however, that you can drop into and never escape. The information in this chapter can keep you from getting lost.

Interrupts have been around for years. Part of their unsavory reputation was gained when they were first introduced as a major part of system design. On early computer systems, interrupts were often a major headache because programmers had no experience working with them and took unjustified shortcuts.

Interrupts have been the domain of systems programmers and hardware engineers for so long that many programmers are afraid to touch them. Luckily, a PC is a relatively benign place to work with interrupts. The problems you may have are managed simply if you write your interrupt handlers according to some general guidelines. As you gain experience, you will be able to control interrupts without thinking about it.

This chapter starts with a description of interrupts. It includes a discussion of interrupts generated by internal and external hardware in addition to those generated in software. As the discussion proceeds, you should begin to develop a feel for how interrupts can serve you. Some practical examples round out the interrupt-handling discussion.

After you learn about interrupts, the chapter returns to a discussion that was begun in the last chapter—the discussion of terminate-and-stay-resident (TSR) utilities. Nearly every TSR attaches itself in some way to an interrupt and responds to it as an interrupt service routine (ISR). This chapter describes what makes a good TSR and discusses instances when using one does not make sense.

Let's start at the most basic level by trying to find out what an interrupt is.

What Is an Interrupt?

An *interrupt* is a signal to the processor that an event needing special attention has happened. It is used to catch the processor's attention for something important. If you did not have interrupts, you would have to *poll* every device periodically and check whether it had something for you.

If you have 60 devices on a polled system and checking a device takes one second, every device is checked one time per minute. If you need a faster response to a condition in this example, polling is just not suitable. That is the reason that interrupts were invented: to eliminate the need for polling and the resulting slow service for external events.

An interrupt may occur, for example, when a disk drive signals that it has a sector of information ready to transfer to main memory. If the processor is slow in responding to the interrupt, the block is lost, so the processor is forced to put "on hold" whatever it is doing and immediately pick up the interrupt.

Interrupts such as the one in the preceding example are caused by external events. They can be caused also by internal events, such as a divide-by-zero error in a calculation or a program's specific request to execute a software interrupt—including the ubiquitous Int 21h, used for virtually every DOS function.

Whenever your computer senses an interrupt condition, it saves whatever it is doing, "marks its place" in the program, and transfers control to an interrupt handler, which is expected to service the condition and then return. Some processors provide only restricted interrupt identification and depend on the interrupt handler to identify the interrupt and take appropriate action.

Interrupts are handled more efficiently on the 8086 family of processors by using *interrupt vectors* to speed you on your way to a specific interrupt handler. An interrupt vector is a far pointer (32 bits, in offset:segment form) to the actual handler routine; in the 8086 family, the first 1,024 bytes of RAM are dedicated to providing 256 such vectors for the interrupts the processor can recognize.

Programming interrupt handlers has been a somewhat arcane art, known to only an enlightened few, especially on some older computer systems. Interrupt handling on some systems involved issues of precise timing and a knowledge of the intricacies of processor and computer design that went far beyond what typical programmers ever encountered. On systems in which interrupts can occur, multilevel interrupt errors are the bane of all programmers' existence because the path to an error may be random at best and nearly impossible to find.

Interrupts on PCs, however, are relatively well behaved both because PCs are single-user, single-process systems and because the interrupt structure is much more sophisticated. You still have to be careful, but you can use this standard interrupt structure to handle the following situations:

1. Save anything that the processor did not save automatically when the interrupt occurred. (On a PC, this means all registers that might be changed during the handler's operation; it is safest to just save all of them, except CS, IP, SS, and SP, by pushing them onto the stack.)

2. Block any interrupts that might interfere with the handler's operation.

3. Enable interrupts that can occur safely during the handler's operation.

4. Handle the interrupt.

5. Restore the processor registers saved in step 1.

6. Reenable interrupts.

7. Return to normal processing.

Although this prescription does not guarantee good interrupt handling, it does guide you through this nest of vipers with your eyes open.

You already have encountered one situation, serial I/O, that cannot be handled effectively unless you tie an interrupt handler to the serial port. Microsoft BASIC provides an internal interrupt handler for communications that enables you to do serial I/O. In C, Pascal, or assembly language, you have to write your own handler.

The Ctrl-Break/Ctrl-C handler is another useful interrupt handler. For many programs, Ctrl-Break leaves the program in a bad state—with files not updated and so forth. To close down the program in an orderly manner, a Ctrl-Break handler lets your program control the exit.

How Interrupts Work

When an interrupt occurs, the processor can be in any state. A processor is designed so that it always completes any step in progress before it responds to an interrupt. When the processor recognizes an interrupt, it responds by pushing the flag register (the program status word), the instruction pointer (IP), and the code segment register (CS) on the stack and disabling interrupts.

After this critical machine-state information is saved, the processor looks to the system bus for an 8-bit number, the *interrupt request level* (IRQ). This level identifies exactly which device has issued the interrupt and lets the processor know which vector to use in response. As already explained, interrupt vectors are pointers to the actual handler routines for specific functions.

In the PC (and its successors), a fixed offset of 8 is added to the number supplied by the interrupting device to determine the interrupt that is signaled. IRQ level 0 generates Int 08h, for example, and IRQ level 7 generates Int 0Fh. (This process is modified somewhat in the AT and PS/2 designs, which recognize more than eight levels of interrupt request, but the principle remains the same.)

The processor multiplies the Int number by 4 to obtain the offset into the *interrupt vector table* and then looks in segment 0000h to find the vector. The contents of the vector are put in CS:IP, and control automatically transfers to the first instruction of the program that processes the interrupt (the interrupt handler).

After the processor is in the interrupt handler, the handler controls the processor. Most handlers first reenable interrupts so that higher-priority interrupts can be serviced. They also save any other registers they use and then carry out their own operations as quickly as possible. For some devices, a special acknowledgment signal must be passed so that the device knows that it has been serviced. The handler must provide this where necessary.

Interrupt handlers generally must be written to be as tight and as fast as possible. Most of them are written in assembly language to eliminate all possible overhead and to ensure that the routine runs as quickly as possible. You can write handlers in C (some C examples are in this chapter), but time-critical interrupts should be handled with as little overhead as possible.

Interrupts triggered through the 8259A Programmable Interrupt Controller (PIC)—the hardware interrupts generated by IRQ levels—must send an end-of-interrupt signal to the PIC when the processing is finished. All interrupts must restore the machine state by first restoring any registers saved and then executing an interrupt return (IRET) instruction that restores the flag register, CS, and IP to the values that existed before the interrupt occurred.

The Intel 8086 Family Interrupts

Interrupts on the 8086 microprocessor family come in three basic classes. This section describes all three types of interrupts:

- Internal hardware
- External hardware
- Software

Internal Hardware Interrupts

Internal hardware interrupts are designed into a processor to handle special cases, such as a divide-by-zero error or other conditions in which a processor has recognized an error. These conditions are listed in Table 11.1.

Table 11.1 Internal Hardware Interrupts

Interrupt Level	Vector Offset Address	Meaning
8086 Processor Hardware Interrupts		
00h	00h	Divide by zero
01h	04h	Single step
02h	08h	Non-maskable interrupt
03h	0Ch	Break point
04h	10h	Overflow
80286 Processor Hardware Interrupts		
05h	14h	Bound range exceeded
06h	18h	Invalid opcode
07h	1Ch	Processor extension not available
08h	20h	Double exception
09h	24h	Segment overrun
0Ah	28h	Invalid task-state segment
0Bh	2Ch	Segment not present
0Ch	30h	Stack segment overrun
0Dh	34h	General-protection fault

We do not program directly with any of these interrupts. In the basic PC design, IBM reassigned some of these interrupts (which were not used by the original 8086/8088 design but were reserved for future expansion) to deal with other conditions. When the next-generation chip (80186) appeared, a conflict arose, and remains to this day, between what is designed into the 8086 family chips and what IBM has used the interrupt vectors for. This situation is not a good one, but you have to deal with it. Table 11.2 lists the IBM-assigned interrupt vectors. Compare Tables 11.1 and 11.2 to see the conflicts.

Table 11.2 Interrupt Vectors

Vector	Action
00h	Divide by zero
01h	Single step
02h	Non-maskable interrupt

continues

337

Table 11.2 Continued

Vector	Action
03h	Break point
04h	Overflow
05h	Print screen
06h	Unused
07h	Unused
08h	Hardware IRQ0 (timer tick)
09h	Keyboard input interrupt
0Ah	Reserved
0Bh	Asynchronous port controller 1 (COM2)
0Ch	Asynchronous port controller 0 (COM1)
0Dh	Fixed disk controller
0Eh	Floppy disk controller
0Fh	Printer controller
10h	Video driver
11h	Equipment-configuration check
12h	Memory-size check
13h	Floppy disk/fixed disk (PC/XT)
14h	Comm port driver
15h	Cassette/network service
16h	Keyboard driver
17h	Printer driver
18h	ROM BASIC
19h	Restart system
1Ah	Set/read real-time clock
1Bh	Ctrl-Break handler
1Ch	Timer tick (user defined)
1Dh	Video parameter table
1Eh	Disk parameter table
1Fh	Graphics character table (characters 80h–FFh)
20h	Program terminate
21h	DOS function dispatcher
22h	Terminate vector

Vector	Action
23h	Ctrl-C vector
24h	Critical-error vector
25h	Absolute disk read
26h	Absolute disk write
27h	Terminate and stay resident
28h	DOS OK interrupt
2Fh	Multiplex interrupt (see reference section)
40h	Floppy disk driver (PC/XT)
41h	Fixed disk parameter table
43h	Graphics character table

External Hardware Interrupts

External hardware can be tied to the processor to allow the device to signal an interrupt. Most early microcomputer systems that used interrupts were built this way. Two connections are available: the non-maskable interrupt (NMI) and the maskable interrupt (INTR). As the names imply, you can turn off the INTR, but you cannot turn off the NMI.

NMI interrupts are used for problems in which you do not want the interrupt turned off for any reason. On some systems, a physical reset switch wired to an NMI interrupt lets operators get the processor's attention—no matter what.

INTR interrupts are wired through the 8259A PIC to take advantage of the chip's capability to prioritize and control interrupts under software control. Processor instructions can directly enable or disable interrupts, and instructions to the PIC can selectively enable and disable interrupts.

The interrupts, however, are set at the hardware level. In some cases, manufacturers set the interrupt levels, and nothing can change them. Some devices provide switches or jumpers that can reset the interrupt level within a limited range of values.

Software Interrupts

Software interrupts are caused by a program issuing the software interrupt instruction to make the processor act as though it received a hardware interrupt. This method is convenient for accessing DOS and BIOS services independent of any one program. The services can be linked to specific interrupts and changed at will without affecting applications programs that call them.

Interrupt Vectors

The interrupt vector table is stored in the lowest 1,024 bytes of system memory with 4 bytes per interrupt, for a total of 256 distinct interrupt vectors. Every 4-byte entry is composed of the segment number and offset of the interrupt handler for that function. In several cases, a vector contains the address of a table of data values rather than the address of a routine—such as the graphics-character table pointed to by Int 1Fh.

Getting and Setting Interrupt Vectors

All the cautions about interrupt vectors should warn you that anything affecting the interrupt vectors can have damaging side effects. Imagine that you are two bytes into changing an interrupt vector four bytes long and you are interrupted by another process that needs the vector you are changing; the CPU jumps to an incomplete vector address and can end up virtually anywhere in memory. This situation most often results in "hanging" your computer, but *could* erase your hard disk.

How realistic is this scenario? DOS is a single-task system, in which only one operation can happen at a time. Another interrupt service routine, however, responding to a hardware interrupt, simply takes control and leaves your program halfway through it. Many TSRs take control of interrupts when the TSR is activated and then return the interrupts to their original settings when the TSR is finished. This situation *can* happen. In programming, anything that *can* happen eventually *will*; the only question is whether it will happen sooner or later.

More important is the upward-compatibility issue. Modifying an interrupt vector directly is not compatible with future DOS upgrades (including OS/2, if you want to view it as an upgrade). Although direct modification works now, it is guaranteed not to work on a multitasking system. DOS, however, provides a safe way to change the interrupt vectors by using Int 21h, Functions 25h (Set Interrupt Vector) and 35h (Get Interrupt Vector).

To set an interrupt vector, follow these steps:

1. Use Function 35h to get the current vector value and store it for later use in chaining to any routine already using the interrupt and in restoring the interrupt.

2. Use Function 25h to set the new vector.

This process is simple in assembly language (see Listing 11.1).

Listing 11.1

```
; GetSet.asm

;----- Get the Ctrl-C vector -----
        mov     ah,35h          ;Get vector
        mov     al,23h          ;Ctrl-C
```

```
        int     21h
        mov     oldseg,es           ;Store old vector
        mov     oldoff,bx

;----- Set the Ctrl-C vector -----
        mov     ah,25h              ;Set vector
        mov     al,23h              ;Ctrl-C
        mov     dx, seg c_hand
        mov     ds,dx
        mov     dx, offset c_hand
        int     21h
```

You do not have to go down to the DOS level to set the interrupts. The available high-level language services help set them cleanly and eliminate concern about encountering a problem. These high-level language routines are more convenient ways of performing the Int 21h, Functions 25h and 35h services.

Borland C/C++ provides two functions, `getvect` and `setvect`, that do the same thing as DOS Functions 35h and 25h without calling the DOS functions. In Microsoft C/C++, the `_dos_getvect` and `_dos_setvect` functions perform the same actions. In Turbo Pascal, the `GetIntVec` and `SetIntVec` functions perform the same actions.

When Should You Write an Interrupt Handler?

Creating an interrupt handler of your own makes sense in the following situations:

- *When you have to trap an interrupt to keep your program from failing in unusual cases.* When you write commercial programs, you should never let users "bomb out" of your program on a divide-by-zero error or on some other error. Your program should handle the error. Furthermore, if your program performs any "fancy" operations, you should trap Ctrl-C and Ctrl-Break events and handle them rather than let the system cut you off.

- *When you have to link into an interrupt chain.* Here are two examples: writing a TSR that executes on certain keystrokes and writing a special timing routine you want to do in a program.

- *When you have to control the serial port.* As mentioned, DOS does not provide adequate service for the serial ports. If you want to write a real terminal program, it must have an interrupt-driven, serial-port servicing routine.

In cases other than the ones just described, you should attempt to make your code as high-level as possible. If you can code the interrupt handler in a high-level language, by all means, do so, unless the interrupt handler simply does not run fast enough in your program. Debugging is much easier in a high-level language than in assembly language. You can always recode the handler if it is not fast enough.

341

Wherever possible, take advantage of the high-level language facilities for interrupt handling. Borland C/C++ provides the `ctrlbrk()` function for setting a Ctrl-C interrupt handler from a high-level code module. Microsoft C/C++ provides the UNIX-compatible `signal()` function for handling signal traps. QuickBASIC provides the ON KEY and TIMER commands (in addition to others) for handling events. Turbo Pascal can handle interrupts that have in-line assembly code or that use the `Interrupt` directive. Choose the highest level that can do the job.

When you write an interrupt handler, do not use DOS-type functions unless special care is taken. DOS is not reentrant; if it is interrupted while it is doing something, you can easily cause the system to lock up by calling DOS functions again.

One way not to invoke DOS functions is to have the interrupt handler do some setup processing (copy data to a memory buffer, for example). It can set a flag that can be recognized by the program currently using the system to do some additional processing, which might involve DOS calls. More to the point, DOS has some hidden ways to determine when DOS calls are safe. Hackers who spend their time trying to determine how other people perform computer techniques have discovered and published some ways to learn what DOS does.

First, an Int 21h function (Function 34h) returns a pointer in the ES:BX registers. This pointer points to a DOS busy flag, called the *InDOS flag*. The flag is a single byte buried in the operating-system kernel. Whenever an Int 21h function starts, the flag is incremented by one. When the function ends, the flag is decremented by one. Whenever the flag is zero, no DOS functions are executing.

TSRs check for this flag whenever their hot key is pressed. If the flag is nonzero, the TSR sets a hot-key flag in the TSR. TSRs that do this tie into the clock interrupt and check the status of InDOS 18.2 times per second until the flag clears. When InDOS is clear and the hot-key flag is set, the TSR starts its operations.

That process is good, but it leaves you hanging when the command processor is waiting for you to type a command line. Because the command processor uses DOS functions for command-line input, the InDOS flag is set while DOS waits for characters. Clearly, DOS is in a safe position and can be interrupted for other operations if you do not use the DOS functions to do any console I/O. To allow console I/O to occur, DOS has another interrupt, 28h, which is called repeatedly by the console input routines while they are waiting. This is the DOS Idle (or DOSOK) interrupt.

The DOS Idle interrupt normally does an IRET, which returns control to the console input routine. If a TSR is tied to the interrupt and notices that the hot-key flag is on, the body of the TSR can be executed immediately.

When you work with interrupts, be sure to follow a simple rule: *Always* assume that other programs may be involved. For example, you should never set interrupt vectors directly. Int 21h, Function 25h is provided for this purpose and prevents any mix-ups between programs setting the vectors. Unless you write something such as a Ctrl-C handler, you should preserve the original handler vector and branch to it when you complete your processing. You also can install another handler, which needs to be activated. If you do not observe this simple rule, you can get into trouble.

When your program ends, it must clear any interrupt handlers it has set (the system automatically takes care of critical error and Ctrl-C handlers). If you write a terminal program, for example, you should restore the original interrupt handlers before you leave the program, therefore preventing an interrupt from branching to where your handler *used* to be. If your program is setting up a resident handler, you should use the TSR exit so that the handler will be permanently allocated the memory it needs and will not be overwritten.

Writing a Ctrl-C Handler

A simple Ctrl-C handler serves as an example of interrupt handling. This handler is presented in several stages to show you several methods for handling the interrupt problem.

In the first example, `handler.c`, the `ctrlbrk()` function has been used in Borland C/C++ to create a handler totally in C (see Listing 11.2). `Handler.c` enables you to interrupt the process in progress and determine whether to leave. Because the `ctrlbrk()` function handles aborts, you return the appropriate code to the routine, depending on the answer to the question. This method of writing the routine is particularly convenient because it is high level, works the first time, and involves no arcane programming. Furthermore, Borland C/C++ indicates that this routine may use `longjmp` and other functions to interact directly with the program at a high level.

Listing 11.2

```
/* handler.c
   Listing 11.2 of DOS Programmer's Reference */

#include <stdlib.h>
#include <stdio.h>
#include <conio.h>
#include <dos.h>

#define     CR    0x0D
#define     LF    0x0A

int handler(void);

void main()
{
   int    c;
   int    i;
   if(getcbrk()==0)
      printf("BREAK checking is OFF\n");
   else
      printf("BREAK checking is ON\n");
   ctrlbrk(handler);
   for(i=0;  i<250;  i++){
      printf("%4.4d:Testing Ctrl-Break\n",i);
   }
```

continues

Listing 11.2 Continued

```
        printf("\nCharacter input\n");
        printf("Press any key; test Ctrl-Break\n");
        printf("(if all else fails, press Esc to exit)\n\n");
        while((c=getche())!=27)
            if(c==CR || c==LF)
                putchar(LF);
}

handler()
{
    int    c;
    printf("\nCtrl-Break handler\n");
    printf("Do you want to quit? ");
    while((c = getch())!='y' && c!='Y' && c!='n' && c!='N');
    printf("\n");
    return(((c=='Y'||c=='y')?0:1));
}
```

Handler.c does two things to enable you to test the Ctrl-C handling:

1. It displays on the screen 250 lines you can break into with Ctrl-C or Ctrl-Break.

2. It accepts characters from the keyboard so that you can try Ctrl-C or Ctrl-Break during keyboard input.

You also can code directly in assembly language a function that works much the same as ctrlbrk(), although the assembly language function is greatly simplified. You must work in assembly language because you have to complete your handler with a return from interrupt (IRET) rather than the normal function return. The handler could be in-line code, but producing something that can be assembled is more instructive.

A good assembly language programmer can produce an interrupt handler directly, but you might be unsure about how to put one together. To build this assembly language routine, start with an empty C routine and compile it to assembly language source code:

```
set_brk()

{
}

brk()

{
    handler();
}
```

With Borland C/C++, you compile the code like this:

```
C>bcc -S set_brk.c
```

to get the assembly language source code in Listing 11.3.

344

Listing 11.3

```
            ifndef   ??version
?debug      macro
            endm
publicdll macro name
            public   name
            endm
$comm       macro    name,dist,size,count
            comm     dist name:BYTE:count*size
            endm
            else
$comm       macro    name,dist,size,count
            comm     dist name[size]:BYTE:count
            endm
            endif
            ?debug   V 300h
            ?debug   S "set_brk.c"
            ?debug   C E9EC837A1A097365745F62726B2E63
_TEXT       segment byte public 'CODE'
_TEXT       ends
DGROUP      group    _DATA,_BSS
            assume   cs:_TEXT,ds:DGROUP
_DATA       segment word public 'DATA'
d@          label    byte
d@w         label    word
_DATA       ends
_BSS        segment word public 'BSS'
b@          label    byte
b@w         label    word
_BSS        ends
_TEXT       segment byte public 'CODE'
    ;
    ;       set_brk()
    ;
            assume   cs:_TEXT
_set_brk            proc     near
            push     bp
            mov      bp,sp
    ;
    ;       {
    ;       }
    ;
            pop      bp
            ret
_set_brk            endp
    ;
    ;       brk()
    ;
            assume   cs:_TEXT
_brk        proc     near
            push     bp
            mov      bp,sp
    ;
    ;       {
    ;           handler();
    ;
```

continues

Listing 11.3 Continued

```
        call    near ptr _handler
    ;
    ;       }
    ;
        pop     bp
        ret
_brk    endp
        ?debug  C E9
        ?debug  C FA00000000
_TEXT   ends
_DATA   segment word public 'DATA'
s@      label   byte
_DATA   ends
_TEXT   segment byte public 'CODE'
_TEXT   ends
        extrn   _handler:near
        public  _brk
        public  _set_brk
_s@     equ     s@
        end
```

This empty C program (sometimes called a NULL program) produces a kind of fill-in-the-blank routine with which you can build an interrupt handler. You may need to wade through some extraneous information inserted by the C compiler (such as the debug information), but if you are not familiar or comfortable with assembly language, it can save you a little time. Some assembly language "hot shots" might laugh at this type of approach, but professional programmers have been using the method for years to learn how a compiler generates code or to provide a way for recoding a function in assembly language to save processing time.

Building an Assembly Language Routine

Serious assembly language programmers might cringe at the thought, but you can prepare an assembly language routine by first writing it in a high-level language such as C and then compiling with an option that produces assembly language source code. In the example from Listing 11.3, development time has been reduced significantly because the skeleton of the routine was produced from the compiler.

This technique is good to remember if you have to produce an assembly language program or if you want to optimize a program already in a high-level language. Converting the program to assembly code and editing the resulting file gives you a working program in a minimum amount of time.

In Turbo Pascal 4.0 and beyond, you can declare a procedure with the `interrupt` directive to be an interrupt handler. The compiler automatically handles the registers and the IRET instruction. The resulting procedure saves all registers; if you need to save only a few, in-line code still might be more efficient.

Listing 11.4

```
_TEXT       segment byte public 'CODE'
_TEXT       ends
DGROUP      group   _DATA,_BSS
            assume  cs:_TEXT,ds:DGROUP
_DATA       segment word public 'DATA'
d@          label   byte
d@w         label   word
_DATA       ends
_BSS        segment word public 'BSS'
b@          label   byte
b@w         label   word
_BSS        ends
_TEXT       segment byte public 'CODE'
    ;
    ;       set_brk()
    ;
            assume  cs:_TEXT
_set_brk        proc    near
    ;
    ;       {
                push    bp          ;Save the registers
                push    ds
                push    di
                push    si

                mov     dx,cs
                mov     ds,dx
                mov     dx,offset _brk
                mov     ah,25h      ;Set interrupt vector
                mov     al,23h      ;Ctrl-C handler
                int     21h

                pop     si          ;Retrieve the registers
                pop     di
                pop     ds
                pop     bp
                ret
    ;       }
    ;
_set_brk        endp
    ;
    ;       brk()
    ;
            assume  cs:_TEXT
_brk        proc    near
                push    ax          ;Save the registers
                push    bx
                push    cx
                push    dx
                push    di
                push    si
                push    bp
```

continues

347

Listing 11.4   Continued

```
        ;
        ;   {
        ;       handler();
        ;
            call    near ptr _handler
        ;
        ;   }
        ;
            pop     bp              ;Retrieve the registers
            pop     si
            pop     di
            pop     dx
            pop     cx
            pop     bx
            pop     ax
            iret
_brk        endp
_TEXT       ends
_DATA       segment word public 'DATA'
s@          label   byte
_DATA       ends
_TEXT       segment byte public 'CODE'
_TEXT       ends
            extrn   _handler:near
            public  _brk
            public  _set_brk
_s@         equ     s@
            end
```

Notice that no effort has been made to clean up the code beyond what was provided by the compiler, with the exception of removing the obvious debugging code. Some additional chaff could have been cleaned out (hot-shot assembly language programmers will do so), but it is not necessary. The only requirement is that the code works. It does.

Finally, the revision is added to the handler.c program (see Listing 11.5).

Listing 11.5

```
/* handler2.c
   Listing 11.5 of DOS Programmer's Reference */

#include <stdlib.h>
#include <stdio.h>
#include <conio.h>
#include <dos.h>

#define    CR    0x0D
#define    LF    0x0A

int handler(void);

void main()
```

```
    {
        void  set_brk(void);
        int   c;
        int   i;

        if(getcbrk()==0)
            printf("BREAK checking is OFF\n");
        else
            printf("BREAK checking is ON\n");

        set_brk();
        for(i=0; i<250; i++){
            printf("%4.4d:Testing Ctrl-Break\n",i);
        }
        printf("\nCharacter input\n");
        printf("Press any key; test Ctrl-Break\n");
        printf("(if all else fails, press Esc to exit)\n\n");
        while((c=getche())!=27)
            if(c==CR || c==LF)
                putchar(LF);
    }

handler()
{
    int    c;

    printf("\nCtrl-Break handler\n");
    printf("Do you want to quit? ");
    while((c = getch())!='y' && c!='Y' && c!='n' && c!='N');
    printf("\n");
    if(c=='Y'||c=='y')
        exit(0);
    return(0);
}
```

Compiling the program and linking it to the assembly language routine yields a working Ctrl-C handler. You should use the following command line to compile it with the Borland C/C++ compiler:

```
bcc handler2.c set_brk2.asm
```

Writing a Critical Error Handler

A critical error handler is perhaps one of the most involved interrupt handlers you can write. The critical error handler is invoked by DOS when an error occurs and DOS gives the user the ability to decide whether to go gamely past the problem or to stop the program. The standard DOS manifestation is the famous Abort, Retry, Fail? prompt. As a programmer, you should see this message as a catastrophe; it pays no attention to your carefully crafted screens, and it pays only a small amount of attention to exactly what happened. DOS provides the critical error handler with a great deal of information about what happened. The code in Listing 11.6 is a TASM module that can be incorporated into a complete application; it takes advantage of this wealth of information.

Listing 11.6

```
page  55,132

; CritErr.asm
; functions for creating a pop-up critical error handler

criterr_data    segment

MAXLINES     equ  19

        OldCritErrOffset            dw   (?)  ; Old critical error address
        OldCritErrSegment           dw   (?)
        DeviceDriverHeaderOffset    dw   (?)  ; Device driver address
        DeviceDriverHeaderSegment   dw   (?)
        ErrorCode                   dw   (?)  ; Error code on entry
        Line                        dw MAXLINES dup (?) ; Pointers to menu lines
        DOS_MajorVersion            db   (?)  ; DOS major version
        IO_Type                     db   (?)  ; I/O type of error
        DriveNumber                 db   (?)  ; Which drive had error
        MenuLines                   db   (?)  ; Number of lines on screen - 1
        CurrentOption               db   (?)  ; Currently selected option
        MaximumOption               db   (?)  ; Number of valid options - 1
        ReturnCodes                 dw   (?)  ; Pointer to list of valid return codes
        TopLine                     db   (?)  ; Top line of window
        BottomLine                  db   (?)  ; Bottom line of window
        LeftRow                     db   (?)  ; Left line of window
        RightRow                    db   (?)  ; Right line of window
        ActiveDisplayPage           db   (?)  ; Active display video page
        OriginalRow                 db   (?)  ; Where cursor was
        OriginalColumn              db   (?)

Set__2_    db   2
Set__23    db   2,3
Set_12_    db   1,2
Set_123    db   1,2,3
Set0_2_    db   0,2
Set0_23    db   0,2,3
Set012_    db   0,1,2
Set0123    db   0,1,2,3

ATTRIBUTE equ  17H  ; WHITE ON BLUE

TopMenu             db  " ┌──────────────┤Critical Error├──────────────┐ "
UnknownFunction     db  " │Unknown DOS Function                         │ "
Fn_00               db  " │Terminate Program Line                       │ "
Fn_01               db  " │Keyboard Input With Echo                     │ "
Fn_02               db  " │Display Output                               │ "
Fn_03               db  " │Auxiliary Input                              │ "
Fn_04               db  " │Auxiliary Output                             │ "
Fn_05               db  " │Printer Output                               │ "
```

```
Fn_06        db   " Direct Console I/O                                      "
Fn_07        db   " Direct STDIN Input                                      "
Fn_08        db   " STDIN Input                                             "
Fn_09        db   " Display String                                          "
Fn_0A        db   " Buffered STDIN Input                                    "
Fn_0B        db   " Check STDIN Status                                      "
Fn_0C        db   " Clear Buffer And Input                                  "
Fn_0D        db   " Reset Disk                                              "
Fn_0E        db   " Select Disk                                             "
Fn_0F        db   " Open File (FCB)                                         "
Fn_10        db   " Close File (FCB)                                        "
Fn_11        db   " Search For First Entry (FCB)                            "
Fn_12        db   " Search For Next Entry (FCB)                             "
Fn_13        db   " Delete File (FCB)                                       "
Fn_14        db   " Read Sequential File (FCB)                              "
Fn_15        db   " Write Sequential File (FCB)                             "
Fn_16        db   " Create File (FCB)                                       "
Fn_17        db   " Rename File (FCB)                                       "
Fn_19        db   " Get Default Drive                                       "
Fn_1A        db   " Set DTA Address                                         "
Fn_1B        db   " Get Allocation Table Information                        "
Fn_1C        db   " Get Allocation Table Information For Specific Drive     "
Fn_1F        db   " Get Default Disk Parameter Block                        "
Fn_21        db   " Random File Read (FCB)                                  "
Fn_22        db   " Random File Write (FCB)                                 "
Fn_23        db   " Get File Size (FCB)                                     "
Fn_24        db   " Set Random Record Field (FCB)                           "
Fn_25        db   " Set Interrupt Vector                                    "
Fn_26        db   " Create PSP                                              "
Fn_27        db   " Random Block Read (FCB)                                 "
Fn_28        db   " Random Block Write (FCB)                                "
Fn_29        db   " Parse File Name                                         "
Fn_2A        db   " Get System Date                                         "
Fn_2B        db   " Set System Date                                         "
Fn_2C        db   " Get System Time                                         "
Fn_2D        db   " Set System Time                                         "
Fn_2E        db   " Set Verify Flag                                         "
Fn_2F        db   " Get DTA Address                                         "
Fn_30        db   " Get DOS Version Number                                  "
Fn_31        db   " Terminate And Stay Resident                             "
Fn_32        db   " Get Drive Parameter Block                               "
Fn_3300      db   " Get Ctrl-Break Flag                                     "
Fn_3301      db   " Set Ctrl-Break Flag                                     "
Fn_3305      db   " Get Boot Drive Code                                     "
Fn_34        db   " Return Address Of InDOS Flag                            "
Fn_35        db   " Get Interrupt Vector                                    "
Fn_36        db   " Get Free Disk Space                                     "
Fn_3700      db   " Get Switchchar                                          "
Fn_3701      db   " Set Switchchar                                          "
Fn_3702      db   " Read Device Availability                                "
Fn_3703      db   " Set Device Availability                                 "
Fn_38        db   " Get Set Country Information                             "
Fn_39        db   " Create Subdirectory                                     "
Fn_3A        db   " Remove Subdirectory                                     "
Fn_3B        db   " Set Directory                                           "
Fn_3C        db   " Create Truncate File Handle                             "
```

continues

Listing 11.6   Continued

```
        Fn_3D       db  " Open File Handle                        "
        Fn_3E       db  " Close File Handle                       "
        Fn_3F       db  " Read File Or Device Handle              "
        Fn_40       db  " Write To File Or Device Handle          "
        Fn_41       db  " Delete File                             "
        Fn_42       db  " Move File Pointer                       "
        Fn_4300     db  " Get File Attributes                     "
        Fn_4301     db  " Set File Attributes                     "
        Fn_4400     db  " Get Device Information                  "
        Fn_4401     db  " Set Device Information                  "
        Fn_4402     db  " Device IOCTL Read                       "
        Fn_4403     db  " Device IOCTL Write                      "
        Fn_4404     db  " Block Driver IOCTL Read                 "
        Fn_4405     db  " Block Driver IOCTL Write                "
        Fn_4406     db  " Get Input Status                        "
        Fn_4407     db  " Get Output Status                       "
        Fn_4408     db  " Block Device Removable                  "
        Fn_4409     db  " Block Device Local                      "
        Fn_440A     db  " Handle Local                            "
        Fn_440B     db  " Set Sharing Retry Count                 "
        Fn_440C     db  " Generic IOCTL Handles                   "
        Fn_440D     db  " Generic IOCTL Block Devices             "
        Fn_440E     db  " Get Logical Drive Map                   "
        Fn_440F     db  " Set Logical Drive Map                   "
        Fn_4410     db  " Query IOCTL Handle                      "
        Fn_4411     db  " Query IOCTL Device                      "
        Fn_45       db  " Duplicate Handle                        "
        Fn_46       db  " Force Duplicate Handle                  "
        Fn_47       db  " Get Current Directory                   "
        Fn_48       db  " Allocate Memory                         "
        Fn_49       db  " Release Memory                          "
        Fn_4A       db  " Modify Memory Allocation                "
        Fn_4B00     db  " Execute Program                         "
        Fn_4B01     db  " Load Program                            "
        Fn_4B03     db  " Load Overlay                            "
        Fn_4B05     db  " Enter Exec State                        "
        Fn_4C       db  " Terminate With Return Code              "
        Fn_4D       db  " Get Return Code                         "
        Fn_4E       db  " Search For First Match                  "
        Fn_4F       db  " Search For Next Match                   "
        Fn_50       db  " Set PSP Segment                         "
        Fn_51       db  " Get PSP Segment                         "
        Fn_52       db  " Get Disk List                           "
        Fn_53       db  " Translate BPB To DPB                    "
        Fn_54       db  " Get Verify Flag                         "
        Fn_55       db  " Create PSP                              "
        Fn_56       db  " Rename File                             "
        Fn_5700     db  " Get File Date And Time                  "
        Fn_5701     db  " Set File Date And Time                  "
        Fn_5800     db  " Get Allocation Strategy                 "
        Fn_5801     db  " Set Allocation Strategy                 "
        Fn_5802     db  " Get UMB Link Status                     "
        Fn_5803     db  " Set UMB Link                            "
        Fn_59       db  " Get Extended Error Information          "
        Fn_5A       db  " Create Uniquely Named File              "
```

```
Fn_5B              db  " ‖Create New File                            ‖"
Fn_5C00            db  " ‖Set File Access Locks                      ‖"
Fn_5C01            db  " ‖Clear File Access Locks                    ‖"
Fn_5D00            db  " ‖Copy Data To DOS Save Area                 ‖"
Fn_5D06            db  " ‖Get Critical Error Flag Address            ‖"
Fn_5D0A            db  " ‖Set Error Data Values                      ‖"
Fn_5E00            db  " ‖Get Machine Name                           ‖"
Fn_5E01            db  " ‖Set Machine Name                           ‖"
Fn_5E02            db  " ‖Set Network Printer Setup                  ‖"
Fn_5E03            db  " ‖Get Network Printer Setup                  ‖"
Fn_5F02            db  " ‖Get Redirection List Entry                 ‖"
Fn_5F03            db  " ‖Set Redirection List Entry                 ‖"
Fn_5F04            db  " ‖Cancel Redirection List Entry              ‖"
Fn_60              db  " ‖Expand Path Name String                    ‖"
Fn_62              db  " ‖Get PSP Address                            ‖"
Fn_6300            db  " ‖Get System Lead Byte Table                 ‖"
Fn_6301            db  " ‖Set/Clear Interim Console Flag             ‖"
Fn_6302            db  " ‖Get Value Of Interim Console Flag          ‖"
Fn_64              db  " ‖Set Current Country Byte                   ‖"
Fn_65              db  " ‖Set Extended Country Information           ‖"
Fn_6600            db  " ‖Get Global Code Page                       ‖"
Fn_6602            db  " ‖Set Global Code Page                       ‖"
Fn_67              db  " ‖Set Handle Count                           ‖"
Fn_68              db  " ‖Flush Buffer                               ‖"
Fn_6A              db  " ‖Allocate Memory                            ‖"
Fn_6C              db  " ‖Extended Open Create                       ‖"
UnknownErrorCode   db  " ‖Error Code: Unknown                        ‖"
ErrorCode00        db  " ‖Error Code: Write Protect Error            ‖"
ErrorCode01        db  " ‖Error Code: Unknown Unit                   ‖"
ErrorCode02        db  " ‖Error Code: Drive Not Ready                ‖"
ErrorCode03        db  " ‖Error Code: Unknown Command                ‖"
ErrorCode04        db  " ‖Error Code: Data Error                     ‖"
ErrorCode05        db  " ‖Error Code: Bad Request Structure Length   ‖"
ErrorCode06        db  " ‖Error Code: Seek Error                     ‖"
ErrorCode07        db  " ‖Error Code: Unknown Media Type             ‖"
ErrorCode08        db  " ‖Error Code: Sector Not Found               ‖"
ErrorCode09        db  " ‖Error Code: Printer Out Of Paper           ‖"
ErrorCode0A        db  " ‖Error Code: Write Fault                    ‖"
ErrorCode0B        db  " ‖Error Code: Read Fault                     ‖"
ErrorCode0C        db  " ‖Error Code: General Failure                ‖"
ErrorCode0F        db  " ‖Error Code: Invalid Disk Change            ‖"
L2                 db  " ‖        AX = "
L2AX               db  "0000 BX = "
L2BX               db  "0000 CX = "
L2CX               db  "0000 DX = "
L2DX               db  "0000        ‖"
L3                 db  " ‖        DI = "
L3DI               db  "0000 SI = "
L3SI               db  "0000 BP = "
L3BP               db  "0000 SP = "
L3SP               db  "0000        ‖"
L4                 db  " ‖             DS = "
L4DS               db  "0000 ES = "
L4ES               db  "0000 SS = "
L4SS               db  "0000               ‖"
L5                 db  " ‖          CS:IP = "
```

continues

353

Listing 11.6   Continued

```
L5CS             db    "0000:"
L5IP             db    "0000 Flags = "
L5Flags          db    "---------       ||"
L7_Char          db    "||Device: "
L7_Device        db    "                        ||"
L7_UnknownChar   db    "||Unknown Character (?) Device              "
DiskError0       db    "||Drive  : Error Reading MS-DOS Area        "
DiskError1       db    "||Drive  : Error Writing MS-DOS Area        "
DiskError2       db    "||Drive  : Error Reading FAT                "
DiskError3       db    "||Drive  : Error Writing FAT                "
DiskError4       db    "||Drive  : Error Reading Root Directory     "
DiskError5       db    "||Drive  : Error Writing Root Directory     "
DiskError6       db    "||Drive  : Error Reading Files Area         "
DiskError7       db    "||Drive  : Error Writing Files Area         "
DRIVE_OFFSET     equ   7
Bridge2Line      db    "||------------------T------------------------||"
EEC_01           db    "||Extended Error Code|Invalid Function Number    "
EEC_02           db    "||Extended Error Code|File Not Found             "
EEC_03           db    "||Extended Error Code|Path Not Found             "
EEC_04           db    "||Extended Error Code|No Handles Available       "
EEC_05           db    "||Extended Error Code|Access Denied              "
EEC_06           db    "||Extended Error Code|Invalid Handle             "
EEC_07           db    "||Extended Error Code|Memory Ctrl Blocks Destroyed"
EEC_08           db    "||Extended Error Code|Insufficient Memory        "
EEC_09           db    "||Extended Error Code|Invalid Memory Block Address"
EEC_0A           db    "||Extended Error Code|Invalid Environment        "
EEC_0B           db    "||Extended Error Code|Invalid Format             "
EEC_0C           db    "||Extended Error Code|Invalid Access Code        "
EEC_0D           db    "||Extended Error Code|Invalid Data               "
EEC_0F           db    "||Extended Error Code|Invalid Drive              "
EEC_10           db    "||Extended Error Code|Remove Current Directory   "
EEC_11           db    "||Extended Error Code|Not the Same Device        "
EEC_12           db    "||Extended Error Code|No More Files              "
EEC_13           db    "||Extended Error Code|Disk Write-Protected       "
EEC_14           db    "||Extended Error Code|Unknown Unit               "
EEC_15           db    "||Extended Error Code|Drive Not Ready            "
EEC_16           db    "||Extended Error Code|Unknown Command            "
EEC_17           db    "||Extended Error Code|CRC Error                  "
EEC_18           db    "||Extended Error Code|Bad Request Structure Length"
EEC_19           db    "||Extended Error Code|Seek Error                 "
EEC_1A           db    "||Extended Error Code|Unknown Media Type         "
EEC_1B           db    "||Extended Error Code|Sector Not Found           "
EEC_1C           db    "||Extended Error Code|Out of Paper               "
EEC_1D           db    "||Extended Error Code|Write Fault                "
EEC_1E           db    "||Extended Error Code|Read Fault                 "
EEC_1F           db    "||Extended Error Code|General Failure            "
EEC_20           db    "||Extended Error Code|Sharing Violation          "
EEC_21           db    "||Extended Error Code|Lock Violation             "
EEC_22           db    "||Extended Error Code|Invalid Disk Change        "
EEC_23           db    "||Extended Error Code|FCB Unavailable            "
EEC_24           db    "||Extended Error Code|Sharing Buffer overflow     "
EEC_26           db    "||Extended Error Code|Can't Complete File Operation"
EEC_32           db    "||Extended Error Code|Network Request Not Supported"
EEC_33           db    "||Extended Error Code|Remote Computer Not Listening"
EEC_34           db    "||Extended Error Code|Duplicate Name on Network  "
EEC_35           db    "||Extended Error Code|Network Name Not Found       "
```

```
EEC_36        db   " Extended Error Code | Network Busy                             ||"
EEC_37        db   " Extended Error Code | Network Device No Longer Exists          ||"
EEC_38        db   " Extended Error Code | NetBIOS Command Limit Exceeded           ||"
EEC_39        db   " Extended Error Code | Network Adapter Error                     "
EEC_3A        db   " Extended Error Code | Incorrect Network Response                "
EEC_3B        db   " Extended Error Code | Unexpected Network Error                  "
EEC_3C        db   " Extended Error Code | Incompatible Remote Adapter               "
EEC_3D        db   " Extended Error Code | Print Queue Full                          "
EEC_3E        db   " Extended Error Code | Not Enough Room For Print File            "
EEC_3F        db   " Extended Error Code | Print File Deleted                        "
EEC_40        db   " Extended Error Code | Network Name Deleted                      "
EEC_41        db   " Extended Error Code | Access Denied                            "
EEC_42        db   " Extended Error Code | Network Device Type Incorrect             "
EEC_43        db   " Extended Error Code | Network Name Not Found                    "
EEC_44        db   " Extended Error Code | Network Name Limit Exceeded               "
EEC_45        db   " Extended Error Code | NetBIOS Session Limit Exceeded            "
EEC_46        db   " Extended Error Code | Sharing Temporarily Paused                "
EEC_47        db   " Extended Error Code | Network Request Not Accepted              "
EEC_48        db   " Extended Error Code | Print/Disk Redirection Paused             "
EEC_50        db   " Extended Error Code | File Already Exists                       "
EEC_52        db   " Extended Error Code | Cannot Make Directory Entry               "
EEC_53        db   " Extended Error Code | Fail on Int 24                            "
EEC_54        db   " Extended Error Code | Too Many Redirections                     "
EEC_55        db   " Extended Error Code | Duplicate Redirection                     "
EEC_56        db   " Extended Error Code | Invalid Password                          "
EEC_57        db   " Extended Error Code | Invalid Parameter                         "
EEC_58        db   " Extended Error Code | Network Data Fault                        "
EEC_59        db   " Extended Error Code | Fn Not Supported By Network               "
EEC_5A        db   " Extended Error Code | Req'd Sys. Comp. Not Installed            "
EEC_Unknown   db   " Extended Error Code | Unknown                                   "
ECC_01        db   "     Error Class Code | Out Of Resource                         "
ECC_02        db   "     Error Class Code | Temporary Situation                     "
ECC_03        db   "     Error Class Code | Authorization                          "
ECC_04        db   "     Error Class Code | Internal                               "
ECC_05        db   "     Error Class Code | Hardware Failure                       "
ECC_06        db   "     Error Class Code | System Failure                         "
ECC_07        db   "     Error Class Code | Application Program Error               "
ECC_08        db   "     Error Class Code | Not Found                              "
ECC_09        db   "     Error Class Code | Bad Format                             "
ECC_0A        db   "     Error Class Code | Locked                                 "
ECC_0B        db   "     Error Class Code | Media                                  "
ECC_0C        db   "     Error Class Code | Already Exists                         "
ECC_Unknown   db   "     Error Class Code | Unknown                                "
RAC_1         db   " Recommended Action | Retry Then Abort/Ignore                   "
RAC_2         db   " Recommended Action | Delay & Retry Then Abort/Ignore           "
RAC_3         db   " Recommended Action | Get Correct Data From User                "
RAC_4         db   " Recommended Action | Abort Application With Cleanup            "
RAC_5         db   " Recommended Action | Abort Without Cleanup Attempt             "
RAC_6         db   " Recommended Action | Ignore Error                             "
RAC_7         db   " Recommended Action | Correct Error Then Retry                  "
RAC_Unknown   db   " Recommended Action | Unknown                                  "
Locus_2       db   "              Locus | Block Device                             "
Locus_3       db   "              Locus | Network                                  "
Locus_4       db   "              Locus | Serial Device                            "
```

continues

355

Listing 11.6 Continued

```
Locus_5            db    "              Locus│Memory Related        "
Locus_Unknown      db    "              Locus│Unknown               "
BridgeLine         db    " - - - - - - - - - -│- - - - - - - - - - -"
IgnoreOption       db    " │Ignore Error                            "
RetryOption        db    " │Retry Function Call                     "
TerminateOption    db    " │Terminate Program                       "
FailCallOption     db    " │Fail Function Call                      "
BottomMenu         db    "                                          "
LINEWIDTH     equ  $-BottomMenu
ScreenSave    db   (LINEWIDTH * MAXLINES * 2) dup (?)

MainTable dw   Fn_00
          dw   Fn_01
          dw   Fn_02
          dw   Fn_03
          dw   Fn_04
          dw   Fn_05
          dw   Fn_06
          dw   Fn_07
          dw   Fn_08
          dw   Fn_09
          dw   Fn_0A
          dw   Fn_0B
          dw   Fn_0C
          dw   Fn_0D
          dw   Fn_0E
          dw   Fn_0F
          dw   Fn_10
          dw   Fn_11
          dw   Fn_12
          dw   Fn_13
          dw   Fn_14
          dw   Fn_15
          dw   Fn_16
          dw   Fn_17
          dw   UnknownFunction
          dw   Fn_19
          dw   Fn_1A
          dw   Fn_1B
          dw   Fn_1C
          dw   UnknownFunction
          dw   UnknownFunction
          dw   Fn_1F
          dw   UnknownFunction
          dw   Fn_21
          dw   Fn_22
          dw   Fn_23
          dw   Fn_24
          dw   Fn_25
          dw   Fn_26
          dw   Fn_27
          dw   Fn_28
          dw   Fn_29
          dw   Fn_2A
          dw   Fn_2B
```

```
dw    Fn_2C
dw    Fn_2D
dw    Fn_2E
dw    Fn_2F
dw    Fn_30
dw    Fn_31
dw    Fn_32
dw    -1
dw    Fn_34
dw    Fn_35
dw    Fn_36
dw    -1
dw    Fn_38
dw    Fn_39
dw    Fn_3A
dw    Fn_3B
dw    Fn_3C
dw    Fn_3D
dw    Fn_3E
dw    Fn_3F
dw    Fn_40
dw    Fn_41
dw    Fn_42
dw    -1
dw    -1
dw    Fn_45
dw    Fn_46
dw    Fn_47
dw    Fn_48
dw    Fn_49
dw    Fn_4A
dw    -1
dw    Fn_4C
dw    Fn_4D
dw    Fn_4E
dw    Fn_4F
dw    Fn_50
dw    Fn_51
dw    Fn_52
dw    Fn_53
dw    Fn_54
dw    Fn_55
dw    Fn_56
dw    -1
dw    -1
dw    Fn_59
dw    Fn_5A
dw    Fn_5B
dw    -1
dw    -1
dw    -1
dw    -1
dw    Fn_60
dw    UnknownFunction
dw    Fn_62
dw    -1
```

continues

357

Listing 11.6   Continued

```
              dw    Fn_64
              dw    Fn_65
              dw    -1
              dw    Fn_67
              dw    Fn_68
              dw    UnknownFunction
              dw    Fn_6A
              dw    UnknownFunction
              dw    Fn_6C
Table33       dw    Fn_3300
              dw    Fn_3301
              dw    UnknownFunction
              dw    UnknownFunction
              dw    UnknownFunction
              dw    Fn_3305
Table37       dw    Fn_3700
              dw    Fn_3701
              dw    Fn_3702
              dw    Fn_3703
Table43       dw    Fn_4300
              dw    Fn_4301
Table44       dw    Fn_4400
              dw    Fn_4401
              dw    Fn_4402
              dw    Fn_4403
              dw    Fn_4404
              dw    Fn_4405
              dw    Fn_4406
              dw    Fn_4407
              dw    Fn_4408
              dw    Fn_4409
              dw    Fn_440A
              dw    Fn_440B
              dw    Fn_440C
              dw    Fn_440D
              dw    Fn_440E
              dw    Fn_440F
              dw    Fn_4410
              dw    Fn_4411
Table4B       dw    Fn_4B00
              dw    Fn_4B01
              dw    UnknownFunction
              dw    Fn_4B03
              dw    UnknownFunction
              dw    Fn_4B05
Table57       dw    Fn_5700
              dw    Fn_5701
Table58       dw    Fn_5800
              dw    Fn_5801
              dw    Fn_5802
              dw    Fn_5803
Table5C       dw    Fn_5C00
              dw    Fn_5C01
Table5D       dw    Fn_5D00
              dw    UnknownFunction
```

```
                    dw    UnknownFunction
                    dw    UnknownFunction
                    dw    UnknownFunction
                    dw    UnknownFunction
                    dw    Fn_5D06
                    dw    UnknownFunction
                    dw    UnknownFunction
                    dw    UnknownFunction
                    dw    Fn_5D0A
Table5E       dw    Fn_5E00
                    dw    Fn_5E01
                    dw    Fn_5E02
                    dw    Fn_5E03
Table5F       dw    UnknownFunction
                    dw    UnknownFunction
                    dw    Fn_5F02
                    dw    Fn_5F03
                    dw    Fn_5F04
Table63       dw    Fn_6300
                    dw    Fn_6301
                    dw    Fn_6302
Table66       dw    Fn_6600
                    dw    UnknownFunction
                    dw    Fn_6602
ECTable       dw    ErrorCode00
                    dw    ErrorCode01
                    dw    ErrorCode02
                    dw    ErrorCode03
                    dw    ErrorCode04
                    dw    ErrorCode05
                    dw    ErrorCode06
                    dw    ErrorCode07
                    dw    ErrorCode08
                    dw    ErrorCode09
                    dw    ErrorCode0A
                    dw    ErrorCode0B
                    dw    ErrorCode0C
                    dw    UnknownErrorCode
                    dw    UnknownErrorCode
                    dw    ErrorCode0F
DiskErrorTable dw    DiskError0
                    dw    DiskError1
                    dw    DiskError2
                    dw    DiskError3
                    dw    DiskError4
                    dw    DiskError5
                    dw    DiskError6
                    dw    DiskError7
EEC_Table dw    EEC_Unknown
            dw    EEC_01
            dw    EEC_02
            dw    EEC_03
            dw    EEC_04
            dw    EEC_05
            dw    EEC_06
            dw    EEC_07
```

continues

359

Listing 11.6 Continued

```
        dw    EEC_08
        dw    EEC_09
        dw    EEC_0A
        dw    EEC_0B
        dw    EEC_0C
        dw    EEC_0D
        dw    EEC_Unknown
        dw    EEC_0F
        dw    EEC_10
        dw    EEC_11
        dw    EEC_12
        dw    EEC_13
        dw    EEC_14
        dw    EEC_15
        dw    EEC_16
        dw    EEC_17
        dw    EEC_18
        dw    EEC_19
        dw    EEC_1A
        dw    EEC_1B
        dw    EEC_1C
        dw    EEC_1D
        dw    EEC_1E
        dw    EEC_1F
        dw    EEC_20
        dw    EEC_21
        dw    EEC_22
        dw    EEC_23
        dw    EEC_24
        dw    EEC_Unknown
        dw    EEC_26
        dw    EEC_Unknown
        dw    EEC_Unknown
        dw    EEC_Unknown
        dw    EEC_Unknown
        dw    EEC_Unknown
        dw    EEC_Unknown
        dw    EEC_Unknown
        dw    EEC_Unknown
        dw    EEC_Unknown
        dw    EEC_Unknown
        dw    EEC_Unknown
        dw    EEC_32
        dw    EEC_33
        dw    EEC_34
        dw    EEC_35
        dw    EEC_36
        dw    EEC_37
        dw    EEC_38
        dw    EEC_39
        dw    EEC_3A
        dw    EEC_3B
        dw    EEC_3C
        dw    EEC_3D
```

```
              dw    EEC_3E
              dw    EEC_3F
              dw    EEC_40
              dw    EEC_41
              dw    EEC_42
              dw    EEC_43
              dw    EEC_44
              dw    EEC_45
              dw    EEC_46
              dw    EEC_47
              dw    EEC_48
              dw    EEC_Unknown
              dw    EEC_Unknown
              dw    EEC_Unknown
              dw    EEC_Unknown
              dw    EEC_Unknown
              dw    EEC_Unknown
              dw    EEC_Unknown
              dw    EEC_50
              dw    EEC_Unknown
              dw    EEC_52
              dw    EEC_53
              dw    EEC_54
              dw    EEC_55
              dw    EEC_56
              dw    EEC_57
              dw    EEC_58
              dw    EEC_59
              dw    EEC_5A
ECC_Table dw    EEC_Unknown
              dw    ECC_01
              dw    ECC_02
              dw    ECC_03
              dw    ECC_04
              dw    ECC_05
              dw    ECC_06
              dw    ECC_07
              dw    ECC_08
              dw    ECC_09
              dw    ECC_0A
              dw    ECC_0B
              dw    ECC_0C
RAC_Table dw    RAC_Unknown
              dw    RAC_1
              dw    RAC_2
              dw    RAC_3
              dw    RAC_4
              dw    RAC_5
              dw    RAC_6
              dw    RAC_7
Locus_Table    dw    Locus_Unknown
               dw    Locus_Unknown
               dw    Locus_2
               dw    Locus_3
               dw    Locus_4
               dw    Locus_5
```

continues

361

Listing 11.6 Continued

```
criterr_data    ends

;    Stack structure in CritErr

CE_CallerStack struc
        OldDS           dw    (?)   ; DS on entry
        OldES           dw    (?)   ; ES on entry
        OldBP           dw    (?)   ; BP on entry
        OldSI           dw    (?)   ; SI on entry
        OldDI           dw    (?)   ; DI on entry
        OldBX           dw    (?)   ; BX on entry
        OldCX           dw    (?)   ; CX on entry
        OldDX           dw    (?)   ; DX on entry
        Int21IP         dw    (?)   ; Int 21 IP
        Int21CS         dw    (?)   ; Int 21 CS
        Int21Flags      dw    (?)   ; Int 21 Flags
        UsersAX         dw    (?)   ; Caller's AX
        UsersBX         dw    (?)   ; Caller's BX
        UsersCX         dw    (?)   ; Caller's CX
        UsersDX         dw    (?)   ; Caller's DX
        UsersSI         dw    (?)   ; Caller's SI
        UsersDI         dw    (?)   ; Caller's DI
        UsersBP         dw    (?)   ; Caller's BP
        UsersDS         dw    (?)   ; Caller's DS
        UsersES         dw    (?)   ; Caller's ES
        UsersIP         dw    (?)   ; Caller's IP
        UsersCS         dw    (?)   ; Caller's CS
        UsersFlags      dw    (?)   ; Caller's Flags
CE_CallerStack ends

criterr_code    segment

assume      CS:criterr_code
assume      DS:nothing
assume      ES:nothing
assume      SS:nothing

CritErr     proc
            push DX         ; Save registers
            push CX
            push BX
            push DI
            push SI
            push BP
            push ES
            push DS
            mov  BX,seg criterr_data  ; Set DS to local data
            mov  DS,BX

            assume     DS:criterr_data

            mov  IO_Type,AH           ; Save special values
            mov  DriveNumber,AL
            mov  ErrorCode,DI
            mov  DeviceDriverHeaderSegment,BP
```

```
                mov    DeviceDriverHeaderOffset,SI
                mov    BP,SP                   ; Let BP point to stack structure
                mov    Line,offset DS:TopMenu
                mov    Line + 2,offset DS:UnknownFunction
                mov    AX,[BP.UsersAX]         ; Get caller's AX value
                cmp    AH,6CH                  ; Out of known range?
                jbe    ValidFunction
                jmp    DumpRegistersIsle
ValidFunction:
                cmp    AH,33H                  ; Identify subfunction?
                jne    Not_Fn33
                jmp    Fn33
Not_Fn33:
                cmp    AH,37H
                jne    Not_Fn37
                jmp    Fn37
Not_Fn37:
                cmp    AH,43H
                jne    Not_Fn43
                jmp    Fn43
Not_Fn43:
                cmp    AH,44H
                jne    Not_Fn44
                jmp    Fn44
Not_Fn44:
                cmp    AH,4BH
                jne    Not_Fn4B
                jmp    Fn4B
Not_Fn4B:
                cmp    AH,57H
                jne    Not_Fn57
                jmp    Fn57
Not_Fn57:
                cmp    AH,58H
                jne    Not_Fn58
                jmp    Fn58
Not_Fn58:
                cmp    AH,5CH
                je     Fn5C
                cmp    AH,5DH
                je     Fn5D
                cmp    AH,5EH
                je     Fn5E
                cmp    AH,5FH
                je     Fn5F
                cmp    AH,63H
                je     Fn63
                cmp    AH,66H
                je     Fn66
                shl    AH,1         ; Double the index
                mov    BL,AH        ; Put in BX
                xor    BH,BH
                mov    AX,MainTable[ BX ]
                jmp    SetFunction
Fn66:
```

continues

Listing 11.6 Continued

```
                cmp   AL,02H    ; Undefined?
                ja    DumpRegistersIsle
                shl   AL,1
                mov   BL,AL
                xor   BH,BH
                mov   AX,Table66[ BX ]
                jmp   SetFunction
        Fn63:
                cmp   AL,02H    ; Undefined?
                ja    DumpRegistersIsle
                shl   AL,1
                mov   BL,AL
                xor   BH,BH
                mov   AX,Table63[ BX ]
                jmp   SetFunction
        Fn5F:
                cmp   AL,04H    ; Undefined?
                ja    DumpRegistersIsle
                shl   AL,1
                mov   BL,AL
                xor   BH,BH
                mov   AX,Table5F[ BX ]
                jmp   SetFunction
        Fn5E:
                cmp   AL,03H    ; Undefined?
                ja    DumpRegistersIsle
                shl   AL,1
                mov   BL,AL
                xor   BH,BH
                mov   AX,Table5E[ BX ]
                jmp   SetFunction
        Fn5D:
                cmp   AL,0AH    ; Undefined?
                jbe   Fn5D_1
        DumpRegistersIsle:
                jmp   DumpRegisters
        Fn5D_1:
                shl   AL,1
                mov   BL,AL
                xor   BH,BH
                mov   AX,Table5D[ BX ]
                jmp   short SetFunction
        Fn5C:
                cmp   AL,01H    ; Undefined?
                ja    DumpRegisters
                shl   AL,1
                mov   BL,AL
                xor   BH,BH
                mov   AX,Table5C[ BX ]
                jmp   short SetFunction
        Fn58:
                cmp   AL,03H    ; Undefined?
                ja    DumpRegisters
                shl   AL,1
                mov   BL,AL
```

```
                xor   BH,BH
                mov   AX,Table58[ BX ]
                jmp   short SetFunction
        Fn57:
                cmp   AL,01H     ; Undefined?
                ja    DumpRegisters
                shl   AL,1
                mov   BL,AL
                xor   BH,BH
                mov   AX,Table57[ BX ]
                jmp   short SetFunction
        Fn4B:
                cmp   AL,05H     ; Undefined?
                ja    DumpRegisters
                shl   AL,1
                mov   BL,AL
                xor   BH,BH
                mov   AX,Table4B[ BX ]
                jmp   short SetFunction
        Fn44:
                cmp   AL,11H     ; Undefined?
                ja    DumpRegisters
                shl   AL,1
                mov   BL,AL
                xor   BH,BH
                mov   AX,Table44[ BX ]
                jmp   short SetFunction
        Fn43:
                cmp   AL,01H     ; Undefined?
                ja    DumpRegisters
                shl   AL,1
                mov   BL,AL
                xor   BH,BH
                mov   AX,Table43[ BX ]
                jmp   short SetFunction
        Fn37:
                cmp   AL,03H     ; Undefined?
                ja    DumpRegisters
                shl   AL,1
                mov   BL,AL
                xor   BH,BH
                mov   AX,Table37[ BX ]
                jmp   short SetFunction
        Fn33:
                cmp   AL,05H     ; Undefined?
                ja    DumpRegisters
                shl   AL,1
                mov   BL,AL
                xor   BH,BH
                mov   AX,Table33[ BX ]
        SetFunction:
                mov   Line + 2,AX
        DumpRegisters:
                mov   BX,offset L2AX
                mov   AX,[ BP.UsersAX ]
                call  FillWord
```

continues

Listing 11.6 Continued

```
                mov   BX,offset L2BX
                mov   AX,[ BP.UsersBX ]
                call  FillWord
                mov   BX,offset L2CX
                mov   AX,[ BP.UsersCX ]
                call  FillWord
                mov   BX,offset L2DX
                mov   AX,[ BP.UsersDX ]
                call  FillWord
                mov   Line + 4,offset L2
                mov   BX,offset L3DI
                mov   AX,[ BP.UsersDI ]
                call  FillWord
                mov   BX,offset L3SI
                mov   AX,[ BP.UsersSI ]
                call  FillWord
                mov   BX,offset L3BP
                mov   AX,[ BP.UsersBP ]
                call  FillWord
                mov   BX,offset L3SP
                mov   AX,BP
                add   AX,size CE_CallerStack
                call  FillWord
                mov   Line + 6,offset L3
                mov   BX,offset L4DS
                mov   AX,[ BP.UsersDS ]
                call  FillWord
                mov   BX,offset L4ES
                mov   AX,[ BP.UsersES ]
                call  FillWord
                mov   BX,offset L4SS
                mov   AX,SS
                call  FillWord
                mov   Line + 8,offset L4
                mov   BX,offset L5CS
                mov   AX,[ BP.UsersCS ]
                call  FillWord
                mov   BX,offset L5IP
                mov   AX,[ BP.UsersIP ]
                call  FillWord
                mov   BX,offset L5Flags
                mov   AX,[ BP.UsersFlags ]
                test  AX,0800H
                jz    OF_Clear
                mov   byte ptr [ BX ],'O'
OF_Clear:
                inc   BX
                test  AX,0400H
                jz    DF_Clear
                mov   byte ptr [ BX ],'D'
DF_Clear:
                inc   BX
                test  AX,0200H
                jz    IF_Clear
                mov   byte ptr [ BX ],'I'
```

```
        IF_Clear:
                inc   BX
                test  AX,0100H
                jz    TF_Clear
                mov   byte ptr [ BX ],'T'
        TF_Clear:
                inc   BX
                test  AX,0080H
                jz    SF_Clear
                mov   byte ptr [ BX ], 'S'
        SF_Clear:
                inc   BX
                test  AX,0040H
                jz    ZF_Clear
                mov   byte ptr [ BX ],'Z'
        ZF_Clear:
                inc   BX
                test  AX,0010H
                jz    AF_Clear
                mov   byte ptr [ BX ],'A'
        AF_Clear:
                inc   BX
                test  AX,0004H
                jz    PF_Clear
                mov   byte ptr [ BX ],'P'
        PF_Clear:
                inc   BX
                test  AX,0001H
                jz    CF_Clear
                mov   byte ptr [ BX ],'C'
        CF_Clear:
                mov   Line + 10,offset L5
                mov   AX,offset UnknownErrorCode
                mov   BX,ErrorCode
                xor   BH,BH
                cmp   BX,0FH
                ja    SetErrorCode
                shl   BX,1
                mov   AX,ECTable[ BX ]
        SetErrorCode:
                mov   Line + 12,AX
                test  IO_Type,80H
                jz    DiskError
                mov   AX,DeviceDriverHeaderSegment
                mov   ES,AX
                mov   BX,DeviceDriverHeaderOffset
                test  word ptr ES:[ BX + 4 ],8000H
                jz    UnknownDevice
                push  DS
                push  ES
                mov   DS,AX
                lea   SI,[ BX + 10 ]
                mov   AX,seg criterr_data
                mov   ES,AX
                mov   DI,offset criterr_data:L7_Device
                mov   CX,8
```

continues

367

DOS
PROGRAMMING

Listing 11.6 Continued

```
                cld
                rep   movsb
                pop   ES
                pop   DS
                mov   Line + 14,offset L7_Char
                jmp   short SetBridge
UnknownDevice:
                mov   Line + 14,offset L7_UnknownChar
                jmp   short SetBridge
DiskError:
                mov   BL,IO_Type
                and   BL,7
                xor   BH,BH
                shl   BX,1
                mov   BX,DiskErrorTable[ BX ]
                mov   Line + 14,BX
                mov   AL,DriveNumber
                add   AL,'A'
                mov   [ BX + DRIVE_OFFSET ],AL
SetBridge:
                mov   Line + 16,offset Bridge2Line
                push  DS
                mov   AH,59H
                xor   BX,BX
                int   21H
                pop   DS
                mov   Line + 18,offset EEC_Unknown
                cmp   AX,5AH
                ja    No_EEC
                push  BX
                mov   BX,AX
                shl   BX,1
                mov   AX,EEC_Table[ BX ]
                pop   BX
                mov   Line + 18,AX
No_EEC:
                mov   Line + 20,offset ECC_Unknown
                cmp   BH,0CH
                ja    No_ECC
                push  BX
                mov   BL,BH
                xor   BH,BH
                shl   BX,1
                mov   AX,ECC_Table[ BX ]
                mov   Line + 20,AX
                pop   BX
No_ECC:
                mov   Line + 22,offset RAC_Unknown
                cmp   BL,7
                ja    No_RAC
                xor   BH,BH
                shl   BX,1
                mov   AX,RAC_Table[ BX ]
                mov   Line + 22,AX
```

```
No_RAC:
        mov     Line + 24,offset Locus_Unknown
        cmp     CH,5
        ja      No_Locus
        mov     BL,CH
        xor     BH,BH
        shl     BX,1
        mov     AX,Locus_Table[ BX ]
        mov     Line + 24,AX
No_Locus:
        mov     Line + 26,offset BridgeLine
        cmp     DOS_MajorVersion,2
        ja      NotARF
        jmp     SetARF
NotARF:
        mov     AL,IO_Type
        and     AL,38H
        cmp     AL,00H
        jne     NotOption0
        mov     Line + 28,offset TerminateOption
        mov     Line + 30,offset BottomMenu
        mov     MenuLines,15
        mov     MaximumOption,0
        mov     ReturnCodes,offset Set__2_
        jmp     DrawScreen
NotOption0:
        cmp     AL,08H
        jne     NotOption1
        mov     Line + 28,offset TerminateOption
        mov     Line + 30,offset FailCallOption
        mov     Line + 32,offset BottomMenu
        mov     MenuLines,16
        mov     MaximumOption,1
        mov     ReturnCodes,offset Set__23
        jmp     DrawScreen
NotOption1:
        cmp     AL,10H
        jne     NotOption2
        mov     Line + 28,offset RetryOption
        mov     Line + 30,offset TerminateOption
        mov     Line + 32,offset BottomMenu
        mov     MenuLines,16
        mov     MaximumOption,1
        mov     ReturnCodes,offset Set_12_
        jmp     DrawScreen
NotOption2:
        cmp     AL,18H
        jne     NotOption3
        mov     Line + 28,offset RetryOption
        mov     Line + 30,offset TerminateOption
        mov     Line + 32,offset FailCallOption
        mov     Line + 34,offset BottomMenu
        mov     MenuLines,17
        mov     MaximumOption,2
        mov     ReturnCodes,offset Set_123
        jmp     DrawScreen
```

continues

369

Listing 11.6 Continued

```
NotOption3:
        cmp   AL,20H
        jne   NotOption4
        mov   Line + 28,offset IgnoreOption
        mov   Line + 30,offset TerminateOption
        mov   Line + 32,offset BottomMenu
        mov   MenuLines,16
        mov   MaximumOption,1
        mov   ReturnCodes,offset Set0_2_
        jmp   DrawScreen
NotOption4:
        cmp   AL,28H
        jne   NotOption5
        mov   Line + 28,offset IgnoreOption
        mov   Line + 30,offset TerminateOption
        mov   Line + 32,offset FailCallOption
        mov   Line + 34,offset BottomMenu
        mov   MenuLines,17
        mov   MaximumOption,2
        mov   ReturnCodes,offset Set0_23
        jmp   short DrawScreen
NotOption5:
        cmp   AL,30H
        jne   NotOption6
SetARF:
        mov   Line + 28,offset IgnoreOption
        mov   Line + 30,offset RetryOption
        mov   Line + 32,offset TerminateOption
        mov   Line + 34,offset BottomMenu
        mov   MenuLines,17
        mov   MaximumOption,2
        mov   ReturnCodes,offset Set012_
        jmp   short DrawScreen
NotOption6:
        mov   Line + 28,offset IgnoreOption
        mov   Line + 30,offset RetryOption
        mov   Line + 32,offset TerminateOption
        mov   Line + 34,offset FailCallOption
        mov   Line + 36,offset BottomMenu
        mov   MenuLines,18
        mov   MaximumOption,3
        mov   ReturnCodes,offset Set0123
DrawScreen:
        mov   AX,0040H
        mov   ES,AX
        mov   AL,ES:84H
        sub   AL,MenuLines
        shr   AL,1
        mov   TopLine,AL
        add   AL,MenuLines
        mov   BottomLine,AL
        mov   AL,ES:4AH
        sub   AL,LINEWIDTH
        shr   AL,1
        mov   LeftRow,AL
        add   AL,LINEWIDTH - 1
```

```
              mov   RightRow,AL
              mov   AH,0FH     ; Get current display mode
              int   10H
              mov   ActiveDisplayPage,BH
              mov   AH,3        ; Read cursor position and configuration
              int   10
              mov   OriginalRow,DH
              mov   OriginalColumn,DL
              mov   SI,offset ScreenSave
              mov   DI,offset Line
              mov   DH,TopLine
OuterLoop:
              mov   DL,LeftRow
InnerLoop:
              mov   AH,2       ; Set cursor position
              int   10H
              mov   AH,8       ; Read character and attribute
              int   10H
              mov   [ SI ],AH
              inc   SI
              mov   [ SI ],AL
              inc   SI
              mov   AH,9       ; Write character and attribute
              push  SI
              mov   SI,DS:[ DI ]
              mov   AL,[ SI ]
              inc   SI
              mov   DS:[ DI ],SI
              pop   SI
              mov   BL,ATTRIBUTE
              mov   CX,1
              int   10H
              inc   DL          ; Next row
              cmp   DL,RightRow
              jbe   InnerLoop
              inc   DI
              inc   DI
              inc   DH          ; Next line
              cmp   DH,BottomLine
              jbe   OuterLoop
              mov   CurrentOption,0
              mov   AH,2       ; Set cursor position
              mov   DH,TopLine
              add   DH,14
              mov   DL,LeftRow
              inc   DL
              int   10H
              mov   AH,9       ; Write character and attribute
              mov   AL,10H
              mov   BL,ATTRIBUTE
              mov   CX,1
              int   10H
GetKey:
              xor   AH,AH       ; Get keyboard character
              int   16H
              or    AL,AL       ; Character code 0?
```

continues

Listing 11.6 Continued

```
            jz      CheckScanCode
            cmp     AL,13       ; Return?
            jne     GetKey
            jmp     Return
CheckScanCode:
            cmp     AH,47H      ; Home?
            je      GoHome
            cmp     AH,48H      ; CursorUp?
            je      GoUp
            cmp     AH,49H      ; PageUp?
            je      GoUp
            cmp     AH,4BH      ; CursorLeft?
            je      GoUp
            cmp     AH,4DH      ; CursorRight?
            je      GoDown
            cmp     AH,4FH      ; End?
            je      GoEnd
            cmp     AH,50H      ; CursorDown?
            je      GoDown
            cmp     AH,51H      ; PageDown?
            jne     GetKey
GoDown:
            mov     AH,9        ; Write character and attribute
            mov     AL,' '
            mov     BL,ATTRIBUTE
            mov     CX,1
            int     10H
            mov     AL,CurrentOption
            cmp     AL,MaximumOption
            jne     MoveDown
            xor     AL,AL
MoveCursor:
            mov     CurrentOption,AL
            mov     AH,2
            mov     BH,ActiveDisplayPage
            mov     DH,TopLine
            add     DH,14
            add     DH,AL
            mov     DL,LeftRow
            inc     DL
            int     10H
            mov     AH,9        ; Write character and attribute
            mov     AL,10H
            mov     BL,ATTRIBUTE
            mov     CX,1
            int     10H
            jmp     GetKey
MoveDown:
            inc     AL
            jmp     MoveCursor
GoHome:
            cmp     CurrentOption,0
            je      GetKey
            mov     AH,9        ; Write character and attribute
            mov     AL,' '
```

```
                mov    BL,ATTRIBUTE
                mov    CX,1
                int    10H
                xor    AL,Al
                jmp    MoveCursor
        GoUp:
                mov    AH,9       ; Write character and attribute
                mov    AL,' '
                mov    BL,ATTRIBUTE
                mov    CX,1
                int    10H
                mov    AL,CurrentOption
                or     AL,AL
                jnz    MoveUp
                mov    AL,MaximumOption
                jmp    MoveCursor
        MoveUp:
                dec    AL
                jmp    MoveCursor
        GoEnd:
                mov    AL,MaximumOption
                cmp    AL,CurrentOption
                jne    EraseOption
                jmp    GetKey
        EraseOption:
                mov    AH,9       ; Write character and attribute
                mov    AL,' '
                mov    BL,ATTRIBUTE
                mov    CX,1
                int    10H
                mov    AL,MaximumOption
                jmp    MoveCursor
        Return:
                mov    SI,offset ScreenSave
                mov    DH,TopLine
        OuterLoop2:
                mov    DL,LeftRow
        InnerLoop2:
                mov    AH,2       ; Set cursor position
                int    10H
                mov    AH,9       ; Write character and attribute
                mov    BH,ActiveDisplayPage
                mov    BL,[ SI ]
                inc    SI
                mov    AL,[ SI ]
                inc    SI
                mov    CX,1
                int    10H
                inc    DL         ; Next row
                cmp    DL,RightRow
                jbe    InnerLoop2
                inc    DI
                inc    DI
                inc    DH         ; Next line
                cmp    DH,BottomLine
                jbe    OuterLoop2
```

continues

373

Listing 11.6 Continued

```
                mov   AH,2
                mov   BH,ActiveDisplayPage
                mov   DH,OriginalRow
                mov   DL,OriginalColumn
                int   10H
                mov   AL,CurrentOption
                xor   AH,AH
                mov   BX,ReturnCodes
                add   BX,AX
                mov   AL,[ BX ]
                pop   DS          ; Restore registers
                pop   ES
                pop   BP
                pop   SI
                pop   DI
                pop   BX
                pop   CX
                pop   DX
                iret              ; Interrupt return
CritErr         endp

assume          DS:criterr_data

FillWord        proc near
                xchg AH,AL
                call FillByte
                xchg AH,AL
                call FillByte
                ret
FillWord        endp

FillByte        proc near
                push CX
                push AX
                mov   CL,4
                shr   AL,CL
                call FillNibble
                pop   AX
                call FillNibble
                pop   CX
                ret
FillByte        endp

FillNibble      proc    near
                push AX
                and   AL,0FH
                cmp   AL,9
                jbe   FillNibble_1
                add   AL,7
FillNibble_1:
                add   AL,'0'
                mov   [ BX ],AL
                inc   BX
                pop   AX
                ret
```

```
FillNibble    endp

assume    DS:nothing
assume    ES:nothing
assume    SS:nothing

;    Install the new critical error handler

_CritErrInit    proc far
          push DS          ; Save old registers
          push ES
          push AX
          push BX
          push CX
          push DX
          mov  AX,seg criterr_data
          mov  DS,AX        ; Set DS to local data

          assume    DS:criterr_data

          mov  AH,30H       ; Get DOS version
          int  21H
          mov  DOS_MajorVersion,AL
          mov  AH,35H       ; Get old critical error handler address
          mov  AL,24H
          int  21H
          mov  OldCritErrOffset,BX
          mov  OldCritErrSegment,ES
          mov  AH,25H       ; Set new critical error handler address
          mov  AL,24H
          mov  DX,seg criterr_code
          mov  DS,DX
          mov  DX,offset CS:CritErr
          int  21H
          pop  DX           ; Restore old registers
          pop  CX
          pop  BX
          pop  AX
          pop  ES
          pop  DS
          ret               ; Return to caller
_CritErrInit    endp

assume    DS:nothing

;    Reinstall the critical error handler (as after
;    returning from a DOS shell)

_CritErrReInit  proc    far
          push DS          ; Save old registers
          push AX
          push DX
          mov  AH,25H       ; Set new critical error handler address
          mov  AL,24H
          mov  DX,seg criterr_code
          mov  DS,DX
```

continues

Listing 11.6 Continued

```
              mov   DX,offset CS:CritErr
              int   21H
              pop   DX         ; Restore old registers
              pop   AX
              pop   DS
              ret              ; Return to caller
    _CritErrReInit  endp

    ;     Uninstall the critical error handler (as before,
    ;     invoking a DOS shell)

    _CritErrUnInit  proc     far
              push  DS         ; Save old registers
              push  AX
              push  DX
              mov   AX,seg criterr_data
              mov   DS,AX      ; Set DS to local data

              assume    DS:criterr_data

              mov   AX,OldCritErrOffset
              mov   DX,OldCritErrSegment
              mov   DS,DX

              assume    DS:nothing

              mov   AH,25H     ; Set old critical error handler address
              mov   AL,24H
              int   21H
              pop   DX         ; Restore old registers
              pop   AX
              pop   DS
              ret              ; Return to caller
    _CritErrUnInit  endp

    public     _CritErrInit
    public     _CritErrReInit
    public     _CritErrUnInit

    criterr_code    ends
              end
```

Now that you have learned something about interrupts and how TSRs are activated, let's see how TSRs work.

Revisiting TSRs

TSRs originally were intended to be a convenient way to add ISRs to DOS by allowing programs to initialize themselves and link into the system-interrupt structure. Service routines that sort, search, and perform other utility functions were envisioned as normal uses for this function—and with good reason.

When DOS first entered the market, operating systems such as CP/M and TRSDOS had no TSR facility. But programmers had discovered how to build utilities and stash them in memory for other programs to use. Several popular packages with sorting utilities, display-handling utilities, and programmers' tools were available then; it seems likely that the designers of MS-DOS were aware of them and wanted to make building such utilities an easier process.

As users gained experience with DOS, they learned that they could tie an interrupt service routine into the keyboard interrupt and see what was happening. Because early copies of the PC's *Technical Reference Manual* included a ROM BIOS listing, it was easy to see how things worked and the effect of linking into the keyboard interrupt. On PCs, no effect would be visible to users; but for the TSR, it was another story.

When the TSR was linked to the keyboard interrupt, it no longer was a *passive* TSR. It became *active* because it could decide on its own when to do something; an active TSR took on an existence of its own.

A passive TSR would sit quietly in memory and respond only when a program passed a specific request for service. This type of TSR is easy to write because it needs no special coding tricks. When the TSR is called, you know that DOS is not active because the application program that invoked the interrupt had to have control of the machine. In this situation, anything the machine could do was legal. That stopped, however, with active TSRs.

An active TSR could interrupt the machine at any time. Knowing what the machine was executing when the TSR got control was impossible. Because DOS and PCs were designed as single-user, single-task systems, no provision had ever been made for the possibility that someone might run more than one program at the same time. BIOS and DOS, therefore, store large amounts of information in global tables. Intermediate results of data entry and calculations all use the same buffers. When you interrupt the system, the implication is that control *might* be inside DOS at the time of the interrupt. If you then call DOS again, you lose what DOS is doing and probably crash the system.

Early TSRs continually caused system crashes. They interfered not only with DOS but also with each other. Some were as tenacious as bulldogs in taking control of the machine. Hard-won experience has led to the following unofficial rules for writing TSRs:

- Never call DOS functions unless you have no other way to get what you want. (File system access is the major reason for having to call DOS.)

- If you *have* to do I/O, you can do the following:

  Use something other than DOS console I/O functions (Int 21h, Functions 01h–0Ch). Better ways of getting to the console are available.

  Monitor the InDOS flag. When this flag is nonzero, DOS is executing an Int 21h function. Do not run your process when this flag is nonzero. (See the discussion of Int 21h, Function 34h in the "DOS Reference" section for information about how to access this flag.)

Monitor Int 28h. This interrupt tells you that even though DOS is doing Int 21h functions, it is in a "busy wait" for console I/O. If you do your own console I/O below DOS, you can safely execute anything else. (See Int 28h in the "DOS Reference" section for more information.)

Provide a check function that lets your TSR indicate whether it is already installed. Linking to an unused interrupt vector lets the TSR check for the presence of an earlier copy in memory, but is rife with danger because the machine has only a limited number of vectors available. You can link into the Multiplex interrupt chain DOS provides for its *own* TSRs (PRINT, APPEND, SHARE, and so on) to use, and that will be much safer. Refer to Appendix C, "A Standard TSR-Identification Technique," for a standardized method of using Multiplex interrupt 2Fh to identify TSRs.

Put a signature inside the executable code to tell whether the TSR is present.

Always assume that other TSRs are present. Chain any interrupts used by your TSR by passing control to the interrupt vector your TSR found when it started.

Use your own stack rather than the one controlled by the interrupted program. You have no way of knowing what might be on that stack, nor do you know the *size* of the stack or the amount of space that is left before you crash into something.

Because of all the conflicts, a group of leading independent TSR authors banded together in early 1986 to try to develop a standard for TSRs. Although the original goal (providing a total Application Package Interface that could be accepted by all commercial vendors in addition to independent authors) could not be met, some members of the group persisted. In 1988, they released a set of library functions—compatible with C, Turbo Pascal 4.0 and above, and assembler—that handles the difficult parts of TSR design for you.

This package, TesSeRact, is available as a shareware package on CompuServe and from many local bulletin-board systems. An overview, including the means by which it standardizes conflict resolution, is included as Appendix C. It is only fair to point out, though, that Jim Kyle was a charter member of the team and one of the two still participating in the project.

A number of commercial developers have accepted this interface standard even though they write their own internal routines rather than use the library. The team encourages this; the idea is to avoid conflicts by agreeing on a standard rather than promote the use of any single code package to the exclusion of all others.

Interrupts Essential to TSRs

Some of the many interrupts are documented. Interrupts are important to anyone who writes a TSR. The "DOS Reference" section gives as much detail as we know about each of them. This section introduces you to the interrupts so that you can see the kinds of assistance they can provide.

The Keyboard Interrupt

The keyboard interrupt (Int 09h) is the way an active TSR takes control. By monitoring what happens at the keyboard, the TSR can tell when the hot key is pressed and activated. The following code shows the basic method:

```
Int 09h activates on keystroke
Handler activates and reads keystroke
if(hot key has been found){
    throw away the keystroke
    check DOS
    if(in DOS){
        set a hot key flag
        return from the interrupt
    } else {
        activate the TSR
        when the TSR is done, return
            from the interrupt
    }
} else {
    chain to the next handler on Int 09h
}
```

What's this about "check DOS"? Remember that DOS is not reentrant. If you call DOS for anything, you might crash the system. To check DOS, use Int 21h, Function 34h, which is described in the next section.

The InDOS Flag, DOSOK Interrupt, and Timer Interrupt

Calling Int 21h, Function 34h returns a pointer to the InDOS flag (DOS busy flag). If this flag is nonzero, DOS was interrupted to execute a function. If your TSR did interrupt DOS, the function usually returns in a fraction of a second. The preceding pseudocode for Int 09h shows where you would check the InDOS flag. After you set the hot-key flag, you must have a way to pick it up. For this purpose, you have the DOSOK interrupt and the timer interrupt.

When your program starts up, it must initialize a special interrupt handler for Int 28h such as the following:

```
Int 28h activates
check hot key flag
if(hot key flag is set){
    turn hot key flag off
    activate the TSR
}
call the next Int 28h service routine
return from the interrupt
```

Int 28h (the DOSOK interrupt) activates when DOS is waiting for console input in Int 21h, Functions 01h–0Ch. If you see this interrupt, you know that you can safely use other DOS

379

functions. (Two exceptions to this statement when you run under DOS V2 are the undocumented functions 50h and 51h; see the reference section for details and how you can use them safely at this point.)

If DOS is not waiting for input, you use the timer interrupt. The timer interrupt (1Ch) ticks 18.2 times per second. You can attach to this interrupt the following service routine that checks the hot-key flag also:

```
Timer Interrupt activates
call next timer interrupt service
check hot key flag
if(hot key flag is set){
    turn hot key flag off
    activate the TSR
}
return from the interrupt
```

After you get control, you have other problems. Your TSR wants to work as simply as possible, but you do not know the state of the machine you are interrupting. How deep is the stack? How much space below the stack pointer is free for growth? More important, you do not want the TSR to be grabbed by a system error.

To make your TSR as robust as possible, you want to have it take control of the Critical-Error interrupt (Int 24h) and the Ctrl-Break interrupt (Int 23h). The TSR can also insert itself into the interrupt chain of the BIOS disk driver (Int 13h) and any other routines that might cause problems. Then, if a problem occurs, the TSR can correct it and you can shift to an internal stack and execute your functions.

Some programmers advocate *context switching*, where the DOS pointer to the active process's PSP is changed to point to the TSR's PSP. You use Int 21h, Function 51h to get the segment address of the interrupted program, save that address, and then use Int 21h, Function 50h to tell DOS that the TSR's program segment prefix (PSP) is the current active process. Under V2, this process is fraught with danger if it is executed during service of Int 28h, because 50h and 51h use the same DOS stack space as 28h and, as a result, the system hangs.

Context switching is a useful technique if you do file I/O or otherwise want to have total control. You can avoid the danger in V2 by setting the DOS *critical error* flag before calling either function (therefore causing DOS to use an alternate stack area), and then clearing the flag on return from the function so that DOS acts normally. Unfortunately, this process in turn creates more problems because the location of the critical error flag differs from one version of DOS to another. The best solution is to avoid context switching unless it is absolutely necessary (as for handle-based file I/O); if you must use it, see Functions 50h and 51h in the reference section for details.

When the TSR finishes with its main business, it must "clean itself up," restore the interrupts, and reset the stack to normal. Then it can return to the interrupted program.

To demonstrate basic TSR operation, some of the concepts have been put to work in a simple clock program (clock.c) that sets itself up and then waits for a clock tick to activate (see Listing 11.7).

Listing 11.7

```
/* clock.c
   Listing 11.7 of DOS Programmer's Reference */

#include <stdio.h>
#include <stdlib.h>
#include <dos.h>
#include <string.h>

/*   Define needed constants */
#define      BOOL        int
#define      FALSE       0
#define      TRUE        !FALSE

/*   Define program size for the system */
#define      PGMSIZE     3000

/*   Define base address for video display */
#define      MONOBASE    0xb000
#define      COLORBASE   0xb800

/*   Define interrupt vectors for BIOS and DOS needed by program */
#define      GOTOXY      0x02
#define      GETXY       0x03
#define      TELETYPE    0x0e
#define      VIDEO       0x10
#define      CLOCK       0x1a
#define      TIMER       0x1c
#define      DOS         0x21
#define      TSR         0x31
#define      TEST        0x66

void interrupt clock();              /* Declare clock() */
void interrupt (*orig_clock)();      /* Original clock vector */
void interrupt test();               /* Declare test()  */

BOOL inclock = FALSE;                /* Clock processing flag */
BOOL extra = FALSE;                  /* Extra tick flag */
int count = 0;                       /* Clock tick counter */
char buf[20];                        /* Time buffer */
char far *clkptr;                    /* Pointer to screen location */

int  sp;                             /* Stack pointer */
int  ss;                             /* Stack segment */

int  hr, min, sec;                   /* Current time */

void main(argc,argv)
```

continues

Listing 11.7 Continued

```
            char argc;
            char *argv[];

    {
            union REGS regs;
            int  mode;

            int  streql(char *str1, char *str2);
            void readclock(int *hr, int *min, int *sec);
            void tsrexit(void);
            int  getmode(void);

    /*  Initialize clock output buffer with a string for printing */
            strcpy(buf,"   TEST   ");

            orig_clock = getvect(TEST);

            if(streql(argv[1],"-u") && orig_clock!=0){
                    printf("Updating the clock\n");
                    int86(TEST,&regs,&regs);
                    exit(0);
            }

            if(orig_clock != 0){
                    printf("Already installed ... exiting\n");
                    exit(0);
            }

            setvect(TEST,test);

    /*  Read the initial value of the clock at start-up, and
        then set the clock pointer to the screen address */
            orig_clock = getvect(CLOCK);
            setvect(CLOCK,clock);
            readclock(&hr,&min,&sec);
            mode = getmode();
            printf("Display mode is %d\n",mode);
            if(mode==7)
                    clkptr = MK_FP(MONOBASE,120);
            else
                    clkptr = MK_FP(COLORBASE,120);

    /*  TSR exit to save the memory for the program */
            tsrexit();
    }

    void interrupt clock()
        {
        void displayclk(char *str);

        (*orig_clock)();

        count++;
        if(sec%5==0 && count%18==0 && !extra){
                extra=TRUE;
                count--;
```

```
        } else {
            extra=FALSE;
        }

        if(count%18 == 0){
            disable();
            sp = _SP;
            ss = _SS;
            _SS = _CS;
            _SP = PGMSIZE;
            enable();

            sec++;
            if(sec>=60){
                sec=0; min++;
            }
            if(min>=60){
                min=0;hr++;
            }
            if(hr>=24) hr = 0;

            if(!inclock){
                inclock = TRUE;
                sprintf(buf+6,"%02.2d:%02.2d:%02.2d ",hr,min,sec);
                displayclk(buf);
                inclock = FALSE;
            }

            disable();
            _SP = sp;
            _SS = ss;
            enable();
        }
    }

void tsrexit(void)
    {
        union REGS regs;

        regs.h.ah = TSR;
        regs.h.al = 0;
        regs.x.dx = PGMSIZE;
        int86(DOS,&regs,&regs);
    }

void displayclk(str)
    char        *str;
    {
        char far        *ptr;
        ptr = clkptr;
        while(*str){
            *ptr++ = *str++;
            ptr++;
        }
    }

void readclock(hr,min,sec)
```

continues

Listing 11.7 Continued

```c
int  *hr, *min, *sec;
{
        union REGS regs;
        unsigned long  clock;
        unsigned long  remain;
        unsigned long  x1, x2;

        regs.h.ah = 0;
        int86(CLOCK,&regs,&regs);
        x1 = regs.x.cx * 65536L; x2 = regs.x.dx;
        clock = x1 + x2;
        *hr = (int) (clock / 65543L);
        remain = clock % 65543L;
        *min = (int) (remain / 1092);
        remain = remain % 1092;
        *sec = remain / 18.21;
}

void interrupt test()
    {
        register int ds;

        disable();
        sp = _SP;
        ss = _SS;
        _SS = _CS;
        _SP = PGMSIZE;
        ds = _DS;
        _DS = _CS;
        readclock(&hr,&min,&sec);
        _DS = ds;
        _SP = sp;
        _SS = ss;
        enable();
    }

int streql(str1,str2)
    char *str1, *str2;
    {
        return(strcmp(str1,str2)==0);
    }

int getmode()
    {
        union REGS regs;

        regs.h.ah = 0x0f;
        int86(VIDEO,&regs,&regs);
        return(regs.h.al);
    }
```

Let's go over the program to see how it works.

Notice that part of the setup involves putting the word TEST at the beginning of the clock output buffer so that it is displayed when the clock is updated. (This is just a convenience for the demonstration program.)

Standard Turbo C functions are used to access the interrupt vector table (rather than make the calls directly). First, however, you have to see whether the TSR is already installed. A simple way to do this was chosen: Int 66h was used as a marker because it is unused by most TSRs and its value normally is zero. If Int 66h is nonzero, the program assumes that the TSR has set it. If the value is zero, you know that it has not been set.

Int 66h is used also to force the clock program to reset its current time from the system. Rather than write a new program to do that, simply start the TSR with a -u flag. If the first argument is -u, reset the clock and leave.

The Turbo C getvect() function is used to get the value of the vector. Next, the program checks for the -u flag if the Int 66h vector has been set. If it finds the -u flag and if the vector is nonzero, an Int 66h is issued to reset the clock and exit.

If there is no -u flag, the program checks whether the vector is nonzero. If it is, the program assumes that the clock program has already started. If another TSR that uses Int 66h is active, you cannot start the clock program (because of the Int 66h vector).

If, after all your checks, you find that the vector is zero, you set the vector to point to the test() interrupt function (which forces the TSR to read the BIOS clock) and set up the clock function.

To set up the clock function, you first get the original clock vector, save it for future use, and reset the vector to point to the clock() interrupt function. Then you read the initial clock time from the BIOS clock function, get the current display mode to identify a monochrome versus a color monitor, and establish a pointer (clkptr) to point to the screen location at which you will write the clock. To eliminate the use of BIOS or DOS functions while the TSR is operating, you put the clock directly to the screen display buffer. *This process works only in text modes; programs that shift the display to graphics modes will show garbage from the clock.*

After everything is set up, the TSR exit is called and the program is resident. The clock interrupt handler, clock(), is the heart of the TSR. Let's go over it step by step to see how it operates.

First, you call the original clock timer so that it does whatever is required on each clock tick. Then you can proceed. The count variable keeps track of timer ticks (which occur at a rate of 18.2 per second). The clock advances one second every 18 ticks. Every five seconds, one extra tick is allowed to bring the average over 5-second periods to 18.2 ticks per second. After advancing the count, check whether you are at a five-second interval. If you are, you decrease the count by one to force a wait of one extra tick (giving you 19 ticks on this second). The extra flag tells you that you are doing the extra tick and prevents you from decrementing the count whenever you come back at the fifth second.

With the period between seconds covered, you now check for every 18th tick. When you find it, you reset the stack to your internal stack and advance the timer by one second (sec++). Then, to keep the clock running correctly, you check for 60 seconds, 60 minutes, and 24 hours. After everything else is finished, you display the clock.

If you are not already in the clock display section (inclock is set to FALSE), you enter that portion of the program, set inclock to TRUE, and set up and display the clock. Finally, you re-set the stack to its status when the clock() function was called.

The clock display is simple. You write directly to the screen memory and advance the screen buffer pointer by 2 to get past the attribute byte for every byte of the clock you write to the screen. The remainder of the clock program is made up of some simple, self-explanatory functions.

The program is compiled with the Borland C/C++ compiler, by using the MAKE utility provided with the software. The makefile that compiles the program correctly is shown in Listing 11.8.

Listing 11.8

```
# clock.mak
clock.exe:      clock.obj
     tlink /x c0t clock, clock,, emu maths cs

clock.obj:      clock.c
     bcc -c -mt clock.c
```

The MAKE utility recompiles the program only when necessary. This type of utility, although of minimal use here, is especially useful on large projects. Use the following command line to execute the MAKE utility:

```
make -fclock
```

The important thing about the compilation is that the program is compiled with the TINY memory model (the same as a COM program, so that Code, Data, and Stack segments are all the same). Consult your *Borland C/C++ User's Guide* for details about how to use the compiler switches.

If you are using Microsoft C, you can modify the program to handle segment registers within the limits of the Microsoft system and establish similar compilation switches for control of the program compilation.

Summary

This chapter showed you how to work with interrupts. By using utilities provided as part of DOS Int 21h, you can change an interrupt vector to point to a function you design. You have written a sample handler in C with an assembly language front end to handle the interfacing. Turbo Pascal 4.0 provides a specific way for you to create interrupt handlers as Pascal functions.

Terminate-and-stay-resident utilities can be written to trigger on interrupts (the keyboard and clock interrupts, for example). These utilities can be extremely dangerous to programs, however, because DOS never was intended to handle multitasking operations. DOS is a purely nonreentrant system and can fail when a TSR calls functions that were in progress when the TSR got control of the computer.

You learned several ways to minimize problems with TSRs. You know not to call DOS functions unless absolutely necessary and to use BIOS or direct calls for keyboard and screen I/O. You know about monitoring the InDOS flag to see when performing DOS functions is safe, and you know about monitoring Int 28h to determine when the system is waiting for keyboard input. You learned to provide a check function that lets the TSR check to see whether it is already loaded and to always assume that another TSR is present. And, you know that using an internal stack is a good way to prevent problems in stack operations.

12

Device Drivers

In the early days of computing, programmers wrote all types of programs directly at the hardware level. Every program had to deal directly with the intricacies of card readers, printers, tape drives, and other equipment connected to computers. Programmers, therefore, had to master all kinds of arcane information about handling each type of error, processing correct input and output, and so on.

As computers developed, programmers saw that their time for this sort of repetitive work was at a premium. Handlers for external devices gradually became standard items that programmers added to their programs. Before long, these handlers were collected in a primitive operating system in which *all* programs could use the same set of device handlers, or *drivers*.

In the earliest operating systems, the different *device drivers* were coded as integral parts of the system and interacted in intricate ways with the rest of the system. As a result of attempts to make device drivers more independent, systems programmers can install device drivers as necessary during start-up.

Although most significant operating systems have some such flexibility, DOS provides the most flexibility for *users* to install drivers. Many microcomputer operating systems required tedious patching to accomplish what can be done with a prewritten driver and the system configuration file.

For most people who work with DOS, their only contact with drivers is to load them from distribution disks and make the required entry in the CONFIG.SYS file. (These entries are described later in this chapter.) Users follow written instructions that tell them, line for line, how to make the changes. In some systems, you do not have even this much contact because an installation program makes the changes for you.

Most programmers eventually begin to feel rather confident about their skills and decide to write a device driver. Experienced assembly language programmers find this task to be relatively easy—they just have to follow a formula. If you follow the formula correctly, your driver will work correctly. Many programmers fail because they do not stick to the rigid outline of what a driver must do and how it must be laid out. The purpose of this chapter is to show you how to write good device drivers.

For maximum speed and coding convenience, device drivers usually are written in assembly language on PCs. Although parts of a device driver can be written in a language such as C, problems can occur in getting the correct structure and in minimizing overhead. Because of a device driver's rigid structure, modules compiled in C can provide only functional services to the driver. If you use C to build functions for a driver, you must start with an assembly language section that gets initial control and then calls C routines as necessary. You *cannot* call C library functions because many of them refer to DOS functions. (A driver is not allowed to call DOS services. You can read more about this subject in this chapter's "Driver Initialization" section.)

Here are three good reasons for using assembly language to code the entire driver:

- Because a device driver is at the heart of all access to a device, it must be coded as tightly as possible to save execution time and memory space.

- The driver layout is rigidly defined; only assembly language gives you the required layout control.

- You must manipulate specified CPU registers at specific times, which is difficult to do from C.

Coding device drivers in C is common in the UNIX world, but the interface requirements are different. An assembly language front end that you do not see links and controls the operating system. Coding a driver in C can be fun (and frustrating), if you want to try it.

Before you learn how to build a device driver, you should understand how a device driver is laid out and how it works. Implementation flows naturally from what you learn.

As you learn about drivers, you will build a driver shell into which you can drop additional code to make real drivers for real devices. You start by learning about types of drivers and how they work.

Driver Types

The two basic types of device drivers—character devices and block devices—are fundamentally different. Before you continue, you should understand how they differ.

Character Device Drivers

Character devices are byte-oriented devices such as printer ports or serial ports. All communication with the device occurs on a character-by-character basis.

I/O from a character device occurs in one of two basic modes: cooked and raw. In *cooked mode*, DOS requests one character at a time from the driver and buffers the input internally. Special keystrokes such as Ctrl-C and the carriage return are processed by DOS. In *raw mode*, DOS does not buffer the data nor does it look for and respond to Ctrl-C or the carriage return. Rather, requests for input of a fixed number of characters are passed directly to the driver; the return is made up of the characters read by the driver.

Character devices are given names (CON, AUX, and LPT, for example) that can be as long as eight characters (like file names). The 8-character limitation occurs because the driver's name held in the device header is only eight characters. (The header is discussed in the "Device Header" section later in this chapter.) This limitation was deliberately designed in DOS to make it possible to use the same I/O routines to deal with both named files and named devices. It also makes it impossible to access a file that has the same name as any driver present in the system; the routines access the driver instead.

Block Device Drivers

Block devices process blocks of data such as those on tapes and disks. Every access to a block device *always* transfers data in the appropriate block sizes. With block devices, there is no equivalent to the character device drivers' cooked and raw modes.

Block devices are assigned drive letters and become one or more of the system's logical drives (A, B, and C, for example). A single block device driver can handle more than one hardware unit or map one hardware unit into multiple logical devices. Every logical device is structured with a base-file system that includes a FAT (file allocation table) and root directory. (For additional information about these structures, see Chapter 2, "The Structure of a DOS System," and Chapter 8, "Disks.")

How Device Drivers Work

When an applications program calls DOS Int 21h to perform any I/O function, device drivers get involved in almost every case (except for such system functions as extended error processing). Consider an example in which you try to write to a file on the disk.

Whether you explicitly code the file-writing operation as a call to DOS or use a library function, the applications program sets up the registers and makes a call to Int 21h (DOS service routines) to handle the disk I/O. When the service routine gets control, it in turn sets up and makes a call to Int 26h (Absolute Disk Write). Int 26h sets up a request header (a command buffer for the driver) in a reserved area of memory and calls the strategy routine for the device driver that handles the disk. The strategy routine simply saves the address of the request header and returns control to the interrupt handler.

Next, DOS calls the interrupt portion of the driver. (Its name, like that of the strategy routine, does not reflect its function.) The interrupt portion of the driver reads the request header and determines what is requested. The interrupt portion then transfers control to the appropriate internal routine and executes the disk write by calling the BIOS disk write function, Int 13h. When the disk write is completed, control returns through the chain to the applications program, and status codes are adjusted to reflect what each calling routine expects.

Figure 12.1 shows the sequence of events. Every step of the operation involves a transfer of control to successively lower-level routines until the disk write occurs.

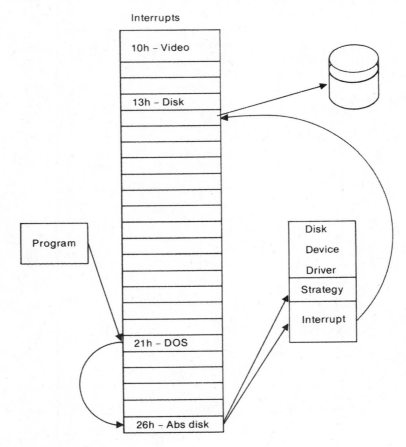

Figure 12.1   Calling for a disk write.

All these steps take place for every individual operation of the disk; there can be many such calls to the driver. If you use high-level language resources in the file call, you might need additional access to the disk to read the FAT, allocate space, and update parameters on the disk. Drivers can be extremely busy.

Although this example of a disk write is complicated, you can handle it with a call to the BIOS. You do not have to worry about the "down and dirty" interfacing details (the hardware operation). On each PC and compatible, the BIOS is supposed to make all devices look like a set of standard devices. But, what if you add a custom piece of equipment? Figure 12.2 shows what happens. The driver must manipulate the new hardware directly. There is no BIOS to handle the interfacing details.

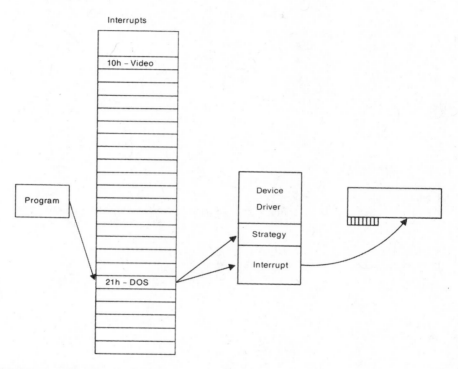

Figure 12.2   A custom device driver.

When you add a board that adds a new capability to the system, you must add a new device driver. When you add a CD-ROM drive, a mouse, a local area network, or a music synthesizer, you add hardware the PC system software was never designed to handle. MS-DOS has no software to handle a mouse device. The driver that comes with the mouse has to work directly with the hardware. The complexity begins here. To interface this hardware to the system, you need a driver.

The example of disk access through the driver (refer to Fig. 12.1) hid one important fact: the BIOS already has taken care of the hardware details. All the timing details, bit manipulations, and so on are handled by the BIOS. For a custom add-on, your driver must handle the hardware details directly.

When you add a piece of hardware to the system and write the driver for it, *you* must complete all the interfacing details. If you add an analog-digital converter so that you can read some instrumentation, you must service the chips on the hardware level. If you have to observe timing restrictions or deal with other problems, *you* must know about them.

A demonstration of a working interface to a special board is beyond the scope of this book. To perform a successful interface, you must have an intimate knowledge of the hardware you want to run. Nothing less is acceptable. This book tries to give you a framework in which to make your driver work, whether you are writing a driver for a new piece of hardware to be added to a system or for some existing hardware.

Device Driver Structure

A device driver is made up of three parts: the device header, the strategy routine, and the interrupt routine. In DOS V2, the driver had to be a memory image (or a COM program) with no origin (ORG 0, or no statement). And, it had to be coded as a FAR procedure. The EXE2BIN program converts the assembled driver to an image file, and the system loads the image during the boot operation. By convention, drivers usually have the extension .SYS (or sometimes .BIN). The file extension is changed to .SYS to prevent someone from accidentally executing the driver as a program.

In DOS V3.0 and later versions, drivers can be object files in EXE format. The operating system loads them correctly. To maintain backward compatibility with DOS V2, however, most people who write drivers work with the COM format. (DOS V1 had no provision for loadable drivers.) The examples in this chapter are COM-type drivers.

This section examines the structure of the driver. It looks first at the device header—the first important part of a working driver.

Device Header

The device header is an 18-byte area divided into five fields (see Fig. 12.3).

This list describes the five fields:

- *Next driver pointer.* Four bytes are initialized to –1 (FFFFFFFFh). DOS uses this field to load a pointer to the next driver in the list of drivers. The last driver in the list is marked with –1. (Only the *offset* half of this pointer must be –1; the *segment* half can be 0.)

- *Driver attribute word.* Two bytes that specify the driver characteristics (see Table 12.1).

- *Strategy routine offset.* A 2-byte offset to the strategy routine within the driver.

- *Interrupt routine offset.* A 2-byte offset to the interrupt routine within the driver.
- *Device name.* If the device is a character device, an 8-character, left-justified, blank-filled device name appears next. If the name is the same as the name of an existing device, the new driver replaces the existing device. If the device is a block device, the first byte in this field is the number of logical devices associated with the driver; the other bytes are ignored (some versions of DOS include special information about the boot block device here).

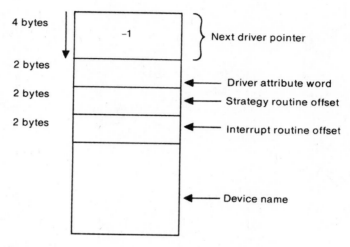

Figure 12.3   The device header.

Table 12.1   Driver Attribute Word

Bits		Meaning
FEDCBA98	76543210	
....	1	Standard input device
....	0	Not standard input device
....	......1.	Character device: Standard output device
		Block device: Can handle 32-bit sector numbers (V4 only)
....	......0.	Character device: Not standard output device
		Block device: Cannot handle 32-bit sector numbers (V4 only)
....	.....1..	NUL device
....	.....0..	Not NUL device

continues

395

Table 12.1 Continued

——— Bits ———		Meaning
FEDCBA98	76543210	
....	....1...	Clock device
....	....0...	Not clock device
....	...1....	Driver services Int 29h
....000	000.....	Reserved before V3.2 (set to zero)
....	..0.....	Reserved in V3.2 and higher (set to zero)
....	.1......	Driver supports generic IOCTL (V3.2 and higher)
....	.0......	Driver does not support generic IOCTL (V3.2 and higher)
....000	0.......	Reserved in V3.2 and higher (set to zero)
....0...	....	OPEN/CLOSE/Removable media supported (V3 and higher)
....1...	....	OPEN/CLOSE/Removable media not supported (V3 and higher)
...0....	....	Reserved (set to zero)
..1.....	....	Character device: Device does not support output-till-busy operation
		Block device: IBM block format
..0.....	....	Character device: Device supports output-till-busy operation
		Block device: Not IBM block format
.1......	....	IOCTL supported
.0......	....	IOCTL not supported
1.......	....	Character device
0.......	....	Block device

As DOS initializes itself, it establishes a chain of the standard device drivers; the next driver pointer in every driver gives the address of the next driver in the chain (see Fig. 12.4). The last driver in the chain has a pointer of –1 to indicate the end of the chain.

When DOS finally reads the CONFIG.SYS file, a driver chain already has been set up. New drivers are added at the head of the chain (see Fig. 12.5).

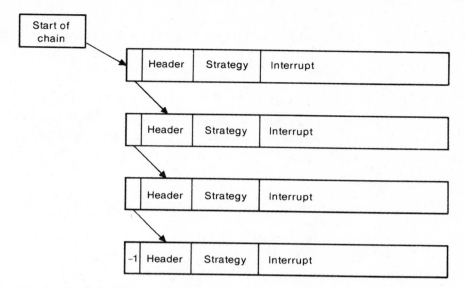

Figure 12.4 The driver chain.

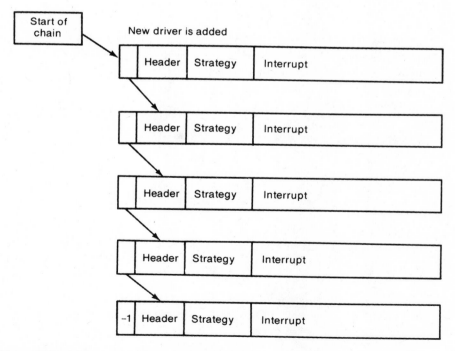

Figure 12.5 Adding a new driver to the driver chain.

DOS looks for a character device driver by searching through the chain of drivers for a driver name that matches the name that is called for. Starting at the beginning of the driver list, DOS checks the name of the first driver to see whether it matches the requested name. If not, the Next Driver Pointer field is consulted to find the next driver in the list and DOS checks there. DOS checks every driver in the chain (it skips over block device drivers) until it finds either the requested driver or the end of the list (marked by a –1 in the Next Driver Pointer field).

A new driver is always added to the beginning of the chain (refer to Fig. 12.5). Then, when DOS searches for a driver, it checks the new driver first. If you add a driver with the same name as an existing driver (for example, you add a new driver with the name PRN—the same name as that of the printer driver), the new driver "replaces" the existing one because a search always results in the new driver, never the old one, being used.

The ANSI.SYS driver works this way when it is included in the CONFIG.SYS file. It has the same name (CON) as the console driver; when the ANSI.SYS driver is added to the driver chain, it is found first whenever a console operation occurs. All console operations then work through the ANSI.SYS driver rather than through the normal DOS console driver.

To illustrate how you set up and work with a driver, let's create a practical example (or at least a *working* shell for a real driver). Listing 12.1 is the header for a real driver called drvr.asm. Later in this chapter, this driver is assembled into one that does not really do anything. The driver is a shell to which more code for actual applications can be added.

Listing 12.1

```
CR          EQU   0Dh          ;Carriage return
LF          EQU   0Ah          ;Line feed
MAXCMD      EQU   16           ;DOS 3.0, 12 DOS 2.0
ERROR       EQU   8000h        ;Set error bit
BUSY        EQU   0200h        ;Set busy bit
DONE        EQU   0100h        ;Set completion bit
UNKNOWN     EQU   8003h        ;Set unknown status

cseg segment    public 'code' ;Start the code segment
     org        0             ;Zero origin
     assume     cs:cseg,ds:cseg,es:cseg
```

The first part of the driver is made up of instructions to the assembler. First, for convenience during the program, define several constants such as CR (carriage return), LF (line feed), MAXCMD (the maximum command number: 16 for DOS V3.0 and V3.1, 12 for V2.X), and so on. These definitions simplify your programming as you continue.

As mentioned earlier in this chapter, Listing 12.1 has been defined as a code segment with a 0 origin (ORG 0). All the segment registers are set the same as the code segment so that you can assemble the driver as a binary image (COM format) file.

The first part of the driver that affects memory begins with the label drvr, where you declare that this is a FAR procedure. This is necessary because all drivers will be called by DOS with a FAR subroutine call. A FAR subroutine call is one that can cross segment boundaries—it pushes the return address (both segment and offset) on the stack as part of the call. By declaring this to be a FAR procedure, you ensure that the assembler uses a FAR return (which gets both segment and offset off the stack) to return control to DOS.

The first field in the header (a double word, or eight bytes) initially is declared to be –1. DOS sets this word to the address of the next driver in the chain. You then set the attribute word to 8000h to indicate that this character driver has no special capabilities (refer to Table 12.1). This step is followed by the pointers (offsets only) to the driver's strategy and interrupt procedures and then by this driver's 8-character name.

The header is critical to proper driver operation. When DOS needs to refer to the driver, it checks the attribute word to see what the driver can do and then uses the strategy and interrupt pointers to locate the routines. If the header is not right, the driver fails before it starts. Because the header is all bookkeeping and the assembler does the bookkeeping for you, let's move on to the strategy routine.

Strategy Routine

A strategy routine has little to do with what usually is considered "strategy"—it does not try to devise the best way to drive the device or anything of that sort. You can write the strategy routine in as little as five lines; its purpose is to "remember" where in memory the operating system has assigned the location of the device's *request header* (RH). The RH serves the following two functions:

- It is a data area for DOS's internal operations.

- It is a communication area in which DOS tells the driver what to do and the driver responds with the result of the operation.

When a driver is asked to output data, the data address comes by way of the RH. The driver responds by performing its output task and then setting a flag or status byte in the request header to indicate completion.

When a driver is about to be called by DOS, the request header is built in a reserved area of memory and its address is passed to the strategy routine in ES:BX. Although every call to the driver can have a new address, in practice the address generally is the same. The strategy routine saves this value for future use by the driver's interrupt routine.

Request headers vary in length but always have a fixed 13-byte header (sometimes called the "static portion" of the request header). The structure of the request header is shown in Table 12.2.

Table 12.2 Request Header Leading Bytes

Byte Offset	Field Length	Meaning
00h	Byte	Length of the request header
01h	Byte	Unit code: the device number for block devices
02h	Byte	Command code: the number of the most recent command sent to the driver
03h	Word	Status: status code set by the driver after every call. If bit 15 is set, an error code is in the low-order eight bits. A status code of 0 means a successful completion.
05h	8 bytes	Reserved for use by DOS
0Dh	Variable	Data required by the driver

Most of the fields in the request header are self-explanatory. The status word (bytes 03–04h), however, needs clarification.

The status word passes the completion status of a request back to DOS in the format shown in Table 12.3.

Table 12.3 Request Header Status Word

Bits FEDCBA98 76543210	Meaning
1....... 00000000	Write-protect violation error
1....... 00000001	Unknown unit error
1....... 00000010	Drive not ready error
1....... 00000011	Unknown
1....... 00000100	CRC error
1....... 00000101	Bad drive request structure length error
1....... 00000110	Seek error
1....... 00000111	Unknown media error
1....... 00001000	Sector not found error
1....... 00001001	Printer out of paper error
1....... 00001010	Write fault
1....... 00001011	Read fault
1....... 00001100	General failure

Bits		Meaning
FEDCBA98	76543210	
1.......	00001101	Reserved
1.......	00001110	Reserved
1.......	00001111	Invalid disk change
.......x	....	Done
......x.	....	Busy
.xxxxx..	....	Reserved
0.......	....	No error

The error bit in the status word is set to indicate that an error occurred in the operation of the driver. The error code is returned in the lower eight bits of the status word. When the error bit is not set, the error code should be set to zero to indicate satisfactory completion of the operation.

The busy bit is set to indicate that the device was busy when called. The done bit is set when the driver has completed the operation. The driver sets the bits to indicate the status of whatever operation is requested. All functions should set the done bit to indicate completion.

The strategy routine for the sample driver (drvr.asm) looks like Listing 12.2.

Listing 12.2

```
rh_seg      dw   ?              ;RH segment address
rh_off      dw   ?              ;RH offset address
strategy:
            mov  cs:rh_seg,es
            mov  cs:rh_off,bx
            ret
```

Listing 12.2 allocates space in which to store the segment and the offset of the request header. The entire strategy routine consists of saving the request header pointer (the segment address in the ES register and the offset address in the BX register). Why doesn't it do more? A more pointed question might be "Why have two entry points?" Why not pass the pointer to the interrupt routine in ES:BX and be done with it?

The answer involves the operating system's compatibility and internal mechanisms. The driver structure was designed to be compatible with a future extension intended to convert DOS to a multitasking structure. When the operating system runs multiple tasks, more than one request might be sent to a specific driver before a single request can be handled. In other words, the requests might have to be queued.

401

If you make requests for disk-sector reads, for example, multiple requests might arrive before the first request can be satisfied, especially if the requested sector is far from the present location on the disk. You can add intelligence to the strategy routine and let it try to optimize access to a disk device by sequencing multiple requests to minimize head movement. None of this, however, is applicable to DOS through V4.01.

Because DOS is a single-user, single-task system, the potential capability for multiple processes accessing any driver does not exist. The structure is in place, however, to allow an extension in that direction (if that type of an extension is ever deemed to be necessary).

After the request header's address is stored safely, you can return to DOS and await the call to the interrupt routine: It occurs immediately in a single-task system.

Interrupt Routine

The major portion of the driver, called the interrupt routine, does all the work. It is poorly named because it does not act like an interrupt, and it ends with RET rather than with IRET. The name reflects plans that have not materialized; the intention was that the queued requests would be serviced by interrupt handlers. Each device would interrupt DOS when it could take care of its next task, and then the handler would direct control to the interrupt routine. Like the strategy design, however, this does not yet apply to DOS.

The interrupt routine contains code for as many as 21 functions required by the DOS system (13 on DOS V2, 17 on DOS V3, 20 on DOS V3.2, and 21 on DOS 5.0). Whenever the device driver is called, it gets the address of the request header and looks at the byte at offset 02h of the header to find the command code that indicates which function the driver will perform.

Most drivers create a table with pointers to the driver's functions. The command code is used as an index into the table to locate the desired function. Listing 12.3 shows such a dispatch table for the sample driver.

Listing 12.3

```
d_tbl:
        dw    s_init       ;Initialization
        dw    s_mchk       ;Media check
        dw    s_bpb        ;BIOS parameter block
        dw    s_ird        ;IOCTL read
        dw    s_read       ;Read
        dw    s_nrd        ;Nondestructive read
        dw    s_inst       ;Current input status
        dw    s_infl       ;Flush input buffer
        dw    s_write      ;Write
        dw    s_vwrite     ;Write with verify
        dw    s_ostat      ;Current output status
        dw    s_oflush     ;Flush output buffers
        dw    s_iwrt       ;IOCTL write
        dw    s_open       ;Open
        dw    s_close      ;Close
```

```
        dw    s_media              ;Removable media
        dw    s_busy               ;Output until busy
```

The table is particularly easy to lay out because the assembler keeps track of the functions and automatically inserts the correct offset addresses in the table. This driver (as written) does not support the special functions introduced after DOS V3.0: Generic IOCTL, Get Logical Device, Set Logical Device, and IOCTL Query. This is not a problem because most programs, to run with older versions of DOS, do not use the calls that depend on these functions.

The body of the interrupt routine determines the nature of the request to be served. It branches from the dispatch table to the appropriate function. Listing 12.4 shows the rest of the body of the interrupt routine.

Listing 12.4

```
interrupt:
        cld                        ;Save machine state
        push es                    ;Save all registers
        push ds
        push ax
        push bx
        push cx
        push dx
        push si
        push di
        push bp

        mov   dx,cs:rh_seg
        mov   es,dx
        mov   bx,cs:rh_off

        mov   al,es:[bx]+2         ;Command code
        xor   ah,ah
        cmp   ax,MAXCMD            ;Legal command?
        jle   ok                   ;Jump if okay
        mov   ax,UNKNOWN           ;Unknown command
        jmp   finish

ok:
        shl   ax,1                 ;Multiply by 2
        mov   bx,ax
        jmp   word ptr [bx + d_tbl]

finish:

        mov   dx,cs:rh_seg
        mov   es,dx
        mov   bx,cs:rh_off

        or    ax,DONE              ;Set the DONE bit
        mov   es:[bx]+3,ax
```

continues

Listing 12.4 Continued

```
        pop   bp                      ;Restore the registers
        pop   di
        pop   si
        pop   dx
        pop   cx
        pop   bx
        pop   ax
        pop   ds
        pop   es
        ret                           ;Back to DOS
```

The interrupt routine starts by saving the present machine state on the stack. Then it gets the pointer to the request header from the location at which the strategy routine stored it. The interrupt routine determines what it is supposed to do by looking at offset 02h in the request header. The routine then checks to make sure that the command is legal: if it is, the routine branches to the location at which it handles the function. An illegal command (one that is larger than the maximum command number) results in the driver's returning an error flag set to indicate that the command was unknown.

When the command number is determined to be less than MAXCMD (the number of commands the driver supports), the driver multiplies the command number by two (by means of a left shift, which is the same as multiplying by two) to obtain the offset of the command code within the dispatch table. The shift is necessary because two bytes are stored for every table entry in the dispatch table. Then the offset is added to the dispatch table's base address, and the driver jumps to the designated routine.

When the function finishes, the driver retrieves the pointer to the request header and sets the done bit in the status word to reflect the operation's completion. The registers saved at the beginning of the driver are restored and control is returned to the DOS kernel.

Before you look at each separate driver function, let's look at the sample driver's remaining code. As in any driver, only some functions have to be implemented. In cases in which a function is not needed, the driver can simply return a status code and do nothing. Some people advocate returning a zero code that indicates successful operation; others suggest returning an error code 3 (Command Unknown). If you write your own driver to use with your own software, you can make your own choice. If you write a driver to replace an existing one, however, the new return codes should be consistent with the ones returned by the original driver.

Listing 12.5 gives the remainder of `drvr.asm`.

Listing 12.5

```
    s_mchk:                           ;Media check
    s_bpb:                            ;BIOS parameter block
    s_ird:                            ;IOCTL read
```

```
s_read:                              ;Read
s_nrd:                               ;Nondestructive read
s_inst:                              ;Current input status
s_infl:                              ;Flush input buffers
s_vwrite:                            ;Current output status
s_ostat:                             ;Current output status
s_oflush:                            ;Flush output buffers
s_iwrt:                              ;IOCTL write
s_open:                              ;Open
s_close:                             ;Close
s_media:                             ;Removable media
s_busy:                              ;Output until busy
            MOV  AX, UNKNOWN         ;Set error bits
            jmp  finish

ident:
    db    CR,LF
    db    'Sample Device Driver -- Version '
    db    '0.0'
    db    CR,LF,LF,'$'
s_init:
    mov   ah,9                   ;Print string
    mov   dx, offset ident
    int   21h

;   Retrieve the rh pointer

    mov   dx,cs:rh_seg
    mov   es,dx
    mov   bx,cs:rh_off

    lea   ax,end_driver         ;Get end of driver address
    mov   es:[bx]+14,ax
    mov   es:[bx]+16,cs

xor ax,ax                       ;Zero the AX register
    jmp   finish

s_write:
    xor   ax,ax                 ;Zero the AX register
    jmp   finish

end_driver:
drvr endp
cseg ends
    end
```

When you write a driver, you can ignore all the functions that you do not need to do something with. In drvr.asm, for example, only the initialization function and the write function do anything. All the remaining functions are handled with a single section that returns a code which tells DOS that the requested function was unknown. A driver that needs only read and write could provide only those functions.

The only function that *must* be included in all drivers is the initialization function: It must put the address of the end of the driver into the request header at offset 0Eh for use by the operating system's initialization code. If this address is zero, for a block device driver, the entire driver header is removed from memory during installation. This removal might be advisable if a fatal error was encountered while initializing; one enterprising developer used this feature to create a driver that merely displayed data on-screen and then vanished. A character device driver, however, cannot do this; its "end" address *must* leave in place at least the entire header. If it does not, all subsequent character devices are disabled.

To ignore the functions, you simply return a code which says that you do not know what DOS is requesting. Then you jump to the part of the interrupt routine that closes out the operation and sets the done bit (bit 8) in the request header's status word (offset 03h).

Initialization is next. You print a string to the screen (so that you know that the driver is there) and then determine the address of the end of the driver. (The label `end_driver` is the end of this routine.) This address must be stored in the request header so that DOS knows where to load the next driver. Because drivers are loaded from low to high memory, the next driver is loaded after the ending address of the current driver (see Fig. 12.6).

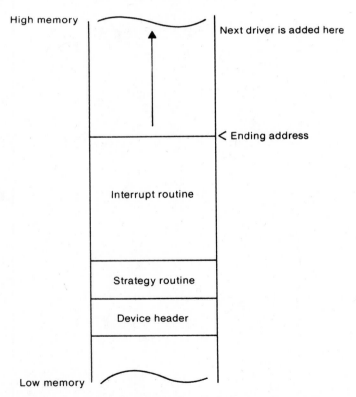

Figure 12.6 The next driver is loaded after the ending address of the current driver.

Finally, the write routine sets the AX register to zero (the function return status for the driver) to indicate no errors in the operation of the driver. This type of simple function setup is typical of most drivers. Most drivers require only a few of the functions to do anything. As you will learn when you read about the functions individually, some of them make sense for only one type of driver. The BIOS Parameter Block function, for example, is meaningless for a driver that deals with the keyboard.

Table 12.4 lists the device driver functions and indicates which ones are applicable to specific versions of DOS. Each function is examined in detail to see how it works.

Table 12.4 Device Driver Functions

Function	Meaning	DOS Versions
00h	Driver initialization	2, 3, 4, 5, 6
01h	Media check	2, 3, 4, 5, 6
02h	Build BIOS parameter block	2, 3, 4, 5, 6
03h	I/O control read	2, 3, 4, 5, 6
04h	Read	2, 3, 4, 5, 6
05h	Nondestructive read	2, 3, 4, 5, 6
06h	Input status	2, 3, 4, 5, 6
07h	Flush input buffers	2, 3, 4, 5, 6
08h	Write	2, 3, 4, 5, 6
09h	Write with verify	2, 3, 4, 5, 6
0Ah	Output status	2, 3, 4, 5, 6
0Bh	Flush output buffers	2, 3, 4, 5, 6
0Ch	I/O control write	2, 3, 4, 5, 6
0Dh	Open	3, 4, 5, 6
0Eh	Device close	3, 4, 5, 6
0Fh	Removable media	3, 4, 5, 6
10h	Output until busy	3, 4, 5, 6
11h	Generic IOCTL	3.2, 3.3
13h	Generic IOCTL	4, 5, 6
17h	Get logical device	3.2, 3.3, 4, 5, 6
18h	Set logical device	3.2, 3.3, 4, 5, 6
19h	IOCTL query	5, 6

Driver Initialization

The initialization function is the one function that *must* be present in all drivers. It performs any necessary setup for the driver. One task of the initialization function is essential to DOS: It must set the address of the end of the driver into byte offset 0Eh of the request header. If your driver were driving a hard disk system, the initialization section would have to check for the presence and proper operation of the disk, initialize the disk parameters, and so forth. For a serial port, it should initialize the port and establish default settings.

The driver's initialization section is the only section that can call DOS functions legally. No other part of the driver is allowed to call DOS. (Remember that DOS is not reentrant. While your program is inside the driver, it *is* DOS!) Only Functions 01h through 0Ch (Limited Console I/O) and 30h (Get DOS Version) are available for use. Because other parts of DOS have not been initialized when driver initialization occurs, calls to disk drives (and so on) fail and lock up the system.

To permit parameters to be passed to the driver by means of the CONFIG.SYS command line, a pointer to the command line is passed to the driver in the RH. This pointer points to the first character after the equal sign in the `"DEVICE="` line; the initialization code is permitted only to read the data, not to change it.

In keeping with the improved error reporting throughout DOS V4 (and later versions), a flag was added to the initialization function's RH format to permit display of the `Error in CONFIG.SYS` message. If you want the message displayed if installation fails, pass any nonzero value in this 16-bit field; a zero value prevents the display, and operation is the same as in earlier DOS versions.

The initialization process must update the request header by adding the following information:

Byte Offset	Contents
03h	Return status
0Dh	Number of units (for block devices)
0Eh	Address of first free memory above driver
12h	BIOS parameter block pointer (block devices)

Figure 12.7 shows the request header as it enters the initialization function; Figure 12.8 shows the request header coming out of the function.

Because the initialization code is called only once, many programmers save memory by placing it at the end of the driver module and then setting the first free memory address to the start of the initialization code. Big drivers with large initialization sections can gain a great deal of space this way. The example in this chapter is not that sophisticated, however. It simply uses a defined address at the end of the code segment to define the end of the driver.

Request header
Offset | | Contents

00h	00	Length
01h	01	Unit number
02h	02	Command code
03h	03	
04h	04	Return status
05h	05	
06h	06	
07h	07	
08h	08	Reserved for DOS
09h	09	
0Ah	10	
0Bh	11	
0Ch	12	
0Dh	13	
0Eh	14	
0Fh	15	
10h	16	
11h	17	
12h	18	Offset of CONFIG.SYS command line
13h	19	
14h	20	Segment of CONFIG.SYS command line
15h	21	
16h	22	First unit #
17h	23	CONFIG.SYS Error Msg control Flag word (V4 only)
18h	24	
19h	25	
1Ah	26	
1Bh	27	
1Ch	28	
1Dh	29	
1Eh	30	
1Fh	31	

Figure 12.7 The request header on entry to the initialization function.

Media Check

DOS gives the media check function the following information in the request header:

Byte Offset	Contents
01h	Unit code
02h	Command code (1 for media check)
0Dh	Media descriptor byte

The media check function is supposed to check whether the disk medium on a block device has been changed since the last access. For a character device, the routine should always return DONE (the request header status word is set to 0100h; the done bit, bit 8, is set; all other bits are zero). This means "complete" (see Listing 12.1 for a definition). For a fixed block device (such as a hard disk), the routine should always indicate that the medium has not changed by placing a 1 at byte offset 0Eh in the request header. But, how can you tell whether a removable disk has been changed?

Request header

Offset		Contents
00h	00	Length
01h	01	Unit number
02h	02	Command code
03h	03	
04h	04	Return status
05h	05	
06h	06	
07h	07	
08h	08	Reserved for DOS
09h	09	
0Ah	10	
0Bh	11	
0Ch	12	
0Dh	13	# units
0Eh	14	Offset of free memory
0Fh	15	
10h	16	Segment of free memory
11h	17	
12h	18	Offset of BPB
13h	19	
14h	20	Segment of BPB
15h	21	
16h	22	
17h	23	
18h	24	
19h	25	
1Ah	26	
1Bh	27	
1Ch	28	
1Dh	29	
1Eh	30	
1Fh	31	

Figure 12.8   The request header on return from initialization.

Many programmers have wrestled with this problem. Because the DOS world never had standards (before V4) for insisting on volume labels and so on, however, no one has been able to come up with a truly reliable answer. Here are some ideas that have been attempted:

- Go back for another disk access so fast that the disk could not have been removed. So far, no one has figured out how fast is fast enough (as soon as someone does, the Olympics will have a new event—opening disk drive doors); the IBM manuals for V4 specify two seconds as the time to use.

- If opening of the drive door can be sensed, and if it *has* been opened, you could assume that the medium has been changed. (But what if the door opened accidentally and was simply reclosed?)

- If the volume ID has changed since the last disk access, you know that the medium is not the same. Unfortunately, the inverse of this statement is not true. (How many disks do you have with the same volume ID?)

- If you are using at least DOS V4 and the volume serial number has changed, the medium has changed. This method is the most reliable, but it works in only V4 or later; earlier versions do not have volume serial numbers.

Clearly, no foolproof ways to determine that the disk has not been changed work across all versions of DOS. On the Macintosh, disks cannot be changed except through the operating system. There is no way (other than by a series of manipulations with a paper clip) to remove the disk without the operating system being involved. Because the PC is not this restrictive, DOS programmers are left holding the proverbial "bag." In general, you can never really be sure whether the disk you write to is the one intended.

DOS's reaction depends on the return code placed in byte offset 0Eh of the request header. If the value is 1, DOS assumes that the device has not been changed and proceeds to write without rereading the FAT from the disk. A code of –1 tells DOS that the disk has been changed and forces DOS to dump any write buffers and then reread the FAT and directory from the device. When DOS dumps its buffers, the information in them is simply thrown away.

A code of 0 means "maybe" (the driver cannot tell whether the media has been changed). In this case, DOS assumes that everything is OK and flushes any buffers directly to the disk. If the buffers are empty, DOS rereads the FAT and the directory to be sure that the buffers are empty. Generally, this response is the safest. If any doubt exists, DOS at least tries to save the information (if the disk has been changed, this process usually results in disk sectors being overwritten).

Beginning with DOS V3, this function also returns a pointer to the last volume ID read from the disk. Figure 12.9 shows the request header on entry to the media check function; Figure 12.10 shows the request header on return.

The safe course of action for a disk driver is to always return NOT CHANGED (a value of 1 at byte offset 0Eh in the request header) for a hard disk and DON'T KNOW (a value of 0 at byte offset 0Eh in the request header) for a floppy disk.

Build BIOS Parameter Block

For block devices only, build BIOS parameter block (BPB) functions and return a pointer to them at offset 12h in the request header. Character devices should just return DONE. In DOS V3 and later systems, this routine should also read and store the device volume ID for later use by the media check function, which must return a pointer to the volume label in DOS V3 and later (refer to Fig. 12.10).

On entry to the build BPB function, the request header contains the following information:

Byte Offset	Meaning
01h	Unit code
02h	Command code (2)
0Dh	Media descriptor byte
0Eh	Buffer address

411

Request header

Offset		Contents
00h	00	Length
01h	01	Unit number
02h	02	Command code
03h	03	Return status
04h	04	
05h	05	
06h	06	
07h	07	
08h	08	Reserved for DOS
09h	09	
0Ah	10	
0Bh	11	
0Ch	12	
0Dh	13	Media ID
0Eh	14	
0Fh	15	
10h	16	
11h	17	
12h	18	
13h	19	
14h	20	
15h	21	
16h	22	
17h	23	
18h	24	
19h	25	
1Ah	26	
1Bh	27	
1Ch	28	
1Dh	29	
1Eh	30	
1Fh	31	

Figure 12.9 The request header on entry to the media check function.

A 1-sector buffer is passed to this routine. If the non-IBM format bit in the device attribute word is zero, the buffer contains the first sector of the FAT and should not be changed. If the bit is set, the buffer can be used as a scratch area in which to build the BPB.

Whenever the media check detects a disk change or "thinks" that the disk might have been changed, DOS calls the BPB routine to rebuild its BPB from the disk. The BPB's layout is shown in Table 12.5. The original BPB structure was extended in V3.2 to permit use of sector numbers requiring 32-bit storage, but the extended structure did not come into general use until V4. Version 4 uses the original BPB for drives with less than 64K sectors and the extended one for those that exceed this size.

Table 12.5 BIOS Parameter Block (BPB) Layout

Byte Offset	Field Length	Meaning
00h	Word	Number of bytes per sector
02h	Byte	Number of sectors per cluster

Byte Offset	Field Length	Meaning
03h	Word	Number of reserved sectors that start at sector 0
05h	Byte	Number of FATs
06h	Word	Maximum number of root directory entries
08h	Word	Total number of sectors (0 in V3 and higher if greater than 65,535)
0Ah	Byte	Media descriptor
0Bh	Word	Number of sectors per FAT
0Dh	Word	Number of sectors per track (DOS V3 or later)
0Fh	Word	Number of heads (DOS V3 or later)
11h	Double word	Number of hidden sectors (DOS V3 or later)
15h	Double word	Total sectors if word at 08h is zero (DOS V3 or later)
19h	Seven bytes	Reserved

Request header

Offset		Contents
00h	00	Length
01h	01	Unit number
02h	02	Command code
03h	03	
04h	04	Return status
05h	05	
06h	06	
07h	07	
08h	08	Reserved for DOS
09h	09	
0Ah	10	
0Bh	11	
0Ch	12	
0Dh	13	
0Eh	14	Media change code
0Fh	15	Offset of volume label
10h	16	
11h	17	Segment of volume label
12h	18	
13h	19	
14h	20	
15h	21	
16h	22	
17h	23	
18h	24	
19h	25	
1Ah	26	
1Bh	27	
1Ch	28	
1Dh	29	
1Eh	30	
1Fh	31	

DOS V3 & later

Figure 12.10 The request header on return from the media check function.

The request header on entry to the function is shown in Figure 12.11; Figure 12.12 shows it on return.

Request header
Offset | | Contents

Offset		Contents
00h	00	Length
01h	01	Unit number
02h	02	Command code
03h	03	
04h	04	Return status
05h	05	
06h	06	
07h	07	
08h	08	Reserved for DOS
09h	09	
0Ah	10	
0Bh	11	
0Ch	12	
0Dh	13	Media ID
0Eh	14	Offset of FAT buffer
0Fh	15	
10h	16	Segment of FAT buffer
11h	17	
12h	18	
13h	19	
14h	20	
15h	21	
16h	22	
17h	23	
18h	24	
19h	25	
1Ah	26	
1Bh	27	
1Ch	28	
1Dh	29	
1Eh	30	
1Fh	31	

Figure 12.11   The request header on entry to the build BPB function.

I/O Control Read

The I/O control (IOCTL) read function enables a program to access the device directly by means of the IOCTL call. This function is called *only* when the IOCTL bit is set in the attribute word of the device header. The request header includes the following information:

Byte Offset	Meaning
01h	Unit code
02h	Command code (3)
0Dh	Media descriptor byte
0Eh	Transfer address
12h	Byte/sector count

Request header

Offset		Contents
00h	00	Length
01h	01	Unit number
02h	02	Command code
03h	03	Return status
04h	04	Return status
05h	05	
06h	06	
07h	07	
08h	08	Reserved for DOS
09h	09	
0Ah	10	
0Bh	11	
0Ch	12	
0Dh	13	
0Eh	14	
0Fh	15	
10h	16	
11h	17	
12h	18	Offset of BPB
13h	19	
14h	20	Segment of BPB
15h	21	
16h	22	
17h	23	
18h	24	
19h	25	
1Ah	26	
1Bh	27	
1Ch	28	
1Dh	29	
1Eh	30	
1Fh	31	

Figure 12.12 The request header on return from the build BPB function.

The routine should return the status word at offset 03h and the number of bytes transferred at offset 12h. DOS does no error checking on the call.

All IOCTL calls (read, write, and the generic call added in DOS V3.2) communicate with the *driver*, not with the device. Programs use these calls to tell the driver what to do or how to configure itself. With a serial driver, for example, you might use an IOCTL write to set the baud rate, word length, stop bits, and parity; you could use an IOCTL read to determine the current settings. The problem is that IOCTL calls are extremely specific to the driver.

An IOCTL command has no DOS-defined structure. The command (in any form in which the application puts it) is stored at the transfer address. If a program wants to configure a serial port, it might place this string:

```
WORD=8,BAUD=1200,STOP=1,PARITY=N
```

at the transfer address to indicate eight bits, 1200 baud, one stop bit, and no parity (for a discussion of the meaning of these terms, see Chapter 7, "Serial Devices"). *But, there is no guarantee that the driver will understand the control string.*

415

If you were to try an IOCTL call to the sample driver (refer to Listing 12.5), the driver would ignore any information passed and the IOCTL call would be unsuccessful. The IOCTL call would never reach the driver because the IOCTL-supported bit (bit 14 in the device attribute word in Table 12.1) has not been set. Furthermore, even if the driver is reached, the unknown function error from the IOCTL read and write functions is returned. The sample driver has not been written to respond to IOCTL calls.

In most books, information about IOCTL is vague or undefined. IOCTL information that is defined is included in the "DOS Reference" section of this book.

Read

The read function reads data from the device and returns the data to a designated buffer. The function also returns a completion code and the number of bytes or sectors transferred. All of these *must* be passed, even if an error occurs. In DOS V3 (and later versions), the driver must also return a pointer to the volume ID if error 0Fh is returned.

The read function communicates with the device by reading from it and making what it reads available to the program that called the device driver. On entry to the function, the request header contains the following information:

Byte Offset	Meaning
01h	Unit code
02h	Command code (3)
0Dh	Media descriptor byte
0Eh	Transfer address
12h	Byte/sector count
14h	Starting sector number (block devices); if it is –1 with DOS V4, use value at 16h instead if the driver can deal with 32-bit sector numbers
16h	32-bit starting sector number (V4 only)

The read function is called to read both character and block devices. When a single character read is supposed to take place, the driver is given a byte count of 1. Parameters that have no meaning for the driver are ignored. (The same principle applies also in the write calls.)

Nondestructive Read

A nondestructive read is a look-ahead read for character devices only. This command is meaningless for block drivers; they should return DONE. On entry, the request header contains only the command code (05h) at position 02h (see Fig. 12.13). The driver should read the next character but leave it in the input buffer to be used by the read function when it is called. The character should be returned in the request header at position 0Dh, as shown in Figure 12.14.

Request header
Offset | | Contents

Offset		Contents
00h	00	Length
01h	01	Unit number
02h	02	Command code
03h	03	
04h	04	Return status
05h	05	
06h	06	
07h	07	
08h	08	Reserved for DOS
09h	09	
0Ah	10	
0Bh	11	
0Ch	12	
0Dh	13	
0Eh	14	
0Fh	15	
10h	16	
11h	17	
12h	18	
13h	19	
14h	20	
15h	21	
16h	22	
17h	23	
18h	24	
19h	25	
1Ah	26	
1Bh	27	
1Ch	28	
1Dh	29	
1Eh	30	
1Fh	31	

Figure 12.13   The request header on entry to the nondestructive read function.

DOS uses the nondestructive read function for a look-ahead read during keyboard operations. DOS uses this function to look for a Ctrl-C character in the input stream from the keyboard.

Input Status

DOS uses the input status function to check whether characters are waiting in the input buffer on a character device. Block devices automatically return DONE for this routine. Character devices return their status at position 03h of the request header. This function, unlike a nondestructive read, does not read any characters; it simply returns the busy status of the device.

When this function is available, DOS uses it to check whether the device is busy before attempting to read. On entry, the request header contains only the command code (06h) at position 02h.

Request header
Offset		Contents
00h	00	Length
01h	01	Unit number
02h	02	Command code
03h	03	Return status
04h	04	
05h	05	
06h	06	
07h	07	
08h	08	Reserved for DOS
09h	09	
0Ah	10	
0Bh	11	
0Ch	12	
0Dh	13	Character
0Eh	14	
0Fh	15	
10h	16	
11h	17	
12h	18	
13h	19	
14h	20	
15h	21	
16h	22	
17h	23	
18h	24	
19h	25	
1Ah	26	
1Bh	27	
1Ch	28	
1Dh	29	
1Eh	30	
1Fh	31	

Figure 12.14 The request header on return from the nondestructive read function.

Flush Input Buffers

The flush input buffers command code (07h, at position 02h in the request header on entry to the function) tells the driver to dump any characters waiting to be input from the device. The function should return the return status code at position 03h in the request header. Block drivers should always return DONE.

Write

The write function (command code 08h at position 02h in the request header) takes characters out of the buffer passed with the request header and outputs them to the device. The function returns the return status (at position 03h), the number of bytes or sectors transferred (at position 12h), and (with DOS V3.0 and later versions) a pointer to the volume ID (at position 16h) if the 0Fh error code is returned. The error status and number of bytes transferred *must* be returned.

The layout of the request header is identical to that of the read function (and the write with verify function).

418

Write with Verify

The write with verify function (command code 09h at position 02h in the request header), the format of which is identical to that of the write function, should also verify the completed write. Verification can consist of anything from an outright lie (that is, no verification, as the normal CON drivers do) to performing a complete byte-by-byte comparison of the data that was written to the data that was read back after writing. The standard block device driver performs only a cyclic redundancy check (CRC) of data written in response to this command.

Any device incapable of performing verification should respond to this request with the nonverifying write action. If the DOS verify flag is ON, all write requests are converted automatically to write with verify; it is essential, therefore, that the function be supported.

Output Status

The output status function (command code 0Ah at position 02h in the request header) returns the status of a character device. To determine whether a device is busy, DOS calls this function before outputting to the device. When data to be printed is passed to the printer driver, the driver sees this call. The return status word (bytes 03h–04h in the request header) is used to return the device status. If the lower eight bits are zero, the device is ready. If the device is not ready, its status is coded from the standard code in Table 12.3.

Flush Output Buffers

The flush output buffers function (command code 0Bh at position 02h in the segment header) dumps the contents of the output buffers. Like the flush-input function, it is for character devices only. Block devices should return DONE.

I/O Control Write

Like the I/O control read function, the I/O control (IOCTL) write function (command code 0Ch at position 02h in the request header) accesses the device directly. It is called only if the IOCTL bit is set in the device header's attribute word. Everything (except the command code) said about the IOCTL read function applies here, but in reverse—the IOCTL write passes information *to* the driver, for example. As with the read function, the driver *and* the application must agree on what should be sent and its format.

Open

If the OPEN/CLOSE/RM bit is set in the device attribute word, the open function (command code 0Dh at position 02h in the request header) is called when an open is attempted on the device. For block devices, the call can be used to keep track of the number of open files on the device. Unfortunately, FCB function calls can leave this count hanging because files opened with the FCB may not be closed. When you deal with handles, DOS automatically closes the files when a process ends. With FCB functions, however, there is no call to the FCB CLOSE function

419

unless the process closes it. On character devices, the situation is easier because this call is commonly used to pass special start-up strings (such as printer-initialization strings) to the device, or to deny simultaneous access to more than one process.

On entry to the function, the request header contains the unit code (at position 01h) and the command code (0Dh, at position 02h). On return from the function, you pass the status word at position 03h.

Device Close

The device close function (command code 0Eh at position 02h in the request header) can help keep track of whether the device is currently open to one or more processes. If the open function (command code 0Dh) increments an internal counter whenever it is called, the close function can decrement the count and flush buffers when the count reaches zero. But the problems with FCB open functions remain. Termination strings (such as final form feeds) can be sent to character devices. The entry parameters for this function are like those of the open functions: the unit code at position 01h and the command code (0Eh) at position 02h.

Removable Media

If the OPEN/CLOSE/RM bit is set in the device header, the removable media call (command code 0Fh at position 02h of the request header) is used in DOS V3 and later versions to determine whether the device has removable media. If not, DOS can optimize its strategy for dealing with the device by loading disk tables into memory for faster access. Character devices should simply return DONE. Status codes are selected from Table 12.3 to return in the status word at position 03h of the request header.

If the device has removable media, this call returns a 0 in the BUSY bit of the status word; a 1 indicates nonremovable media.

Output Until Busy

The output until busy function (command code 10h at position 02h in the request header) was provided primarily for print spooling. Some types of devices, most notably printers with large internal buffers or separate printer buffers, can accept characters at an extremely high rate— higher than the computer can feed them. The driver, if allowed to do so, can transfer continuously a large number of bytes to the device without the device becoming busy. That is the purpose of this function.

When this function is called, it transfers bytes to the device as fast as it can. It transfers as many bytes as it can, either until the device becomes busy or until all the bytes it was given to transfer have been transferred. On entry to the function, the request header has the command code at position 02h, the transfer address (where the bytes to write to the device are located) at position 0Eh, and the byte count to be transferred at position 12h.

On return from the function, the request header must have the return status at position 03h and the number of bytes transferred at position 12h. If the number of bytes transferred is less than the number to be transferred, there is no error. Block devices should return DONE for this function.

Generic IOCTL

Like the IOCTL read and IOCTL write functions, the generic IOCTL function (command code 11h at position 02h in the request header with V3, and command code 13h at the same position for V4 or later) depends on the use of an agreed-on set of signals between the driver and the applications program. Because there are no rules, this function usually works best for programmers who write their own drivers. Generic IOCTL supports some of the new IOCTL functions introduced with DOS V3.3. (These functions are described in detail in the "DOS Reference" section.)

Figure 12.15 shows the layout of the request header on entry to the function; the layout on return is shown in Figure 12.16.

Request header

Offset		Contents
00h	00	Length
01h	01	Unit number
02h	02	Command code
03h	03	Return status
04h	04	
05h	05	
06h	06	
07h	07	
08h	08	Reserved for DOS
09h	09	
0Ah	10	
0Bh	11	
0Ch	12	
0Dh	13	Category (major) code
0Eh	14	Function (minor) code
0Fh	15	SI register
10h	16	
11h	17	DI register
12h	18	
13h	19	Offset of IOCTL data packet
14h	20	
15h	21	Segment of IOCTL data packet
16h	22	
17h	23	
18h	24	
19h	25	
1Ah	26	
1Bh	27	
1Ch	28	
1Dh	29	
1Eh	30	
1Fh	31	

Figure 12.15 The request header on entry to the generic IOCTL.

Request header
Offset   Contents

Offset	Dec	Contents
00h	00	Length
01h	01	Unit number
02h	02	Command code
03h	03	Return status
04h	04	
05h	05	
06h	06	
07h	07	
08h	08	Reserved for DOS
09h	09	
0Ah	10	
0Bh	11	
0Ch	12	
0Dh	13	
0Eh	14	
0Fh	15	
10h	16	
11h	17	
12h	18	
13h	19	
14h	20	
15h	21	
16h	22	
17h	23	
18h	24	
19h	25	
1Ah	26	
1Bh	27	
1Ch	28	
1Dh	29	
1Eh	30	
1Fh	31	

Figure 12.16   The request header on return from the generic IOCTL.

Get and Set Logical Device

The get and set logical device functions (command codes 12h and 13h in V3 or 17h and 18h in V4 or later, at position 02h in the request header) support the operation of Int 21h, Function 44h (Subfunctions 0Eh and 0Fh). They determine which block device name was last used to refer to a given device, and they tell the driver which device name will be used next. For additional information about these functions, see the "DOS Reference" section.

The get and set logical device functions are called with the unit number at position 01h of the request header and the command code at position 02h. On return, the last device unit code is returned at position 01h, and the device status is returned at position 03h.

The Whole Driver

The sample driver (drvr.asm) is listed in full in Listing 12.6. You can produce a working driver by typing this listing and assembling it according to the directions in the following section. (Although this driver does not do much, it is a beginning.) Be careful, though: Although this driver has been tested, you can mess up your system if you mistype something, if a smudge in your book hides an important step, or if a step does not complete properly (and you miss it). Whenever you test drivers, be sure to work on a floppy rather than on your main system. Be sure to follow the precautions listed in the following section.

Listing 12.6

```
; drvr.asm

CR          EQU   0Dh              ;Carriage return
LF          EQU   0Ah              ;Line feed
MAXCMD      EQU   16               ;DOS 3.0, 12 DOS 2.0
ERROR       EQU   8000h            ;Set error bit
BUSY        EQU   0200h            ;Set busy bit
DONE        EQU   0100h            ;Set completion bit
UNKNOWN     EQU   8003h            ;Set unknown status

cseg segment    public 'code'  ;Start the code segment
     org        0              ;Zero origin
     assume     cs:cseg,ds:cseg,es:cseg

;=========================================================
drvr        proc       far        ;FAR procedure
            dd         -1         ;Next driver pointer
            dw         8000h      ;Attribute
            dw         strategy   ;Pointer to strategy
            dw         interrupt  ;Pointer to interrupt
            db         'DRVR  '   ;Device name

;=========================================================

rh_seg      dw    ?               ;RH segment address
rh_off      dw    ?               ;RH offset address
strategy:
            mov   cs:rh_seg,es
            mov   cs:rh_off,bx
            ret

;=========================================================
; dispatch table
;=========================================================

d_tbl:
      dw    s_init          ;Initialization
      dw    s_mchk          ;Media check
      dw    s_bpb           ;BIOS parameter block
```

continues

Listing 12.6 Continued

```
        dw    s_ird           ;IOCTL read
        dw    s_read          ;Read
        dw    s_nrd           ;Nondestructive read
        dw    s_inst          ;Current input status
        dw    s_infl          ;Flush input buffer
        dw    s_write         ;Write
        dw    s_vwrite        ;Write with verify
        dw    s_ostat         ;Current output status
        dw    s_oflush        ;Flush output buffers
        dw    s_iwrt          ;IOCTL write
        dw    s_open          ;Open
        dw    s_close         ;Close
        dw    s_media         ;Removable media
        dw    s_busy          ;Output until busy


;===========================================================
; interrupt routine
;===========================================================

interrupt:
        cld                   ;Save machine state
        push es               ;Save all registers
        push ds
        push ax
        push bx
        push cx
        push dx
        push si
        push di
        push bp

        mov   dx,cs:rh_seg
        mov   es,dx
        mov   bx,cs:rh_off

        mov   al,es:[bx]+2      ;Command code
        xor   ah,ah
        cmp   ax,MAXCMD        ;Legal command?
        jle   ok              ;Jump if OK
        mov   ax,UNKNOWN      ;Unknown command
        jmp   finish

ok:
        shl   ax,1            ;Multiply by 2
        mov   bx,ax
        jmp   word ptr [bx + d_tbl]

finish:

        mov   dx,cs:rh_seg
        mov   es,dx
        mov   bx,cs:rh_off
```

```
        or    ax,DONE              ;Set the DONE bit
        mov   es:[bx]+3,ax

        pop   bp                   ;Restore the registers
        pop   di
        pop   si
        pop   dx
        pop   cx
        pop   bx
        pop   ax
        pop   ds
        pop   es
        ret                        ;Back to DOS


;==========================================================
; main body of driver
;==========================================================

s_mchk:                            ;Media check
s_bpb:                             ;BIOS parameter block
s_ird:                             ;IOCTL read
s_read:                            ;Read
s_nrd:                             ;Nondestructive read
s_inst:                            ;Current input status
s_infl:                            ;Flush input buffers
s_vwrite:                          ;Current output status
s_ostat:                           ;Current output status
s_oflush:                          ;Flush output buffers
s_iwrt:                            ;IOCTL write
s_open:                            ;Open
s_close:                           ;Close
s_media:                           ;Removable media
s_busy:                            ;Output until busy
        MOV   AX, UNKNOWN          ;Set error bits
        jmp   finish

ident:
        db    CR,LF
        db    'Sample Device Driver -- Version '
        db    '0.0'
        db    CR,LF,LF,'$'
s_init:
        mov   ah,9                 ;Print string
        mov   dx, offset ident
        int   21h

;    Retrieve the rh pointer

        mov   dx,cs:rh_seg
        mov   es,dx
        mov   bx,cs:rh_off

        lea   ax,end_driver        ;Get end of driver address
        mov   es:[bx]+14,ax
        mov   es:[bx]+16,cs
```

continues

Listing 12.6   Continued

```
xor ax,ax                    ;Zero the AX register
    jmp   finish

s_write:
    xor   ax,ax              ;Zero the AX register
    jmp   finish

end_driver:
drvr endp
cseg ends
    end
;========================================================
```

Assembling the Driver

To assemble the driver, you need to run the macro assembler and linker (`ml` beginning with MASM 6.0), and then the EXE2BIN program to create the driver as a binary image. These steps have been combined in a standard batch file that also copies the driver to drive A (in case you forget to do so). Listing 12.7 is the MAKEDRVR.BAT file.

Listing 12.7

```
;========================================================
@echo off
ml /Fo%1 %1.asm
exe2bin %1 %1.sys
copy %1.sys a:
```

The batch file first assembles the driver. If the driver assembles properly, it gets linked. If the link is successful, EXE2BIN is executed to convert the driver to a memory-image format. When the program ends, the driver is copied to drive A.

When most programmers work on a driver, they repeatedly reassemble. The batch file helps ease the tension that surrounds repeated failures with *nothing* visible and no clear way to get output. If you write a driver, expect to lock up the system a few times before you get it right.

To use the batch file, you must give it the name of the driver's source file (without the extension). To execute the `drvr.asm` program, you type this line:

```
C:> makedrvr drvr
```

The batch file sees automatically that the output is a file (called DRVR.SYS) that can be added to the CONFIG.SYS file.

Installing the Driver

The operating system installs device drivers when it processes the CONFIG.SYS file during the system boot procedure. If DRVR.SYS (your driver) is stored in the root directory on drive A, you can add it to the system by editing the CONFIG.SYS file to include the following line:

```
DEVICE=A:DRVR.SYS
```

Debugging the Driver

If your driver works the first time you run it, you are better than most programmers. Even the best programmers must test and retest the driver until they "get it right." Sometimes the problem is not something the programmer did wrong; it might be something he or she did not understand (or know) about the device.

To debug a device driver, you have to do a great deal of intensive head-scratching. A minor error in address modes during initialization can lock up a DOS system if the pointers it is looking for are somewhere else in memory. A call to a driver can disappear down a black hole, never to return again. Applications programs can be given incorrect responses to a function call because the driver returned the wrong count.

Because printing from inside a driver is not easy, getting information about an error is a nightmare. Sometimes, when an error is time-critical, just putting in the debugging code causes the driver to work perfectly. One driver that worked for a UNIX system would not work unless a certain amount of undetermined time was eaten up in the middle of the driver. Although many systems programmers have worked on the function, the delay is still there. DOS can get you in the same way.

To debug a driver, remember the following guidelines:

- *Never test a new driver on your hard disk.* Make a bootable floppy disk and copy the driver and the CONFIG.SYS file to the floppy for testing. If you test on the hard disk and the driver fails on initialization, you cannot boot the hard disk directly. You will have to boot to a floppy to change CONFIG.SYS on the hard disk.

- *If you have a system without a hard disk, do the testing there.* Even a simple problem can have damaging consequences at the driver level. (What if your driver scrambles your hard disk's FAT?)

- *Use BIOS calls to print the driver's status at critical points.* If you want to understand the output, be careful not to include so many debugging outputs that you cannot read them as they go by.

- *Anything that records the screen display during testing and can be played back at slow speed can help.* Small computers, the system printer, or even a videotape can help if they can be configured to record what is happening.

Making a Practical Driver

You can make the sample driver more concrete by adding some substance to it. A write function is added to make the driver capable of writing to the printer as it gets characters. If you want this driver to replace the default printer driver, you can change its name (to PRN) in the device header.

Everything in drvr.asm remains the same, but the write function is expanded (see Listing 12.8).

Listing 12.8

```
        mov   cx,es:[bx]+12h      ;Number of bytes to print
        mov   di,es:[bx]+0eh      ;Offset of data buffer
        mov   ax,es:[bx]+10h      ;Segment address of data buffer
        mov   es,ax

        mov   dl,0                ;Printer 0
        mov   bx,0                ;Count 0 bytes printed

s_prt1:
        cmp   bx,cx               ;Printed all characters yet?
        je    s_done              ;All done

        mov   al,es:[di]          ;Get a character
        inc   di                  ;Point to the next one

        mov   ah,2                ;Check printer status
        int   17h
        test  ah,80h             ;Busy?
        jne   s_prtch             ;Print it
        jmp   s_err               ;Busy device, exit
s_prtch:
        cmp   al,LF               ;Is the character a line feed?
        je    s_bxinc             ;Skip it
        mov   ah,0                ;Print character
        int   17h
        test  ah,09h             ;I/O error?
        jne   s_err               ;Handle it
s_bxinc:
        inc   bx                 ;Count one printed
        jmp   s_prt1
s_err:
        mov   ax,800ch           ;General failure error
        jmp   s_end
s_done:
        mov   ax,bx              ;Save count
        mov   bx,cs:rh_off       ;Get req.hdr
        mov   es:[bx]+12h,ax     ;Store byte count
        xor   ax,ax              ;Zero AX register
s_end:
        jmp   finish
```

The new code prints characters to the printer and ignores line-feed characters on their way out. This function is useful if you want to use one of the older printers that interprets carriage returns or line feeds as a "carriage return and line feed" pair.

The function is simple. It begins by locating the request header pointer to the data buffer (offset 0Eh and 10h) and the number of bytes to transfer (offset 12h). Then it checks the printer status and, if the printer is busy, returns an error. If the printer is not busy, it prints the character. In this simplistic routine, any error that prevents you from writing the characters to the device causes the function to set an error code in the AX register (the device return status).

You can expand the entire function to do more sophisticated error processing—such as recognizing which errors are which and returning appropriate codes—but the basic function is sound.

Using the Device Driver

To test the device driver, you have to use it. There are several simple ways to use it from a program or directly from the command-line prompt.

The sample driver is named DRVR (refer to Listing 12.6). Like all other devices, this driver is activated when it is called by name. To redirect something to the printer with the normal driver (PRN), you can type this line:

```
C:\>type autoexec.bat >prn:
```

This line directs a copy of the AUTOEXEC.BAT file out to the printer. To use the driver, you can type this line:

```
C:\>type autoexec.bat >drvr:
```

When you attempt to write to drvr, DOS checks the driver chain to locate the name DRVR and then uses the driver to print the data.

You also can access the driver from a program by opening the device as you would open a file. You can use a handle function call to open the device (see Listing 12.9).

Listing 12.9

```
/* example.c
   Listing 12.9 of DOS Programmer's Reference */

union REGS regs;

regs.h.ah = 0x3d;       /* Open-file function       */
regs.h.al = 0x01;       /* Write access             */
regs.x.dx = (int)"drvr"; /* Creates pointer to string */
intdos(&regs,&regs);    /* Call DOS function int    */
handle = regs.x.ax;     /* Save the file handle     */
```

Regardless of the way you choose to access the driver, you can test its operation according to its design. In the case of `drvr`, you want to be able to test whether it prints characters to the printer and whether it eliminates line feeds from the character stream.

Summary

This chapter has discussed what most programmers find to be the most difficult part of programming in DOS: creating device drivers. You have learned that you can create device drivers by following a standard "mold" for a driver.

All drivers are built in three primary sections:

- The device header
- The strategy routine
- The interrupt routine

Each section has its own structure. The device header contains the name of the driver and the pointer to the next driver in the chain of system drivers. The strategy routine provides only for remembering where the system request header will be stored for communication between the driver and the operating system kernel.

Most of the driver is contained in the individual functions (as many as 21 of them) that make up the interrupt routine. Any given driver can implement only a few of these functions and ignores the rest, returning a suitable completion code if such a request is made to the driver.

430

13

Miscellaneous Functions

This chapter focuses on three basic types of functions: DOS information functions, date and time functions, and extended error processing. The first two types are simple and do not require extensive treatment. The third type of function is an extremely powerful extension to DOS's error-processing capabilities. Because this type of function tends to be extremely program dependent, this chapter does not include a practical example of its usefulness.

DOS Version Information

A function was added in DOS V2.0 to let you retrieve the DOS version number. This information can be essential to knowing which functions to use in running a system. Fortunately, because DOS versions earlier than V2.0 (in other words, V1.x) reliably return a 0, any return value less than 2 indicates a DOS V1.x system. You cannot tell V1.0 from V1.1, but at least you know that the major change point at which full DOS came into existence has not been reached.

If detecting the DOS version does not seem important, remember that, in all likelihood, many people have never upgraded from DOS V1.0 or V1.1. For example, a couple stopped at a Seattle computer store to buy extra hardware so that they could expand their two-disk *original* IBM PC to a hard disk system. They were still running DOS V1.1 and had to be told that it would not run the equipment they were buying. They left the store with their hardware and DOS V3.2.

To maintain perfect compatibility across the different versions of DOS, you would have to restrict your programming to only those functions available in DOS V1—a laudable but silly goal. Most programming these days requires *at least* DOS V2.0; with earlier versions, such features as directories cannot even be used.

We recommend that you use the DOS version number in one of two ways:

1. Check for the proper DOS level and tell the user if it is not high enough to support the program.

2. Check for the DOS level and compensate as necessary.

The second approach creates considerable overhead, unless you are limiting DOS-specific code to overlays (with a separate overlay for each DOS version) or doing an installation that will patch in the correct code version for the DOS in use.

The following lines of code paragraph check for minimum functionality (at least DOS V2). The function returns two numbers: AL is the major version number (02h is DOS V2, 03h is DOS V3) and AH is the minor version number (10 is .10, 20 is .20, and so forth). Save registers BX and CX if you will need them after the call—the interrupt destroys them.

```
Int 21h, Function 30h: Get DOS Version Number
mov        ah,30h    ; DOS version
int        21h
cmp        al,2      ; Check for greater than or equal to V2
jl         wrong     ; Wrong version
```

You can create (and use as a library function) a C subroutine that gives you the DOS version number. If you simply want to check for a minimum version of DOS, for example, you can use the chkver() subroutine in Listing 13.1.

Listing 13.1

```c
/* chkver.c
   Listing 13.1 of DOS Programmer's Reference */

#include <stdio.h>
#include <stdlib.h>
#include <dos.h>

void main()
{
    int  ver;
    unsigned int chkver(void);

    if((ver = chkver()) < 3){
        printf("ERROR -- Version MUST use at least DOS 3.0\n");
        printf("         Yours is only version %d\n",ver);
        exit(0);
    }
    printf("Thanks ... you have version %d of DOS\n",ver);
}

unsigned int chkver()
{
```

```
      union REGS regs;
      regs.h.ah = 0x30;
      intdos(&regs,&regs);
      if(regs.h.al == 0) regs.h.al = 1;
      return(regs.h.al);
}
```

Because of the way this program is written, you can pull out the `chkver()` subroutine, place it in a subroutine library, and use it with other C programs. At the beginning of the program, be sure to add this statement:

```
#include <stdio.h>
```

so that standard I/O functions are declared for the subroutine.

The subroutine simply calls Function 30h. Although the function returns both the major and minor numbers of the version (in registers AL and AH, respectively), only the major number is important.

Listing 13.2 is a BASIC version of the same program.

Listing 13.2

```
' chkver.bas
' $INCLUDE: 'REGNAMES.INC'

DEF fnchkver
'Determine the DOS version from Int 21h, Function 30h
     ToRegs.ax = &h3000
     call interrupt (&h21, ToRegs, FromRegs)

     if FromRegs.ax and &h00ff = 0 then FromRegs.ax = &h0001
     fnchkver = FromRegs.ax and &h00ff
END DEF

'MAIN PROGRAM
'
'Use the check version function to print the
'system's version number

Ver=fnChkVer
PRINT "You are using DOS";Ver
IF fnchkver < 3 THEN
     PRINT "OOPS -- You have an operating system version"
     PRINT "Earlier than 3.0.  You need to upgrade."
END IF
END
```

If you want to print the DOS version number, you can use the `getversion()` subroutine shown in Listing 13.3.

Listing 13.3

```
/* getver.c
   Listing 13.3 of DOS Programmer's Reference */

#include <stdio.h>
#include <dos.h>

char *getversion()
{
    static char buffer[5];
    union REGS regs;
    regs.h.ah = 0x30;
    intdos(&regs,&regs);
    if(regs.h.al == 0) regs.h.al = 1;
    sprintf(buffer,"%d.%d",regs.h.al,regs.h.ah);
    return(buffer);
}
```

The getversion() subroutine, which uses the DOS version's major and minor numbers, is more complex than the chkver() subroutine. To make the version numbers accessible for printing, you create a static character buffer in which the version string is written in the proper format. Be careful, because the static buffer is only five characters (the last of which *must* be a NULL character). A 5-character buffer will work until versions of DOS have 3-digit minor numbers or 2-digit major numbers; if version numbers get too high, you have to make the buffer larger. (Note that programs running in the DOS compatibility box of OS/2 now return a DOS version number of 10!)

Because you return a pointer to the static character buffer, your main routine can simply print the return value and—voilà—you have the DOS version. You can include this getversion() subroutine in a library and use it, as necessary, for other programs.

Listing 13.4 is a BASIC version of the subroutine. The BASIC function is substantially the same as the C routine but (because of the way BASIC works) seems quite different.

Listing 13.4

```
' getver.bas
' $INCLUDE: 'REGNAMES.INC'

DEF fngetver
'Determine the DOS version from Int 21h, Function 30h
'     vn = version number
'     rn = revision number

      ToRegs.ax = &H3000
      CALL interrupt(&H21, ToRegs, FromRegs)

      IF FromRegs.ax AND &HFF = 0 THEN FromRegs.ax = &H1
      vn = (FromRegs.ax AND &HFF)
```

```
        rn = (FromRegs.ax AND &HFF00) / 256
        fngetver = vn + rn / 100
END DEF

' MAIN PROGRAM

' Use the get version function to print the
' system's version number
' NOTE: You must use PRINT USING to get the
'       proper number of decimal places

    CLS
    PRINT USING "Version Number: #.##"; fngetver

END
```

Equipment Information

You may want to know which equipment is included on your system in addition to the DOS version number. BIOS Int 11h returns a code in register AX that indicates the equipment installed on the computer. Table 13.1 shows how the information is coded.

Table 13.1 BIOS Int 11h Return Code

Bit(s)	Meaning
0	Set if disk drives installed (bits 6–7 significant)
1	Set if math co-processor installed (AT only)
2–3	Memory configuration (not meaningful for AT)
	0 = 16K system board RAM
	1 = 32K system board RAM
	2 = 48K system board RAM
	3 = 64K system board RAM
4–5	Initial video mode
	1 = 40 × 25, text, color
	2 = 80 × 25, text, color
	3 = 80 × 25, text, mono
6–7	Number of disk drives minus 1
	(Valid only if bit 0 is 1)
8	Not used

continues

Table 13.1   Continued

Bit(s)	Meaning
9–11	Number of RS232 ports
12	Set if game adapter installed (PC only)
13	Set if internal modem installed (AT only)
14–15	Number of printers attached

To determine the equipment in a computer, you simply invoke Int 11h and then interpret the return code. The C program in Listing 13.5 uses the interrupt in a subroutine. (Note, however, that the video information returned by this routine is not adequate to determine the exact type of video system in use; if that is essential to your program, this is only a starting point that can eliminate certain possibilities.)

Listing 13.5

```
/* equip.c
   Listing 13.5 of DOS Programmer's Reference */

#include <stdio.h>
#include <dos.h>

#define   BOOL      int
#define   FALSE     0
#define   TRUE      !FALSE
#define   EQUIPMENT 0x11

void main()
{
    unsigned int eqpt;
    unsigned int equipment(int print);

    eqpt = equipment(TRUE);
    printf("Equipment Value is %x\n",eqpt);
}

unsigned int equipment(print)
    BOOL print;
{
    union REGS regs;
    int  eqpt;

    int86(EQUIPMENT,&regs,&regs);
    if(print){
        eqpt = regs.x.ax;
        if(eqpt & 0x01)
            printf("Floppy Drives are attached\n");
        if((eqpt>>1) & 0x01)
            printf("Math Coprocessor installed (AT only)\n");
```

```
        switch((eqpt>>4) & 0x03){
            case 1:
                printf("Initial video mode 40X25 color\n");
                break;
            case 2:
                printf("Initial video mode 80X25 color\n");
                break;
            case 3:
                printf("Initial video mode 80X25 mono\n");
                break;
        }
        if((eqpt>>6) & 0x01)
            printf("Number of disk drives is %d\n",
                ((eqpt>>6) & 0x03) + 1);
        printf("Number of RS-232 ports is %d\n",
            (eqpt>>9) & 0x07);
        if((eqpt>>12) & 0x01)
            printf("Game adapter installed\n");
        if((eqpt>>13) & 0x01)
            printf("Internal modem installed (AT only)\n");
        printf("Number of printers is %d\n",
            (eqpt>>14) & 0x03);
    }
    return(regs.x.ax);
}
```

The equipment() function can be pulled from this program and added to a function library of useful routines.

Notice the use of the EQUIPMENT definition in the interrupt call. By defining constants such as EQUIPMENT (0x11), you can simplify program maintenance and make your code much more readable.

Listing 13.6 shows the equipment program written in BASIC.

Listing 13.6

```
' equip.bas

DECLARE SUB printeqpt (n%)
' $INCLUDE: 'REGNAMES.INC'

' Get the installed equipment and interpret it
' with the subroutine printeqpt
    CALL interrupt(&H11, ToRegs, FromRegs)
    eq% = FromRegs.ax
    CLS
    PRINT "System Equipment Installed"
    PRINT "    Equipment code = "; HEX$(eq%)
    CALL printeqpt(eq%)
END
```

continues

437

Listing 13.6 Continued

```
SUB printeqpt (n%)
' This procedure prints the installed equipment list
' given the equipment code number
    IF n% AND &H1 THEN PRINT "Floppy drives attached"
    IF n% AND &H2 THEN PRINT "Math coprocessor installed"
    IF n% AND &H1000 THEN PRINT "Game adapter installed"
    vm = (n% AND &H30) / 16
    SELECT CASE vm
        CASE 1
            PRINT "40 x 25 text, color"
        CASE 2
            PRINT "80 x 25 text, color"
        CASE 3
            PRINT "80 x 25 text, mono"
    END SELECT
    IF n% AND &H1 THEN
        dd = (n% AND &HC0) / 64 + 1
        PRINT "Number of disk drives: "; dd
    ENDIF
    rs = (n% AND &HE00) / 512
    PRINT "Number of RS-232 ports: "; rs
END SUB
```

Date and Time Functions

During system start-up, the date and time are initialized to their default values. If your system does not have an internal hardware clock (a rare occurrence these days), the default date is 1/1/80 and the default time is 00:00:00.00 (midnight). If your computer has an internal clock, the date and time are set from the values in the internal clock. From this point, the time is kept in the BIOS data area and the date is kept in COMMAND.COM. If your computer does not have an internal clock, the system date and time are reset with the DOS commands DATE and TIME.

In some versions of DOS V3, a bug prevents the date from changing when midnight rolls around. The bug was present in early versions, and then was fixed, but reappeared later. In MS-DOS V3.2, the BIOS code returned the "passed-midnight" flag to DOS when called, but the DOS code ignored the result.

If your system suffers from this bug, the only reliable solution is to use one of the public domain replacement CLOCK$ device drivers, such as CLKFIX.SYS, available from commercial services or BBSs. These drivers essentially replace the faulty code with a corrected version and reroute all affected interrupt vectors to the new code.

Even with the correction, however, a design flaw in the date routines can cause entire days to be skipped. For example, if a computer is left running over the weekend and no one uses it for more than 24 hours, including two midnight passages, only one of the passages is recognized.

438

The passing of midnight sets a flag rather than a counter; DOS does not know, therefore, when more than one midnight has gone by since the last time it asked. Unlike the other bug, this one has no simple correction. The most direct cure is to reboot the computer every Monday morning to reset the system date.

The best way to access the time and date is to use the DOS functions provided for that purpose. In DOS V1.1 and later versions, the system date function gets the day, month, year, and day of the week as follows:

```
Int 21h, Function 2Ah: Get System Date
mov         ah,2ah       ; Get date
int         21h
mov         dow,al       ; Day of week
mov         mo,dh        ; Month
mov         dy,dl        ; Day
mov         yr,cx        ; Year
```

The returned values are in the following ranges:

Day	1–31
Month	1–12
Year	1980–2099
Day of week	0–6 (0=Sunday, 1=Monday, and so on)

These ranges are used when you set the system date with DOS Int 21h, Function 2Bh. DOS returns AL=0 if the date is set successfully, or FFh if the date is not valid.

You can also set the system date under program control through the use of the following DOS function:

```
Int 21h, Function 2Bh: Set System Date
mov         ah,2bh       ; Set date
mov         cx,yr        ; Year
mov         dh,mo        ; Month
mov         dl,dy        ; Day
int         21h
or          al,al        ; Test for invalid
jnz         error        ; Jump on  error
```

In addition to the functions provided for getting and setting the system date, DOS includes functions for getting and setting the system time. When it gets the system time, DOS returns values in the following ranges:

Hours (CH)	0–23
Minutes (CL)	0–59
Seconds (DH)	0–59
Hundredths of seconds (DL)	0–99

439

Because of the relatively slow speed of some computer systems, the real-time clock may not have an accurate resolution of 100ths of seconds. On these systems, the DL value should not be used for accurate or critical timing.

You get the system time by executing the following DOS interrupt and function:

```
Int 21h, Function 2Ch: Get System Time
mov        ah,2ch      ; Get time
int        21h
mov        hr,ch       ; Hours
mov        mn,cl       ; Minutes
mov        sc,dh       ; Seconds
mov        hn,dl       ; Hundredths of seconds
```

The range restrictions for setting the time are the same as those for getting the time. To set the time, use DOS Int 21h, Function 2Dh. The system returns AL=0 if the time is set successfully, or AL=FFh if the time set is not valid.

```
Int 21h, Function 2Dh: Set System Time
mov        ah,2dh      ; Set time
mov        ch,hr       ; Hour
mov        cl,mn       ; Minutes
mov        dx,0        ; Seconds = 0
int        21h
or         al,al       ; Error?
jnz        error
```

Listing 13.7 includes a set of C functions for getting the time and date. The `cdate()` and `ctime()` subroutines can be pulled out of the listing and added to your library of functions. Each returns a string pointer to a static buffer inside the function, with the date or time formatted appropriately in this buffer.

Listing 13.7

```
/* DateTime.c
   Listing 13.7 of DOS Programmer's Reference */

#include <stdio.h>
#include <dos.h>

void main()
{
    char *cdate(void);
    char *ctime(void);
    printf("Date: %s Time: %s\n",cdate(), ctime());
}

char *cdate()
{
    static char buffer[9];
    union REGS regs;
```

```
        regs.h.ah = 0x2a;
        intdos(&regs,&regs);

        sprintf(buffer,"%02.2d/%02.2d/%02.2d",
            regs.h.dh, regs.h.dl, regs.x.cx-1900);
        return(buffer);
}

char *ctime()
{
        static char    buffer[9];
        union REGS regs;

        regs.h.ah = 0x2c;
        intdos(&regs,&regs);

        sprintf(buffer,"%02.2d:%02.2d:%02.2d",
            regs.h.ch, regs.h.cl, regs.h.dh);
        return(buffer);
}
```

Each function is put together to hold the string representation of the date or time until you can use the string. Such static variables are permanently allocated and can occupy a great deal of memory that will be used only infrequently. Be careful not to use too many of them.

Listing 13.8, the Pascal program `clock.pas`, is another example of the use of the date and time functions. This program displays an on-screen clock until you press the Escape key (Esc).

Listing 13.8

```
{ clock.pas }

{ Turbo Pascal 4.0 or greater. For 3.0, omit next  }
{ code line and declare the Registers record type. }

uses crt, Dos;

const    cr:  char = ^M;

var hour,min,sec,month,day,year : byte;
    ch : char;

Procedure get_time( var hr,mi,se : byte );

var
    I: Integer;
    Regs: Registers;

begin { get_time }
    With Regs Do
        begin
            AH:=$2C;
```

continues

Listing 13.8 Continued

```
                    Flags:=0;
                    MsDos(Regs);     {execute software interrupt}
                    hr:=CH;
                    mi:=CL;
                    se:=DH;
          end; { With Regs }
end; { end get_time }


Procedure get_date( var mo, da, yr : byte);

var
     I: Integer;
     Regs: Registers;

begin { get_date }
     With Regs Do
          begin
                AH:=$2A;
                Flags:=0;
                MsDos(Dos.Registers(Regs));   {execute software interrupt}
                yr:=(CX mod 100);
                da:=DL;
                mo:=DH;
          end; { With Regs }
end; { end get_date }

procedure print_time( hr,mi,se,mo,dy,yr : byte);

begin { procedure print_time }
     write(mo:2,'/',dy:2,'/',yr:2);
     write(' ',hr:2,':',mi:2,':',se:2);
     write(cr);
end; { end print_time }

begin { Main Routine }
     repeat
          get_time(hour,min,sec);
          get_date(month,day,year);
          print_time(hour,min,sec,month,day,year);
          delay(10);
     until keypressed;
     { flush the input buffer }
     while keypressed do ch := readkey;
     { for version 3.0, replace preceding line with }
     {     while keypressed do read(kbd,ch); }
end. { end Main Routine }
```

Clock.pas is a simplistic program. The main part of the program occurs at the end, between the begin-end pair marked as Main Routine. This main routine sets up a continuous loop (repeat-until) that gets the date and time and prints them every ten seconds until a key is pressed. (Whenever a key is pressed, keypressed is set to TRUE so that Turbo Pascal can recognize it.)

After the clock loop ends, the program clears any keystrokes in the input buffer by simply reading characters as long as keypressed remains TRUE. Then the program ends.

Extended Error Processing

A DOS function, introduced with DOS V3, lets you determine extended error information. *Extended error information* provides detailed information about an error that has just occurred (after a DOS service call) and suggests action to remedy the error. Although this function is most useful at the assembly language level, you also can get suggested recovery actions by using the routine from a high-level language.

If you are working in assembly language, you should save any essential registers before you call Function 59h because this special function destroys most of your register setups while it is processing. (If you are working in a high-level language, you do not need to save the registers.)

The following DOS function saves the registers and then gets the extended error information:

```
Int 21h, Function 59h: Get Extended Error Information
push     ax          ; Save registers before call
push     bx
push     cx
push     dx
push     si
push     di
push     bp
push     ds
push     es
mov      ah,59h       ; Extended error info
mov      bx,0
int      21h
```

The routine returns the following codes:

AX = Extended error code

BH = Error class

BL = Recommended action

CH = Error locus

The meaning of these codes is detailed in the following tables. The codes are self-explanatory; how you respond to them depends on the program and the nature of the call that generated the problem.

Table 13.2 lists the error codes with the primary error indication—in other words, the "what happened?" This type of error indication is familiar to programmers accustomed to working with operating system calls. Informational messages (maybe we should call them "semi-informational") give us something to tell the user but are not much help to us unless only one

443

thing could possibly be wrong. If there is more than one possible cause for an error, the informational message is only marginally helpful. In most cases, if you can expect the error, you should have programmed around it in the first place.

Table 13.2 Extended Error Codes Returned in AX

Code	Meaning
1	Invalid function
2	File not found
3	Path not found
4	No handles available
5	Access denied
6	Invalid handle
7	Memory control blocks destroyed
8	Insufficient memory
9	Invalid memory block address
10	Invalid environment
11	Invalid format
12	Invalid access code
13	Invalid data
14	Reserved
15	Invalid drive
16	Attempt to remove current directory
17	Not the same device
18	No more files
19	Disk write-protected
20	Unknown unit
21	Drive not ready
22	Unknown command
23	CRC error
24	Bad request structure length
25	Seek error
26	Unknown media type
27	Sector not found
28	Out of paper
29	Write fault

Code	Meaning
30	Read fault
31	General failure
32	Sharing violation
33	Lock violation
34	Invalid disk change
35	FCB unavailable
36	Sharing buffer overflow
37	Code page mismatch
38	Error handling EOF
39	Handle disk full
40–49	Reserved
50	Network request not supported
51	Remote computer not listening
52	Duplicate name on network
53	Network name not found
54	Network busy
55	Network device no longer exists
56	Net BIOS command limit exceeded
57	Network adapter error
58	Incorrect network response
59	Unexpected network error
60	Incompatible remote adapter
61	Print queue full
62	Not enough space for print file
63	Print file deleted
64	Network name deleted
65	Access denied
66	Network device type incorrect
67	Network name not found
68	Network name limit exceeded
69	Net BIOS session limit exceeded
70	Temporarily paused

continues

Table 13.2 Continued

Code	Meaning
71	Network request not accepted
72	Print or disk redirection is paused
73–79	Reserved
80	File already exists
81	Reserved
82	Cannot make directory entry
83	Fail on Int 24
84	Too many redirections
85	Duplicate redirection
86	Invalid password
87	Invalid parameter
88	Network data fault

The error class codes in Table 13.3 go one step beyond the error codes themselves. Error class codes classify the error, based on internal knowledge of the operating system.

Table 13.3 Error Class Codes Returned in BH

Class	Meaning
1	Out of resource
2	Temporary situation
3	Authorization
4	Internal
5	Hardware failure
6	System failure
7	Application program error
8	Not found
9	Bad format
10	Locked
11	Media
12	Already exists
13	Unknown

With most systems, an operating system error can occur because of so many causes that the program must be extremely sophisticated in its error handling if it is to shield the user from problems. All experienced programmers have thought that "it must be an operating system bug" as they have butted heads against a seemingly intractable problem. DOS tries to tell you if there seems to be such an error—but do you trust DOS to admit its own mistakes? If, when you are running a program intended for commercial use, you get an indication of an error that cannot be corrected by the software, you can help minimize your own support problems if you make sure that the program clearly tells the user the source of the error. If you can point out a hardware failure, your customer service group will thank you for every call it does *not* have to take.

Most experienced programmers have wondered what to do when certain errors occur. The recommended action codes shown in Table 13.4 are meant to help, but are not a total solution. By suggesting possible actions to the programmer, the designers of DOS have applied their knowledge of the system to your problems. You can take reasonable action based on the action codes.

Table 13.4   Recommended Action Codes Returned in BL

Action Code	Meaning
1	Retry; if not cleared in a reasonable number of attempts, prompt user to `Abort` or `Ignore`
2	Delay, and then retry; if not cleared in reasonable number of attempts, prompt user to `Abort` or `Ignore`
3	Get corrected information from user (bad file name or disk drive)
4	Abort application with cleanup
5	Abort application without cleanup (cleanup may increase problems)
6	Ignore error
7	Prompt user to correct error and then retry

Errors that involve the user are especially prone to difficulties in error correction, particularly if the user does not understand your error message and prompts (`Abort or Ignore error`, for example). Suggested actions do not eliminate the programmer's responsibility for making the program as user-friendly as possible.

Action codes should be used as the basis for error recovery when an error condition is recognized. In most situations, only one or two of the recommended actions make sense—you can ignore the others. Be careful, however—provide a graceful way to exit from a program if an error (that cannot be corrected by software) occurs. If the user has to reboot the system to get out of an error-correction loop, the error has not been corrected. Always include an override to allow frustrated users to get out.

The error locus codes shown in Table 13.5 expand information about an error and attempt to tell you something about the origin of the error—in other words, which device caused the error. (You can determine the area of DOS from which an error originated because these values are stored internally by DOS, as each functional area of the DOS code is entered. In this way, a common error-detection routine can process errors with different locus codes.)

Table 13.5 Error Locus Codes Returned in CH

Locus Code	Meaning
1	Unknown
2	Block device (disk or disk emulator)
3	Network
4	Serial device
5	Memory related

On a single-user system, error locus code information is marginally useful because, in most cases, the original error code has told you what caused the error. This type of error information becomes useful in situations that deal with the possibilities inherent in redirection and device independence.

If you write a program that works with the standard input and output devices, for example, a user can redirect the output to a disk drive, a network, or the RS-232 port without the program being aware of the change. The error locus code can give you the key to interpreting and correcting the error.

Some programmers have reported that the Extended Error function has returned inappropriate information when called after errors occur on a character (rather than block) device by using DOS V3. A study of the actual code used in V4 shows that three of the four items returned (the class, action, and locus) are set at entry to other DOS functions so that they can be used later in case of error and are never explicitly returned to zero if no error occurs. Not all are set by every function; some functions set only one or two.

The remaining item, the extended error code itself, is mapped by a straight table-lookup procedure from the older error codes, but only when an error is detected. This item *is* set to zero at the start of each DOS function to indicate that no error has occurred yet.

When the Extended Error function is called, it merely gets the four values stored earlier and returns them to the caller. No analysis is performed on these values. It is possible, therefore, although unlikely, that a call to the function might return values stored by DOS functions that are different from the one in which the error occurred. If so, it would be a significant bug in DOS; with the exception of a few scattered reports that might have been due to errors in the calling programs, no such verifiable bug has been reported. Still, if you find inconsistent results, be aware that others have reported problems.

Undocumented Features

No discussion of the miscellaneous functions of DOS can be complete without touching on the famed "undocumented features" that Microsoft and IBM tenaciously show as "reserved" in the official reference manuals. These types of features have been a significant part of DOS from the beginning. Most authorities tell you to avoid them because they are never guaranteed to stay the same from one version to the next or to be present in any specific OEM version of DOS.

These features span a wide range. Some are so intimately connected with the internals of how DOS does its job that they are essentially useless outside of DOS itself. Others provide hooks for things that are not yet fully implemented. A few have moved into the twilight zone of semi-respectability (they were discussed earlier, in connection with TSR programming).

The reference section of this book tells you all that has been learned about these intriguing bits of mystery. In every case, a disclaimer states that the feature may behave differently, or even be absent, on your machine. This was more true of V2 than it has been since the introduction of network support in V3, because at that time Microsoft changed its OEM contracts to require that certain areas (including many of the "reserved" functions) not be changed; they are necessary now for network support.

Note, however, that the use of these functions is still risky. Despite literally years of study by some of the best analytical minds in the industry, no one outside Microsoft and IBM knows exactly what all of them are supposed to do. This means that any of them can have serious hidden side effects under relatively rare circumstances; when such side effects are known, you are told, but not everything is known.

Still, experimenting with these things is fun, and the risk can be minimized by following the rules set forth for testing device drivers: Limit your exposure, and keep a good set of backups in case things go wrong.

Rather than provide examples of the use of undocumented functions in this chapter, we have added them as Appendix D. You can use the programs described there to do your own snooping inside DOS.

Summary

This chapter has discussed a group of special functions that do not fit neatly into a single category: the DOS version functions, BIOS equipment function, DOS date and time functions, and DOS error-information function. All these standard functions are valuable additions to a personal function library. You have learned how to build a few sample routines (in C, BASIC, and Pascal) for each of these functions.

Finally, this chapter briefly discussed the subject of the "reserved" functions listed in all official reference manuals. At this point, you are ready to start using the rest of this book and what you have learned so far to design and build your own programs.

Part V

Reference

Reference Overview

The remainder of this book documents the great mass of BIOS, DOS, and miscellaneous API functions and services available to you, as the programmer. The information in each reference section of this book was compiled from the widest available range of sources. Every effort was made to ensure the technical accuracy and timeliness of this information; if you find discrepancies, Que Corporation is interested in your comments.

The following sections follow this brief overview:

- BIOS Reference
- DOS Reference
- Mouse Reference
- EMS Reference
- XMS Reference
- DPMI Reference
- Task Switching Reference
- DoubleSpace Reference

How Services Are Presented

In each reference section, a standard format is used to present each interrupt or function. All services are organized in ascending numeric order by interrupt and function number. A sample of this presentation format follows:

Int 21h	Function 44h Subfunction 08h	V3
	Block Device Removable?	

The first line for every function lists the interrupt number, the function number (if any), the subfunction number (if any), and possibly the version number at which the service became available. The second line lists the purpose of the function. Additional information includes a quick description, calling registers, return registers, and comments. Let's examine each element of this format.

Interrupt Number

The interrupt number is the one used to invoke the service. A wide range of interrupts are discussed, as you can see by looking at the information in Table Ref.1.

Table Ref.1   Interrupts Discussed in *DOS Programmer's Reference*

Interrupt	Purpose
00h	Divide-by-Zero Interrupt
01h	Single Step Interrupt
02h	Non-Maskable Interrupt
03h	Breakpoint Interrupt
04h	Arithmetic Overflow Interrupt
05h	Print Screen
06h	Reserved
07h	Reserved
08h	System Timer
09h	Keyboard Interrupt
0Ah	Reserved
0Bh	Communications
0Ch	Communications
0Dh	Hard Disk Controller
0Eh	Floppy Disk Management
0Fh	Printer Management
10h	Video
11h	Get Equipment Status
12h	Get Memory Size
13h	Diskette
14h	Asynchronous Communications
15h	System Services
16h	Keyboard

Interrupt	Purpose
17h	Printer
18h	Execute ROM BASIC
19h	System Warm Boot
1Ah	System Timer/Real-Time Clock Services
1Bh	Ctrl-Break Address
1Ch	Timer Tick Interrupt
1Dh	Video-Initialization Parameter Table
1Eh	Disk-Initialization Parameter Table
1Fh	Graphics Display Character Bit-Map Table
20h	Program Termination
21h	DOS Function Dispatcher
22h	Terminate Address
23h	Ctrl-C Interrupt Vector
24h	Critical-Error Vector
25h	Absolute Disk Read
26h	Absolute Disk Write
27h	Terminate and Stay Resident
28h	Keyboard Busy Loop
29h	Fast Putchar
2Ah	Network Interface
2Eh	Execute Command
2Fh	Multiplex Interface
31h	DPMI Interface
33h	Mouse Interface
4Fh	VESA BIOS Services
67h	LIM-EMS Interface
70h	Real-Time Clock Interrupt

DOS PROGRAMMING

Function Number

The function number, a designator almost universally loaded in the AH register, is used by the interrupt handlers to determine which service is desired. Although the function number is optional depending on the interrupt being invoked, in reality it is almost a necessity. For instance, Int 21h has more than 150 functions available. Without the function number, the interrupt handlers would be lost regarding what you wanted done.

Subfunction Number

Like the function number, the subfunction is an optional designator that may further define the desired service. Only a few functions are divided into subfunctions. If the DOS function being selected requires the specification of a subfunction, the subfunction number typically is loaded into the AL register before the interrupt is invoked. If no subfunctions are supported by the function, the use of AL may not be defined, or it may be used to pass other parameters to the service.

Version Availability

Version availability is not included for all functions in this book. Where it is included, it is a designation of the software version number in which the service became available. This information may be of vital importance in developing your programs because you do not want to try to invoke a service that may not be supported by the system on which your program is running.

Purpose

The next portion is simply a statement of the meaning of the service. It is designed to give a quick overview of what the service is designed to accomplish. In most instances, the purpose is garnered from technical publications from IBM, Microsoft, or other vendors. In a few instances, however, the vendor's listed purposes may be unclear, ambiguous, or imprecise. In these cases, the stated purposes have been semantically modified for greater clarity.

Description

The description is a quick, one- or two-sentence indication of what the service can do. It is similar to the "Purpose" section but is expanded to provide a brief explanation of the scope of the service.

Calling Registers

Next is a list of the CPU register settings needed by the service to function properly. Usually, these settings are referred to as *parameters* although they can include pointers to required parameter tables. This portion of the function listing is a quick checklist of register settings required for the service.

Return Registers

Like the "Calling Registers" section, "Return Registers" is a quick checklist of the values returned in registers by the service. It gives a good listing of what is provided by the particular service.

Comments

The "Comments" section is the body of each service listing. It provides a narrative explanation of what the function does, how it is used, possible uses, and any quirks that should be noted. If the function requires the use of parameter tables, either they are described in this section or information that helps you determine the table content is provided.

A Detailed Function Summary

The following is a detailed listing of the functions covered in this book. You may want to use it as a quick reference guide to finding information about a particular service.

Note: Undocumented functions are marked with an asterisk (*).

Int	Func	Sub	Purpose	Page
00			Divide-by-zero interrupt	485
01			Single step interrupt	486
02			Non-maskable interrupt	486
03			Breakpoint interrupt	487
04			Arithmetic overflow interrupt	488
05			Print screen	488
06			Reserved	

continues

457

continues

459

Int	Func	Sub	Purpose	Page
	00		Reset disk system	523
	01		Get disk system status	523
	02		Read disk sectors	524
	03		Write disk sectors	525
	04		Verify disk sectors	526
	05		Format disk track	527
	06		Format cylinder and set bad sector flags	528
	07		Format drive from specified cylinder	529
	08		Return disk drive parameters	529
	09		Initialize hard disk table	531
	0A		Read long sector	531
	0B		Write long sector	533
	0C		Seek cylinder	534
	0D		Alternate disk reset	535
	0E		Read sector buffer	535
	0F		Write sector buffer	536
	10		Test hard disk system status	536
	11		Recalibrate hard disk drive	537
	12		Diagnose controller RAM	537
	13		Diagnose drive	538
	14		Diagnose controller	538
	15		Return DASD type	538
	16		Read disk change line status	539
	17		Set DASD type for disk format	540
	18		Set media type for format	540
	19		Park heads	541

continues

461

Int	Func	Sub	Purpose	Page
	85		System request key pressed	556
	86		Delay	557
	87		Move block	557
	88		Extended memory size determination	559
	89		Switch processor to protected mode	559
	90		Device wait	560
	91		Interrupt complete	561
	C0		Return system configuration parameters	562
	C1		Return extended BIOS data area segment address	564
	C2		Pointing device BIOS interface	565
	C3		Enable/disable watchdog time-out	567
	C4		Programmable option select	567
	D8	00	Read EISA Slot Information	568
		01	Read EISA Function Information	569
		02	Clear EISA CMOS	570
		03	Write to EISA CMOS	570
16			Keyboard	571
	00		Read keyboard character	571
	01		Read keyboard status	572
	02		Return keyboard flags	572
	03		Adjust keyboard repeat rate	573
	04		Key-click on/off	574
	05		Write to keyboard buffer	574
	10		Get keystroke	575

462

continues

Int	Func	Sub	Purpose	Page
1E			Disk-initialization parameter table	587
1F			Graphics display character bit-map table	587
20			Terminate program	595
21			DOS function dispatcher	596
	00		Terminate program	596
	01		Keyboard input with Echo	597
	02		Display output	598
	03		Auxiliary input	598
	04		Auxiliary output	599
	05		Printer output	600
	06		Direct console I/O	600
	07		Direct STDIN input	601
	08		STDIN input	602
	09		Display string	602
	0A		Buffered STDIN input	603
	0B		Check STDIN status	604
	0C		Clear buffer and input	605
	0D		Reset disk	606
	0E		Select disk	606
	0F		Open file (FCB)	607
	10		Close file (FCB)	608
	11		Search for first entry (FCB)	609
	12		Search for next entry (FCB)	610
	13		Delete file (FCB)	611
	14		Read sequential file (FCB)	611
	15		Write sequential file (FCB)	612

continues

465

continues

Int	Func	Sub	Purpose	Page
	4D		Get return code	689
	4E		Search for first match	690
	4F		Search for next match	692
	50		Set PSP segment	693
	51		Get PSP segment	694
	52*		Get disk list	695
	53*		Translate BPB to DPB	698
	54		Get verify flag	701
	55*		Create PSP	701
	56		Rename file	701
	57	00	Get file date and time	702
		01	Set file date and time	703
	58	00	Get allocation strategy	704
		01	Set allocation strategy	705
		02	Get UMB link status	706
		03	Set UMB link status	707
	59		Get extended error information	707
	5A		Create uniquely named file	713
	5B		Create new file	714
	5C	00	Set file access locks	715
	5C	01	Clear file access locks	716
	5D	00*	Copy data to DOS save area	717
		06*	Get critical-error flag address	717
		0A	Set error data values	718
	5E	00	Get machine name	719
		01*	Set machine name	719
		02	Set network printer setup	720

continues

469

Int	Func	Sub	Purpose	Page
26			Absolute disk write	743
27			Terminate and stay resident	745
28*			DOS safe to use	746
29*			Fast putchar	746
2A*			Microsoft Networks interface	747
2B			Reserved	-
2C			Reserved	-
2D			Reserved	-
2E*			Primary shell program loader	747
2F			Multiplex service interrupt	748
	01	00	Print installation check	748
		01	Submit file to print spooler	749
		02	Remove file from print queue	749
		03	Cancel all files in print queue	750
		04	Hold print jobs	750
		05	End print hold	751
		06	Get printer device	751
	05*		Get outboard critical-error handler installation status	752
	06		Get ASSIGN.COM/ASSIGN.EXE installation status	752
	08*		Get DRIVER.SYS installation status	752
	10		Get SHARE.EXE installation status	753
	11		Get network redirector installation status	753
	12	00*	Get DOS installation status	753
		01*	Flush file	754
		02*	Get interrupt vector address	754

continues

continues

Int	Func	Sub	Purpose	Page
	00	0F	Set multiple descriptors	884
	01	00	Allocate DOS memory block	885
	01	01	Free DOS memory block	886
	01	02	Resize DOS memory block	886
	02	00	Get real mode interrupt vector	887
	02	01	Set real mode interrupt vector	887
	02	02	Get processor exception handler vector	888
	02	03	Set processor exception handler vector	888
	02	04	Get protected mode interrupt vector	889
	02	05	Set protected mode interrupt vector	889
	02	10	Get extended processor exception handler vector (protected mode)	890
	02	11	Get extended processor exception handler vector (real mode)	890
	02	12	Set extended processor exception handler vector (protected mode)	891
	02	13	Set extended processor exception handler vector (real mode)	891
	03	00	Simulate real mode interrupt	892
	03	01	Call real mode procedure with far return frame	893
	03	02	Call real mode procedure with IRET frame	895
	03	03	Allocate real mode callback address	896
	03	04	Free real mode callback address	897
	03	05	Get state save/restore addresses	897
	03	06	Get raw mode switch addresses	898
	04	00	Get version	899

Int	Func	Sub	Purpose	Page
	04	01	Get DPMI capabilities	899
	05	00	Get free memory information	901
	05	01	Allocate memory block	902
	05	02	Free memory block	903
	05	03	Resize memory block	903
	05	04	Allocate linear memory block	904
	05	05	Resize linear memory block	905
	05	06	Get page attributes	906
	05	07	Set page attributes	907
	05	08	Map device in memory block	908
	05	09	Map conventional memory in memory block	909
	05	0A	Get memory block size and base	910
	05	0B	Get memory information	910
	06	00	Lock linear region	912
	06	01	Unlock linear region	912
	06	02	Mark real mode region as pageable	913
	06	03	Relock real mode region	913
	06	04	Get page size	914
	07	02	Mark page as demand paging candidate	914
	07	03	Discard page contents	915
	08	00	Physical address mapping	915
	08	01	Free physical address mapping	916
	09	00	Get and disable virtual interrupt state	916
	09	01	Get and enable virtual interrupt state	917
	09	02	Get virtual interrupt state	917

continues

475

Int	Func	Sub	Purpose	Page
	0A	00	Get vendor-specific API entry point	917
	0B	00	Set debug watchpoint	918
	0B	01	Clear debug watchpoint	919
	0B	02	Get state of debug watchpoint	919
	0B	03	Reset debug watchpoint	920
	0C	00	Install resident service provider callback	920
	0C	01	Terminate and stay resident	921
	0D	00	Allocate shared memory	922
	0D	01	Free shared memory	923
	0D	02	Serialize on shared memory	923
	0D	03	Free serialization on shared memory	924
	0E	00	Get co-processor status	925
	0E	01	Set processor emulation	926
33			Mouse interrupt	786
	00		Initialize the mouse	786
	01		Show mouse cursor	787
	02		Hide mouse cursor	787
	03		Get mouse position	787
	04		Set mouse position	789
	05		Get button-press information	789
	06		Get button-release information	790
	07		Set mouse X limits	790
	08		Set mouse Y limits	791
	09		Set graphics cursor shape	791
	0A		Set text cursor type	794
	0B		Read motion counters	794
	0C		Set user-defined event handler	795

476

Int	Func	Sub	Purpose	Page
	0D		Start light-pen emulation	796
	0E		Stop light-pen emulation	797
	0F		Set mickey-to-pixel ratio	797
	10		Conditional cursor off	797
	13		Set double speed threshold	798
	14		Swap user event handlers	798
	15		Get save-state storage size	799
	16		Save mouse driver state	800
	17		Restore mouse driver state	800
	18		Set alternate mouse user handler	800
	19		Get user alternate interrupt vector	802
	1A		Set mouse sensitivity	802
	1B		Get mouse sensitivity	802
	1C		Set interrupt rate	803
	1D		Set CRT page number	803
	1E		Get CRT page number	803
	1F		Disable mouse driver	804
	20		Enable mouse driver	804
	21		Software reset	804
	22		Set message language	805
	23		Get message language	805
	24		Get mouse information	806
	25		Get general driver information	806
	26		Get maximum virtual coordinates	807
	27		Get cursor masks and mickey counts	808
	28		Set video mode	808
	29		Get supported video modes	808

continues

477

Int	Func	Sub	Purpose	Page
	2A		Get cursor hot spot	809
	2B		Set acceleration curves	809
	2C		Get acceleration curves	811
	2D		Set or get active acceleration curve	811
	2F		Mouse hardware reset	812
	30		Set or get ballpoint information	812
	31		Get virtual coordinates	813
	32		Get active advanced functions	813
	33		Get switch settings	814
	34		Get MOUSE.INI path	815
	4A		Real-time clock alarm interrupt	588
67			LIM-EMS interface	822
	40		Get manager status	822
	41		Get page frame segment	822
	42		Get page counts	823
	43		Get handle and allocate memory	824
	44		Map/unmap memory	824
	45		De-allocate handle and memory	825
	46		Get EMM version	826
	47		Save page map	826
	48		Restore page map	827
	49		Reserved	828
	4A		Reserved	828
	4B		Get handle count	829
	4C		Get pages owned by handle	829
	4D		Get pages for all handles	830
	4E	00	Get page map registers	831

478

Int	Func	Sub	Purpose	Page
		01	Set page map registers	831
		02	Get and set page map registers	832
		03	Get size for page map array	832
	4F	00	Get partial page map	833
		01	Set partial page map	834
		02	Get partial page map size	834
	50	00	Map/unmap multiple handle pages (physical page number mode)	835
		01	Map/unmap multiple handle pages (segment address mode)	835
	51		Re-allocate pages	836
	52	00	Get handle attribute	837
		01	Set handle attribute	837
		02	Get attribute capability	838
	53	00	Get handle name	839
		01	Set handle name	839
	54	00	Get handle directory	840
		01	Find named handle	840
		02	Get handle count	841
	55		Alter page map and jump	841
	56		Alter page map and call	843
		02	Get stack space size	844
	57	00	Move memory region	845
		01	Exchange memory regions	846
	58	00	Get mappable physical address array	848
		01	Get mappable physical address array size	849

continues

479

BIOS Reference

BIOS (basic input/output system) functions are the fundamental level of any PC or compatible computer. BIOS functions embody the basic operations needed for successful use of the computer's hardware resources. These functions are used also by DOS to carry out its own operations. Most programming on PCs or compatibles is performed above the BIOS level. Programmers who need special functions call BIOS functions directly when no other method will work. In some cases, even the BIOS does not provide the services needed, and programmers have to go below it to the hardware.

The BIOS in a PC or compatible is contained largely in ROM (thus, the term *ROM BIOS*) as part of the hardware system. Ordinarily, the manufacturer of a system provides the BIOS, according to Microsoft's specifications for MS-DOS. Extensions of the ROM BIOS for EGA monitors or other devices can be added easily to the system. These extensions serve as one of the foundations of the PC environment's extendable nature. Some parts of the BIOS are loaded from disk when the system boots (a hidden system file, typically called either IO.SYS or IBMBIO.COM). See Chapter 3, "The Dynamics of DOS," for a detailed description of how DOS is booted.

The ROM release date is located in the eight bytes starting at F000:FFF5h. Some important BIOS release dates include the ones in Table BIOS.1:

Table BIOS.1   BIOS Release Dates

Date	Machine Type
04/24/81	PC
10/19/81	Revised PC with bug fixes
08/16/82	PC XT
10/27/82	PC to XT upgrade
11/08/82	Portable PC
06/01/83	PC*jr*
01/10/84	Personal Computer AT
09/13/85	Convertible PC
04/21/86	PC XT 286
09/02/86	PS/2 line

These dates, which cover only the IBM ROM BIOS, are meaningful only if you are working with an IBM PC. Systems that do not have the true IBM ROM are likely to have different dates. The table does not cover *all* releases of the ROM BIOS. From time to time, notes in magazines or on bulletin boards (mostly reporting bugs) refer to other dates for ROM but, as far as has been determined, no comprehensive list of dates exists.

A model-identification byte (located at F000:FFFEh) can be used to differentiate between models (see Table BIOS.2). The PS/2 family continues to support this model-identification byte. For non-IBM machines, however, this byte cannot be relied on; no standard set of values has ever been established.

Table BIOS.2   Model Identification Bytes

Byte	System
9Ah	COMPAQ Plus
FFh	IBM PC
FEh	PC XT, Portable PC
FDh	PC*jr*
FCh	Personal Computer AT, PS/1, PS/2 Models 50 and 60
FBh	PC XT (after 1/10/86)

Byte	System
FAh	PS/2 Model 30
F9h	Convertible PC
F8h	PS/2 Model 80

For additional information about the BIOS release dates and model identification, refer to the description of Int 15, Function C0h, later in this section.

On the PS/2, no BIOS stands between OS/2 and the hardware. All hardware interfacing is performed through device drivers. (See Chapter 12, "Device Drivers," for a discussion of device drivers.) The BIOS remains in the PS/2 system for three reasons: to bootstrap the operating system, to support DOS (if DOS is being used), and to support the Compatibility Box for running DOS programs.

Device drivers are direct interfaces linked into the operating system to control access to hardware. In a multitasking operating system such as Windows, UNIX, or OS/2, these drivers can handle multiple requests from processes (programs) and keep everything in order. Access through drivers is essential in a multitasking environment because any program with direct access to the hardware or to an all-encompassing BIOS can destroy what other programs are trying to do.

A BIOS originally written to support DOS would have trouble running under OS/2 because the BIOS does not run in protected mode. Some processor instructions are not allowed in protected mode, and programs are prevented from accessing portions of memory assigned to other programs. Protected mode makes multitasking operations possible because you can write a program and not worry about its effect on other programs. The IBM PS/2 includes an advanced BIOS (ABIOS) that can work with a device driver in real and protected modes, support multitasking, and address as much as 16M of memory.

On the PS/2, BIOS calls are supported for programs running in the Compatibility Box. Even Borland's SideKick (which uses undocumented system calls) runs on the PS/2, although the official position of Microsoft and IBM is to support only *documented* DOS calls. Under OS/2, however, DOS programs that must run in the background are suspended. The OS/2 developers made the worst-case assumption that DOS programs are not compatible with multitasking because they directly access memory (and write directly to the screen, for example).

Readers moving into the OS/2 environment will find that this section indicates (wherever possible) the PS/2 aspects of interrupt processing in the BIOS. Keep in mind that IBM is not publishing the BIOS listing for the PS/2, as it did for the original PC. Instead, it is publishing only the entry points, which are almost entirely compatible with the old PC BIOS. Programs built on a BIOS foundation will continue to work with the PS/2. Programs whose timing depends on the speed of the BIOS work much faster on the PS/2 family than they do on a PC.

The major changes in the PS/2 BIOS are shown in Table BIOS.3.

Table BIOS.3 Personal System/2 Differences

Interrupt	Meaning
0Bh	Reserved, no longer communications
0Ch	Reserved, no longer communications
0Dh	Reserved
0Fh	Reserved
15h	System services (cassette I/O)
40h	Diskette BIOS revector
41h	Hard disk parameters
46h	Hard disk parameters
4Ah	User alarm
71h–74h	Reserved
76h–77h	Reserved
F1h–FFh	User program interrupts

Except for communications programs that customarily take control of interrupts 0Bh and 0Ch, these changes should have no effect on most programs.

If you have any question about how the functions in this section are presented, refer to the "Reference Overview" section of this book.

Int 00h

Divide-by-Zero Interrupt (Hardware Error)

Called by the CPU if an attempt is made to divide by a zero value

Calling registers: None

Return registers: Nothing

Comments: The divide-by-zero interrupt is invoked automatically when the processor attempts to perform the illegal divide-by-zero operation. Because the division process in the computer can never end if the divisor is zero, the operation is always treated as an error on any computer. The interrupt handler automatically deals with this error.

At start-up, the BIOS sets this interrupt to point to an IRET instruction. DOS resets the interrupt, however, to point to a handler that generates the message `Divide by Zero` and then aborts the program that caused the error. This process is handled at the DOS level because a corresponding handler does not exist at the BIOS level. A divide-by-zero error can leave the operating system unstable and result in other errors. If a divide-by-zero error occurs, the best course is to restart the system manually or create a better handler (such as the one for DOS Int 24h).

If you are writing a program in which user input can cause this type of error, you should trap the interrupt and handle it in a routine of your own. It is good programming practice to write your programs so that they screen user input and never allow this error trap to occur. Sometimes, however, your program can generate the divide-by-zero error in ways you hadn't considered.

A divide-by-zero error can occur unexpectedly during operation of a program in which a stack problem results in attempts by the processor to execute Int 00h. Occasionally, a divide-by-zero error occurs when particularly intricate stack manipulation takes place during the process of debugging a program.

In addition to these causes, some versions of DOS generate a divide-by-zero error when an attempt is made to access a file that does not exist; the error apparently occurs in the calculations DOS performs to convert a cluster number to the track/head/sector address format required by all disk controllers. This error is especially mystifying because no *apparent* relation exists between the user's actions and the error message.

Int 01h

Single Step Interrupt

Called by the CPU if the trap flag is set

Calling registers: None

Return registers: Nothing

Comments: Whenever the trap flag (TF) is set, Int 01h is called after each instruction has been executed. The debugger uses this interrupt to handle program single stepping. (Other types of programs should not call this interrupt.)

If you are writing a debugger, take special care with the STI (Set Interrupt Flag) instruction to prevent trapping your own interrupt handler. When you enter your handler, interrupts are off and the trap flag is set. If you reenable interrupts before you turn off the trap flag, your interrupt handler will be single stepped. You have to reboot to regain control.

Int 02h

Non-Maskable Interrupt (NMI)

Called by the CPU on a memory parity error

Calling registers: None

Return registers: Nothing

Comments: From the programmer's standpoint, the non-maskable interrupt (NMI) is one of the least useful interrupts because it represents a major system failure in progress. When an NMI occurs, you probably will not have time to recover. The NMI cannot be blocked or turned off — it simply must be accepted.

On the PC family of computers (including the PS/2 Model 30), this interrupt reports parity errors. When a memory parity error occurs on the system board, ROM BIOS displays PARITY CHECK 1 and then locks up the machine. PARITY CHECK 2 indicates an I/O channel parity error. A display of PARITY CHECK 3 indicates an intermittent-read problem with memory.

Although you could trap the interrupt to shut down the system in an orderly manner, the interrupt handler might not be in good memory because this interrupt arises from a memory parity error. More important, any attempt to flush disk buffers or update your files can damage an otherwise good file. Several public domain and shareware programs are available, however, to trap the interrupt and give you a choice of action rather than force a reboot.

This interrupt is used for parity checks on the PS/2 family (except the Model 30) but the error messages are numeric codes taken from the following table:

Code	Meaning
110	System-board memory failure
111	I/O channel-check activated
112	Watchdog time-out
113	Direct memory access bus time-out

A fault in I/O channel memory causes error 111. The watchdog time-out is used to detect a missed IRQ0 (system timer) interrupt. When such an interrupt occurs with the watchdog time-out enabled, NMI error 112 is generated. On systems driven by direct memory access (DMA), error 113 is generated if a DMA device is given control of the system bus for more than 7.8 microseconds.

Int 03h

Breakpoint Interrupt

Used by debuggers to trap program breakpoints

Calling registers: None

Return registers: Nothing

Comments: Debugging programs put at this interrupt a vector that points to their breakpoint-handling routines. Debuggers place an Int 03h (using the special single-byte synonym opcode 0CCh) at the desired breakpoint and allow the program to run. When the program reaches the breakpoint, the interrupt handler returns control to the debugger.

Such a special single-byte opcode might sound foreign to some programmers, but Intel provided this alternative to 0CDh 03h (the normal coding for Int 03h) to facilitate easy placement of breakpoints in executable code.

Interrupts 03h and 01h are the primary hardware tools available for debugging assembly language programs.

Int 04h

Arithmetic Overflow Interrupt

Called by the CPU when an arithmetic operation overflows

Calling registers: None

Return registers: Nothing

Comments: When arithmetic operations generate results larger than the data type allows, you can call this interrupt by executing the INTO (Interrupt on Overflow) instruction. To enable the instruction, the overflow bit (bit 11) in the flag register must be set before the arithmetic instruction (such as MUL or IMUL) is executed.

Because arithmetic overflow is not much of a problem for most programs, no action is usually taken. The default for the interrupt is to point to an IRET instruction and return immediately from the interrupt. No special handler is used to deal with overflow because the Intel microprocessor instruction set includes the JO and JNO (Jump if Overflow and Jump if Not Overflow) instructions, which ordinarily are used for handling overflow.

Int 05h

Print Screen

Prints the text screen to the printer

Calling registers: None

Return registers: Nothing

Comments: To trigger this function, which prints the current screen display to the printer, you press the PrtSc key (usually Shift-PrtSc). Function 05h transfers to a routine that sends to the printer the ASCII contents of the video screen buffer. Notice the use of the phrase *ASCII contents*—if you are working with a graphics screen, this interrupt causes printing to occur, but what is printed is unpredictable.

Most versions of DOS include the GRAPHICS.COM utility, which installs a substitute print-screen interrupt handler capable of dealing with graphics. Versions before V4 worked properly only with IBM (Epson-compatible) graphics printers; with V4, support was extended to all current IBM printer models.

Several other alternative Int 05h routines are widely distributed. Intel, for example, provides a replacement handler as part of the software supplied with the Above Board Plus EMS-memory board, which gives you control of its software print-buffering facility and retains the print-screen feature.

You can call Int 05h from your own programs if you want to provide a way to print the screen display. Printing the screen display can be particularly useful in database programs, for example — you can print the contents of the screen rather than have to print records.

In some cases, you might need to replace the interrupt vector with a special handler that deals with special screen conditions or performs a completely different function. The standard function saves the cursor position and then prints the screen to printer 1 on the system. It runs with interrupts enabled so that any interrupt (except another print screen) can take control of the system.

This function, which does not modify any registers, maintains a status byte at memory location 0050:0000h. If this status byte is 1, printing is in progress. If the value is 0, a successful print operation has occurred; FFh indicates that the last print operation was unsuccessful.

Int 08h

System Timer

Called by the system clock approximately 18.2 times per second (65,536 times per hour)

Calling registers: None

Return registers: Nothing

Comments: Int 08h, which is called 18.2 times per second to advance the time-of-day counter, is tied directly to channel 0 of the system timer chip. People who write TSRs with utilities such as SideKick, for example, find Int 08h particularly useful for time-related triggering (as with a clock or alarm). This interrupt calls Int 1Ch (Timer Tick). Most TSRs should connect to Int 1Ch rather than to Int 08h.

Because this interrupt is called every 55 milliseconds, all handlers for it must execute as quickly as possible. Interrupt processing should be a small part of the normal use of the processor system. And, because the timer is attached as IRQ0 (the highest-priority hardware interrupt), servicing this interrupt takes precedence over all other interrupts on the system. If this interrupt is handled poorly, it can lead to problems in servicing other important interrupts, such as disk servicing.

Note that because Int 1Ch (the user hook for the timer) is called *before* the Int 08h handler completes its processing, all actions performed in a handler for it *also* take precedence over any other hardware interrupt requests. Experienced software designers often overlook this fact.

Address 0040:006Ch is a 32-bit time-of-day indicator, counting the number of ticks since power-up. Position 0040:0070h is set to 1 every time the count reaches 24 hours and is cleared to 0 when the BIOS reads it. If another 24 hours elapse with no intervening read action, an entire day vanishes from the computer's time system.

This interrupt also provides an automatic motor-off function for disks, by decrementing location 0040:0040h. When location 0040:0040h reaches zero, the motor-running flag in the motor status at 0040:003Fh is reset to turn off the disk motor.

The reason for the odd frequency with which the timer calls Int 08h (18.2 times per second) is that the designers attempted to simplify their time-display chores by setting them up so that the high word of the 32-bit value at 0040:006Ch would increment exactly one time per hour, which permitted a simple comparison to 24 (decimal) to detect the midnight rollover.

Dividing 65,536 (the count at which the low word rolls over) by 3,600 (the number of seconds in one hour) results in exactly 18.20, which was the target frequency. Unfortunately, the timer chip's countdown frequency was slightly lower, and the actual number of counts detected in the BIOS is 11 more than the goal would indicate. Because, in practice, the frequency varies slightly between systems, the clocks must be reset from time to time. This process normally happens every time the system is booted; on some systems with separate real-time clocks, however, those clocks also gain or lose several seconds per week.

Int 09h

Keyboard Interrupt

The primary keystroke interrupt, called whenever a key is pressed or released

Calling registers: None

Return registers: Nothing

Comments: Whenever a key is pressed or released, the keyboard sends a signal (IRQ1) that triggers this interrupt. The handler for this interrupt reads the key information from the keyboard port (port 60h) and processes that information into character and scan code information, which it then puts into the 32-byte input character queue (normally stored at 0040:001Eh). The two codes are placed at the location pointed to by 0040:001Ch (keyboard buffer tail pointer), and the pointer is incremented by 2. If the buffer is already full, the pointer is recycled to the beginning of the buffer. Rather than access the keyboard directly, the BIOS console-input routines access this input queue, thereby allowing programmers some type-ahead room and considerable flexibility in keyboard handling.

Special keystrokes are interpreted by the handler as follows:

Keystroke	Handling
Ctrl	0040:0017h and 0040:0018h (keyboard control bytes) are updated and 0040:0096h (keyboard mode flags) are updated
Alt	Same as Ctrl
Shift	Same as Ctrl

Keystroke	Handling
Ctrl-Alt-Del	0040:0072h (reset flag) is set to 1234h, and system control is transferred to the POST (Power-On Self Test) routines; POST bypasses the normal start-up memory tests when this flag is set
Pause	Causes the handler to loop until it gets a valid character
Print Screen	Issues Int 05h to call the print-screen routine
Ctrl-Break	Issues Int 1Bh to call the Control-Break processor
System Request	PC XT BIOS systems (dates after 1/10/86), Personal Computer AT systems, PC XT 286 systems, PC Convertibles, and PS/2 systems issue an Int 15h, Function 85h (SysReq key pressed)

If you are using a PC XT with a BIOS release date after 1/10/86, or if you are using a Personal Computer AT, a PC XT 286, PC Convertible, or PS/2 system, this interrupt also issues an Int 15h, Function 91h (Interrupt Complete) with AL set to 02h after the keystroke has been processed. (See Int 15h, Function 91h for more information.)

TSRs (terminate-and-stay-resident utilities) that provide immediate response to keypresses frequently intercept and act on this interrupt. Because the keyboard routines have to do a great deal of processing, intercepting keyboard requests from the normal BIOS keyboard routines is preferable to intercepting operations at this interrupt. If immediate responsiveness is essential, Int 09h is the best one to use.

Int 0Bh

COM1 and COM3 Interrupt Service (PC, PC XT)
COM2 and COM4 Interrupt Service (Personal Computer AT)
Reserved (PS/2)

Called when the serial-port hardware issues an interrupt on IRQ3

Calling registers: None

Return registers: Nothing

Comments: Telecommunications programs generally intercept this interrupt vector. All other methods of accessing the serial port (BIOS or DOS functions) are not fast enough to handle speeds greater than 1200 bps. (See Chapter 7, "Serial Devices," and Chapter 11, "Interrupt Handlers," for a more detailed discussion.) By tying a custom interrupt handler here, the programmer can handle speeds up to the capacity of the machine (about 38.4K bits per second) if the interrupt handler is programmed carefully.

Int 0Ch handles the COM ports not handled by this interrupt.

Unfortunately, this interrupt is listed as reserved on the PS/2. Communications programs that rely on this interrupt for speed have to be rewritten on the PS/2.

Int 0Ch

COM2 and COM4 Interrupt Service (PC, PC XT)
COM1 and COM3 Interrupt Service (Personal Computer AT)
Reserved (PS/2)

Called when the serial port hardware issues an interrupt on IRQ4

Calling registers: None

Return registers: Nothing

Comments: Telecommunications programs generally intercept this interrupt vector. All other methods of accessing the serial port (BIOS or DOS functions) are not fast enough to handle speeds greater than 1200 bps. (See Chapters 7, "Serial Devices," and Chapter 11, "Interrupt Handlers," for a more detailed discussion.) By tying a custom interrupt handler here, the programmer can handle speeds up to the capacity of the machine (about 38.4K bits per second) if the interrupt handler is programmed carefully.

Int 0Bh handles the COM ports not handled by this handler.

Unfortunately, this interrupt is marked as reserved on the PS/2. Communications programs that rely on this interrupt for speed have to be rewritten on the PS/2.

Int 0Dh

Hard Disk Management (Disk Controller) (PC XT)
LPT2 Control (Personal Computer AT)
Reserved (PS/2)

Called by the designated hardware controllers using hardware-interrupt request line IRQ5

Calling registers: None

Return registers: Nothing

Comments: This interrupt handler was added only in later versions of the ROM BIOS. It represents a function that is available beginning with the PC XT.

On the Personal Computer AT, Int 0Dh is used for LPT2 handling. (See Int 0Fh for a discussion of printer services.)

On the PS/2, Int 0Dh is reserved; its functions are redistributed elsewhere. Because few (if any) programs make direct use of this interrupt, this change does not affect most programmers.

Int 0Eh

Floppy Disk Management

Called by the floppy disk controller (hardware) using hardware request line IRQ6

Calling registers: None

Return registers: Nothing

Comments: Int 0Eh is used by the floppy disk controller to detect disk transfer completions. Typically, because the operations available through this interrupt are attainable through other BIOS functions, this interrupt can be ignored. Most programmers do not use this interrupt.

Int 0Fh

Printer Management (LPT1)
Reserved (PS/2)

Internal printer-control interrupt using hardware request line IRQ7

Calling registers: None

Return registers: Nothing

Comments: On the PC, Int 0Fh was assigned to the printer controller to detect printer errors and print completion. Programmers typically do not use it because many printer controllers do not generate it reliably. Generally, you can ignore this interrupt.

The IRQ7 request (because it is the lowest priority level request) can also be generated as a default by the 8259 Priority Interrupt Controller, if the controller cannot determine which device requested service. It is never safe, therefore, to assume that an interrupt reaching this handler was originated by the printer; it could have originated anywhere.

On the PS/2, Int 0Fh is marked as reserved; its functions are allocated elsewhere.

Int 10h   Function 00h

Set Video Mode

Sets the display mode used by the video adapter

Calling registers: AH   00h
                        AL   Display mode (see Table BIOS.4)

Return registers: Nothing

Table BIOS.4 Video Display Modes

Video Mode	Mode Type	Display Adapter	Pixel Resolution	Box Size	Characters	Colors
00h	Text	CGA	320×200	8×8	40×25	16 (gray)
		EGA[2]	320×350	8×14	40×25	16 (gray)
		MCGA	320×400	8×16	40×25	16
		VGA[1]	360×400	9×16	40×25	16
01h	Text	CGA	320×200	8×8	40×25	16
		EGA[2]	320×350	8×14	40×25	16
		MCGA	320×400	8×16	40×25	16
		VGA[1]	360×400	9×16	40×25	16
02h	Text	CGA	640×200	8×8	80×25	16 (gray)
		EGA[2]	640×350	8×14	80×25	16 (gray)
		MCGA	640×400	8×16	80×25	16
		VGA[1]	720×400	9×16	80×25	16
03h	Text	CGA	640×200	8×8	80×25	16
		EGA[2]	640×350	8×14	80×25	16
		MCGA	640×400	8×16	80×25	16
		VGA[1]	720×400	9×16	80×25	16
04h	Graph	CGA/EGA/ MCGA/VGA	320×200	8×8	40×25	4
05h	Graph	CGA/EGA/ MCGA/VGA	320×200 320×200	8×8 8×8	40×25 40×25	4 (gray) 4
06h	Graph	CGA/EGA/ MCGA/VGA	640×200	8×8	80×25	2
07h	Text	MDA/EGA	720×350	9×14	80×25	Mono
		VGA[1]	720×400	9×16	80×25	Mono
08h	Graph	PCjr	160×200	8×8	20×25	16
09h	Graph	PCjr	320×200	8×8	40×25	16

Video Mode	Mode Type	Display Adapter	Pixel Resolution	Box Size	Characters	Colors
0Ah	Graph	PC*jr*	640×200	8×8	80×25	4
0Bh		——R E S E R V E D ——				
	0Ch	——R E S E R V E D ——				
0Dh	Graph	EGA/VGA	320×200	8×8	40×25	16
0Eh	Graph	EGA/VGA	640×200	8×8	80×25	16
0Fh	Graph	EGA/VGA	640×350	8×14	80×25	Mono
10h	Graph	EGA/VGA	640×350	8×14	80×25	16
11h	Graph	MCGA/VGA	640×480	8×16	80×30	2
12h	Graph	VGA	640×480	8×16	80×30	16
13h	Graph	MCGA/VGA	320×200	8×8	40×25	256

[1] *Enhanced VGA mode; otherwise, the VGA can emulate either the CGA or the EGA characteristics for this mode.*

[2] *EGA mode when connected to an enhanced color display; otherwise, emulates the CGA characteristics for this mode.*

Comments: This function sets the video mode, clears the screen, and selects the video adapter (if more than one is present). To prevent the screen-clear on EGA, MCGA, and VGA systems, set bit 7 of AL to 1.

Int 10h   Function 01h

Set Cursor Type

Used to set the height of the video cursor

Calling registers: AH   01h
CH   Starting (top) scan line for cursor in bits 0–4
CL   Ending (bottom) scan line for cursor in bits 0–4

Return registers: Nothing

Comments: This function sets the type of the text-mode cursor by specifying the cursor's starting and ending scan lines. The video-display system displays a blinking cursor by turning scan lines on and off. A character cell has 8 scan lines in the CGA and 14 in the EGA. To specify the cursor size, the scan lines are numbered from the top, beginning with 0.

495

Cursor size in text mode is controlled by specifying the start and end scan line numbers of the character box, starting with line 0. The starting scan line is specified in CH; the ending scan line, in CL. On a CGA-equipped machine, for example, to produce a two-line cursor that occupies the lower two lines of the character cell, you set CX to 0607h.

Many programmers do not realize that the cursor wraps around inside the character cell on many video adapters. If CH is less than CL, a normal one-piece cursor is displayed. By setting CH greater than CL, you can create a two-piece cursor. On some adapters, attempting this type of wrap-around disables the cursor display. To disable the cursor on those systems that permit wrap-around, set CH=20h (the value for CL does not need to be changed). On other adapters, you might need to position the cursor to a nondisplayable address such as line 25, column 0.

There is only one cursor type for all video pages. When a program uses different cursors on different video pages, it has to do the bookkeeping and explicitly change the cursor when it changes screen pages.

For monochrome video modes, the default starting cursor scan line is 0Bh and the ending scan line is 0Ch. For color video modes, the default starting scan line is 06h and the ending scan line is 07h. These values provide an underline cursor two scan lines high; for a full block cursor, change the starting line number in both cases to 0.

Int 10h   Function 02h

Set Cursor Position

Used to specify the cursor coordinates for the video display

Calling registers:	AH	02h
	BH	Page number (0 for graphics modes)
	DH	Row (zero based)
	DL	Column (zero based)

Return registers: Nothing

Comments: This function positions the cursor for the specified page at a specific location on the text screen. The system permits the tracking of separate cursor locations for each possible display page, to a maximum of eight pages in text mode.

Positions are defined relative to the upper left corner (position 0,0) when the screen is in text mode. The lower left corner is position 79,24 in 80×25 text mode and position 39,24 in 40×25 modes. The valid ranges for DL and DH, depending on the video mode, are shown in this table:

80-column Text Mode	*40-column Text Mode*
DL = 0 to 79	DL = 0 to 39
DH = 0 to 24	DH = 0 to 24

496

You can usually turn off the cursor by placing it off the screen (position 0,25 is often used). Be careful about using this trick if you expect to run your programs on an EGA-equipped system in 43-line mode or on a VGA's 50-line display; it might backfire.

You can position the cursor on any page to allow a program to do extensive work on a page that is not displayed on the screen. Then, when the completed screen is ready, you can present it almost instantaneously to the user. Table BIOS.5 shows the valid page numbers for different display types. You can display only those pages for which a specific video adapter has adequate memory. The MDA, for example, has only one display page; other display adapters (depending on their mode) can have as many as seven display pages.

Table BIOS.5   Valid Page Numbers

Page Numbers	Modes	Adapters
0–7	00–01h	CGA, EGA, MCGA, VGA
0–3	02–03h	CGA
0–7	02–03h	EGA, MCGA, VGA
0	07h	MDA
0–7	07h	EGA, VGA

If you are working in graphics modes, you should set the page number to 0. Use Function 05h to set the currently displayed page.

Int 10h   **Function 03h**

Read Cursor Position and Configuration

Returns the cursor coordinates and type

Calling registers:	AH	03h
	BH	Page number
Return registers:	BH	Video page number
	CH	Starting line for cursor
	CL	Ending line for cursor
	DH	Row
	DL	Column

Comments: This function gets the current cursor position and returns the same values that were used to position the cursor with Function 02h. In 80×25 mode, position 0,0 is the upper left corner and position 79,24 is the lower right corner; in 40×25 mode, position 39,24 is the lower right corner.

This function also returns the starting and ending rows for the cursor (see Function 01h for information about setting these values). You can use this function to determine the exact cursor type before you change it (so that you can restore it after your program has completed its work). If your program has to coexist in a mixed program environment, restoring the cursor type to what it was when your program began is good programming practice.

Not all programs use the BIOS to handle their cursor positioning. TSR pop-up programs are prone to bypass BIOS and go directly to the video controller chip; when this is done, the information you get back by using this BIOS call is meaningless. There is little you can do to make other programs behave, but at least you can keep your own program from adding to the chaos. *Always* do cursor positioning through the BIOS, at least for the last character written at each operation, so that other programs can restore your position and type properly.

Int 10h   Function 04h

Read Light Pen Position

Returns the coordinates of the light pen

Calling registers:	AH	04h
Return registers:	AH	0, light pen not down or not triggered
		1, light pen down or triggered
	BX	Pixel column (0–319 or 0–639, depending on mode)
	CH	Pixel row (0–199)
	CX	Pixel row (0–*nnn*, depending on mode)
	DH	Character row (0–24)
	DL	Character column (0–79 or 0–39, depending on mode)

Comments: This function reads the light pen's status and position. Although the mouse is more widely used than the light pen on the PC system, some applications use the light pen (and others can use it). Before using the light pen, you must check to see whether it has been triggered (AH=1). If the light pen has been triggered, its location is given in the other registers; if it has not been triggered, the information contained in the other return registers has no meaning and should be ignored.

The light pen returns a vertical position that is accurate to only two scan lines. Horizontal accuracy of the light pen is no better than 2 pixels (320 pixels per scan line) or 4 pixels (640 pixels per scan line). The light pen is not suitable, therefore, for high-resolution graphics control. On most monochrome monitors, use of the light pen is not effective because of the long image-retention time of the display phosphors.

The vertical resolution of some video modes is greater than 200 pixels. In such modes, the pixel row is returned in CX rather than in CH. Be sure to check the video mode to ascertain which register (CH or CX) will contain the value you should use.

PS/2 systems (MCGA or VGA) do not support the light pen (AH always returns 00h).

Int 10h   Function 05h

Select Active Display Page

Used to select the video display page to be viewed

Calling registers: AH   05h

AL   Page number selected (see Table BIOS.6)

Return registers: Nothing

Comments: This function, which selects the active (displayed) video page, works with the CGA, MCGA, EGA, and VGA. It cannot be used with monochrome adapters, which have only one display page of memory. Table BIOS.6 shows the valid page numbers.

Table BIOS.6 Valid Page Numbers

Page Numbers	Modes	Adapters
0–7	00h, 01h	CGA, EGA, MCGA, VGA
0–3	02h, 03h	CGA
0–7	02h, 03h	EGA, MCGA, VGA
0–7	07h, 0Dh	EGA, VGA
0–3	0Eh	EGA, VGA
0–1	0Fh, 10h	EGA, VGA

Note that this function operates differently with the PC*jr* than it does with all other models; the AL register contains a subfunction code rather than a page number, and BX contains CRT and CPU page numbers. The differences are major, and reliable information is absent from most PC reference manuals. See the PC*jr Technical Reference Manual* if you need to do animation on that machine, and don't worry about it otherwise.

This function is particularly useful for building spectacular text-screen displays. By building a screen in a nondisplayed page and then calling this function to display it, you can create an instantaneous screen change that gives your program an impressive, snappy look. Most of the important output functions can write to any page.

DOS
PROGRAMMING

Int 10h   Function 06h

Scroll Window Up

Used to blank the screen or scroll the text screen up by a specified number of lines in a defined area of the screen

Calling registers:

AH	06h
AL	Number of lines to scroll (if zero, entire window is blanked)
BH	Attribute used for blanked area
CH	Row, upper left corner
CL	Column, upper left corner
DH	Row, lower right corner
DL	Column, lower right corner

Return registers: Nothing

Comments: This function (which is the opposite of Int 10h; Function 07h) initializes a window to blank with a specified attribute or scrolls the window up a specified number of lines. The scroll function moves all lines in the window up one line, adds a blank line (with the designated attribute) at the bottom of the window, and eliminates the line that previously was at the top of the window. (If the new line is to be filled with text, your program must do the work.)

You can use this window-oriented function to define rectangular areas to clear (or scroll) on the screen and to set attribute values for the cleared line or lines within a window.

To clear the window, set AL either to 0 or to a value greater than the number of lines in the window. The BIOS listing in early versions of the *IBM Technical Reference Manual* shows this function implemented as a "clear a line, decrement the counter" function until the counter reaches zero. (IBM does not include BIOS listings in the current editions of the technical reference manuals.) Given this algorithm, a "clear window" performed by setting AL to 0 takes longer than if you set AL to 25 (or some other value greater than the height of the rectangle being cleared). Unless your application is extremely screen-intensive, the time differential introduced by setting AL to 0 is not noticeable.

You should understand that, on some BIOS implementations, only setting AL to 0 results in the screen's being cleared. If you set AL to a value other than 0 but greater than the number of screen lines, the results will be unpredictable. With this in mind, if you want to clear the entire screen, you might want to simply set the screen mode (Function 00h). If you are clearing a portion of the screen (just a specific window), make sure that you have AL set to 0, to ensure compatibility with all BIOS implementations your program might encounter.

This function affects only the active display page.

Int 10h   Function 07h

Scroll Window Down

Used to scroll the text screen down by a specified number of lines in a defined area of the screen

Calling registers: AH   07h

	AL	Number of lines to scroll
		(if zero, entire window is blanked)
	BH	Attribute used for blanked area
	CH	Row, upper left corner
	CL	Column, upper left corner
	DH	Row, lower right corner
	DL	Column, lower right corner

Return registers: Nothing

Comments: This function initializes a window to blank with a specified attribute or scrolls the window down a specified number of lines. Use this function (which is the opposite of Int 10h, Function 06h) to scroll down the screen. The scroll function moves all lines in the window down one line, adds a blank line (with the designated attribute) at the top of the window, and eliminates the line that previously was at the bottom. (If the new line is to be filled with text, your program must do the work.)

You can use this window-oriented function to define rectangular areas to clear (or scroll) on the screen and to set attribute values for the cleared line or lines within the window.

To clear the window, set AL either to 0 or to a value greater than the number of lines in the window. The BIOS listing in earlier versions of the *IBM Technical Reference Manual* shows this function implemented as a "clear a line, decrement the counter" function until the counter reaches zero. (IBM does not include BIOS listings in the current editions of the technical reference manuals.) Given this algorithm, a "clear window" performed by setting AL to 0 takes longer than if you set AL to 25 (or some other value greater than the height of the rectangle being cleared). Unless your application is extremely screen-intensive, the time differential introduced by setting AL to 0 is not noticeable. In any event, a simpler, faster way to clear the entire screen is to set the screen mode (Function 00h).

This function affects only the currently active display page.

Int 10h   Function 08h

Read Character and Attribute

Returns the character and attribute at the current cursor position

Calling registers: AH   08h

	BH	Display page

Return registers: AH   Attribute byte

AL   ASCII character

Comments: This function reads the character and attribute bytes (for a specified display page) at the cursor's current position. Because you can get this information directly from the screen, you do not have to store information about the screen in your program, nor do you need tricky techniques to pass the screen display from one program to the next. The screen is in the screen memory.

TSR spelling and thesaurus utilities use this function to read the screen so that they can determine which word to check. If you are writing this type of utility, however, be careful. Because some programs access screen memory directly, without updating the screen cursor, the cursor mentioned in the descriptions of Functions 01h through 03h may *not* indicate the word you want.

Int 10h   Function 09h

Write Character and Attribute

Stores a specific number of copies of a single character with a defined attribute, starting at the cursor position

Calling registers: AH   09h

AL   Character

BH   Display page

BL   Attribute byte of character in AL

CX   Number of characters to write

Return registers: Nothing

Comments: This function writes character and attribute bytes to the display, starting at the cursor's current position on a specified display page. Use it to write many characters quickly to the screen (the characters and attribute all must be the same).

In text mode, the function writes as many as 65,536 characters to the screen. (The largest normal text-mode display, 132 columns by 50 rows, can hold only 6,600 characters on one display page; the rest overflow on following display pages if they exist.) As the function writes characters, it wraps lines — continuing from the end of one line to the beginning of the next without stopping. In graphics mode, the function goes only to the end of the line it was on at the beginning. While each character appears on the screen, the cursor position does not change.

An interesting way to use this function is to clear an area on-screen for text entry just before you call the input character function. You can set this area with a different color attribute to make it stand out. Because this function can clear an area much larger than the screen, the area can be as large as necessary for data entry. Because the cursor does not move, you do not need to reposition it before you enter data.

In graphics modes, use the video attribute byte in BL to determine the color of the character that is written. If bit 7 is set, however, the value in BL is XORed with the background color when the character is displayed (which can be extremely useful). You can erase a character from the screen by writing it to the display in graphics mode and then rewriting it with bit 7 on.

In graphics modes, the characters for codes 80 – FFh come from a bit-map table whose address is stored in interrupt vector 1Fh. By resetting this pointer to a table of your own, you can create your own table of characters. (See Function 1Fh for a discussion of the bit-map character table.) The characters for codes 00 – 7Fh are generated from a ROM character table that cannot be reset (EGA and VGA users *can* reset normal display fonts; see Int 10h Function 11h).

Int 10h	Function 0Ah
	Write Character at Cursor

Stores a specific number of copies of a single character, starting at the cursor position

Calling registers:

AH	0Ah
AL	Character
BH	Display page number
BL	Color of character in AL (in graphics modes only)
CX	Number of characters and attribute words to write

Return registers: Nothing

Comments: This function (which is identical to Function 09h, except that you cannot set the attribute byte for the character in text mode) writes a number of characters at the cursor's current position on a specified display page. The attribute at the position at which each character is written remains unchanged.

Use this function when you want to write many characters quickly to the screen. In text mode, the function writes as many as 65,536 characters to the screen. As the function writes characters, it wraps lines (continuing from the end of one line to the beginning of the next without stopping). In graphics modes, the function goes only to the end of the line on which it started. The cursor position remains unchanged throughout the operation.

In graphics modes, BL determines the color of the character that is written. If bit 7 is set, however, the value in BL is XORed with the background color when the character is displayed. This feature can be extremely useful for erasing a character from the screen—you simply write a character to the display in graphics mode and then rewrite it with bit 7 on.

In graphics modes, the characters for codes 80–FFh come from a bit-map table whose address is stored in interrupt vector 1Fh. By resetting this pointer to a table of your own, you can create your own table of characters. (See Function 1Fh for a discussion of the bit-map character table.) The characters for codes 00 – 7Fh are generated from a ROM character table that cannot be reset (EGA/VGA users *can* reset normal display fonts; see Int 10h Function 11h).

Int 10h   Function 0Bh

Set Color Palette

Selects colors for the graphics display

Calling registers: AH   0Bh
                          BH   Color palette ID being set
                                          0, BL has background and border color
                                          1, BL has palette color
                          BL   Color value to be used for that color ID

Return registers: Nothing

Comments: This function, when BH=1, selects or sets the contents of the color palette for medium-resolution (4-color) graphics displays, such as mode 4. The function has no direct effect on memory. Rather, by interpreting the codes and changing the colors, this function affects the way the 6845 CRT controller interprets the video memory. By using this function to rapidly change the palette, you can produce a flashing display. Function 10h provides additional palette control for the PC*jr*, EGA, VGA, and MCGA.

In text mode (BH=0), this function sets the screen's border color.

Table BIOS.7 lists the valid color palettes the function can set.

Table BIOS.7   Color Palettes

Palette	Pixel	Color
0	0	Same as background
	1	Green
	2	Red
	3	Brown
1	0	Same as background
	1	Cyan
	2	Magenta
	3	White

504

Int 10h   **Function 0Ch**

Write Graphics Pixel

Writes a single pixel to the screen at the current cursor position

Calling registers: AH   0Ch

                         AL   Color value

                         BH   Page number

                         CX   Pixel column number

                         DX   Pixel row number

Return registers: Nothing

Comments: This function, which writes a single pixel to the screen at a specified graphics coordinate, is the most basic graphics-plotting service. Complex graphics-handling functions are built up by collections of operations that set the value of screen pixels.

In medium-resolution modes, the exact effect of the function depends on the palette in use. High-resolution CGA (mode 6) can show only black and white colors for pixels; mode 4 or 5 allows the pixels to be set from a 4-color palette. With this function, if bit 7 of AL is set to 1, the new color is XORed with the current pixel; you can erase that pixel by writing it a second time.

The limits on the screen position this function can address are 0–199 or 0–349 in the vertical and 0–319 or 0–639 in the horizontal, depending on the graphics mode. Refer to Table BIOS.4 for details on screen limits by mode. Table BIOS.8 gives the valid page numbers (BH register) used by this function.

Table BIOS.8   Valid Page Numbers

Page Numbers	Modes	Adapters
0–7	0Dh	EGA, VGA
0–3	0Eh	EGA, VGA
0–1	0Fh, 10h	EGA, VGA

DOS
PROGRAMMING

Int 10h   Function 0Dh

Read Graphics Pixel

Returns the color of the pixel at a specific screen coordinate

Calling registers: AH   0Dh
                        BH   Page number
                        CX   Pixel column number
                        DX   Pixel row number

Return registers: AL   Color value

Comments: This function, which gets the value of the pixel at the specified graphics coordinates, is often used in video games and advanced graphics applications. In video games, it is useful for collision detection. When advanced graphics programs move a graphics object on the screen, they can use this function to detect boundaries.

The limits for addressing are 0–199 or 0–349 in the vertical and 0–319 or 0–639 in the horizontal, depending on the video mode. Refer to table BIOS.4 for details about the addressing limits of the various video modes. Refer to Table BIOS.8 for the valid page numbers that can be set in BH.

Int 10h   Function 0Eh

Write Text in Teletype Mode

Outputs characters with limited control processing

Calling registers: AH   0Eh
                        AL   Character
                        BH   Display page (alpha modes)
                        BL   Foreground color (graphics modes)

Return registers: Nothing

Comments: This function writes text to the screen as though the screen were an old-fashioned Teletype machine. The function interprets the ASCII character codes for the bell (07h), backspace (08h), carriage return (0Dh), and line feed (0Ah) in order to ring the console bell, backspace the cursor, move the cursor to the beginning of the line, or move to the next line, respectively. All other control characters, including the tab and form-feed characters, are displayed (smiley faces, pointing arrows, and so on) rather than acted on. After the write, the cursor moves to the next character position.

Despite its somewhat archaic designation (which might make you think of the old teletype-writer machines), this function is useful. DOS uses it in the console driver to put operating-system text and messages on the screen.

For Function 0Eh to work on PC BIOS ROMs dated 4/24/81 and 10/19/81, the BH register *must* point to the currently displayed page. With later ROMs, this function works on either displayed or nondisplayed pages.

The significant difference between this and other display functions is that Function 0Eh automatically handles the normal control functions of the bell, backspace, line feed, and carriage return, in addition to line wrap and scrolling. Although it does not allow you to change the video attributes of what you write, this function is the best one for simple output.

Even if you are working on a nondisplayed page, the bell character sounds the system bell to call attention to any background operations. Unfortunately, this function does *not* expand tab characters to spaces.

Int 10h	Function 0Fh
	Get Current Display Mode

Returns the video display mode, screen width, and active page

Calling registers: AH   0Fh

Return registers: AH   Number of columns on the screen
                         AL   Display mode (refer to Table BIOS.4)
                         BH   Active display page

Comments: This function, which gets the video controller's display mode, including the number of character columns and the current display page, is most useful during program initialization. You use it to determine the current setting of the display system so that, when your program is finished, it can return the display system to its original display mode.

Knowing the current display mode is especially important if you are writing TSR (terminate-and-stay-resident) utilities that pop up on the screen during another application. Your utility may be working with a character screen, but the program that had control when your utility started might have been using a mode that is not what you need to use. Early TSRs failed to handle the screen display properly—in many cases, the resulting display looked as though a bomb had exploded inside the computer.

Although you can use Function 0Fh to determine the width of the screen, it is recommended that you set the mode you want rather than try to work out what is already there.

507

Int 10h   Function 10h

Set Palette Registers

Controls operations on the color-palette registers in PC*jr*, EGA, VGA, and MCGA video controllers

Calling registers:	AH	10h
	AL	00h, set palette register
	BX	0712h is only allowable value (MCGA only)
	BH	Color value
	BL	Palette register to set
	AL	01h, set border color register (not on MCGA)
	BH	Color value
	AL	02h, set all registers and border (not on MCGA)
	ES:DX	Pointer to 17-byte color list
	AL	03h, toggle blink/intensity
	BL	Blink/intensity bit
		00h Enable intensity
		01h Enable blinking
	AL	07h, read palette register (VGA only)
	BL	Palette register to read (0–15)
	AL	08h, read overscan (border) register (VGA only)
	AL	09h, read palette registers and border (VGA only)
	ES:DX	Pointer to 17-byte table for values
	AL	10h, set individual color register (MCGA and VGA only)
	BX	Color register to set
	CH	Green value to set
	CL	Blue value to set
	DH	Red value to set
	AL	12h, set block of color registers (MCGA and VGA only)
	BX	First color register to set
	CX	Number of color registers to set
	ES:DX	Pointer to color values
	AL	13h, select color page (VGA only)
	BL	00h, select paging mode
	BH	Paging mode
		00h 4 register blocks of 64 registers
		01h 16 register blocks of 16 registers
	AL	13h, select color page (VGA only)
	BL	01h, select page
	BH	Page number
		00–03h for 64 register blocks
		00–0Fh for 16 register blocks

AL	15h, read color register (MCGA and VGA only)	
BX	Color register to read	
AL	17h, read block of color registers (MCGA and VGA only)	
BX	First color register to read	
CX	Number of color registers to read	
ES:DX	Pointer to buffer to hold color register values	
AL	18h, update video DAC mask register (MCGA and VGA only)	
BL	DAC mask register value	
AL	19h, read video DAC mask register (MCGA and VGA only)	
AL	1Ah, read color page state (VGA only)	
AL	1Bh, sum color values to gray shades (MCGA and VGA only)	
BX	First color register to sum	
CX	Number of color registers to sum	

Return registers: Subfunctions 07h–08h

BH	Value read
	Subfunction 09h
ES:DX	Pointer to 17-byte table
	Subfunction 15h
CH	Green value read
CL	Blue value read
DH	Red value read
	Subfunction 17h
ES:DX	Pointer to color table
	Subfunction 19h
BL	Value read
	Subfunction 1Ah
BL	Current paging mode
CX	Current page

Comments: On the PC*jr*, MCGA, EGA, and VGA display systems, this function, with its 17 subfunctions, controls the correspondence of colors to pixel values. Although listed as reserved in the IBM Personal Computer AT BIOS, this function is an extension to the BIOS, applicable to EGA and VGA display systems.

A detailed explanation of this function is beyond the scope of this book. If you are interested in programming display systems directly, refer to the bibliography for more guidance.

Some subfunctions (as designated by the contents of AL when calling this function) are not available on the PS/2 Model 30 system. These subfunctions are 01h, 02h, 07h, 08h, 09h, 13h, and 1Ah.

Int 10h   Function 11h

Character Generator

Supports the graphics character-generator functions, allowing a program to set up its own character-generator tables

Calling registers:	AL	00h, user alpha load (EGA, VGA, and MCGA)
	BH	Number of bytes per character
	BL	Block to load
	CX	Count to store
	DX	Character offset into table
	ES:BP	Pointer to user table
	AL	01h, ROM monochrome set (EGA and VGA)
	BL	Block to load
	AL	02h, ROM 8 × 8 double dot (EGA, VGA, and MCGA)
	BL	Block to load
	AL	03h, set block specifier (PC*jr*, EGA, VGA, and MCGA)
	BL	Character-generator block selection
	AL	04h, load 8 × 16 ROM (VGA and MCGA)
	AL	10h, user alpha load (EGA, VGA, and MCGA)
	BH	Number of bytes per character
	BL	Block to load
	CX	Count to store
	DX	Character offset into table
	ES:BP	Pointer to user table
	AL	11h, ROM monochrome set (EGA and VGA)
	BL	Block to load
	AL	12h, ROM 8 × 8 double dot (EGA, VGA, and MCGA)
	BL	Block to load
	AL	14h, load 8×16 ROM (VGA and MCGA)
	AL	20h, set user graphics character pointer at 1Fh (EGA, VGA, and MCGA)
	ES:BP	Pointer to user table
	AL	21h, set user graphics character pointer at 43h (EGA, VGA, and MCGA)
	BL	Row specifier

CX	Bytes per character
ES:BP	Pointer to user table
AL	22h, ROM 8 × 14 set (EGA, VGA, and MCGA)
BL	Row specifier
AL	23h, ROM 8 × 8 double dot (EGA, VGA, and MCGA)
BL	Row specifier
AL	24h, ROM 8 × 16 (VGA)
BL	Row specifier
BH	Rows per screen
AL	30h, font information (EGA, VGA, and MCGA)
BH	Font pointer

Return registers: Varies by subfunction

Comments: Although listed as reserved in the IBM Personal Computer AT BIOS, this function is an extension to the BIOS, applicable to EGA and VGA display systems.

A detailed explanation of this function is beyond the scope of this book. If you are interested in programming display systems directly, refer to the bibliography for more guidance.

Some subfunctions (as designated by the contents of AL when calling this function) are not available on the PS/2 Model 30 system. These subfunctions are 01h, 10h, 11h, 12h, and 22h.

Int 10h   Function 12h

Alternate Select

Provides additional control of EGA (and PS/2 emulations of EGA).

Calling registers:	AH	12h
	AL	00h, enable subfunctions 31h–34h and 36h
		01h, disable subfunctions 31h–34h and 36h
	BL	10h, return EGA information
	BL	20h, select alternate print-screen routine
	BL	30h, select scan lines for A/N modes
	AL	Number of scan lines
		00h 200 scan lines
		01h 350 scan lines
		02h 400 scan lines
	BL	31h, control palette loading during set mode command operation
	BL	32h, video on/off
	BL	33h, summing to gray shades on/off

511

BL	34h, cursor emulation
BL	35h, video display switching
AL	00h, initial adapter video off
	01h, initial planar video on
	02h, switch active video off
	03h, switch inactive video on
ES:DX	Pointer to 128-byte save area (for AL = 00h, 02h, or 03h)
BL	36h, video refresh control

Return registers: Subfunction 10h

BH	Default BIOS video mode
00h	Color
01h	Monochrome
BL	Amount of EGA video RAM
00h	64K
01h	128K
02h	192K
03h	256K
CH	Feature bits
CL	Configuration switch setting

Subfunctions 30h–36h

AL	12h

Comments: Although this function is listed as reserved in the IBM Personal Computer AT BIOS, it is an extension to the BIOS, applicable to EGA/VGA display systems.

A detailed explanation of this function is beyond the scope of this book. If you are interested in programming display systems directly, refer to the bibliography for more guidance.

Int 10h   Function 13h

Write String

Writes an ASCII string to the display

Calling registers:

AH	13h
AL	Write mode (see Table BIOS.9)
BH	Video page
BL	Attribute (write modes 0 and 1)
CX	Length of string
DH	Row at which to write string
DL	Column at which to write string
ES:BP	Pointer to string

Return registers: Nothing

Table BIOS.9   Write String Modes

Mode	Comments
0	Attribute in BL. String is characters only. Cursor not updated.
1	Attribute in BL. String is characters only. Cursor updated.
2	String alternates characters and attributes. Cursor not updated.
3	String alternates characters and attributes. Cursor updated.

Comments: This function, *available on only PC XTs with BIOS dates of 1/10/86 or later, on the Personal Computer AT, and on machines in the PS/2 family,* writes a string of characters to the currently active display.

Use this function to designate a string (with embedded or global attributes for the characters) and then write it to the screen. Because it relies on other BIOS functions to write the string, this function is not particularly fast.

Because this function uses the Teletype interrupt (Int 10h, Function 0Eh) for output, it responds to the backspace (ASCII 08h), bell (ASCII 07h), line feed (ASCII 0Ah), and carriage return (ASCII 0Dh) characters by moving the cursor back one space, ringing the console bell, moving down one line, or moving the cursor to the beginning of the current line, respectively. It also performs line wrap and scrolling.

Int 10h   Function 1Ah

Read/Write Display Codes

Reads or writes display codes

Calling registers: AH   1Ah
                        AL   00h, read display codes
                        BH   Alternate display code
                        AL   01h, write display codes
                        BL   Active display code

Return registers: If reading display codes:
                        BH   Alternate display code
                        BL   Active display code

                        If writing display codes:
                        AL   1Ah, codes were changed

513

Comments: This function, supported on only the PS/2 models, permits the display codes to be read or written. The codes used are shown in this table:

Value	Meaning
00h	No display
01h	Mono with mono monitor
02h	CGA with color monitor
03h	Reserved
04h	EGA with color monitor
05h	EGA with mono monitor
06h	Professional Graphics System with color monitor
07h	VGA with analog mono monitor (not on Model 30)
08h	VGA with analog color monitor (not on Model 30)
09h	Reserved
0Ah	Reserved
0Bh	MCGA with analog mono monitor (Model 30)
0Ch	MCGA with analog color monitor (Model 30)
0Dh–FEh	Reserved for expansion
FFh	Unknown type of monitor

These codes are most useful in determining the type of monitor connected to a system.

Int 10h   Function 1Bh

Get Display State

Provides 51 bytes of detailed information concerning the video system

Calling registers:	AH	1Bh
	ES:DI	Point to 64-byte buffer to receive video state information
Return registers:	AL	1Bh if buffer content valid

Comments: This function works on only the PS/2 series of computers. Even though only 51 bytes of defined data are returned, you need a 64-byte buffer because 13 bytes of reserved space are in the buffer. Perhaps this amount is for future system expansion use.

514

A detailed explanation of this function is beyond the scope of this book. If you are interested in programming display systems directly, refer to the bibliography for more guidance.

Int 10h   Function 1Ch

Save/Restore Display State

Saves or restores the status of the VGA display system

Calling registers:	AH	1Ch
	AL	00h, return buffer size needed
		01h, save video state
		02h, restore video state
	CX	Bit map of requested states:

```
FEDCBA98 76543210
........ .......1 Video hardware
........ ......1. Video BIOS
........ .....1.. Video DAC and color registers
00000000 00000... Not used
```

	ES:BX	If AL=01 or 02, point to buffer for video state information
Return registers:	AL	1Ch (if results are valid)
	BL	Number of 64-byte blocks required for save buffer

Comments: This function works on only the PS/2 series, models 50, 60, and 80. It is used to save or restore VGA-specific status information such as the state of the video digital-to-analog converters, the color registers, and the driver data area. The state of the VGA is altered while saving; you should follow saves with a restore operation.

This function returns 1Ch in AL if the results are valid; any other value indicates that the function is not supported (a VGA is not installed or a non-standard VGA is installed, for example).

A more detailed explanation of this function is beyond the scope of this book. If you are interested in programming display systems directly, refer to the bibliography for more guidance.

Int 10h   Function 4Fh   Subfunction 00h

Return SuperVGA Information

VESA function that returns data about supported SuperVGA capabilities

Calling registers:	AH	4Fh
	AL	00h
	ES:DI	Address of a 256-byte buffer

Return registers: AX   Status (see Table BIOS.10)

ES:DI   Address of a 256-byte buffer, structured as follows:

        Bytes 0–3, signature ('VESA')

        Byte 4, minor version number

        Byte 5, major version number

        Bytes 6–9, pointer to ASCIIZ

        OEM string

        Bytes 10–13, capabilities bit map currently undefined and unused—should be zero

        Bytes 14–17, pointer to list of supported modes, represented by a list of words terminated by FFFFh. (See Table BIOS.11 for standard VESA display modes.)

Comments: Before calling the other VESA functions (all accessed through Int 10h, Function 4Fh), this function should be called to determine whether VESA is supported.

Table BIOS.10 VESA Status Return Values

Register	Meaning
AL = 4Fh	Function is supported
AH = 0	Function returned successfully
AH = 1	Function failed
AH = 2–FF	Reserved (should be treated as a failure)

Table BIOS.11 Standard VESA display modes

Mode	Resolution	Colors
100h	640×400	256
101h	640×480	256
102h	800×600	16
103h	800×600	256
104h	1024×768	16
105h	1024×768	256

Mode	Resolution	Colors
106h	1280×1024	16
107h	1280×1024	256
6Ah	800×600	16

Note: 6Ah, if supported, can be set by using the standard VGA BIOS mode Select call (Function 00).

Int 10h　　　　**Function 4Fh**　　　　　　　　　　　**Subfunction 01h**

Return SuperVGA Mode Information

VESA function that returns information about the specified mode

Calling registers:　　AX　　　　4F01h
　　　　　　　　　　　　CX　　　　Desired mode
　　　　　　　　　　　　ES:DI　　Address of a 256-byte buffer

Return registers:　　AX　　　　Status (see Table BIOS.10)
　　　　　　　　　　　　ES:DI　　Address of a 256-byte buffer, structured as follows:

Bytes 0–1, mode attributes that are bit-mapped as follows:

Bit 0　　Mode is supported by current display
Bit 1　　Optional info block is valid
Bit 2　　BIOS text functions are supported
Bit 3　　Color mode
Bit 4　　Graphics mode

Byte 2, window A attributes that are bit-mapped as follows:

Bit 0　　Window is supported
Bit 1　　Window is readable
Bit 2　　Window is writable

Byte 3, window B attributes that are bit-mapped as above

Bytes 4–5, window granularity (the smallest increment that can be used in selecting the start address of a display window page)

Bytes 6–7, window size (the size of a page of display
    memory in kilobytes)
Bytes 8–9, window A segment
Bytes 10–11, window B segment
Bytes 12–15, pointer to display memory windowing
    function
Bytes 16–17, bytes per scan line

The following are optional fields:

Bytes 18–19, horizontal resolution in pixels (graphics)
    or characters (text)
Bytes 20–21, vertical resolution in pixels (graphics)
    or characters (text)
Byte 22, character cell width in pixels
Byte 23, character cell height in pixels
Byte 24, number of memory planes
Byte 25, bits per pixel
Byte 26, number of banks
Byte 27, memory model
    0 = text mode
    1 = CGA graphics
    2 = Hercules graphics
    3 = 4-plane graphics
    4 = packed pixel graphics
    5 = nonchain 4, 256-color graphics
    6–0F, reserved by VESA
    10–FF, manufacturer defined
Byte 28, bank size

Comments: Because the options fields are predefined, they are not required for standard
VESA video modes.

Int 10h	Function 4Fh	Subfunction 02h
	Set SuperVGA Display Mode	

VESA function that sets the display mode

Calling registers: AX   4F02h
                          BX   Display mode number

Return registers: AX   Status (See Table BIOS.10)

Comments: The mode value should follow VESA numbering conventions:

Bits 0 – 8   Mode number

Bits 9 – 14   Reserved for future expansion (should be 0)

Bit 15   0, clear memory
               1, preserve memory

Int 10h	Function 4Fh	Subfunction 03h
	Return SuperVGA Display Mode	

VESA function that gets the current display mode

Calling registers: AX   4F03h

Return registers: AX   Status (See Table BIOS.10)
                      BX   Current display mode

Comments: The mode value should follow VESA numbering conventions:

Bits 0 – 8   Mode number

Bits 9 – 14   Reserved for future expansion (should be 0)

Bit 15   0, clear memory
               1, preserve memory

Int 10h	Function 4Fh	Subfunction 04h
	Save/Restore SuperVGA Video State	

VESA function that saves and restores the video state information

Calling registers: AX   4F04h
                      DL   Subfunction
                                  0, return state buffer size
                                  1, save state
                                  2, restore state
                      CX   States to be saved or restored
                                  Bit 0, video hardware
                                  Bit 1, video BIOS data
                                  Bit 2, video DAC state
                                  Bit 3, SuperVGA state
                     ES:BX   Pointer to save buffer (Subfunctions 1 and 2)

Return registers: AX   Status (see Table BIOS.10)

                            BX   Number of 64-byte blocks needed to save
                                            specified state or states (Subfunction 0 only)

Comments: Subfunction 0 should be called by the program to determine the size of the buffer required, and then Subfunctions 1 and 2 can be called safely.

Int 10h   **Function 4Fh**   **Subfunction 05h**

Display Memory Window Control

VESA function that selects a page of display memory or determines which page is displayed

Calling registers: AX   4F05h

                           BH   Subfunction
                                         0, select display memory page
                                       1, return current display memory page

                           BL   Window number
                                         0, A
                                       1, B

                           DX   Page starting address in granularity units
                                         (Subfunction 0 only)

Return registers: AX   Status (see Table BIOS.10)

                           DX   Current page starting address in granularity units
                                         (Subfunction 1 only)

Comments: This function can be called directly by a far call. The address is obtained by executing Function 1, and is a double-word pointer at offset 12 (0Ch) in the buffer. If called directly, AX does not need to be set; no status is returned, and AX and DX are destroyed.

Int 11h

Get Equipment Status

Returns a rudimentary list of equipment attached to the computer

Calling registers: None

Return registers: AX   Equipment status word (see Table BIOS.12)

Table BIOS.12 Equipment Status Word

Bits	Meaning
0	Disk drive installed = 1
1	Math coprocessor installed = 1
2–3	System board RAM
	00 = 16K
	01 = 32K
	10 = 48K
	11 = 64K
2	Pointing device installed = 1 (PS/2 line only)
3	Not used (PS/2 line only)
4–5	Initial video mode
	01 = 40×25 color
	10 = 80×25 color
	11 = 80×25 mono
6–7	Number of disk drives (if bit 0 = 1)
	00 = 1 drive attached
	01 = 2 drives attached
	10 = 3 drives attached
	11 = 4 drives attached
8	Not used
9–11	Number of serial cards attached
12	Game adapter installed = 1
12	Not used (PS/2 line only)
13	Not used
13	Internal modem installed = 1 (PS/2 line only)
14–15	Number of printers attached

521

Comments: During the booting process, the hardware status byte is set to indicate which equipment is attached to the computer. Bits 6 and 7, for example, represent the number of floppy disk drives attached to the system. This status byte does not change after you boot the system.

This function is particularly useful to programmers who must adapt their programs to existing equipment. By checking for serial ports, disk drives, printers, and other equipment, your program can simplify the user's interaction with the program. Programs that have to ask for the characteristics of the system rely on the user to understand the PC well enough to answer the questions. The fewer questions your program has to ask, the easier it is to use.

As you can see from Table BIOS.12, the meaning of the different bits varies according to computer type. To determine which type of machine you are using, check the computer's signature byte at address FFFF:FFFE.

Int 12h

Get Memory Size

Returns the number of contiguous 1K memory blocks available

Calling registers: None

Return registers: AX   Number of 1K memory blocks

Comments: This interrupt returns the number of *contiguous* 1K memory blocks found during start-up memory checks of the system. Contrary to what has been written about this interrupt, it has nothing to do with the switches on the motherboard of a standard PC or compatible.

Because the memory is determined from the Power-On Self Test (POST), an incorrect number may be returned if defective memory causes the memory test to fail. (If this happens, the interrupt returns the number of blocks found before the error.) The POST assumes that all installed memory is functional and that memory in the range of 0 to 640K is contiguous.

The method used to determine available memory depends on the system, but generally consists of an attempt to write to and then read from a memory block. As soon as the write-then-read cycle fails, the end of memory is assumed to have been reached.

When there is more than 640K of memory, Int 15h, Function 88h must be called to determine extended memory size.

On PS/2 systems, this interrupt returns a maximum amount of memory of as much as 640K, minus the amount of memory set aside for the extended BIOS data area (EBDA). The EBDA can be as little as 1K. (See Int 15h, Function C1h for more information.)

Int 13h   Function 00h

Reset Disk System

Resets the controller for the disk drive

Calling registers: AH   00h

DL   Drive number (zero based)

Bit 7 = 0 for a diskette, 1 for a hard disk

Return registers: Carry flag clear if successful

Carry flag set if error

AH   Return code (see Table BIOS.13)

Comments: This function resets the disk controller in preparation for disk I/O. (A reset of the disk system is essential for handling critical disk-access errors.) This function recalibrates the disk by forcing the drive to pull the heads to track 0 and to start the next I/O operation from track 0.

Invoking this operation does not cause the disk system to react immediately. Rather, a reset flag is set in the disk controller to recalibrate the drives the next time they are used. The recalibration causes the grinding sound you sometimes hear after a disk error.

When the drive number in DL has the high bit set, the floppy disk system is reset, and then the hard disk (fixed disk) is reset. The error return refers to the hard disk reset. The floppy disk status can be found in the BIOS data area, at 0040:0041h.

This function is best used when an error has been returned in an attempt to use the floppy disk system. When a problem occurs, the reset function should be called and the function tried again. Depending on the program, you might want to do several retries. If you get consistent failure, you should notify the user and end the retry cycle.

Int 13h   Function 01h

Get Disk System Status

Returns the disk status byte

Calling registers: AH   01h

DL   Drive code (PS/2 and extended BIOS only)

Return registers: AH   Status byte (see Table BIOS.13)

Table BIOS.13 Disk Controller Status Bits

Bit 76543210	Meaning
. 1	Illegal command to driver
. . . . . .1.	Address mark not located (bad sector)
. 11	Write-protected disk
. . . . .1..	Requested sector not found
. . . . 11.	Diskette change line active
. . . .1...	DMA overrun
. . . .1..1	DMA attempt across 64K boundary
. . . 11..	Invalid media
. . .1....	CRC error on disk read
. .1.....	Controller error
.1......	Seek failure
1.......	Disk time-out (failure to respond, drive not ready)

Comments: The status of the controller is set after every disk operation. With this function, your program can get the status of the disk as of the most recent disk operation. You can use this function to detect, for example, a write-protected disk in the drive by examining bit 1.

Int 13h	Function 02h
	Read Disk Sectors

Retrieves a specific number of disk sectors

Calling registers:	AH	02h
	AL	Number of sectors to transfer
	ES:BX	Pointer to user's disk buffer
	CH	Track number (see comments)
	CL	Sector number
	DH	Head number
	DL	Drive number (bit 7 set if hard disk)
Return registers:	Carry flag clear if successful	
	AH	0
	AL	Number of sectors transferred

Carry flag set if error
AH   Status byte (refer to Table BIOS.13)

Comments: This function transfers one or more sectors from the disk into memory. Reading the disk is such a standard operation that the lack of any error checking beyond the disk drive number is surprising. All input parameters should be checked carefully before you issue a call for service because passing an invalid value can lead to unpredictable results.

When this function is used with a hard disk, the track number is ten bits rather than eight. The upper two bits are passed to the function in the high two bits of the CL register.

 Note: When you use this function, a peculiarity of the system is that the error code AH=9 (DMA Boundary Error) can occur when the DMA operation crosses a memory offset address that ends in three zeros. This type of memory boundary must correspond to a sector boundary in the disk read.

This DMA boundary problem is especially troublesome with the FORMAT.COM program supplied with some versions of DOS; it generates an error message that track 0 is bad and the disk is unusable. If the message appears, it can be corrected by adding or removing FILES= or BUFFERS= values from the CONFIG.SYS file and rebooting to change the position in memory of the disk buffer used by FORMAT.COM.

Int 13h   Function 03h

Write Disk Sectors

Writes a specified area of memory to a designated number of disk sectors

Calling registers:	AH	03h
	AL	Number of sectors to transfer
	ES:BX	Pointer to user's disk buffer
	CH	Track number (see comments)
	CL	Sector number
	DH	Head number
	DL	Drive number (bit 7 set if hard disk)
Return registers:	Carry flag clear if successful	
	AH	0
	AL	Number of sectors transferred
	Carry flag set if error	
	AH	Status byte (refer to Table BIOS.13)

Comments: This function writes one or more sectors from memory to the disk. Except for the disk drive number, none of the values passed to this function is checked for validity. Checking for validity is the programmer's responsibility. Writing to the disk is such a standard operation that this lack of error checking is surprising. You should check all input parameters carefully before you issue a call for service because passing an invalid value may lead to unpredictable results.

When this function is used with a hard disk, the track number is ten bits rather than eight. The upper two bits are passed to the function in the high two bits of the CL register.

IBM documentation indicates that the number of sectors stored in AL is not required when you use this function on the PC XT 286. Leaving AL set does not matter in this case because the passed values are not checked for validity.

> **Note:** When you use this function, a peculiarity of the system is that the error code AH=9 (DMA Boundary Error) can occur when the DMA operation crosses a memory offset address that ends in three zeros. This type of memory boundary must correspond to a sector boundary in the disk write.

Int 13h   Function 04h

Verify Disk Sectors

Checks accuracy of the CRC values of a specified number of disk sectors

Calling registers:	AH	04h
	AL	Number of sectors to verify
	CH	Track number (see comments)
	CL	Sector number
	DH	Head number
	DL	Drive number (bit 7 set if hard disk)
Return registers:	Carry flag clear if successful	
	AH	0
	Carry flag set if error	
	AH	Status byte (refer to Table BIOS.13)

Comments: Use this function to verify the address fields of the specified disk sectors. No data is transferred to or from the disk during this operation. When this function is used with a hard disk, the track number is ten bits rather than eight. The upper two bits are passed to the function in the high two bits of the CL register.

Disk verification, which takes place on the disk, does not (as some people believe) involve verification of the data on the disk against the data in memory. This function does not read or write a disk; rather, it causes the system to read the data in the designated sector or sectors and to check its computed cyclic redundancy check (CRC) against data stored on the disk.

When a sector is written to disk, the CRC is computed and stored on the disk as part of the sector header information. Because the verify operation checks this value, it is highly probable, but never *certain*, that the data in the disk sector is good.

As with most of the other disk functions, the disk drive number is the only input data checked for errors. Errors in input cause unpredictable results.

This function can be used to check the disk drive for the presence of a readable disk. If the drive does not contain a properly formatted disk, the function returns an error.

Int 13h	Function 05h
	Format Disk Track

Formats a single disk track

Calling registers:

AH	05h
ES:BX	Pointer to track address field list
CH	Track number
DH	Head number
DL	Drive number

Return registers:

AH	Return code (refer to Table BIOS.13)

Comments: This function formats a disk track by initializing the disk address fields and data sectors. (See Chapter 8, "Disks," for more information.) Be sure to use this function very carefully; it can cause the loss of some of or all the disk storage on your machine. Test it on a stripped-down system (floppy disk only) until you are absolutely certain of its correctness.

Formatting a disk track is only one part of formatting a disk. To format a disk, you must format each track correctly; if the disk is to be used with DOS, however, you must also write the basic DOS disk structure to the disk (including the boot sector, initial FAT tables, and the disk's root directory).

The disk formatting operation is controlled by the track address field list (pointed to by ES:BX). The table is laid out as a series of 4-byte entries, one for each sector on the track. Each 4-byte entry is laid out like this:

Byte Offset	Meaning
00h	Track number
01h	Head number
02h	Sector number
03h	Size code

If this function is used with a hard disk, the track number is ten bits rather than eight. The upper two bits are passed to the function in the high two bits of the sector number.

Table BIOS.14 shows allowable size codes; the entries are laid out in the order in which the sectors appear on disk. This order does not need to be sequential; the sectors can be interleaved to improve disk access performance (see Chapter 8, "Disks").

Table BIOS.14 Track Address Field Size Code

Size Code	Bytes per Sector
0	128
1	256
2	512
3	1,024

Int 13h   Function 06h

Format Cylinder and Set Bad Sector Flags

Formats the specified cylinder only and sets flags for any bad sectors found in the process

Calling registers:
	AH	08h
	AL	Interleave factor
	CH	Cylinder to format
	CL	Sector number
	DH	Head number
	DL	Drive number (zero based)
		Bit 7 = 0 for a floppy disk, 1 for a hard disk

Return registers: Carry flag clear if successful
Carry flag set if error
	AH	Error status (refer to Table BIOS.13)

Comments: This function, *available on only PC XTs with BIOS dates of 1/10/86 or later, on the Personal Computer AT, and on machines in the PS/2 family,* reformats only the specified cylinder of a drive. All data in the reformatted area will be lost. Extreme care should be taken in the use of this function.

Int 13h   Function 07h

Format Drive from Specified Cylinder

Formats only the specified cylinder and sets flags for any bad sectors found in the process

Calling registers: AH   08h
AL   Interleave factor
CH   Cylinder to format
CL   Sector number
DH   Head number
DL   Drive number (zero based)
Bit 7 = 0 for a floppy disk, 1 for a hard disk

Return registers: Carry flag clear if successful
Carry flag set if error
AH   Error status (refer to Table BIOS.13)

Comments: This function, *available on only PC XTs with BIOS dates of 1/10/86 or later, on the Personal Computer AT, and on machines in the PS/2 family,* reformats the specified cylinder and all higher-numbered cylinders of a drive. All data in the reformatted area will be lost. Extreme care should be taken in the use of this function.

Int 13h   Function 08h

Return Disk Drive Parameters

Returns information about a specified disk drive

Calling registers: AH   08h
DL   Drive number (zero based)
Bit 7 = 0 for a floppy disk, 1 for a hard disk

Return registers: Carry flag clear if successful
CH   Number of tracks per side
CL   Number of sectors per track
DH   Number of sides
DL   Number of consecutive drives attached
ES:DI   Pointer to 11-byte diskette parameter table
BL   Valid drive-type value from CMOS
01h   5 1/4 inch, 360K, 40 track
02h   5 1/4 inch, 1.2M, 80 track
03h   3 1/2 inch, 720K, 80 track
04h   3 1/2 inch, 1.44M, 80 track

Carry flag set if error

AH   Error status (refer to Table BIOS.13)

Comments: This function, *available on only the Personal Computer AT and the PS/2*, is used to obtain the physical parameters of the disk.

Setting bit 7 of the DL register on calling the function refers to hard disks.

This function enables you to check the characteristics of the disk in the designated drive. On return, the table pointed to by ES:DI has the format shown in Table BIOS.15.

Table BIOS.15   Disk Media Characteristic Table

Offset	Meaning
00h	First specify byte
01h	Second specify byte
02h	Number of timer ticks to wait before turning off drive motor
03h	Number of bytes per sector
	00h = 128
	01h = 256
	02h = 512
	03h = 1024
04h	Sectors per track
05h	Gap length
06h	Data length
07h	Gap length for format
08h	Fill byte for format
09h	Head settle time in milliseconds
0Ah	Motor start-up time in 1/8ths seconds

Int 13h   Function 09h

Initialize Hard Disk Table

Sets the values in the specified hard disk table to their default values

Calling registers: AH   09h
                         DL   Hard disk drive number

Return registers: Carry flag clear if successful
                        AH   0

                        Carry flag set if error
                        AH   Status byte (refer to Table BIOS.13)

Comments: Use this function, *which is available on only the Personal Computer AT and PS/2 line and works on only fixed (hard) disks,* to set the hard disk drive's physical parameters. The drive numbers used are not the standard BIOS drive numbers; rather, they are taken from a special series of numbers for fixed disks only (80h corresponds to the first disk, 81h to the second, and so on). Using an out-of-range disk drive number leads to unpredictable results.

Initialization information for the drive is taken from the hard disk parameter tables. Interrupt vector 41h points to the table for disk 1; vector 46h points to the table for disk 2. If a reference is made for any other disk, the function returns an "invalid command" status byte in AH.

Int 13h   Function 0Ah

Read Long Sector

Reads a specified number of long sectors from a hard disk

Calling registers: AH   0Ah
                         AL   Number of sectors
                         ES:BX   Pointer to data buffer
                         CH   Track (see comments)
                         CL   Sector
                         DH   Head number
                         DL   Hard disk drive number

Return registers: Carry flag clear if successful
                        AH   0
                        Carry flag set if error
                        AH   Status byte (refer to Table BIOS.13)

531

Comments: This function, *which is available on only the Personal Computer AT and works on only fixed (hard) disks,* reads long sectors from the hard disk into memory. Long sectors are standard sectors that contain four bytes of error-correcting code in addition to regular data.

This function, like the other read/write functions, is susceptible to the DMA boundary error (AH=9) that can occur when a DMA crosses a memory offset that ends in three zeros. Because there is no error checking of parameters with this function, errors in parameter values can lead to unexpected results.

The drive numbers used are not the standard BIOS drive numbers; rather, they are taken from a special series of numbers for hard disks only (80h corresponds to the first disk, 81h to the second, and so on). Using an out-of-range disk drive number leads to unpredictable results.

Table BIOS.16 gives the valid ranges for all parameters that can be passed to the function. *Note especially that the track number (CH and CL registers) is a 10-bit number stored with the high-order bits in bits 6 and 7 of register CL and the eight low-order bits in register CH. The sector address (register CL) is a 6-bit number stored in bits 0–5 (the bits not used by the track number).*

Table BIOS.16 Valid Parameter Ranges

Register	Parameter	Valid range
AL	Number of sectors	1–121
CH/CL	Track	0–1023
CL	Sector	1–17
DH	Head	0–15
DL	Drive	80h, 81h, etc.

Figure BIOS.1 shows how the bits in CH and CL are interpreted by this function.

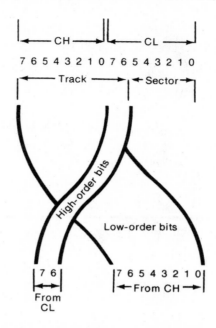

Figure BIOS.1   Bits in CH and CL, as interpreted by Int 13h, Function 0Ah.

Int 13h	**Function 0Bh**
	Write Long Sector

Writes a specified number of long sectors to the hard disk

Calling registers: AH   0Bh
AL   Number of sectors
ES:BX   Pointer to data buffer
CH   Track (see comments)
CL   Sector
DH   Head number
DL   Hard disk drive number

Return registers: Carry flag clear if successful
AH   0

Carry flag set if error

AH   Status byte (refer to Table BIOS.13)

Comments: *This function is available on only the Personal Computer AT and works on only fixed (hard) disks.* Long sectors are standard sectors that contain four bytes of error-correcting code in addition to regular data. This function, like the other read/write functions, is susceptible to the DMA boundary error (AH=9), which can occur when a DMA crosses a memory offset that ends in three zeros. Because there is no error checking of parameters, errors in parameter values can lead to unexpected results.

The drive numbers used are not the standard BIOS drive numbers; rather, they are taken from a special series of numbers for hard disks only (80h corresponds to the first disk, 81h to the second, and so on). Using an out-of-range disk drive number leads to unpredictable results.

The track number is ten bits rather than eight. The upper two bits are passed to the function in the high two bits of the sector number.

Int 13h   Function 0Ch

Seek Cylinder

Moves read/write head to a specified cylinder

Calling registers: AH   0Ch
                        CH   Low-order track
                        CL   High-order track
                        DH   Head number
                        DL   Hard disk drive number

Return registers: Carry flag clear if successful
                        AH   0

                        Carry flag set if error
                        AH   Status byte (refer to Table BIOS.13)

Comments: This function, *which is available on only the Personal Computer AT and works on only fixed (hard) disks,* moves the read/write heads to a specified cylinder. The drive numbers used are not the standard BIOS drive numbers; rather, they are taken from a special series of numbers for hard disks only (80h corresponds to the first disk, 81h to the second, and so on). Using an out-of-range disk drive number leads to unpredictable results. Unpredictable results can occur also from invalid parameter settings when the function is called.

This function is automatically called when the BIOS performs a read or write function; it does not need to be called separately. Its only use is to pre-position the heads when no I/O transfer is expected immediately.

Int 13h   Function 0Dh

Alternate Disk Reset

Resets the hard disk controller

Calling registers: AH   0Dh

                          DL   Hard disk drive number

Return registers: Carry flag clear if successful

                          AH   0

                          Carry flag set if error

                          AH   Status byte (refer to Table BIOS.13)

Comments: *This function is available on only the Personal Computer AT and works on only fixed (hard) disks.* The drive numbers used are not the standard BIOS drive numbers; rather, they are taken from a special series of numbers for hard disks only (80h corresponds to the first disk, 81h to the second, and so on). Using an out-of-range disk drive number leads to unpredictable results.

This function is identical to Int 13h, Function 00h, except that in the newer BIOS versions it does not reset the floppy disk controller. Both are used by critical-error handlers to force recalibration (by causing the disk heads to be repositioned to track 0 before the next I/O operation is started). In older BIOS versions, this handler is coded to go to the same routine address as Int 13h, Function 00h.

Int 13h   Function 0Eh

Read Sector Buffer

Reads the sector buffer

Calling registers: AH   0Eh

                          ES:BX   Point to RAM buffer area

Return registers: Carry flag clear if successful

                          Carry flag set if error

                          AX   Error code

Comments: *This function is available on only XT models with the original 10M hard disk controller.* It is undefined for all other versions of BIOS, and you should avoid its use.

This function is a carryover from IBM S/360 usage. The 10M disk controller simply transfers 512 bytes (one sector) of data from an internal sector buffer (on the controller) to RAM, starting at the address contained in ES:BX. This function is obsolete and should not be used by programmers.

Int 13h   Function 0Fh

Write Sector Buffer

Writes the sector buffer

Calling registers: AH   0Fh
                        ES:BX   Point to RAM buffer area

Return registers: Carry flag clear if successful
                        Carry flag set if error
                        AX   Error code

Comments: *This function is available on only XT models with the original 10M hard disk controller.* It is undefined for all other versions of BIOS, and you should avoid using it if possible.

This function is a carryover from IBM S/360 usage. The 10M disk controller simply transfers 512 bytes (one sector) of data from RAM, starting at the address contained in ES:BX, to an internal sector buffer (on the controller). When formatting the 10M XT drive, this function should be used to initialize the controller's buffer before using Function 05h. This function is obsolete and should not be used by programmers.

Int 13h   Function 10h

Test Hard Disk System Status

Returns the disk status byte (hard disks only)

Calling registers: AH   10h
                        DL   Hard disk drive number

Return registers: Carry flag clear if successful
                        AH   Status byte (see Table BIOS.13)
                        Carry flag set if error
                        AX   Error code

Comments: *This function is the same as Function 01, but works on only fixed (hard) disks.* It returns the disk status as 00h if no error is present.

536

The drive numbers used are not the standard BIOS drive numbers; rather, they are taken from a special series of numbers for hard disks only (80h corresponds to the first disk, 81h to the second, and so on). Using an out-of-range disk drive number leads to unpredictable results.

Int 13h   Function 11h

Recalibrate Hard Disk Drive

Returns the hard disk's heads to cylinder 00 and reports the drive status

Calling registers: AH   11h
                         DL   Hard disk drive number

Return registers: Carry flag clear if successful
                         AH   Status byte (see Table BIOS.13)
                         Carry flag set if error
                         AX   Error code

Comments: *This function works on only fixed (hard) disks.* It returns the disk status as 00h if no error is present.

The drive numbers used are not the standard BIOS drive numbers; rather, they are taken from a special series of numbers for hard disks only (80h corresponds to the first disk, 81h to the second, and so on). Using an out-of-range disk drive number leads to unpredictable results.

Int 13h   Function 12h

Diagnose Controller RAM

Performs built-in diagnostic tests on the internal sector buffer RAM of the hard disk controller in XT models only

Calling registers: AH   12h

Return registers: Carry flag clear if successful
                         Carry flag set if error
                         AX   Error code

Comments: *This function is available on only XT models with the original 10M hard disk controller.* It is undefined for all other versions of BIOS, and its use should be avoided if possible.

Int 13h   Function 13h

Diagnose Drive

Performs built-in diagnostic tests on the hard disk in XT models only

Calling registers: AH   13h

Return registers: Carry flag clear if successful
                         Carry flag set if error
                         AX   Error code

Comments: *This function is available on only XT models with the original 10M hard disk controller.* It is undefined for all other versions of BIOS, and its use should be avoided if possible.

Int 13h   Function 14h

Diagnose Controller

Performs built-in diagnostic tests on the hard disk controller in XT models only

Calling registers: AH   14h

Return registers: Carry flag clear if successful
                         Carry flag set if error
                         AX   Error code

Comments: *This function is available on only XT models with the original 10M hard disk controller.* It is undefined for all other versions of BIOS, and its use should be avoided if possible.

Int 13h   Function 15h

Return DASD Type

Gets the driver's DASD (direct access storage device) type and number of sectors

Calling registers: AH   15h
                                       DLDrive number

Return registers: Carry flag clear if successful
                         AH   DASD type of drive
                         CX   Number of hard disk sectors (high word)
                         DX   Number of hard disk sectors (low word)
                         Carry flag set if error
                         AH   Status byte (refer to Table BIOS.13)

Comments: This function, *available on only the PC XT (BIOS dated 1/10/86 or later), PC XT 286, Personal Computer AT, or PS/2 line*, can use either the standard series of BIOS drive numbers (0 = drive A, 1 = drive B, and so on) or the hard disk numbers (80h = first drive, 81h = second drive, and so on).

This function is used to determine whether Function 16h can be used to test the drive to see whether the floppy disk in the drive has been changed since the last access. Table BIOS.17 lists the function's valid return codes, which indicate whether you can tell anything about the status of the disk in the drive.

Table BIOS.17 DASD Types

Code	DASD Type
0	Drive requested is not available
1	Drive present, cannot detect disk change
2	Drive present, can detect disk change
3	Hard disk

The value returned in CX:DX is valid only if the DASD type returned in AH is 3.

Int 13h   **Function 16h**

Read Disk Change Line Status

Determines whether the disk in a specific drive has been changed

Calling registers: AH   16h
                         DL   Drive number

Return registers: Carry flag clear
                        AH   00h, disk not changed
                        Carry flag set
                        AH   06h, disk changed
                        AH   00h, error

Comments: Use this function, *available on only the PC XT (BIOS dated 1/10/86 or later), PC XT 286, Personal Computer AT, or PS/2 line*, to determine whether the disk in a drive has been changed or removed. This function can use either the standard series of BIOS drive numbers (0 = drive A, 1 = drive B, and so on) or the hard-disk-only numbers (80h = first drive, 81h = second drive, and so on).

539

In this function, note the unfortunate use of the carry flag, which is confusing and inconsistent with its use in the interrupt's other functions. In this one instance, the presence of the carry flag does *not* indicate that an error has occurred. Rather, it indicates one of two possible conditions: an error has occurred or the disk has been removed. All other disk-access functions use the carry flag to indicate that an error has occurred.

Int 13h   Function 17h

Set DASD Type for Disk Format

Specifies the DASD (Direct Access Storage Device) type for use by BIOS disk-formatting functions

Calling registers: AH   17h
                         AL   DASD format type (see Table BIOS.18)
                         DL   Drive number (zero based)

Return registers: Nothing

Comments: This function, *available on only the PC XT (BIOS dated 1/10/86 or later), PC XT 286, Personal Computer AT, or PS/2 line*, must be called before you format a disk. Its purpose is to tell the format function the DASD format type for formatting operations.

Table BIOS.18 lists the valid disk types that can be formatted on the Personal Computer AT system.

Table BIOS.18   DASD Format Types

Type	Meaning
1	Formatting 320/360K disk in 320/360K drive
2	Formatting 320/360K disk in 1.2M drive
3	Formatting 1.2M disk in 1.2M drive
4	Formatting 720K floppy disk in 720K drive

The diskette status is kept in the BIOS data area at 0004:0041.

Int 13h   Function 18h

Set Media Type for Format

Specifies the type of media for the BIOS to use in disk-formatting functions

Calling registers: AH   18h
                          CH   Number of tracks (zero based)
                          CL   Sectors per track
                          DL   Drive number (zero based)
                                        Bit 7 = 0 for a floppy disk, 1 for a hard disk

Return registers: Carry flag clear if successful
                          ES:DI   Pointer to 11-byte parameter table (refer to Table
                                        BIOS.15)
                          Carry flag set if error
                          AH   Return code

Comments: This function, *available on only the Personal Computer AT (BIOS dated after 11/15/86), PC XT (BIOS dated after 1/10/86), PC XT Model 286, and the PS/2 line,* is intended to be used before Int 13h, Function 05h is used to format a disk track. This function specifies to the BIOS the type of media it can expect to find in the disk drive.

Before using this function, you should note the use of the CH and CL registers to specify the track and sector information. The track can be a 10-bit value; as such, it requires the two high-order bits of CL. (Refer to Figure BIOS.1, which shows how this information is stored in the two registers.)

Int 13h   Function 19h

Park Heads

Moves the hard disk drive's read/write heads to a "safe" position on the disk drive

Calling registers: AH   18h
                          DL   Drive number (zero based, PS/2 series only)
                                        Bit 7 = 0 for a floppy disk, 1 for a hard disk

Return registers: Carry flag clear if successful
                          AH   Status byte (see Table BIOS.13)
                          Carry flag set if error
                          AX   Error code

Comments: This function, *available on only the Personal Computer AT (BIOS dated after 11/15/86), PC XT (BIOS dated after 1/10/86), PC XT Model 286, and the PS/2 line,* moves the disk heads to the manufacturer-specified landing zone. It is intended for use before powering down or moving the system, to prevent damage to data.

541

Int 13h   **Function 1Ah**

Format ESDI Unit

Formats an ESDI-compatible disk drive connected to a PS/2 system

Calling registers: AH   18h
                        AL   0, no defect table used
                                  < > 0, use defect table
                        ES:BX   Point to defect table
                        CL   Modifier bits (see comments)
                        DL   Drive number (zero based)
                                  Bit 7 = 1 for a hard disk

Return registers: Nothing

Comments: This function, *available on only the PS/2 line, models 50, 60, and 80,* formats an ESDI disk. All data on the disk is lost when this function is used. Be extremely careful when you use it. If this function is used to format a floppy drive, the results are unknown.

The CL register contains modifier bits with the following significance when this function is called:

Bits 76543210	*Meaning*
. . . . 1	Ignore primary defect map
. . . . . . 1 .	Ignore secondary defect map
. . . . . 1 . .	Update secondary defect map
. . . . 1 . . .	Perform extended surface analysis
. . . 1	Periodic interrupts ON
xxx	Reserved

Int 14h   **Function 00h**

Initialize Communications Port

Sets serial port parameters

Calling registers: AH   00h
                        AL   Initialization parameter
                        DX   Port number (0=COM1, 1=COM2) (2=COM3, 3=COM4
                                  on Personal Computer AT)

Return registers: AH   Port status
                           AL   Modem status

Comments: Use this function to initialize the communications port specified in DX. You can use the function to initialize COM ports 1 and 2 (DX = 0–1); on Personal Computer AT systems, COM ports 1–4 are allowed.

In AL, you specify how the communications port should be initialized. Use the parameters shown in Table BIOS.19 to specify the baud rate, parity, word length, and stop bits.

Table BIOS.19   Serial Port Initialization Parameters

7,6,5 *Baud Rate*	4,3 *Parity*	2 *Stop Bits*	1,0 *Word Length*
000= 110 baud	x0=none	0=1 bit	10=7 bits
001= 150 baud	01=odd	1=2 bits	11=8 bits
010= 300 baud	10=none		
011= 600 baud	11=even		
100=1200 baud			
101=2400 baud			
110=4800 baud			
111=9600 baud			

The interrupt returns the status of the port (see Table BIOS.20) and the modem (see Table BIOS.21). The BIOS adds bit 7 of the port status bits (time-out) to indicate excessive time spent waiting for a response. Otherwise, the status is what you would get directly from the hardware.

Table BIOS.20   Port Status Bits

Bit *76543210*	*Meaning*
. 1	Data ready
. . . . . .1.	Overrun error
. . . . .1. .	Parity error
. . . .1. . .	Framing error

continues

Table BIOS.20   Continued

Bit 76543210	Meaning
...1....	Break detected
..1.....	Transmit holding register (THR) empty
.1......	Transmit shift register (TSR) empty
1.......	Time-out

Table BIOS.21   Modem Status Bits

Bit 76543210	Meaning
.......1	Change in Clear to Send (CTS) status
......1.	Change in Data Set Ready (DSR) status
.....1..	Trailing edge ring indicator
....1...	Change in receive line signal
...1....	Clear to Send (CTS)
..1.....	Data Set Ready (DSR)
.1......	Ring Indicator (RI)
1.......	Receive line signal detected

No matter how you want to use a communications port, initializing the port with this function gives you direct control over important parameters without involving many chip-dependent details. Even programmers who access the serial chips directly through their I/O port addresses will find this function a convenient way to control parameters with minimum complexity.

Int 14h   Function 01h

Write Character to Communications Port

Outputs a character to a serial port

Calling registers: AH   01h

AL   Character to write

	DX	Communications port (0=COM1, 1=COM2) (2=COM3, 3=COM4 on Personal Computer AT)
Return registers:	AH bit 7	0 (function successful)
	AH bit 7	1 (function failed)
		Bits 0–6 show cause of failure (refer to Table BIOS.20)

Comments: This function writes a character to and returns the status of the specified communications port. Ordinarily, writing a character to a serial port is not a time-critical task. It can be done whenever the character is ready. This function can write to serial ports 1 and 2 (COM1 and COM2). Before you call this function, be sure to use Int 14h, Function 00h to initialize the port. (On the Personal Computer AT, you can access ports COM1 to COM4.)

Although communications programs that depend on BIOS read functions can seldom exceed 1200 baud operation, this is not true for the write function. The only effect of failing to supply a new output character as soon as the previous one is sent is a reduction in the effective throughput of the system. No data is lost.

Table BIOS.20 shows the meaning of bits 0–6 in the AH register on return from the function (if the function failed).

Int 14h   Function 02h

Read Character from Communications Port

Inputs a character from a serial port

Calling registers:	AH	02h
	DX	Communications port (0=COM1, 1=COM2) (2=COM3, 3=COM4 on Personal Computer AT)
Return registers:	AH bit 7	0 (function successful)
	AL	Character
	AH bit 7	1 (function failed)
		Bits 0–6 show cause of failure (refer to Table BIOS.20)

Comments: This function reads a character from the specified communications port, returns the port's status, and can read from serial ports 1 and 2 (COM1 and COM2). (On the Personal Computer AT, you can access ports COM1 to COM4.) Before calling this function, be sure to initialize the port.

In any communications application, receiving characters is an extremely time-critical operation. When characters are coming in at uncontrolled intervals from an external device, the computer must be ready to respond to them immediately. Although output is controlled by the computer (but intimately tied to input in a communications program), input must respond to the external system. If the computer is not ready to respond before a new character arrives, that character will be lost.

Communications programs that depend on this function can seldom exceed 300 baud for continuous operation. In most cases, a rate of 1200 baud can transfer only a few characters at a time and will lose several characters every time the display fills and has to scroll up one line.

This function is useless in most commercial applications because direct access to the I/O ports is required in order to achieve the speed necessary for continued operation. Programs that do not depend on human interaction can work acceptably using this function. Reading a serial device with this function is often practical and useful in controlling and monitoring applications with relatively slow speeds.

Table BIOS.20 shows the meaning of bits 0–6 in the AH register on return from the function (if the function failed).

Int 14h   Function 03h

Request Communications Port Status

Returns status information about a serial port

Calling registers: AH   03h
                         DX   Communications port (0=COM1, 1=COM2) (2=COM3, 3=COM4 on Personal Computer AT)

Return registers: AH   Port status (refer to Table BIOS.20)
                         AL   Modem status (refer to Table BIOS.21)

Comments: This function, which returns the current status of the specified communications port, requests the status without doing any I/O or affecting the serial port in any other way. The function can access communications ports 1 and 2 (DX = 0–1). (On the Personal Computer AT, this function can access ports COM1–COM4.)

Tables BIOS.17 and BIOS.18 show the meaning of the status bits in the AH and AL registers on return from the call. Table BIOS.17 specifies the bits for the serial port, whereas Table BIOS.18 gives the bits for the modem connected to the serial port.

Int 14h   Function 04h

Extended Initialization

Initializes serial port parameters

Calling registers: AH   04h
                         AL   Break setting
                         BH   Parity
                         BL   Stop bits
                         CH   Data length
                         CL   Transmission rate (bps)
                         DX   Communications port (0=COM1, 1=COM2, 2=COM3, 3=COM4)

Return registers: AH   Port status (refer to Table BIOS.17)

AL   Modem status (refer to Table BIOS.21)

Comments: This function, *available on only the PS/2 line,* provides (in a simpler manner than that used by Function 00h) for RS-232 port initialization directly at the BIOS level. Table BIOS.22 shows the possible register settings for this function.

Table BIOS.22   Possible Register Settings

Register	Meaning	Settings	Meaning
AL	Break	00h	No break
		01h	Break
BH	Parity	00h	No parity
		01h	Odd parity
		02h	Even parity
		03h	Stick parity odd
		04h	Stick parity even
BL	Stop Bits	00h	One stop bit
		01h	Two stop bits (1 1/2 if data length setting in CH is 00h)
CH	Data Length	00h	5-bit word length
		01h	6-bit word length
		02h	7-bit word length
		03h	8-bit word length
CL	BPS Rate	00h	110 baud
		01h	150 baud
		02h	300 baud
		03h	600 baud
		04h	1200 baud
		05h	2400 baud
		06h	4800 baud
		07h	9600 baud
		08h	19,200 baud

On return from the function, the AH and AL registers reflect the current status of the port. Tables BIOS.17 and BIOS.18 give the meaning of each bit in the registers.

Int 14h   Function 05h

Extended Communications Port Control

Allows extended control of the modem control register

Calling registers:	AH	05h
	AL	00h, read modem control register
	DX	Communications port (0=COM1, 1=COM2, 2=COM3, 3=COM4)
	AL	01h, write modem control register
	BL	Modem control register (if AL = 01h, see Table BIOS.23)
	DX	Communications port (0=COM1, 1=COM2, 2=COM3, 3=COM4)
Return registers:	AH	Port status (refer to Table BIOS.20)
	AL	Modem status (refer to Table BIOS.21)
	BL	Modem control register (see Table BIOS.23)

Comments: This function, *available on only the PS/2 line,* enables you to read or write the modem-control register associated with the desired RS-232 port. This gives you direct access from the BIOS level to the port's modem-control lines. In a read operation, you get the status of these lines; in a write operation, you set the status. The bits in the BL register are defined in Table BIOS.23.

Table BIOS.23   Modem-Control Register Bits

Bit *76543210*	*Meaning*
. . . . 1	Data Terminal Ready (DTR)
. . . . . . 1 .	Request to Send (RTS)
. . . . . 1 . .	Out1
. . . . 1 . . .	Out2
. . . 1	Loopback test
111	Reserved

When this function is called, it also returns the current status of the serial port and modem in registers AH and AL. Tables BIOS.17 and BIOS.18 give the meaning of each bit on return from the call.

Int 15h   Function 00h

Turn On Cassette Motor

Turns on the motor of the cassette tape machine

Calling registers: AH   00h

Return registers: Carry flag clear if successful
Carry flag set if error
AH   Return code (see Table BIOS.24)

Comments: Because *this function works on only older PC models,* using it on PC XT, Personal Computer AT, or PS/2 systems results in the carry flag's being set and the return of AH=86h (see Table BIOS.24).

Table BIOS.24   Cassette Services Return Codes

Code	Meaning
00h	Invalid command
01h	CRC error
02h	Data transitions lost
03h	No data located on tape
04h	Data not found (PC*jr* only)
86h	No cassette port available

Some owners of older systems with cassette relays have rewired the relays for other control functions. This step should be taken carefully, with a full understanding of the equipment's loading and other electrical requirements.

Int 15h   Function 01h

Turn Off Cassette Motor

Turns off the motor of the cassette tape machine

Calling registers: AH   01h

Return registers: Carry flag clear if successful

Carry flag set if error

AH   Return code (refer to Table BIOS.24)

Comments: Because *this function works on only older PC models,* using it on a PC XT, Personal Computer AT, or PS/2 system results in the carry flag's being set and the return of AH=86h (refer to Table BIOS.24).

Some owners of older systems with cassette relays have rewired the relays for other control functions. This step should be taken carefully, with a full understanding of the equipment's loading and other electrical requirements.

Int 15h   Function 02h

Read Data Blocks from Cassette Drive

Reads a specified number of bytes from the cassette

Calling registers: AH   02h

ES:BX   Pointer to data buffer

CX   Number of bytes to read

Return registers: Carry flag clear if successful

DX   Number of bytes read

ES:BX   Pointer to byte following last byte read

Carry flag set if error

AH   Return code (refer to Table BIOS.24)

Comments: Because *this function works on only older PC models,* using it on a PC XT, Personal Computer AT, or PS/2 system results in the carry flag's being set and the return of AH=86h (refer to Table BIOS.24).

If you are using a cassette on a system with a cassette port, this function transfers data from the cassette in 256-byte blocks but delivers to the buffer only the number of bytes called for.

Some owners of older systems with cassette relays have rewired the relays for other control functions. This step should be taken carefully, with a full understanding of the equipment's loading and other electrical requirements.

Int 15h   Function 03h

Write Data Blocks to Cassette Drive

Writes a specified number of bytes to the cassette

Calling registers: AH   03h

ES:BX   Pointer to data buffer

CX   Number of bytes to write

Return registers: Carry flag clear if successful
   ES:BX   Pointer to byte following last byte written
   Carry flag set if error
   AH   Return code (refer to Table BIOS.24)

Comments: Because *this function works on only older PC models,* using it on a PC XT, Personal Computer AT, or PS/2 system results in the carry flag's being set and the return of AH=86h (refer to Table BIOS.24).

All transfers to the tape occur in 256-byte blocks, but only the number of bytes specified in the CX register are transferred from the data buffer. Errors during the transfer indicate command, not transfer, errors. If you are writing an application that will use a cassette, the program should provide a way to verify the tape write before destroying the data in memory.

Some owners of older systems with cassette relays have rewired the relays for other control functions. This step should be taken carefully, with a full understanding of the equipment's loading and other electrical requirements.

Int 15h   Function 0Fh

ESDI Unit Format Periodic Interrupt

Called by formatting routines at the end of formatting each cylinder

Calling registers: AH   0Fh
   AL   Phase code
               00h   Reserved
               01h   Surface analysis
               02h   Formatting

Return registers: Carry flag set, end of formatting or scanning
   Carry flag clear, continue formatting or scanning

Comments: This function, *available on only PS/2 machines,* is used by programmers who want to gain control after formatting or scanning each disk cylinder. At that time, the format routine calls this interrupt.

If this function is invoked from any machine other than a PS/2, the carry flag is set and AH contains 80h (PC and PC*jr*) or 86h (all others) on return.

Int 15h   **Function 21h**

Power-On Self-Test Error Log

Updates or reads the POST error log

Calling registers:	AH	21h
	AL	00h, read POST error log
		01h, write error code to POST error log
	BX	POST error code if AL=01h
	BH	Device code
	BL	Device error

Return registers:	If *reading* POST error log (AL = 0)	
	Carry flag clear if successful	
	AH	00h
	BX	Number of POST error codes stored
	ES:DI	Pointer to POST error log
	Carry flag set if error	
	AH	80h (PC*jr* and PC)
	AH	86h (all others)
	If *writing* to POST error log (AL = 1)	
	Carry flag clear if successful	
	AH	00h
	Carry flag set if error	
	AH	01h, POST error log full
	AH	80h (PC*jr* and PC)
	AH	86h (all others)

Comments: This function is used by the POST primarily to write information to the internal error log or by diagnostic routines to gain information about the error codes detected during the POST. The values returned depend on whether you are posting or reading. A discussion of the use of the POST error log is beyond the scope of this book.

This function works on only PS/2 machines (except the Model 30). If this function is invoked from any machine other than a PS/2, the carry flag is set and AH contains 80h (PC and PC*jr*) or 86h (all others, including PS/2 Model 30) on return.

Int 15h   Function 4Fh

Keyboard Intercept

Called by keyboard routines during I/O processing

Calling registers: AH   4Fh
                          AL   Keyboard scan code
                          Carry flag set

Return registers: PC, PC*jr:*
                          Carry flag set, AH=80h
                          PC XT BIOS 11/08/82, Personal Computer AT
                          BIOS 1/10/84:
                          Carry flag set, AH=86h

                          All others:
                          Carry flag set
                          AL   New keyboard scan code
                          Carry flag clear
                          AL   Original keyboard scan code

Comments: *This function is available on only the Personal Computer AT (BIOS dated after 1/10/84), PC XT (BIOS dated after 11/8/82), PC XT Model 286, and PS/2 series computers.* You can determine whether this function is available by using Int 15h, Function C0h. If it is available, this function is called by Int 09h every time a key is pressed and before Int 09h processes the keystroke. This function normally returns the scan code in the AL register with the carry flag set. By providing a function to replace this one, a programmer can change scan codes to do character translations (such as you might do with an alternate keyboard layout).

If the function returns with the carry flag clear, Int 09h ignores the character. In addition to doing character translations, a replacement function can use this to cause the system to ignore certain keystrokes.

Int 15h   Function 80h

Device Open

Opens a device for a specific process

Calling registers: AH   80h
                          BX   Device ID
                          CX   Process ID

Return registers: Carry flag clear if successful
Carry flag set if error
AH 80h (PC, PC*jr*)
AH 86h (PC XT with BIOS 11/8/82)

Comments: *This function is available on only the Personal Computer AT, PC XT (BIOS dated after 11/8/82), PC XT Model 286, and PS/2 series computers.* It is intended for use in rudimentary multitasking operations and is beyond the scope of this book.

Int 15h Function 81h

Device Close

Closes a device associated with a specific process

Calling registers: AH 81h
BX Device ID
CX Process ID

Return registers: Carry flag clear if successful
Carry flag set if error
AH 80h (PC, PCjr)
AH 86h (PC XT with BIOS 11/8/82)

Comments: *This function is available on only the Personal Computer AT, PC XT (BIOS dated after 11/8/82), PC XT Model 286, and PS/2 series computers.* It is intended for use in rudimentary multitasking operations and is beyond the scope of this book.

Int 15h Function 82h

Program Termination

Used to terminate a process

Calling registers: AH 82h
BX Process ID

Return registers: Carry flag clear if successful
Carry flag set if error
AH 80h (PC, PC*jr*)
AH 86h (PC XT with BIOS 11/8/82)

Comments: *This function is available on only the Personal Computer AT, PC XT (BIOS dated after 11/8/82), PC XT Model 286, and PS/2 series computers.* It is intended for use in rudimentary multitasking operations and is beyond the scope of this book.

Int 15h   Function 83h

Event Wait

Waits for a process event to occur

Calling registers: AH   83h
AL   00h, set interval
CX:DX   Microseconds until posting
ES:BX   Pointer to byte with high-order bit set as soon as possible after end of interval
AL   01h, cancel set interval (PS/2 only)

Return registers: Carry flag clear if successful
Carry flag set if error
AH   80h (PC)
AH   86h (PC XT, Personal Computer AT—BIOS dated after 1/10/84

Comments: *This function is available on only the Personal Computer AT (BIOS dated after 1/10/84) and PS/2 series computers, except the Model 30.* The function is intended for use in rudimentary multitasking operations and is beyond the scope of this book.

Int 15h   Function 84h

Joystick Support

Returns the status and coordinates of the joystick

Calling registers: AH   84h
DX   00h, read switch settings
01h, read joystick position

Return registers: PC, PC*jr:*
Carry flag set
AH   80h
PC XT BIOS 11/08/82:
Carry flag set
AH   86h

All others:
If reading switch settings (DX = 0)
AL   Switch settings (bits 4–7)
Carry flag set if error

DOS
PROGRAMMING

If reading joystick position (DX = 1)

AX	A(X) value
BX	A(Y) value
CX	B(X) value
DX	B(Y) value

Comments: This function is used to control the operations of the joystick on all IBM computers (including the PS/2 line) *except* the PC, PC*jr*, and early PC XT (BIOS dated 11/08/82). On these computers, the function returns with the carry flag set, which indicates an error. AH will contain the error code: either 80h or 86h (for the PC XT).

The value in DX is used to indicate the type of information you want from the joystick. If DX is 0, this function returns the switch settings in the four most-significant bits of AL. If DX is 1, the position of the joystick is returned in the four general-purpose registers: AX, BX, CX, and DX. If no joystick is attached to the computer, the carry flag is set on return.

Int 15h   Function 85h

System Request Key Pressed

Called whenever the SysRq (System Request) key is pressed

Calling registers: AH   85h

Return registers: PC, PC*jr:*
Carry flag set
AH   80h
PX XT BIOS 11/08/82:
Carry flag set
AH   86h

All others:
AL   00h, key pressed
01h, key released

Comments: BIOS calls this function whenever the System Request key (Alt-Print Screen) is pressed or released. *Only the more recent versions of the BIOS support this function, which is accessible only from keyboards with a System Request key.*

If a computer's BIOS does not support this function, the carry flag is set and AH contains either 80h or 86h (early PC XT) on return.

Ordinarily, the System Request key returns with the flags and registers set. This is of no value, but your program can intercept this function to make effective use of the key. To program the System Request key, you simply revector Int 15h and save the old address. Then your routine should check the contents of AH. If AH does not contain 85h, you should pass control to the original Int 15h handler. If AH does contain 85h, the System Request key was either pressed or released. AL reflects the key's state: If it is 00h, the key was just pressed; if it is 01h, the key was just released.

Int 15h   Function 86h

Delay

Pauses a certain amount of time before returning

Calling registers:	AH	86h
	CX,DX	Time before return in microseconds (accurate to within 976 microseconds)

Return registers:	PC, PC*jr*:	
	Carry flag set	
	AH	80h
	PC XT:	
	Carry flag set	
	AH	86h
	All others:	
	Carry flag set (wait in progress)	
	Carry flag clear (successful wait)	

Comments: This function, *which works on only the Personal Computer AT and PS/2 line*, is designed to be used (within operating system software) for setting system waits. It is not intended for use by applications programs.

Int 15h   Function 87h

Move Block

Transfers a specified block of memory on 80286 and 80386 machines

Calling registers:	AH	87h
	CX	Word count of storage to be moved
	ES:SI	Pointer to global descriptor table

Return registers:	PC, PC*jr*:	
	Carry flag set	
	AH	80h
	PC XT, PS/2 Model 30:	
	Carry flag set	
	AH	86h
	All others:	
	Carry flag clear, zero flag set	

Operation successful

AH	00h

Carry flag set, zero flag clear

Operation failed

AH	01h	RAM parity error
	02h	Other exception occurred
	03h	Gate address line 20h failed

Comments: With this function, IBM computers based on 80286 or 80386 microprocessors can transfer blocks of data to and from memory. (There must be more than 1M of memory.) The computer switches from the processor's real mode to protected mode. No interrupts are allowed during this type of transfer (interrupts may be missed if the move is a large one).

The global descriptor table pointed to by ES:SI is laid out as shown in Table BIOS.25.

Table BIOS.25   Global Descriptor Table

Offset	Description
00h	Dummy; set to zero.
08h	GDT data segment location; set to zero.
10h	Source GDT. Points to a GDT for the source memory block.
18h	Target GDT. Points to a GDT for the target memory block.
20h	Pointer to BIOS code segment; initialized to zero. BIOS uses this area to create the protected mode code segment.
28h	Pointer to BIOS stack segment; initialized to zero. BIOS uses this area to create the protected mode stack segment.

Source/Target GDT Layout

Offset	Description
00h	Segment limit
02h	24-bit segment physical address
05h	Data access rights (set to 93h)
06h	Reserved word (must be zero)

Because the word count loaded in CX has a limit of 8000h, this routine cannot transfer more than 64K bytes of data.

Int 15h   Function 88h

Extended Memory Size Determination

Returns the number of contiguous 1K memory blocks available in extended memory

Calling registers: AH   88h

Return registers: PC, PC*jr:*
                         Carry flag set
                         AH   80h
                         PC XT, PS/2 Model 30:
                         Carry flag set
                         AH   86h

                         All others:
                         AX   Contiguous 1K blocks of memory beginning at 100000h

Comments: Returns the amount of memory determined available by POST checks above address 100000h. This function is available only for machines using either the 80286 or 80386 microprocessor.

Int 15h   Function 89h

Switch Processor to Protected Mode

Switches the processor to protected mode so that it can access extended memory and take advantage of protected mode instructions

Calling registers: AH   89h
                         BL   IRQ0 interrupt vector offset
                         BH   IRQ8 interrupt vector offset
                         ES:SI   Pointer to Global Descriptor Table (GDT)
                         CX   Offset into protected mode CS to jump to

Return registers: Carry flag clear if successful
                         Carry flag set if error

Comments: For a programmer with access to a system with extended memory, the capability of switching the processor to protected mode is potentially very interesting. Although protected mode gives you access to additional memory and instructions, the price you pay is incompatibility with many existing systems. Only machines with a 286 or 386 processor have this capability (and they do not necessarily have the extra memory). Furthermore, DOS itself does not use protected mode. Subtle bugs may crop up unless you write all your own handling for this situation.

To use this function, you first must set up the global descriptor table (GDT) for the call. (Refer to Table BIOS.25 for the GDT layout.)

While Function 89h is in use, the normal BIOS functions are not available to the user. Programs running in protected mode must create their own I/O commands. Furthermore, the standard interrupt vectors must be moved to accommodate the 80286 interrupt definitions that overlay some of the interrupt vectors assigned for real-mode use of the system. Interrupt handlers for the hardware interrupts also must be defined.

Interrupt handling is a major part of any shift to protected mode using this function. A more detailed discussion of 80286/80386 interrupts is beyond the scope of this book. For details about the operation of protected mode interrupts and the design of handlers for them, you should consult a reference on the 80286 and 80386 processors.

Int 15h   Function 90h

Device Wait

Used by the BIOS to indicate a waiting state

Calling registers:	AH	90h
	AL	Device type code
	ES:BX	Pointer to network control block if waiting for a network
Return registers:	PC, PCjr:	
	Carry flag set	
	AH	80h
	PC XT BIOS (11/08/82):	
	Carry flag set	
	AH	86h
	All others:	
	Carry flag set (minimum wait satisfied)	
	Carry flag clear (wait not satisfied)	

Comments: Use this function to tell the operating system that a program is about to wait for a device. This function is designed for developing multitasking software; it is not meant for use by applications programmers. Whenever the BIOS is about to enter a busy loop (when it must wait for a device), it calls this function. Table BIOS.26 lists the type codes passed to the routine in AL.

Table BIOS.26   Type Codes Passed in AL

AL	Type Code
00h	Disk time-out
01h	Diskette time-out
.02h	Keyboard (no time-out)
03h	Pointing device (time-out)
80h	Network (no time-out)
FCh	Hard disk reset (PS/2 only)
FDh	Diskette drive motor start (time-out)
FEh	Printer (time-out)

This function (called at the beginning of an interrupt) is the opposite of Int 15h, Function 91h (called when the interrupt is complete). If you want to do other things while the computer is busy, you can hook into the Int 15h vector, which passes all functions (except 90h and 91h) to the original handler. After you save the machine's status, you are free to do another task.

Int 15h	Function 91h
	Interrupt Complete

Used by the BIOS to indicate the end of a waiting state

Calling registers: AH   91h

Return registers: PC, PC*jr:*
                         Carry flag set
                         AH   80h
                         PC XT BIOS (11/08/82):
                         Carry flag set
                         AH   86h

                         All others:
                         AL   Type code

Comments: The BIOS uses this function to report that the device interrupt is complete, according to the type code given in table BIOS.27. This function is not meant to be called by applications programmers; it is intended to be used internally by the operating system or to develop multitasking systems. Device interrupts use Int 91h to indicate to the operating system that they are complete (see the comments for Int 09h).

Table BIOS.27   Type Codes on Return from Function 91h

AL	Type Code
00h	Disk time-out
01h	Diskette time-out
02h	Keyboard (no time-out)
03h	Pointing device (time-out)
80h	Network (no time-out)
FCh	Hard disk reset (PS/2 only)
FDh	Diskette drive motor start (time-out)
FEh	Printer (time-out)

This function, which is called when an interrupt is complete, is the opposite of Int 15h, Function 90h (called when the interrupt begins).

Int 15h   Function C0h

Return System Configuration Parameters

Returns a pointer to system descriptor information

Calling registers: AH   C0h

Return registers: PC, PC*jr*:
Carry flag set
AH   80h
PC XT BIOS (11/08/82), Personal Computer AT
BIOS (1/10/84):
Carry flag set
AH   86h

All others:
ES:BX   Pointer to system descriptor table in ROM

Comments: The ROM system descriptor table contains useful information about the system. Table BIOS.28 shows the meaning of the entries.

Table BIOS.28   System Descriptor Table

Offset	Meaning
00h	Byte count of data that follows (minimum 8)
02h	Model byte
03h	Submodel byte
04h	BIOS revision level (00 = first release)
05h	Feature information (see Table BIOS.29 for meaning)
06–09h	Reserved

The feature information byte is interpreted as shown in Table BIOS.29.

Table BIOS.29   Feature Information Byte

Bit 76543210	Meaning
.......x	Reserved
......0.	PC bus I/O channel
......1.	MicroChannel Architecture
.....1..	Extended BIOS data area (EBDA) allocated
....1...	Wait for external event is supported
...1....	Keyboard intercept (Int 15h, Function 4Fh) called by Int 09h
..1.....	Real-time clock present
.1......	Second interrupt chip present
1.......	DMA channel 3 used by hard disk BIOS

The model byte contained at offset 02h of the system descriptor table should be the same as the system ID byte (stored at F000:FFFE). The submodel byte (offset 03h) can be used for additional system identification. From the information shown in Table BIOS.30, you can determine which type of IBM computer is being used. (The BIOS date is provided to indicate differences between table entries for the same type of computer.)

DOS
PROGRAMMING

Table BIOS.30 System Model Identifications

Computer Type	Model Byte (offset 02h)	Submodel (offset 03h)	BIOS Revision (offset 04h)	BIOS Date
PC	FFh			
PC XT	FEh			
PC XT	FBh		00h	01h 1/10/86
PC XT	FBh		00h	02h 5/09/86
PC*jr*	FDh			
AT	FCh			
AT	FCh		00h	01h 6/10/85
AT, COMPAQ 286		FCh	01h	00h 11/15/85
PC XT 286	FCh		02h	00h
PC Convertible	F9h	00h	00h	09/13/85
PS/1	FCh	0Bh	05	12/1/89
PS/2 Model 30	FAh	00h	00h	9/2/86
PS/2 Model 50	FCh	04h	00h	
PS/2 Model 60	FCh	05h	00h	
PS/2 Model 80	F8h	00h	00h	

Int 15h   Function C1h

Return Extended BIOS Data Area Segment Address

Returns the segment address of the EBDA

Calling registers: AH   C1h

Return registers: PC, PC*jr:*
Carry flag set
AH   80h

PC XT, Personal Computer AT:
Carry flag set
AH   86h

PS/2:

Carry flag clear if successful

ES   Extended BIOS data area segment address

Carry flag set if error

Comments: This function is used to determine the segment address of the extended BIOS data area (EBDA). Notice that this area is used (so far) only by the PS/2 line. You can determine whether it is supported on your system through Int 15h, Function C0h (refer to bit 2 of the feature information byte).

The EBDA is used internally by the BIOS on the Personal System/2 line. It is allocated by the POST routines and resides at the top of the user memory area (usually as the last 1K of the 640K main memory area). POST adjusts the amount of free memory to allow for the EBDA. To determine the amount of free memory available, refer to Int 12h.

Int 15h   Function C2h

Pointing Device BIOS Interface

Interface function for auxiliary pointing devices

Calling registers:	AH	C2h
	AL	00h, enable/disable pointing device
	BH	00h, enable
		01h, disable
	AL	01h, reset pointing device
	AL	02h, set sample rate
	AL	03h, set resolution
	AL	04h, read device type
	AL	05h, pointing device interface initialization
	AL	06h, extended commands
	AL	07h, pointing device far call initialization

Return registers: PC, PC*jr:*

Carry flag set

AH   80h

PC XT, Personal Computer AT:

Carry flag set

AH   86h

PS/2:

Carry flag clear if successful

Other registers vary by subfunction (see comments)

Carry flag set if error

AH	01h, invalid function call
	02h, invalid input
	03h, interface error
	04h, resend
	05h, no far call installed

Comments: This function, *which works on only the PS/2 line,* is designed to interface pointing devices (such as a mouse, digitizer, or puck) to DOS. Because most mouse software is interfaced through an Int 33h device driver, information about the mouse is covered under that interrupt. (Later versions of the Int 33h device driver furnished by Microsoft use this BIOS interrupt, if it is available, to accomplish their functions, but programs universally use the Int 33h interface because it has become a standard.)

Although a discussion of the detailed use of this function is beyond the scope of this book, we quickly discuss the parameters for each subfunction. Before you issue a subfunction, you should tell BIOS about the interrupt handler for the pointing device (set AL to 7 and ES:BX to the interrupt handler's far address). Next, enable the pointing device by setting AL and BH to 0 and calling this function.

After you have enabled the pointing device, you can reset it by setting AL to 1 and calling the function. On successful completion, BH is set to the device ID of the pointing device and the device's parameters are reset.

Note that a similar subfunction (AL=5) is used to initialize the pointer device's interface. This subfunction is invoked with BH set to a number in the range of 1–8, which represents the number of bytes to be used for the data package size.

To allow for setting the pointing device's sampling rate, set AL to 2. A code that indicates the desired sampling rate is loaded in BH as follows:

Code	Sample Rate
00h	10 reports per second
01h	20 reports per second
02h	40 reports per second
03h	60 reports per second
04h	80 reports per second
05h	100 reports per second
06h	200 reports per second

To set the resolution of the pointing device, set AL to 3 and BH to the desired resolution (0 = 1 count per millimeter (cpm), 1 = 2 cpm, 2 = 4 cpm, and 3 = 8 cpm).

By setting AL to 4, you cause the device ID (returned in BH) to be read. This return value is the same as that returned when you reset the device (see AL = 5).

Int 15h   Function C3h

Enable/Disable Watchdog Time-out

Provides control for the PS/2 watchdog timer

Calling registers: AH   C3h
                        AL   00h, disable watchdog time-out
                                    01h, enable watchdog time-out
                        BX   Watchdog timer count (1–255)

Return registers: PC, PCjr:
                        Carry flag set
                        AH   80h
                        PC XT, Personal Computer AT, PS/2 Model 30:
                        Carry flag set
                        AH   86h

                        PS/2:
                        Carry flag clear if successful
                        Carry flag set if error

Comments: This function is used to enable or disable the watchdog timer available with the PS/2 line of computers that use 80286 or 80386 microprocessors. On non-PS/2 computers, this function returns with the carry flag set and an error code in AH.

The watchdog timer uses timer channel 3 and is tied to the IRQ 0 line. When IRQ 0 is active for more than one cycle of the channel 0 timer (main system timer), the watchdog timer count is decremented. When the watchdog timer count reaches 0, a non-maskable interrupt (NMI) is generated. The main purpose of this function (and the watchdog timer) is to help in the detection of and recovery from errors.

Int 15h   Function C4h

Programmable Option Select

Provides access to PS/2 system programmable registers on option boards

Calling registers: AH   C4h
                        AL   00h, return base POS adapter register address
                                    01h, enable slot for setup
                                    02h, adapter enable

Return registers: PC, PC*jr:*
Carry flag set
AH   80h
PC XT, Personal Computer AT, PS/2 Model 30:
Carry flag set
AH   86h
PS/2:
Carry flag clear if successful
DL   Base POS adapter register address (function 0)
BL   Slot number (function 1)
Carry flag set if error

Comments: Programmable Option Select (POS), which is available on PS/2 models that use the 80286 and 80386 microprocessors, eliminates the need for system-board and adapter switches. The function of the switches is replaced by programmable registers accessible through this function.

On non-PS/2 systems, this function returns an error. The carry flag is set and AH contains an error code.

This function is intended primarily for use by system configuration software, not by applications programs. If you decide to use it, be aware that *improper use of the POS can cause loss of system integrity and might damage some adapter boards.* A discussion of the process for Personal System/2 system configuration and setup is beyond the scope of this book.

Int 15h	**Function D8h**	**Subfunction 00h**

Read EISA Slot Information

On an EISA system, returns information about an EISA device in the specified slot

Calling registers: AH   D8h
AL   00h, read slot information
CL   Slot number (0-63)

Return registers: Carry flag clear if successful
AH   00h, successful
AL   Vendor information byte
BH   Major revision number
BL   Minor revision number
CX   Checksum for configuration file
DH   Number of device functions
DL   Combined function information
SI:DI   4-byte vendor ID
Carry flag set if error
AH   80h, Invalid slot number
82h, Extended CMOS RAM corrupted

83h, Slot is empty

86h, Invalid BIOS call

87h, Invalid system configuration

Comments: EISA bus computers are an extension of ISA bus computers and an alternative to MCA bus computers introduced several years ago by IBM. This function is used by EISA setup routines. It enables you to read device information for a device in a specific expansion slot. If the program using this utility is running in 32-bit mode (CS is 32-bits), the value used in AH when calling this function should be set to 80h.

This function is intended primarily for use by system configuration software, not by applications programs. A discussion of the process for EISA system configuration and setup is beyond the scope of this book.

Int 15h	Function D8h	Subfunction 01h
	Read EISA Function Information	

On an EISA system, returns information about a specific EISA function for a device in the specified slot

Calling registers:

AH	D8h	
AL	01h, read function information	
CH	Function number	
CL	Slot number (0-63)	
DS:SI	320-byte buffer address	

Return registers: Carry flag clear if successful

AH   00h, successful

Carry flag set if error

AH

80h, Invalid slot number

81h, Invalid function number

82h, Extended CMOS RAM corrupted

83h, Slot is empty

86h, Invalid BIOS call

87h, Invalid system configuration

Comments: EISA bus computers are an extension of ISA bus computers and an alternative to MCA bus computers introduced several years ago by IBM. This function is used by EISA setup routines. It enables you to read function information for a specific device in a specific expansion slot. The information is returned in a 320-byte data block pointed to by DS:SI. If the program using this utility is running in 32-bit mode (CS is 32 bits), the value used in AH when calling this function should be set to 81h, and DS:ESI should point to the data buffer.

This function is intended primarily for use by system configuration software, not by applications programs. A discussion of the process for EISA system configuration and setup is beyond the scope of this book.

569

Int 15h | **Function D8h** | **Subfunction 02h**

Clear EISA CMOS

On an EISA system, initializes the CMOS RAM

Calling registers: AH   D8h
AL   02h, clear CMOS
BH   Major revision number
BL   Minor revision number

Return registers: Carry flag clear if successful
AH   00h, successful
Carry flag set if error
AH   84h, Error writing to CMOS
86h, Invalid BIOS call
88h, Configuration utility unsupported

Comments: EISA bus computers are an extension of ISA bus computers and an alternative to MCA bus computers introduced several years ago by IBM. This function is used by EISA setup routines. It enables you to erase the extended CMOS area, if the configuration utility specified by the revision number in BX is supported by the system. If the program using this utility is running in 32-bit mode (CS is 32 bits), the value used in AH when calling this function should be set to 82h.

This function is intended primarily for use by system configuration software, not by applications programs. A discussion of the process for EISA system configuration and setup is beyond the scope of this book.

Int 15h | **Function D8h** | **Subfunction 03h**

Write to EISA CMOS

On an EISA system, writes a block of information to the CMOS RAM

Calling registers: AH   D8h
AL   03h, write to CMOS
CX   Length of data
DS:SI   Address of data buffer

Return registers: Carry flag clear if successful
AH   00h, successful
Carry flag set if error
AH   84h, Error writing to CMOS
85h, CMOS area is full
86h, Invalid BIOS call

Comments: EISA bus computers are an extension of ISA bus computers and an alternative to MCA bus computers introduced several years ago by IBM. This function is used by EISA setup routines. It enables you to write a block of configuration information to the extended CMOS area. If the program using this utility is running in 32-bit mode (CS is 32 bits), the value used in AH when calling this function should be set to 83h, and the data area should be pointed to by DS:ESI.

This function is intended primarily for use by system configuration software, not by applications programs. A discussion of the process for EISA system configuration and setup is beyond the scope of this book.

Int 16h — Function 00h

Read Keyboard Character

Returns an ASCII value and a scan code from the keyboard buffer

Calling registers:	AH	00h
Return registers:	AH	Keyboard scan code
	AL	ASCII character code

Comments: This function, which reads a single character from the keyboard buffer and returns the character and its scan code, is the one you most likely will use when you write a TSR that needs a hot key to trigger its operation. By watching requests to this interrupt, you can trap and respond directly to occurrences of the hot key. The keyboard buffer is usually located at 0040:001Ah.

This function waits until a key is pressed and then returns the keyboard scan code and the ASCII code of the keystroke. If a key has no defined ASCII code, a value of 0 is returned for the ASCII code. (The arrow keys and function keys are examples of keys with no defined ASCII code.)

Although the Ctrl, Alt, and Shift keys return no code for themselves, they modify other keystrokes to produce unique codes. (See Int 16h, Function 02h for a way to determine the status of these keys.)

The special keystrokes Ctrl-Alt-Del (press and hold the Ctrl, Alt, and Del keys simultaneously) and PrtSc (press and hold the Shift key and the PrtSc key simultaneously) are not returned. BIOS recognizes these special keystrokes and immediately passes control to other interrupt-servicing routines.

This function enables you to enter any character by holding down the Alt key while you type its corresponding ASCII code on the keypad. If you hold down the Alt key while you type 156, for example, the scan code 156 is returned. If you type a number greater than 256, the returned code is the number modulo 256 (the number entered is divided by 256; the code is the remainder).

Int 16h   Function 01h

Read Keyboard Status

Checks for availability of a keystroke and returns the ASCII code and scan code if available

Calling registers: AH   01h

Return registers: Zero flag clear (Key waiting)
                         AH   Scan code
                         AL   ASCII character
                         Zero flag set (No key waiting)

Comments: Unlike Function 00h of Int 16h, this function does a quick check of the keyboard and then returns immediately. If a keystroke is ready, the function clears the zero flag and returns the keystroke's ASCII code and the keyboard scan code. If there is no keystroke to be processed, the function sets the zero flag. If the key has no defined ASCII code, a value of 0 is returned for the ASCII code. (The arrow keys and function keys are examples of keys with no defined ASCII code.)

Although the Ctrl, Alt, and Shift keys return no code for themselves, they modify other keystrokes to produce unique codes. (See Function 02h for a way to tell the status of these keys.) The special Ctrl-Alt-Del and PrtSc keystrokes are not returned, but cause other interrupts to occur immediately.

You can enter any ASCII code by holding down the Alt key while typing its corresponding 3-digit code number. Holding down the Alt key while typing 156, for example, returns the scan code 156. If you type a number greater than 256, the returned code is the number modulo 256 (the number entered is divided by 256; the code is the remainder).

Int 16, Function 01h does not end with an IRET instruction, as other interrupt handlers do; rather, it uses a RET instruction with an option that allows the function to flush bytes from the stack. By returning in this way, the function can use the zero flag for a return flag. It is not apparent why the programmer chose to do this, but it works. Perhaps the intent was to mimic the old CP/M keyboard-status function, which operated in approximately the same way.

Int 16h   Function 02h

Return Keyboard Flags

Returns a status byte indicating the condition of the Shift keys

Calling registers: AH   02h

Return registers: AL   ROM BIOS keyboard flags byte

Comments: This function returns the status of keyboard toggles and Shift keys from the BIOS status register kept in memory location 0000:0417h.

Unusual key combinations make good triggers for special actions. In older programs, the Escape key (Esc) was often used for getting out of an application. Esc is not a safe choice for irrevocable actions, however: The key is too easily pressed. To prevent accidental triggering, you would have to add an `Are you sure?` question if your program found the Esc key. You can provide a more positive initiator by triggering on a key sequence that is unlikely to occur accidentally (Ctrl-Left Shift-Right Shift, for example). Just be careful not to use key sequences that require double-jointed fingers or other unusual characteristics!

Table BIOS.31 shows the meaning of the bits in the AL register on return from the function.

Table BIOS.31 BIOS Keyboard Status Flags

Bit 76543210	Meaning
.......1	Right Shift key is depressed
......1.	Left Shift key is depressed
.....1..	Ctrl key is depressed
....1...	Alt key is depressed
...1....	Scroll Lock is enabled
..1.....	Num Lock is enabled
.1......	Caps Lock is enabled
1.......	Insert key has been toggled

Int 16h   Function 03h

Adjust Keyboard Repeat Rate

Sets the keyboard repeat delay time and repeat rate

Calling registers: AH   03h

AL   Subfunction:

00h, Restore default rate and delay (PC*jr* only)

01h, Increase initial delay (PC*jr* only)

02h, Cut repeat rate in half (PC*jr* only)

03h, Increase initial delay and cut repeat rate in half (PC*jr* only)

04h, Turn off keyboard repeat (PC*jr* only)

05h, Set repeat rate and delay (Personal Computer AT only)

573

BH	Repeat delay (AT and PS/2 only)
	($0-3 \times 250$ ms)
BL	Repeat rate (AT and PS/2 only)
	(00h-1Fh, lower values give higher rates)

Return registers: Nothing

Comments: This function is not available on the PC or the PC/XT. For details of its use, either experiment or refer to the bibliography.

Int 16h Function 04h

Key-Click On/Off

Turns the key-click sound (issued when a key is struck) on or off

Calling registers:	AH	04h
	AL	00h, key-click off
		01h, key-click on

Return registers: Nothing

Comments: *This function is available on only the PCjr;* it is not available on the PC, the PC/XT, the Personal Computer AT, or the PS/2.

Int 16h Function 05h

Write to Keyboard Buffer

Writes to an enhanced keyboard's buffer

Calling registers:	AH	05h
	CH	Scan code
	CL	Character

| **Return registers:** | AL | 1 if buffer is full |

Comments: *This function works on only Personal Computer ATs and PS/2s with enhanced keyboards.* To determine whether a system has an enhanced keyboard, follow these steps:

1. Use Function 05h to write FFFFh to the keyboard's buffer.

2. Use Function 10h to read from the keyboard.

If you do not get FFFFh back within 16 tries (the size of the keyboard buffer), you do not have an enhanced keyboard.

Int 16h   Function 10h

Get Keystroke

Gets a keystroke from an enhanced keyboard

Calling registers:	AH	10h
Return registers:	AH	Scan code
	AL	Character

Comments: This function, *which works on only Personal Computer ATs and PS/2s with enhanced keyboards,* adds to keyboard processing a recognition of similarly named keys. For example, the keyboard has two Alt keys (left and right); this function adds recognition of the left versus the right Alt key. (For a table of additional available key identifications, see Int 16h, Function 12h.) The discussion of Int 16h, Function 05h tells you how to determine whether an enhanced keyboard is present.

Int 16h   Function 11h

Check Keyboard

Checks an enhanced keyboard for a keystroke

Calling registers:	AH	11h
Return registers:	Zero flag clear if keystroke is available	
	AH	Scan code
	AL	Character
	Zero flag set if no keystroke is available	

Comments: *This function works on only Personal Computer ATs and PS/2s with enhanced keyboards.* Like other keyboard input routines, this function returns the character and scan code if a character is available and returns the zero flag set if no character is available. This function can be used to implement input routines that poll the keyboard regularly but do other work while waiting for input.

Int 16h   Function 12h

Get Keyboard Status Flags

Returns the status of enhanced keyboard Shift keys

Calling registers:	AH	12h
Return registers:	AL	Status flag 1
	AH	Status flag 2

Comments: This function, *which works on only Personal Computer ATs and PS/2s with enhanced keyboards,* is similar in purpose and operation to Int 16h, Function 02h, except that extended information is returned. The meaning of the status flags returned by this function is shown in tables BIOS.29 and BIOS.30. Notice that the information provided in Table BIOS.32 (returned in AL) is the same as that returned in AL by Int 16h, Function 02h (see Table BIOS.33).

Table BIOS.32   BIOS Keyboard Status Flag 1

Bit 76543210	Meaning
.......1	Right Shift key is depressed
......1.	Left Shift key is depressed
.....1..	Either Ctrl key is depressed
....1...	Either Alt key is depressed
...1....	Scroll Lock is enabled
..1.....	Num Lock is enabled
.1......	Caps Lock is enabled
1.......	Insert key has been toggled

Table BIOS.33   BIOS Keyboard Status Flag 2

Bit 76543210	Meaning
.......1	Left Ctrl key is depressed
......1.	Left Alt key is depressed
.....1..	Right Ctrl key is depressed
....1...	Right Alt key is depressed
...1....	Scroll Lock is depressed
..1.....	Num Lock key is depressed
.1......	Caps Lock key is depressed
1.......	SysReq Key is depressed

Int 17h   Function 00h

Write Character to Printer

Outputs a character to a parallel printer port

Calling registers: AH   00h
                          AL   Character
                          DX   Printer number (0–2)

Return registers: AH   Printer status (see Table BIOS.34)

Comments: This function writes the specified character to the printer port and returns the printer's current status, as shown in Table BIOS.34.

Table BIOS.34   Print Status Bits

Bit 76543210	Meaning
. . . . 1	Time-out
. . . . . xx.	Unused
. . . . 1 . . .	I/O error
. . . 1	Printer selected
. . 1	Out of paper
. 1	Acknowledged
1	Printer *not* busy

Not all printers return the specified items of status information. Because of this lack of standardization among printer manufacturers, it is not advisable to depend on status information unless genuine IBM printers are involved. In particular, if no printer is connected, the BIOS functions often (but not always) report a status indicating that the printer is ready and data is being successfully transferred; if the printer is connected but is either powered down or off-line, the "ready" indication is normally *not* given.

Int 17h   Function 01h

Initialize Printer Port

Sends a reset sequence to a parallel printer port

577

Calling registers: AH   01h
                      DX   Printer number (0–2)

Return registers: AH   Printer status (refer to Table BIOS.34)

Comments: This function initializes the parallel printer port and returns the port's status (refer to Table BIOS.34). The function outputs the byte sequence 08h 0Ch to the printer port (note that these are control signals, not data characters). Epson and IBM printers respond to this sequence by performing a reset. Other printers, however, may not respond correctly and, if they are not Epson- or IBM-compatible, may even exhibit undesirable effects from the code sequence.

Int 17h   Function 02h

Request Printer Port Status

Returns the status of a parallel printer port

Calling registers: AH   02h
                      DX   Printer number (0–2)

Return registers: AH   Printer status (refer to Table BIOS.34)

Comments: This function returns the current status of the specified parallel printer port (refer to Table BIOS.34).

Note that if you are using a Personal Computer AT, a PC XT 286, or a Personal System/2 machine, and the BIOS determines that the printer is busy (see bit 7 of Table BIOS.34), the BIOS executes an Int 15h, Function 90h. (See the description of that function for additional information.)

Int 18h

Execute ROM BASIC

Starts BASIC from ROM

Calling registers: None

Return registers: Nothing

Comments: On IBM systems, the ROM BASIC interpreter is still included in all BIOS ROM sets. During the boot process, if a floppy disk is not found and no hard disk is present, this interrupt is triggered to execute ROM BASIC (a cassette BASIC interpreter). This interrupt is rarely used directly. User-written software should not trigger this interrupt.

ROM BASIC is still necessary, however, because the BASICA interpreter on IBM distribution disks uses ROM BASIC for many of its routines. Because ROM BASIC is not present on compatibles, you cannot start IBM BASIC on a compatible.

On PS/2 systems, ROM BASIC is still included in the BIOS.

Int 19h

System Warm Boot

Initiates a boot sequence

Calling registers: None

Return registers: Nothing

Comments: This function, which is similar to Ctrl-Alt-Del, performs a warm boot of the computer without losing the present status of memory. (Ctrl-Alt-Del performs a warm boot and also resets the machine state and the memory allocations.)

Contrary to some references, neither of these methods is the same as a power-off restart, which causes the entire system to be reset and power-on checks (including memory checks) to be performed.

When this interrupt is executed, it reads track 0, sector 1 (the boot code) from the disk to memory, starting at address 0000:7C00. The DL register is set to the drive number from which the boot is taking place, and then the boot code at that address (0000:7C00h) is executed. If there is a hardware error (the BIOS cannot locate a boot sector that can be loaded), an Int 18h is executed.

Int 1Ah   Function 00h

Get Clock Counter

Returns the value of the system clock counter

Calling registers: AH   00h

Return registers: AL   Midnight flag
CX   High-order word clock count
DX   Low-order word clock count

Comments: This interrupt retrieves the system clock counter, which ticks 18.2065 times per second, starting with zero (at midnight).

Midnight is determined as the number of ticks in a complete day of 86,400 seconds (1,573,040 ticks of the clock, for a total elapsed time of 86,399.9121 seconds). A flag byte in RAM is set to 1 when midnight passes, and calling this function returns the content of that flag byte in the AL register. Note that if midnight passes *twice* before this function is called, the second event is ignored.

You reset AL to zero by executing this function. Be careful, however—other date routines might need the midnight-passage information.

Int 1Ah   Function 01h

Set Clock Counter

Sets the value of the system clock counter

Calling registers: AH   01h
CX   High-order word clock count
DX   Low-order word clock count

Return registers: Nothing

Comments: This interrupt sets the system clock counter. To set the clock to a particular time, you compute the number of ticks (since midnight) you want to represent. This number becomes the new setting for the clock.

To determine the number of ticks, you compute the number of seconds since midnight for the desired time setting and multiply that number by 18.2065 (the number of ticks per second). Be careful, however—the BIOS does not protect you from illegal values. If you specify a value outside a normal day's range (24 hours, or 1800Bh ticks), the BIOS accepts it.

Int 1Ah   Function 02h

Read Real-Time Clock

Returns the time maintained by the real-time clock

Calling registers: AH   02h

Return registers: Carry flag clear if successful
CH   Hours (BCD)
CL   Minutes (BCD)
DH   Seconds (BCD)
DL   Daylight savings time flag (not supported in all BIOS
versions)
Carry flag set if error

Comments: This function, *available on only the PC XT 286, Personal Computer AT, or PS/2 line,* returns the clock values in BCD (binary-coded decimal). If the Personal Computer AT BIOS is dated before 6/10/85, the value in DL, which indicates the presence of the daylight savings time option, is not returned.

BCD means that each 4-bit nibble is interpreted as a single decimal digit and that hexadecimal digits A through F are ignored. Table BIOS.35 shows the decimal values that correspond to the range of hexadecimal values in a 4-bit nibble representing BCD digits.

Table BIOS.35   BCD Correspondence Table

Hex Value	Decimal Value
0	0
1	1
2	2
3	3
4	4
5	5
6	6
7	7
8	8
9	9
A	Undefined
B	Undefined
C	Undefined
D	Undefined
E	Undefined
F	Undefined

To use Table BIOS.35, determine which digits correspond to a byte that has been coded BCD and then look at each nibble of the byte. A byte value of 34h, for example, represents a decimal value of 34 in BCD. The byte A3h is undefined in BCD coding because the first nibble (A) is outside the range of allowed BCD representations.

If the carry flag is set, the clock is not functioning and the return values should be ignored.

Int 1Ah   **Function 03h**

Set Real-Time Clock

Sets the time maintained by the real-time clock

Calling registers: AH   03h
                         CH   Hours (BCD)

581

CL	Minutes (BCD)
DH	Seconds (BCD)
DL	Daylight savings time (not supported in all BIOS versions)

Return registers: Nothing

Comments: *This function is available on only the PC XT 286, Personal Computer AT, or PS/2 line.* Clock values should be set in BCD (binary coded decimal). Each 4-bit nibble is interpreted as a single decimal digit; hexadecimal digits A through F are ignored. Table BIOS.35 shows the decimal values that correspond to the full range of hexadecimal values in a 4-bit nibble representing a BCD digit.

Register DL is coded to indicate whether the clock is keeping standard time (DL=0) or daylight savings time (DL=1). If the Personal Computer AT BIOS is dated before 6/10/85, the value in DL, which indicates the presence of the daylight savings time option, is not acted on and does not need to be set.

Int 1Ah   Function 04h

Read Date from Real-Time Clock

Returns the date maintained by the real-time clock

Calling registers: AH   04h

Return registers: Carry flag clear if successful

CH	Century (BCD)
CL	Year (BCD)
DH	Month (BCD)
DL	Day (BCD)

Carry flag set if error

Comments: This function, *available on only the PC XT 286, Personal Computer AT, and PS/2 line,* returns the clock values in BCD (binary coded decimal). Each 4-bit nibble is interpreted as a single decimal digit; hexadecimal digits A through F are ignored. Table BIOS.35 shows the decimal values that correspond to the full range of hexadecimal values in a 4-bit nibble representing a BCD digit.

If the carry flag is set, the clock is not functioning. Return values should be ignored.

Int 1Ah   Function 05h

Set Date of Real-Time Clock

Sets the date maintained by the real-time clock

Calling registers:

AH	05h
CH	Century (BCD) (19 or 20)
CL	Year (BCD)
DH	Month (BCD)
DL	Day (BCD)

Return registers: Nothing

Comments: *This function is available on only the PC XT 286, Personal Computer AT, or PS/2 line.* Clock values should be set in BCD (binary coded decimal). Each 4-bit nibble is interpreted as a single decimal digit; hexadecimal digits A through F are ignored. Table BIOS.35 shows the decimal values that correspond to the full range of hexadecimal values in a 4-bit nibble representing a BCD digit.

The values provided to the BIOS must be correct because no range checking is done on them. Incorrect values cause unpredictable settings of the clock.

Int 1Ah — Function 06h

Set System Alarm

Sets the system alarm timer to generate an interrupt at a future time

Calling registers:

AH	06h
CH	Hours (BCD)
CL	Minutes (BCD)
DH	Seconds (BCD)

Return registers: Carry flag clear if successful
Carry flag set if error

Comments: *This function is available on only the PC XT 286, Personal Computer AT, or PS/2 line.* The alarm settings must be in BCD (binary coded decimal). Each 4-bit nibble is interpreted as a single decimal digit; hexadecimal digits A through F are ignored. Table BIOS.35 shows the decimal values that correspond to the full range of hexadecimal values in a 4-bit nibble representing a BCD digit.

The alarm setting is an offset time from the present time. When the time runs out, the system triggers Int 04h (arithmetic overflow). The program that sets the alarm must check the validity of the values provided because BIOS does no checking. Before you reset an alarm, you must disable it with function 07h and set up an interrupt handler to deal with the alarm.

On return, a set carry flag indicates that an error has occurred. Either the alarm has been set previously without being disabled or the clock is not functioning.

Int 1Ah   Function 07h

Disable Real-Time Clock Alarm

Turns off the system alarm timer

Calling registers: AH   07h

Return registers: Nothing

Comments: This function, *available on only the PC XT, Personal Computer AT, or PS/2 line,* disables the real-time alarm clock. If you have already set the alarm, this function must be called before you can reset it.

Int 1Ah   Function 09h

Read Real-Time Clock Alarm

Returns the status of the system alarm timer

Calling registers: AH   09h

Return registers: CH   BCD hours
                         CL   BCD minutes
                         DH   BCD seconds
                         DL   Alarm status:
                                     0, not enabled
                                     1, enabled, no power on
                                     2, enabled, will power on system (Convertible only)

Comments: This function, *available on only the PC Convertible and the PS/2 Model 30,* reports the setting and status of the real-time alarm clock.

Int 1Ah   Function 0Ah

Get Day Count

Returns a count of the days since 01-01-1980

Calling registers: AH   0Ah

Return registers: CX   Total count of days since 01-01-1980

Comments: This function, *which is available on only the PC XT with BIOS dated 01/10/86 or later and on the PS/2 line,* returns in the CX register the total count of days since January 1, 1980.

Int 1Ah   Function 0Bh

Set Day Count

Sets the number of days since 01-01-1980

Calling registers: AH   0Ah
                         CX   Total count of days since 01-01-1980

Return registers: Nothing

Comments: This function, *available on only the PC XT with BIOS dated 01/10/86 or later and on the PS/2 line,* passes to the BIOS in the CX register the total count of days since January 1, 1980. This value is stored internally to maintain the system calendar; the effect is to change the calendar setting.

Int 1Ah   Function 80h

Set Sound Source

Selects a sound source to be used by the system

Calling registers: AH   80h
                         AL   Sound source:
                                     00h, 8253 chip, channel 2
                                     01h, cassette input
                                     02h, audio in line of I/O channel
                                     03h, sound generator chip

Return registers: Nothing

Comments: This function, *available on only the PC*jr, selects one of four sources for the internal sound system. No other computer in the PC line has this type of sound capabilities.

Int 1Bh

Ctrl-Break Address

Address of the Ctrl-Break interrupt handler

Calling registers: None

Return registers: Nothing

Comments: Interrupt vector 1Bh contains the address of the Ctrl-Break interrupt handler. Control is transferred to this address when a program is terminated by a Ctrl-Break key sequence. When the ROM BIOS finds the Ctrl-Break character during keyboard input, the BIOS calls the handler immediately. Because this process takes place during the character scan of the keyboard at the BIOS level, it is not guaranteed to be safe with respect to DOS. (See Chapter 11, "Interrupt Handlers," for a discussion of safe interrupt handling.)

During initialization, the ROM BIOS sets this vector to point to an IRET instruction. DOS resets the vector to point to a handler in DOS, which forces a Ctrl-C character into the keyboard buffer that DOS maintains (separate from the one maintained by the BIOS). DOS then discovers that Ctrl-C the next time it checks for one.

This makes the effects of both handlers identical but delays action on the Ctrl-Break keystroke until it is safe to do something. The Ctrl-C interrupt (Int 23h) is a DOS-level action and is not executed until DOS is in a "safe" position. Ctrl-Break, being handled at the ROM BIOS level, cannot tell whether DOS conditions are safe.

The simplest Ctrl-Break (or Ctrl-C) handler for a program points the interrupt to another IRET instruction so that the Ctrl-Break (or Ctrl-C) character is ignored. Then the program can process these characters as they arrive in the input stream.

Int 1Ch

Timer Tick Interrupt

Interrupt called by the system timer interrupts on each clock tick

Calling registers: None

Return registers: Nothing

Comments: Vector 1Ch, the timer tick interrupt called by Int 08h (System Metronome), is initialized to point to an IRET instruction. A TSR that needs to be triggered at each clock tick can reset the vector for this interrupt to point to a custom interrupt handler.

Because this function is called from inside the Int 08h code, before the handling of that top-priority action is completed, it shares the top priority and prevents the system from responding to any other hardware interrupt requests, including those from serial devices or disk units, while it executes. It is necessary, therefore, to keep to an absolute minimum the time spent in any handler for this function or you risk the loss of data when time-sensitive applications are running.

The best practice for a TSR is merely to set a flag from this function and then inspect the flag from another handler hooked into the Int 28h (DosOK) chain, which has ample time to take care of any necessary processing without blocking hardware interrupts.

Int 1Dh

Video-Initialization Parameter Table

Pointer to a parameter table used for video controller initialization

Calling registers: None

Return registers: Nothing

Comments: Int 1Dh (which is not a true interrupt) points to a table of initialization parameters for the video controller. Because Int 1Dh is *not* executable code, this interrupt should not be called by a program. The results of an attempt to execute code at this interrupt are unpredictable—most likely a system lockup.

Int 1Eh

Disk-Initialization Parameter Table

Pointer to a diskette base table used for disk controller initialization

Calling registers: None

Return registers: Nothing

Comments: Int 1Eh (which is not a true interrupt) points to the diskette base table, a table of initialization parameters for the disk controller. Because Int 1Eh is *not* executable code, this interrupt should not be called by a program. The results of an attempt to execute code at this interrupt are unpredictable—most likely a system lockup.

Although this table can be modified to optimize disk accesses and tune a system, *any modification should be done with extreme care because the procedure can destroy anything and everything you have stored on disk.*

Int 1Fh

Graphics Display Character Bit-Map Table

Pointer to a bit-map table used for video character generation

Calling registers: None

Return registers: Nothing

Comments: Int 1Fh (which is not a true interrupt) points to a table of character bit maps for the graphics mode representations of ASCII characters 128 to 255. Because Int 1Fh is *not* executable code, this interrupt should not be called by a program. The results of an attempt to execute code at this interrupt are unpredictable—most likely a system lockup.

The bit-map table contains 128 characters (a total area of 1K) and is simply constructed. Each entry is eight bytes long and represents one 8-by-8 character. Each byte corresponds to one scan line in the character.

The following sample character represents an uppercase *I*—the coding includes a blank scan line at the top and bottom, one scan line apiece for the top and bottom bars, and four scan lines for the central vertical bar:

```
  1 2 3 4 5 6 7 8

1 0 0 0 0 0 0 0 0

2 0 1 1 1 1 1 1 0

3 0 0 0 1 1 0 0 0

4 0 0 0 1 1 0 0 0

5 0 0 0 1 1 0 0 0

6 0 0 0 1 1 0 0 0

7 0 1 1 1 1 1 1 0

8 0 0 0 0 0 0 0 0
```

Byte string: 00h, 7Eh, 14h, 14h, 14h, 14h, 7Eh, 00h

By resetting the pointer, you can create your own characters for use in CGA graphics modes.

Int 4Ah

Real-Time Clock Alarm Interrupt

Called when a real-time clock alarm occurs

Calling registers: None

Return registers: Nothing

Comments: *This function applies to only Personal Computer AT, PC XT 286, and PS/2 product lines.* When you set a real-time clock alarm (see Int 1Ah, Function 06h) and the specified time is encountered, an alarm is generated and this interrupt is invoked. You can provide a routine to be executed by the alarm by intercepting this interrupt.

If you use this interrupt, you must be sure to reset it to its original vector before returning to DOS.

Int 70h

Real-Time Clock Interrupt

Called 1,024 times per second to control periodic and alarm functions

Calling registers: None

Return registers: Nothing

Comments: *This function applies to only Personal Computer AT, PC XT 286, and PS/2 product lines.* (The periodic function is not included on the PS/2 Model 30.)

The real-time clock interrupt is called nearly 1,024 times per second. Whenever the interrupt is called, a double-word counter is decremented by 976 microseconds (1/1024 of a second). The initial value of this counter is set by calls to Int 15h, Function 83h (Event Wait) or Function 86h (Delay) as part of the call. When the counter reaches a value less than or equal to zero, bit 7 of the designated wait flag is set. For Function 83h, the wait flag is specified by the ES:BX register pointer. For Function 86h, the flag is at BIOS data area location 0040:00A0h (Delay Active Flag).

If the real-time clock is activated as an alarm function by a call to Int 1Ah, Function 06h, when the time runs out, Int 4Ah is called by Int 70h to activate the alarm handler. (The alarm handler must be set up before issuing the call to Int 1Ah.)

589

DOS Reference

This section covers services offered by DOS. These services are interrupts in the range of 20–2Fh and include many functions that are important for proper program execution. Separate reference sections cover the use of Int 33h for mouse functions and Int 67h for expanded memory management, in addition to DOS extenders, extended memory management, and DOS task-switching.

Before getting into the specifics of the DOS services, you should understand a few concepts so that you can have a solid understanding of how the services are used.

How DOS Services Are Invoked

DOS services are invoked in much the same manner as the BIOS services—through the use of software interrupts. How interrupts are directly executed depends on the programming language you are using and, in many cases, on the dialect or implementation of that language. Examples throughout this book are in different languages, such as assembler, BASIC, C, and Pascal.

If the DOS interrupt is used for many different functions, the desired function number is loaded in the AH register before the interrupt is called. This procedure may be modified if the same function number is used for several different subfunctions. In this case, the subfunction number is loaded into the AL register before the interrupt is called.

In addition to the interrupt, function, and subfunction numbers, each DOS service generally requires specific parameters. These parameters usually are provided through the use of CPU registers. Their use varies depending on the needs of the DOS service and even on the version of DOS in use.

To recap — in order to use DOS services successfully, you must follow these general steps:

1. Load the necessary registers with the proper parameters for the DOS service.

2. If the DOS interrupt is used for multiple functions, load AH with the proper function number.

3. If the DOS function is used for multiple subfunctions, load AL with the proper subfunction number.

4. Invoke the DOS interrupt.

5. Examine any returned values for validity and use.

Reentrancy

Because DOS was designed as a single-user, single-task system, DOS services are not reentrant. This means that DOS services cannot be called from within other DOS services without running the risk of really mucking things up. For example, if you have developed an interrupt-driven, whiz-bang system and have installed it as a terminate-and-stay-resident (TSR) utility, it is possible that, while one interrupt is being handled by your software, another interrupt of the same nature can occur. What do you do? If DOS were reentrant, you could process merrily away and handle each interrupt as it occurred. This is not possible, however, because DOS is not reentrant. Figure DOS.1 illustrates the possible consequences of this type of action.

Notice that, at step D, while a DOS command was already in progress, a new interrupt was sensed that began the handler process over again. The handling of that interrupt was completed with the execution of step I, and control was returned to the original point in the first iteration of the DOS command (step J). At this point, however, all the DOS variables and stack positions previously in use during step C have been changed by steps F and G. The result is predictable: Your program loses control of the system, which has locked up in trying to return to the point from which DOS originally was called (at step B) but actually going back to the second call point (at step E).

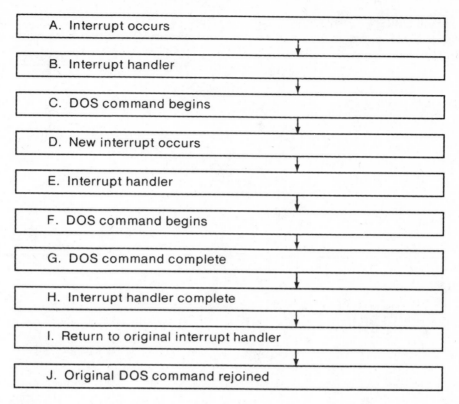

Figure DOS. 1 The effects of nonreentrancy in DOS.

Reserved Functions

The functions listed in Table DOS.1 are considered reserved by IBM and Microsoft. According to Tim Paterson (the author of MS-DOS's immediate ancestor, 86-DOS), the first four functions were included in 86-DOS specifically for compatibility with the older CP/M operating system, but IBM chose not to document them in its original DOS version. The functions have survived to provide backward compatibility to V1. These functions, which are invoked through Int 21h, are not included in the DOS service reference listings later in this section. The reason for the existence of Function 61h is not known, but it uses the same two-instruction code sequence as do the older four.

Table DOS.1 Reserved Functions

Int	Function
21h	18h
	1Dh
	1Eh
	20h
	61h
2Bh	
2Ch	
2Dh	

Undocumented Functions

Other functions undocumented by IBM or Microsoft, but whose meaning and use have been documented by programmers over time, are listed in Table DOS.2. Many times, the function's meaning and use have been accrued by tedious trial-and-error and poring over code listings. The functions are presented here and later in the DOS service reference listings for your information. Keep in mind that, because the functions are officially undocumented, IBM, Microsoft, or other DOS vendors may change them at any time without notice. You should test their operation on your system and verify that the same results are returned for your particular applications. See also Appendix D, "The Reserved DOS Functions," which presents additional information about the undocumented and reserved functions.

Table DOS.2 Undocumented Interrupts and Functions

Int	Function	Purpose
21h	37h	Get/set switchchar
	52h	Get disk list
	53h	Translate BPB
	55h	Create PSP
	5Dh	Get critical-error flag address
	60h	Expand to full path name

Int	Function	Purpose
29h		Fast putchar
2Eh		Execute command

Later in this section, as each reserved function is presented, you will notice the "stop sign" icon beside the function. This icon indicates that extreme caution should be used with the function that is presented. No other warning about the function is provided.

DOS Services

If you have any question about how the functions in this section are presented, refer to the "Reference Overview" section of this book.

Int 20h V1

Terminate Program

Terminates a program's operation and returns control to the process that spawned the program, normally COMMAND.COM

Calling registers: None

Return registers: None

Comments: Old DOS hands will recognize this function because it was the standard way to terminate programs on DOS V1. It performs the same basic operations as those provided by Function 00h. With the introduction of DOS Functions 4Ch and 31h, this is no longer the recommended way to terminate a program unless it must maintain compatibility with DOS V1 systems. The newer functions allow exit codes to be returned from higher-level programs or batch files. The newer versions of DOS handle the Int 20h action by converting it to a call to Int 21h with AX set to 4C00h. On those systems, therefore, this interrupt results in an exit code of 00h.

Microsoft recommends that this function no longer be used, unless it is needed to maintain older software. Support for this function may end at any time. Function 4Ch should be used instead.

In addition to terminating the program and freeing the memory space occupied by the program, this interrupt does the following:

- Restores the termination-handler vector from the program segment prefix (offset 0Ah)

- Restores the Ctrl-C vector from the program segment prefix (offset 0Eh)

- In V2 and higher, restores the critical-error handler vector from the program segment prefix (offset 12h)

- Flushes to disk the file buffers used by DOS itself (*not* those within any programs)

- Frees any memory owned by the terminating program

Item 3 is not performed by versions of DOS before V2. After these items are completed, system control is transferred to the termination-handler address as restored in item 1.

Although this process sounds complete, it is not complete enough if you are using file control block (FCB) file-handling functions. With FCB functions, the files are not closed by use of this command. Even though the information in the buffers that DOS keeps for itself is written to the disk (they have been flushed), the directory information is *not* updated to reflect changes to the file, nor is there any guarantee that file buffers inside an application have been flushed. Only the close file function for FCBs (Function 10h) properly closes the file, updates the directory, and frees the buffer space for use by other programs. As a result, and to practice good programming style, you should explicitly close any open files before using this program-termination function.

EXE programs calling this function must take extra care because the CS register must point to the segment the program segment prefix (PSP) is in. With COM programs, this is usually the case, but there is no such assurance with EXE programs. In most cases, this is not a problem, and a call without explicitly setting the CS register will work.

On completion of the program-termination function, system control is returned to the parent program that invoked the recently terminated child with the EXEC function (DOS Function 4Bh). Normally, this parent is COMMAND.COM, but it can be any other program. If returning to DOS, control is passed to the resident portion of COMMAND.COM, where a memory test is performed to determine whether the transient section needs to be reloaded. If this checksum test fails, the transient portion is reloaded. Finally, if a batch file is in progress, the next line of the batch file is retrieved and executed.

Int 21h   **Function 00h**   **V1**

Terminate Program

Terminates a program and returns control to the process that spawned the program

Calling registers: AH   00h

                 CS   PSP segment address

Return registers: None

Comments: This function is operationally identical to Int 20h. Refer to the "Comments" section of the Int 20h description for more information.

Int 21h   **Function 01h**   **V1**

Keyboard Input with Echo

Reads a character from the keyboard (STDIN beginning with DOS V2) and echoes the character to the video display (STDOUT beginning with DOS V2)

Calling registers: AH   01h

Return registers: AL   8-bit data

Comments: This is the simplest method of keyboard input that programmers are likely to use. The function simply waits for a character to be entered from the keyboard, echoes the character to the video display, and returns it to the program.

With DOS V1, it was this simple: The function retrieved characters only from the keyboard and displayed them only on the video display. Starting with DOS V2, however, the process was complicated by the introduction of redirection. Now a character is retrieved from the standard input device (STDIN) and displayed on the standard output device (STDOUT). Normally, STDIN is the keyboard and STDOUT is the video display, but these can be redirected by the user.

If no character is available at STDIN, this function waits until one is available. If STDIN has been redirected to a device other than the keyboard, this can cause problems if the input is variable or sporadic. When you are working with the keyboard, however, this method of operation is reasonable and usually desirable.

When a character is available and has been displayed, its ASCII value is returned. If the character is an extended ASCII character, a zero is returned, and another call to this function is required to return the scan code of the key pressed. The extended ASCII codes are detailed in Appendix A, "The ASCII Character Set."

When STDIN and STDOUT are redirected, problems can occur when you are using this function:

- If input is coming from a file, a zero byte that does not correspond to an extended keyboard code may be returned.

- The function cannot detect the end of a file in DOS versions before V4. With V4, a fatal error (Out of Data) is reported at the end of file when input is redirected.

These considerations may cause significant problems when STDIN has been redirected so that input is retrieved from a file. Because of this, you may want to use a different DOS input function: 06h, 07h, 08h, or 3Fh (when you are using handle 0, STDIN).

When you use this function, pressing Ctrl-C or Ctrl-Break causes Int 23h to be invoked before returning from the function.

Like all DOS keyboard input functions that perform Ctrl-C checks, this function can be misled by certain Alt-key input combinations (those that return a scan code with a bit pattern DOS misinterprets, and responds to, as being Ctrl-Q, Ctrl-S, or Ctrl-P; these keys are, respectively, Alt-W, Alt-R, and Alt-Q).

Microsoft recommends that this function no longer be used, unless it is needed to maintain older software. Support for this function may end at any time. Function 3Fh should be used instead.

Int 21h   Function 02h   V1
Display Output

Outputs a character to the video display (STDOUT beginning with DOS V2.0)

Calling registers: AH   02h
                         DL   8-bit character data

Return registers: None

Comments: Like most of the other low-numbered I/O functions accessed through Int 21h, this function's use depends on the version of DOS being used. Under DOS V1, this function directs output to only the video display. Beginning with DOS V2, output is directed to the standard output device (STDOUT), which defaults to the video display.

The system properly handles a backspace character as a nondestructive backspace on the screen. Ctrl-C and Ctrl-Break are also handled (through Int 23h) if either is detected during the operation.

If output is redirected by the user, this function can cause problems. If output is sent to a file, a disk error can "hang" your system because there is no intrinsic method (before V4) for this function to sense or handle disk errors. (V4 introduced improved error handling that can force a fatal error termination of your program.) Notice that there are no return values for this function, and therefore no way to indicate an error while attempting to output a character. Because of this consideration, you may want to use a different DOS output function, such as Function 40h, by using the predefined handle 1 (STDOUT).

Microsoft recommends that you no longer use this function, unless it is needed to maintain older software. Support for this function may end at any time. Function 40h should be used instead.

Int 21h   Function 03h   V1
Auxiliary Input

Reads a character from the first serial port (STDAUX beginning with DOS V2)

Calling registers: AH   03h

Return registers: AL   8-bit input data from STDAUX

Comments: Unlike the keyboard, a serial device is unbuffered, which means that it handles characters one at a time as they are available. If characters become available faster than they can be handled by your software, they are lost. This function retrieves a character from the serial port. If no character is available, the function waits until one is available before returning.

Beginning with DOS V2, this function retrieves characters from the standard auxiliary device (STDAUX), which defaults to COM1. Under IBM's version of DOS, COM1 has a default initialization of 2400 bps, 8 data bits, no parity, and 1 stop bit. The DOS MODE command can be used to redirect STDAUX, and the data format settings can be changed either with BIOS functions (see Chapter 7, "Serial Devices," and the BIOS Reference) or directly at a hardware level. A discussion of the latter method is beyond the scope of this book.

Unfortunately, there is no access to information about the status of the serial port through this DOS function. You cannot tell whether a character is waiting or has been lost, nor can you set the parameters for the port. This is a major flaw in a system with serial devices. To do anything serious with serial ports, you must go at least to the BIOS level and generally to the hardware level with custom interrupt-handling software to run the port.

Ctrl-C and Ctrl-Break processing is enabled during this function. If either Ctrl-C or Ctrl-Break is detected, Int 23h is executed immediately.

In addition to this function, you can also use Function 3Fh with the predefined handle 3 (STDAUX) to read information from the serial port.

Microsoft recommends that you no longer use this function, unless it is needed to maintain older software. Support for this function may end at any time. Function 3Fh should be used instead.

Int 21h	Function 04h	V1
	Auxiliary Output	

Outputs a character to the first serial port (STDAUX beginning with DOS V2)

Calling registers: AH   04h
                        DL   8-bit data to output to STDAUX

Return registers: None

Comments: This function is used to send a character out the serial port. Beginning with DOS V2, output is directed to the standard auxiliary device (STDAUX), which defaults to the first serial port. IBM's version of DOS initializes COM1 as the default STDAUX at 2400 bps, 8 data bits, no parity, and 1 stop bit. Although other versions of DOS can differ in the default data format, all should default to COM1 as the standard auxiliary device.

If the STDAUX device is not free when output is attempted, this function waits until it is. "Hanging" the computer is relatively easy, therefore, if this function is invoked while STDAUX is not available. A more useful function would return information about the status of the serial port. This function now is of limited value to serious programmers. To do anything serious with

DOS
PROGRAMMING

serial ports, you must go at least to the BIOS level and generally to the hardware level with custom interrupt-handling software to run the port.

Fortunately, Ctrl-C and Ctrl-Break processing is enabled during this call. On detection of either a Ctrl-C or Ctrl-Break, Int 23h is invoked. By intercepting the Ctrl-Break handler, it may be possible to recover from a "hung" computer that is waiting for a serial port which will never be available. This process, however, is unwieldy and cumbersome. It is better (and more user friendly) to program other methods of controlling the serial port.

As with other DOS device control functions, you can send a character out STDAUX by using DOS Function 40h with the predefined handle 3 (STDAUX).

Microsoft recommends that you no longer use this function, unless it is needed to maintain older software. Support for this function may end at any time. Function 40h should be used instead.

Int 21h	Function 05h	V1
	Printer Output	

Outputs a character to the printer (STDPRN beginning with DOS V2)

Calling registers: AH   05h
                         DL   8-bit data to print to STDPRN

Return registers: None

Comments: This function waits until the printer is ready and then sends a byte. Because no printer-status information is returned, the computer could "hang" while waiting for a printer that is not attached to the system or not ready. You can achieve more satisfactory results with the BIOS printer functions (Int 17h) or through DOS Function 40h by using the predefined handle 04.

Ctrl-C and Ctrl-Break are detected during this function and cause the execution of Int 23h.

Microsoft recommends that you no longer use this function, unless it is needed to maintain older software. Support for this function may end at any time. Function 40h should be used instead.

Int 21h	Function 06h	V1
	Direct Console I/O	

Reads and writes the console without processing by DOS

Calling registers: AH   06h
                         DL   Function requested
                                 00h through 0FEh, character to output
                                 0FFh, input character request

Return registers: If outputting a character, nothing is returned
If inputting a character:

Zero flag set (ZF = 1) if no character is available
Zero flag cleared (ZF = 0) if character is available
AL   8-bit data

Comments: This function is unique in that it inputs or outputs characters depending on the setting of the DL register. Because FFh in the DL register says "input," this function clearly cannot be used to output an FFh character—not a major limitation but, in some cases, significant.

If not being able to output all possible ASCII codes is a drawback for your application, you can accomplish the same type of input and output by using DOS Functions 3Fh and 40h with pre-defined handles 1 (STDIN) and 2 (STDOUT).

This function is sometimes referred to as the *raw* I/O function: It reads characters without echo and ignores Ctrl-C and Ctrl-Break characters, and then passes them to the program rather than branching to an interrupt handler. Editing, word processing, and other programs that need complete keyboard control because they have to interpret all keystrokes generally use this function. (The opposite of raw I/O is *cooked* I/O; these terms come from the UNIX terminal-handler world, where they have specific meanings. See Chapter 12, "Device Drivers," for a discussion of raw and cooked I/O as it relates to character-oriented device drivers.)

As with Function 01h, the codes returned from the keyboard are ASCII codes, except when there is no corresponding ASCII code for the key pressed. If this function returns a zero in AL, calling the function again returns the scan code corresponding to the key that is pressed. See Appendix A, "The ASCII Character Set," for extended ASCII code information. This DOS function is the only one that properly reads certain Alt-key input combinations (those that return as the scan code a bit pattern DOS misinterprets, and responds to, as being Ctrl-Q, Ctrl-S, or Ctrl-P; these keys are, respectively, Alt-W, Alt-R, and Alt-Q).

Int 21h	Function 07h	V1
	Direct STDIN Input	

Reads a character from the standard input device (STDIN) without Ctrl-C intercepting

Calling registers: AH   07h

Return registers: AL   8-bit input data

Comments: This function handles input similarly to Function 01h, except that the character is not echoed to the video display, and no Ctrl-C or Ctrl-Break handling is supported. On DOS V1 systems, a character is read only from the keyboard. If no character is ready, it waits for one to become available. On DOS V2 and higher, the function reads from the standard input device (STDIN) and therefore supports redirection.

When a character is available, its ASCII value is returned. If the character is an extended ASCII character, a zero is returned and another call to this function is required to return the scan code of the key pressed. The extended ASCII codes are detailed in Appendix A, "The ASCII Character Set."

This function does not echo characters to the display screen, allowing the program to control this function as necessary. As with direct I/O (Function 06h), this function ignores Ctrl-C and Ctrl-Break characters. If Ctrl-C or Ctrl-Break intervention is required, use Function 08h.

Int 21h	Function 08h	V1
	STDIN Input	

Reads a character from the standard input device (STDIN)

Calling registers: AH   08h

Return registers: AL   8-bit input data

Comments: This function handles input like other DOS input functions. It is most similar to Function 07h, except that Ctrl-C and Ctrl-Break interception is supported.

On DOS V1 systems, a character is read only from the keyboard. If no character is ready, the function waits for one. On DOS V2 and higher, the function reads from the standard input device (STDIN) and therefore supports redirection.

When a character is available, its ASCII value is returned. If the character is an extended ASCII character, a zero is returned and another call to this function is required to return the scan code of the key pressed. The extended ASCII codes are detailed in Appendix A, "The ASCII Character Set."

This function does not echo characters to the display screen, allowing the program to control this function as necessary. If either Ctrl-C or Ctrl-Break is detected, an Int 23h is executed.

Like all DOS keyboard input functions that perform Ctrl-C checks, this function can be misled by certain Alt-key input combinations (those that return as the scan code a bit pattern DOS misinterprets, and responds to, as being Ctrl-Q, Ctrl-S, or Ctrl-P; these keys are, respectively, Alt-W, Alt-R, and Alt-Q).

Int 21h	Function 09h	V1
	Display String	

Outputs a string of characters to the standard output device (STDOUT)

Calling registers: AH   09h
                        DS:DX   Pointer to string terminated by a dollar sign ($, ASCII code 24h)

Return registers: None

Comments: The display of strings of characters on the screen is such a normal operation that it would seem strange if a function were not provided for this purpose. Function 09h allows string output operations by outputting a contiguous series of characters in the same way that Function 02h displays single characters. All characters beginning at the specified address are output until a dollar sign ($, ASCII code 24h) is encountered.

The strings handled by this function are unlike strings handled by any high-level language; they must be terminated by a dollar sign. C functions terminate strings with a NUL character, and Pascal and BASIC strings have a length byte (or word). Because of the choice of string terminator, which is a carryover from CP/M days, you cannot output a dollar sign with this function. This severely limits the usefulness of this function in applications programs. Better results generally are achieved by using one of the other DOS output functions to write an efficient string-output routine matched to your high-level language requirements.

Microsoft recommends that you no longer use this function, unless it is needed to maintain older software. Support for this function may end at any time. Function 40h should be used instead.

Int 21h	Function 0Ah	V1
	Buffered STDIN Input	

Reads characters from the standard input device (STDIN) and places them in a user-specified buffer

Calling registers:

AH	0Ah
DS:DX	Pointer to input buffer
Byte 0	Number of bytes the buffer can hold
Byte 1	Number of bytes read
Byte 2–?	Returned characters

Return registers: None

Comments: Buffered STDIN input is a useful, commonly used function that gives you the full power of the normal input functions for keyboard handling. Input is taken from STDIN, which defaults to the keyboard, and is placed in a user-defined buffer area. The keyboard input buffer, which must be specified from the calling program, is set up as follows:

Byte Offset	Contents
0	Maximum number of bytes to read
1	Number of bytes read
2–?	Actual bytes from the keyboard

To use this function, simply store the number of bytes allowed for input in the first byte of the buffer pointed to by DS:DX. Because the buffer size must allow space for a terminating carriage return (ASCII 0Dh), the minimum buffer size is necessarily 1. In use, this would not allow for any actual keyboard input because the 1 byte set aside for the buffer would be used by the terminating carriage return—not very useful. The realistic minimum buffer size is 2 bytes (1 byte of input plus the carriage return). The maximum buffer size is 255, which is logical because the buffer length specifier is only a single byte.

The function reads in characters from the keyboard and places them in the buffer, beginning with the third byte of the buffer. Every ASCII character requires one byte of buffer space. When the actual number of characters read reaches one less than the size of the buffer, new characters are ignored and the bell rings with every keystroke. When the Enter key is finally pressed, the number of bytes retrieved and stored is placed in the second byte of the buffer, and control is returned to the calling program.

The input itself allows type-ahead, and all keyboard editing commands are active. Ctrl-C and Ctrl-Break functions are active also, which results in the execution of Int 23h.

Notice that the size of the string is determined by the value returned in the length byte. This length does not include the terminating carriage return.

Like all DOS keyboard input functions that perform Ctrl-C checks, this function can be misled by certain Alt-key input combinations (those that return as the scan code a bit pattern DOS misinterprets, and responds to, as being Ctrl-Q, Ctrl-S, or Ctrl-P; these keys are, respectively, Alt-W, Alt-R, and Alt-Q).

Microsoft recommends that you no longer use this function, unless it is needed to maintain older software. Support for this function may end at any time. Function 3Fh should be used instead.

Int 21h	Function 0Bh	V1
	Check STDIN Status	

Checks whether a character is available from the standard input device (STDIN)

Calling registers: AH   0Bh

Return registers: AL   FFh, character available from STDIN
                                  00h, character not available from STDIN (before V4)
                                  < > FFh, character not available from STDIN (V4)

Comments: This function checks whether a character is available from STDIN. Because STDIN normally is set to the keyboard, this function ordinarily is used to determine whether a keystroke is waiting in the keyboard buffer.

When this function is called, it returns immediately with a status in register AL indicating whether a character is waiting to be read. If a character is available, AL contains FFh. Notice that the actual character is not returned by this function, which merely provides an indication of availability. This function continues to return the same status on successive calls until one of the DOS input functions (01h, 06h, 07h, 08h, or 0Ah) is used to read the character.

If a Ctrl-C or Ctrl-Break is detected during the execution of this function, an Int 23 is invoked.

Int 21h   Function 0Ch   V1

Clear Buffer and Input

Clears the standard input device (STDIN) buffer and then executes the designated input function call

Calling registers:	AH	0Ch
	AL	Function number to perform after clearing the buffer
		01h, wait for keyboard input
		06h, direct console I/O
		DL = FFh, direct console input
		DL < > FFh, char to write to STDOUT
		07h, direct console input without echo
		08h, console input without echo
Return registers:	Return defined by function:	
		01h, wait for keyboard input
	AL	Character from STDIN
		06h, direct console I/O
	ZF	1, no character available from STDIN
	ZF	0, AL = character from STDIN
		07h, direct console input without echo
	AL	Character from STDIN
		08h, console input without echo
	AL	Character from STDIN

Comments: This function is provided to enable the programmer to prevent type-ahead mistakes, which often occur during program operation. It prevents a user from accidentally typing past critical program input points. A good example might be a program that formats a disk. You want to ask the user whether he or she really wants to format the disk, because starting the operation destroys the disk. By using this function, you can prevent problems caused by accidental type-ahead.

This is an alternative entry point for earlier DOS input functions: 01h, 06h, 07h, and 08h. The function's only operation is to clear the input buffer; then control is passed to the DOS input function requested in AL. Return values and programming considerations of each of the available DOS input functions apply when you are using this function.

Microsoft now states that Subfunction 0AH is reserved and should not be used.

Int 21h   **Function 0Dh**   **V1**

Reset Disk

Flushes all disk-buffer contents (if modified) to the appropriate disk files

Calling registers: AH   0Dh

Return registers: None

Comments: This function writes the contents of the disk buffers to their corresponding disk files (flushes the disk buffers). It does not update the disk directory and should not be used in place of a file-close operation. No other disk operations are affected, nor are any other disk parameters reset.

On a 3Com network, this function forces a new copy of the network volume file allocation table (FAT) to be loaded into memory when all files are closed.

Int 21h   **Function 0Eh**   **V1**

Select Disk

Changes the default disk drive

Calling registers: AH   0Eh
                         DL   Drive number (A = 0 through Z = 25)

Return registers: AL   Number of logical drives

Comments: In addition to selecting the default drive, this function can be used to determine the number of logical drives associated with the system. Logical drives are block-oriented devices — RAM disks, hard disks, disk emulators, and so forth — installed on the system.

This function always returns a minimum value of 2, indicating the presence of two logical drives (DOS always views a single, physical, floppy disk drive as two logical drives, A and B). If you want to determine the number of physical floppy disk drives attached to the system, use BIOS Function 11h.

Beginning with DOS V3, this function returns a minimum last drive value equal to the number of logical drives or the LASTDRIVE value from the CONFIG.SYS file, whichever is greater. If there are only three logical drives and CONFIG.SYS does not specify a LASTDRIVE value, the default LASTDRIVE value of 5 is returned.

The value returned does not necessarily map to a drive letter; a return value of 5, for example, does not mean that there are A, B, C, D, and E drives.

The maximum number of drive designators has varied from one DOS version to another, as shown in the following table:

DOS Version	Available Designators
1	16 (00 – 0Fh)
2	63 (00 – 3Fh)
3	26 (00 – 19h)

When compatibility with all versions of DOS is required, applications should be limited to a maximum of 16 drives (the maximum number allowed for DOS V1). Those needing compatibility with only V2 and higher should be limited to 26. In most cases, the number used is much smaller.

Notice a peculiarity of this function: The value returned in AL is one-based and represents the number of disk drives attached to the system, but the value used to call the function is zero-based and represents the desired default disk drive. If you want, therefore, to set the default drive to the last logical drive, you must complete the following steps:

1. Determine the current default drive (use Function 19h).

2. Call this function with DL set to the current default drive retrieved from step 1.

3. Decrement the value returned from step 2 (make it zero-based).

4. Call this function with the derived value from step 3.

Int 21h	Function 0Fh	V1
	Open File (FCB)	

Searches the current directory for the named file; if the named file is found, it is opened and the file control block (FCB) is filled in

Calling registers: AH   0Fh
                           DS:DX   Pointer to unopened FCB

Return registers: AL   00h, file opened successfully
                                     FFh, file not opened

Comments: This function is used to open an existing disk file that uses an FCB. This function does not create a file; that operation is left to Function 16h. Chapter 9, "Directories and Files," discusses files and explains FCBs in more detail. The open function is called after filling in the drive, file name, and extension fields of the FCB.

You should note that the proper drive designations are 0 for the default drive, 1 for A, 2 for B, and so on. If the function is called with the drive field set for the default drive (0), the field value is automatically changed to the correct drive number so that subsequent calls to the file remain correct even if the default drive is changed. In addition, the function sets the FCB block field

607

to zero; the record size to 80h (128-character record length); and the file size, date, and time from the requested file's directory entry. If your file operations require the use of a different block number or record size, these values should be changed after this function is completed but before any other FCB file operations.

For applications operating in a network environment, it is important to note that this function automatically opens a file in compatibility mode. If a different mode is required, the handle operations should be used. If a file was created in a different mode and is subsequently opened in compatibility mode (as with this function), a DOS critical error is generated and Int 24h is executed.

As with other FCB file operations, an error is indicated by the status code returned in the AL register. If AL is 0, no error was detected; if AL is FFh, there was an error during the operation.

Microsoft recommends that you no longer use this function, unless it is needed to maintain older software. Support for this function may end at any time. Function 3Dh should be used instead.

Int 21h	Function 10h	V1
	Close File (FCB)	

Closes a previously opened file that uses a file control block (FCB)

Calling registers: AH   10h
                          DS:DX   Pointer to opened FCB

Return registers: AL   00h, file closed successfully
                                      FFh, file not closed

Comments: This function is used to close a previously opened disk file that uses an FCB. The close function is essential to proper operation in FCB files because there is no other way to force DOS to update the file's directory entry. Without properly closing a file, data can be lost. Chapter 9, "Directories and Files," discusses files and explains FCBs in more detail.

To use the function, you must provide information in the FCB's file-name, extension, and drive-designator fields. If you are working with a previously opened file, all this information should already be in place.

A feature of the close command is that the system checks for the position of the file within the directory. If it is not the same, the system is supposed to assume that the disk has changed, and AL will have an FFh character on return. It has been documented that this function does not work as advertised on DOS V2. It does, in fact, overwrite the file allocation table (FAT) and directory, thereby damaging the new disk.

As with other FCB file operations, an error is indicated by the status code returned in the AL register. If AL is 0, no error was detected; if it is FFh, there was an error during the operation. For V3 and higher, Get Extended Error (Function 59h) may be used to determine the exact error if one is reported.

Microsoft recommends that you no longer use this function, unless it is needed to maintain older software. Support for this function may end at any time. Function 3Eh should be used instead.

Int 21h	Function 11h	V1
	Search for First Entry (FCB)	

Searches for the first matching entry in the current directory

Calling registers: AH   11h
                                DS:DX   Pointer to unopened FCB

Return registers: AL   00h, match was found
                                        FFh, no match was found

Comments: This function is used to search for the first occurrence of a specified directory entry that uses a file control block (FCB). Chapter 9, "Directories and Files," explains FCBs in detail. This function is powerful and makes it easy to look for files in a consistent way without damaging the directory structure.

To use this function, you must provide the file name, extension, and drive designators in the appropriate FCB fields. Beginning with DOS V2.1, the question mark (?) is supported as a wild-card character in file-name specifications. Asterisks (*) are allowed as wild cards only under DOS V3 and higher.

To search for a file with a specific attribute, you must use an extended FCB (see Chapter 9). Valid attributes are derived from the various attribute bit settings and include the following:

Value	File Types Matched
00h	Normal
02h	Normal and hidden
04h	Normal and system
06h	Normal, hidden, and system
08h	Volume labels
10h	Directories

When the function completes successfully, the disk transfer area (DTA) holds an unopened FCB for the file that was found. If the search is called with an extended FCB, the DTA has an extended FCB; otherwise, it has a normal FCB. For more information about the DTA, refer to Chapter 9 and Function 1Ah.

609

As with other FCB file operations, an error is indicated by the status code returned in the AL register. If AL is 0, no error was detected; if AL is FFh, there was an error during the operation. For V3 and higher, Get Extended Error (Function 59h) can be used to determine the exact error if one is reported.

If you are using wild-card characters to search for files and no error was returned from this function, you can continue the search for the next matching file by using Function 12h.

Microsoft recommends that you no longer use this function, unless it is needed to maintain older software. Support for this function may end at any time. Function 4Eh should be used instead.

Int 21h	Function 12h	V1
	Search for Next Entry (FCB)	

Searches for the next matching entry in the current directory

Calling registers: AH   12h
                               DS:DX   Pointer to FCB returned by either Function 11h or 12h

Return registers: AL   00h, match was found
                                       FFh, no match was found

Comments: This function, which continues a search begun with Function 11h, can be called as many times as necessary to locate a given file specification in a directory; it searches only for the next matching entry, however, not for the first entry. See Function 11h for more information.

Clearly, this function is of value only if the directory entry being searched uses wild-card characters. The file control block (FCB) pointed to by DS:DX should be the same FCB pointed to when Function 11h was called. Again, see the Function 11h comments for more information.

When this function completes successfully, the disk transfer area (DTA) holds an unopened FCB for the file that was found. If the search originally was initiated with an extended FCB, the DTA has an extended FCB; otherwise, it has a normal FCB. For more information about the DTA, refer to Chapter 9, "Directories and Files," and Function 1Ah.

As with other FCB file operations, an error is indicated by the status code returned in the AL register. If AL is 0, no error was detected; if AL is FFh, there was an error during the operation. For V3 and higher, Get Extended Error (Function 59h) can be used to determine the exact error if one is reported.

If you are using wild-card characters to search for files and no error was returned from this function, you can continue the search for the next matching file by using this function again.

Microsoft recommends that you no longer use this function, unless it is needed to maintain older software. Support for this function may end at any time. Function 4Fh should be used instead.

Int 21h   **Function 13h**   **V1**

Delete File (FCB)

Deletes all allowable directory entries that match the file specifications provided

Calling registers: AH   13h

                                DS:DX   Pointer to an unopened FCB

Return registers: AL   00h, file was deleted

                                                     FFh, file was not deleted

Comments: This function is used to delete files through a file control block (FCB). Chapter 9, "Directories and Files," discusses files and explains FCBs in more detail. Only normal files can be deleted. Read-only files, system files, hidden files, volume labels, or directories cannot be deleted with this function.

To use this function, you must provide the file name, extension, and drive designators in the appropriate FCB fields. Beginning with DOS V2.1, the question mark (?) is supported as a wild-card character in file-name specifications. Asterisks (*) are allowed as wild cards only if you are running under DOS V3 or above.

Files deleted with this function are not cleared from the disk. The directory entry is modified to indicate that the file has been deleted and that the directory entry is available for use; the data clusters previously used by the file are made available to other files. The data that was contained in the file is left untouched and may be recovered with special file-recovery programs, such as the Norton Utilities, the Mace Utilities, or PC Tools.

As with other FCB file operations, an error is indicated by the status code returned in the AL register. If AL is 0, no error was detected; if AL is FFh, there was an error during the operation. Possible causes for error include trying to delete an illegal file or not finding the specified file name. For V3 and higher, Get Extended Error (Function 59h) can be used to determine the exact error if one is reported.

Do not try to delete an open file. This can cause problems later when you try to close the file or during program termination when DOS attempts to flush the disk buffer to the deleted file. Files must be closed before you delete them.

In a network environment, you must have create-access rights to delete files.

Microsoft recommends that you no longer use this function, unless it is needed to maintain older software. Support for this function may end at any time. Function 41h should be used instead.

Int 21h   **Function 14h**   **V1**

Read Sequential File (FCB)

Beginning at the file pointer's current location, reads the next block of data and updates the file pointer

611

Calling registers: AH   14h
                          DS:DX   Pointer to an opened FCB

Return registers: AL   00h, read was successful
                                       01h, no read, already at EOF
                                       02h, read canceled, DTA boundary error
                                       03h, partial read, now at EOF

Comments: This function facilitates the sequential reading of information from a disk file using a file control block (FCB). You can read information only from a file that has been previously opened (Function 0Fh). Chapter 9, "Directories and Files," discusses files and explains FCBs in more detail.

To use this function, you should ensure that DS:DX points to an FCB created after a file was opened successfully. Sequential reads are controlled by the parameters set in the FCB. The length of the read is given in the record-size field. The location is given by the current block number and the current record number. Before issuing this function, you can change the values of these FCB fields to values appropriate for your application.

When the read is completed, the information read from the disk is placed in the disk transfer area (DTA), and the record address in the FCB is automatically incremented. For more information about the DTA, refer to Chapter 9 and Function 1Ah.

Because the information read from the disk is placed in the DTA, be sure that the DTA is large enough to receive the information. Otherwise, information from the disk could overwrite other data.

As with other FCB file operations, an error is indicated by the status code returned in the AL register. If AL is 0, no error was detected; any other value denotes an error during the operation. If the amount of data read by this function results in crossing a memory segment boundary in the DTA (a memory address ending in 000), a failure is indicated with AL = 2. Partial records (AL = 3) are read and padded with zero characters to the end. For V3 and higher, Get Extended Error (Function 59h) can be used to determine the exact error if one is reported.

In a network environment, you must have read-access rights in order to use this function.

Microsoft recommends that you no longer use this function, unless it is needed to maintain older software. Support for this function may end at any time. Function 3Fh should be used instead.

Int 21h   **Function 15h**   **V1**

Write Sequential File (FCB)

Writes the record to the current block and record locations from the file control block (FCB)

Calling registers: AH   15h
                          DS:DX   Pointer to an opened FCB

Return registers: AL   00h, write was successful
                                 01h, no write attempted, disk full or read-only file
                                 02h, write canceled, DTA boundary error

Comments: This function facilitates the sequential writing of data to a disk file using an FCB. You can write data only to a previously opened (Function 0Fh) or created (Function 16h) file. Chapter 9, "Directories and Files," discusses files and explains FCBs in more detail.

To use this function, you should ensure that DS:DX points to an FCB created after a file was opened or created successfully. The parameters set in the FCB control sequential writes. The length of the write is given in the record-size field. The location is given by the current block number and the current record number. Before issuing this function, you can change the values of these FCB fields to values appropriate for your application.

Because information written to disk comes from the disk transfer area (DTA), take care that the record size being written is the amount of data you want. Otherwise, other data (garbage) could be written inadvertently to the disk file. For more information about the DTA, refer to Chapter 9 and Function 1Ah.

If the amount of data being written does not fill the entire DOS disk buffer (internal to DOS), the data is simply added to that already in the disk buffer, pending a need to write it to the disk. When this function is completed successfully, the record address in the FCB is updated automatically.

As with other FCB file operations, an error is indicated by the status code returned in the AL register. If AL is 0, no error was detected; any other value denotes an error during the operation. If the disk is full or you try to write to a read-only file, AL is equal to 1. If a memory-segment boundary in the DTA (a memory address ending in 000) is crossed during a write operation, the function fails and returns AL = 2.

In a network environment, you must have write-access rights to use this function.

Microsoft recommends that you no longer use this function, unless it is needed to maintain older software. Support for this function may end at any time. Function 40h should be used instead.

Int 21h	**Function 16h**	**V1**
	Create File (FCB)	

Creates a disk file based on the information provided in the file control block (FCB)

Calling registers: AH   16h
                             DS:DX   Pointer to an unopened FCB

Return registers: AL   00h, file was created
                                 FFh, file was not created

Comments: This function serves as a complement to opening a file (Function 0Fh). It creates the specified file and leaves it open for subsequent use with an FCB. Chapter 9, "Directories and Files," discusses files and explains FCBs in more detail.

Why not use this function all the time? Because file creation also truncates files that already exist — without warning! First, the function searches the current directory for the specified file. If the file is found, it is truncated and the FCB is updated; the file is open as though it were newly created. If the file doesn't exist, it is created and the FCB is set for access to the new file.

To use this function, the FCB's drive, file-name, and extension fields must be provided. When you use an extended FCB, you also can assign an attribute to create a hidden file or a volume label. For information about file attributes, refer to Chapter 9.

As with other FCB file operations, an error is indicated by the status code returned in the AL register. If AL is 0, no error was detected; if AL is FFh, there was an error during the operation. For V3 and higher, Get Extended Error (Function 59h) can be used to determine the exact error if one is reported.

In a network environment, you must have create-access rights to use this function.

Microsoft recommends that you no longer use this function, unless it is needed to maintain older software. Support for this function may end at any time. Function 3Ch should be used instead.

Int 21h	Function 17h	V1
	Rename File (FCB)	

Renames an existing file

Calling registers: AH   17h
DS:DX   Pointer to a modified FCB

Return registers: AL   00h, file was renamed
FFh, file was not renamed

Comments: This function enables you to change the name of existing disk files by using a modified file control block (FCB). Only normal files can be renamed; therefore, read-only files, system files, hidden files, volume labels, or directories cannot be renamed with this function.

This function uses a modified FCB with the following format:

Offset	Meaning
00h	Drive designation
01h	Original file name
09h	Original file extension
11h	New file name
19h	New file extension

614

Notice that only three pieces of information are required: a drive designator (all renaming must occur on the same drive) and the old and new file names. Beginning with DOS V2.1, the question mark (?) is supported as a wild-card character in file-name specifications. Only under DOS V3 and higher are asterisks (*) allowed as wild cards. Putting wild cards in the original file name causes the function to try to rename every file that matches the pattern. Putting wild cards in the new file name causes those character positions to remain unchanged in the new file.

Because file names in any given directory must be unique, this function stops and returns an error if it is asked to rename a file to a name that already exists. Through effective use of wild-card matching, you can build a sophisticated, multifile renamer. Suppose that you have a series of files named ABC01.DAT, ABC02.DAT, ABC03.DAT, and so on, and that you want to rename them with the extension .OLD. If you choose the original file name ABC??.DAT and the new file name *.OLD, the rename process proceeds smoothly.

As with other FCB file operations, an error is indicated by the status code returned in the AL register. If AL is 0, no error was detected; if AL is FFh, there was an error during the operation. For V3 and higher, Get Extended Error (Function 59h) can be used to determine the exact error if one is reported.

In a network environment, you must have create-access rights to use this function.

Microsoft recommends that you no longer use this function, unless it is needed to maintain older software. Support for this function may end at any time. Function 56h should be used instead.

Int 21h	Function 19h	V1
	Get Default Drive	

Returns the number of the current default drive

Calling registers: AH   19h

Return registers: AL   Current drive number (A = 0 through Z = 25)

Comments: This function is used to determine which disk drive DOS is using as the default drive. A number, representing the default drive, is returned in the AL register. The number is zero-based, with 0 for drive A, 1 for drive B, and so on. This is a little different from other functions where a 0 may be used to specify the default drive. This function is related to Function 0Eh, which is used to set the default drive.

Int 21h	Function 1Ah	V1
	Set DTA Address	

Establishes an address that DOS uses as the beginning of the disk transfer area (DTA)

615

Calling registers: AH   1Ah

                           DS:DX   Pointer to a new DTA

Return registers: None

Comments: This function is used to specify a DTA to be used by DOS for disk operations. The DTA is used by many of the DOS functions, most notably the file control block (FCB) file functions. The handle functions used for file searching (Functions 4Eh and 4Fh) and Int 25h and Int 26h also use the DTA. When a program is started, a default DTA of 128 bytes is set aside at offset 80h in the program segment prefix (PSP). The converse of this function is Function 2Fh, which is used to get the current DTA address.

The programmer is responsible for seeing that the DTA used for disk operations is adequate for the tasks that are undertaken. Because DOS keeps track of only the DTA's beginning address, the system has no way of knowing whether it has reached the end of the DTA during disk operations. The upshot is that program data or code can easily be overwritten by information transferred from the disk if the amount of data being transferred is more than the DTA can hold.

Int 21h	Function 1Bh	V1
	Get Allocation Table Information	

Gets basic information about disk allocation for the disk in the default drive

Calling registers: AH   1Bh

Return registers: AL   Sectors per cluster

                           CX   Bytes per physical sector

                           DX   Clusters per disk

                           DS:BX   Pointer to media descriptor byte

Comments: This function returns the information basic to a knowledge of the capacity of the disk in the default drive. The information is seldom used as much as the combination of $CX \times AL \times DX$, which gives the disk's total capacity (in bytes). Function 1Ch returns identical information for a disk in a specific drive, and Function 36h is used to determine the amount of free space on a disk.

Beginning with DOS V2, DS:BX points to the media descriptor byte, contained in the file allocation table (FAT), but on DOS V1 it points to the FAT in memory. The media descriptor (or FAT ID) byte can be used to identify the media's formatting from the following table:

Value	Meaning
F0h	Not identifiable
F8h	Fixed disk
F9h	Double sided, 15 sectors per track (1.2M)

Value	Meaning
F9h	Double sided, 9 sectors per track (720K)
FCh	Single sided, 9 sectors per track
FDh	Double sided, 9 sectors per track (360K)
FEh	Single sided, 8 sectors per track
FFh	Double sided, 8 sectors per track

Notice that the F9h FAT ID byte lets you know only that the disk was formatted in a high-capacity disk drive. You must examine the other information returned by this function to determine the disk's actual capacity. Furthermore, FAT IDs are not supported uniformly by all versions of DOS. The standard as given is from the technical manual for the IBM version of DOS and may not apply to a particular manufacturer's version of DOS.

Microsoft recommends that you no longer use this function, unless it is needed to maintain older software. Support for this function may end at any time. Function 36h should be used instead.

Int 21h	**Function 1Ch**	**V2**
	Get Allocation Table Information for Specific Drive	

Gets the basic information about disk allocation for the disk in a specified drive

Calling registers:	AH	1Ch
	DL	Drive number (current drive = 0, A = 1 through Z = 26)
Return registers:	AL	Sectors per cluster
	CX	Bytes per physical sector
	DX	Clusters per disk
	DS:BX	Pointer to media descriptor byte

Comments: This function returns the information basic to a knowledge of the capacity of the disk in a specific drive. The information is exactly the same as that returned by Function 1Bh for the default drive. See the comments on Function 1Bh for details.

Microsoft recommends that you no longer use this function, unless it is needed to maintain older software. Support for this function may end at any time. Function 36h should be used instead.

Int 21h	**Function 1Fh**	**V2**
	Get Default Disk Parameter Block	

Returns the address of the disk parameter block for the default drive

Calling registers:	AH	1Fh
Return registers:	AL	00h, no error
		FFh, error
	DS:BX	Address of drive parameter block

Comments: Use this function to return, in DS:BX, the address of the disk parameter block (DPB) used by DOS to determine specific structural information about the disk in the default drive. The structure of the DPB is shown in Table DOS.3.

Table DOS.3 Drive Parameter Block (DPB)

Offset Byte	Field Length	Meaning
All Versions		
00h	Byte	Drive number (0 = A, 1 = B, and so on)
01h	Byte	Device driver unit number
02h	Word	Bytes per sector
04h	Byte	Sectors per cluster (zero based)
05h	Byte	Shift factor
06h	Word	First sector containing FAT
08h	Byte	Number of FAT copies
09h	Word	Number of root directory entries
0Bh	Word	First data sector number
0Dh	Word	Highest cluster number plus 1
Version 2 or 3 Only		
0Fh	Byte	Sectors per FAT (0–255)
10h	Word	Root directory starting sector number
12h	Double word	Drive's device driver address
16h	Byte	Media descriptor byte
17h	Byte	Disk parameter block access flag (0FFh indicates need to rebuild)
18h	Double word	Address of next device parameter block
Version 2 Only		
1Ch	Word	Starting cluster number for current directory
1Eh	64 bytes	ASCIIZ of current directory path

Offset Byte	Field Length	Meaning
Version 3 Only		
1Ch	Word	Last cluster number allocated from this drive
1Eh	Word	Purpose unknown; normally FFFFh
Version 4		
0Fh	Word	Sectors per FAT (0–65,535)
11h	Word	Root directory starting sector number
13h	Double word	Drive's device driver address
17h	Byte	Media descriptor byte
18h	Byte	Disk parameter block access flag (0FFh indicates need to rebuild)
19h	Double word	Address of next device parameter block
1Dh	Word	Last cluster number allocated from this drive
1Fh	Word	Purpose unknown; normally FFFFh
Version 5		
0Fh	Word	Sectors per FAT (0–65,535)
11h	Word	Root directory's starting sector number
13h	Double word	Drive's device driver address
17h	Byte	Media descriptor byte
18h	Byte	Disk parameter block access flag (0FFh indicates need to rebuild)
19h	Double word	Address of next device parameter block
1Dh	Word	Last cluster number allocated from this drive
1Fh	Word	Number of free clusters

Note that the DPB structure is different for each DOS version. The purpose of each item in the table should be self-explanatory.

Because this function returns a value in the DS register, you should save the value of DS before you call the function.

Int 21h   Function 21h   V1

Random File Read (FCB)

Reads the record specified by the current-block and current-record fields of an FCB from a disk file, placing the information in the disk transfer area (DTA)

Calling registers: AH   21h
                         DS:DX   Pointer to open FCB

Return registers: AL   00h, read was successful
                                     01h, no read, EOF encountered
                                     02h, read canceled, DTA boundary error
                                     03h, partial record read, EOF encountered

Comments: This function facilitates the reading of random (nonsequential) information from a disk file with a file control block (FCB). Chapter 9, "Directories and Files," discusses files and explains FCBs in more detail. You can read information only from a file that has been previously opened (Function 0Fh).

To use this function, be sure that DS:DX points to an FCB created after a file was opened successfully. Random reads are controlled by parameters set in the FCB. The record to read is specified in the FCB by setting the random-record field, and the amount of data is controlled by the record-size field. Before issuing this function, you can change the values of these FCB fields to values appropriate for your application. DOS uses these two values to calculate the file position at which reading is begun.

When this function is completed, the information read from the disk is in the DTA. For more information about the DTA, refer to Chapter 9, "Directories and Files," and Function 1Ah. The FCB current-position field is not updated by this function as it is with sequential functions. Unless the random-record field is changed, subsequent accesses of the file return the same data.

Because information read from the disk is placed in the DTA, take care that the DTA is large enough to receive the data. Otherwise, information from the disk may overwrite other data.

As with other FCB file operations, an error is indicated by the status code returned in the AL register. If AL is 0, no error was detected; any other value denotes an error during the operation. If the amount of data read by this function results in crossing a memory segment boundary in the DTA (a memory address ending in 000), the function fails and returns AL = 2. Partial records (AL = 3) are read and padded with zero characters to the end.

In a network environment, you must have read-access rights to use this function.

Microsoft recommends that you no longer use this function, unless it is needed to maintain older software. Support for this function may end at any time. Function 3Fh should be used instead.

Int 21h   Function 22h   V1

Random File Write (FCB)

Writes the record specified by the current-block and current-record fields of an FCB to a disk file, transferring the information from the disk transfer area (DTA)

Calling registers: AH   22h
                         DS:DX   Pointer to open FCB

Return registers: AL   00h, write was successful
                                         01h, no write attempted, disk full or read-only file
                                         02h, write canceled, DTA boundary error

Comments: This function facilitates the writing of random (nonsequential) information to a disk file that uses a file control block (FCB). You can write information only to a previously opened (Function 0Fh) or created (Function 16h) file. Chapter 9, "Directories and Files," discusses files and explains FCBs in more detail.

To use this function, make sure that DS:DX points to an FCB created after a file is opened or created successfully. Parameters set in the FCB control random writes. The record to write is specified in the FCB by setting the random-record field; the amount of data is controlled by the record-size field. Before issuing this function, you can change the values of these FCB fields to values appropriate for your application. DOS uses these values to calculate the file position at which writing begins.

Because the information written to disk comes from the DTA, you must be careful that the record size being written is the amount of data you want. Otherwise, other data (garbage) can inadvertently be written to the disk file. For more information about the DTA, refer to Chapter 9 and Function 1Ah.

If the data being written does not fill the entire DOS disk buffer (internal to DOS), it is added to the data already in the disk buffer, pending a need to write it to the disk.

Unlike sequential functions, this function does not update the FCB current-position field. Subsequent random writing to the file transfers information to the same file record unless the random-record field is changed.

As with other FCB file operations, an error is indicated by the status code returned in the AL register. If AL is 0, no error was detected; any other value denotes an error during the operation. If the disk was full or if you attempted to write to a read-only file, AL is equal to 1. If, during a write operation, a memory segment boundary in the DTA (a memory address ending in 000) is crossed, the function fails and returns AL = 2.

In a network environment, you must have write-access rights to use this function.

Microsoft recommends that you no longer use this function, unless it is needed to maintain older software. Support for this function may end at any time. Function 40h should be used instead.

Int 21h   Function 23h   V1

Get File Size (FCB)

Searches a directory for a matching file name; if the file is found, fills in the size information in the designated file control block (FCB)

Calling registers: AH   23h

                        DS:DX   Pointer to unopened FCB

Return registers: AL   00h, matching file found

                                FFh, no matching file found

Comments: This function is used to determine the number of records in a specified file through the use of an FCB. Chapter 9, "Directories and Files," discusses files and explains FCBs in more detail. The file should be unopened when you are using this function.

This function can be used after filling in the drive, file-name, extension, and record-size fields of the FCB. The supplied file name must be complete and unique; wild-card characters are not allowed. To find the size of the file in bytes, simply set the record-size field to 1.

If a file is located that matches the specified file name, the random-record field of the FCB pointed to by DS:DX is updated to indicate the number of records in the file. This number is determined by dividing the file size (in bytes) by the record size, resulting in the number of records. If there is any remainder from the division, the number of records is rounded up. If you forget to set the record-size field before calling this function, or for files in which the file-size portion of the directory entry may be incorrect or rounded to reflect a full sector, the information returned by this function may be of questionable value.

As with other FCB file operations, an error is indicated by the status code returned in the AL register. If AL is 0, no error was detected; if AL is FFh, an error occurred during the operation (generally, this means that the specified file was not found).

Microsoft recommends that you no longer use this function, unless it is needed to maintain older software. Support for this function may end at any time. Function 42h should be used instead.

Int 21h   Function 24h   V1

Set Random Record Field (FCB)

When switching from sequential to random file I/O, used to set the file control block (FCB) random-record field based on the current file position

Calling registers: AH   24h

                        DS:DX   Pointer to open FCB

Return registers: None

Comments: This function modifies an open FCB to prepare it for random-access functions. This function can be used after filling in the record-size, record-number, and block-number fields of the FCB. The function modifies the random-record field based on these field values. Chapter 9, "Directories and Files," discusses files and explains FCBs in more detail.

Microsoft recommends that you no longer use this function, unless it is needed to maintain older software. Support for this function may end at any time. Function 42h should be used instead.

Int 21h	Function 25h	V1
	Set Interrupt Vector	

Safely modifies an interrupt vector to point to a specified interrupt handler

Calling registers: AH   25h
AL   Interrupt number
DS:DX Pointer to interrupt handler

Return registers: None

Comments: This function makes quick work of what otherwise can be a delicate operation—changing interrupt vectors. Because interrupt vectors are maintained in a table in low memory (see Chapter 11, "Interrupt Handlers"), they could easily be changed directly. This process can be dangerous, however, if an interrupt occurs during the process — particularly while only a portion of the address has been transferred to the table.

Rather than write your own code to safely manage setting interrupts, you can use this function, which guarantees to safely update the interrupt vector table to an address you supply. This method is the only approved one for altering interrupt vectors.

Changing interrupt vectors can lead to some special problems. Interrupts 22h, 23h, and 24h are reset automatically to their original values when a program terminates in a normal manner (see Int 20h, Int 27h, and Functions 00h, 31h, and 4Ch). If the program modifies any other interrupt vectors, these remain at their changed values, even after the program terminates. This can cause problems; an interrupt condition that occurs after the program has terminated can cause a jump to a nonexistent interrupt handler.

To prevent this type of situation, programs that change the interrupt vectors should first use Function 35h to get the original vector value and store it. The original vector value can be restored when the program ends. This has even greater implications for programs that change interrupt vectors. A program that changes vectors to interrupts other than 22h, 23h, or 24h must be capable also of trapping all the ways in which the program can be terminated abnormally — this means Ctrl-C and Ctrl-Break interrupt servicing, DOS critical-error servicing, and servicing for any other potential interrupt that might cause the program to terminate, such as dividing by zero.

If the program does not intercept any and all methods that might terminate it, hanging interrupt vectors can remain. If a program crashes without being able to reset the interrupt vectors, the only safe course is to reset the system before you do anything else.

623

Int 21h   Function 26h   V1

Create PSP

Copies the program segment prefix (PSP) from the currently executing program to the specified segment address and then updates it for use by a new program

Calling registers: AH   26h

DX   Segment address for new PSP

Return registers: None

Comments: This function creates a PSP preparatory to running another program. A copy is made of the current program's PSP at the specified memory segment address. The PSP is discussed in detail in Chapter 3, "The Dynamics of DOS."

In theory, you could copy a COM file directly into the memory space after the new PSP and execute the program, but it would not be a good practice for the simple reason that this function is out of date. It has been superseded, in V2 and later versions, by the more sophisticated EXEC function (Function 4Bh), which is much easier to use. All Microsoft and IBM documentation recommends the use of the EXEC function in preference to Function 26h when you are spawning programs. EXEC better handles the details of program loading and execution and insulates the program from potential errors in operation. This function does not load or execute another program; it simply prepares a PSP for one. The function invoking the program still must load and execute the program.

If your program has changed the interrupt vectors for Int 22h, 23h, and 24h, the new vectors are copied into the newly created PSP. In addition, the memory-allocation information is updated appropriately.

Microsoft recommends that you no longer use this function, unless it is needed to maintain older software. Support for this function may end at any time. Function 4Bh, Subfunction 00h, should be used instead.

Int 21h   Function 27h   V1

Random Block Read (FCB)

Reads one or more consecutive random records from a disk file to the disk transfer area (DTA)

Calling registers: AH   27h

CX   Number of records to read

DS:DX   Pointer to opened FCB

Return registers: AL   00h, all records read successfully

01h, no read, EOF encountered

02h, read canceled, DTA boundary error
03h, partial record read, EOF encountered

CX Number of records read

Comments: This function facilitates the reading of a group of consecutive random records from a disk file by using a file control block (FCB). You can read information only from a file that has been previously opened (Function 0Fh). Chapter 9, "Directories and Files," discusses files and explains FCBs in more detail.

To use this function, make sure that CX contains the number of records you want and that DS:DX points to an FCB created after a file was opened successfully. Parameters set in the FCB control random reads. The beginning record to read is specified in the FCB by setting the random-record field, and the size of each record is controlled by the record-size field. Before issuing this function, you can change the values of these FCB fields to values appropriate for your application. DOS uses these values to calculate the file position at which reading begins.

When this function is completed, the information read from the disk is in the DTA. (For more information about the DTA, refer to Chapter 9 and Function 1Ah.) When the function is successfully completed, the random-record, current-block, and current-record fields of the FCB are updated.

Because the information read from the disk is placed in the DTA, you must be careful that the DTA is large enough to receive the total block of information. Otherwise, other data or program code can be overwritten with information from the disk.

As with other FCB file operations, an error is indicated by the status code returned in the AL register. If AL is 0, no error was detected; any other value denotes an error during the operation. If the amount of data being read by this function results in crossing a memory segment boundary in the DTA (a memory address ending in 000), the function fails and returns AL = 2. Partial records (AL = 3) are read and padded to the end with zero characters.

In a network environment, you must have read-access rights to use this function.

Microsoft recommends that you no longer use this function, unless it is needed to maintain older software. Support for this function may end at any time. Functions 3Fh and 42h should be used instead.

Int 21h	Function 28h	V1

Random Block Write (FCB)

Writes one or more consecutive random records to a disk file from the disk transfer area (DTA)

Calling registers: AH 28h
CX Number of records to write
DS:DX Pointer to opened FCB

Return registers: AL   00h, all records successfully written

01h, no write attempted, disk full or read-only file

02h, write canceled, DTA boundary error

CX   Number of records written

Comments: This function facilitates the writing of a group of consecutive random records to a disk file by using a file control block (FCB). You can write information only to a previously opened (Function 0Fh) or created (Function 16h) file. Chapter 9, "Directories and Files," discusses files and explains FCBs in more detail.

To use this function, make sure that CX contains the number of records to write and that DS:DX points to an FCB created after a file was successfully opened or created. Parameters set in the FCB control random writes. The beginning record to write is specified in the FCB by setting the random-record field, and the size of each record is controlled by the record-size field. Before issuing this function, you can change the values of these FCB fields to values appropriate for your application. DOS uses these values to calculate the file position at which reading begins.

Because the information written to disk comes from the DTA, you must be careful that the record size and number of records being written correspond to the amount of data you want. Otherwise, other data (garbage) can inadvertently be written to the disk file. For more information about the DTA, refer to Chapter 9, "Directories and Files," and Function 1Ah.

If the amount of data being written does not fill the entire DOS disk buffer (internal to DOS), the data is simply added to that already in the disk buffer, pending a need to write it to the disk.

When the function has been completed successfully, the FCB's random-record, current-block, and current-record fields are updated.

As with other FCB file operations, an error is indicated by the status code returned in the AL register. If AL is 0, no error was detected; any other value denotes an error during the operation. If the disk was full or if you attempted to write to a read-only file, AL is equal to 1. During a write operation, if a memory segment boundary in the DTA (a memory address ending in 000) is crossed, the function fails and returns AL = 2.

In a network environment, you must have write-access rights to use this function.

Microsoft recommends that you no longer use this function, unless it is needed to maintain older software. Support for this function may end at any time. Functions 40h and 42h should be used instead.

Int 21h   **Function 29h**   **V1**

Parse File Name

Parses a file-name string into a file control block (FCB) for use

Calling registers: AH   29h

AL   Parse control flag (see Table DOS.4)

	DS:SI	Pointer to text string
	ES:DI	Pointer to FCB
Return registers:	AL	00h, no wild cards encountered
		01h, wild cards found
		FFh, drive specifier invalid
	DS:SI	Pointer to the first character after the parsed file name
	ES:DI	Pointer to the updated, unopened FCB

Comments: Originally, the purpose of this function was to extract file names from command lines and place them in the proper format for opening an FCB. To do so, you start with the pointer to the file-name string and a pointer to the FCB you plan to use. This FCB does not have to be in any sort of format — it can be a block of memory sufficient to hold an FCB.

Separator characters in all versions are the period (.), comma (,), colon (:), semicolon (;), equal sign (=), plus sign (+), tab, and space. In DOS V1, the following additional characters serve as separators: the double quotation mark ("), slash (/), left bracket ([ ), and right bracket ( ]).

The function returns a proper, unopened FCB for the desired file and a pointer to the first characters after the file name (clearly useful if you are parsing a command line within which the file name is one of several). Asterisk characters are converted automatically into one or more question-mark characters to the end of the file name or extension in this function.

Because this is an FCB function, it is not compatible with path names; therefore, you cannot include directories in file names. This function can refer only to files in the current directory. The interpretation of the file name is controlled by a parse flag, shown in Table DOS.4.

Table DOS.4   Parse Control Flag

Bit *76543210*	*Meaning*
. . . . 0	Stop parsing if a file separator is encountered
. . . . 1	Ignore leading separators
. . . . . . 0 .	Sets the drive ID in the FCB to 0 (default drive) if the string does not contain a drive letter
. . . . . . 1 .	The drive ID in the FCB is left alone if the string does not contain a drive letter
. . . . . 0 . .	The file name in the FCB is set to eight spaces (20H) if the string contains no file name
. . . . . 1 . .	The file name in the FCB is left alone if the string contains no file name

continues

627

Table DOS.4 Continued

Bit 76543210	Meaning
....0...	The extension field in the FCB is set to three spaces if the string contains no extension
....1...	The extension field in the FCB is left alone if the string contains no extension

When you work with FCB functions, this function is useful for setting up the FCB properly. This function results in a properly formatted FCB, ready to be opened. To use the FCB open or create functions, the pointer in ES must be moved to DS:DX.

If there is no valid file name to parse, the function returns the pointer ES:DI so that ES:DI+1 points to a blank character.

Int 21h	**Function 2Ah**	**V1**
	Get System Date	

Gets the year, month, day, and day of the week from the system

Calling registers:	AH	2Ah
Return registers:	CX	Year (1980–2099)
	DH	Month (1–12)
	DL	Day (1–31)
	AL	Day of week (0 = Sunday, 1 = Monday, and so on), DOS V1.1 or later

Comments: This function returns information about DOS's understanding of the current system date. This is simply a check of the DOS internal clock, not an access to a real-time clock/calendar if one is installed. As a general rule, if the system has an installed clock/calendar, it is checked from the AUTOEXEC.BAT file when the system is started or it is set manually by an operator.

Systems that run for days at a time can drift from accurate time in unexpected ways. The system date or time may not be properly updated, or processes may interfere with or change the internal system time. This function might therefore return an incorrect date (without access to a clock/calendar chip, however, you cannot check it).

A common error that affects the accuracy of this function afflicts systems that are left running and unused for more than 24 consecutive hours (over a weekend, for instance). Because the date is advanced only when DOS detects that the midnight flag has been set, and this can happen only when one of a limited number of functions is called, the date does not advance while the system is unused. On the next use, the midnight flag is detected, but it has no record of how many midnights have gone by; therefore, only one day is added to the date. Note that BIOS function 1Ah (Get Clock Count) resets the midnight flag as part of its activity. It is a simple matter to check and change the date the first time the system is used after an extended period without use.

The function uses the same register format as Function 2Bh (Set System Date) for ease of use.

Int 21h	Function 2Bh	V1
	Set System Date	

Sets the system date to the specified value without affecting the system time

Calling registers: AH   2Bh
CX   Year (1980–2099)
DH   Month (1–12)
DL   Day (1–31)

Return registers: AL   00h, date set successfully
FFh, date invalid, not set

Comments: This function uses the same register format as the Get System Date function. If you have a clock/calendar, you can access it to get the current date and update the system date by using this function. Without a clock/calendar, you can prompt the user for input and then correct it in the operating system so that calls to the Get System Date function return the correct date.

The date set with this function is used to mark files during file operations.

If your computer system has a CMOS clock, this function causes its date to be set.

Int 21h	Function 2Ch	V1
	Get System Time	

Gets the system time in hours, minutes, seconds, and hundredths of seconds

Calling registers: AH   2Ch

Return registers: CH   Hour (0–23)
CL   Minutes (0–59)
DH   Seconds (0–59)
DL   Hundredths of seconds (0–99)

Comments: Like getting the system date, getting the system time is a clearly useful function we do not pay much attention to. You frequently need this information for reports or screen displays. You need to be aware, however, of the following points:

629

- This function does not retrieve time from a clock/calendar chip. It gets the DOS internal time, which is only as accurate as its setting.

- On many systems, the system's real-time clock is not accurate enough to provide hundredths-of-a-second resolution. In this type of situation, the function could return a discontinuous time value for the hundredths-of-a-second value.

Applications that use the time function for other than actual system time do not need to worry about the time setting. An application such as a timer that is started by setting the DOS time to zero and then checking elapsed time can be useful in some programs. If you write this type of program, however, be aware that other programs expect to get the time of day from this clock. If you use it for elapsed time by setting it to zero and then leave it, the person using your program will be upset when other programs return the wrong system time.

The register format is the same as that used for Function 2Dh (Set System Time).

Int 21h	Function 2Dh	V1
	Set System Time	

Sets the system time to the specified hour, minute, second, and hundredth of a second without affecting the system date

Calling registers:

AH	2Dh
CH	Hour (0–23)
CL	Minutes (0–59)
DH	Seconds (0–59)
DL	Hundredths of seconds (0–99)

Return registers:

AL	00h, time set successfully
	FFh, time invalid, not set

Comments: Setting the system time can be useful in a number of cases:

- Your program works with a clock/calendar and can set the date and time exactly from the chip

- Your program queries the user for a time to set

- You are using the clock as an elapsed time clock; you can reset it to zero and display or monitor it in terms of elapsed time rather than system time

The register format, which is the same as that used for Function 2Ch (Get System Time), enables you to get the time, ask about it, and then update only what has changed. It is often best to set to an accuracy of no greater than plus or minus one second when working with a person. Trying to set hundredths of a second goes beyond what the typical user wants. Setting the time to a greater accuracy (for applications in astronomy, for example) requires special synchronizing techniques.

Programs working from a clock/calendar chip or from a time service, such as a WWV radio link, can set the time to hundredths-of-a-second accuracy. Some computers cannot return this accuracy on a consistent basis because the real-time clock is not accurate enough.

If your computer system has a CMOS clock, this function causes its time to be set.

Int 21h	Function 2Eh	V1
	Set Verify Flag	

Toggles the DOS verify flag; turning it on results in an additional CRC (cyclic redundancy check) when writing to disk and increases disk transfer time

Calling registers: AH   2Eh
                         AL   00h, turn off verify
                                 01h, turn on verify
                         DH   00h   (DOS version earlier than 3.0)

Return registers: None

Comments: How could you *not* want to verify your disk writes to make sure that they are correct? Forcing a disk verify of all data written to a disk, however, increases by a factor of 2 the time necessary to do the operation. On some non-IBM BIOS variants, the operation is not supported.

So, why not do it? Time, obviously. When you do not need absolute assurance that every disk write is correct, leaving the verify flag off makes sense. Only for truly critical functions should you bother to set the flag, and then it should be turned off afterward.

Even when the verify flag is turned on, you do not have absolute assurance that data was properly written because the verification process does not perform a byte-by-byte comparison of the data that was written with the data that was supposed to be written. It waits one revolution, reads the data that was written and has the disk controller calculate its CRC value again, and then compares the calculated CRC while reading the value that was calculated and written to the disk the first time.

This process offers no protection against any data error that might occur between memory and the disk controller; it verifies only that the controller wrote to disk the same value it used to calculate the first CRC and that it then performed the same calculation two times running. Because most disk errors involve failure of the media, however, which would prevent the readback CRC from matching that which was written, the test does offer some benefit. For critical work, though, such as archival transfer of data that then will be erased from the hard disk, a byte-by-byte comparison of the copy with the original is the only absolute assurance that the copy was performed successfully.

Function 54h can be used to determine the current setting of the verify flag.

631

Int 21h   Function 2Fh   V2

Get DTA Address

Gets the current value of the disk transfer area (DTA) pointer for file control block (FCB) file operations

Calling registers: AH   2Fh

Return registers: ES:BX   Pointer to DTA

Comments: The default DTA is a 128-byte buffer at offset 80h in the program segment prefix (PSP). Most programs do not need more than this amount for their operations. If you are working with larger record sizes or have special disk transfer requirements, however, setting up another DTA is useful.

Function 1Ah sets the DTA; this function (2Fh) tells you where it is. This function does *not* tell you, however, how large the DTA is (and the information is essential). If you are not sure whether the DTA is big enough for what you are doing, you have no choice but to set it yourself to a block of memory large enough to handle the expected operations.

Int 21h   Function 30h   V2

Get DOS Version Number

Returns the DOS version number for reference so that an application can determine the capabilities of the software system; DOS versions earlier than 2.0 should return a version number of 0

Calling registers: AH   30h
                           AL   Version flag
                           00h   OEM number
                           01h   DOS version flag

Return registers: AL   Major version number (2, 3)
                           AH   Minor version number (2.1 = 10)
                           BH   OEM number or DOS version flag
                           BL:CX   24-bit serial number

Comments: The DOS version number is important to programmers who deal directly with DOS; it enables them to customize a program to the system version installed. This function, which was added with DOS V2.0, gives you the major and minor version numbers for the DOS under which your program is expected to run. This is a good way to verify at the beginning of a program that the system can support the DOS calls you need. (***Note:*** With Microsoft C and Borland C++, these values are available as global variables.)

If your program works under a DOS earlier than V2.0, the function returns 0 for both major and minor version numbers. This immediately gives you such important information as no path names, no directories, and no hard disk support. If you are writing programs for DOS V2.0 and then later find yourself on DOS 1.x versions, you should do the following:

1. Display an error message with Int 21h, Function 09h.

2. Exit from the program with Int 21h, Function 00h.

If you intend to support DOS versions earlier than 2.0, use this information to restrict your use of DOS functions.

DOS V1.x restrictions are not the only ones of concern when you program. Programmers customarily use functions that extend their abilities, as those functions become available. DOS V3.3 added functions that enable you to increase the number of open files and to flush file buffers to disk. By using these functions in a database program, you can make that database easier to write. A user without DOS V3.3, however, would be left out (and would not be a prospective buyer) if you did not provide alternative ways to deal with the problems for earlier versions of DOS.

If the DOS version flag is returned, bit 3 set means that MS-DOS runs in ROM; otherwise, it runs in RAM. The other bits are undefined. If the OEM number is returned, the OEM-dependent serial number in BL:CX, if unused, is set to zero.

The DOS version number is the value set by the MS-DOS SETVER command, and may be different from the version number returned by Function 3306h.

Int 21h	**Function 31h**	**V2**
	Terminate and Stay Resident	

Terminates a process and returns control to the parent process

Calling registers:	AH	31h
	AL	Return code
	DX	Memory size to reserve (in paragraphs)

Return registers: None

Comments: Terminate-and-stay-resident (TSR) utilities are so common that you would be hard-pressed to find a system which does not use one or more of them. In addition to utilities such as pop-up calculators, calendars, and notepads, TSRs can be used to provide common subroutine services for a series of programs. By building a library of functions activated by calls to a specific interrupt, you can provide standard utility routines for several programs without having to link the routines directly to the program. This ability reduces the size of such modules and speeds up the process of loading them.

The purpose of the TSR function is to terminate (like Function 4Ch) the operation of a program but *not* to return the program's assigned memory to the pool of memory managed by DOS. This allows the program to remain active and to activate if it ties itself to an interrupt of some kind. For example, you could have a program activate and display a clock on the screen if it tied itself

633

to the clock interrupt. Also, the program could be activated if a key is pressed or if a program calls the interrupt function.

This function replaces the Int 27h TSR function originally provided with DOS V1. The original TSR function allowed only 64K of memory for the function and could not provide a return code. This function allows more than 64K of memory and allows control of the return code, which is available to the parent program through Function 4Dh. This allows batch files to control execution with the ERRORLEVEL parameter available inside the batch file.

The TSR function attempts to allocate the memory requested in the DX register out of the memory allocated when the program was started. It does not deal with memory assigned to the process by a call to Function 48h.

This function does not close any files the program opened; files opened by the program remain open. Handle functions are associated with the currently active process through an undocumented area of the program segment prefix (PSP). When the TSR function is not the active process, the files it might refer to by using handles are those opened by the real currently active process. This does not apply to file control block (FCB) functions, which are buffered through the process's own memory area. (See Chapter 9, "Directories and Files," for a discussion of FCB functions.)

Any TSR, therefore, that uses handle functions to deal with files or devices — and needs to use those functions when popped up or otherwise active — must switch DOS's definition of the currently active process by using undocumented Functions 50h and 51h, before using the handles. Otherwise, results will not be what you expect and could do severe damage to other programs or data.

Int 21h	Function 32h	V2
	Get Drive Parameter Block	

Retrieves the drive parameter block that defines the characteristics of the designated disk drive; if called with DL = 0, this function is identical to Function 1Fh

Calling registers: AH   32h
                         DL   Drive number (0 = default, 1 = A, and so on)

Return registers: AL   FFh if drive number invalid
                         DS:BX   Address of drive parameter block

Comments: Use this function to return, in DS:BX, the address of the disk parameter block (DPB) used by DOS to determine specific structural information about the disk in the drive specified by DL at entry.

The structure of the DPB is shown in Table DOS.3 (see Function 1Fh). Note that the DPB structure is different for every DOS version. The purpose of each item in the table should be self-explanatory.

Because this function returns a value in the DS register, you should save the value of DS before you call the function.

Int 21h   **Function 33h**   **Subfunction: 00h**   **V2**

Get Ctrl-Break Flag

Gets the status of the Ctrl-Break/Ctrl-C check flag

Calling registers:	AH	33h
	AL	00h, getting flag status
Return registers:	DL	00h, Ctrl-Break checking off
		01h, Ctrl-Break checking on

Comments: Except for a few I/O functions (see character I/O Functions 01h–0Ch for the exceptions), checking for Ctrl-Break or Ctrl-C characters is normally not done during much of the Int 21h function handling. When this checking is turned on, the check is performed for *all* Int 21h functions except the few that merely set or get flag data. This subfunction returns in DL the current state of the Ctrl-Break check flag; see Subfunction 01h to change its state.

When checking is enabled, if a Ctrl-Break or Ctrl-C is found, control is turned over to the handler for Int 23h. You can replace the Int 23h handler and deal with the Ctrl-Break or Ctrl-C in a function of your own rather than disable it.

Be aware that the Ctrl-Break/Ctrl-C flag is a system global that affects all processes running on a DOS system. As a system global, some care must be taken with its handling because it is possible to affect processes other than the one activating or deactivating the function.

Int 21h   **Function 33h**   **Subfunction 01h**   **V2**

Set Ctrl-Break Flag

Sets the status of the Ctrl-Break/Ctrl-C check flag

Calling registers:	AH	33h
	AL	01h, setting flag status
	DL	00h, Ctrl-Break checking off
		01h, Ctrl-Break checking on
Return registers:	None	

Comments: Except for a few I/O functions (see character I/O Functions 01h–0Ch for the exceptions), checking for Ctrl-Break or Ctrl-C characters is normally not done during much of the Int 21h function handling. When this checking is turned on, the check is performed for *all* Int 21h functions except the few that merely set or get flag data. This subfunction establishes the current state of the Ctrl-Break check flag; see Subfunction 00h to test its state.

When checking is enabled, if a Ctrl-Break or Ctrl-C is found, control is turned over to the handler for Int 23h. You can replace the Int 23h handler and deal with the Ctrl-Break or Ctrl-C in a function of your own rather than disable it.

Be aware that the Ctrl-Break/Ctrl-C flag is a system global that affects all processes running on a DOS system. As a system global, some care must be taken with its handling because it is possible to affect processes other than the one activating or deactivating the function.

Int 21h	Function 33h	Subfunction 05h	V4

Get Boot Drive Code

Returns a code telling from which drive the system was most recently booted

Calling registers: AH   33h
                 AL   05h, get boot drive code

Return registers: DL   Boot drive code (1 = A, 2 = B, 3 = C, and so on)

Comments: With this function, added in V4, the program can determine from which drive the system was booted. This information is stored in the DOS kernel area every time the system initializes itself.

Int 21h	Function 33h	Subfunction 06h	V5

Get MS-DOS Version

Returns the MS-DOS version number, revision number, and version flags

Calling registers: AH   33h
                 AL   06h, get MS-DOS version number

Return registers: BL   Major version number
                 BH   Minor version number
                 DL   Revision number in bits 0–2; the other bits are reserved and set to zero
                 DH   Version flag. Bit 3, if set, indicates that MS-DOS is running from ROM; otherwise, MS-DOS is running from RAM. Bit 4, if set, indicates that MS-DOS is running from the high memory area (HMA); otherwise, MS-DOS is running from conventional memory. All other bits are reserved and set to zero.

Comments: This version number is not changed by SETVER.

Int 21h   Function 34h   V2

Return Address of InDOS Flag

An internal DOS flag used to tell when DOS is processing an Int 21h function

Calling registers: AH   34h

Return registers: ES:BX   Pointer to InDOS flag

Comments: When DOS enters an Int 21h function, DOS increments the InDOS flag; when DOS leaves, it decrements the flag. This flag is used by DOS and by terminate-and-stay-resident (TSR) utilities to determine whether DOS is inside the kernel and processing an Int 21h function. When a TSR utility determines that DOS is in a function, it can do one of two things:

- Continue with processing because no Int 21h function is necessary.

- Refuse to process because Int 21h functions are necessary.

This need arises because the operating system kernel is not fully reentrant. If an interrupt occurs while the operating system is already inside the kernel, therefore, the servicing routine cannot use Int 21h functions for processing because a call to a function might conflict with the previous call. In this case, you can easily crash the system, but not necessarily in any way that can be traced directly to the interrupt handler.

For operational necessity, a few portions of the DOS kernel code *do* make use of other parts through the Int 21h interface, and the InDOS flag serves as a signal to prevent that code from causing problems. It also permits official TSR programs such as PRINT.COM and its kin to operate properly. At times, however, this flag is misleading.

When DOS waits for keyboard input, it idles in a loop and reads characters as they come in. As long as DOS is waiting at this point, it is safe to use the file-handling and other functions, even though the InDOS flag indicates otherwise. To let you know that you can safely use these functions, DOS continually invokes Int 28h (Keyboard Busy Loop) during its input loop. A TSR can intercept Int 28h, which defaults to a pointer to an IRET and checks for things to do when it comes alive.

If your TSR is started by pressing a hot key, for example, but it finds that DOS is executing an Int 21h function because the InDOS flag is set, the TSR can set an internal flag that means, "I've been invoked, but I can't do anything." Whenever Int 28h is called, this flag can be checked. If the flag is set, the handler can branch immediately to the TSR part that performs the requested function.

A TSR may also intercept the clock interrupt and check the InDOS and TSR invocation flags during clock ticks. The purpose of this is to take care of the situation in which an Int 21h function (other than a character I/O function) was active when the TSR was first called. In this case, the clock interrupt detects that the InDOS flag is clear and the TSR invocation flag is set. The interrupt then determines that the requested function can be performed.

637

With DOS V2, however, using Int 28h still can cause the system to crash mysteriously. The reason is that V2 switches to its own internal stack before dispatching control to any requested function; if any function is called while DOS is already processing another function in the range from 00 through 0Ch (which it nearly always *is*, when Int 28h is invoked), the second stack switch that results can destroy information needed by the original function call.

The cure is equally simple but extremely subtle: You can trick DOS into believing that it is processing a critical error by manipulating its critical error (CritErr) flag. Setting the CritErr flag before calling a function forces DOS to use its alternate internal stack. You must restore the flag to its original value after returning from the function.

In V3, the DOS dispatch code was modified to test for the affected functions before doing any stack switching; if one of them is requested, DOS simply uses the caller's own stack and avoids the problem. This code remains unchanged in V4.

The CritErr flag is a byte which indicates that DOS has encountered a serious error condition and is processing an Int 24h (Critical Error) handler routine. To let such handlers use as many DOS functions as possible, the flag is set and causes the DOS dispatching code to use an alternate internal stack rather than the normal stack space. Although this is not full reentrant coding, it permits a limited capability to reuse the code.

In all versions of DOS from V2 through V4, the CritErr flag is adjacent to the InDOS flag. Unfortunately, its location flipped between V2 and V3. In V2, it is the byte at the next higher address; in V3 and V4, it is the next lower byte.

 Note: This function can cause problems when it is called from an Int 28h handler. The proper use of this is when you install a TSR, before it is resident. At this point, you can make use of all DOS facilities to determine which correction should be applied for the CritErr address. Use this function to get and save the InDOS flag address, determine the DOS version, apply the increment or decrement as required, and save the CritErr flag address in a separate pointer.

Then, when the TSR pops up, it can use its own InDOS pointer to determine whether DOS is active and, if necessary, it can use its own CritErr pointer to get the current value of that flag, save the value, set the flag to force use of the alternate stack, do any processing needed, and restore the original flag value before exiting.

Int 21h	Function 35h	V2
	Get Interrupt Vector	

Gets the interrupt handler address for the specified interrupt

Calling registers: AH   35h

AL   Interrupt number

Return registers: ES:BX   Pointer to interrupt handler

Comments: Although the interrupt handler address is readily available for a given interrupt, this is the only *approved* way to get the current setting of an interrupt vector. This function is guaranteed to work cleanly and return a reliable value for the vector. Another program, a terminate-and-stay-resident (TSR) utility, for example, can change the interrupt vector after this function has returned the value. This happens when a single-user, single-tasking operating system is pushed beyond its limits.

When you set up a program that will work from an interrupt, you should use this function to determine the original setting of the interrupt so that you can restore it when you finish. You must be careful in doing this because you can come into conflict with TSRs or other interrupt handlers. If you remember an interrupt value, and a TSR starts and changes it, you might replace the interrupt vector in a way that would disable the TSR.

To guard against such a happening, you should always compare the current contents of any interrupt vector you are about to restore to the value your program originally set into it. If these values are not the same, some other program has modified the interrupt vector since you saved it and it is not safe to perform the restore or to remove your program from memory. If they do match, you can restore the original value with no danger.

Int 21h	Function 36h	V2
	Get Free Disk Space	

Gets the amount of space available on a designated disk drive in addition to other selected information about the drive

Calling registers: AH   36h
                          DL   Disk drive (0 = default, 1 = A, and so on)

Return registers: AX   Sectors per cluster (FFFFh if the drive was invalid)
                         BX   Number of available clusters
                         CX   Bytes per sector
                         DX   Clusters on the drive

Comments: This function, which is similar to Functions 1Bh and 1Ch, returns basic information that can be used to determine the available space on a disk.

You start by specifying the disk drive you want to check. You get back the following raw information:

- Number of sectors per cluster

- Number of available clusters

- Number of bytes per sector

- Number of clusters on the drive

639

Using this information, the amount of space available is

(Available clusters) × (sectors per cluster) × (bytes per sector)

This returns the number of bytes available on the drive. Divide by 1,024 to get the number of kilobytes, or divide by a record length to get the available space in numbers of records for a database, and so on.

To get the total usable space on a disk, use the following:

(Clusters on the drive) × (sectors per cluster) × (bytes per sector)

With this, you can write a function that prints something like this:

```
XXX bytes free out of YYY
```

Functions 1Bh and 1Ch return similar information.

Int 21h	Function 37h	Subfunction 00h	V2
	Get Switchchar		

Gets the current switchchar

Calling registers: AH 37h
AL 00h

Return registers: AL FFh, AL subfunction was not in the range 0–3
DL Switch character

Comments: The switchchar is the character used by DOS during parsing of strings to designated command switches. Normally, the switchchar is set to be the slash (/), but you can set it to some other character if your application requires it.

Int 21h	Function 37h	Subfunction 01h	V2
	Set Switchchar		

Enables you to reset the current switchchar

Calling registers: AH 37h
AL 01h
DL Switch character

Return registers: AL FFh, AL subfunction was not in the range 0–3

Comments: The switchchar is the character used by DOS during parsing of strings to designated command switches. Normally, the switchchar is set to be the slash (/), but you can set it to some other character if your application requires it.

If you use this function, you should determine the current switchchar (Subfunction 0) and store it so that you can restore the original switchchar when your program is completed.

Int 21h   **Function 37h**   **Subfunction 02h**   **V2 and 4.0 only**

Read Device Availability

Indicates whether device names must be preceded by the pseudopath name /DEV/

Calling registers:	AH	37h
	AL	02h
Return registers:	AL	FFh, AL subfunction was not in the range 0–3
	DL	0, /DEV/ must precede device names
		<> 0, /DEV/ does not need to precede device names

Comments: The device availability flag, present in V2 only, controlled a UNIX-like feature that permitted files and devices to have identical names by forcing all devices to be in the pseudo-directory DEV. When the flag is 00, devices can be opened or closed only in the DEV directory; any nonzero flag permits devices to take precedence over file names, which means that no file anywhere in the system can have a name identical to any device. In V3, the flag was set permanently to nonzero, and Subfunction 3 was disabled.

Int 21h   **Function 37h**   **Subfunction 03h**   **V2 only**

Sets Device Availability

Determines whether device names must be preceded by the pseudopathname /DEV/

Calling registers:	AH	37h
	AL	03h
	DL	0, /DEV/ must precede device names
		<> 0, /DEV/ need not precede device names
Return registers:	AL	FFh, AL subfunction was not in the range 0–3
	DL	Device availability flag (same as input)

Comments: The device availability flag, present in V2 only, controlled a UNIX-like feature that permitted files and devices to have identical names, by forcing all devices to be in the pseudo-directory DEV. When the flag is 00, devices can be opened or closed only in the DEV directory; any nonzero flag permits devices to take precedence over file names, which means that no file anywhere in the system can have a name identical to any device. In V3, the flag was set permanently to nonzero, and Subfunction 3 was disabled.

Int 21h   **Function 38h**   **V2**

Get/Set Current Country Information

Gets the current country information; with DOS V3.0 and later, allows the country information to be set also

Calling registers:	AH	38h
	AL	00, get current country information
		With DOS V3.0 and later:
		01 to FEh, specified country code less than 255
		FFh, country code is in BX register
	BX	Country code if AL=FFh
	DS:DX	Pointer to buffer for information
	DX	FFFFh to set country code (DOS V3.0 and later)
Return registers:	Carry flag clear if successful	
	BX	Country code (DOS V3 only)
	DS:DX	Pointer to returned country information
	Carry flag set if error	
	AX	Error code
		02h, invalid country (file not found)

Comments: Because DOS is an international disk operating system, programs sold for DOS may be expected to work in an international setting. This function tells your program what to use for many of the country-dependent parameters used for display of information. For example, a date format typical of a certain country is encoded in bytes 0 and 1.

When the function gets the country-dependent information, it returns a pointer to a 32-byte buffer with the information. On DOS V3 and later, the function can be used also to set the country information for use by other programs.

The country code is usually the international telephone prefix code (DOS V3 and later). Some typical codes (American Samoa is 684 and Portugal is 351, for example) can be found at the front of almost any telephone book. The important point to notice is that the numbers can be higher than 255. To accommodate this, the function provides for using the BX register to hold the country code when the AL register is set to FFh.

Table DOS.5 gives the format of the country information table, which is pointed to by DS:DX.

Table DOS.5   Country Information Buffer

Bit Offset	Length	Meaning
DOS V2		
00h	Word	Date and time format
	0 = USA	m d y, hh:mm:ss
	1 = Europe	d m y, hh:mm:ss
	2 = Japan	y m d, hh:mm:ss
02h	Byte	Currency symbol

Bit Offset	Length	Meaning
03h	Byte	Zero
04h	Byte	Thousands separator
05h	Byte	Zero
06h	Byte	Decimal separator
07h	Byte	Zero
08h	18 bytes	Reserved

DOS V3 or V4

Bit Offset	Length	Meaning
00h	Word	Date format
	0 = USA	m d y
	1 = Europe	d m y
	2 = Japan	y m d
02h	5 bytes	Currency symbol string (ASCIIZ)
07h	Byte	Thousands separator
08h	Byte	Zero
09h	Byte	Decimal separator
0Ah	Byte	Zero
0Bh	Byte	Date separator
0Ch	Byte	Zero
0Dh	Byte	Time separator
0Eh	Byte	Zero
0Fh	Byte	Currency format
		00h = symbol leads currency, no space
		01h = symbol follows currency, no space
		02h = symbol leads currency, one space
		03h = symbol follows currency, one space
		04h = symbol replaces decimal separator
10h	Byte	Number of digits after decimal

continues

Table DOS.5 Continued

Bit Offset	Length	Meaning
11h	Byte	Time format
		Bit 0 = 0, 12-hour clock
		Bit 0 = 1, 24-hour clock
12h	Double word	Case map call address
16h	Byte	Data list separator
17h	Byte	Zero
18h	8 bytes	Reserved
DOS V5		
00h	Word	Date format
	0 = USA	m d y
	1 = Europe	d m y
	2 = Japan	y m d
02h	5 bytes	Currency symbol string (ASCIIZ)
07h	2 bytes	Thousands separator (ASCIIZ)
09h	2 bytes	Decimal separator (ASCIIZ)
0Bh	2 bytes	Date separator (ASCIIZ)
0Dh	2 bytes	Time separator (ASCIIZ)
0Fh	Byte	Currency format
		00h = symbol leads currency, no space
		01h = symbol follows currency, no space
		02h = symbol leads currency, one space
		03h = symbol follows currency, one space
		04h = symbol replaces decimal separator
10h	Byte	Number of digits after decimal
11h	Byte	Time format
		Bit 0 = 0, 12-hour clock
		Bit 0 = 1, 24-hour clock

Bit Offset	Length	Meaning
12h	Double word	Case map call address
16h	2 bytes	Data list separator (ASCIIZ)
18h	10 bytes	Reserved

The case map call address listed at offset 12h in the table is the far address (segment:offset) of a format procedure that performs country-specific, lower- to uppercase mapping for character values higher than 7Fh. The mapping procedure should be called with the characters to be mapped in the AL register. The adjusted values are returned in the AL register.

Int 21h   **Function 39h**   **V2**

Create Subdirectory

Creates a subdirectory at the specified drive and path location

Calling registers: AH   39h
                          DS:DX   Pointer to ASCIIZ path specification

Return registers: Carry flag clear if successful
                          Carry flag set if error
                          AX   Error code
                                         03h, path not found
                                       05h, access denied

Comments: DOS does not provide a way to manipulate directory entries other than through this function and the other directory functions (Functions 3Ah and 3Bh). This particular function enables you to create a new directory, which takes the path name of the directory and the drive designation if necessary.

This function returns an error and does not create the requested directory if the directory already exists, if any element of the path name does not exist, or if the directory is from the root and the root is full.

In a network environment, you must have create-access rights to be allowed to create a subdirectory.

Int 21h   **Function 3Ah**   **V2**

Remove Subdirectory

Removes a subdirectory if it is empty

645

Calling registers: AH   3Ah
                         DS:DX   Pointer to ASCIIZ path specification

Return registers: Carry flag clear if successful
                         Carry flag set if error
                         AX   Error code
                                     03h, path not found
                                     05h, access denied
                                     10h, current directory

Comments: This is one of only three functions provided to manipulate directory entries in other directories. It enables you to delete the specified directory but only if the directory exists and is empty and if the directory to be deleted is not the default directory.

In a network environment, you must have create-access rights to be allowed to delete a sub-directory.

Int 21h   Function 3Bh   V2

Set Directory

Sets the current or default directory to match the designated string

Calling registers: AH   3Bh
                         DS:DX   Pointer to ASCIIZ path string

Return registers: Carry flag clear if successful
                         Carry flag set if error
                         AX   Error code
                                     03h, path not found

Comments: This function enables you to place your program in a designated location in the directory system.

A useful technique for a program that works in a special directory is to use Function 47h to determine the current directory and save that information before using this function to set a new directory area. Then, when the program is finished, it can return to the original directory. Too few programs perform this simple step.

Int 21h   Function 3Ch   V2

Create/Truncate File (handle)

Creates the designated file if it does not exist or truncates it to zero length if it does exist

Calling registers: AH   3Ch
                         CX   File attribute
                         DS:DX   Pointer to ASCIIZ file specification

Return registers: Carry flag clear if successful
AX   File handle
Carry flag set if error
AX   Error code
                        03h, path not found
                        04h, no handles available
                        05h, access denied

Comments: This function is basic to file operations. It does for handle-oriented functions what Function 16h does for file control block (FCB) functions. It creates the named file if it does not exist or truncates it to zero length if it does exist. The desired file is named by an ASCIIZ string, which may contain drive and path specifiers. A 16-bit file handle is returned. The file handle is used for further access to the file. The new file will have the file attributes set in the CX register. The following table describes the file types that are matched according to the different values:

Value	File Types Matched
00h	Normal
02h	Hidden
04h	System
06h	Hidden and system

When the truncate function is not wanted, you have three options, depending on which DOS version is running:

- With DOS V2, try to open the file with Function 3Dh. If the function fails, call this function to create the file.

- With DOS V3, try to create the file with Function 5Bh. If the function fails, call Function 3Dh to open the file.

- With DOS V4, you also can use Function 6Ch, which provides all file-open options in a single function.

Either way, you need to think carefully about the use of this function. More than one programmer has called this function at the wrong time and destroyed important data.

This function fails if any element of the path name does not exist, if the file is being created in the root directory and the root is full, or if a read-only file exists with the same name.

The file is created as a normal file with read/write permission returned. Function 43h can be used to change the file's attributes if you want. You cannot use this function to create either subdirectories or volume labels.

In a network environment, you must have create-access rights to be allowed to create or truncate a file.

647

Int 21h   Function 3Dh   V2

Open File (handle)

Opens the designated file and returns a file handle (16-bit number) used to reference the opened file

Calling registers: AH   3Dh

AL   Access mode (DOS V2)

Access and file-sharing mode (DOS V3 and above)

DS:DX   Pointer to ASCIIZ file specification

Return registers: Carry flag clear if successful

AX   File handle

Carry flag set if error

AX   Error code

01h, invalid function

02h, file not found

03h, path not found

04h, no handles available

05h, access denied

0Ch, invalid access code

Comments: To open a file, specify the file name as an ASCIIZ string. Normal, hidden, or system files are accessible to the function. Register AL tells the function what access you want to the file. Table DOS.6 shows how to set the AL register for DOS V2 and V3.

Table DOS.6   Access and File-Sharing Modes

Bit	Meaning
76543210	

DOS V2

.....000	Read access
.....001	Write access
.....010	Read/write access

DOS V3 or V4

.....000	Read access
.....001	Write access

648

Bit 76543210	Meaning
....010	Read/write access
....x...	Reserved
.000....	Sharing mode—compatibility mode
.001....	Sharing mode—read/write access denied
.010....	Sharing mode—write access denied
.011....	Sharing mode—read access denied
.100....	Sharing mode—full access permitted
0.......	Inherited by child processes
1.......	Private to current process

In DOS V3 and higher, in addition to requesting read/write access, you can request network access (file-sharing modes) and indicate whether the file is to be inherited by any children that this process may execute.

On return, the file is opened for access in the desired mode unless the file cannot be found or the desired access mode is not allowed (accessing a read-only file with the access mode set to read/write, for example). If the file-open function is successful, the read/write pointer will be at the beginning of the file.

In DOS V2, only bits 0–2 of the AL register are significant in this function. The remaining bits should be set to zero. In DOS V3 and higher with the file-sharing software loaded, four bits of the AL register are devoted to permissions for other processes (bits 4–6, the sharing mode, and bit 7, the inherit bit). On the dark side, a file-sharing error results in an Int 24h (Critical Error) with error code 02h (Drive Not Ready).

The inherit bit, if set to 1, makes the file private to the process that opened it; it does not pass to any child processes. If this bit is 0, the file passes on to any process spawned after the file is opened. If a file handle is inherited by a child or duplicated by a process, all its file-sharing modes also are inherited.

Compatibility mode (bits 3–7 set to zero) is the normal mode for most DOS software written before DOS V3, as well as for much of the software written afterward. As long as the software is running on a single workstation, there is no conflict in file access. When networking software is introduced and file sharing becomes a reality, compatibility mode no longer is suitable for file control.

To work with other programs in a network environment, programs will have to use sharing modes in the open call to provide for access within the limits of the programming task involved.

Files opened by using FCB functions are assumed to be in compatibility mode unless they are opened for read-only access, in which case they are assigned deny-write sharing mode. Files opened by handle functions with read-only access also are considered to be in deny-write sharing mode. All other compatibility access modes will deny all outside file access.

To use this function properly, the programmer must carefully think through the required access to the file and the implications of unrestricted write access to the file. The resulting possible modes are shown in the following list:

- *Deny read/write.* Files opened in this mode cannot be opened again by another program (or the current program) either on the current machine or on another machine on the network. This type of access is necessary for control of database operations for critical updating.

- *Deny write.* Files opened in this mode can be opened only for reading by other programs.

- *Deny read.* Files opened in this mode cannot be opened for reading by other programs.

- *Deny none.* No access (read or write) is denied to other programs.

Multiple-program access to data files is a serious concern in a network environment. Databases can be corrupted by programs trying to update the same file record simultaneously. Methods of coordinating file access among different programs are beyond the scope of this book. You should consult books on networked databases or operating systems to learn about such coordination mechanisms.

Int 21h	Function 3Eh	V2
	Close File (handle)	

Closes a file previously opened with file handles

Calling registers:	AH	3Eh
	BX	File handle

Return registers:	Carry flag clear if successful	
	Carry flag set if error	
	AX	Error code
		06h, invalid handle

Comments: This function is used to close a previously opened or created file by using the DOS file-handling functions. The handle is returned to the system for use, and any updates to the file are performed. The file's date, as recorded in its directory entry, is updated if changes are made.

Good programming practice dictates that a program should always close any files it opens to force the operating system to update the file system properly. DOS automatically closes active file handles when a program terminates, but you should not rely on it, particularly if you want your programs to be portable.

Note: Be especially careful about closing file handle zero, which is the standard input device (normally, the keyboard). If you accidentally close file handle zero, you will lose communication through the keyboard unless you immediately reopen the CON device.

Int 21h   Function 3Fh   V2

Read File or Device (handle)

Reads data from the file or device specified by the file-handle argument; this data is written to a designated memory location

Calling registers:	AH	3Fh
	BX	File handle
	CX	Number of bytes
	DS:DX	Pointer to buffer area

Return registers:	Carry flag clear if successful	
	AX	Number of bytes read
	Carry flag set if error	
	AX	Error code
		05h, access denied
		06h, invalid handle

Comments: A basic file read gets a designated number of bytes from the file to the buffer as specified. If a read completes successfully, but AX is less than CX, a partial read occurred before the end of file (EOF) was detected. If the EOF already has been reached when this function is called, the carry flag will be set, but the AX register will be zero.

As with all file-handle calls, devices can be treated exactly the same as files. You can use this function to read from character devices such as the keyboard. Some special restrictions apply, however, when you are dealing with a character device. If a character device is in cooked mode (see Function 44h), the read is terminated by a carriage return (it reads only a single line).

In a network environment, you must have read-access rights to read a file or device.

Int 21h   Function 40h   V2

Write to a File or Device (handle)

Writes data to a file specified in the handle

Calling registers:	AH	40h
	BX	File handle
	CX	Number of bytes to write
	DS:DX	Pointer to buffer of data to write

Return registers: Carry flag clear if successful

AX   Number of bytes written

Carry flag set if error

AX   Error code

                           05h, access denied

                           06h, invalid handle

Comments: Using the file-handle function to write to a file is as simple as specifying the file handle and the number of bytes and pointing to the data buffer. The function then writes that number of bytes to the current position in the file.

Register AX returns the number of bytes written or, if the function failed, an error code. Normally, the number of bytes returned in AX is the same as the number of bytes to write (CX register). If the write was successful and if AX is less than CX, a partial record was written. Partial-record writes could result if the disk is out of space; in this case, a check of available space with Function 36h, 1Bh, or 1Ch is a good test. An error code is returned if the file is marked as read-only.

In a network environment, you must have write-access rights to write to a file or device.

Int 21h   **Function 41h**   **V2**

               Delete File

Deletes the specified file from the system

Calling registers: AH   41h

                      DS:DX   Pointer to ASCIIZ file specification

Return registers: Carry flag clear if successful

Carry flag set if error

AX   Error code

                           02h, file not found

                           05h, access denied

Comments: This function deletes the file by marking the directory entry with an E5h in the first byte of the file name. This makes it possible to recover the "deleted" file if no other files are created or changed after the deletion. Nothing else is changed in the directory entry. The clusters allocated to the file are returned to the system for reuse. The actual file is not over-written.

Unlike the file control block (FCB) delete function (13h), wild cards are not allowed here. If you want to delete a group of files by matching a file name that uses wild cards, you must use the search functions (4Eh and 4Fh) to locate the files one by one. Because this function allows access to files in subdirectories, this restriction is easy to live with.

If the file exists but has the read-only attribute, or if the file cannot be found, this function fails.

To delete a file in a network environment, you must have create-access rights.

Int 21h   **Function 42h**   **V2**

Move File Pointer

Changes the current location in the file, the file pointer, to a position relative to the start of file, end of file, or current position

Calling registers:	AH	42h
	AL	Method code
		00h, offset from beginning of file
		01h, offset from current position
		02h, offset from end of file
	BX	File handle
	CX	Most significant part of offset
	DX	Least significant part of offset
Return registers:	Carry flag clear if successful	
	DX:AX	New file-pointer location
	Carry flag set if error	
	AX	Error code
		01h, invalid function (file sharing)
		06h, invalid handle

Comments: The file read/write pointer is adjusted by this function to a new position set from the beginning, end, or current position in the file. The offset can be specified as a 32-bit number (ranges up to 4,096M). Before V4, you could not practically use files of this size because the operating system restricted you to a maximum 32M disk capacity for a single disk volume. In V4, this limit was removed. When the file pointer is moved, this becomes the next point at which data is written into or read from the file.

A practical use of this function, other than setting the file position, is to determine the file size. You can get this by setting register AL to 2 (relative to end of file) and the CX and DX registers to 0 (offset from end of file). The location returned in the AX and DX registers represents the actual size of the file in bytes. Of course, this leaves the pointer at the end of the file. If this is not satisfactory, you must reset the position to the desired location before a read or write.

Another important use of the function is to implement an open-at-end-of-file or append function. You can use Function 3Dh to open the file and then use this function to reset immediately the read/write pointer to the end of file by the same method used to determine the file size (AL = 2, CX and DX = 0).

With this function, you can set the file pointer to a position before the beginning of the file or after the end of it. Setting the file pointer after the end of the file does not result in an error except when a read is attempted from this nonexistent location. A write to a location past the end of the file causes space to be allocated to the file and makes the file large enough to accommodate the write. Setting the file pointer before the beginning of the file results in an error when a read or write is attempted.

653

If this function is used on a network system with a file in deny-read or deny-none sharing mode, the file-pointer information is adjusted on the computer that has the file. If the file is in any other sharing mode, the file-pointer information is kept on the remote computer.

| **Int 21h** | **Function 43h** | **Subfunction 00h** | **V2** |

Get File Attributes

Gets the attributes of a file

Calling registers:

	AH	43h
	AL	00, get file attributes
	DS:DX	Pointer to ASCIIZ file specification

Return registers: Carry flag clear if successful

	CX	Attribute byte (see Table DOS.7)
	Carry flag set if error	
	AX	Error code
		01h, invalid function (file sharing)
		02h, file not found
		03h, path not found
		05h, access denied

Comments: The file attributes for a directory entry are bit-mapped as shown in Table DOS.7.

Table DOS.7   Bit Meanings for Attribute Byte Returned by Function 43h, Subfunction 00h

Bit 76543210	Meaning
.......1	Read only
......1.	Hidden
.....1..	System
....1...	Volume label
...1....	Directory
..1.....	Archive
xx......	Unused

Attributes of directory entries for the volume label or for subdirectories are not accessible with this function.

Int 21h	Function 43h	Subfunction 01h	V2
	Set File Attributes		

Sets the attributes of a file

Calling registers:

AH	43h
AL	01, set file attributes
CX	New attribute (see Table DOS.8)
DS:DX	Pointer to ASCIIZ file specification

Return registers:

Carry flag clear if successful
Carry flag set if error

AX	Error code
	01h, invalid function (file sharing)
	02h, file not found
	03h, path not found
	05h, access denied

Comments: The attributes for a file can be set to the values shown in the Table DOS.8.

Table DOS.8   Attribute Settings Used for Function 43h, Subfunction 00h

Bit 654 3210	Meaning
... ...1	Read only
... ..1.	Hidden
... .1..	System
.1.	Archive

You cannot set the subdirectory or volume label attributes with this function. To create a volume label, you must use the file control block (FCB) file-creation function and an extended FCB. Function 39h is the only function that enables you to create a directory.

In a network environment, you must have create-access rights to change any file-attribute bit except the archive bit. Changing the archive bit does not require any restrictive rights.

Int 21h	Function 44h	V2

Device Driver Control (IOCTL)

Passes or retrieves control information to and from a device driver

Calling registers:

AH	44h
AL	Device subfunction code (see Table DOS.9)
BX	Handle (Subfunction codes 00h, 01h, 02h, 03h, 06h, 07h, 0Ah, 0Ch, and 10h)
BL	Drive code, 0 = default, 1 = A, and so on (Subfunction codes 04h, 05h, 08h, 09h, 0Dh, and 11h)
CX	Number of bytes to read or write
CH	Category code (Subfunction codes 0Ch, 0Dh, 10h, and 11h)
CL	Function code (Subfunction codes 0Ch, 0Dh, 10h, and 11h)
DS:DX	Pointer to buffer area (Subfunction codes 02h–05h)
DS:DX	Pointer to parameter block (Subfunction codes 0Ch, 0Dh, 10h, and 11h)
DX	Device information (Subfunction code 01h) (see Table DOS.9)

Return registers:

Carry flag clear if successful

AX	Number of bytes transferred (Subfunction codes 02h–05h)
AL	Status (Subfunction codes 06h–07h)
00h	Not ready
FFh	Ready
AX	Value (Subfunction code 08h)
00h	Removable
01h	Fixed
DX	Device information (Subfunction code 00)

Carry flag set if error

AX	Error code
	01h, invalid function (file sharing)
	04h, no handles available
	05h, access denied
	06h, invalid handle
	0Dh, invalid data
	0Fh, invalid drive

656

Comments: The IOCTL function is one of the most comprehensive functions available under DOS. There are 18 separate subfunctions to this function. Table DOS.9 gives an overview of the subfunctions and the DOS version in which the subfunction was officially activated. The meaning of the information passed depends on which specific device driver is addressed.

Table DOS.9 Device Function Codes

AL	Meaning	DOS Version
00h	Get device information	2.0
01h	Set device information	2.0
02h	Character device read	2.0
03h	Character device write	2.0
04h	Block device read	2.0
05h	Block device write	2.0
06h	Get input status	2.0
07h	Get output status	2.0
08h	Block device changeable?	3.0
09h	Block device local or remote?	3.1
0Ah	Handle local or remote?	3.1
0Bh	Set sharing retry count	3.0
0Ch	Generic I/O control for handles	3.2
0Dh	Generic I/O control for block devices	3.2
0Eh	Get logical drive map	3.2
0Fh	Set logical drive map	3.2
10h	Query IOCTL handle	5.0
11h	Query IOCTL device	5.0

The IOCTL function is a generalized device-driver interface program. Its purpose is not to transfer data but to communicate with a driver and tell it how to work.

657

Int 21h   Function 44h   Subfunction 00h   V2

Get Device Information

Gets information about the device or file referred to by the handle

Calling registers: AH   44h
AL   00h
BX   Handle

Return registers: Carry flag clear if successful
DX   Device information (see Table DOS.10)
Carry flag set if error
AX   Error code
01h, invalid function
05h, access denied
06h, invalid handle

Comments: The DX register returns coded information from the system about the character device or file referenced by the file handle in the BX register. Table DOS.10 shows the codes and their meaning. The handle must refer to an open file or character device.

Table DOS.10   Device Information Codes

Bit Settings FEDCBA98 76543210	Meaning
Character Device	
....1	Standard input device
....1.	Standard output device
....1..	NUL device
....1...	Clock device
....0....	Device does not support Int 28h
....1....	Device supports Int 28h
....0.....	Cooked mode
....1.....	Raw (binary) mode
.... .0......	End of file for input
.... .1......	Not end of file for input
.... 1.......	Character device

Bit Settings FEDCBA98 76543210	Meaning
..xxxxxx	Reserved
.1......	Device can process control strings sent with Subfunctions 02h and 03h. This bit can be read only, not set.
x.......	Reserved

Block Device (Disk File)

....xxxxxx	Block device number (0 = A, 1 = B, and so on for first block driver; sequence proceeds for subsequent drivers)
.... .0......	File has been written to
.... .1......	File has not been written to
.... 0.......	Block device (disk file)
..xxxxxx	Reserved; must be set to zero when function is called
.1......	Device can process control strings sent with Subfunctions 02h and 03h; this bit can be read-only, not set
x.......	Reserved

Bit 5 for character devices is a particularly useful information bit. UNIX programmers are familiar with the terms *cooked mode* and *raw mode* when they deal with terminal devices. In DOS, *cooked mode* means that Ctrl-C, Ctrl-P, Ctrl-Q, Ctrl-S, and Ctrl-Z are processed and also that input is terminated on detection of a carriage return rather than of the specified number of characters. *Cooked mode* is the full-editing entry mode that many reference manuals describe as the only console input mode.

In raw mode, the supplied I/O system drivers ignore the special meanings of these characters and wait until the full specified number of bytes has been received before returning from a read operation. All bytes received are passed directly to the applications program with no interpretation by either the I/O system or DOS. Similar differences exist in output processing (expansion of tab characters, automatic addition of carriage return before line feed, and so forth).

The handle in the BX register must refer to an open file or device. If not, the function returns error code 06h (invalid handle).

Bits 8–15 of the DX register on return correspond to the same bits in the device driver's attribute word (see Chapter 12, "Device Drivers," for a more complete discussion of the attribute word and the driver header).

Int 21h Function 44h Subfunction 01h V2

Set Device Information

The complement of Subfunction 00h for character devices only, this subfunction allows setting device information codes

Calling registers: AH   44h
                        AL   01h
                        BX   Handle
                        DX   Device data word

Return registers: Carry flag clear if successful
                        Carry flag set if error
                        AX   Error code
                                 01h, invalid function
                                 05h, access denied
                                 06h, invalid handle
                                 0Dh, invalid data

Comments: Subfunction 01h enables you to set a limited portion of the device data word for character devices only. The only bit normally modified in this call is bit 5. (For an explanation of raw mode and cooked mode, see the discussion for Subfunction 00h.)

If the DH register is not zero, the subfunction returns error code 01h (invalid function). This subfunction also requires that the handle refer to an open device. If the handle is a file, no information is updated. Table DOS.11 shows the interpretation of the Device Data Word (DX register).

Table DOS.11   Device Data Word

Bit Settings FEDCBA98 76543210	Meaning
....1	Standard input device
....1.	Standard output device
....1..	NUL device
....1...	Clock device
....1....	Device supports Int 28h
....0.....	Cooked mode

Bit Settings	Meaning
....1.....	Raw (binary) mode
.... .0......	End of file for input
.... 1.......	Character device
xxxxxxx	Reserved

Int 21h   Function 44h   Subfunction 02h   V2
Device IOCTL Read

Gets control string information from the driver for use by the calling program

Calling registers: AH   44h
               AL   02h
               BX   Handle
               CX   Number of bytes to get
               DS:DX   Pointer to data buffer

Return registers: Carry flag clear if successful
               AX   Number of bytes transferred
               Carry flag set if error
               AX   Error code
                             01h, invalid function
                             05h, access denied
                             06h, invalid handle
                             0Dh, invalid data

Comments: Arbitrary information about a driver can be passed to the calling program in a control string. This can be any kind of information the driver is written to support; there are no standards for format or content of these messages. The way the driver responds to the request is up to the driver. Chapter 12, "Device Drivers," discusses control strings in more detail.

Bit 0Eh of Subfunction 00h indicates whether the driver can provide or respond to control strings.

Int 21h   Function 44h   Subfunction 03h   V2
Device IOCTL Write

Sends control-string information to the driver

Calling registers:	AH	44h
	AL	03h
	BX	Handle
	CX	Number of bytes to send
	DS:DX	Pointer to data buffer

Return registers:	Carry flag clear if successful	
	AX	Number of bytes transferred
	Carry flag set if error	
	AX	Error code
		01h, invalid function
		05h, access denied
		06h, invalid handle
		0Dh, invalid data

Comments: Arbitrary information about a driver can be passed to the driver in a control string. This can be whatever kind of information the driver is written to support; there are no standards for format or content of these messages. The way the driver responds to the request is up to the driver. Chapter 12, "Device Drivers," discusses control strings in more detail. This subfunction is often used to pass configuration information, such as baud rate or word length, to a driver.

Bit 0Eh of Subfunction 00h indicates whether the driver can provide or respond to control strings.

Int 21h   Function 44h   Subfunction 04h   V2
Block Driver IOCTL Read

Gets control information from a block driver (disk type)

Calling registers:	AH	44h
	AL	04h
	BL	Drive number
	CX	Number of bytes to get
	DS:DX	Pointer to data buffer

Return registers:	Carry flag clear if successful	
	AX	Number of bytes transferred
	Carry flag set if error	
	AX	Error code
		01h, invalid function
		05h, access denied
		06h, invalid handle
		0Dh, invalid data

Comments: Arbitrary information about a block driver can be passed from it in a control string. This can be status information or whatever kind of information the driver is written to support. There are no standards for format or content of these messages.

The way the driver responds to the request is up to the driver. Chapter 12, "Device Drivers," discusses control strings in more detail. A frequent use of this subfunction involves readiness for the operation of block devices. Devices such as CD-ROM drives, tape drives, or other devices can be queried if the driver is written for it.

Bit 0Eh of Subfunction 00h indicates whether the driver can provide or respond to control strings. Block device drivers are not required to support this subfunction. If the driver called does not support it, error code 01h (Invalid Function) is returned.

Int 21h	Function 44h	Subfunction 05h	V2

Block Driver IOCTL Write

Sends controlling information to a block device (disk type)

Calling registers:

AH	44h	
AL	05h	
BL	Drive number	
CX	Number of bytes to send	
DS:DX	Pointer to data buffer	

Return registers:

Carry flag clear if successful

AX	Number of bytes transferred	

Carry flag set if error

AX	Error code	
	01h, invalid function	
	05h, access denied	
	06h, invalid handle	
	0Dh, invalid data	

Comments: Arbitrary information about a block driver can be passed to it in a control string. This can include commands or whatever kind of information the driver is written to support. There are no standards for format or content of these messages.

The way the driver responds to the request is up to the driver. Chapter 12, "Device Drivers," discusses control strings in more detail. Frequent uses of this subfunction include non-I/O device functions, such as tape rewind and disk eject.

Bit 0Eh of Subfunction 00h indicates whether the driver can provide or respond to control strings. Block device drivers are not required to support this subfunction. If the driver called does not support it, error code 01h (Invalid Function) is returned.

Int 21h   Function 44h   Subfunction 06h   V2
Get Input Status

Returns status of the device or file for input operations

Calling registers: AH   44h
                               AL   06h
                               BX   Handle

Return registers: Carry flag clear if successful
                             AL   Input status code (see Table DOS.12)
                         Carry flag set if error
                           AX   Error code
                                             01h, invalid function
                                           05h, access denied
                                           06h, invalid handle

Comments: With this subfunction, you can tell whether a particular device or file is ready for an input operation. You can test files for position at EOF except when positioned by Function 42h, or you can test whether character devices are ready to operate. Table DOS.12 gives the input status code (register AH) interpretation.

Table DOS.12   Input Status Code for Function 44h, Subfunction 06h

Code	File	Device
00h	At EOF	Not ready
FFh	Not at EOF	Ready

(***Special case:*** *A file does not return EOF if positioned at EOF using Int 21h, Function 42h.*)

Int 21h   Function 44h   Subfunction 07h   V2
Get Output Status

Returns status of the device or file for output operations

Calling registers: AH   44h
                               AL   07h
                               BX   Handle

Return registers: Carry flag clear if successful
                        AL   Output status code (see Table DOS.13)
                        Carry flag set if error
                        AX   Error code
                                            01h, invalid function
                                            05h, access denied
                                            06h, invalid handle

Comments: With this subfunction, you can tell whether a particular device or file is ready for an output operation. As shown in the following table, files always return ready for output; character devices do not.

Table DOS.13   Input Status Code for Function 44h, Subfunction 07h

Code	File	Device
00h	At EOF	Not ready
FFh	Not at EOF	Ready

Int 21h	Function 44h Subfunction 08h	V3

Block Device Removable?

Used to determine whether a block device is removable

Calling registers: AH   44h
                         AL   08h
                         BL   Drive number

Return registers: Carry flag clear if successful
                        AX   00h, removable media
                                            01h, nonremovable media
                        Carry flag set if error
                        AX   Error code
                                            01h, invalid function
                                            0Fh, invalid drive

Comments: Applications that need to locate data files or overlays on a particular device can determine with this subfunction whether the device is removable. If the desired file is not located on the device and the device is removable, the program should prompt the user to insert the correct disk in order to continue.

Bit 0Bh of the device driver's attribute word indicates whether the driver can support this function. Some drivers do not. In this case, the subfunction returns error code 01h.

665

Int 21h   **Function 44h   Subfunction 09h**   **V3.1**

Block Device Local or Remote?

Determines whether the block device is local or remote

Calling registers: AH   44h
AL   09h
BL   Drive number

Return registers: Carry flag clear if successful
DX   Device attribute word
Bit 12 = 1, drive is remote
Bit 12 = 0, drive is local
Carry flag set if error
AX   Error code
01h, invalid function
0Fh, invalid drive

Comments: If the network has not been started, this subfunction returns error code 01h, invalid function.

It is good programming practice to avoid this function. Programs should be written in such a way that they are not dependent on a particular device's location on a network. Certain undocumented functions operate properly, however, only with respect to local files and cannot be used with remote files; if such a function must be used in a program, this subfunction permits you to avoid some error conditions.

If bit 12 of DX is 0, indicating that the drive is local, other bits in DX have the following meaning:

Bit 1   1 = Drive uses 32-bit sector addressing

Bit 6   1 = Drive supports Function 44h, Subfunctions 0Dh, 0Eh, and 0Fh

Bit 7   1 = Drive supports Function 44h, Subfunction 11h

Bit 9   1 = Drive is local, but is shared by other computers in the network

Bit 11   1 = Drive supports Function 44h, Subfunction 08h

Bit 13   1 = Drive requires media descriptor in FAT

Bit 14   1 = Drive supports Function 44h, Subfunctions 04h and 05h

Bit 15   1 = Substitution drive (that is, set by the SUBST command)

All other bits are zero.

Int 21h   **Function 44h**   **Subfunction 0Ah**   **V3.1**

Handle Local or Remote?

Determines whether the handle is local or remote

Calling registers: AH   44h
                         AL   0Ah
                         BX   Handle

Return registers: Carry flag clear if successful
                         DX   Device attribute word
                         Bit 15 = 1, handle is remote
                         Bit 15 = 0, handle is local
                         Carry flag set if error
                         AX   Error code
                                       01h, invalid function
                                       06h, invalid handle

Comments: If the network has not been started, this subfunction returns error code 01h, invalid function.

It is good programming practice to avoid this function. Programs should be written in such a way that they are not dependent on a particular device's location on a network. Certain undocumented functions operate properly, however, only with respect to local handles and cannot be used with remote handles; if such a function must be used in a program, this subfunction permits you to avoid some error conditions.

If bit 7 of DX is clear, the handle identifies a file, and other bits in DX have the following meaning:

Bits 0–5	*Drive number (0 = A, 1 = B, and so on)*
Bit 6	1 = File has not been written to
Bit 12	1 = No inherit
Bit 14	1 = Date/time not set at close

All other bits are zero.

If bit 7 of DX is set, the handle is a device handle, and other bits in DX have the following meaning:

Bit 0	1 = Console input device
Bit 1	1 = Console output device
Bit 2	1 = Null device

Bit 3	1 = Clock device
Bit 4	1 = Special device
Bit 5	1 = Binary mode
	0 = ASCII mode
Bit 6	0 = EOF returned if device is read
Bit 11	1 = Network spooler
Bit 12	1 = No inherit
Bit 13	1 = Named pipe

All other bits are zero.

Int 21h	**Function 44h** **Subfunction 0Bh**	**V3.0**
	Set Sharing Retry Count	

Changes the retry parameters for file sharing across a network

Calling registers: AH 44h
AL 0Bh
CX Pause between retries
DX Number of retries

Return registers: Carry flag clear if successful
Carry flag set if error
AX Error code
01h, invalid function

Comments: When you are working with multiple PCs over a network, the retry parameters are associated with file-locking mechanisms. It is assumed that file locks are temporary and will be cleared after a short update. Such built-in mechanisms automatically retry to establish access to a file if the file is locked when the first attempt is made.

The two parameters (retry count and pause between retries) are dependent on the system. Differences in CPU and clock speed have a significant effect on the length of the pause. The CX register controls the pause by giving the number of times a tight timing loop is executed. The timing loop repeats 65,536 times whenever it is called. Clearly, the retry count is the number of times the access is attempted before failure is reported. Defaults are PAUSE = 1 and RETRY = 3.

These parameters can be used to tune the system to minimize file-sharing problems. If you expect long periods during which a desired file will be locked, you can extend the pause period when you make another attempt to access the file. If you change any of the defaults, however, restoring the defaults to prevent side effects on other programs is prudent.

Int 21h   Function 44h   Subfunction 0Ch   V3.2

Generic I/O Control for Handles

In DOS V3.2, sets or gets the iteration count for a character-oriented device. In DOS V3.3 and above, the function also performs code-page switching. In DOS V5.0, the function also gets and sets the display mode.

Calling registers:	AH	44h
	AL	0Ch
	BX	Handle
	CH	Category code (device type)
DOS V3.2		
		05h, printer
DOS V3.3 and above		
		00h, unknown
		01h, COMx
		03h, CON
		05h, LPTx
	CL	Minor function code
DOS V3.2 and above		
		45h, set iteration count
		65h, get iteration count
DOS V3.3 and above		
		4Ah, select
		4Ch, prepare start
		4Dh, prepare end
		6Ah, query select
		6Bh, query prepare list
DOS V5.0		
		5Fh, set display mode
		7Fh, get display mode
	DS:DX	Pointer to iteration count word (minor codes 45h and 65h)
		Pointer to parameter block (minor codes 4Ah, 4Ch, 4Dh, 5Fh, 6Ah, 6Bh and 7Fh)
Return registers:	Carry flag clear if successful	
	Carry flag set if error	
	AX	Error code
		01h, invalid function

Comments: The iteration count word specifies the number of times an operation is attempted before giving up. With DOS V3.2, only category code 05h (printer) was allowed.

669

With DOS V3.3 and higher, this subfunction changed to handle code-page switching for devices. The minor functions include the following:

- Prepare Start (4Ch) tells the driver to be ready for code-page font loading through Subfunction 03h. A special start operation is a "refresh," which is generated by setting all code-page IDs to FFFFh.

- Prepare End (4Dh) tells the driver that the code-page font loading is complete.

- Select Code Page (4Ah) selects the code page to use.

- Set Display Mode (5Fh) sets the display mode for the device.

- Query Selected Code Page (6Ah) determines the status of the code page from the device.

- Query Prepare List (6Bh) determines the list of code pages on the device.

- Get Display Mode (7Fh) gets the display mode for the device.

Table DOS.14 defines the parameter block, pointed to by DS:DX.

Table DOS.14   Parameter Block

Bytes	Meaning
Minor Functions 4Ah, 4Dh, 6Ah	
0–1	Length of following data
2–3	Code-page ID
Minor Function 4Ch	
0–1	Flags
2–3	Length of parameter block (after this point)
4–5	Number of code pages
.	
.	Code-page designations
.	
Minor Function 6Ah	
0–1	Length of parameter block (after this point)
2–3	Number of hardware code pages
.	
.	Hardware code-page designations

Bytes	Meaning
n–n+1	Number of prepared code pages
.	Prepared code-page designations

Minor Functions 5Fh, 7Fh

Bytes	Meaning
0	Information level (must be zero)
1	Reserved
2–3	Length of parameter block (after this point)
4–5	Control flags
	0 = Intensity off
	1 = Intensity on
6	Display mode
	1 = Text mode
	2 = Graphics mode
7	Reserved
8–9	Number of colors
0A–0B	Screen width, in pixels (graphics mode only)
0C–0D	Screen length, in pixels (graphics mode only)
0E–0F	Columns
10–11	Rows

Int 21h	Function 44h Subfunction 0Dh	V3.2
	Generic I/O Control for Block Devices	

A collection of six input/output functions for handling special functions on block devices

Calling registers: AH   44h
                          AL   0Dh

671

BL	Drive number
CH	Category code
	08h, disk drive
CL	Minor function code
	40h, set parameters for block device
	41h, write track on logical drive
	42h, format and verify track on logical drive
	46h, set media ID
	60h, get parameters for block device
	61h, read track on logical device
	62h, verify track on logical drive
	66h, get media ID
	68h, sense media type
DS:DX	Pointer to parameter block

Return registers: Carry flag clear if successful
Carry flag set if error

AX	Error code
	01h, invalid function
	02h, invalid drive

Comments: This subfunction is provided to extend the capability to control block devices. A number of primitive operations can be controlled through this IOCTL call in a device-independent manner. Each minor function is examined individually.

Minor Function 40h (set device parameters) must be called before the other minor functions for a given device.

Minor Function 40h: Set Device Parameters

The parameter block for this minor function indicates the complete layout of the block device, including physical characteristics, media type, and so forth.

Parameter Block Layout

Byte Offset	Meaning
00h	Special function codes
01h	Device type code
02–03h	Device attributes code
04–05h	Number of cylinders
06	Media type code
07–25h	Device BPB
26h–?	Track layout table

Special Function Codes

Bit 76543210	Meaning
. . . . 0	BPB entry is a new BPB
. . . . 1	Use current BPB
. . . . . . 0 .	Use all fields in parameter block
. . . . . . 1 .	Use only track layout field
. . . . . 0 . .	Sectors in track may be different sizes
. . . . . 1 . .	Sectors in track are all the same size
0 0 0 0 0 . . .	Reserved

Device Type Codes

Code	Meaning
00h	320/360K, 5 1/4-inch disk
01h	1.2M, 5 1/4-inch disk
02h	720K, 3 1/2-inch disk
03h	Single-density, 8-inch disk
04h	Double-density, 8-inch disk
05h	Fixed disk
06h	Tape drive
07h	Other block device

Device Attribute Codes

Bit 76543210	Meaning
. . . . 0	Removable storage
. . . . 1	Nonremovable storage
. . . . . . 0 .	Device does not indicate change-line status

continues

Bit	Meaning
......1.	Device does indicate change-line status
xxxxxx..	Reserved

Media Type Code

Code	Meaning
00h	1.2M, 5 1/4-inch disk
01h	320/360K, 5 1/4-inch disk

BIOS Parameter Block (BPB) Layout

Offset Byte	Field Length	Meaning
00h	Word	Number of bytes per sector
02h	Byte	Number of sectors per cluster
03h	Word	Number of reserved sectors starting at sector 0
05h	Byte	Number of FATs
06h	Word	Maximum number of root directory entries
08h	Word	Total number of sectors
0Ah	Byte	Media descriptor
0Bh	Word	Number of sectors per FAT
0Dh	Word	Number of sectors per track
0Fh	Word	Number of heads
11h	Double word	Number of hidden sectors
15h	11 bytes	Reserved

Track Layout Table

Length	Meaning
Word	Number of sectors in track
Word	Number of first sector in track

Length	Meaning
Word	Size of first sector in track
.	
.	
.	
Word	Number of last sector in track
Word	Size of last sector in track

Minor Function 41h: Write Track

The write-track function allows specification of all important parameters for a track (head, cylinder, sector, number of sectors, and location of data). For counting, the sector numbers and cylinder numbers start at zero.

Parameter Block

Offset	Meaning
00h	Special function = 0
01–02h	Number of disk head to use
03–04h	Number of disk cylinder to use
05–06h	First sector to use
07–08h	Number of sectors to transfer
09–0Ch	Pointer to data transfer buffer

Minor Function 42h: Format and Verify Track

This function formats and verifies a track on the disk. You have to specify only the disk head and cylinder to use; all the rest is handled by the driver.

Parameter Block—Format Track

Offset	Meaning
00h	Special function = 0
01–02h	Number of disk head to use
03–04h	Number of disk cylinder to use

675

Parameter Block—Verify Format Status

Offset	Meaning
00h	Special function = 1
01–02h	Number of disk head to use
03–04h	Number of disk cylinder to use

On completion, if the special function field is checked for status, the following return values are possible:

0 = Supported by ROM BIOS, heads/cylinders allowed

1 = Not supported by ROM BIOS

2 = Specified number of heads/cylinders not allowed

3 = Drive is empty

Minor Function 46h: Set Media ID

This function sets the serial number, volume label, and file system type for the specified drive.

Parameter Block

Offset	Meaning
00–01h	Information level
02–05h	Serial number
06–10h	ASCII volume label
11–18h	File system type
"FAT12"	12-bit FAT
"FAT16"	16-bit FAT

Minor Function 60h: Get Parameters

This function is the complement to minor Function 40h. This minor function uses the same parameter-block format as minor Function 40h to retrieve information about the device from the driver.

Minor Function 61h: Read Track

This function reads the track into the memory buffer provided in the parameter block. As with the write-track minor function, the location information is provided to the driver.

Parameter Block

Offset	Meaning
00h	Special function = 0
01–02h	Number of disk head to use
03–04h	Number of disk cylinder to use
05–06h	First sector to use
07–08h	Number of sectors to transfer
09–0Ch	Pointer to data transfer buffer

Minor Function 62h: Verify Track

This function performs the track-verify operation part of format/verify in minor Function 62h.

Parameter Block

Offset	Meaning
00h	Special function = 0
01–02h	Number of disk head to use
03–04h	Number of disk cylinder to use

Minor Function 66h: Get Media ID

This function gets the serial number, volume label, and file system type for the specified drive.

Parameter Block

Offset	Meaning
00–01h	Information level
02–05h	Serial number
06–10h	ASCII volume label
11–18h	File system type
"FAT12"	12-bit FAT
"FAT16"	16-bit FAT

677

Minor Function 68h: Sense Media Type

This function returns the media type for the specified drive.

Parameter Block

Offset	Meaning
00h	Default flag
	0 = Media is not default type
	1 = Media is default type
01h	Media type
	2 = 720K disk
	7 = 1.44M disk
	9 = 2.88M disk

Int 21h	Function 44h	Subfunction 0Eh	V3.2

Get Logical Drive Map

Determines whether more than one logical drive name is assigned to a device

Calling registers: AH   44h
                     AL   0Eh
                     BL   Drive number

Return registers: Carry flag clear if successful
                     AL   Drive number
                                  0 = Only one logical drive assigned
                                  1 = A, 2 = B, and so on
                   Carry flag set if error
                     AX   Error code
                                  01h, invalid function
                                  05h, access denied
                                  0Fh, invalid drive

Comments: The drive number returned by this call tells you the last drive designation used to access the drive if more than one logical drive designation applies to the device.

Int 21h   **Function 44h**   **Subfunction 0Fh**   **V3.2**

Set Logical Drive Map

Sets the logical drive name that is used to access this device next

Calling registers: AH   44h
AL   0Fh
BL   Drive number

Return registers: Carry flag clear if successful
AL   Drive number
0 = Only one logical drive assigned
1 = A, 2 = B, and so on
Carry flag set if error
AX   Error code
01h, invalid function
05h, access denied
0Fh, invalid drive

Comments: When you copy files between two disks, each of which corresponds to a different logical device but both of which must use the same physical device, you normally are prompted to change the disks when you do I/O to the device that is not currently in the drive. This function enables you to force the switch without getting the operating system prompt.

The function works by setting the next drive letter that would be issued to refer to this device. DOS then will not issue the `Insert Disk` prompt to the user. Subfunction 0Eh determines the name of the last logical drive used to access the device.

Int 21h   **Function 44h**   **Subfunction 10h**   **V5**

Query IOCTL handle

Determines whether a specific IOCTL capability is supported by the device specified by the handle

Calling registers: AH   44h
AL   10h
BX   Device handle
CH   Category code
CL   Function code
DS:DX   Pointer to parameter block

Return registers: Carry flag clear if successful

AX   0

Carry flag set if error

AL   01h, function not supported

05h, access denied

Comments: The parameter block is set up as it would be for the generic IOCTL call. If the device in question supports Query IOCTL, this can be used to determine whether the specified generic IOCTL call is supported by the driver. Typically, an application interrogates the driver before making a generic IOCTL call.

Int 21h   Function 44h   Subfunction 11h   V5

Query IOCTL device

Determines whether a specific IOCTL capability is supported by the device specified by the handle

Calling registers: AH   44h

AL   11h

BL   Drive number

CH   Category code

CL   Function code

DS:DX   Pointer to parameter block

Return registers: Carry flag clear if successful

AX   0

Carry flag set if error

AL   01h, function not supported

05h, access denied

0Fh, invalid drive

Comments: The parameter block is set up as it would be for the generic IOCTL call. If the device in question supports Query IOCTL, this can be used to determine whether the specified generic IOCTL call is supported by the driver. Typically, an application interrogates the driver before making a generic IOCTL call.

The following functions are supported in DOS 5.0:

40h   Set device parameters

41h   Write track on logical drive

42h   Format track on logical drive

46h   Set media ID

60h   Get device parameters

61h   Read track on logical drive

62h	Verify track on logical drive
66h	Get media ID
68h	Sense media type

Int 21h   Function 45h   V2

Duplicate Handle

Provides a new handle for an already opened device or file

Calling registers: AH   45h
                         BX   File handle

Return registers: Carry flag clear if successful
                        AX   New handle
                        Carry flag set if error
                        AX   Error code
                                    04h, no handles available
                                    06h, invalid handle

Comments: Duplicating a file handle provides another handle for the same file. The file pointers move together. If you move the file pointer of one file, the file pointer for the other moves also.

The most common use for this function is to force an update to a file's directory entry without having to incur the overhead of a file open and close. In DOS versions earlier than 3.3, this was the only way to force the update. DOS V3.3 introduced the new Function 68h to do the same thing more easily.

Int 21h   Function 46h   V2

Force Duplicate Handle

Makes two file handles refer to the same opened file at the same location

Calling registers: AH   46h
                         BX   First file handle
                         CX   Second file handle

Return registers: Carry flag clear if successful
                        Carry flag set if error
                        AX   Error code
                                    04h, no handles available
                                    06h, invalid handle

681

Comments: The result of this function is similar to that of Function 45h: It causes two file handles to refer to the same file and move together. The most significant use of this function is to provide for device redirection. You can control the redirection process from inside another program and then return the device to normal with the following steps:

1. Use Function 45h to duplicate the handle to be redirected. Save the new handle for later restoration.

2. Use Function 46h for redirection by putting the "handle to be redirected" into CX and the "handle to be redirected to" in BX.

When you want to return conditions to normal, call Function 46h again with the redirected handle in CX and the duplicated handle returned by Function 45h in the BX register.

In the calling registers, if the handle in CX refers to an open file, the file is closed first before the function starts.

Int 21h	Function 47h	V2
	Get Current Directory	

Returns an ASCIIZ string with the full path of the current directory, not including the drive and the leading backslash character (\)

Calling registers: AH   47h
                         DL   Drive code (0 = default, 1 = A, and so on)
                         DS:SI   Pointer to 65-byte scratch buffer

Return registers: Carry flag clear if successful
                         DS:SI   Unchanged, buffer contains current directory path as
                                         ASCIIZ string
                         Carry flag set if error
                         AX   Error code
                                     0Fh, invalid drive

Comments: This function returns the path name of the current directory without the drive designator or the leading backslash (\). Because you set the drive code when you call the function, the absence of the drive designator and backslash is OK. (If you want to use the return from this function to build a file name, you have to supply the drive and initial backslash for the file name.) If the directory is the root directory, the string returned is NUL (first byte 0).

Many programs could benefit from using this function before changing the directory so that the user could be returned to the original directory when the program is complete. Programmers must be careful because an invalid drive code causes the function to fail. To set the current directory, refer to Function 3Bh.

Int 21h	Function 48h	V2
	Allocate Memory	

Allocates a block of memory for use and returns a pointer to the beginning of the block

Calling registers: AH   48h
                                BX   Number of paragraphs needed

Return registers: Carry flag clear if successful
                                AX   Initial segment of allocated block
                                Carry flag set if error
                                AX   Error code
                                                07h, memory control blocks destroyed
                                                08h, insufficient memory
                                BX   Size of largest available block if function failed

Comments: The pointer is the segment address of the base of the block (the base address is AX:0000h). Because COM programs are always allocated all of memory, this function always fails when it is called from a COM program unless memory has first been released after entering the program. (For more information, see Chapter 3, "The Dynamics of DOS," and Chapter 10, "Program and Memory Management.")

In multitasking environments, the top of memory seen by the process may not be the actual top of memory. Programs such as DESQview and Windows give each program only as much space as the program is allowed in the program information files.

If the attempt to get space fails, the function returns the size of the largest available memory block. Another call requesting no more than this amount of space will be successful. The EXEC loader function uses this technique to assign all available RAM to a COM program. First, it loads BX with FFFFh, which asks for 1,048,560 bytes of RAM (more than can ever be available). Because error code 8 is certain to result, no check is performed. The Function 48h call is simply repeated; the first call returned in BX is the amount actually available, which the second call allocates.

This same technique can be used in your own programs if you need to know the amount of RAM available (not reserved by any program). If you use Function 48h with BX = FFFFh, the value returned in BX is the number of blocks available.

Int 21h	Function 49h	V2
	Release Memory	

Releases a block of memory to the pool managed by DOS (makes the memory available for other programs)

Calling registers: AH   49h
                         ES   Segment of block to be released

Return registers: Carry flag clear if successful
                         Carry flag set if error
                         AX   Error code
                                     07h, memory control blocks destroyed
                                     09h, invalid memory block address

Comments: This function assumes that the block of memory being freed was acquired from Function 48h. If the block was not acquired from Function 48h, the function may simply fail (if you are lucky), or it may cause unpredictable errors in the program's freeing of the memory or in other programs residing in memory. The problem occurs because the system, in being told to free memory, is expecting the address given to refer to a defined memory block as part of the overall memory-allocation scheme. Chapter 10, "Program and Memory Management," discusses memory management in more detail.

Int 21h	Function 4Ah	V2
	Modify Memory Allocation	

Expands or shrinks a memory block previously allocated by Function 48h

Calling registers: AH   4Ah
                         BX   New requested block size in paragraphs
                         ES   Segment of block to be modified

Return registers: Carry flag clear if successful
                         Carry flag set if error
                         AX   Error code
                                     07h, memory control blocks destroyed
                                     08h, insufficient memory
                                     09h, invalid memory block address
                         BX   Maximum block size available (if AX = 08h)

Comments: Programs can use this function call to modify a memory block they received from a call to Function 48h or to modify their own memory allocation. Because COM programs are allocated all memory when they run, they must call this function if they expect to be able to EXEC other programs. EXE programs also need to call this function to free memory unless their MAXALLOC parameter in the EXE header has been modified to request less than all memory. Chapter 10, "Program and Memory Management," discusses in more detail the subject of memory management for program execution.

This function is frequently referred to as SETBLOCK.

Int 21h   **Function 4Bh**   **V2**

Execute Program (EXEC)

Executes a program under control of another program

Calling registers: AH   4Bh
                       AL   00, loading and executing a program
                                   01, loading but not executing a program
                                   03, loading an overlay
                                   05, enter Exec state
                       ES:BX   Pointer to parameter block
                       DS:DX   Pointer to program specification
                       DS:DX   Pointer to ExecState structure, defined as follows
                                       (Subfunction code 05h only):
                                   00h (word), reserved; should be zero
                                   02h (word) type flags; bit 0 = program is an EXE,
                                       bit 1= program is an overlay
                                   04h (dword), pointer to ASCIIZ program name
                                       (can include path specification)
                                   08h (word), PSP segment for new program
                                   0Ah (dword), CS:IP of new program
                                   0Eh (dword), program size (including PSP)

Return registers: Carry flag clear if successful. All registers except CS and IP are de-
                      stroyed, including the stack pointers. SS and SP must be stored
                      locally, in a CS-addressable location, before calling this function and
                      restored after it returns.

                      Carry flag set if error
                      AX   Error code
                                  01h, invalid function
                                  02h, file not found
                                  05h, access denied
                                  08h, insufficient memory
                                  0Ah, invalid environment
                                  0Bh, invalid format

Comments: The EXEC function provides for executing programs and managing overlays in the system. The originating program (the parent process) regains control when the new program (the child process) has been completed. The parent may receive an exit code from the child if the child uses a DOS-termination function that transfers return codes.

This function can also load overlays. Overlays can consist of program segments or data. A major difference between program execution and overlay operation is that programs are allocated memory from whatever is free in the system, and overlays are loaded to memory already owned by the program invoking the overlay function. If necessary, a program should release memory (a necessity for COM programs) before executing another program.

685

The primary control for the operation is the parameter block pointed to by the ES:BX registers. The format of the parameter block is shown in Table DOS.15.

Table DOS.15   Parameter Block Layout

Offset Byte	Field Length	Contents
EXEC Function (AL = 00h)		
00h	Word	Segment pointer to environment block
02h	Word	Offset of command tail
04h	Word	Segment of command tail
06h	Word	Offset of first FCB (offset 5Ch)
08h	Word	Segment of first FCB
0Ah	Word	Offset of second FCB (offset 6Ch)
0Ch	Word	Segment of second FCB
Debug Function (AL = 01h)		
00h	Word	Segment pointer to environment block
02h	Word	Offset of command tail
04h	Word	Segment of command tail
06h	Word	Offset of first FCB (offset 5Ch)
08h	Word	Segment of first FCB
0Ah	Word	Offset of second FCB (offset 6Ch)
0Ch	Word	Segment of second FCB
0Eh	Word	SP of loaded program
10h	Word	SS of loaded program
12h	Word	IP of loaded program
14h	Word	CS of loaded program
Overlay Function (AL = 03h)		
00h	Word	Segment pointer to load point for the overlay
02h	Word	Relocation factor to be applied to the code image (EXE files only)

The environment block is a series of ASCIIZ strings used to pass environment information to the program being executed. These strings are set at the command level by the SET function, or they can be created internally in the program. Usually, these strings include the COMSPEC variable (where to find the system command processor, COMMAND.COM), the PATH variable (where to look for executables), in addition to other variables as specified on the system.

A typical environment block might look like this:

```
          1         2         3         4
1234567890123456789012345678901234567890
COMSPEC=C:\COMMAND.COM*PATH=C:\DOS**
```

The asterisks represent NUL or zero bytes. If the environment block pointer is zero, the child inherits the same environment the parent has. In DOS V3 and later, the final zero in the environment block is followed by a 2-byte word with a character count followed by an ASCIIZ string with the drive and path name of the program file being executed.

The command tail is a single string that consists of whatever is typed on the command line after the command to be executed. The format is a single-byte length count, followed by the string of characters and terminated with a carriage return. The total length cannot exceed 128 bytes; it is copied into the program segment prefix (PSP) at offset 80h, giving the command tail only 128 bytes before it runs into the program.

A typical command tail looks like this:

```
         1         2         3         4
1234567890123456789012345678901234567890
#/c CHAPT01.DOC@
```

The # is a single numeric byte with the value 14, and @ represents the single-byte carriage return.

A child process spawned in this way inherits the parent process I/O files unless the parent explicitly specifies otherwise in the file-open call (Function 3Dh). Standard files remain open. If standard files were redirected for the parent, they remain redirected for the child. The parent can redirect the files (see Function 46h).

When you call this function, precautions are in order. During any EXEC function, it must be assumed that all registers are modified in the course of the function call because the purpose of the function is to run another program. When the EXEC function returns, only CS and IP can be assumed to be correct. Before the call, the parent program must store at least SS and SP (plus any other registers you want to retain) in locations that can be addressed by the CS segment register. On return, SS and SP can be restored to their original values, but the restoration must take place with interrupts disabled so that the restoration cannot be stopped in the middle, a condition that would put the system in an unstable state.

The EXEC function cannot complete successfully unless there is sufficient memory to load the desired program. Assembly language programs should release needed memory with Function

687

4Ah before calling EXEC. When a C program starts, unneeded memory has already been released. For a more detailed discussion of memory allocation, see Chapter 10, "Program and Memory Management."

In DOS V2, this function gained a reputation for problems. Many of them were due to programmers attempting to save registers by pushing them onto the stack, but some versions failed to ensure that the CPU direction flag was properly set up and, as a result, the system would hang intermittently. To prevent this problem, simply issue a CLD instruction as part of the setup before calling EXEC. If your program is used only with V3 and later, this is not necessary; the check was added to the DOS code.

An interesting sidelight is that this function in IBM's version of DOS 2.x is not physically located in the IBMDOS.COM file but rather forms part of COMMAND.COM. IBM did this to save space; other V2.x systems included it as part of MSDOS.SYS, as did IBM beginning with 3.0 (when the requirement that both DOS files be unfragmented was finally relaxed).

Subfunction 01h is used by debuggers to load a program into memory and leave it ready for execution. This function is used by Microsoft's DEBUG, SYMDEB, and CODEVIEW debuggers, and by Borland's Turbo Debugger. Of particular use to the debugger is the fact that the loaded program's SS, SP, CS and IP register values are stored at ES:[BX+0Eh] on return. Like the documented Subfunctions 00h and 03h, Subfunction 01h destroys all register contents on return; the programmer must save the ES and BX register values where they can be retrieved relative to CS before the programmer can use the SS:SP and CS:IP values.

Subfunction 05h, which is new to V5, supports programs that intercept the MS-DOS EXEC call and perform the loading themselves. It performs internal fixups such as setting the version number the loaded program will see (the one set by SETVER) and performing load-time patches to the loaded program.

Subfunction 05h should be the last call made before transferring control to the loaded program. In particular, the application should make no MS-DOS or BIOS calls or otherwise issue any software interrupts between the successful return of this function and transferring control to the loaded program.

If DOS is running in the HMA, A20 is turned off on return from the call to Subfunction 05h.

Int 21h	Function 4Ch	V2
	Terminate with Return Code	

Exits a program to its parent task

Calling registers:	AH	4Ch
	AL	Return code
Return registers:	None	

Comments: On exit, DOS does the following:

- Restores the termination handler vector from PSP:000Ah

- Restores the Ctrl-Break handler vector from PSP:000Eh

- Restores the critical-error handler vector from PSP:0012h (DOS V3 and above)

- Flushes the file buffers (handle files)

- Transfers to the termination-handler address

This method is now the approved way to terminate a program. Programs that exist in DOS V2 and later should always use this function in preference to Int 20h or Int 21h, Function 00h. This function has two advantages over the earlier termination functions:

- It allows the return of an exit code, which can be used as the ERRORLEVEL parameter in batch files or by the parent process through Function 4Dh to determine return information.

- It does not rely on any register settings for proper operation, such as the CS register pointing to the segment the PSP is in.

Because this function automatically closes out file handles and updates the disk directory, it protects against inadvertent errors in file handling. It does not, however, do anything for file control block (FCB) files.

Int 21h	Function 4Dh	V2
	Get Return Code	

Gets the return code from a successful EXEC function call

Calling registers:	AH	4Dh
Return registers:	AH	System exit code
		00, normal termination
		01, termination by Ctrl-C
		02, termination by critical device error
		03, termination by call to Function 31h
	AL	Child exit code

Comments: When this function is called, it returns (once and only once) the exit code returned by a child process through the system. The use of this function resets the returned exit code to zero; if you need to pass it on to a parent process, it must be saved and returned as your own process's exit code. The system exit code tells you whether the program terminated normally.

The child exit code tells you anything the program wants to tell you; its interpretation depends on the program you have run.

Int 21h   Function 4Eh   V2

Search for First Match

Locates the first occurrence of a matching file name, given an ASCII string, which can include wild cards

Calling registers:	AH	4Eh
	CX	Attribute to use in search
	DS:DX	Pointer to ASCIIZ file specification
Return registers:	Carry flag clear if successful	
	Carry flag set if error	
	AX	Error code
		02h, file not found
		03h, invalid path
		12h, no more files

Comments: This function, when given an ASCIIZ string that contains the full file name of a desired file (possibly including the * and ? wild cards), fills information about the returned file into the disk transfer area (DTA). The search is limited by the attribute provided to the function. Only those files that match the attributes specified are found. The file attributes for the file can include the following values:

Value	File Types Matched
00h	Normal
02h	Normal and hidden
04h	Normal and system
06h	Normal, hidden, and system
08h	Volume labels
10h	Directories

Because the attribute is a byte, you can set CX by setting CL to the desired attribute and CH to zero. When the function returns, the DTA is set as shown in the following table:

Offset Byte	Field Length	Contents
00h	21 bytes	Reserved for DOS use on subsequent searches
15h	Byte	Attribute of matched file
16h	Word	File time
18h	Word	File date
1Ah	Double word	File size
1Eh	13 bytes	File name and extension as ASCIIZ string; blanks are stripped, and a period is placed in front of the extension

Time and date entries are interpreted as follows:

Bit Settings FEDCBA98 76543210	Meaning
Time Field Encoding	
xxxxx...	Hours (0–23)
.....xxx xxx.....	Minutes (0–59)
....xxxxx	Two-second increments (0–29)
Date Field Encoding	
xxxxxxx.	Year—1980
.......x xxx.....	Month (1–12)
....xxxxx	Day (1–31)

The DTA may be read to retrieve the information about the located file, which after all will have a file name that is different from the search string if it includes wild cards. The DTA should remain inviolate, however, for use in further searches.

Int 21h   Function 4Fh   V2

Search for Next Match

After a successful call to Function 4Eh, this call continues to find files that match the specified criteria. The DTA must retain the information originally placed there by the call to Function 4Eh.

Calling registers: AH   4Fh

Return registers: Carry flag clear if successful
Carry flag set if error
AX   Error code
12h, no more files

Comments: If wild cards are used in a first search (Function 4Eh), additional files that match the wild-card specification can be found by repeatedly calling this function. A failed search (carry flag set on return from the function) indicates that no additional file names match the pattern.

Searches with the "next match" function continue to use the same procedures used for the first match. The function updates the DTA to indicate the name of the file and other data regarding the file located by the search. The DTA must not be modified between calls to allow successive searches. Table DOS.16 shows the layout of the data in the DTA on return from the function.

Table DOS.16   DTA Layout

Offset Byte	Field Length	Contents
00h	21 bytes	Reserved for DOS use on subsequent searches
15h	Byte	Attribute of matched file
16h	Word	File time
18h	Word	File date
1Ah	Double word	File size
1Eh	13 bytes	File name and extension as ASCIIZ string; blanks are stripped, and a period is placed in front of the extension

Time and date entries are interpreted as follows:

Bit Settings FEDCBA98 76543210	Meaning

Time Field Encoding

xxxxx...	Hours (0–23)
.....xxx xxx.....	Minutes (0–59)
....xxxxx	Two-second increments (0–29)

Date Field Encoding

xxxxxxx.	Year—1980
.......x xxx.....	Month (1–12)
....xxxxx	Day (1–31)

The DTA may be read to retrieve the information about the located file, which after all will have a file name that is different from the search string if it includes wild cards. The DTA should remain inviolate, however, for use in further searches.

Int 21h	**Function 50h**	**V2**
	Set PSP Segment	

Sets the address of the currently executing process's program segment prefix (PSP)

Calling registers: AH   50h
                            BX   Segment address of the new PSP

Return registers: None

Comments: Function 50h allows a terminate-and-stay-resident (TSR) program to implement context switching between the TSR process and the interrupted process on a DOS system. *Context switching* involves making the DOS system think that the TSR is the primary process rather than the interrupted process. To do this, you have to record the original PSP's address (Function 51h) and tell DOS that the TSR's PSP is the current one (Function 50h). When you are ready to return to the interrupted program, you return the PSPs to normal.

It has often been reported that this function is unreliable before DOS V3 and that, in particular, it does not work in an Int 28h handler (Keyboard Busy Loop).

The reason for these reports is simple: DOS V2 switches to its own internal stack before dispatching control to any requested function; if this function is called while DOS is already processing another normal input function, the second stack switch that results destroys information needed by that input function.

The cure is equally simple but extremely subtle: You can trick DOS into believing that it is processing a critical error by manipulating its critical error flag. Setting the critical error flag before calling this function forces DOS to use its alternate internal stack. You must restore the flag to its original value after return from this function. See the comments for Int 21h, Function 34h for details of the critical error flag.

In V3, the DOS dispatch code was modified to test for this function before doing any stack switching; if this function was requested, DOS simply uses the caller's own stack and avoids the problem.

The PSP segment address has come to be called the process ID (PID) for the running process. This function is often known as SetPID.

Int 21h	Function 51h	V2
	Get PSP Segment	

Gets the address of the currently executing process's program segment prefix (PSP)

Calling registers: AH   51h

Return registers: BX   PSP of currently executing process

Comments: This function is used to determine the PSP of the process interrupted by a terminate-and-stay-resident (TSR) program. The TSR can save this address and then tell DOS that its own PSP is the executing one for the course of its processing. See Function 50h and Chapter 11, "Interrupt Handlers," for a more detailed discussion.

It has often been reported that this function is unreliable before DOS V3 and that, in particular, it does not work in an Int 28h handler (Keyboard Busy Loop).

The reason for these reports is simple: DOS V2 switches to its own internal stack before dispatching control to any requested function; if this function is called while DOS is already processing another normal input function, the second stack switch that results destroys information needed by that input function.

The cure is equally simple but extremely subtle: You can trick DOS into believing that it is processing a critical error by manipulating its critical error flag. Setting the critical error flag before calling this function forces DOS to use its alternate internal stack. You must restore the flag to its original value after return from this function. See the comments for Int 21h, Function 34h for details of the critical error flag.

In V3, the DOS dispatch code was modified to test for this function before doing any stack switching; if this function was requested, DOS simply uses the caller's own stack, avoiding the problem entirely.

The PSP segment address has come to be called the process ID (PID) for the running process. This function is often known as GetPID. In Version 3, Function 62h was added as a documented function to perform this same task; in all versions examined, both functions execute the self-same code.

Int 21h	Function 52h	V2
	Get Disk List	

This function provides access to the list of drive parameter blocks, where DOS maintains its data about disk configuration, and to many more internal DOS tables

Calling registers: AH   52h

Return registers: ES:BX   Pointer to DOS table as described in the following paragraph

Comments: For internal purposes, DOS keeps track of key parameters for disk drive operations as a linked list of drive parameter blocks. This function returns a pointer to the head of that linked list. The list of DPBs, however, is only one of a number of items about which DOS maintains data internally, and the pointer returned by this function can be used to locate the other items also, as shown in Table DOS.17. This pointer returned by this function is sometimes referred to as the *list of lists* because of the comprehensive nature of the information that can be ascertained. Appendix D, "The Reserved DOS Functions," discusses this function more fully.

Table DOS.17   Configuration Variable Table (CVT)

Offset Byte	Field Length	Meaning
DOS V3.x and Higher		
–08h	Double word	Current buffer in BUFFERS= chain
–04h	Word	Offset within current buffer
DOS V2.x and Higher		
–02h	Word	Segment of first memory control block
00h	Double word	Pointer to first drive parameter block
04h	Double word	Pointer to first DCB (system file table device control block)
08h	Double word	Pointer to CLOCK$ device driver
0Ch	Double word	Pointer to CON device driver

continues

695

Table DOS.17 Continued

Offset Byte	Field Length	Meaning
DOS V2.x Only		
10h	Byte	Number of logical drives
11h	Word	Maximum bytes per sector on any block device
13h	Double word	Pointer to start of disk buffer chain
17h		Beginning of NUL device driver; first device in the device driver chain
DOS V3.x and Higher		
10h	Word	Maximum bytes per sector on any block device
12h	Double word	Pointer to start of disk buffer chain (in V4, points to EMS link record, which in turn points to buffer chain)
16h	Double word	Pointer to logical drive table (see following discussion for layout)
1Ah	Double word	Pointer to start of DOS's FCB chain
1Eh	Word	Number of FCBs to keep when swapping
20h	Byte	Number of block devices
21h	Byte	Number of logical drives, set by value of LASTDRIVE in CONFIG.SYS (defaults to 5 if not specified)
22h		Beginning of NUL device driver; first device in the device driver chain

Notice that the construction of Table DOS.17 varies with the DOS version. Only the data from the DPB pointer −02h up through +0Fh remains constant over all three versions. In V2, the number of logical drives is given by a byte at 10h, which is followed by a word giving the maximum block size in bytes and a double word pointing to the first buffer control block.

In V3, six more bytes were added at the front of the table: a double-word pointer to the current buffer control block at −08h, and a word giving the offset into the current buffer (usually 0000) is at −04h. The byte at 10h in V2 was moved to 21h in V3, and the six following bytes were moved up to fill the gap. Then at 16h, a double-word pointer to the logical drive table was added, followed at 1Ah by a double-word pointer to the system FCB chain and at 1Eh by a word telling how many of the FCBs to keep when swapping out during network operations. The byte at 20h gives the number of block devices present, and the byte at 21h (mentioned earlier) tells how many logical drives are present.

As noted in Table DOS.17, the only change from V3 to V4 is that the BCB pointer at 12h becomes a pointer to a new EMS linkage block for the file buffers, and the current-BCB pointer at –06h gives direct access to the buffer chain.

There are "holes" in many of the data areas reached by Table DOS.17—not because the unknown bytes have no purpose, but because their purpose is not known. What *is* known comes from dedicated DOS hackers who have been digging out the information one piece at a time; Appendix D, "The Reserved DOS Functions," goes into much more detail in this respect. (The format of each DPB is shown in Table DOS.19, which appears with the discussion of Function 53h.)

Table DOS.18 shows what is known about the Logical Drive Table pointed to at offset 16h in Table DOS.17 (DOS V3 and above). The pointer is to the beginning of this table. There is one table for every logical drive on the system, beginning with drive A. The minimum is a default of five (A through E) or the value set in LASTDRIVE of the CONFIG.SYS file. The tables, each of which is 81 bytes long in V3 (and 88 bytes in V4), follow one another in memory.

Table DOS.18   The Logical Drive Table

Offset Byte	Field Length	Meaning
00h	2 bytes	Actual drive designator and :
02h	65 bytes	Current path for this drive as an ASCIIZ string (includes root directory slash and room for terminating 00h byte)
43h	Word	Current status of drive (bit map)
		8000h = unknown
		4000h = ready for use
		2000h = unknown
		1000h = SUBSTed unit
		0000h = logical drive not mapped to a physical drive
45h	Double word	Pointer to DOS DPB for drive
49h	Word	First cluster of current directory (FFFFh if drive was never accessed; 0 if at the root directory)

continues

697

Table DOS.18 Continued

Offset Byte	Field Length	Meaning
4Bh	Word	Unknown
4Dh	Word	Unknown
4Fh	Word	Number of bytes to skip over when reporting directory: 0002 for normal drive, more if SUBSTed unit

DOS V4

51h	7 bytes	Unknown, default values of 0

Int 21h	**Function 53h**	**V2**
	Translate BPB to DPB	

Translates a BIOS parameter block (BPB) into a DOS drive parameter block (DPB)

Calling registers:	AH	53h
	DS:SI	Pointer to BPB
	ES:BP	Pointer to area for DPB

Return registers: None

Comments: Both the BIOS and DOS keep their own information about the disks and drives attached to the system. This function enables you to change the BIOS parameter block (BPB) to a DOS drive parameter block (DPB). See also Int 21h, Functions 1Fh and 32h in addition to Int 21h, Function 44h, Subfunction 0Dh, minor Function 40h. Table DOS.19 gives the layout of a BPB and a DPB. As you will notice, the information is primarily disk oriented, particularly in the BPB.

Table DOS.19 BIOS and DOS Parameter Block Layout

Offset Byte	Field Length	Meaning
BIOS Parameter Block Information		
00h	Word	Number of bytes per sector
02h	Byte	Number of sectors per cluster
03h	Word	Number of reserved sectors starting at sector 0

Offset Byte	Field Length	Meaning
05h	Byte	Number of FATs
06h	Word	Maximum number of root directory entries
08h	Word	Total number of sectors (or 0, in V4 to indicate use of extended BPB format)
0Ah	Byte	Media descriptor
0Bh	Word	Number of sectors per FAT
0Dh	Word	Number of sectors per track
0Fh	Word	Number of heads
11h	Double word	Number of hidden sectors
15h	Double word	In extended BPB format, total number of sectors; used only if word at offset 08h above is zero. Applies to V4 only.
19h	7 bytes	Reserved

DOS Parameter Block Information
All Versions

Offset Byte	Field Length	Meaning
00h	Byte	Drive number (0 = A, 1 = B, and so on)
01h	Byte	Device driver unit number
02h	Word	Bytes per sector
04h	Byte	Sectors per cluster (zero-based)
05h	Byte	Shift factor
06h	Word	Number of reserved boot sectors
08h	Byte	Number of FAT copies
09h	Word	Number of root directory entries
0Bh	Word	First data sector number
0Dh	Word	Highest cluster number plus 1

continues

Table DOS.19 Continued

Offset Byte	Field Length	Meaning
Version 2 or 3 Only		
Fh	Byte	Sectors per FAT (0–255)
0h	Word	Root directory starting sector number
12h	Double word	Drive's device driver address
16h	Byte	Media descriptor byte
17h	Byte	Disk parameter block access flag (0FFh indicates need to rebuild)
18h	Double word	Address of next device parameter block
Version 2 Only		
1Ch	Word	Starting cluster number for current directory
1Eh	64 bytes	ASCIIZ of current directory path
Version 3 Only		
1Ch	Word	Last cluster number allocated from this drive
1Eh	Word	Purpose unknown; normally FFFFh
Version 4 Only		
0Fh	Word	Sectors per FAT (0–65,535)
11h	Word	Root directory starting sector number
13h	Double word	Drive's device driver address
17h	Byte	Media descriptor byte
18h	Byte	Disk parameter block access flag (0FFh indicates need to rebuild)
19h	Double word	Address of next device parameter block
1Dh	Word	Last cluster number allocated from this drive
1Fh	Word	Purpose unknown; normally FFFFh

Int 21h　　　　　Function 54h　　　　　　　　V2

Get Verify Flag

Gets the current value of the read-after-write (verify) flag

Calling registers:　AH　　　　　54h

Return registers:　AL　　　　　00h, verify off
　　　　　　　　　　　　　　　　　　01h, verify on

Comments: The verify flag controls whether the system does a read-after-write verify of disk operations. The default for this flag is OFF (value 00).

Function 2Eh sets the verify flag. The effect of the setting is to slow down disk operations somewhat to allow the verify but increase the assurance that disk operations are successful.

Because network systems do not support the verify function, the return code is meaningless in these cases.

Int 21h　　　　　Function 55h　　　　　　　　V2

Create PSP

Creates a program segment prefix (PSP) at the designated segment-address location

Calling registers:　AH　　　　　55h
　　　　　　　　　　　　　　DX　　　　　Segment at which to set up PSP

Return registers:　None

Comments: This function is similar to Int 21h, Function 26h. The difference is that this function does not simply copy the PSP; it creates a separate and distinct "child" PSP in preparation for running another program. Like Int 21h, Function 26h, the usefulness of this function has been superseded by the EXEC function (Int 21h, Function 4Bh).

Int 21h　　　　　Function 56h　　　　　　　　V2

Rename File

Renames a file or moves it to another directory on the same disk drive

Calling registers:　AH　　　　　56h
　　　　　　　　　　　　　　DS:DX　　　Pointer to ASCIIZ current file name
　　　　　　　　　　　　　　ES:DI　　　Pointer to ASCIIZ new file name

Return registers: Carry flag clear if successful
Carry flag set if error

	AX	Error code
		02h, file not found
		03h, path not found
		05h, access denied
		11h, not the same device

Comments: The present rename function is both more powerful and less powerful than the one provided for use with file control block (FCB) functions. This rename function enables you to use directory path names to locate files and can even move a file between directories. Because it does not allow wild cards, however, renaming groups of files is no longer a possibility.

For most normal work, the limitations are not significant. Renaming files in directories and moving them between directories is much more advantageous for general use. Multiple files can be handled by the calling program.

The function does not work if the path name does not exist or if a file of the desired name is already in the target directory. Nor does the function work across disk drives. If files being renamed are open, they should be closed first. Leaving a file open when you are renaming it can lead to unpredictable results.

In a network environment, you must have create-access rights to rename a file.

Int 21h	**Function 57h**	**Subfunction 00h**	**V2**

Get File Date and Time

Gets the file's last modified date and time in the directory entry

Calling registers:

	AH	57h
	AL	00h, get the date and time
	BX	File handle

Return registers: Carry flag clear if successful

	CX	Time if getting date and time
	DX	Date if getting date and time

Carry flag set if error

	AX	Error code
		01h, invalid function (file sharing)
		06h, invalid handle

Comments: The date and time functions work on files opened with Functions 3Ch, 3Dh, 5Ah, or 5Bh (the handle open or create functions). Table DOS.20 shows the layout of the bits and how they are interpreted for the date and time.

Table DOS.20   Date and Time Bit Layout

Bit Settings FEDCBA98 76543210	Meaning
Time Field Encoding	
xxxxx...	Hours (0–23)
.....xxx xxx.....	Minutes (0–59)
....xxxxx	Two-second increments (0–29)
Date Field Encoding	
xxxxxxx.	Year—1980
.......x xxx.....	Month (1–12)

Int 21h	Function 57h Subfunction 01h	V2
	Set File Date and Time	

Sets the file's last modified date and time in the directory entry

Calling registers: AH   57h
                         AL   01h, set the date and time
                         BX   File handle
                         CX   Time if setting the date and time
                         DX   Date if setting the date and time

Return registers: Carry flag clear if successful
                        Carry flag set if error
                        AX   Error code
                                    01h, invalid function (file sharing)
                                    06h, invalid handle

Comments: The date and time functions work on files opened with Functions 3Ch, 3Dh, 5Ah, or 5Bh (the handle open or create functions). Table DOS.21 shows the layout of the bits and how they are interpreted for the date and time.

Table DOS.21   Date and Time Bit Layout

Bit Settings FEDCBA98 76543210	Meaning
Time Field Encoding	
xxxxx...	Hours (0–23)
.....xxx xxx.....	Minutes (0–59)
....xxxxx	Two-second increments (0–29)
Date Field Encoding	
xxxxxxx.	Year—1980
.......x xxx.....	Month (1–12)
....xxxxx	Day (1–31)

Int 21h	**Function 58h**	**Subfunction 00h**	**V2**

Get Allocation Strategy

Gets the code that tells which strategy to use for memory allocation

Calling registers:	AH	58h
	AL	00h, get strategy code
Return registers:	Carry flag clear if successful	
	AX	Strategy code
		00h, first fit, low 640K first (default)
		01h, best fit, low 640K first
		02h, last fit, low 640K first
		40h, first fit, UMBs only
		41h, best fit, UMBs only
		42h, last fit, UMBs only
		80h, first fit, UMBs first
		81h, best fit, UMBs first
		82h, last fit, UMBs first
	Carry flag set if error	
	AX	Error code
		01h, invalid function (file sharing)

Comments: In V2, Microsoft and IBM officially specified this function as "used internally by DOS." If your copy of DOS V2 is from a third-party vendor, this function may be used for a different purpose. In V3, this function became an official and documented function in Microsoft documentation, but it remains undocumented in IBM versions.

This subfunction permits a program to learn the strategy DOS is using to allocate memory to processes. In general, this type of parameter is meaningless unless you have reason to believe that one strategy will work better than another.

Possible strategies known to DOS include first fit, best fit, and last fit. These strategies can be modified under V5 to include specifying whether to try the UMBs or the low 640K first. The first-fit strategy searches from low memory to high for the first of memory that is as large as, or larger than, the requested memory size, and returns the first one it finds.

The best-fit strategy checks all available memory blocks to find the smallest block that will meet the allocation requested. Although this strategy results in the most efficient utilization of memory for the available processes, it takes more processor time.

The last-fit strategy is the same as the first-fit strategy except that the search proceeds from high memory to low memory rather than from low to high, and returns the last block that will meet the requirement.

Under V5, if the first memory arena checked yields a successful result (regardless of whether the arena is the low 640K or the UMBs), the second arena is not checked. The best-fit strategy, therefore, does not necessarily give the application the best fit. As long as there is at least one block that can be allocated in the first arena, the second arena, which might yield a better fit, is not checked.

Before V5, because the last-fit strategy (code 02) could be any value greater than or equal to 02, a number other than 02 may have been stored. A test for strategy should account for the possibility that the number can be greater than 02.

Int 21h	Function 58h	Subfunction 01h	V2
	Set Allocation Strategy		

Sets the code that tells which strategy to use for memory allocation

Calling registers:

AH   58h
AL   01h, set strategy code
BX   Strategy code
            00h, first fit, low 640K first (default)
            01h, best fit, low 640K first
            02h, last fit, low 640K first
            40h, first fit, UMBs only
            41h, best fit, UMBs only
            42h, last fit, UMbs only
            80h, first fit, UMBs first

81h, best fit, UMBs first

82h, last fit, UMBs first

Return registers: Carry flag clear if successful

Carry flag set if error

AX   Error code

01h, invalid function (file sharing)

Comments: In V2, Microsoft and IBM officially specified this function as "used internally by DOS." If your copy of DOS V2 is from a third-party vendor, this function may be used for an entirely different purpose. In V3, this function became an official and documented function in Microsoft documentation, but it remains undocumented in IBM versions.

This subfunction selects the strategy DOS uses to allocate memory to processes when DOS is asked for memory. In general, this type of tuning parameter is meaningless for most programmers, unless they have some reason to think that one strategy will work better than another.

Possible strategies known to DOS include first fit, best fit, and last fit. These strategies can be modified under V5 to include specifying whether to try the UMBs first or the low 640K first. The first-fit strategy searches from low memory to high for a memory block and returns the first one that is as large as or larger than the requested memory.

The best-fit strategy checks all available memory blocks to find the smallest block that will meet the allocation requested.

The last-fit strategy is the same as the first-fit strategy except that the search proceeds from high memory to low memory rather than from low to high.

Under V5, if the first memory arena checked yields a successful result (regardless of whether the arena is the low 640K or the UMBs), the second arena is not checked. The best-fit strategy, therefore, does not necessarily give the application the best fit. As long as there is at least one block that can be allocated in the first arena, the second arena, which might yield a better fit, is not checked.

Before V5, the last-fit strategy (code 02) could be any value greater than or equal to 02. When you are setting the strategy, a number other than 02 may be stored.

Int 21h   Function 58h   Subfunction 02h   V5

Get UMB link status

Gets the status of the UMB arena link

Calling registers: AH   58h

AL   02h

Return registers: Carry flag clear if successful

AL   Result

706

                              00h, not linked
                              01h, linked
                    Carry flag set if error
                    AX   Error code
                              07h, arena trashed

Comments: This subfunction permits a program to learn whether DOS is using UMBs in its memory-allocation scheme.

Int 21h   **Function 58h**   **Subfunction 03h**   **V5**

                    Set UMB link status

Sets the status of the UMB arena link

Calling registers: AH   58h
                         AL   03h
                         BX   Link status
                                   00h, unlink
                                   01h, link

Return registers: Carry flag clear if successful
                         Carry flag set if error
                         AX   Error code
                                   01h, invalid function when MS-DOS loaded without DOS=UMB
                                   07h, arena trashed

Comments: This subfunction permits a program to select whether DOS will use UMBs in its memory-allocation scheme.

Int 21h   **Function 59h**   **V3**

                    Get Extended Error Information

Gets extended error return information about a failed call to an Int 21h function, including recommended remedial action. This call destroys registers AX, BX, CX, DX, SI, DI, BP, DS, and ES.

Calling registers: AH   59h
                         BX   00

Return registers: AX   Extended error code
                         BH   Error class
                         BL   Recommended action
                         CH   Error locus

707

Comments: Extended error processing provides a significant extension to DOS error handling by making the DOS system a partner in diagnosing and solving run-time problems. This function adds a significant capability for analyzing and isolating an error that occurs from a DOS call. It can be called after an error from any call to Int 21h or from Int 24h when an error status is returned. If there was no error, this function returns AX = 0000h. File control block (FCB) calls that return FFh can also be resolved with this function.

The information returned is classified in the accompanying tables. Register AX returns the extended error code (see Table DOS.22). These are general system errors already familiar as the error returned from many Int 21h functions. Register BH contains the error class, which provides further information about the error (see Table DOS.23).

The BL register returns the most interesting value, the recommended action to resolve the error (see Table DOS.24). Finally, register CH returns the error locus, which helps identify the error's physical location (see Table DOS.25). The only problem with all this information is that the wealth of it can be staggering. A generalized error handler would be out of the question. Some general steps, however, can be taken depending on what type of error has occurred.

If a function indicates an error by setting the carry bit on return, its error handling should be written like this:

1. Load the registers for the function.

2. Issue the Int 21h function call.

3. If the carry flag is clear, continue with normal operations.

4. If the carry flag is set, disregard the error code returned from the function and issue a call to Function 59h.

5. Use the suggested action in the BL register to determine the proper course of action.

Some functions indicate an error by returning a code in the AL register (AL = FFh). For these cases, the call should be written like this:

1. Load the registers for the function.

2. Issue the Int 21h function call.

3. If no error is reported in AL, continue with normal operations.

4. If an error is reported in AL, disregard the error code reported and issue a call to Function 59h.

5. Use the suggested action in the BL register to determine the proper course of action.

You must be careful in using this function. On return, registers AX, BX, CX, DX, SI, DI, BP, DS, and ES are destroyed. You also must call the function *immediately* after an error has occurred. If another DOS function is executed before the call, the return does not correspond to the desired error.

Table DOS.22 Extended Error Codes Returned in AX

Codes Decimal	Hex	Meaning
1	01	Invalid function number
2	02	File not found
3	03	Path not found
4	04	No handles available
5	05	Access denied
6	06	Invalid handle
7	07	Memory control blocks destroyed
8	08	Insufficient memory
9	09	Invalid memory block address
10	0A	Invalid environment
11	0B	Invalid format
12	0C	Invalid access code
13	0D	Invalid data
14	0E	Reserved
15	0F	Invalid drive
16	10	Attempt to remove current directory
17	11	Not the same device
18	12	No more files
19	13	Disk write-protected
20	14	Unknown unit
21	15	Drive not ready
22	16	Unknown command
23	17	CRC error
24	18	Bad request structure length
25	19	Seek error

continues

709

Table DOS.22 Continued

Codes Decimal	Hex	Meaning
26	1A	Unknown media type
27	1B	Sector not found
28	1C	Out of paper
29	1D	Write fault
30	1E	Read fault
31	1F	General failure
32	20	Sharing violation
33	21	Lock violation
34	22	Invalid disk change
35	23	FCB unavailable
36	24	Sharing buffer overflow
37	25	Code page mismatched
38	26	Unable to complete file operation (V4 only)
39	27	Handle disk full
40 – 49	28 – 31	Reserved
50	32	Network request not supported
51	33	Remote computer not listening
52	34	Duplicate name on network
53	35	Network name not found
54	36	Network busy
55	37	Network device no longer exists
56	38	NetBIOS command limit exceeded
57	39	Network adapter error
58	3A	Incorrect network response
59	3B	Unexpected network error

Codes Decimal	Hex	Meaning
60	3C	Incompatible remote adapter
61	3D	Print queue full
62	3E	Not enough space for print file
63	3F	Print file deleted
64	40	Network name deleted
65	41	Access denied
66	42	Network device type incorrect
67	43	Network name not found
68	44	Network name limit exceeded
69	45	NetBIOS session limit exceeded
70	46	Sharing temporarily paused
71	47	Network request not accepted
72	48	Print or disk redirection is paused
73–79	49 – 4F	Reserved
80	50	File already exists
81	51	Duplicate FCB
82	52	Cannot make directory entry
83	53	Fail on Int 24
84	54	Too many redirections
85	55	Duplicate redirection
86	56	Invalid password
87	57	Invalid parameter
88	58	Network data fault
89	59	Function not supported by network (V4 only)
90	5A	Required system component not installed (V4 only)

Table DOS.23 Error Class Codes Returned in BH

Class Codes Decimal	Hex	Meaning
1	01	Out of resource
2	02	Temporary situation
3	03	Authorization
4	04	Internal
5	05	Hardware failure
6	06	System failure
7	07	Application program error
8	08	Not found
9	09	Bad format
10	0A	Locked
11	0B	Media
12	0C	Already exists
13	0D	Unknown

Table DOS.24 Recommended Action Codes Returned in BL

Action Code	Meaning
1	Retry. If not cleared, prompt user to Abort or Ignore.
2	Delay and then retry. If not cleared, prompt user to Abort or Ignore.
3	Get correct data from user (bad file name or disk drive).
4	Abort application with clean-up.
5	Abort without cleanup (clean-up may increase problems).
6	Ignore error.
7	Prompt user to correct error, and then retry.

Table DOS.25   Error Locus Codes Returned in CH

Locus Code	Meaning
1	Unknown
2	Block device (disk or disk emulator)
3	Network
4	Serial device
5	Memory related

Int 21h	Function 5Ah	V3
	Create Uniquely Named File	

Creates a file with a guaranteed unique name in the specified directory

Calling registers: AH   5Ah
                        CX   Attribute
                        DS:DX   Pointer to ASCIIZ path specification ending in a backslash
                                    (\ )

Return registers: Carry flag clear if successful
                        AX   Handle
                        DS:DX   Pointer to ASCIIZ file specification with file name
                                    appended
                        Carry flag set if error
                        AX   Error code
                                    03h, path not found
                                    04h, no handles available
                                    05h, access denied

Comments: Unique files always have uses as temporary files. By using the unique file-creation call, you do not have to worry about the exact name created; you can leave that to the operating system.

To use the function, provide a path name to the directory in which you want the temporary file created. Use a full path name ending in a backslash character (for example, \TMP\, to put the file in the \TMP directory). You also can specify the attribute of the file you want created. The following table shows the valid attributes that can be set by this function. The function returns a unique file name according to its own internal rules.

713

Value	File Types Matched
00h	Normal
02h	Hidden
04h	System
06h	Hidden and system

The only ways to fail are if the path to the desired directory does not exist, if you have already used all the available handles for the current process, or if you are creating the file in the root directory and it is already full. You have to take some care, though. Files created as temporary files have as much existence as files created to have continuing existence. Because these types of files are not automatically deleted when the program ends, your program should clean up after itself by deleting all such files it creates.

In a network environment, you must have create-access rights to use this function.

Int 21h	Function 5Bh	V3
	Create New File	

Creates a new file in the specified directory

Calling registers: AH   5Bh
                  CX   Attribute
                  DS:DX   Pointer to ASCIIZ file specification

Return registers: Carry flag clear if successful
                  AX   Handle
                  Carry flag set if error
                  AX   Error code
                                03h, path not found
                                  04h, no handles available
                                  05h, access denied
                                  50h, file already exists

Comments: This is the normal method of creating a new file you intend to use as more than just a temporary file. The function returns a file handle for access to the file. If the file cannot be created because the path does not exist, because no handles are available, or because you try to create it in the root directory and the root is full, the function fails.

Unlike Function 3Ch, this function fails if the file already exists. You can use this function to test for the existence of a designated file. If creation succeeds, the file did not exist.

The file is created as a normal file with read/write access. You can change the attributes with Function 43h. You cannot, however, create volume labels or subdirectories. The valid attributes are listed in Table DOS.26.

Table DOS.26 Valid attributes for creating files

Value	File Types Matched
00h	Normal
02h	Hidden
04h	System
06h	Hidden and system

An interesting use for this file-creation function is to implement a semaphore mechanism across a PC network. If this function successfully creates a file, the program has the semaphore and can proceed into its critical code section. If it cannot create the file, you can retest the operation periodically.

When the program that created the file is finished with its critical section, it deletes the file and thereby releases the semaphore.

In a network environment, you must have create-access rights to use this function.

Int 21h	Function 5Ch	Subfunction 00h	V3
	Set File Access Locks		

Locks a specified area of a file

Calling registers:
AH   5Ch
AL   00h
BX   File handle
CX   Most significant part of region offset
DX   Least significant part of region offset
SI   Most significant part of region length
DI   Least significant part of region length

Return registers: Carry flag clear if successful

Carry flag set if error

AX		Error code
		01h, invalid function
		06h, invalid handle
		21h, lock violation
		24h, sharing buffer exceeded

Comments: File locking is an essential operation in network environments for database- and other transaction-oriented functions. If more than one process is allowed to write to the same section of a file, the results of two such writes are indeterminate. Record locking enforces an ordering on the operations so that one process must complete its write before another starts. It does not guarantee that the order of writes is sensible — it just makes sure that they do not interfere with each other.

Locks and unlocks are like Begin-End pairs in Pascal or braces ({}) in C; they must always be matched. For every file lock, there must be an exact duplicate file unlock in the same program. Failing to unlock a file results in a file whose state is indeterminate.

Programs that use file locking must take pains to trap all possible error exits from the program so that unlocks can be handled even in abnormal conditions. Programs which access files that are or can be locked should not attempt direct access to the file. The proper procedure for using the locking mechanism is not to rely on it to prevent collisions directly. Rather, an attempt should be made to lock the desired portion of the file and check the resulting error code for successful completion. If the lock can be created, file manipulation can proceed. If the lock cannot be created, the program should delay and try again.

The locking mechanism includes an automatic retry function. By using the IOCTL Function (44h), Subfunction 0Bh, you can change the number of retries and the retry interval.

File handles duplicated with Function 45h inherit access to the locked regions. Programs spawned with the program EXEC Function (4Bh) do not inherit the file locks along with the files.

Int 21h	Function 5Ch	Subfunction 01h	V3
	Clear File Access Locks		

Unlocks a specified area of a file that was locked with Subfunction 00h

Calling registers:	AH	5Ch
	AL	01h
	BX	File handle
	CX	Most significant part of region offset
	DX	Least significant part of region offset
	SI	Most significant part of region length
	DI	Least significant part of region length

Return registers: Carry flag clear if successful
Carry flag set if error
AX Error code
01h, invalid function
06h, invalid handle
21h, lock violation
24h, sharing buffer exceeded

Comments: File locking is an essential operation in network environments for database- and other transaction-oriented functions. If more than one process is allowed to write to the same section of a file, the results of two such writes are indeterminate. Record locking enforces an ordering on the operations so that one process must complete its write before another starts. It does not guarantee that the order of writes is sensible — it just makes sure that they do not interfere with each other.

Locks and unlocks are like Begin-End pairs in Pascal or braces ({ }) in C; they must always be matched. For every file lock, there must be an exact duplicate file unlock in the same program. Failing to unlock a file results in a file whose state is indeterminate.

Refer to the discussion for Subfunction 00h for additional details about this function.

Int 21h	Function 5Dh	Subfunction 00h	V3
	Copy Data to DOS Save Area		

This function copies 18 bytes of data from the location pointed to by DS:SI to the DOS internal register-save area so that it is returned as the register content when DOS returns to the caller

Calling registers: AH 5Dh
AL 00h

Return registers: DS:SI Pointer to data to be copied

Comments: This function replaces all the saved register values kept by DOS and can transfer control to another part of the system. Its intended purpose is not known.

Int 21h	Function 5Dh	Subfunction 06h	V3
	Get Critical-Error Flag Address		

Returns a pointer to the location at which the system critical-error flag is stored

Calling registers: AH 5Dh
AL 06h

Return registers: DS:SI Pointer to critical-error flag

Comments: This function returns a pointer to the error flag used by DOS to determine whether a critical error has occurred.

Int 21h   **Function 5Dh**   **Subfunction 0Ah**   **V3**

Set Error Data Values

Changes the system-error data codes stored internally by each DOS operation

Calling registers: AH   5Dh

                              AL   0Ah

                              DS:SI   Pointer to ERROR structure:

                                                   Word, extended error code

                                                   Byte, action code to set

                                                   Byte, class code to set

                                                   Word, locus code to set

                                                   Word, DX at time error occurred

                                                   Word, SI at time error occurred

                                                   Word, DI at time error occurred

                                                   Word, DS at time error occurred

                                                   Word, ES at time error occurred

                                                   Word, reserved

                                                   Word, computer ID (0 if local)

                                                   Word, program ID (0 if local)

Return registers: None

Comments: This subfunction changes the internal storage locations used by DOS for returning information through Interrupt 21h, Function 59h (Get Extended Error Information). It can be used with Subfunction 06h (Get Critical-Error Flag Address) to save these codes when an error is detected and then restore them after preliminary processing (which might modify the stored codes) is finished.

These functions can also be used in TSR coding to prevent a pop-up action from accidentally changing an error code and producing inaccurate results. To do so, you would use Subfunction 06 first, to get the address, and then save the data to your own storage area. When you do the save, note that the internal DOS structure differs from the one used by Subfunction 0Ah:

                                           Byte, locus code

                                           Word, extended error code

                                           Byte, action code

                                           Byte, class code

                                           Double word, far pointer to driver address

Int 21h   **Function 5Eh**   **Subfunction 00h**   **V3.1**

Get Machine Name

Gets the network machine name

Calling registers: AH   5Eh
                        AL   00h, get machine name
                        DS:DX   Pointer to buffer to receive machine name
                        DS:SI   Pointer to setup string

Return registers: Carry flag clear if successful
                        CH =   00h, name not defined
                        CH >   00h, name defined
                        CL   NetBIOS name number (CH > 00h)
                        DS:DX   Pointer to identifier (CH > 00h)
                        Carry flag set if error
                        AX   Error code
                                    01h, invalid function

Comments: The *machine name* is a 15-byte, ASCIIZ string used to identify the machine to a network. This function requires that the network be running. If the network is not running, the results of the function will be unpredictable.

Int 21h   **Function 5Eh**   **Subfunction 01h**   **V3.1**

Set Machine Name

Sets the network machine name

Calling registers: AH   5Eh
                        AL   01h, set machine name
                        DS:DX   Pointer to buffer containing machine name as ASCIIZ
                                    string

Return registers: Carry flag clear if successful
                        Carry flag set if error
                        AX   Error code
                                    01h, invalid function

Comments: The *machine name* is a 15-byte, ASCIIZ string used to identify the machine to a network. This function requires that the network be running. If the network is not running, the results of the function will be unpredictable. This function should be used only by network software because it modifies information essential to the network's operation.

Int 21h   **Function 5Eh**   **Subfunction 02h**   **V3.1**

Set Network Printer Setup

Sets the printer setup

Calling registers: AH   5Eh
                        AL   02h, set printer setup
                        BX   Redirection list index
                        CX   Length of setup string (maximum of 64 bytes)
                        DS:SI   Pointer to setup string

Return registers: Carry flag clear if successful
                        Carry flag set if error
                        AX   Error code
                                    01h, invalid function

Comments: The printer setup is a string sent before any print job when accessing the network printer. This function allows setting the string.

Int 21h   **Function 5Eh**   **Subfunction 03h**   **V3.1**

Get Network Printer Setup

Gets the printer setup string

Calling registers: AH   5Eh
                        AL   03h, get printer setup
                        BX   Redirection list index
                        ES:DI   Pointer to buffer to receive setup string

Return registers: Carry flag clear if successful
                        CX   Length of printer setup string
                        ES:DI   Pointer to printer setup string
                        Carry flag set if error
                        AX   Error code
                                    01h, invalid function

Comments: The printer setup is a string to be sent before any print job when accessing the network printer. This function allows retrieving the string.

Int 21h   **Function 5Fh**   **Subfunction 02h**   **V3.1**

Get Redirection List Entry

Gets the network redirection list entries

Calling registers:	AH	5Fh
	AL	02h
	BX	Redirection list index
	DS:SI	Pointer to 128-byte buffer for device name
	ES:DI	Pointer to 128-byte buffer for network name

Return registers:	Carry flag clear if successful	
	BH	Device status flag
		Bit 0 = 0, device valid
		Bit 0 = 1, device invalid
	BL	Device type
		03h, printer
		04h, disk drive
	CX	Stored parameter value
	DX	Destroyed
	BP	Destroyed
	DS:SI	Pointer to ASCIIZ local device name
	ES:DI	Pointer to ASCIIZ network name
	Carry flag set if error	
	AX	Error code
		01h, invalid function
		12h, no more files

Comments: This function is used to get network redirection for devices (printers or disk directories) on the network. The network must be running to support this function. Using this function (together with related Subfunction 03h), you can associate a disk-drive identifier with a network directory, for example. You also can assign a remote printer device to be accessed with a local printer device name. The function supports remote passwords for remote disk access.

The file-sharing module must be loaded to use this function. All identifiers are passed as ASCIIZ strings and are thereby compatible with programming in C but not directly compatible with Pascal or BASIC. When you are getting a redirection entry, each call to Subfunction 02h returns a single entry in the redirection table. The entries are ASCIIZ strings representing the local device name, to which DS:SI points, and the network name, to which ES:DI points.

As you make subsequent calls to Subfunction 02h, you can tell that you have reached the end of the list when error code 12h (no more files) is returned. Calling this function destroys the contents of registers DX and BP, even though they are not used to return values.

Despite the sophisticated redirection available, COM devices, STDOUT, and STDERR cannot be redirected.

Int 21h	Function 5Fh	Subfunction 03h	V3.1

Set Redirection List Entry

Gets or modifies the network redirection list entries

Calling registers:

	AH	5Fh
	AL	03h
	BL	Device type
		03h, printer
		04h, disk drive
	CX	Parameter to save for caller
	DS:SI	Pointer to ASCIIZ local device name
	ES:DI	Pointer to ASCIIZ network name followed by ASCIIZ
		password

Return registers: Carry flag clear if successful

Carry flag set if error

	AX	Error code
		01h, invalid function
		03h, path not found
		05h, access denied
		08h, insufficient memory
		0Fh, invalid drive
		12h, no more files
		57h, invalid parameter

Comments: This function is used to set network redirection for devices (printers or disk directories) on the network. It does this by modifying a list of local device names associated with network devices, files, or directories. The network must be running to support this function. Using this function, you can associate a disk-drive identifier with a network directory, for example. You can also assign a remote printer device to be accessed with a local printer device name. The function supports remote passwords for remote disk access.

The file-sharing module must be loaded to use this function. All identifiers are passed as ASCIIZ strings and are thereby compatible with programming in C but not directly compatible with Pascal or BASIC. The entries are ASCIIZ strings representing the local device name, to which DS:SI points, and the network name, to which ES:DI points.

Subfunction 03h enables you to specify a redirection to use. You can specify a printer or disk redirection (BL = device type) and indicate its local name (A, B, and so on for disk redirections; PRN:, LPT1:, and so on for printer redirection). When you redirect a printer, the output for the printer is buffered and sent to the network printer spooler for the desired device. Because this redirection occurs at the Int 17h level, you will trap all but hardware access to the printer itself.

Despite the sophisticated redirection available, COM devices, STDOUT, and STDERR cannot be redirected.

Int 21h	Function 5Fh	Subfunction 04h	V3.1
	Cancel Redirection List Entry		

Cancels network redirection list entries

Calling registers: AH   5Fh
                            AL   04h
                            DS:SI   Pointer to ASCIIZ device name

Return registers: Carry flag clear if successful
                           Carry flag set if error
                           AX   Error code
                                              01h, invalid function
                                                0Fh, invalid drive

Comments: This function is used to cancel network redirection for devices (printers or disk directories) on the network. It does this by modifying a list of local device names associated with network devices, files, or directories. The network must be running to support this function. Using this function, you can associate a disk-drive identifier with a network directory, for example. You can also assign a remote printer device to be accessed with a local printer device name. The function supports remote passwords for remote disk access.

The file-sharing module must be loaded to use this function. All identifiers are passed as ASCIIZ strings and are therefore compatible with programming in C but not directly compatible with Pascal or BASIC.

Subfunction 04h uses only the local device name. The redirection is broken if that device has been reassigned. When the device name is a string starting with two backslashes, the connection between the local machine and the network directory is broken.

Despite the sophisticated redirection available, COM devices, STDOUT, and STDERR cannot be redirected.

Int 21h	Function 60h		V3
	Expand Path Name String		

This function expands a relative path name, which may include reference to a SUBSTed or ASSIGNed drive, into a fully qualified path name that refers to the physical drive involved

Calling registers: AH   60h
                            DS:SI   Points to ASCIIZ relative path name
                            ES:DI   Address of 67-byte work buffer

Return registers: Carry flag clear if successful

ES:DI	Unchanged; work buffer contains fully qualified path name

Carry flag set if error

AX	Error code
	02h, illegal character in input string

Comments: This appears to be the function introduced with V3 to permit the EXEC function to add the full path name of a program file to the end of the Environment area. Some reports have indicated that additional token parsing is performed, but our tests indicated that any string that could be a legal path name (including the use of the wild-card characters ? and *) was interpreted to be one. No checks were made by the function to determine whether the named file existed. The only error reported was due to illegal characters included in the input string.

Int 21h	Function 62h	V3
	Get PSP Address	

Gets the segment address of the program segment prefix (PSP) for the current program

Calling registers: AH 62h

Return registers: BX Segment address of PSP

Comments: The purpose of this function is to allow the program to retrieve the address of its PSP at any time without having to explicitly save it in an accessible area during program startup. Because most access to functions should avoid direct access to the PSP, this function has only marginal utility.

In all DOS versions tested, this function is a duplicate of reserved Function 51h, using the self-same code.

Int 21h	Function 63h	Subfunction 00h	V2.25
	Get System Lead Byte Table		

Gets the address of the system lead byte table

Calling registers: AH 63h
AL 00h

Return registers: DS:SI Pointer to lead byte table

Comments: This function retrieves the address of the system lead byte table. These data structures are associated with handling 2-byte-per-character display systems such as Kanji and Hangeul. This function first applied to DOS V2.25 only, was not available on DOS V3, and then reappeared in V4, but without documentation.

724

In V4, the other subfunctions for Function 63h are not implemented and do not return any error indication if called.

Int 21h Function 63h Subfunction 01h V2.25 Only
Set/Clear Interim Console Flag

Controls the interim console flag

Calling registers: AH 63h
AL 01h
DL 00h, setting interim console flag
01h, clearing interim console flag

Return registers: None

Comments: This function allows control of the interim console flag. These data structures are associated with handling 2-byte-per-character display systems such as Kanji and Hangeul. This function applies to DOS V2.25 only; it is not available on DOS V3 or above.

Int 21h Function 63h Subfunction 02h V2.25 Only
Get Value of Interim Console Flag

Gets the value of the interim console flag

Calling registers: AH 63h
AL 02h

Return registers: DL Value of interim console flag

Comments: This function retrieves the value of the interim console flag. These data structures are associated with handling 2-byte-per-character display systems such as Kanji and Hangeul. This function applies to DOS V2.25 only; it is not available on DOS V3 or higher.

Int 21h Function 64h V3
Set Current Country Byte

Sets DOS's internal current country byte

Calling registers: AH 64h
AL Current country byte value

Return registers: None

Comments: The content of the AL register is stored in the internal current country code location. No tests for validity are made nor is any error condition returned. All flags remain unchanged by this function.

Int 21h   Function 65h   V3.3

Get Extended Country Information

Returns extended information for the specified country

Calling registers: AH   65h

AL   ID of information of interest (1, 2, 4, 5, 6, or 7) or
                         Subfunction (20h, 21h, or 22h)

BX   Code page of interest (–1 = active CON device)

CX   Amount of data to return

DX   Country ID (default –1)

ES:DI   Pointer to buffer to return information to

Return registers: Carry flag clear if successful

ES:DI   Pointer to returned information buffer

Carry flag set if error

AX   Error code

01h, invalid function

02h, file not found

Comments: Programmers working on international systems must have access to a wide range of country-specific information such as the currency symbol and date format. Function 65h retrieves this information for your program, depending on the country you specify.

Table DOS.27 can be retrieved by country ID. The default (–1) represents the United States. The call retrieves only as much data as specified in CX. If the table contains additional data, that data will be truncated and no error will be returned.

Table DOS.27   Extended Country Information

Offset Byte	Field Length	Meaning

Extended Country Information Buffer
Info ID: 01

00h	Byte	Info ID = 01
01h	Word	Size (38 or less)
03h	Word	Country ID
05h	Word	Code page

Offset Byte	Field Length	Meaning
07h	Word	Date and time format code
		0 = USA m d y, hh:mm:ss
		1 = Europe d m y, hh:mm:ss
		2 = Japan y m d, hh:mm:ss
09h	5 bytes	Currency symbol string (ASCIIZ)
0Eh	Byte	Thousands separator
0Fh	Byte	Zero
10h	Byte	Decimal separator
11h	Byte	Zero
12h	Byte	Date separator
13h	Byte	Zero
14h	Byte	Time separator
15h	Byte	Zero
16h	Byte	Currency format
		00h = Symbol leads currency, no space
		01h = Symbol follows currency, no space
		02h = Symbol leads currency, 1 space
		03h = Symbol follows currency, 1 space
		04h = Symbol replaces decimal separator
17h	Byte	Number of digits after decimal
18h	Byte	Time format
		Bit 0 = 0–12 hour clock
		Bit 0 = 1–24 hour clock
19h	Double word	Case map call address
1Dh	Word	Data list separator

continues

727

Table DOS.27 Continued

Offset Byte	Field Length	Meaning
1Eh	Byte	Zero
1Fh	10 bytes	Reserved

Extended Country Uppercase Table
Info ID: 02

00h	Byte	Info ID = 02
01h	Double word	Pointer to uppercase table. Uppercase table is 130 bytes: 2-byte length plus 128 uppercase values.

Extended Country File Name Uppercase Table
Info ID: 04

00h	Byte	Info ID = 04
01h	Double word	Pointer to file name uppercase table. File name uppercase table is 130 bytes: 2-byte length plus 128 uppercase values.

Extended File Name Character Table
Info ID: 05

00h	Byte	Info ID = 05
01h	Double word	Pointer to file name character table. Table starts with a 16-bit length, followed by characters that must not be used in file names for the specified country.

Extended Country Collating Table
Info ID: 06

00h	Byte	Info ID = 06
01h	Double word	Pointer to collating table. Collating table is 258 bytes: 2-byte length plus 256 values in collating order.

Offset Byte	Field Length	Meaning
DBCS Lead Byte Table (V4 only) **Info ID: 07**		
00h	Word	Number of bytes that follow
02h	2 bytes	Start, end of first lead-byte range
04h	2 bytes	Start, end of next lead-byte range
.	2 bytes	(Repeat as necessary)
.	2 bytes	0,0 marks end of table; not included in count

Int 21h	**Function 65h**	**Subfunction 20h**	**V4**
	Convert Character		

Converts the specified character to uppercase using the current uppercase table

Calling registers: AH   65h
                          AL   20h
                          DL   Character

Return registers: Carry flag clear if successful
                         DL   Uppercase character
                         Carry flag set if error

Comments: This function provides a reliable way to convert a character to uppercase for the current country.

Int 21h	**Function 65h**	**Subfunction 21h**	**V4**
	Convert String		

Converts the specified string to uppercase using the current uppercase table

Calling registers: AH   65h
                          AL   21h
                          CX   String length
                          DS:DX   Pointer to string

Return registers: Carry flag clear if successful

Comments: This function provides a reliable way to convert a string to uppercase for the current country.

Int 21h   Function 65h   Subfunction 22h   V4

Convert ASCIIZ String

Converts the specified string to uppercase by using the current uppercase table

Calling registers: AH   65h
                        AL   22h
                        DS:DX   Pointer to ASCIIZ string

Return registers: Carry flag clear if successful

Comments: This function provides a reliable way to convert a string to uppercase for the current country.

Int 21h   Function 66h   Subfunction 01h   V3.3

Get Global Code Page

Gets the code page for the current country

Calling registers: AH   66h
                        AL   01h

Return registers: Carry flag clear if successful
                        BX   Active code page
                        DX   System code page
                        Carry flag set if error
                        AX   Error code
                                    02h, file not found

Comments: This function tells which country data stored in COUNTRY.SYS is in the resident country buffer area, the code page. Devices can be selected automatically for code page switching in the CONFIG.SYS file if the devices support it.

Int 21h   Function 66h   Subfunction 02h   V3.3

Set Global Code Page

Sets the code page for the current country

Calling registers: AH   66h
                        AL   02h
                        BX   Active code page
                        DX   System code page

Return registers: Carry flag clear if successful
Carry flag set if error
AX   Error code
              02h, file not found

Comments: This function moves the country data stored in COUNTRY.SYS into the resident country buffer area, the code page. Devices can be selected automatically for code page switching in the CONFIG.SYS file if the devices support it.

Int 21h   **Function 67h**   **V3.3**

Set Handle Count

Allows a process to modify dynamically the number of file handles (normally 20) allowed for a process

Calling registers: AH   67h
BX   Number of open handles to allow

Return registers: Carry flag clear if successful
Carry flag set if error
AX   Error code

Comments: This function allows a program to control the number of file handles available for use while the program is running. This can be particularly important for complicated database programs, which often require a considerable amount of manipulation to handle the large number of files they need to keep open. Memory is allocated from memory freed by Function 4Ah. If the amount of memory is less than the current number of files open, the memory will become effective when the current number of files drops below the limit.

The CONFIG.SYS entry FILES= can set as many as 255 file handles in DOS V3.3. This function allows the number of file handles to rise to 64K entries. If the number specified is less than 20, the number defaults to 20.

Int 21h   **Function 68h**   **V3**

Flush Buffer

Flushes all buffered data for a file to the device

Calling registers: AH   68h
BX   File handle

Return registers: Carry flag clear if successful
Carry flag set if error
AX   Error code

Comments: The standard way to flush buffers to disk has always been to close a file and then reopen it. A classic improvement on this was first to duplicate the file handle with Function 45h and then close the duplicate. This got the close without incurring the overhead of another open.

Function 68h eliminates the need to be tricky. If you want to flush the buffers, this function will do it faster and in a more secure manner.

This function can be used rather than handle duplication or a close/open sequence to flush data buffers.

Int 21h	Function 6Ah	V4
	Allocate Memory	

Allocates a block of memory for use and returns a pointer to the beginning of the block. This is a duplicate of function 48h.

Calling registers:	AH	6Ah
	BX	File handle
Return registers:	Carry flag clear if successful	
	Carry flag set if error	
	AX	Error code

Comments: In IBM V4.01, this function uses the same code as documented Function 48h.

Int 21h	Function 6Ch	V4
	Extended Open/Create	

Combines functions presently provided by Functions 3Ch, 3Dh, and 5Bh into a single multi-purpose file-open facility

Calling registers:	AH	6Ch
	AL	00h (required)
	BX	Open mode (bit map):

Bit Settings FEDCBA98 76543210	Meaning
....000	Read-only access
....001	Write-only access
....010	Read/write access
....011	Not used, zero

Bit Settings FEDCBA98 76543210	Meaning
....1xx	Not used, zero
....x...	Not used, zero
.... .000....	Compatibility mode
.... .001....	Deny all sharing
.... .010....	Deny write sharing
.... .011....	Deny read sharing
.... .100....	Deny none
.... .101....	Not used, zero
.... .110....	Not used, zero
.... .111....	Not used, zero
.... 0.......	Child inherits handle
.... 1.......	Handle not passed to child
...xxxxx	Not used, zero
..0.....	Use Int 24h handler
..1.....	Return error only
.0......	Writes may be buffered
.1......	All writes execute immediately
x.......	Not used, zero

CX   File attributes (bit map):

Bit Settings FEDCBA98 76543210	Meaning
....0	Read/write
....1	Read only
....0.	Visible
....1.	Hidden

continues

Bit Settings FEDCBA98 76543210	Meaning
....0..	Normal user file
....1..	System file
....0...	Not volume label
....1...	Volume label
....x....	Not used, zero
....0.....	Not modified
....1.....	Modified (archive)
xxxxxxxx xx......	Not used, zero

DX   Action flag (bit map):

Bit Settings FEDCBA98 76543210	Meaning
....0000	Fail if file exists
....0001	Open if file exists
....0010	Replace if file exists
....0011	Not used, zero
....01xx	Not used, zero
....1xxx	Not used, zero
.... 0000....	Fail if file does not exist
.... 0001....	Create file if it does not exist
.... 001x....	Not used, zero
.... 01xx....	Not used, zero
.... 1xxx....	Not used, zero
xxxxxxxx	Not used, zero

DS:SI   Pointer to ASCIIZ path name for file

Return registers: Carry flag clear if successful
    AX   File handle
    CX   Action taken
                    01, file existed and was opened
                    02, file did not exist, created
                    03, file existed, was replaced
    Carry flag set if error
    AX   Error code

Comments: Like the three older handle-based file open/create functions that it combines, this function is called with DS:SI pointing to an ASCIIZ path name for the file to be opened or created, AL containing a bit map of the access privileges desired, and CX containing a bit map of the permanent attributes to be assigned to the file if it is created by the call. But unlike the older functions, this one carries added information in DX telling the system what to do if the file exists and what to do if it does not exist. It also permits the program to specify that the Int 24h Critical Error handler not be used in case of problems with this file, permitting the program to handle all errors without having to modify DOS actions for other programs that might be running at the same time.

The function was added to DOS for compatibility with OS/2, but fills a long-felt need and should be used on any program that can ignore pre-V4 versions of DOS.

The function fails if any part of the specified path cannot be found (except for the file-name portion, which is controlled by the setting of DX at entry). When running on a network, the user must have access rights at least equal to those specified in the call to the function.

Int 22h   V1

Terminate Address

This is not an interrupt but simply the address of the routine to which control is transferred when the executing program ends

Calling registers: Not applicable

Return registers: Not applicable

Comments: When a program is loaded, the contents of this memory location are copied into the program segment prefix (PSP) at offset byte 0Ah. When the program terminates, this value is normally restored from the same location. Because it is purely a storage area, it should never be executed directly.

Int 23h

V1

Ctrl-C Interrupt Handler

This interrupt is the routine that receives control when a Ctrl-C (or, indirectly, a Ctrl-Break) detection occurs

Calling registers: Not applicable

Return registers: Not applicable

Comments: Whenever detection of a Ctrl-C occurs during I/O operations or at other times when BREAK is on, the system branches to the address given in this vector. (The Ctrl-Break service normally forces a Ctrl-C into the DOS input buffer and thus reaches this routine also, but indirectly.) When a program is loaded, this vector is copied into its program segment prefix (PSP) at byte 0Eh; the vector is restored by program termination.

Ctrl-C and Ctrl-Break handlers are two of the most commonly needed special routines programmers must write. Sophisticated programs cannot afford to relinquish control to a default handler. They must control any break operations to allow proper cleanup in the event of a problem. (Telecommunications programs written by inexperienced programmers are particularly subject to this type of error.)

Because of these control problems, you should never issue an Int 23h to activate the handler. The function will come into play soon enough as the system processes Ctrl-C and Ctrl-Break characters.

Ctrl-C and Ctrl-Break handlers have a number of options they can use to process a break condition:

- The handler can set a local flag, which can be polled by the main program for extensive action. Some limited action can be taken directly and then a return from interrupt (IRET) can be executed to return control to DOS. DOS restarts the interrupted function from the beginning and completes the call normally. This is useful for applications in which every millisecond spent servicing the interrupt is important. High-speed communications programs can be written this way.

- The handler can take action on the condition that caused the interrupt and then do a *far return* (ret far) to return control to DOS. The carry flag should be set to indicate that the application must be aborted or cleared if the application is to be allowed to continue.

- The handler can take whatever action it needs and then resume operation of the program directly without ever returning to DOS.

Any of the options are valid; the one you choose depends on what else you are doing. Option 1 should be chosen when it is necessary to minimize the time spent in a handler outside of normal processing. Option 2 is more generally useful as a processing procedure when an abort of the process is a possible option. Option 3 can be used to redirect operation and continue directly when it is not a good idea to return to the original operation in progress. It does no harm, but is not generally a wise idea except in special circumstances for which no other solution exists than a radical break from processing.

While in a Ctrl-C/Ctrl-Break handler, you can use any DOS function needed to process the condition.

Int 24h

V1

Critical-Error Handler

This interrupt is the routine that receives control when a critical error is detected. A critical error generally represents a hardware failure of some sort and is usually the aftermath of a failed device driver call within DOS.

Calling registers:

AH	Error information	
AL	Drive number	
DI	Error code	
BP:SI	Pointer to device driver header	

STACK   Set up as follows:

High Addr	Flags	Original caller's flags register
	CS	Original caller's CS register
	IP	Original caller's IP register
	ES	Original caller's ES register
	DS	Original caller's DS register
	BP	Original caller's BP register
	DI	Original caller's DI register
	SI	Original caller's SI register
	DX	Original caller's DX register
	CX	Original caller's CX register
	BX	Original caller's BX register
	AX	Original caller's AX register
	Flags	DOS's flags register
	CS	DOS's CS register
Low Addr	IP	DOS's IP register

Return registers: AL   Action code

Comments: When a program is loaded, the contents of this vector are read into the program segment prefix (PSP) starting at offset 12h. When the program terminates, this vector is restored by the system termination handler. This interrupt should never be called directly.

When the critical-error handler is invoked by DOS, the AH, AL, and DI registers contain information about the nature of the error. BP:SI points to a device driver header. The SS, SP, DS, ES, BX, CX, and DX registers must be preserved by the critical-error handler.

DOS typically retries the device driver call (normally three times, but this may change in later versions) before invoking the critical-error handler. When the critical-error handler is invoked, it should preserve the necessary registers and then attempt to deal with the error. Only DOS Functions 00h–0Ch (Traditional Character I/O), 30h (Get DOS Version), and 59h (Get Extended Error Information) can be called in the critical-error handler. Other function calls can destroy DOS's internal stack and should be avoided.

The AH register has bit 7 clear if the error was a disk error; otherwise, bit 7 is set. If the error was a disk error, the rest of the AH register will be as shown in Table DOS.28. AL will contain the drive number (0 = A, 1 = B, and so on).

Table DOS.28   AH Register Usage on Disk Errors

Bit(s)	Meaning
7	0, to signify a disk error
6	Reserved
5	0 = ignore response not permitted
	1 = ignore response permitted
4	0 = retry response not permitted
	1 = retry response permitted
3	0 = function call fail response not permitted
	1 = function call fail response permitted
1–2	Disk area where error occurred
	00 = MS-DOS area
	01 = file allocation table
	10 = root directory
	11 = files area

Bit(s)	Meaning
0	0 = read
	1 = write

If the error was a nondisk error, the word at [BP:SI+4] can be examined; if bit 15 is set, the error was due to a character device call. The 8-character name of the device begins at [BP:SI+10].

The error codes returned in the lower byte of DI are the same as the error codes returned in a device driver's request header (see Table DOS.29).

Table DOS.29   Error Code (Lower Byte of DI)

Code	Meaning
00h	Write-protect error
01h	Unknown unit
02h	Drive not ready
03h	Unknown command
04h	Data error (bad CRC)
05h	Bad request structure length
06h	Seek error
07h	Unknown media type
08h	Sector not found
09h	Printer out of paper
0Ah	Write fault
0Bh	Read fault
0Ch	General failure
0Fh	Invalid disk change

When the critical-error handler is ready to return, it should set an action code in the AL register according to Table DOS.30.

Table DOS.30 Action Codes

Code	Meaning
00h	Ignore error
01h	Retry operation
02h	Terminate program
03h	Fail system call in progress (V3 and above)

When the action code is set, the saved registers are restored and a return from interrupt (IRET) is performed.

The handler can return directly to the user program, but if it does, it will be responsible for cleaning up the stack and removing all but the last three words from the stack before issuing an IRET. Control then returns to the statement directly after the I/O function that caused the error. This leaves DOS in an "unstable" condition until a call to an Int 21h function above 0Ch is performed. Specifically, the DOS CritErr flag will remain set, causing potential problems with the DOS internal stacks. It is possible for your handler to overcome this by getting the flag's address and clearing it explicitly; refer to Int 21h, Function 34h for details. Such modification of normal DOS actions is recommended only if absolutely necessary; in most cases, the best action for an Int 24h handler is to return by DOS rather than directly.

A sidelight concerning the handler's action codes: Some programmers have reported that action code 2 does not seem to work in some versions of DOS; efforts to identify precisely which versions are involved, however, have not been successful. All documentation for action code 2 in versions before V4 (including the first edition of this book) said that termination occurred through Interrupt 23h; in the *IBM Technical Reference Manual* for V4, this was changed to 22h, which is the normal termination procedure. Apparently, the earlier versions were the victims of a long-standing typographical error, because none invoked Interrupt 23h.

The extended file open function added to DOS in V4 provides the capability of specifying that the critical-error handler not be used for a file. That is, if you set the appropriate bit in a register when the file is opened, any critical error will result in an automatic exit code 3 return, with no screen dialogue.

Int 25h   V1

Absolute Disk Read

Reads data from a specified disk sector to the designated memory area

Calling registers: AL   Drive number (0 = A, 1 = B, and so on)

CX   > 0, number of sectors to read

−1, use extended format (V4)

DX	Starting relative (logical) sector number
DS:BX	Pointer to DTA if CX > 0
	Pointer to parameters if CX = −1

Return registers: Carry flag clear if successful
Carry flag set if error

AX	Error code
	0207h, wrong format used (V4 only)

Comments: This function reads a disk sector from the disk into memory by accessing the desired logical sector directly. This type of access must be handled with care because it bypasses the DOS directory structure.

Logical sectors are located starting with track 0, head 0. The first sector on this track is disk sector 0. Sectors then go to the next head, and then to the next track, and so on. Logical sectors correspond to the sequence of sector numbers stored magnetically on the disk and may not correspond to the physical sectors. By specifying interleaving factors, logical disk sectors can be physically separated on the disk. This is often done to improve the efficiency of the disk.

If the carry flag is set when the function returns, the AX register is interpreted as shown in the accompanying tables. AH and AL are interpreted as separate error codes (see Table DOS.31).

Table DOS.31   Interpretation of Error Codes Returned by Int 25h

Code	Meaning
AH Register Error Codes	
80h	Attachment failed to respond
40h	Seek operation failed
20h	Controller failed
10h	Data error (bad CRC)
08h	DMA failure
04h	Requested sector not found
03h	Write-protect fault
02h	Bad address mark
01h	Bad command
AL Register Error Codes	
00h	Write-protect error
01h	Unknown unit

continues

DOS
PROGRAMMING

Code	Meaning

AL Register Error Codes

02h	Drive not ready
03h	Unknown command
04h	Data error (bad CRC)
05h	Bad request structure length
06h	Seek error
07h	Unknown media type
08h	Sector not found
09h	Printer out of paper
0Ah	Write fault
0Bh	Read fault
0Ch	General failure

Because the absolute disk read can destroy any registers except the segment registers, you should take care to preserve needed values before the call.

A special problem with this function makes it difficult to use directly from high-level languages. When the function returns, the word containing the CPU flags, originally pushed on the stack by Int 25h, is still there. To get rid of it and restore the stack to its expected condition, you can do a POPF to take the number off the stack, or you can do an ADD SP, 2 to increment the stack pointer past the number. Because high-level languages do not provide direct facilities for this kind of operation, this function has to be called from assembly language to prevent failure of the system. (It could be embedded assembly code, as in Turbo Pascal.)

In DOS V4, the possible size of a logical sector number was extended to 32 bits. To accommodate this larger value, an extended format for Interrupt 25h was created; the extended format must be used when reading from a volume greater than 32M, even if the sector number could be expressed in only 16 bits.

Use of the extended format is indicated by setting CX to FFFFh (–1). DS:BX is interpreted as the address of a parameter block rather than as the address of the buffer to read into. This parameter block is arranged as follows:

Offset	Length	Comments
00h	Double word	Logical sector number, zero-based
04h	Word	Number of sectors to transfer
06h	Double word	Pointer to data buffer

Int 26h

Absolute Disk Write

V1

Writes data from the designated transfer area (DTA) to the disk sectors specified

Calling registers:

AL		Drive number (0 = A, 1 = B, and so on)
CX		> 0, number of sectors to write
		−1, use extended format (V4)
DX		Starting relative (logical) sector number
DS:BX		Pointer to DTA if CX > 0
		Pointer to parameters if CX = −1

Return registers:

Carry flag clear if successful

Carry flag set if error

AX	Error code
	0207h, wrong format used (V4 only)

Comments: This function writes a disk sector from memory by accessing the desired logical sector directly. This type of access must be handled with care because it bypasses the DOS directory structure.

Logical sectors are located starting with track 0, head 0. The first sector on this track is disk sector 0. Sectors then go to the next head, and then to the next track, and so on. Logical sectors correspond to the sequence of sector numbers stored magnetically on the disk and may not correspond to the physical sectors. By specifying interleaving factors, logical disk sectors can be physically separated on the disk. This is sometimes done to improve the disk's efficiency.

If the carry flag is set when the function returns, the AX register is interpreted as shown in the accompanying tables. AH and AL are interpreted as separate error codes (see Table DOS.32).

Table DOS.32 Interpretation of Error Codes Returned by Int 26h

Code	Meaning
AH Register Error Codes	
80h	Attachment failed to respond
40h	Seek operation failed
20h	Controller failed
10h	Data error (bad CRC)
08h	DMA failure
04h	Requested sector not found
03h	Write-protect fault
02h	Bad address mark
01h	Bad command
AL Register Error Codes	
00h	Write-protect error
01h	Unknown unit
02h	Drive not ready
03h	Unknown command
04h	Data error (bad CRC)
05h	Bad request structure length
06h	Seek error
07h	Unknown media type
08h	Sector not found
09h	Printer out of paper
0Ah	Write fault
0Bh	Read fault
0Ch	General failure

A special problem with this function makes it difficult to use directly from high-level languages. When the function returns, the word containing the CPU flags, originally pushed onto the stack by Int 26h, is still there. To get rid of it and restore the stack to its expected condition, you can do a POPF to take the number off the stack, or you can do an ADD SP, 2 to increment the stack pointer past the number. Because high-level languages do not provide direct facilities for this kind of operation, this function has to be called from assembly language to prevent failure of the system. (It could be embedded assembly code, as in Turbo Pascal.)

In DOS V4, the possible size of a logical sector number was extended to 32 bits. To accommodate this larger value, an extended format for Interrupt 26h was created; the extended format must be used when reading from a volume greater than 32M, even if the sector number could be expressed in only 16 bits.

Use of the extended format is indicated by setting CX to FFFFh (−1). DS:BX is interpreted as the address of a parameter block, rather than as the address of the buffer to write from. This parameter block is arranged as follows:

Offset	Length	Comments
00h	Double word	Logical sector number, zero-based
04h	Word	Number of sectors to transfer
06h	Double word	Pointer to data buffer

Int 27h   V1

Terminate and Stay Resident

Terminates the presently running program but preserves its memory area

Calling registers: DX   Offset of last byte plus 1 (relative to PSP) of the program
                                                 to remain resident
                                CS   Segment of the PSP

Return registers: None (does not return)

Comments: Terminate-and-stay-resident (TSR) utilities are familiar to almost all of us working with PCs. Who doesn't have SideKick or some other utility that gives the feeling of multitasking operations without true multitasking? This interrupt was the original (DOS V1) TSR termination procedure, which allowed a program to set aside its memory after connecting itself to whatever interrupt it needed for processing.

On termination, the procedure restores Int 22h (Terminate Address), Int 23h (Ctrl-C Interrupt Vector), and Int 24h (Critical-Error Vector), and then transfers control to the termination address. It allows the program to retain its memory area (DX register sizes the protected area) so that the TSR can remain active.

This termination is subject to some significant limitations. First, you must have the CS register set to the segment of the program segment prefix (PSP) for the program. Generally, this is no

745

problem, but you should make sure. Most significantly, only 64K bytes can be set aside for the TSR program. Under DOS V2 and V3, the preferred TSR termination is Int 21h, Function 31h, which allows any amount of memory and does not require that the CS register be set. Given the improvement in TSR termination handlers, Int 27h should be called only on DOS V1.x systems.

Unlike the normal terminate action, this interrupt does not close any files that may be open. If you want them closed, you must explicitly close them before using this interrupt.

Int 28h   V1

DOS Safe To Use

Called regularly during the DOS console I/O polling loops to let terminate-and-stay-resident (TSR) programs (such as the DOS-supplied utility PRINT.COM) know that it is safe to use file operations and other Int 21h functions above 0Ch

Calling registers: Not applicable

Return registers: Not applicable

Comments: This interrupt is called by DOS at several points in its console input-polling loop, where it is safe to do file system operations or most other DOS functions above 0Ch.

Normally, the vector for Interrupt 28h points to a single IRET instruction, making it a dummy handler stub. Any handler you write should chain to the next handler in line and let the original default IRET take care of returning to DOS. This will ensure that all processes which are depending on it will get an opportunity to run while COMMAND.COM is waiting for input at a command-line prompt.

Note that in DOS V2, not *all* DOS functions above 0Ch are safe to use from this interrupt because of internal stack-usage conflicts. Refer to the comments on Int 21h, Function 34h for a discussion of this problem and a method for overcoming it.

Int 29h   V2

Fast Putchar

DOS output routine interrupt

Calling registers: AL   Character to display

Return registers: Not applicable

Comments: This interrupt is called by DOS output routines if the output is going to a device and the device driver's attribute word has bit 3 set to 1.

All ASCII characters are output as if going to a display, with no processing, except for the carriage return, line feed, and bell characters. These are processed as control characters.

This interrupt is intended for use with DOS device drivers and is not documented as being supported beyond DOS V2.0. Nevertheless, it is the output method used by ANSI.SYS in later versions and thus can be expected to be supported without change. Any use in applications programs, however, is at your own risk.

Int 2Ah   V3

Microsoft Networks Interface

This interrupt, which has many functions, provides protection against interference between multiple users on a networked system

Calling registers: Not applicable

Return registers: Not applicable

Comments: Calls to this interrupt appear frequently in the code of DOS to provide protection against interference between multiple processes when operating in a network. When no network is present, the routines that call it are disabled; when the network is installed, the disabling code is automatically patched out and the interrupt is called to control access to critical regions of code. It is *not* to be used in applications programs. Because it is not a part of DOS unless network software has been installed, a discussion about its actions are beyond the scope of this book.

Int 2Eh   V3

Primary Shell Program Loader

Loads program under primary command interpreter shell for execution

Calling registers: DS:SI   Point to counted, CR-terminated command string identical to that supplied to DOS by Interrupt 21h, Function 0Ah

Return registers: Returns to address pointed to by Int 22h vector

Comments: This function permits access to the main environment area. It has been essentially superceded by EXEC function (Int 21h, Function 4Bh, Subfunction 00h).

The only known reason for using this function rather than EXEC would be to gain access to the master environment area of the system to make changes to it. Programs that make use of this function may not operate in a network or multiuser situation.

Int 2Fh   V3

Multiplex Service Interrupt

Multiplex service, only partially documented; controlled by content of AH register at entry, which may range from 01h through FFh

Comments: Only Function 12h, DOS internal services, is present in "vanilla" DOS operation; additional functions graft themselves into this service when the corresponding program is installed. For example, Function 01h has no meaning unless the resident portion of the DOS print spooler (PRINT.COM) has been installed.

Functions 00h through BFh for this interrupt have been reserved for use by DOS; Functions C0h through FFh are documented as being available for users. The dividing line originally was set at 80h rather than C0h, until Function B7h was taken for use (at V3.3) by the DOS function APPEND. A number of user programs take over functions below C0h. At least one third-party utility searches the Int 2Fh chain looking for any available code and uses the first one it can find.

To preserve some semblance of order, Subfunction 00h (the content of AL) of *all* functions has been officially reserved for use as the "get installed status" operation and returns that status as documented for Function 01h; 00h in AL on return indicates that the function is not yet installed, but may be installed; 01h indicates that the function is not installed and may not be; and FFh indicates that the function is already in place. Adherence to this standard makes it possible to avoid multiple installation of the same resident utility. Unfortunately, not all functions that employ Int 2Fh follow this standard, but the majority seem to do so. One notable exception is described in Appendix C, "A Standard TSR-Identification Technique."

Int 2Fh   Function 01h   Subfunction 00h   V3

Print Installation Check

Interface to resident portion of DOS print spooler (PRINT.COM)

Calling registers: AH   01h
                         AL   00h

Return registers: Carry flag clear if successful
                         AL   Status
                                     00h, okay to install if not installed
                                     01h, not okay to install if not installed
                                     FFh, installed

Comments: Print spooling has become a normal method of operation for many people who are too busy to stop what they are doing to wait for a printout. This function gives a program access to the printer spooler. Subfunction 00h lets a program determine whether the spooler is installed.

Int 2Fh **Function 01h** **Subfunction 01h** **V3**

Submit File to Print Spooler

Interface to resident portion of DOS print spooler (PRINT.COM)

Calling registers: AH   01h
                     AL   01h
                     DS:DX   Pointer to packet address

Return registers: Carry flag clear if successful
                     Carry flag set if error
                     AX   Error code
                                       01h, function invalid
                                       02h, file not found
                                       03h, path not found
                                       04h, too many open files
                                       05h, access denied
                                         08h, queue full
                                         09h, spooler busy
                                         0Ch, name too long
                                         0Fh, drive invalid

Comments: Print spooling has become a normal method of operation for many people who are too busy to stop what they are doing to wait for a printout. This function gives a program access to the printer spooler.

For Subfunction 01h, you provide a 5-byte packet with a priority level in the first byte and a pointer to an ASCIIZ file specification to be printed. The spooler takes over and automatically prints the file unless you intervene.

Int 2Fh **Function 01h** **Subfunction 02h** **V3**

Remove File from Print Queue

Interface to resident portion of DOS print spooler (PRINT.COM)

Calling registers: AH   01h
                     AL   02h
                     DS:DX   Point to ASCIIZ file specification

Return registers: Carry flag clear if successful
                     Carry flag set if error
                     AX   Error code
                                       01h, function invalid
                                     02h, file not found
                                     03h, path not found

04h, too many open files
05h, access denied
08h, queue full
09h, spooler busy
0Ch, name too long
0Fh, drive invalid

Comments: Print spooling has become a normal method of operation for many people who are too busy to stop what they are doing to wait for a printout. This function gives a program access to the printer spooler.

Subfunction 02 accepts wild cards (* and ?) in the file specification, allowing multiple print file terminations from a single call to the function.

Int 2Fh	Function 01h	Subfunction 03h	V3
	Cancel All Files in Print Queue		

Stops the current print job and removes all files from the print queue

Calling registers: AH   01h
                          AL   03h

Return registers: None

Comments: Because this function makes no attempt to clean up the last page of the file that was being printed, you may want the calling program to send a form feed.

Int 2Fh	Function 01h	Subfunction 04h	V3
	Hold Print Jobs		

Interface to resident portion of DOS print spooler (PRINT.COM)

Calling registers: AH   01h
                          AL   04h

Return registers: Carry flag clear if successful
                         DX   Error count
                         DS:SI   Pointer to print queue
                         Carry flag set if error
                         AX   Error code
                                           01h, function invalid
                                           09h, spooler busy

Comments: Print spooling has become a normal method of operation for many people who are too busy to stop what they are doing to wait for a printout. This function gives a program access to the printer spooler.

Subfunction 04 returns a pointer to a series of file-name entries, each 64 bytes long and containing an ASCIIZ string that is the file specification for one of the print files. The first in the list is the file being printed. The last entry has a NUL character in the first byte (zero length file-name string). This function also puts the spooler's action into a HOLD status so that none of the information can become obsolete before the caller can act on it. Subfunction 05 releases the HOLD status.

Int 2Fh	Function 01h	Subfunction 05h	V3
	End Print Hold		

Interface to resident portion of DOS print spooler (PRINT.COM)

Calling registers: AH 01h
AL 05h

Return registers: Carry flag clear if successful
Carry flag set if error
AX Error code
01h, function invalid
09h, spooler busy

Comments: Print spooling has become a normal method of operation for many people who are too busy to stop what they are doing to wait for a printout. This function gives a program access to the printer spooler.

Subfunction 05 cancels the HOLD status established by use of Subfunction 04; all print-spooling action stops between these two calls.

Int 2Fh	Function 01h	Subfunction 06h	V3
	Get Printer Device		

Returns the address of the device header for the current printer

Calling registers: AH 01h
AL 06h

Return registers: Carry flag clear if queue empty
AX 0
Carry flag set if queue not empty
DS:SI Pointer to device header
AX 0008

Comments: This function can be used to determine whether the printer queue is empty.

751

Int 2Fh   Function 05h   V3

Get Outboard Critical-Error Handler Installation Status

Interface to the outboard critical-error handler

Calling registers: AH   05h
                          AL   00h

Return registers: Carry flag clear if successful
                          AL   Status
                                    00h, okay to install if not installed
                                    01h, not okay to install if not installed
                                    FFh, installed

Comments: Action of this undocumented function is not fully understood. It seems to permit direct communication with the DOS critical-error handler routines.

Int 2Fh   Function 06h   V3

Get ASSIGN.COM/ASSIGN.EXE Installation Status

Checks to determine whether ASSIGN.COM or ASSIGN.EXE is loaded

Calling registers: AH   06h
                          AL   00h

Return registers: Carry flag clear if successful
                          AL   Status
                                    00h, OK to install if not installed
                                    01h, not OK to install if not installed
                                    FFh, installed

Comments: This function interfaces to ASSIGN.EXE and does nothing if ASSIGN is not loaded.

Int 2Fh   Function 08h   V3

Get DRIVER.SYS Installation Status

Checks to see whether DRIVER.SYS is installed

Calling registers: AH   08h
                          AL   00h

Return registers: Carry flag clear if successful
                          AL   Status
                                    00h, OK to install if not installed

01h, not OK to install if not installed
FFh, installed

Comments: This function interfaces to DRIVER.SYS and does nothing if that file is not loaded.

Int 2Fh   Function 10h   V3
Get SHARE.EXE Installation Status

Checks to determine whether SHARE.EXE is loaded

Calling registers: AH   10h
                      AL   00h

Return registers: Carry flag clear if successful
                      AL   Status
                                    00h, okay to install if not installed
                                    01h, not okay to install if not installed
                                    FFh, installed

Comments: This function interfaces to SHARE.EXE and does nothing if SHARE is not loaded.

Int 2Fh   Function 11h   V3
Get Network Redirector Installation Status

Checks to see whether the network redirector interface has been installed

Calling registers: AH   11h
                      AL   00h

Return registers: Carry flag clear if successful
                      AL   Status
                                    00h, OK to install if not installed
                                    01h, not OK to install if not installed
                                    FFh, installed

Comments: This function interfaces with the standard network redirector routines and does nothing unless Microsoft Networks or a fully compatible similar program is loaded.

Int 2Fh   Function 12h   Subfunction 00h   V3
Get DOS Installation Status

Checks to see whether DOS is installed; primarily for conformity with other DOS functions

Calling registers: AH   12h
                      AL   00h

Return registers: AL   FFh (function always installed)

Comments: Function 12h provides access to certain DOS internal services (00h–25h in Version 3, 00h–2Fh in Version 4). Note that many of these can be called only when all segment registers are set to the DOS kernel's segment; *if this restriction is not met, damage to data is extremely likely*. Nevertheless, they do provide information that is difficult to obtain by any other means and can be useful to developers who take proper precautions.

Subfunction 00h always returns the *installed* condition because this function is hard-coded into the DOS kernel. It is the standard "Is the function available?" test and seems to have been included for consistency with other DOS functions that do installation checks.

Int 2Fh	Function 12h	Subfunction 01h	V3
	Flush File		

Accesses internal services of DOS to flush a file

Calling registers: AH   12h
                        AL   01h
                        BX   File handle

Return registers: Carry flag clear if successful
                        Carry flag set if error
                        AX   Error code

Comments: Function 12h provides access to certain DOS internal services (00h–25h in Version 3, 00h–2Fh in Version 4). Note that many of these can be called only when all segment registers are set to the DOS kernel's segment; *if this restriction is not met, damage to data is extremely likely*. Nevertheless, they do provide information that is difficult to obtain by any other means and can be useful to developers who take proper precautions.

Subfunction 01h appears to flush the file whose handle is passed to it. That is, it writes to disk all accumulated buffers for the file. It assumes that all segment registers point to the DOS kernel area. It is uncertain whether the file is closed by this action.

Int 2Fh	Function 12h	Subfunction 02h	V3
	Get Interrupt Vector Address		

Accesses internal services of DOS to retrieve an interrupt vector

Calling registers: AH   12h
                        AL   02h
                        STACK   Number of interrupt to get

Return registers: ES:BX   Far pointer to interrupt vector

Comments: Function 12h provides access to certain DOS internal services (00h–25h in Version 3, 00h–2Fh in Version 4). Note that many of these can be called only when all segment registers are set to the DOS kernel's segment; *if this restriction is not met, damage to data is extremely likely.* Nevertheless, they do provide information that is difficult to obtain by any other means and can be useful to developers who take proper precautions.

Subfunction 02h provides direct access to the internal routine used by Interrupt 21h, Functions 25h and 35h to address the interrupt vector table. Subfunction 02h must be passed the number of the interrupt vector desired, in the low byte of the word on top of the stack. It returns a far pointer to the interrupt vector itself (not the interrupt service routine) in ES and BX.

Int 2Fh	Function 12h	Subfunction 03h	V3
	Get DOS Data Segment		

Accesses internal services of DOS to return the DOS-kernel data segment value

Calling registers:	AH	12h
	AL	03h
Return registers:	DS	DOS kernel segment address

Comments: Function 12h provides access to certain DOS internal services (00h–25h in Version 3, 00h–2Fh in Version 4). Note that many of these can be called only when all segment registers are set to the DOS kernel's segment; *if this restriction is not met, damage to data is extremely likely.* Nevertheless, they do provide information that is difficult to obtain by any other means and can be useful to developers who take proper precautions.

Subfunction 03h obtains the segment address of the DOS kernel, which then can be used to make other segment registers point to the DOS kernel area. Because DS is destroyed by this call, the caller's DS value should be saved first so that it can be restored.

Int 2Fh	Function 12h	Subfunction 04h	V3
	Normalize Path Separator		

Accesses internal services of DOS to normalize a path delimiter

Calling registers:	AH	12h
	AL	04h
	STACK	Separator to process (in low byte)
Return registers:	AL	5Ch (ASCII "\")

Comments: Function 12h provides access to certain DOS internal services (00h–25h in Version 3, 00h–2Fh in Version 4). Note that many of these can be called only when all segment registers are set to the DOS kernel's segment; *if this restriction is not met, damage to data*

is extremely likely. Nevertheless, they do provide information that is difficult to obtain by any other means and can be useful to developers who take proper precautions.

Subfunction 04h translates the alternate path delimiter (/) into the DOS standard delimiter (\).

Int 2Fh	**Function 12h**	**Subfunction 05h**	**V3**
	Output a Character		

Accesses internal services of DOS to output a character with Int 29h

Calling registers: AH   12h
AL   05h
STACK   Character to output (in low byte)

Return registers: None

Comments: Function 12h provides access to certain DOS internal services (00h–25h in Version 3, 00h–2Fh in Version 4). Note that many of these can be called only when all segment registers are set to the DOS kernel's segment; *if this restriction is not met, damage to data is extremely likely*. Nevertheless, they do provide information that is difficult to obtain by any other means and can be useful to developers who take proper precautions.

Subfunction 05h sends the character found on top of the stack to the CRT using interrupt 29h. This function is redundant and adds to overhead for programmers who already use Int 29h.

Int 2Fh	**Function 12h**	**Subfunction 06h**	**V3**
	Invoke Critical Error		

Accesses internal services of DOS to invoke the critical-error handler as though an error had been encountered

Calling registers: AH   12h
AL   06h

Return registers: AL   Action code (see interrupt 24h)

Comments: Function 12h provides access to certain DOS internal services (00h–25h in Version 3, 00h–2Fh in Version 4). Note that many of these can be called only when all segment registers are set to the DOS kernel's segment; *if this restriction is not met, damage to data is extremely likely*. Nevertheless, they do provide information that is difficult to obtain by any other means and can be useful to developers who take proper precautions.

Subfunction 06h invokes the critical-error handler as though an error had been detected and then returns its action code.

Int 2Fh **Function 12h** **Subfunction 07h** **V3 only**

Move Disk Buffer

Accesses internal services of DOS to move a disk buffer under DOS V3 (only)

Calling registers: AH 12h
AL 07h

Return registers: DS:DI Point to disk buffer

Comments: Function 12h provides access to certain DOS internal services (00h–25h in Version 3, 00h–2Fh in Version 4). Note that many of these can be called only when all segment registers are set to the DOS kernel's segment; *if this restriction is not met, damage to data is extremely likely.* Nevertheless, they do provide information that is difficult to obtain by any other means and can be useful to developers who take proper precautions.

Subfunction 07h manipulates the internal DOS disk buffers set up by BUFFERS= in CONFIG.SYS. This function should *not* be used unless you are more confident of your knowledge of the buffering algorithms than are the authors of this book; any *mistakes in its use could destroy all data on your hard disk* because the file allocation tables usually reside in these buffers.

Int 2Fh **Function 12h** **Subfunction 08h** **V3**

Decrement User Count

Accesses internal services of DOS to decrement the user count word in a device control block

Calling registers: AH 12h
AL 08h
ES:DI Point to DCB for file or device

Return registers: AX New user count

Comments: Subfunction 08h decrements the user count word in a DOS internal device control block. It is called with ES:DI pointing to the appropriate DCB (because the user count is the first word in the DCB, DI automatically points to the count word), and it returns with the DCB user count decremented and the new user count in AX. This routine usually is called as part of processing the Close Handle function but, by pointing ES:DI to some other word in RAM, it could be used to decrement that word instead. It makes no assumptions about the segment registers.

Int 2Fh **Function 12h** **Subfunction 0Ch** **V3**

IOCTL Open Used by DOS

Accesses internal services of DOS to open a file or device using IOCTL routines

Calling registers: AH   12h
                         AL   0Ch

Return registers: Carry flag clear if successful

Comments: Function 12h provides access to certain DOS internal services (00h–25h in Version 3, 00h–2Fh in Version 4). Note that many of these can be called only when all segment registers are set to the DOS kernel's segment; *if this restriction is not met, damage to data is extremely likely.* Nevertheless, they do provide information that is difficult to obtain by any other means and can be useful to developers who take proper precautions.

Subfunction 0Ch uses the Open subfunction of the IOCTL call to open the device or file previously tagged by DOS internal pointers as being current. It can be used only by DOS or by programs that control all the DOS internal tables and flags.

Int 2Fh	Function 12h	Subfunction 0Dh	V3
	Get Date and Time for File Closing		

Accesses internal services of DOS to retrieve the system date and time for file date and time stamping

Calling registers: AH   12h
                         AL   0Dh

Return registers: AX   System date in packed (file) format
                         DX   System time in packed (file) format

Comments: Function 12h provides access to certain DOS internal services (00h–25h in Version 3, 00h–2Fh in Version 4). Note that many of these can be called only when all segment registers are set to the DOS kernel's segment; *if this restriction is not met, damage to data is extremely likely.* Nevertheless, they do provide information that is difficult to obtain by any other means and can be useful to developers who take proper precautions.

Subfunction 0Dh is used by DOS to obtain the system date and time, in the file-directory format, when closing a modified file. This function assumes that all segment registers point into the DOS kernel.

Int 2Fh	Function 12h	Subfunction 0Eh	V3 only
	Search Buffer Chain		

Accesses internal services of DOS, apparently to search a buffer chain under DOS V3 (only)

Calling registers: AH   12h
                         AL   0Eh

Return registers: Unknown

Comments: Function 12h provides access to certain DOS internal services (00h–25h in Version 3, 00h–2Fh in Version 4). Note that many of these can be called only when all segment registers are set to the DOS kernel's segment; *if this restriction is not met, damage to data is extremely likely*. Nevertheless, they do provide information that is difficult to obtain by any other means and can be useful to developers who take proper precautions.

The purpose of Subfunction 0Eh is not fully known. It *seems* to search the disk buffering used in DOS and should be approached with care. See the comments concerning Subfunction 07h.

Int 2Fh	Function 12h	Subfunction 10h	V3

Find Modified Buffer (V3 only), Time Delay (V4)

Accesses internal services of DOS to either find a disk buffer that had been modified (under DOS V3) or execute a time delay (under DOS V4)

Calling registers: AH   12h
                        AL   10h

Return registers: Carry flag clear if successful

Comments: Function 12h provides access to certain DOS internal services (00h–25h in Version 3, 00h–2Fh in Version 4). Note that many of these can be called only when all segment registers are set to the DOS kernel's segment; *if this restriction is not met, damage to data is extremely likely*. Nevertheless, they do provide information that is difficult to obtain by any other means and can be useful to developers who take proper precautions.

Subfunction 10h was used in V3 to locate a "dirty" buffer (one that had been modified and needed to be written out to disk). With the total rewrite of the buffering scheme introduced in V4, this subfunction became obsolete and was pointed to the time-delay routine to provide a harmless no-op action. It should never be used outside of DOS.

Int 2Fh	Function 12h	Subfunction 11h	V3

Normalize ASCIIZ File Name

Accesses internal services of DOS to perform normalization conversion on a path name

Calling registers: AH   12h
                        AL   11h
                        DS:SI   Point to file name to normalize
                        ES:DI   Point to buffer to receive output

Return registers: ES:DI   Unchanged, point to normalized file name with all alpha characters in uppercase and all / characters changed to \ characters

Comments: Subfunction 11h converts a file or path name into standard format for use by the other DOS functions. All lowercase characters are converted to uppercase and all forward-slash characters are changed to backslashes. Both the input and output are ASCIIZ strings. This function makes no assumptions about the segment registers.

Int 2Fh	Function 12h	Subfunction 12h	V3

Find ASCIIZ String Length

Accesses internal services of DOS to determine the length of the ASCIIZ string pointed to by ES:DI

Calling registers:

	AH	12h
	AL	12h
	ES:DI	Pointer to ASCIIZ string

Return registers: CX — Length of string in bytes

Comments: Function 12h provides access to certain DOS internal services (00h–25h in Version 3, 00h–2Fh in Version 4). Note that many of these can be called only when all segment registers are set to the DOS kernel's segment; *if this restriction is not met, damage to data is extremely likely.* Nevertheless, they do provide information that is difficult to obtain by any other means and can be useful to developers who take proper precautions.

Subfunction 12h counts the number of bytes in the ASCIIZ string pointed to by ES:DI at entry and then returns the count (not including the NUL that terminates the ASCIIZ string) in the CX register. The SS register is assumed to point into the DOS kernel area.

Int 2Fh	Function 12h	Subfunction 13h	V3

Case and Country Conversion

Accesses internal services of DOS to convert the case (and country information, if necessary) of an ASCII character

Calling registers:

	AH	12h
	AL	13h
	STACK	Character to be converted

Return registers: AL — Uppercase (and translated) version of character

Comments: Function 12h provides access to certain DOS internal services (00h–25h in Version 3, 00h–2Fh in Version 4). Note that many of these can be called only when all segment registers are set to the DOS kernel's segment; *if this restriction is not met, damage to data is extremely likely.* Nevertheless, they do provide information that is difficult to obtain by any other means and can be useful to developers who take proper precautions.

Subfunction 13h takes the word from the top of the stack, converts its low byte to uppercase, and if country translation is in effect, translates it from the extended ASCII character set to normal ASCII. The result is returned in AX. This function assumes that the SS register points into the DOS kernel code in order to locate the country conversion tables and the translation flag; for this reason, it is not useful in most cases.

Int 2Fh	Function 12h	Subfunction 14h	V3
	Compare 32-bit Numbers		

Accesses internal services of DOS to compare two 32-bit values (typically pointers)

Calling registers: AH   12h
         AL   14h
         DS:SI First pointer
         ES:DI Second pointer

Return registers: Zero flag set if pointers equal, clear if not equal

Comments: Subfunction 14h can be used to compare any two 32-bit numbers by loading them into the appropriate registers. It is used by DOS as a general pointer-compare function. No assumptions about segment registers are made.

Int 2Fh	Function 12h	Subfunction 16h	V3
	Get DCB Address		

Accesses internal services of DOS to retrieve the device control block address for a specified handle

Calling registers: AH   12h
         AL   16h
         BX   File handle

Return registers: Carry flag clear if successful
         ES:DI Point to DCB that corresponds to the handle
         Carry flag set if error
         AX   Error code

Comments: Function 12h provides access to certain DOS internal services (00h–25h in Version 3, 00h–2Fh in Version 4). Note that many of these can be called only when all segment registers are set to the DOS kernel's segment; *if this restriction is not met, damage to data is extremely likely.* Nevertheless, they do provide information that is difficult to obtain by any other means and can be useful to developers who take proper precautions.

Subfunction 16h provides direct access to the device control block being used by any file or device handle. However, this function assumes that all segment registers point into the DOS kernel and so is useful primarily to DOS.

761

Int 2Fh **Function 12h** **Subfunction 17h** **V3**

Get LDT Address

Accesses internal services of DOS to return an address for the logical drive table

Calling registers: AH 12h
AL 17h
Stack Word, drive code (0 = A, 1 = B, and so on)

Return registers: Carry flag clear if successful
DS:SI Point to logical drive table for that drive (DOS internal
pointers also set)
Carry flag set if error
AX Error code

Comments: Function 12h provides access to certain DOS internal services (00h–25h in Version 3, 00h–2Fh in Version 4). Note that many of these can be called only when all segment registers are set to the DOS kernel's segment; *if this restriction is not met, damage to data is extremely likely*. Nevertheless, they do provide information that is difficult to obtain by any other means and can be useful to developers who take proper precautions.

Subfunction 17h assumes that all segment registers point into the DOS kernel code and so is useful mainly to DOS. This function sets the current drive pointers and returns the address of the logical drive table for the specified drive.

Int 2Fh **Function 12h** **Subfunction 18h** **V3**

Get User Stack Address

Accesses internal services of DOS to retrieve the user's stack address

Calling registers: AH 12h
AL 18h

Return registers: DS:SI Point to area of DOS stack where registers were saved at
entry to Interrupt 21h

Comments: Subfunction 18h loads DS and SI from the locations at which DOS saved SS and SP after pushing all registers at entry to Interrupt 21h. This permits direct control of the values that will be returned by Interrupt 21h (unless subsequent code changes the values again). This function is of limited value and makes no assumptions about segment registers.

Int 2Fh   **Function 12h**   **Subfunction 19h**   **V3**

Set LDT Pointers

Accesses internal services of DOS to set the logical drive table pointers

Calling registers: AH   12h
                          AL   19h

Return registers: None

Comments: Function 12h provides access to certain DOS internal services (00h–25h in Version 3, 00h–2Fh in Version 4). Note that many of these can be called only when all segment registers are set to the DOS kernel's segment; *if this restriction is not met, damage to data is extremely likely.* Nevertheless, they do provide information that is difficult to obtain by any other means and can be useful to developers who take proper precautions.

Subfunction 19h uses the DOS internal data to set up the LDT pointer to correspond to the selected drive. It assumes that all segment registers point into the DOS kernel and is of limited value outside of DOS.

Int 2Fh   **Function 12h**   **Subfunction 1Ah**   **V3**

Get Drive Code from Path Name

Accesses internal services of DOS to parse, from a supplied ASCIIZ path name, the drive code

Calling registers: AH   12h
                          AL   1Ah
                          DS:SI   Point to ASCIIZ path name

Return registers: AL   Drive code (0 = default, 1 = A, and so on)
                          DS:SI   Advanced past drive specification if one was present;
                                          otherwise unchanged

Comments: Subfunction 1Ah determines whether a drive has been specified as part of the path name passed to it and, if so, translates the drive letter into a numeric value and advances SI to point past the drive specification. This function makes no assumptions about segment registers.

Int 2Fh   **Function 12h**   **Subfunction 1Bh**   **V3**

Adjust for Leap Year

Accesses internal services of DOS to set the number of days in February based on whether the supplied year is a leap year

Calling registers: AH 12h
       AL 1Bh
       CX Year (full value, such as 1989)

Return registers: AL 29 if leap year, else 28

Comments: Function 12h provides access to certain DOS internal services (00h–25h in Version 3, 00h–2Fh in Version 4). Note that many of these can be called only when all segment registers are set to the DOS kernel's segment; *if this restriction is not met, damage to data is extremely likely.* Nevertheless, they do provide information that is difficult to obtain by any other means and can be useful to developers who take proper precautions.

Subfunction 1Bh assumes that all segment registers point into the DOS kernel and is of limited usefulness outside of DOS. It tests the value in CL to determine whether the year is a leap year and, if it is, modifies the DOS days-per-month table accordingly. In any event, the number of days in February for the specified year is returned in AL. This function is part of DOS time/date processing.

Int 2Fh   **Function 12h**   **Subfunction 1Ch**   **V3**

Calculate Days since Start-of-Month

Accesses internal services of DOS to return the number of elapsed days since the beginning of the month

Calling registers: AH 12h
       AL 1Ch
       CX Number code of current month
       DX Total days in previous years (0, if day in this year desired)
       DS:SI Point to days-per-month table

Return registers: DX Total days to start of current month

Comments: Function 12h provides access to certain DOS internal services (00h–25h in Version 3, 00h–2Fh in Version 4). Note that many of these can be called only when all segment registers are set to the DOS kernel's segment; *if this restriction is not met, damage to data is extremely likely.* Nevertheless, they do provide information that is difficult to obtain by any other means and can be useful to developers who take proper precautions.

Subfunction 1Ch assumes that all segment registers point into the DOS kernel and is of limited usefulness outside of DOS. It calculates a tally of the total number of days elapsed from the DOS "zero day" (January 1, 1980) or from the start of the current year (if DX = 0) to the start of the current month. This function is part of DOS time/date processing.

Int 2Fh   **Function 12h**   **Subfunction 1Dh**   **V3**

Calculate Date

Accesses internal services of DOS to calculate the month and day of the year when supplied with a count of the number of elapsed days

Calling registers: AH   12h
                         AL   1Dh
                         CX   00h
                         DX   Total day count *this year*
                         DS:SI   Point to days-per-month table

Return registers: CX   Month
                         DX   Day

Comments: Function 12h provides access to certain DOS internal services (00h–25h in Version 3, 00h–2Fh in Version 4). Note that many of these can be called only when all segment registers are set to the DOS kernel's segment; *if this restriction is not met, damage to data is extremely likely.* Nevertheless, they do provide information that is difficult to obtain by any other means and can be useful to developers who take proper precautions.

Subfunction 1Dh assumes that all segment registers point into the DOS kernel and is of limited usefulness outside of DOS. It accepts a count of total days *in the year* and calculates the current month and day values. This function is part of DOS time/date processing.

This function is the inverse of Function 12h, Subfunction 1Ch. It assumes that DX is less than 367 at entry, but no error is reported if this condition is not true. If DX is outside this range, the results are unpredictable. Because this function was never intended for general public use, no error detection was included.

Int 2Fh   **Function 12h**   **Subfunction 1Eh**   **V3**

Compare Strings

Accesses internal services of DOS to provide a comparison test of two ASCIIZ strings

Calling registers: AH   12h
                         AL   1Eh
                         DS:SI   Point to one string
                         ES:DI   Point to other string

Return registers: Zero flag set if strings match identically; clear otherwise

Comments: Subfunction 1Eh provides a generic test for equality of two ASCIIZ strings. It makes no assumptions about segment registers, but, if the two strings differ, it returns no information other than that they *do* differ. In particular, it does not tell you the location at which they differ or the nature of the difference.

Int 2Fh	Function 12h	Subfunction 1Fh	V3
	Initialize LDT		

Accesses internal services of DOS to set up the logical drive table for a specified drive

Calling registers: AH   12h
AL   1Fh
STACK   Drive letter in ASCII

Return registers: Carry flag clear if successful
Carry flag set if error
AX   Error code

Comments: Function 12h provides access to certain DOS internal services (00h–25h in Version 3, 00h–2Fh in Version 4). Note that many of these can be called only when all segment registers are set to the DOS kernel's segment; *if this restriction is not met, damage to data is extremely likely.* Nevertheless, they do provide information that is difficult to obtain by any other means and can be useful to developers who take proper precautions.

Subfunction 1Fh assumes that all segment registers point into the DOS kernel and is of limited usefulness outside of DOS. It is used as a part of the SUBST function, which permits a subdirectory to be identified as a separate logical drive. Because it modifies internal DOS pointers, it should be explored with utmost caution.

Int 2Fh	Function 12h	Subfunction 20h	V3
	Get DCB Number		

Accesses internal services of DOS to return a drive control block number (not address) for a specifed file handle

Calling registers: AH   12h
AL   20h
BX   File handle

Return registers: Carry flag clear if successful
ES:DI   Pointer to appropriate byte in the handle table for the
current process (address of DCB number for that
handle)
Carry flag set if error
AX   Error code

Comments: Subfunction 20h assumes that the SS register points into the DOS kernel, in order to locate the handle table for the current process. No other segment register assumptions are made. Upon successful return, ES:DI points to the byte in the handle table that contains the DCB number for the specified handle. This DCB number, in turn, may be used to locate the DCB by means of Subfunction 16h.

The SS register may be forced into the DOS area by setting SS:SP to offset 40h of the logical drive table for an unused drive; the LDT is always in the DOS kernel. To locate the LDT, refer to the information in Appendix D, "Reserved DOS Functions."

Int 2Fh	Function 12h	Subfunction 21h	V3
	Expand ASCIIZ Path Name		

Accesses internal services of DOS to expand a partial path name to a full path name

Calling registers:	AH	12h
	AL	21h
	DS:SI	Point to path name for expansion
	ES:DI	Point to 65-byte buffer to receive expanded string
Return registers:	Carry flag clear if successful	
	ES:DI	Unchanged, point to expanded string
	Carry flag set if error	
	AX	Error code
		02, illegal character in input string

Comments: Function 12h provides access to certain DOS internal services (00h–25h in Version 3, 00h–2Fh in Version 4). Note that many of these can be called only when all segment registers are set to the DOS kernel's segment; *if this restriction is not met, damage to data is extremely likely.* Nevertheless, they do provide information that is difficult to obtain by any other means and can be useful to developers who take proper precautions.

Subfunction 21h accesses the same routine used by undocumented Function 60h of Interrupt 21h. This function assumes that the SS register points into the DOS kernel, in order to access a number of internal tables used during the expansion. The expanded string includes the drive letter and full path name (if the input string referred to a SUBSTed drive, the physical drive letter replaces it in the output expansion).

Int 2Fh	Function 12h	Subfunction 22h	V3
	Translate Extended Error Codes		

Accesses internal services of DOS to determine the extended error codes of an error

Calling registers:	AH	12h
	AL	22h

Return registers: None

Comments: Function 12h provides access to certain DOS internal services (00h–25h in Version 3, 00h–2Fh in Version 4). Note that many of these can be called only when all segment registers are set to the DOS kernel's segment; *if this restriction is not met, damage to data is extremely likely.* Nevertheless, they do provide information that is difficult to obtain by any other means and can be useful to developers who take proper precautions.

Subfunction 22h is useful only to DOS. This function uses internal DOS tables to translate an error condition into the appropriate extended error code, class code, action code, and locus; it then places those values in the DOS internal storage locations from which Int 21h, Function 59h will retrieve them. It should not be used by other programs.

Int 2Fh	Function 12h	Subfunction 24h	V3
	Execute Delay		

Accesses internal services of DOS to execute a variable-length delay based on internal DOS values

Calling registers: AH   12h
                          AL   24h

Return registers: None

Comments: Function 12h provides access to certain DOS internal services (00h–25h in Version 3, 00h–2Fh in Version 4). Note that many of these can be called only when all segment registers are set to the DOS kernel's segment; *if this restriction is not met, damage to data is extremely likely.* Nevertheless, they do provide information that is difficult to obtain by any other means and can be useful to developers who take proper precautions.

Subfunction 24h executes a delay loop, using delay values stored in the DOS kernel. It assumes that all segment registers point into the DOS kernel and should not be used outside of DOS.

Int 2Fh	Function 12h	Subfunction 25h	V3
	Get ASCIIZ String Length		

Accesses internal services of DOS to determine the length of an ASCIIZ string pointed to by DS:SI

Calling registers: AH   12h
                          AL   25h
                          DS:SI   Point to ASCIIZ string

Return registers: CX   Length of string in bytes

Comments: Function 12h provides access to certain DOS internal services (00h–25h in Version 3, 00h–2Fh in Version 4). Note that many of these can be called only when all segment registers are set to the DOS kernel's segment; *if this restriction is not met, damage to data is extremely likely*. Nevertheless, they do provide information that is difficult to obtain by any other means and can be useful to developers who take proper precautions.

Subfunction 25h counts the number of bytes in the ASCIIZ string pointed to by DS:SI at entry and then returns the count in the CX register. The SS register is assumed to point into the DOS kernel area.

Int 2Fh	Function 12h	Subfunction 26h	V4
	Open File		

Accesses internal services of DOS to open a file through Int 21h, Function 3Dh

Calling registers:

AH 12h
AL 26h
CL Access mode (same as AL for Int 21h, Function 3Dh)
DS:DX Pointer to ASCIIZ file specification

Return registers:

Carry flag clear if successful
AX Handle
Carry flag set if error
AX Error code
01h, invalid function
02h, file not found
03h, path not found
04h, no handles available
05h, access denied
0Ch, invalid access code

Comments: Function 12h provides access to certain DOS internal services (00h–25h in Version 3, 00h–2Fh in Version 4). Note that many of these can be called only when all segment registers are set to the DOS kernel's segment; *if this restriction is not met, damage to data is extremely likely*. Nevertheless, they do provide information that is difficult to obtain by any other means and can be useful to developers who take proper precautions.

Subfunction 26h transfers CL into AL and then executes the same routine reached by Interrupt 21h, Function 3Dh (Open File). It assumes that all segment registers point into the DOS kernel. In most cases, therefore, this function is useful only to DOS.

769

Int 2Fh   **Function 12h**   **Subfunction 27h**   **V4**

Close File

Accesses internal services of DOS to close a file through Int 21h, Function 3E

Calling registers: AH   12h
                         AL   27h
                         BX   File handle

Return registers: Carry flag clear if successful
                         Carry flag set if error
                         AX   Error code

Comments: Function 12h provides access to certain DOS internal services (00h–25h in Version 3, 00h–2Fh in Version 4). Note that many of these can be called only when all segment registers are set to the DOS kernel's segment; *if this restriction is not met, damage to data is extremely likely.* Nevertheless, they do provide information that is difficult to obtain by any other means and can be useful to developers who take proper precautions.

Subfunction 27h executes the same routine reached by Int 21h, Function 3Eh (Close File). It assumes that all segment registers point into the DOS kernel. In most cases, therefore, this function is useful only to DOS.

Int 2Fh   **Function 12h**   **Subfunction 28h**   **V4**

Position File Pointer

Accesses internal services of DOS to position a file pointer through Int 21h, Function 42h

Calling registers: AH   12h
                         AL   28h
                         BX   File handle
                         CX   Most significant part of offset
                         DX   Least significant part of offset
                         BP   Normal values of AX for Int 21h, Function 42h

Return registers: Carry flag clear if successful
                         DX:AX   New file-pointer location
                         Carry flag set if error
                         AX   Error code
                                     01h, invalid function (file sharing)
                                     06h, invalid handle

Comments: Function 12h provides access to certain DOS internal services (00h–25h in Version 3, 00h–2Fh in Version 4). Note that many of these can be called only when all segment registers are set to the DOS kernel's segment; *if this restriction is not met, damage to data is extremely likely.* Nevertheless, they do provide information that is difficult to obtain by any other means and can be useful to developers who take proper precautions.

Subfunction 28h transfers BP into AX and then executes the same routine reached by Int 21h, Function 42h (Move File handle). It assumes that all segment registers point into the DOS kernel. In most cases, therefore, this function is useful only to DOS.

Int 2Fh	Function 12h	Subfunction 29h	V4
	Read File		

Accesses internal services of DOS to read a file through Int 21h, Function 3Fh

Calling registers: AH   12h
                          AL   29h
                          BX   File handle
                          CX   Number of bytes
                          DS:DX   Pointer to buffer area

Return registers: Carry flag clear if successful
                          AX   Number of bytes read
                          Carry flag set if error
                          AX   Error code
                                    05h, access denied
                                    06h, invalid handle

Comments: Function 12h provides access to certain DOS internal services (00h–25h in Version 3, 00h–2Fh in Version 4). Note that many of these can be called only when all segment registers are set to the DOS kernel's segment; *if this restriction is not met, damage to data is extremely likely.* Nevertheless, they do provide information that is difficult to obtain by any other means and can be useful to developers who take proper precautions.

Subfunction 29h executes the same routine reached by Int 21h, Function 3Fh (Read File or Device). It assumes that all segment registers point into the DOS kernel. In most cases, therefore, this function is useful only to DOS.

Int 2Fh	Function 12h	Subfunction 2Bh	V4
	IOCTL Interface		

Accesses internal services of DOS to interface with IOCTL services of Int 21h, Function 44h

Calling registers: AH   12h

AL   2Bh

BX   Handle (Subfunction codes 00h, 01h, 02h, 03h, 06h, 07h, and 0Ah)

BL   Drive code: 0 = default, 1 = A, and so on (Subfunction codes 04h, 05h, 08h, and 09h)

CX   Number of bytes to read or write

BP   Normal values of AX for IOCTL function

DS:DX   Pointer to buffer area (Subfunction codes 02h–05h)

DX   Device information (Subfunction code 01h)

Return registers: Carry flag clear if successful

AX   Number of bytes transferred (Subfunction codes 02h–05h)

AL   Status (Subfunction codes 06h–07h)

00h, not ready

FFh, ready

AX   Value (Subfunction code 08h)

00h, removable

01h, fixed

DX   Device information (Subfunction code 00h)

Carry flag set if error

AX   Error code

01h, invalid function (file sharing)

04h, no handles available

05h, access denied

06h, invalid handle

0Dh, invalid data

0Fh, invalid drive

Comments: Function 12h provides access to certain DOS internal services (00h–25h in Version 3, 00h–2Fh in Version 4). Note that many of these can be called only when all segment registers are set to the DOS kernel's segment; *if this restriction is not met, damage to data is extremely likely.* Nevertheless, they do provide information that is difficult to obtain by any other means and can be useful to developers who take proper precautions.

Subfunction 2Bh transfers BP into AX and then executes the same routine reached by Int 21h, Function 44h (IOCTL). It assumes that all segment registers point into the DOS kernel. In most cases, therefore, this function is useful only to DOS.

Int 2Fh   **Function 12h**   **Subfunction 2Dh**   **V4**

Get Extended Error Code

Accesses internal services of DOS to retrieve extended error code information

Calling registers: AH   12h
                         AL   2Dh

Return registers: AX   Error code

Comments: Function 12h provides access to certain DOS internal services (00h–25h in Version 3, 00h–2Fh in Version 4). Note that many of these can be called only when all segment registers are set to the DOS kernel's segment; *if this restriction is not met, damage to data is extremely likely.* Nevertheless, they do provide information that is difficult to obtain by any other means and can be useful to developers who take proper precautions.

Subfunction 2Dh returns in AX the current value of the extended error code that would be returned by Int 21h, Function 59h. It assumes that the SS and DS registers point into the DOS kernel.

Int 2Fh   **Function 12h**   **Subfunction 2Fh**   **V4**

Store DX

Accesses internal services of DOS to store the value of DX in the DOS kernel

Calling registers: AH   12h
                         AL   2Fh
                         DX   New value to set

Return registers: None

Comments: Function 12h provides access to certain DOS internal services (00h–25h in Version 3, 00h–2Fh in Version 4). Note that many of these can be called only when all segment registers are set to the DOS kernel's segment; *if this restriction is not met, damage to data is extremely likely.* Nevertheless, they do provide information that is difficult to obtain by any other means and can be useful to developers who take proper precautions.

Subfunction 2Fh stores the value in the DX register into an internal DOS word, the purpose of which is not known. Extreme caution should be used when you experiment with this function. It assumes that all segment registers point into the DOS kernel.

Int 2Fh   **Function 14h**   **Subfunction 00h**   **V3**

Get NLSFUNC Installation Status

Interfaces with NLSFUNC.COM and does nothing unless that program is loaded

Calling registers: AH   14h
                        AL   00h

Return registers: Carry flag clear if successful
                        AL   Status
                                    00h, OK to install if not installed
                                    01h, not OK to install if not installed
                                    FFh, installed

Comments: Function 14h, Subfunction 00h is used for interfacing with NLSFUNC.COM. The uses of other subfunctions are not known at this time.

Int 2Fh   **Function 15h**   **V3**

CDROM Interface

Interfaces with the CDROM routines and does nothing unless that program is loaded

Calling registers: AX   1500h, get installed status

Return registers: Carry flag clear if successful
                        AL   Status
                                    00h, not installed, okay to install
                                    01h, not okay to install
                                    FFh, installed

Comments: Used for CD-ROM interface routines, most notably those provided by Microsoft in the CD-ROM extensions. A discussion of these services is beyond the scope of this book.

Int 2Fh   **Function 16h**   **Subfunction 80h**   **V5**

MS-DOS Idle Call

Informs the system that the calling program is idle

Calling registers: AH   16h
                        AL   80h

Return registers: None

Comments: Programs should use this interrupt when they are idle, such as when they are waiting for user input. Before doing so, the calling program should make sure that the Int 2Fh vector is not zero.

The interrupt is nonblocking; if the system does not have another program to run, it returns immediately and the calling program continues to run.

Int 2Fh	Function 1Ah	Subfunction 00h	V4
	Get ANSI.SYS Installed State		

Returns the installation state of ANSI.SYS

Calling registers:	AH	1Ah
	AL	00h
Return registers:	AL	FFh, ANSI.SYS loaded
		00h, ANSI.SYS not loaded

Comments: This function is used to determine whether ANSI.SYS is loaded. The ANSI.SYS driver provides a subset of the ANSI screen-handling codes. Before a program uses such codes, it should call this function to determine whether the codes will be supported.

Int 2Fh	Function 43h	Subfunction 00h	V5
	Get XMS Driver Installed State		

Returns the installation state of an XMS driver

Calling registers:	AH	43h
	AL	00h
Return registers:	AL	80h, XMS driver loaded
		00h, XMS driver not loaded

Comments: This function must be called before calling Function 4310 to verify the presence of the XMS driver.

Int 2Fh	Function 43h	Subfunction 10h	V5
	Get XMS Driver Entry-Point Address		

Returns the address of the XMS driver function call

Calling registers:	AH	43h
	AL	10h
Return registers:	ES:BX	Pointer to function

Comments: This function should be called only after calling Function 43h, Subfunction 00h to verify the installation of an XMS driver.

775

Programs should not take advantage of the XMS driver's HMA and UMB management if MS-DOS is already managing those areas.

Int 2Fh   **Function 48h**   **Subfunction 00h**   **V5**

Get DOSKEY.COM Installed State

Returns the installation state of DOSKEY.COM

Calling registers:	AH	48h
	AL	00h
Return registers:	AL	Nonzero, DOSKEY.COM loaded
		00h, DOSKEY.COM not loaded

Comments: This function is used to determine whether DOSKEY.COM, an enhanced command-line interpreter, is installed.

Int 2Fh   **Function 48h**   **Subfunction 10h**   **V5**

Read Command Line

Reads a line of as many as 126 characters and copies it to the specified buffer

Calling registers:	AH	48h
	AL	10h
	DS:DX	Pointer to buffer
		Byte 0, maximum buffer size
		Byte 1, returned line length
		Byte 2, first byte of input line
Return registers:	AX	0 if successful

Comments: During the call, DOSKEY macros and function keys are enabled. If a macro name is entered, AX will be zero, but a second call must be made to expand the macro.

The returned line has a carriage return (0Dh) added to the end. The returned line length does not include the carriage return.

The line entered is added to the DOSKEY history.

Int 2Fh   **Function 4Bh**   **Subfunction 01h**   **V5**

Build Notification Chain

Creates a linked list of notification function handlers

Calling registers:	AH	4Bh
	AL	01h
	ES:BX	0
	CX:DX	Service function handler address
Return registers:	ES:BX	0, no notification chain

Nonzero, address of SWCALLBACKINFO structure, formatted as follows:

	Dword	Address of next SWCALLBACKINFO struc-ture in chain
	Dword	Address of notification function handler
	Dword	Reserved
	Dword	Address of SWAPIINFO structure

Comments: The client program must handle this call as part of its Int 2Fh handling to support the task switching API. If this call is not handled, the client must jump to the previously installed Int 2Fh handler.

If the client program chooses to handle this call, it must first call the previously loaded Int 2F handler. On return, it should fill its own SWCALLBACKINFO structure, set the address of the next SWCALLBACKINFO structure to the ES:BX value returned by the previous Int 2Fh handler, and set ES:BX to the address of its own SWCALLBACKINFO structure. The most recently loaded client, therefore, is the first in the chain.

Int 2Fh   **Function 4Bh**   **Subfunction 02h**   **V5**

Detect Switcher

Detects the presence of a task switcher

Calling registers:	AH	4Bh
	AL	02h
	BX	0
	DI	0
	ES:BX	0
Return registers:	ES:BX	0 if no task switcher installed

Address of service-function handler if task switcher is installed

Comments: Programs that need to prevent or control the interruptions caused by task switching should call this function during initialization.

Int 2Fh	Function 4Bh	Subfunction 03h	V5
	Allocate Switcher ID		

Returns a unique switcher identifier

Calling registers:	AH	4Bh
	AL	03h
	BX	0
	ES:DI	Service function handler

Return registers:	BX	00, could not allocate an identifier 01h–0Fh, identifier

Comments: This function must be called only by a task switcher, not by a client program.

A task switcher must first find out whether it is the first task switcher installed by calling Function 4B, Subfunction 02h. If it is, it must handle the processing of this call by other task switchers. Otherwise, it must call this function and get a switcher ID. If it fails to do so, it must exit or disable itself.

A task switcher uses its switch ID as the high four bits of any session identifiers it creates, thus ensuring that no two session identifiers are the same.

The task switcher must disable interrupts while examining and changing its record of allocated switch identifiers. At any other time, the task switcher may enable interrupts and call any MS-DOS function. It may modify the AX and BX registers, but it must preserve the other registers.

Int 2Fh	Function 4Bh	Subfunction 04h	V5
	Free Switcher ID		

Frees a switch identifier allocated by Function 4B, Subfunction 03h

Calling registers:	AH	4Bh
	AL	04h
	BX	Identifier
	ES:DI	Service handler address

Return registers:	BX	0, valid identifier freed
		Nonzero, invalid identifier

Comments: When a task switcher exits, it should call this function to free its identifier.

Int 2Fh   **Function 4Bh**   **Subfunction 05h**   **V5**

Identify Instance Data

Identifies instance data maintained by a client program

Calling registers: AH   4Bh
                         AL   05h
                         ES:BX   0
                         CX:DX   Service function handler

Return registers: ES:BX   0, no instance data chain
                         Nonzero, address of SWSTARTUPINFO structure:
                             Word   Version
                             Dword   Previous handler's SWSTARTUPINFO struc-
                                     ture address
                             Dword   Ignored
                             Dword   Ignored
                             Dword   SWINSTANCEITEM structure address

Comments: The client program must handle this call as part of its Int 2Fh handling to support the task switching API. If this call is not handled, the client must jump to the previously installed Int 2Fh handler.

If the client program chooses to handle this call, it must first call the previously loaded Int 2F handler. On return, it should fill its own SWSTARTUPINFO structure, set the address of the previous handler's SWSTARTUPINFO structure to the ES:BX value returned by the previous Int 2Fh handler, and set ES:BX to the address of its own SWSTARTUPINFO structure. The most recently loaded client, therefore, is the first in the chain.

Int 2Fh   **Function ADh**   **Subfunction 80h**   **V3.3**

Get KEYB.COM Version Number

Returns KEYB.COM's version number

Calling registers: AH   ADh
                         AL   80h

Return registers: BH   Major version number
                         BL   Minor version number

Comments: The version number will be zero if KEYB.COM is not installed.

Int 2Fh   **Function ADh**   **Subfunction 81h**   **V3.3**

Set KEYB.COM Active Code Page

Sets the active code page for KEYB.COM

Calling registers: AH   ADh
                         AL   81h
                         BX   Code page id

Return registers: Carry flag clear, if successful
                        Carry flag set, if error
                        AX   0001

Comments: This function is used to select the code page for the keyboard driver.

Int 2Fh   **Function ADh**   **Subfunction 82h**   **V3.3**

Set KEYB.COM Country Flag

Sets the KEYB.COM country flag

Calling registers: AH   ADh
                         AL   82h
                         BL   Country flag
                              00h, domestic
                              FFh, foreign

Return registers: Carry flag clear, if successful
                        Carry flag set, if error

Comments: This function is used to select between USA and non-USA for the country flag.

Int 2Fh   **Function ADh**   **Subfunction 83h**   **V3.3**

Get KEYB.COM Country Flag

Gets the KEYB.COM country flag

Calling registers: AH   ADh
                         AL   83h

Return registers: BL   Country flag

Comments: This function is used to get the country flag. Values are 00h (domestic) and FFh (foreign).

Int 2Fh   **Function B0h**   **Subfunction 00h**   **V3.3**

Get GRAFTABL.COM Installed State

Returns the installation state of GRAFTABL.COM

Calling registers: AH   B0h
                        AL   00h

Return registers: AL   FFh, GRAFTABL.COM loaded
                                00h, GRAFTABL.COM not loaded

Comments: This function determines whether GRAFTABL is installed. GRAFTABL enables MS-DOS to display characters in the range from 80h to FFh in graphics mode.

Int 2Fh   **Function B7h**   **Subfunction 00h**   **V3.3**

Check for APPEND Installation

Returns a value indicating whether APPEND has been installed at the DOS level

Calling registers: AH   B7h
                        AL   00h

Return registers: AH   <> 0 if APPEND installed

Comments: This function is used to determine whether APPEND has been installed by checking the value returned in AH. APPEND is installed at the DOS level through the APPEND command. Because there has been little standardization in networking during the past several years, not all networks respond correctly to this interrupt.

Int 2Fh   **Function B7h**   **Subfunction 02h**   **V4**

Get APPEND Version

Determines which version of APPEND is installed

Calling registers: AH   B7h
                        AL   02h

Return registers: Carry flag clear if successful
                        AX   FFFFh if V4 APPEND installed; otherwise, APPEND is
                                       not MS-DOS V4 version
                      Carry flag set if error
                        AX   Error code

Comments: This function is used to determine whether all the features added to APPEND at V4 are available. Subfunction 00h returns `installed` if any version is present; this function establishes that the version present is V4.

Int 2Fh	Function B7h	Subfunction 04h	V4

Get APPEND Path Pointer

If APPEND is installed, returns a pointer to the currently active APPEND path

Calling registers: AH   B7h
                          AL   04h

Return registers: Carry flag clear if successful
                          ES:DI   Pointer to active APPEND path
                          Carry flag set if error
                          AX   Error code

Comments: This function is used to determine the address of the active APPEND path.

Int 2Fh	Function B7h	Subfunction 06h	V4

Get APPEND Function State

Returns a bit map of the APPEND fuctions in use (if APPEND is installed)

Calling registers: AH   B7h
                          AL   06h

Return registers: Carry flag clear if successful
                          BX   APPEND state (bit map):

Bit Settings	
`FEDCBA98 76543210`	*Meaning*
`........ .......0`	APPEND disabled
`........ .......1`	APPEND enabled
`...xxxxx xxxxxxx.`	Not used (zero)
`..0..... ........`	/PATH inactive
`..1..... ........`	/PATH active
`.0...... ........`	/E switch inactive
`.1...... ........`	/E switch active

Bit Settings

FEDCBA98 76543210	Meaning
0.......	/X switch inactive
1.......	/X switch active

Carry flag set if error
AX   Error code

Comments: This function is used to read the current state of the APPEND function. For details about the various switches, see the DOS V4 documentation for APPEND.

Int 2Fh	Function B7h	Subfunction 07h	V4

Set APPEND Function State

Changes the state of the APPEND functions using bit-mapped codes

Calling registers: AH   B7h
AL   07h
BX   APPEND state (bit map):

Bit Settings

FEDCBA98 76543210	Meaning
....0	APPEND disabled
....1	APPEND enabled
...xxxxx xxxxxxx.	Not used (zero)
..0.....	/PATH inactive
..1.....	/PATH active
.0......	/E switch inactive
.1......	/E switch active
0.......	/X switch inactive
1.......	/X switch active

Return registers: Carry flag clear if successful
Carry flag set if error
AX   Error code

Comments: This function is used to set the state of the APPEND function by passing it a bit map describing the desired state. For details of the various switches, see the DOS V4 documentation for APPEND.

Int 2Fh	Function B7h	Subfunction 11h	V4

Set Return Found Name State

Modifies action of APPEND for the next DOS access only

Calling registers:
AH B7h
AL 11h

Return registers: Carry flag clear if successful
Carry flag set if error
AX   Error code

Comments: This function is used to cause APPEND to modify the action of Functions 3Dh, 43h, and 6Ch of Interrupt 21h. When this function is executed, the next call to any of those functions returns the fully qualified file name, in the same location at which the file name was passed to the function. You must be sure that the buffer is large enough (67 bytes) to accept any possible return value.

After a fully expanded file name has been returned, the flag set by this function is cleared, and operation of the Interrupt 21h functions returns to normal. Each use of this APPEND subfunction, therefore, affects only a single use of the Interrupt 21h functions.

Mouse Reference

The mouse functions operate through an installed driver (MOUSE.SYS or MOUSE.COM) that ties itself to Int 33h for access to the functions. The driver constantly updates the mouse cursor's position on the screen relative to the movement of the mouse. No action by the program is necessary to maintain the driver's action.

At any time, a program can query the driver to find the current status of the mouse.

Several versions of mouse driver software exist; Microsoft has a tendency to update them without warning or notice. Because the drivers from Microsoft are generally accepted as an industry standard, this section describes the functions provided by Microsoft's Version 8.x drivers. Some older drivers and some drivers from other mouse makers omit functions (especially those numbered above 18h). For use with DOS V1, which did not permit installable device drivers, most are supplied also as TSRs; whether installed as a driver (SYS file) or as a TSR (COM file), the functions are identical. Many mouse users use the TSR version with all DOS versions.

Included near the end of this section are some EGA register interface functions that are particularly useful if you are programming the mouse.

If you have any question about how the functions in this section are presented, refer to the "Reference Overview" section of this book.

The Mouse Functions

Int 33h   **Function 00h**   **V2**

Initialize the Mouse

Determines whether a mouse is installed, resets the driver, and returns the number of buttons on the mouse

Calling register:	AX	0000h
Return registers:	AX	0, mouse not installed –1, mouse installed
	BX	Number of buttons (2 for Microsoft, 3 for some other brands)

Comments: When a program in which you want to use the mouse starts, that program must verify the mouse's presence. The usual way to do this is to call Function 00h. This function resets the mouse to the center of the screen, makes sure that the mouse is off, and sets the default mouse cursor and default movement ratios.

In DOS V2.x, it is best to verify that the vector for Interrupt 33h points to code before using this function. If the four bytes of the vector are not all 00, it should be safe to use Function 00h to determine whether the driver is present.

The initial conditions established for the mouse driver by this function are shown in this list:

Display page:	Page 0
Cursor range:	Entire screen (x=0 to 639, y=0 to 199)
Exclusion area:	None
Cursor position:	At screen center (x=320, y=100)
Cursor state:	Hidden
Cursor shape:	Arrow for graphics modes
	Reverse block for text modes
User interrupts:	Disabled
Light-pen emulator:	Enabled
Mickey/pixel ratio:	Horizontal = 8 to 8
	Vertical = 16 to 8
Speed threshold:	Sixty-four mickeys per second. (*Mickey* is the unit of mouse motion. One mickey is approximately 1/200 inch.)

Int 33h   Function 01h   V2

Show Mouse Cursor

Causes the mouse cursor to appear on the display

Calling register: AX   0001h

Return registers: None

Comments: Turns on the mouse cursor, allowing display on the screen. This is not an absolute function; rather, it increments an internal mouse-cursor flag. Initially, this flag is set to –1. Whenever the flag is zero, the mouse cursor is displayed. Function 02h decrements the cursor flag and causes the cursor to disappear if the original value was zero. Multiple calls to Function 02h therefore require multiple calls to this function. The software prevents the flag's value from becoming greater than zero, however.

Int 33h   Function 02h   V2

Hide Mouse Cursor

Turns off display of the mouse cursor

Calling register: AX   0002h

Return registers: None

Comments: This function turns off the display function but does not disable the driver. As noted in the comment for Function 01h, Function 02h decrements a cursor flag. If the value is not zero, the cursor is turned off. Because the flag can never be greater than zero, a single call to this function is guaranteed to hide the cursor.

Int 33h   Function 03h   V2

Get Mouse Position

Returns current mouse position and button status

Calling register: AX   0003h

Return registers: BX   Button status
                                     CX   X-coordinate (horizontal)
                                     DX   Y-coordinate (vertical)

Comments: This function tells you where the mouse is located. No matter which mode the screen is in, Function 03h always returns an x-coordinate (column) between 0 and 639 and a y-coordinate (row) between 0 and 199. Table M.1 shows the mouse cursor's allowable positions for each display mode, in terms of screen (pixel) coordinates.

Table M.1 Mouse Cursor's Position

Screen Mode	Mouse Coordinates
00h, 01h	x = 16 × column
	y = 8 × row
02h, 03h	x = 8 × column
	y = 8 × row
04h, 05h	x = 2 × screen X
	y = screen Y
06h	x = screen X
	y = screen Y
07h	x = 8 × screen column
	y = 8 × screen row
0Eh–10h	x = screen X
	y = screen Y

The status of the mouse buttons is returned in BX; only the low-order bits are significant. Table M.2 illustrates the meaning of the bits. Because each button acts independently, the value can be anything from 0 to 3 for a 2-button mouse or from 0 to 7 for the 3-button version.

Table M.2 Mouse Button Status Bits

Bit 76543210	Meaning
.......0	Left button up
.......1	Left button down
......0.	Right button up
......1.	Right button down
.....0..	Center button (if present) up
.....1..	Center button (if present) down
xxxxx...	Undefined

Int 33h   Function 04h   V2

Set Mouse Position

Sets the mouse's position on the screen

Calling registers:	AX	0004h
	CX	New x-coordinate (horizontal)
	DX	New y-coordinate (vertical)

Return registers: None

Comments: You can use this function to place the mouse cursor anywhere on the screen. (The mouse driver resumes operating from that location.) This function is useful, for example, when you want to start the mouse at the first item on a menu that is brought up on-screen.

If either coordinate has a value that is inappropriate for the current screen mode as defined for Function 03h, it is adjusted to the nearest appropriate value. If the specified position lies outside the display range established by calls to Functions 07h and 08h, the cursor is placed as close as possible to the specified position while remaining within the range limits. If the position lies within an exclusion area defined by Function 10h, it is hidden.

Int 33h   Function 05h   V2

Get Button-Press Information

Returns information about button presses

Calling registers:	AX	0005h
	BX	Button
		0, left
		1, right
		2, center (if present)

Return registers:	AX	Button status (refer to Table M.2)
	BX	Count of button presses (reset to zero at each call)
	CX	Cursor's horizontal position at last button press
	DX	Cursor's vertical position at last button press

Comments: Function 05h provides information about what has happened to the specified cursor button since your last call to this function. You can tell whether the button has been pressed, the number of times it was pressed since this function was called, and the location of the mouse when the button was last pressed.

The button status is returned in register AX. This status is the same as returned in BX for Function 03h (refer to Table M.2).

Int 33h   **Function 06h**   **V2**

Get Button-Release Information

Returns information about button releases

Calling registers:	AX	0006h
	BX	Button
		0, left
		1, right
		2, center (if present)
Return registers:	AX	Button status (refer to Table M.2)
	BX	Count of button releases since last call
	CX	Cursor's horizontal position when button was last released
	DX	Cursor's vertical position when button was last released

Comments: Function 06h returns information about the release of a mouse button. (Function 05h returns information about presses.) A button release (you let go of the button) is distinct from a press (you press down on the button) and can be identified if you use these two functions. Registers for this function contain information corresponding to the release operation.

Int 33h   **Function 07h**   **V2**

Set Mouse X Limits

Sets the X limits of the mouse's travel on-screen

Calling registers:	AX	0007h
	CX	.	Minimum X bound
	DX	Maximum X bound
Return registers:	None

Comments: When you want to limit the movement of the mouse cursor in the X (horizontal) direction, call Function 07h. This function is useful when you want to keep the mouse cursor within a defined area on-screen, as you might, for example, with a menu. Function 08h (Y Limits) is also useful for restricting the mouse cursor's movement.

The mouse driver is initialized to have its X limits set at 0 for a minimum and 639 for a maximum. The values passed to this function should be between those limits. If the value in CX is greater than that in DX, the two values are swapped. If the mouse cursor position is outside the limit after this function is executed, it automatically moves to the limit position.

Int 33h   Function 08h   V2

Set Mouse Y Limits

Sets the Y limits of the mouse's travel on-screen

Calling registers: AX   0008h
                           CX   Minimum Y bound
                           DX   Maximum Y bound

Return registers: None

Comments: When you want to limit the movement of the mouse cursor in the Y (vertical) direction, call Function 08h. This function is useful when you want to keep the mouse cursor within a defined area on-screen, as you might, for example, with a menu. Function 07h (X Limits) is also useful for restricting the mouse cursor's movement.

The mouse driver is initialized to have its Y limits set at 0 for a minimum and 199 for a maximum. The values passed to this function should be between those limits. If the value in CX is greater than that in DX, the two values are swapped. If the mouse cursor position is outside the limit after this function is executed, it automatically moves to the limit position.

Int 33h   Function 09h   V2

Set Graphics Cursor Shape

Sets shape of cursor for use in graphics mode

Calling registers: AX   0009h
                           BX   Hot-spot x position (−16 to 16)
                           CX   Hot-spot y position (−16 to 16)
                           ES:DX   Pointer to screen and cursor masks

Return registers: None

Comments: In graphics mode, the cursor is defined by a *screen mask*, a *cursor mask*, and the *hot spot*. Function 09h specifies them all.

This concept, one of the most confusing items in the mouse driver, requires detailed examination. To provide a framework for the examination, keep in mind that the visible mouse cursor is always defined to the software as a 16-pixel-by-16-pixel area, and the hot spot is a single pixel addressed relative to the upper left corner of this 16 × 16 square, which is the official cursor location. Within the square, the visible pointer shape is established by the screen and cursor masks.

791

When the mouse cursor is generated in graphics mode, the screen mask is ANDed to the screen, and then the cursor mask is XORed with the result. When two bytes are ANDed together, the resulting byte has a 1 bit wherever *both* the two original bytes have a 1; all the other bits are set to 0. An XOR on two bytes results in a byte with a 1 bit wherever *only one* of the original bytes has a 1; all the other bits are set to 0.

As an example, if the screen mask is 9Ch and the byte is 3Bh, the result of ANDing them together is the following:

```
9Ch         10011100
AND 3Bh     00111011
            _____
            00011000
```

If the cursor mask is 9Ch and the byte is 3Bh, the result of XORing them together is as follows:

```
9Ch         10011100
XOR 3Bh     00111011
            _____
            10100111
```

The practical effect of these operations for graphics modes 1 through 6 is as follows for each bit:

		Screen Mask	
C		0	1
u M			
r a	0	0	1
s s			
o k	1	No change	Inverted
r			

For screen modes 7 and over, the effect is as follows:

		Screen Mask	
C		0	1
u M			
r a	0	Black	White
s s			
o k	1	No change	No change
r			

The masks stored at the location pointed to by ES:DX are bit-mapped blocks of 16-bit words. Each word of the bit map corresponds to one of the 16 rows of the cursor (beginning at the top row, screen mask first). Words 0 through 15 are the screen mask; words 16 through 31 are the cursor mask. Figure M.1 shows how the bytes correspond to cursor locations.

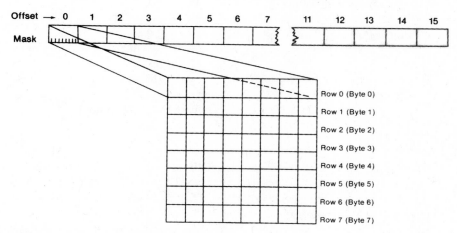

Figure M.1 Bytes corresponding to cursor locations.

There are two bits per cursor pixel in graphics modes 4–6 and 14–16, even though the cursor size may differ.

The screen mask temporarily erases anything behind the cursor area; the cursor mask then draws the pointer shape within the space that remains. This makes the mouse pointer appear to overlay on-screen data. By providing several sets of masks and using this function to switch between them, you can use different pointer shapes in different parts of your programs.

The hot-spot coordinates are always relative to the upper left corner of the 16 × 16 pixel area covered by the two masks and define the specific coordinates that are returned as the mouse position whenever any function requests that information.

Setting the hot spot to 0,0 causes the upper left corner of the image to be the official mouse position (the tip of the default arrow image); a setting of 8,8 makes the center of the area the official position; and 16,16 moves it to the lower right corner. Because –16,–16 is a valid hot-spot setting, it can even be moved outside the actual image—although it is difficult to envision any good reason for doing so.

Int 33h   Function 0Ah   V2

Set Text Cursor Type

Sets up the text mode cursor

Calling registers:	AX	000Ah
	BX	0, select attribute cursor
		1, select hardware cursor
	CX	Screen mask (AND value) if BX = 0
		Starting scan line if BX = 1
	DX	Cursor mask (XOR value) if BX = 0
		Ending scan line if BX = 1

Return registers: None

Comments: In text mode, the cursor is an attribute cursor or a hardware cursor, depending on how BX is set. With the attribute cursor, the CX and DX registers are screen and cursor masks, respectively, which operate on the CRT attribute-character byte pairs in the same way the graphics-mode masks operate on pixels. The screen mask preserves most of the original character's attributes. The cursor mask determines which attributes will be changed. To preserve the character unchanged, the low byte of the screen mask should be FFh, and the low byte of the cursor mask should be 00h.

The attribute and character bytes at the mouse cursor's location are ANDed with the screen mask and XORed with the cursor mask.

If the hardware mode of operation is selected, the CX and DX registers select the start and stop scan lines for the mouse cursor in the same way that CH and CL do for Int 10h, Function 01h. With this option, set the mouse cursor to a different shape than the normal text cursor so that they are easy to distinguish on-screen. Because the number of usable shapes is limited, the attribute mode usually is used instead.

Int 33h   Function 0Bh   V2

Read Motion Counters

Determines the amount of actual mouse motion, if any, since the last call to this function

Calling register:	AX	000Bh

Return registers:	CX	Number of mickeys moved horizontally
		(–32768 to 32767, negative means to left)
	DX	Number of mickeys moved vertically
		(–32768 to 32767, negative means up)

Comments: Function 0Bh tells you the *relative* movement of the mouse cursor between calls. The internal software keeps track of the mouse cursor's location at all times and records its location at each call to this function.

The CX and DX registers return the relative movement (positive values correspond to right and down the screen). The numbers returned are in mickeys, the unit of mouse motion. Every mickey is equal to approximately 0.5 millimeters (0.02 inches).

Int 33h	Function 0Ch	V2
	Set User-Defined Event Handler	

Establishes a vector to a function that will be called by the device driver whenever a condition defined by the supplied call mask occurs

Calling registers:

	AX	000Ch
	CX	Call mask (see "Comments")
	ES:DX	Pointer to user-interrupt routine

Return registers: None

Comments: This function sets up a special handler for conditions recognized by the mouse device driver. A function can be written to respond to button presses, button releases, changes in the cursor's position, or any combination of these events. Operation is essentially identical to that of an interrupt handler, particularly in that the routine can be invoked during the execution of any program as long as it is active; all details are in the mouse driver, however, and the handler does not need to be concerned with them.

Operation of the handler is controlled by a *call mask* in CX that identifies which conditions will trigger the handler's invocation. Wherever the call mask has a 1 bit, the function pointed to by ES:DX is executed when the condition occurs. A 0 bit in the same position cancels the function. Table M.3 shows the assignment of bits in the call mask, and Table M.4 shows the state of the CPU registers on entry to the user's event-handler routine.

Table M.3 Call Mask Bit Values

Bit 76543210	Meaning
.......1	Mouse moved
......1.	Left button pressed
.....1..	Left button released

continues

Table M.3   Continued

Bit 76543210	Meaning
....1...	Right button pressed
...1....	Right button released
..1.....	Center button (if present) pressed
.1......	Center button (if present) released

Table M.4   Register Setup When User Function Is Called

Register	Contents
AX	Event trigger bit (same as condition mask presented in Table M.3, but only the bit that triggered this call is present)
BX	Button state (same as Functions 05h and 06h)
CX	Cursor's horizontal coordinate (same as Function 03h)
DX	Cursor's vertical coordinate (same as Function 03h)
DI	Horizontal counts (same as CX for Function 0Bh)
SI	Vertical counts (same as DX for Function 0Bh)

When Function 00h is called, the entire call mask is reset to zero. Before a program that sets up a special handler for these conditions ends, the call mask should be reset by a call to Function 00h, 0Ch, or 14h. Remember to restore the initial value of the call mask and subroutine addresses before you end your program.

Int 33h	Function 0Dh	V2
	Start Light Pen Emulation	

Turns on light-pen emulation mode

Calling register: AX   000Dh

Return registers: None

Comments: In light-pen emulation mode, the mouse position is the light-pen position. Pressing both mouse buttons corresponds to pressing the light pen to the screen. Not all mouse-driver programs provide this interface.

Int 33h   Function 0Eh   V2

Stop Light Pen Emulation

Turns off light-pen emulation mode

Calling register: AX   000Eh

Return registers: None

Comments: This function is used to instruct the device driver to stop handling the mouse inputs as though they originated from a light pen. Function 0Eh causes the mouse to work in its normal manner, without driver translation. Not all mouse-driver programs provide this interface.

Int 33h   Function 0Fh   V2

Set Mickey-to-Pixel Ratio

Sets the ratio between physical movement of the cursor (in mickeys, 1/200th of an inch) and coordinate changes (in pixels)

Calling registers: AX   000Fh
                          CX   Number of mickeys required to cause an 8-pixel change
                                              in horizontal position (default 8)
                          DX   Number of mickeys required to cause an 8-pixel change
                                              in vertical position (default 16)

Return registers: None

Comments: In both the CX and DX registers, the high bit must be zero. The minimum value for each ratio is 1. The higher the ratio, the slower the mouse cursor moves on-screen.

Int 33h   Function 10h   V2

Conditional Cursor Off

Defines a screen area (exclusion area) in which the cursor is hidden

Calling registers: AX   0010h
                          CX   Upper x screen coordinate

DX	Upper y screen coordinate
SI	Lower x screen coordinate
DI	Lower y screen coordinate

Return registers: None

Comments: Function 10h specifies an area on-screen in which the cursor disappears. After using this function, be sure to call Function 01h again when the cursor has moved out of the hidden region to restore the cursor's visibility.

Int 33h	Function 13h	V2
	Set Double Speed Threshold	

Sets the threshold speed above which the cursor moves at twice the normal rate

| **Calling registers:** | AX | 0013h |
| | DX | Threshold speed in mickeys per second (default is 64) |

Return registers: None

Comments: When the mouse moves at or above the threshold value (of mickeys per second), the cursor-movement factor across the screen is increased by a factor of 2.

Int 33h	Function 14h	V2
	Swap User Event Handlers	

Sets the user-interrupt function and call mask while returning their previous values

Calling registers:	AX	0014h
	CX	User-interrupt call mask
	ES:DX	Point to user-interrupt routine
Return registers:	CX	Old user-interrupt mask
	ES:DX	Old user-interrupt vector

Comments: Like Function 0Ch, this function sets a user-defined handling function to respond to special events recognized by the mouse device driver. The call mask is the same one used in Function 0Ch (see Table M.5). Function 14h is enabled when the call-mask bit is set to 1; when it is set to 0, the function is disabled.

Table M.5 Call Mask Bits

Bit 76543210	Meaning
. . . . 1	Mouse moved
. . . . . . 1 .	Left button pressed
. . . . . 1 . .	Left button released
. . . . 1 . . .	Right button pressed
. . . 1	Right button released
. . 1	Center button (if present) pressed
. 1	Center button (if present) released

Unlike Function 0Ch, with this function you get the old values in return, permitting you to save them and restore them later. Except for this, the two functions are identical.

When the handler is called, the CPU registers are set up with the information shown in Table M.4. The DS register points to the mouse-driver data segment. If the user function needs to get its own data, the function has to set DS to its own data segment.

The major difference between this function and Function 0Ch is that you can save the original values of the call mask and user-interrupt vector. Remember to restore them before you end your program.

Int 33h **Function 15h** **V2**

Get Save-State Storage Size

Returns the size of the buffer for the current state of the mouse device driver

Calling register:	AX	0015h
Return register:	BX	Buffer size (bytes) necessary to hold current mouse state

Comments: This function, which is used in preparation for Function 16h or 17h, determines the amount of memory necessary to save the mouse's current state before you use another program that also needs the mouse. The value returned is the exact number of bytes necessary to save the driver state.

Int 33h   Function 16h   V2

Save Mouse Driver State

Copies the state of the mouse driver to the buffer pointed to by ES:DX

Calling registers: AX   0016h
                        ES:DX   Pointer to buffer to hold mouse state

Return registers: None

Comments: This function copies the mouse's current state to the buffer pointed to by ES:DX. The buffer size necessary is determined by a call to Function 15h.

Use this function whenever you suspend one program that is using the mouse and execute another such program. When the second program ends, you can restore the mouse's state to what it was before the second program started.

Int 33h   Function 17h   V2

Restore Mouse Driver State

Restores the mouse driver to the state saved by Function 16h

Calling registers: AX   0017h
                        ES:DX   Pointer to buffer in which mouse state is saved

Return registers: None

Comments: When one program resumes after having executed another program that used the mouse, this function enables you to restore the mouse's state as it was immediately before the second program was executed (if you saved the state by using Function 16h).

Int 33h   Function 18h   V2

Set Alternate Mouse User Handler

Allows setup of as many as three special-event handlers (similar to those defined in Function 0Ch or 14h)

Calling registers: AX   0018h
                        CX   Call mask (see "Comments")
                        ES:DX   Address offset to function

Return register: AX   0018h if function successful
                                    FFFFh if function failed

Comments: This function creates a special handler for conditions recognized by the mouse device driver. A function can be written to respond to button presses or releases or to changes in cursor position. As many as three such handlers can be defined by separate calls to Function 18h. The difference between the handler established by this function and one established by Function 0Ch or 14h is that this handler responds when the Shift, Alt, or Ctrl key is pressed. The driver permits a total of four handlers simultaneously: the three permitted by this function and the one set by Function 0Ch. Combinations such as Shift-Alt and Ctrl-Alt are *not* supported, contrary to descriptions published elsewhere.

The operation of the interrupt is controlled by a *call mask* that identifies which conditions will trigger the special handler. Wherever the call mask has a 1 bit, the function pointed to by the DX register is executed when the condition occurs. A 0 bit in the same position cancels the function. Table M.6 shows the assignment of bits in the call mask. Note that because the bits to specify the center button on a 3-button mouse in the call mask are used for the Shift and Ctrl key indicators, this function cannot respond to the center button on a 3-button mouse.

Table M.6 Call Mask Bits

Bit 76543210	Meaning
. . . . 1	Mouse moved
. . . . . . 1 .	Left-button down event
. . . . . 1 . .	Left-button up event
. . . . 1 . . .	Right-button down event
. . . 1	Right-button up event
. . 1	Shift button pressed during event
. 1	Ctrl key pressed during event
1	Alt key pressed during event

The entire call mask is reset to zero when Function 00h is called. Before it ends, a program that sets up a special handler for these conditions should reset the call mask by calling Function 18h or Function 00h.

When the handler is called, the CPU registers are set up with the information shown in Table M.4.

Int 33h   Function 19h   V2

Get User Alternate Interrupt Vector

Returns a pointer to a function defined by a call to Function 18h

Calling registers: AX   0019h
                          CX   Call mask

Return registers: BX:DX   User interrupt vector
                          CX   Call mask (0 if no match was found)

Comments: This function searches the event handlers defined by Function 18h for one whose call mask matches the CX register. When one is found, it returns its segment in BX and offset in DX.

Int 33h   Function 1Ah   V2

Set Mouse Sensitivity

Sets the mouse speed *and* double-speed threshold values

Calling registers: AX   001Ah
                          BX   Horizontal mickeys (1–100, default is 8)
                          CX   Vertical mickeys (1–100, default is 16)
                          DX   Double-speed threshold (default is 64)

Return registers: None

Comments: This function combines Functions 0F and 13h in a single call. The values are not reset by a call to Function 00h. The maximum value for BX and CX is 100.

Int 33h   Function 1Bh   V2

Get Mouse Sensitivity

Returns the sensitivity values set by Function 1Ah

Calling register: AX   001Bh

Return registers: BX   Horizontal mickeys per pixel
                          CX   Vertical mickeys per pixel
                          DX   Double-speed threshold

Comments: This function returns the sensitivity of the mouse, represented as the number of mickeys (horizontal and vertical) the mouse must move in order to move the cursor one pixel on the screen.

Int 33h   **Function 1Ch**   **V2**

Set interrupt rate

Sets the rate at which the mouse driver polls the mouse status

Calling registers: AX   001Ch
                        BX   Interrupt rate code:
                                    1, no polling
                                    2, poll 30 times per second
                                    4, poll 50 times per second
                                    8, poll 100 times per second
                                    16, poll 200 times per second

Return registers: None

Comments: *This function applies only to the Microsoft InPort mouse.* If any value other than those listed is put in BX, the lowest bit applies (3 = no polling, for example, because it contains the bit for 1).

Int 33h   **Function 1Dh**   **V2**

Set CRT Page Number

Sets the page on which the mouse cursor is displayed

Calling registers: AX   001Dh
                        BX   CRT page number

Return registers: None

Comments: This function is used to set the screen page on which the mouse cursor is displayed. Valid page numbers depend on both the video hardware in place and the display mode; refer to the discussion of Interrupt 10h, Function 05h for valid combinations.

Int 33h   **Function 1Eh**   **V2**

Get CRT Page Number

Gets the CRT page number on which the mouse cursor is displayed

Calling register: AX   001Eh

Return register: BX   CRT page number

Comments: This function is used to determine the screen page on which the mouse cursor is displayed. Valid page numbers depend on both the video hardware in place and the display mode; refer to the discussion of Interrupt 10h, Function 05h for valid combinations.

Int 33h   Function 1Fh   V2

Disable Mouse Driver

Disables the mouse driver by restoring interrupt vectors used by the mouse driver

Calling register: AX   001Fh

Return registers: AX   001Fh, successful
                                 FFFFh, unsuccessful

ES:BX   Previous vector for Int 33h (only if successful)

Comments: This function disables mouse operation by restoring the interrupt vectors for Int 10h and either Int 71h (8086-processor-based systems) or Int 74h (80286- or 80386-based systems). Int 33h (the mouse function interrupt) is not affected directly by this call. But the original value of the Int 33h vector is returned in the ES:BX register pair. This value can be used to restore Int 33h to its original value, which disables the handler.

Disabling any interrupt handler can be tricky. There is no way of knowing whether another handler has also attached itself to these interrupts after the mouse handler installed itself. The restored interrupt vectors are the values from when the mouse driver was first installed. If another handler attached itself after that, calling this function disables the other handler also. This could lead to a system crash or worse.

Int 33h   Function 20h   V2

Enable Mouse Driver

Reinstalls the mouse driver for use

Calling register: AX   0020h

Return registers: None

Comments: If the Interrupt 33h vector was left alone, this function restores the interrupt vectors for Int 10h and 71h or 74h, which were removed by the call to Function 1Fh.

Int 33h   Function 21h   V2

Software Reset

Resets the mouse software (but not the mouse)

Calling register: AX   0021h

Return registers: AX   FFFFh, mouse driver installed
                                 0021h, mouse driver not installed

BX   Number of buttons mouse has (2 for Microsoft mice, can be 3 for other makes)

Comments: This function is identical to Function 00h except that it does not reset the mouse hardware.

Int 33h	Function 22h	V2
	Set Message Language	

Selects language used by mouse driver for prompts and error messages (not in all versions)

Calling registers: AX   0022h

                      BX   Language number

                                      0, English
                                      1, French
                                      2, Dutch
                                      3, German
                                      4, Swedish
                                      5, Finnish
                                      6, Spanish
                                      7, Portuguese
                                      8, Italian

Return registers: None

Comments: This function is available only in international versions of the mouse drivers.

Int 33h	Function 23h	V2
	Get Message Language	

Returns language used by mouse driver for prompts and error messages (not in all versions)

Calling register: AX   0023h

Return register: BX   Language number

                                      0, English
                                      1, French
                                      2, Dutch
                                      3, German
                                      4, Swedish
                                      5, Finnish
                                      6, Spanish
                                      7, Portuguese
                                      8, Italian

Comments: This function is available only in international versions of the mouse drivers.

Int 33h   Function 24h   V2

Get Mouse Information

Returns driver version number, mouse type, and IRQ number being used

Calling register:	AX	0024h

Return registers:	BH	Major version (6 for 6.11, for example)
	BL	Minor version (11 for 6.11, for example)
	CH	Mouse type
		1, bus mouse
		2, serial mouse
		3, InPort mouse
		4, PS/2 mouse
		5, HP mouse
	CL	IRQ being used
		0, PS/2 system
		2–7, IRQ number

Comments: This function returns the version number of the driver, the mouse type, and the interrupt request line in use for the standard Microsoft drivers. Additional information is returned in function 25h. Drivers from other firms might not support this function or might return different results.

Int 33h   Function 25h

Get General Driver Information

Returns information about the environment in which the mouse is functioning.

Calling register:	AX	0025h

Return register:	AX	Driver information

Comments: This function, used with function 24h, provides a better picture of the mouse environment. Different bits of the value returned in AX have different meanings. Table M.7 indicates the specific bit meanings.

Table M.7   Bit Meanings Returned by Function 25h

Bit Settings	
FEDCBA98 76543210	*Meaning*
xxxxxxxx	Currently active MDD count (used only if bit 14 is 1)
xxxx	Mouse driver interrupt rate
00	Software text cursor active
01	Hardware text cursor active
10	Graphics cursor active
11	Graphics cursor active
1	Integrated mouse display driver (MDD)
0	Non-integrated mouse driver
1	Driver was loaded as a SYS file
0	Driver was loaded as a COM file

Int 33h   Function 26h

Get Maximum Virtual Coordinates

Returns information on driver status and the highest available coordinate range

Calling register:	AX	0026h
Return registers:	BX	Mouse driver status
		0, enabled
		< >0, disabled with function 1Fh
	CX	Maximum horizontal coordinate
	DX	Maximum vertical coordinate

Comments: This function returns two pieces of useful information. First, the value returned in BX indicates whether the mouse driver has been disabled. Second, the values returned in CX and DX indicate the maximum horizontal and vertical mouse coordinates for the active display mode. The minimum coordinates are assumed to be 0,0.

Int 33h   Function 27h

Get Cursor Masks and Mickey Counts

Returns text screen mask, cursor mask, and accumulated mickey count

Calling register: AX   0027h

Return registers: AX   Screen mask or starting scan line
                       BX   Cursor mask or ending scan line
                       CX   Horizontal mickey count
                       DX   Vertical mickey count

Comments: This function returns the text cursor and screen masks if you are using the hardware text cursor. If you are using the software text cursor, it returns the beginning and ending scan lines. These scan lines or masks can be set with function 0Ah.

In addition to the cursor information, the values in CX and DX indicate the number of mickeys accumulated since the last time a function was used to read the mickey count.

Int 33h   Function 28h

Set Video Mode

Sets the video mode used by both the video card and mouse driver

Calling registers: AX   0028h
                        CX   Video mode
                        DX   Font size

Return register: CX   Status (0 if successful, otherwise unchanged)

Comments: This function lets you specify the video mode the mouse driver should use. Because this function changes your video mode, the value you specify in CX should be a mode supported by your video card. Use function 29h to determine which video modes are supported by your system. If your video card supports font definitions for the mode you are going to set, you can specify a font size in DX.

Int 33h   Function 29h

Get Supported Video Modes

Returns information about video modes supported by the mouse driver

Calling registers: AX   0029h
                        CX   Search flag
                                 0, find first
                                 < >0, find next

Return registers: BX   Segment for description

CX   Mode number (0 if unsuccessful)

DX   Offset for description

Comments: If supported by your driver, this function returns information about the video modes available. It searches an internal list (maintained by the mouse driver) of supported video modes.

The address returned in BX:DX indicates an optional ASCIIZ description of the video mode. If no description is available, then BX and DX are 0.

Int 33h   Function 2Ah

Get Cursor Hot Spot

Returns hot-spot coordinate, display flag, and mouse type

Calling register: AX   002Ah

Return registers: AX   Display flag

0, cursor is displayed

< >0, cursor is hidden

BX   Horizontal hot spot

CX   Vertical hot spot

DX   Mouse type

1, bus mouse

2, serial mouse

3, InPort mouse

4, PS/2 mouse

5, HP mouse

Comments: This function is used to get information originally set with function 09h. The values returned in BX and CX represent a pixel offset from the upper left corner of the graphics cursor mask. This offset is the place where the cursor is considered positioned when you click the button; it is also returned when you use a function that indicates the position of the mouse cursor.

Int 33h   Function 2Bh

Set Acceleration Curves

Sets the address of the acceleration curve table

Calling registers: AX   002Bh

BX   Curve number

ES:SI   Buffer address

Return register: AX   Status

0, successful

< >0, unsuccessful

Comments: Acceleration curves are used by the mouse driver to control how raw mouse-movement data is translated into actual cursor movement. This function is used to set the acceleration curves. ES:SI points to a 324-byte buffer containing the acceleration table (see Table M.8). BX is used to indicate which curve to use after the acceleration table is loaded. Four possible curves (1 through 4) are defined by the table, or you can set BX to –1 to leave the curve selector unchanged.

Table M.8   Acceleration Curve Table Layout

Offset	Length	Meaning
00h	1 byte	Curve 1 counts and factors
01h	1 byte	Curve 2 counts and factors
02h	1 byte	Curve 3 counts and factors
03h	1 byte	Curve 4 counts and factors
04h	20h bytes	Curve 1 mouse-count threshold array
24h	20h bytes	Curve 2 mouse-count threshold array
44h	20h bytes	Curve 3 mouse-count threshold array
64h	20h bytes	Curve 4 mouse-count threshold array
84h	20h bytes	Curve 1 scale factor array
A4h	20h bytes	Curve 2 scale factor array
C4h	20h bytes	Curve 3 scale factor array
E4h	20h bytes	Curve 4 scale factor array
104h	10h bytes	Curve 1 name (right-padded ASCII)
114h	10h bytes	Curve 2 name (right-padded ASCII)
124h	10h bytes	Curve 3 name (right-padded ASCII)
134h	10h bytes	Curve 4 name (right-padded ASCII)

To understand better how the acceleration curve table is used, assume that you specify that curve 2 should be used. When the mouse driver goes to position the cursor on-screen, it looks at the byte at offset 01h. This value indicates the number of entries in the other two table arrays for acceleration curve 2. The driver then begins searching the array at offset 24h until it finds a value greater than the number of mickeys moved. The corresponding value is loaded from the array at offset A4h, and this value is multiplied by the raw movement data to determine where the cursor should be displayed.

Int 33h   Function 2Ch

Get Acceleration Curves

Returns the acceleration curve table address

Calling register:	AX	002Ch
Return registers:	AX	Status
		0, successful
		< >0, unsuccessful
	BX	Current curve
	ES:SI	Curve table address

Comments: This function is used to retrieve the address of the acceleration curve being used by the mouse driver. If you plan to change the acceleration curve table (function 2Bh), you should first find the address of the current table so that you can transfer the table to a buffer area where you can reset it when your program ends.

Int 33h   Function 2Dh

Set or Get Active Acceleration Curve

Sets or returns the number and name of the active acceleration curve

Return registers:	AX	2Dh
	BX	Action flag
		1–4, set acceleration curve
		–1, get acceleration curve
Return registers:	AX	Status
		0, successful
		< >0, unsuccessful
	BX	Current curve
	ES:SI	Curve name address

Comments: If you want to know which acceleration curve is being used, or you want to set which curve is used but do not want to redefine the entire acceleration curve table, you can use this function. The address returned in ES:SI is for the 16-byte name contained in the acceleration curve table.

811

Int 33h   Function 2Fh

Mouse Hardware Reset

Sets all hardware-related mouse driver information back to default conditions

Calling register: AX   002Fh

Return register: AX   Status
  −1, successful
  0, unsuccessful

Comments: This function operates in a similar manner to function 00h, except that only a few variables maintained by the mouse driver are reset, along with a reset of the physical mouse. The only variables reset by this function have to do with the CRT page number and the light-pen emulation. All other variables maintained by the mouse driver are considered software variables and can be reset by using function 21h.

Int 33h   Function 30h

Set or Get BallPoint Information

Sets or returns information used to configure the Ballpoint Mouse

Calling registers: AX   0030h
  BX   Rotation angle
  CX   Command
    0, read mouse status
    < >0, set mask values to this value

Return registers: AX   Status
    −1, unsuccessful
    Otherwise, button state
  BX   Rotation angle
  CX   Button masks

Comments: The latest type of mouse available from Microsoft is called the *BallPoint Mouse*. Used primarily for laptop and portable computers, it attaches to the left or right side of the computer case, next to the keyboard. It looks almost like an upside-down mouse, and users can manipulate the mouse cursor by twiddling the mouse ball with their thumb. The BallPoint mouse has four buttons, but only two of them at a time can be active.

Based on the value you set in CX, this function enables you to either read the status of the BallPoint mouse or change the internal rotational pointer and button status maintained by the mouse driver.

Int 33h   Function 31h

Get Virtual Coordinates

Returns the current minimum and maximum limits on the mouse's on-screen travel

Calling register: AX   0031h

Return registers: AX   Minimum X bound
                         BX   Minimum Y bound
                         CX   Maximum X bound
                         DX   Maximum Y bound

Comments: This function enables you to determine the minimum and maximum virtual bounds that were set with functions 07h and 08h. See those functions for more information about virtual bounds.

Int 33h   Function 32h

Get Active Advanced Functions

Returns flags indicating the advanced mouse functions available

Calling register: AX   0032h

Return register: AX   Feature flag

Comments: This function is used to determine the advanced functions available with your mouse driver. Each bit of the value returned in AX indicates whether a specific function is available. Table M.9 lists the meaning of each bit. (If the bit is set, the related function is available.)

Table M.9   Bit Meanings for Value Returned in AX for Function 32h

Bit Settings	
FEDCBA98 76543210	*Meaning*
x	Is function 34h available?
x	Is function 33h available?
x	Is function 32h available?
x	Is function 31h available?
x	Is function 30h available?

continues

Table M.9 Continued

Bit Settings FEDCBA98 76543210	Meaning
x	Is function 2Fh available?
x	Is function 2Eh available?
x	Is function 2Dh available?
x	Is function 2Ch available?
x	Is function 2Bh available?
x	Is function 2Ah available?
x	Is function 29h available?
x	Is function 28h available?
x	Is function 27h available?
x	Is function 26h available?
x	Is function 25h available?

Int 33h   Function 33h

Get Switch Settings

Returns the address of a switch-setting buffer maintained by the mouse driver

Calling registers:	AX	0033h
	CX	Buffer length
	ES:DX	Buffer address
Return registers:	CX	Actual bytes in buffer
	ES:DX	Buffer address

Comments: When you start the mouse driver from the command line, you can include command-line switches that affect the way the driver operates. This function enables you to inspect the settings of these switches. Upon calling, ES:DX should point to a 340-byte buffer. If you use a smaller buffer, not all switch values are returned. On return, the buffer at ES:DX contains the information shown in Table M.10.

Table M.10   Buffer Information Returned by Function 33h

Offset	Length	Meaning
00h	1 byte	Mouse type and port
01h	1 byte	Language
02h	1 byte	Horizontal sensitivity
03h	1 byte	Vertical sensitivity
04h	1 byte	Double-speed threshold
05h	1 byte	Ballistic curve
06h	1 byte	Interrupt rate
07h	1 byte	Cursor mask
08h	1 byte	Laptop adjustment
09h	1 byte	Memory type
0Ah	1 byte	Super VGA flag
0Bh	2 bytes	Rotation angle
0Dh	1 byte	Primary button
0Eh	1 byte	Secondary button
0Fh	1 byte	Click lock enabled
10h	324 bytes	Acceleration curve tables

Int 33h   Function 34h

Get MOUSE.INI Path

Returns the address of the full path for the MOUSE.INI file used in configuring the mouse

Calling register: AX   0034h

Return register: ES:DX   Path address

Comments: This function returns, in ES:DX, the address of a buffer containing the full path name for the MOUSE.INI file. This file is used to set configuration defaults for the mouse driver.

The Mouse Driver's EGA Register Interface

Unlike its predecessors and successors, much of the EGA hardware is controlled through write-only registers, which makes control of the video unusually difficult. To simplify the task of keeping track of the EGA controller's registers, the mouse driver creates a virtual EGA controller through which it controls the physical EGA hardware. An interface to the mouse driver's virtual EGA controller, the EGA register interface, is provided to the programmer through new Video BIOS functions (Interrupt 10h). If an application uses the mouse and intends to manipulate either the EGA or VGA registers, it should manipulate the registers through this interface.

Int 10h   Function F0h

Read One Register

Returns data from a specified EGA register

Calling registers:
	AH	F0h
	BX	Index for pointer/data chips
	BH	0
	BL	Index (this register is ignored for single registers)
	DX	Port number (see Table M.11)

Return register: BL   Data

Comments: Drivers from firms other than Microsoft may not support this function.

Table M.11   EGA Register Values

Port Number	EGA Register
00h	CRT Controller
08h	Sequencer
10h	Graphics Controller
18h	Attribute Controller
20h	Miscellaneous Output Register
28h	Feature Control Register
30h	Graphics 1 Control Register
38h	Graphics 2 Control Register

816

Int 10h   Function F1h

Write One Register

Writes data to a specified EGA register

Calling registers: AH   F1h
                         BL   Index for pointer/data chips or data for single registers
                         BH   Data for pointer/data chips (ignored for single registers)
                         DX   Port number (refer to Table M.11)

Return registers: BH   Contents modified
                         DX   Contents modified

Comments: Drivers from firms other than Microsoft may not support this function. *The function does not check the values used; be sure of your input values before making this function call. Some combinations of register values can cause physical damage to the EGA adapter or monitor.* The contents of the BH and DX registers are not preserved by this function call.

Int 10h   Function F2h

Read Register Range

Returns data from a specified range of EGA registers (several registers on a single chip with consecutive indexes)

Calling registers: AH   F2h
                         CH   Starting index
                         CL   Number of registers (must be greater than 1)
                         DX   Port number
                                     00h, CRT controller
                                     08h, sequencer
                                     10h, graphics controller
                                     18h, attribute controller
                         ES:BX   Pointer to a table of 1-byte entries whose length is the
                                         value in CL

Return register: CX   Contents modified

Comments: Drivers from firms other than Microsoft may not support this function. The contents of the CX register are not preserved by this function call.

817

Int 10h   Function F3h

Write Register Range

Writes data to a specified range of EGA registers (several registers on a single chip with consecutive indexes)

Calling registers: AH   F3h

                            CH   Starting index

                            CL   Number of registers (must be greater than 1)

                            DX   Port number

                                             00h, CRT controller

                                           08h, sequencer

                                           10h, graphics controller

                                           18h, attribute controller

                            ES:BX   Pointer to a table of 1-byte entries whose length is the value in CL

Return registers: BX   Contents modified

                            CX   Contents modified

                            DX   Contents modified

Comments: Drivers from firms other than Microsoft may not support this function. *The function does not check the values used; be sure of your input values before making this function call. Some combinations of register values can cause physical damage to the EGA adapter or monitor.* The contents of the BX, CX, and DX registers are not preserved by this function call.

Int 10h   Function F4h

Read Register Set

Returns data from a specified set of EGA registers (several registers that may not be on the same chip and, if they are on the same chip, may not have consecutive indexes)

Calling registers: AH   F4h

                              CX   Number of registers (must be greater than 1)

                              ES:BX   Pointer to a table of records whose format is as follows:

                                           Byte 0 Port number (refer to Table M.11)

                                           Byte 1 Must be zero

                                           Byte 2   Index value for pointer registers, 0 for single registers

                                           Byte 3 Data is written here

Return register: CX   Contents modified

Comments: Drivers from firms other than Microsoft may not support this function. The contents of the CX register are not preserved by this function call.

Int 10h   Function F5h

Write Register Set

Writes data to a specified set of EGA registers (several registers that may not be on the same chip and, if they are on the same chip, may not have consecutive indexes)

Calling registers: AH   F5h

CX   Number of registers (must be greater than 1)

ES:BX   Pointer to a table of records whose format is as follows:

    Byte 0 Port number (refer to Table M.11)

    Byte 1 Must be zero

    Byte 2 Index value for pointer registers, 0 for single registers

    Byte 3 Data to be written

Return register: CX   Contents modified

Comments: Drivers from firms other than Microsoft may not support this function. *The function does not check the values used; be sure of your input values before making this function call. Some combinations of register values can cause physical damage to the EGA adapter or monitor.* The contents of the CX register are not preserved by this function call.

Int 10h   Function F6h

Revert to Default Registers

Restores the default settings of any registers that were changed through the EGA Register Interface. The default values are those set up by calls to Function F7h.

Calling register: AH   F6h

Return registers: None

Comments: Drivers from firms other than Microsoft may not support this function. If Int 10h, Function 00h is used to set the display mode, the default register values are the BIOS values for the selected mode.

Int 10h   Function F7h

Define Default Register Table

Defines the default settings of a single register or for all the registers in a pointer/data chip

Calling registers:	AH	F7h
	CX	VGA color select flag 5448h: Byte offset 14h of the table pointed to by ES:BX is the value for the VGA color select register
	DX	Port number (refer to Table M.11)
	ES:BX	Pointer to a table of one-byte entries; the table must contain values for all registers in a pointer/data chip
Return registers:	BX	Contents modified
	DX	Contents modified

Comments: Drivers from firms other than Microsoft may not support this function. *The function does not check the values used; be sure of your input values before making this function call. Some combinations of register values can cause physical damage to the EGA adapter or monitor.* The contents of the BH and DX registers are not preserved by this function call.

Int 10h   Function FAh

Interrogate Driver

Interrogates the mouse driver to determine whether the EGA Register Interface is present

Calling registers:	AH	FAh
	BX	0
Return registers:	BX	0 if the EGA Register Interface is not present
	ES:BX	Points to the EGA Register Interface version number. The format is as follows;
		Byte 0 Major release number
		Byte 1 Minor release number (in 100ths)

Comments: Drivers from firms other than Microsoft may not support this function.

EMS Reference

Expanded memory (EMS memory, as explained in Chapter 2) allows as much as eight megabytes of RAM to be accessed through a technique called *bank switching*.

In this technique, you define small sections of an extra memory area (the EMS memory) that can be switched into a processor's physical address area. Each section is called a *bank*. Bank switching has been used on computers for years as a way to extend access to high-speed temporary storage. With EMS memory, the 16K banks (referred to as *pages* in the EMS documentation) are switched to appear as normal memory in a defined *page frame*. (See Chapter 2, "The Structure of a DOS System," and Chapter 10, "Program and Memory Management," for more detailed descriptions of the operation of EMS memory.)

A special driver is loaded to enable programs to access EMS memory. You access EMS memory in the same way you access a file. After opening access to EMS memory with Int 67h, Function 43h, you tell the board (with Int 67h, Function 44h) which memory pages to make accessible. Although a memory page is accessible, you can read from and write to the page. When you are finished, you use Int 67h, Function 45h to close the handle.

Version 3.0 of the EMS standard (the earlier versions never saw public use) was developed jointly by *L*otus, *I*ntel, and *M*icrosoft (therefore the name LIM memory). Version 3.2 added support for such multitasking operating systems as Windows and DESQview. Later, a new version (4.0) was defined. Under the new version, you can run programs from and store information in expanded memory. This reference section was developed using information applicable to LIM Version 4.0; functions present in earlier versions are indicated by the line "LIM Specification Version" at the top of each description.

The only drawback to expanded memory is that programmers must keep track of where things are located in expanded memory. A great deal of effort has gone into creating programming languages that hide the way memory works. You do not have to remember, for example, which memory block your variables are stored in. Even in assembly language, if you use labels to refer to the variables, an assembler keeps track of which one you are dealing with.

With expanded memory, however, you—the programmer—must remember which expanded memory blocks are in the page frame and which blocks contain data. You must ask to have the correct block moved into the page frame when you want something that is not there. In other words, you are responsible for whether the correct piece of memory is in use. Assembly language programmers who use multiple data segments have the same sorts of problems, but high-level language programmers do not.

If you have any question about how the functions in this section are presented, refer to the "Reference Overview" section of this book.

Int 67h	Function 40h	LIM Spec V3.0
	Get Manager Status	

Tests whether expanded memory hardware (if installed) is functional

Calling register:	AH	40h
Return register:	AH	00h, no error
		80h, internal error in EMS software
		81h, malfunction in EMS hardware
		84h, requested function not defined

Comments: When you are sure that an expanded memory board is installed, this function tests to see whether it is functional. (Chapter 10 contains some techniques for determining whether a board is installed.)

Int 67h	Function 41h	LIM Spec V3.0
	Get Page Frame Segment	

Gets the segment address of the page frame used by the EMS

Calling register:	AH	41h
Return registers:	If successful	
	AH	00h
	BX	Segment of page frame

If unsuccessful

AH	80h, internal error in EMS software
	81h, malfunction in EMS hardware
	84h, undefined function

Comments: After you have determined that a board is installed and functional, you must determine its location in memory. The board maps four 16K pages (a total of 64K) into an area of memory between 640K (segment A000h) and 1M (segment 10000h). From the memory maps of as much as 1M on the PC shown in Chapter 2, you can see that most of this space is occupied by video displays and ROMs and that substantial amounts of free space are unused in any single system. When the board is installed, you usually select the address of the EMS window with switches on the board. You must be careful to select memory not being used for any other purposes.

The segment address returned is the base of the first 16K page. All other pages are offset from this location.

Int 67h	**Function 42h**	**LIM Spec V3.0**
	Get Page Counts	

Gets the total number of pages of EMS memory in the system and the number of pages available

Calling register: AH   42h

Return registers: If successful

AH	00h
BX	Number of unallocated pages
DX	Total number of pages in system

If unsuccessful

AH	80h, internal error in EMS software
	81h, malfunction in EMS hardware
	84h, undefined function

Comments: Use this function to determine whether there is enough memory for your application (or to scale the application to the memory). With a single call, you can tell how much memory there is and how much of it is available. Regardless of the number of pages returned in DX, for instance, if BX is equal to 0, all the expanded memory has been allocated and none is available for other uses.

Note that this function might return inaccurate results when it runs under DOS V4.0x because the operating system might take pages from EMS and mark them as allocated to protect them from normal programs, if the /X (EMS) switches are used in any of the CONFIG.SYS commands. If the pages taken happen to be used for disk buffers and contain part of the FAT for your hard disk when some other program uses them, your data will be lost. For this reason, you should avoid the /X switch in DOS V4.

Int 67h   **Function 43h**   **LIM Spec V3.0**

Get Handle and Allocate Memory

Opens an EMS handle for use and allocates a specified number of pages for the process

Calling registers: AH   43h

BX   Number of logical pages to allocate

Return registers: If successful

AH   00h

DX   Handle (0001h to 00FEh)

If unsuccessful

AH   80h, internal error in EMS software

81h, malfunction in EMS hardware

84h, undefined function

85h, no more handles available

87h, allocation requested more pages than are
physically available; no pages allocated

88h, specified more logical pages than are available; no
pages allocated

89h, zero pages requested

Comments: Use this function as a file open for EMS memory. Although it does not perform the same functions as a regular file open call, this function does provide a file-like interface to memory.

The handle returned in this call is used for all accesses to the board. This call associates the handle with a specified number of EMS memory pages you can control with Function 44h.

More than one EMS handle can be assigned to a single process during operation, but the process must close each handle properly by calling Function 45h. Otherwise, the memory assigned to the handle simply disappears and is unavailable for reuse until you restart the system.

One handle, 0000h, is reserved for use by the operating system and is never returned by this function.

Int 67h   **Function 44h**   **LIM Spec V3.0**

Map/Unmap Memory

Maps one of the EMS pages assigned to the handle into one of the four physical pages in the calling process's page frame; also can unmap a page and make it inaccessible, by setting its logical page to FFFFh

Calling registers:	AH	44h
	AL	Physical page number (0–3)
	BX	Logical page number (zero-based, FFFFh to unmap physical page)
	DX	Handle

Return registers:	If successful	
	AH	00h
	If unsuccessful	
	AH	80h, internal error in EMS software
		81h, malfunction in EMS hardware
		83h, invalid handle
		84h, undefined function
		8Ah, logical page not assigned to this handle
		8Bh, physical page number invalid

Comments: The logical pages are the EMS memory pages assigned to the handle by function call 43h. Logical pages are numbered from 0 to $n-1$, where n is the number of pages requested. The special logical page number FFFFh is used to specify unmapping.

On the EMS board, the pages are not accessible to the program because they are outside the computer's physical address space. This function maps one logical page into the computer's physical address space so that memory instructions can be used to manipulate information in the page area. As many as four physical pages can be mapped from a single board (number 0–3).

Int 67h	**Function 45h**	**LIM Spec V3.0**
	De-allocate Handle and Memory	

Closes the specified handle and returns the memory for use by other processes

| **Calling registers:** | AH | 45h |
| | DX | EMS handle |

Return registers:	If successful	
	AH	00h
	If unsuccessful	
	AH	80h, internal error in EMS software
		81h, malfunction in EMS hardware
		83h, invalid handle
		84h, undefined function
		86h, error in save or restore of mapping context

Comments: The EMS memory equivalent of a file close operation, this simple function is particularly important. Because the EMS memory manager functions as an add-on driver to the operating system, the operating system does not close an open EMS handle for you when your program ends. Before a program terminates, it *must* close all EMS handles allocated to it. If it does not, the memory it has allocated *remains allocated* and cannot be used by any other program. The only way to free up the memory is to reboot the computer.

When the close function is executed, the memory that was assigned to the handle is returned to the pool of available EMS memory. If the function does not complete successfully, the memory has not been returned to the pool—you must keep trying.

Most programs simply close files without checking whether the function was successful. Generally, this does not pose a problem for files (handle files, anyway) because DOS closes the file when the program terminates. With EMS memory, however, you must verify the proper exit code and respond with a retry if the function was not successful.

Int 67h	Function 46h	LIM Spec V3.0
	Get EMM Version	

Returns the software version number

Calling register:	AH	46h
Return registers:	If successful	
	AH	00h
	AL	EMM version number
	If unsuccessful	
	AH	80h, internal error in EMS software
		81h, malfunction in EMS hardware
		84h, undefined function

Comments: This function returns (in BCD) the version number of the EMM (expanded memory management) software. The upper four bits of the AL register represent the major version number (the part to the left of the decimal point); the lower four bits represent the minor version number (the part to the right of the decimal). Version 3.2 returns 32h in AL, for example, and 4.0 returns 40h. A program should always be prepared to accept a version number *greater* than that for which it was designed; the EMS specification requires drivers to be upwardly compatible.

Int 67h	Function 47h	LIM Spec V3.0
	Save Page Map	

Saves the current state of the EMS hardware map

Calling registers: AH   47h

                              DX   Handle

Return registers: If successful

                              AH   00h

                              If unsuccessful

                              AH   80h, internal error in EMS software

                                            81h, malfunction in EMS hardware

                                            83h, invalid handle

                                            84h, undefined function

                                            8Ch, page-mapping hardware state save area full

                                            8Dh, save of mapping context failed because one is
already associated with the specified handle

Comments: If you are writing a resident program (TSR), an interrupt service routine, or a device driver that uses EMS memory, you must save the state of the mapping hardware before you do any EMS operations so that other programs do not interfere with your use of the memory. This function saves the state of the mapping hardware. Int 67h, Function 48h is used to restore the hardware map.

This function saves the map register states for only the 64K page frame defined by Version 3.x of the LIM specification. Applications that use a mappable memory region outside the LIM-3.x page frame should use Functions 4Eh and 4Fh to save and restore the state of the map registers.

Int 67h	**Function 48h**	**LIM Spec V3.0**
	Restore Page Map	

Restores the EMS hardware map associated with the designated file handle

Calling registers: AH   48h

                              DX   Handle

Return registers: If successful

                              AH   00h

                              If unsuccessful

                              AH   80h, internal error in EMS software

                                            81h, malfunction in EMS hardware

                                            83h, invalid handle

                                            84h, undefined function

                                            8Eh, restore failed, save area has no context for
the handle

Comments: If you are writing a resident program (TSR), an interrupt service routine, or a device driver that uses EMS memory, you must restore the state of the mapping hardware upon completion of your program. Failure to do so can cause unpredictable results. While your software executes, for example, an applications program that uses EMS memory may be running and expecting the EMS mapping registers to be unchanged. This function restores the state of the mapping hardware. Int 67h, Function 47h is used to save the state of the hardware map.

This function restores the map register states for only the 64K page frame defined by Version 3.x of the LIM specification. Applications that use a mappable memory region outside the LIM-3.x page frame should use Functions 4Eh and 4Fh to save and restore the state of the map registers.

Int 67h	Function 49h	LIM Spec V3.0
	Reserved	

Undefined in Version 3.2 and higher of the EMS standard

Comments: In previous versions of LIM/EMS, this function was used to retrieve the page-mapping register I/O array from the EMS hardware. This function is now reserved. New software should not use it.

Functions 49h and 4Ah were removed from the specification because they were specific to the hardware on certain Intel EMS boards and could not be guaranteed to work with boards from other companies. Programs that use the new functions added in Version 4 of the LIM specification must not use either of these two functions. Programs that do use these functions will not be compatible with the IBM MicroChannel Architecture, but might work with other hardware.

Int 67h	Function 4Ah	LIM Spec V3.0
	Reserved	

Undefined in Version 3.2 and higher of the EMS standard

Comments: In previous versions of LIM/EMS, this function was used to retrieve the logical-to-physical page translation array from the EMS hardware. This function is now reserved. New software should not use it.

Functions 49h and 4Ah were removed from the specification because they were specific to the hardware on certain Intel EMS boards and could not be guaranteed to work with boards from other companies. Programs that use the new functions added in Version 4 of the LIM specification must not use either of these two functions. Programs that do use these functions will not be compatible with the IBM MicroChannel Architecture, but might work with other hardware.

828

Int 67h   **Function 4Bh**   **LIM Spec V3.0**

Get Handle Count

Returns the number of active EMS handles

Calling register: AH   4Bh

Return registers: If successful
                        AH   00h
                        BX   Number of active EMS handles (0–255)
                        If unsuccessful
                        AH   80h, internal error in EMS software
                                      81h, malfunction in EMS hardware
                                      84h, undefined function

Comments: This function tells you how many handles are in active use at any time. If BX=0, expanded memory is not being used. BX can range from 0 to 255 (the maximum number of EMS handles).

Your program's interpretation of this number is less clear than it may seem. The number of active handles is not necessarily the same as the number of programs using expanded memory. Nothing restricts a program from using more than one EMS handle to access expanded memory. Some programs, in fact, use more than one handle to simplify bookkeeping for the data they are managing. Perhaps a more reasonable use of this function is to determine the number of handles still available, which is derived by subtracting the value in BX from 255. A program that knows how many EMS handles it needs to function properly can quickly determine whether it will be capable of functioning with the number of handles remaining in EMS.

Int 67h   **Function 4Ch**   **LIM Spec V3.0**

Get Pages Owned by Handle

Determines the number of pages associated with a specific handle

Calling registers: AH   4Ch
                         DX   Handle

Return registers: If successful
                         AH   00h
                         BX   Number of logical pages (1–2,048)
                         If unsuccessful
                         AH   80h, internal error in EMS software
                                       81h, malfunction in EMS hardware
                                       83h, invalid handle
                                       84h, undefined function

Comments: Any single handle can refer to from 1 to 2,048 (512 before LIM 4) pages of expanded memory. Because every page represents 16K of memory, a single handle can access from 16K to 32M (8M before LIM 4). This function never returns 0 pages because at least 1 page must be assigned to a handle by the expanded memory manager.

Int 67h	**Function 4Dh**	**LIM Spec V3.0**
	Get Pages for All Handles	

Returns the handles and the number of logical pages for all handles

Calling registers: AH   4Dh
                         ES:DI   Pointer to array to hold information (may need to be
                                   1,020 bytes in size)

Return registers: If successful
                         AH   00h
                         BX   Number of active EMS handles (1–255)
                         ES:DI   Pointer to filled array
                         If unsuccessful
                         AH   80h, internal error in EMS software
                                   81h, malfunction in EMS hardware
                                   84h, undefined function

Comments: This function returns an array of values that indicate the current handles and the number of pages assigned to each handle. The EMS handle table is composed of a variable number of 2-word entries, each arranged as follows:

Word	Meaning
0	EMS handle
1	Number of pages

The formula for determining the amount of memory required for the table can be expressed as $4 \times BX$. Because there can be a maximum of 255 handles, 4×255 (or 1,020 bytes) is the maximum reasonable allocation for the table. BX tells you the number of valid table entries. In LIM 4 systems, BX cannot be less than 1 because of the special operating system handles that are always reserved; in earlier versions, if BX is 0, the EMS manager is idle.

Be careful not to place the table (as specified by ES:DI) so that it causes a segment wrap when the table is transferred to memory. This results in an error.

Int 67h   **Function 4Eh**   **Subfunction 00h**   **LIM Spec V3.2**

Get Page Map Registers

Gets the EMS page-mapping registers into a local array without using a handle

Calling registers: AH   4Eh
                         AL   00h
                         ES:DI   Pointer to array to receive information

Return registers: If successful
                         AH   00h
                         ES:DI   Pointer to array filled with information
                         If unsuccessful
                         AH   80h, internal error in EMS software
                                     81h, malfunction in EMS hardware
                                     84h, undefined function
                                     8Fh, subfunction parameter invalid

Comments: This function was added in Version 3.2 of the EMM software to support multitasking systems such as Windows and DESQview. Function 4Eh gives the program direct access to the page-mapping information used internally by the EMS board, information that is extremely hardware-dependent. The array holds information about the page-mapping registers and additional control information.

Multitasking systems are the only programs that should use this type of information—they cannot work effectively without it. Single programs cannot use this type of information.

Be careful not to place the table (as specified by ES:DI) so that it causes a segment wrap when the table is transferred to memory. This results in an error.

Int 67h   **Function 4Eh**   **Subfunction 01h**   **LIM Spec V3.2**

Set Page Map Registers

Sets the EMS page-mapping registers from a local array without using a handle

Calling registers: AH   4Eh
                         AL   01h
                         DS:SI   Pointer to array from which to set information

Return registers: If successful
                         AH   00h
                         If unsuccessful
                         AH   80h, internal error in EMS software
                                     81h, malfunction in EMS hardware
                                     84h, undefined function
                                     8Fh, subfunction parameter invalid

Comments: This function was added in Version 3.2 of the EMM software to support multitasking systems such as Windows and DESQview. Function 4Eh gives the program direct access to the page-mapping information used internally by the EMS board—information that is extremely hardware-dependent. The array holds information about the page-mapping registers and additional control information.

Int 67h	Function 4Eh Subfunction 02h	LIM Spec V3.2
	Get and Set Page Map Registers	

Simultaneously gets the EMS page-mapping registers from a local array and sets them from another, without using handles

Calling registers: AH   4Eh
                        AL   02h
                        DS:SI   Pointer to array from which to set information
                        ES:DI   Pointer to array to receive information

Return registers: If successful
                        AH   00h
                        ES:DI   Pointer to filled array
                        If unsuccessful
                        AH   80h, internal error in EMS software
                                  81h, malfunction in EMS hardware
                                  84h, undefined function
                                  8Fh, subfunction parameter invalid

Comments: This function was added in Version 3.2 of the EMM software to support multitasking systems such as Windows and DESQview. Function 4Eh gives the program direct access to the page-mapping information used internally by the EMS board—information that is extremely hardware-dependent. The array holds information about the page-mapping registers and additional control information.

Int 67h	Function 4Eh Subfunction 03h	LIM Spec V3.2
	Get Size for Page Map Array	

Gets the size needed for a local array to hold the EMS page-mapping registers

Calling registers: AH   4Eh
                        AL   03h

Return registers: If successful
                        AH   00h
                        AL   Bytes in page-mapping array

If unsuccessful

AH   80h, internal error in EMS software

81h, malfunction in EMS hardware

84h, undefined function

8Fh, subfunction parameter invalid

Comments: This function was added in Version 3.2 of the EMM software to support multitasking systems such as Windows and DESQview. Function 4Eh gives the program direct access to the page-mapping information used internally by the EMS board—information that is extremely hardware-dependent. The array holds information about the page-mapping registers and additional control information.

Subfunction 03h can be used to get the array size needed, before using either Subfunctions 00h and 01h separately or 02h to swap the registers in one operation.

Int 67h	Function 4Fh	Subfunction 00h	LIM Spec V4.0
	Get Partial Page Map		

Saves partial mapping context for only specified mappable memory regions; can be much faster than Function 4E, which deals with all mappable memory

Calling registers: AH   4Fh

AL   00h

DS:SI   Pointer to page list

ES:DI   Pointer to destination array

Return registers: If successful

AH   00h

ES:DI   Pointer to filled array

If unsuccessful

AH   80h, internal error in EMS software

81h, malfunction in EMS hardware

84h, undefined function

8Bh, one of the specified segments is not mappable

8Fh, subfunction parameter invalid

A3h, partial page-map structure corrupt

Comments: This function is passed two pointers, one to a list of segments to be mapped and the other to an array in which the maps are to be saved. The page list consists of one word that holds the count of the number of pages in the list, followed by that many additional words, each of which contains the number of a page to be mapped.

The destination array must contain at least the number of bytes returned by Subfunction 03h (Get Partial Page Map Size). Its format is not specified by LIM 4 because the only use of this array is to provide input to Subfunction 01h (Set Partial Page Map).

Int 67h   **Function 4Fh   Subfunction 01h**   **LIM Spec V4.0**

Set Partial Page Map

Restores partial mapping context saved by Subfunction 00h; can be much faster than Function 4E, which deals with all mappable memory

Calling registers: AH   4Fh
                         AL   01h
                         DS:SI   Point to source array

Return registers: If successful
                         AH   00h
                         If unsuccessful
                         AH   80h, internal error in EMS software
                                     81h, malfunction in EMS hardware
                                     84h, undefined function
                                     8Fh, subfunction parameter invalid

Comments: This function is passed a pointer to an array in which the maps were saved by Subfunction 00h. Its format is not specified by LIM 4 because the only use of this array is to provide input to this subfunction. The subfunction then restores the mapping for every page that was saved in the array.

Int 67h   **Function 4Fh   Subfunction 02h**   **LIM Spec V4.0**

Get Partial Page Map Size

Returns the byte count that tells how large an array is required to save page maps using Subfunction 00h

Calling registers: AH   4Fh
                         AL   02h
                         BX   Number of pages in page list

Return registers: If successful
                         AH   00h
                         AL   Number of bytes required for array used by
                                         Subfunctions 00h and 01h
                         If unsuccessful
                         AH   80h, internal error in EMS software
                                     81h, malfunction in EMS hardware
                                     84h, undefined function
                                     8Bh, specified number of pages is outside the range of
                                         physical pages in the system
                                     8Fh, subfunction parameter invalid

834

Comments: This function indicates the array size required to perform partial page mapping. It should be called before a partial page-mapping function to verify that the array passed to that function is of adequate size.

Int 67h   Function 50h   Subfunction 00h   LIM Spec V4.0

Map/Unmap Multiple Handle Pages (Physical Page Number Mode)

Maps or unmaps logical pages into physical pages by using the physical page-number method

Calling registers:

	AH	50h
	AL	00h
	CX	Number of pages to process
	DX	EMM handle
	DS:SI	Point to logical/physical page correspondence list

Return registers:

	If successful	
	AH	00h
	If unsuccessful	
	AH	80h, internal error in EMS software
		81h, malfunction in EMS hardware
		83h, could not find specified EMM handle
		84h, undefined function
		8Ah, logical page out of range
		8Bh, one of the segments is not mappable
		8Fh, subfunction parameter invalid

Comments: This function, an extension of the LIM 3.2 function that mapped a single page for a handle, can deal with multiple pages at one call. The correspondence list pointed to by DS:SI consists of one word pair for every page to be mapped or unmapped; the first word of every pair is the logical page number to be assigned or FFFFh if the page is to be unmapped, and the second word is the corresponding physical page number. Both values are zero-based.

Int 67h   Function 50h   Subfunction 01h   LIM Spec V4.0

Map/Unmap Multiple Handle Pages (Segment Address Mode)

Maps or unmaps logical pages into physical pages by using the segment address method

Calling registers:

	AH	50h
	AL	01h
	CX	Number of pages to process
	DX	EMM handle
	DS:SI	Point to logical page/segment address correspondence list

Return registers: If successful

AH	00h

If unsuccessful

AH	80h, internal error in EMS software
	81h, malfunction in EMS hardware
	83h, could not find specified EMM handle
	84h, undefined function
	8Ah, logical page out of range
	8Bh, one of the segments is not mappable
	8Fh, subfunction parameter invalid

Comments: This function is an alternative for Subfunction 00h, which produces identical results but is sometimes easier to work with. The correspondence list pointed to by DS:SI consists of one word pair for every page to be mapped or unmapped; the first word of every pair is the logical page number to be assigned or FFFFh if the page is to be unmapped, and the second word is the segment address at which that page is to be mapped or unmapped. The logical page values are zero-based, but the segment addresses are those obtained with Function 58h (Get Mappable Physical Address Array) and must correspond exactly.

Int 67h	Function 51h	LIM Spec V4.0
	Re-allocate Pages	

Enables an application to increase or decrease the number of logical pages allocated to an EMM handle

Calling registers:

AH	51h
BX	Number of logical pages desired
DX	EMM handle

Return registers: If successful

AH	00h
BX	Number of logical pages allocated

If unsuccessful

AH	80h, internal error in EMS software
	81h, malfunction in EMS hardware
	83h, could not find specified EMM handle
	84h, undefined function
	87h, not enough pages in system
	88h, not enough pages available

Comments: This function permits one of four cases: The new page count can be zero, smaller than the original page count, equal to the original count, or greater than the original count. If the page count is zero, the handle remains open but all its pages are returned to the available pool. In the other three cases, all allocated pages after the function is completed form a continuous sequence of page numbers based at zero.

The handle determines which type of logical pages are allocated; if its pages were originally allocated using Function 43h or Function 5Ah, Subfunction 00h, they are 16K standard pages. If they were originally allocated with Function 5Ah, Subfunction 01h, they are raw pages and their size is defined by the EMS software.

Int 67h	Function 52h	Subfunction 00h	LIM Spec V4.0
	Get Handle Attribute		

Returns attribute associated with a handle

Calling registers: AH   52h
                            AL   00h
                            DX   EMM handle

Return registers: If successful
                            AH   00h
                            AL   Attribute associated with specified EMM handle
                                           0, volatile
                                           1, nonvolatile
                          If unsuccessful
                            AH   80h, internal error in EMS software
                                         81h, malfunction in EMS hardware
                                         83h, could not find specified EMM handle
                                         84h, undefined function
                                         8Fh, subfunction parameter invalid
                                         91h, feature not supported

Comments: This function is an option that probably is not available in most systems because the hardware prevents memory content from surviving a warm boot operation. If it is not available, the function returns AH=91h.

If the function is available, Subfunction 00h returns in AL the current attribute associated with the specified handle. Volatile (AL=0) indicates that the handle's content will not survive a warm boot operation, and nonvolatile (AL=1) indicates that it will.

Int 67h	Function 52h	Subfunction 01h	LIM Spec V4.0
	Set Handle Attribute		

Sets attribute associated with a handle

Calling registers: AH   52h
                            AL   01h

BL	New attribute for specified EMM handle
	0, volatile
	1, nonvolatile
DX	EMM handle

Return registers: If successful

AH	00h

If unsuccessful

AH	80h, internal error in EMS software
	81h, malfunction in EMS hardware
	83h, could not find specified EMM handle
	84h, undefined function
	8Fh, subfunction parameter invalid
	90h, attribute not 0 or 1
	91h, feature not supported

Comments: This function is an option that probably is not available in most systems because the hardware prevents memory content from surviving a warm boot operation. If it is not available, the function returns AH=91h.

If the function is available, Subfunction 01h sets the current attribute associated with the specified handle to the value specified by BL. Volatile (BL=0) indicates that the handle's content will not survive a warm boot operation, and nonvolatile (BL=1) indicates that it will.

Int 67h	Function 52h	Subfunction 02h	LIM Spec V4.0
	Get Attribute Capability		

Returns system's attribute capability

Calling registers:

AH	52h
AL	02h

Return registers: If successful

AH	00h
ES:DI	Pointer to filled array
AL	Attribute capability of EMS software and hardware
	0, only volatile handles supported
	1, nonvolatile and volatile both supported

If unsuccessful

AH	80h, internal error in EMS software
	81h, malfunction in EMS hardware
	84h, undefined function
	8Fh, subfunction parameter invalid

Comments: Subfunction 02h returns in AL the attribute capability of the EMS software and hardware. A value of zero indicates that only volatile handles are supported, and a value of one indicates that both volatile and nonvolatile support are provided.

Int 67h   **Function 53h**   **Subfunction 00h**   **LIM Spec V4.0**

Get Handle Name

Gets the 8-character name associated with the specified EMM handle

Calling registers: AH   53h

AL   00h

DX   EMM handle

ES:DI   Point to 8-byte buffer to accept handle name

Return registers: If successful

AH   00h

If unsuccessful

AH   80h, internal error in EMS software

81h, malfunction in EMS hardware

83h, could not find specified EMM handle

84h, undefined function

8Fh, subfunction parameter invalid

Comments: This function gets the name associated with the specified handle. The name's length is always eight characters, and each character can be any 8-bit value; it is not restricted to the ASCII character set. The system initializes the name to eight NUL (00h) characters when a handle is allocated or de-allocated; by definition, a handle which has that character string associated with it has no name. When a handle is assigned a name, at least one of the eight bytes must be nonzero to distinguish it from the "no name" case.

Int 67h   **Function 53h**   **Subfunction 01h**   **LIM Spec V4.0**

Set Handle Name

Sets 8-character name associated with specified EMM handle

Calling registers: AH   53h

AL   01h

DX   EMM handle

ES:DI   Point to 8-byte handle name

Return registers: If successful

AH   00h

If unsuccessful

AH   80h, internal error in EMS software

81h, malfunction in EMS hardware

83h, could not find specified EMM handle

84h, undefined function

8Fh, subfunction parameter invalid

A1h, duplicates existing name

Comments: This function sets the name associated with the specified handle. The name's length is always eight characters, and each character can be any 8-bit value; it is not restricted to the ASCII character set. The system initializes the name to eight NUL (00h) characters when a handle is allocated or de-allocated; by definition, a handle which has that character string associated with it has no name. When a handle is assigned a name, at least one of the eight bytes must be nonzero to distinguish it from the "no name" case.

Int 67h	Function 54h	Subfunction 00h	LIM Spec V4.0

Get Handle Directory

Makes local copy of handle directory for all open EMM handles

Calling registers:

	AH	54h
	AL	00h
	ES:DI	Point to destination array

Return registers: If successful

	AH	00h
	AL	Number of entries in the array (same as number of open handles)
	ES:DI	Pointer to filled array

If unsuccessful

	AH	80h, internal error in EMS software
		81h, malfunction in EMS hardware
		84h, undefined function
		8Fh, subfunction parameter invalid

Comments: Subfunction 00h copies into an array all active handles and the name associated with each one (a copy of the EMM handle-to-name directory). The format of each entry in the array is a word containing the EMM handle, followed by eight bytes that contain the name. The array size in bytes is ten times the number of open handles at the time this function is called.

Int 67h	Function 54h	Subfunction 01h	LIM Spec V4.0

Find Named Handle

Given a handle name, this function returns handle value

Calling registers:

	AH	54h
	AL	01h
	DS:SI	Point to handle name

Return registers: If successful

AH	00h
DX	EMM handle associated with name

If unsuccessful

AH	80h, internal error in EMS software
	81h, malfunction in EMS hardware
	84h, undefined function
	8Fh, subfunction parameter invalid
	A0h, no handle could be found
	A1h, handle had no name

Comments: Subfunction 01h searches the handle-name directory for the specified name and, if found, returns the associated handle value. At entry to this function, DS:SI points to an 8-byte string that is the name for which to search.

Int 67h	Function 54h	Subfunction 02h	LIM Spec V4.0
	Get Handle Count		

Return total number of handles supported by the memory-manager system

Calling registers:

AH	54h
AL	02h

Return registers: If successful

AH	00h
BX	Number of handles supported

If unsuccessful

AH	80h, internal error in EMS software
	81h, malfunction in EMS hardware
	84h, undefined function
	8Fh, subfunction parameter invalid

Comments: Subfunction 02h returns the maximum number of handles the system is capable of allocating, including the reserved operating system handle 0. This function can be used to determine the maximum array size that may be necessary to support Subfunction 00h (Get Handle Directory).

Int 67h	Function 55h	LIM Spec V4.0
	Alter Page Map and Jump	

Alters page mapping permanently and transfers control

Calling registers: AH   55h

	AL	Physical page/segment selector
		0, physical page numbers used
		1, segment addresses used
	DX	EMM handle
	DS:SI	Point to map/jump structure
Return registers:	If successful	
	AH	00h
	If unsuccessful	
	AH	80h, internal error in EMS software
		81h, malfunction in EMS hardware
		83h, could not find specified EMM handle
		84h, undefined function
		8Ah, logical page out of range
		8Bh, physical page out of range
		8Fh, subfunction parameter invalid

Comments: This function permits applications programs to run from EMS memory by altering a page map and then transferring control into the mapped area. It is the equivalent of the assembly language FAR JUMP operation. The memory-mapping context that existed before the use of this function is lost.

At entry to function 55h, DX contains the EMM handle, and DS:SI points to a structure that has the layout shown in this table:

Byte Offset	Field Length	Meaning
00h	Double word	Far pointer to address to which control is to transfer
04h	Byte	Number of word pairs in map array
05h	Double word	Far pointer to map array

The map array is a variable-sized set of word pairs that map logical pages into either physical page numbers or segment addresses, depending on the value passed in AL. Its arrangement is shown in this table:

Byte Offset	Field Length	Meaning
00h	Word	Number of the logical page to be mapped
04h	Word	Physical page number or segment address, depending on value in AL

Values in all registers not containing required parameters maintain their values across the jump, as do the flag conditions.

Int 67h	Function 56h	LIM Spec V4.0
	Alter Page Map and Call	

Alters page mapping temporarily and transfers control; mapping is restored upon return

Calling registers: AH   56h
AL   Physical page/segment selector
0, physical page numbers used
1, segment addresses used
DX   EMM handle
DS:SI   Point to map/jump structure

Return registers: If successful
AH   00h
If unsuccessful
AH   80h, internal error in EMS software
81h, malfunction in EMS hardware
83h, could not find specified EMM handle
84h, undefined function
8Ah, logical page out of range
8Bh, physical page out of range
8Fh, subfunction parameter invalid

Comments: This function permits applications programs to run from EMS memory by altering a page map and then transferring control into the mapped area. It is the equivalent of the assembly language FAR CALL operation. The memory-mapping context that existed before the use of this function is saved; it is restored upon return from the called procedure by means of a normal RETF (RET FAR) operation.

At entry to this function, DX contains the EMM handle, and DS:SI points to a structure that has the following layout:

Byte Offset	Field Length	Meaning
00h	Double word	Far pointer to address to which control is to transfer
04h	Byte	Number of word pairs in new map array
05h	Double word	Far pointer to new map array

continues

Byte Offset	Field Length	Meaning
09h	Byte	Number of word pairs in old map array
0Ah	Double word	Far pointer to old map array
0Eh	4 words	Reserved; used by EMS software

Every map array is a variable-sized set of word pairs that map logical pages into either physical page numbers or segment addresses, depending on the value passed in AL. The new map array specifies the context to be used during the CALL, and the old map array preserves the original context so that it can be restored. Their arrangement is as follows:

Byte Offset	Field Length	Meaning
00h	Word	Number of the logical page to be mapped
04h	Word	Physical page number or segment address, depending on value in AL

Values in all registers not containing required parameters maintain their values across the jump, as do the flag conditions.

Int 67h	Function 56h Subfunction 02h	LIM Spec V4.0
	Get Stack Space Size	

Returns number of bytes of additional stack space required for use of Function 56h

Calling registers: AH   56h
                     AL   02h

Return registers: If successful
                    AH   00h
                    BX   Number of bytes of stack space required by Alter Page Map and Call subfunctions
                  If unsuccessful
                    AH   80h, internal error in EMS software
                                       81h, malfunction in EMS hardware
                                       84h, undefined function
                                       8Fh, subfunction parameter invalid

Comments: This function returns in BX the number that must be added to the stack pointer to remove all saved elements from the stack. It should be called before using the Alter Page Map and Call function in order to correct the value of SP upon returning from that function.

Int 67h	Function 57h	Subfunction 00h	LIM Spec V4.0
	Move Memory Region		

Moves memory region

Calling registers:

	AH	57h
	AL	00h
	DS:SI	Point to parameter block for move

Return registers: If successful

	AH	00h, no problem encountered
		92h, overlap, source destroyed

If unsuccessful

	AH	80h, internal error in EMS software
		81h, malfunction in EMS hardware
		83h, could not find specified EMM handle
		84h, undefined function
		8Ah, logical page out of range
		8Fh, subfunction parameter invalid
		93h, region too big for handle
		94h, conventional and expanded regions overlap
		95h, offset in logical page is outside logical page
		96h, length exceeds 1M bytes
		98h, source and destination types not defined
		A2h, 1M wrap-around occurred; no data was moved

Comments: This function moves the content of one region of memory to another region and overwrites what was originally located at the destination. The move can be any combination of conventional and expanded areas: conventional to conventional, conventional to expanded, expanded to conventional, or expanded to expanded.

It is not necessary to modify page mapping to perform this function; the current context is maintained throughout the operation. Length of the region moved can be from 0 to 1M bytes, but generally is some multiple of 16K bytes.

If source and destination handles are identical, the source and destination regions are tested for overlap before the move. If overlap exists, the move is done in such a way that the destination receives an intact copy of the source although the source might be destroyed in the process. A status code indicating that overlap has occurred is returned in this case.

845

Operation of this function is controlled by a parameter block pointed to by DS:SI. The layout of this block is as follows:

Byte Offset	Field Length	Meaning
00h	Double word	Number of bytes to be moved
04h	Byte	Source memory type (0=conventional, 1=expanded, others undefined)
05h	Word	Source handle
07h	Word	Source initial offset
09h	Word	Source segment or page; if type is conventional, this is a segment address; if type is expanded, this is a logical page number
0Bh	Byte	Destination memory type (0=conventional, 1=expanded, others undefined)
0Ch	Word	Destination handle
0Eh	Word	Destination initial offset
10h	Word	Destination segment or page; if type is conventional, this is a segment address; if type is expanded, this a logical page number

Int 67h	Function 57h Subfunction 01h	LIM Spec V4.0
	Exchange Memory Regions	

Exchanges two memory regions

Calling registers: AH   57h
                        AL   01h
                        DS:SI   Point to parameter block for move

Return registers: If successful
                        AH   00h No problem encountered
                        If unsuccessful
                        AH   80h, internal error in EMS software
                                 81h, malfunction in EMS hardware
                                 83h, could not find specified EMM handle
                                 84h, undefined function

8Ah, logical page out of range
8Fh, subfunction parameter invalid
93h, region too big for handle
94h, conventional and expanded regions overlap
95h, offset in logical page is outside logical page
96h, length exceeds 1M bytes
97h, source and destination overlap
98h, source and destination types not defined
A2h, 1M wrap-around occurred; no data was moved

Comments: This function exchanges the content of one region of memory with that of another. They can be any combination of conventional and expanded areas: conventional and conventional, conventional and expanded, expanded and conventional, or expanded and expanded.

It is not necessary to modify page mapping to perform this function; the current context is maintained throughout the operation. Length of the region moved can be from 0 to 1M bytes, but generally is some multiple of 16K bytes.

If source and destination handles are identical, the source and destination regions are tested for overlap before the move. If overlap exists, no exchange takes place and an error status is returned.

Operation of this function is controlled by a parameter block pointed to by DS:SI. The layout of this block is as follows:

Byte Offset	Field Length	Meaning
00h	Double word	Number of bytes to be moved
04h	Byte	Source memory type (0=conventional, 1=expanded, others undefined)
05h	Word	Source handle
07h	Word	Source initial offset
09h	Word	Source segment or page; if type is conventional, this is a segment address; if type is expanded, this is a logical page number
0Bh	Byte	Destination memory type (0=conventional, 1=expanded, others undefined)
0Ch	Word	Destination handle
0Eh	Word	Destination initial offset

continues

Byte Offset	Field Length	Meaning
10h	Word	Destination segment or page; if type is conventional, this is a segment address; if type is expanded, this is a logical page number

Int 67h   Function 58h   Subfunction 00h   LIM Spec V4.0

Get Mappable Physical Address Array

Returns an array containing the segment address and physical page number for every mappable physical page in a system

Calling registers:
AH   58h
AL   00h
ES:DI   Point to destination array

Return registers:
If successful
AH   00h
CX   Number of entries in array
ES:DI   Pointer to filled array
If unsuccessful
AH   80h, internal error in EMS software
        81h, malfunction in EMS hardware
        84h, undefined function
        8Fh, subfunction parameter invalid

Comments: This function fills a user-supplied array with word pairs that correlate actual segment addresses to physical page numbers. The array is sorted into segment sequence, which does not imply any sequence in the physical page numbers. Every word pair in the array has the following structure:

Byte Offset	Field Length	Meaning
00h	Word	Segment address of mappable physical page
02h	Word	Logical page number associated with page

Int 67h   **Function 58h   Subfunction 01h**   **LIM Spec V4.0**

Get Mappable Physical Address Array Size

Returns the number of entries that a call to Subfunction 00h will return

Calling registers: AH   58h
                         AL   01h

Return registers: If successful
                         AH   00h
                         CX   Number of entries in array
                         If unsuccessful
                         AH   80h, internal error in EMS software
                                   81h, malfunction in EMS hardware
                                   84h, undefined function
                                   8Fh, subfunction parameter invalid

Comments: This function returns in CX the number of entries that a call to Subfunction 00h will return. Multiplying the returned value by 4 yields the size in bytes required for the array to be supplied to Subfunction 00h.

Int 67h   **Function 59h   Subfunction 00h**   **LIM Spec V4.0**

Get Expanded Memory Hardware Information

Returns hardware-configuration array

Calling registers: AH   59h
                         AL   00h
                         ES:DI   Point to destination array

Return registers: If successful
                         AH   00h
                         If unsuccessful
                         AH   80h, internal error in EMS software
                                   81h, malfunction in EMS hardware
                                   84h, undefined function
                                   8Fh, subfunction parameter invalid
                                   A4h, access to function denied by operating system

Comments: This function fills in a 5-word array with details of the system's hardware configuration. The layout of the destination array, pointed to by ES:DI at entry to the function, is shown in this table:

849

Byte Offset	Field Length	Meaning
00h	Word	Size of a raw mappable physical page in paragraphs (16 bytes).
02h	Word	Number of alternate mapping register sets available.
04h	Word	Number of bytes required to save a mapping context.
06h	Word	Number of register sets that can be assigned to DMA channels.
08h	Word	0 if DMA register sets behave as described for Function 5Bh; 1 if hardware has only one DMA register set. LIM standard boards have 0 value here.

Int 67h	Function 59h Subfunction 01h	LIM Spec V4.0

Get Unallocated Raw Page Count

Returns the number of unallocated raw mappable pages and the total number of raw pages

Calling registers: AH 59h

AL 01h

Return registers: If successful

AH 00h

BX Number of raw pages available for use

DX Total number of raw pages in EMS

If unsuccessful

AH 80h, internal error in EMS software

81h, malfunction in EMS hardware

84h, undefined function

8Fh, subfunction parameter invalid

Comments: Some EMS hardware has a page size that is a submultiple of the standard 16K bytes. This type of nonstandard page size is termed a *raw page*. This function returns the counts of raw pages available. For hardware using the standard page size, this function is identical to Function 42h, Get Page Counts.

Int 67h   **Function 5Ah**   **Subfunction 00h**   **LIM Spec V4.0**

Allocate Standard Pages

Returns handle after allocating the requested number of standard pages to process

Calling registers: AH   5Ah
                         AL   00h
                         BX   Number of pages desired

Return registers: If successful
                         AH   00h
                         DX   EMM handle
                         If unsuccessful
                         AH   80h, internal error in EMS software
                                     81h, malfunction in EMS hardware
                                     84h, undefined function
                                     85h, all EMM handles in use
                                     87h, not enough pages in system
                                     88h, not enough pages available
                                     8Fh, subfunction parameter invalid

Comments: This function allocates the requested number of standard (16K) pages for use by the calling process and returns a unique handle the process uses to refer to the assigned memory. This is analogous to the file-open process.

Int 67h   **Function 5Ah**   **Subfunction 01h**   **LIM Spec V4.0**

Allocate Raw Pages

Returns handle after allocating the requested number of raw pages to process

Calling registers: AH   5Ah
                         AL   01h
                         BX   Number of pages desired

Return registers: If successful
                         AH   00h
                         DX   EMM raw handle
                         If unsuccessful
                         AH   80h, internal error in EMS software
                                     81h, malfunction in EMS hardware
                                     84h, undefined function
                                     85h, all EMM handles in use

87h, not enough pages in system

88h, not enough pages available

8Fh, subfunction parameter invalid

Comments: This function allocates the requested number of raw (nonstandard) pages for use by the calling process and returns a unique handle the process uses to refer to the assigned memory. This is analogous to the file-open process. Applications should not use this subfunction because the size of a raw page can vary from one make of EMS board to another; by using only standard pages, portability is retained.

Int 67h	Function 5Bh	Subfunction 00h	LIM Spec V4.0

Get Alternate Map Registers

Operating-system-only function to control use of EMS hardware; gets alternate map register set

Calling registers: AH   5Bh

AL   00h

Return registers: If successful

AH   00h

BL   If nonzero, this is the current alternate map register set number, and ES:DI is not affected by this function. If zero, ES:DI is set as described here.

ES:DI   Point to operating-system-supplied context save area that has the state of all map registers for all boards in the system and any additional data necessary to restore the boards' original state

If unsuccessful

AH   80h, internal error in EMS software

81h, malfunction in EMS hardware

84h, undefined function

8Fh, subfunction parameter invalid

A4h, operating system denied access to this function

Comments: This function is for use by only the operating system and can be disabled by the operating system at any time by means of Function 5Dh, OS/E Functions. Details of its operation are extremely complex, and implementors should refer to the official LIM 4 specification.

Int 67h	Function 5Bh	Subfunction 01h	LIM Spec V4.0

Set Alternate Map Registers

Operating-system-only function to control use of EMS hardware; sets alternate map

Calling registers: AH   5Bh

AL   01h

BL   New alternate map register set number 0, ES:DI contains pointer to save area that has all required information

< >0, specifies alternate map register set to activate; function responds by activating it if possible. Content of ES:DI is unaffected and ignored.

ES:DI   Point to map-register-context restore area originally supplied by Subfunction 00h of this function

Return registers: If successful

AH   00h

If unsuccessful

AH   80h, internal error in EMS software

81h, malfunction in EMS hardware

84h, undefined function

8Fh, subfunction parameter invalid

9Ah, requested register set not supported

9Ch, no alternate register sets are supported, and BL was nonzero

9Dh, requested register set either undefined or unallocated

A3h, restore array, or pointer to it, is corrupted

A4h, operating system denied access to this function

Comments: This function is for use by only the operating system and can be disabled by the operating system at any time by means of Function 5Dh, OS/E Functions. Details of its operation are extremely complex, and implementors should refer to the official LIM 4 specification.

Int 67h	Function 5Bh	Subfunction 02h	LIM Spec V4.0
	Get Alternate Map Register Set Size		

Operating-system-only function to control use of EMS hardware; gets alternate map save array size

Calling registers: AH   5Bh

AL   02h

Return registers: If successful

AH   00h

DX   Number of bytes that will be transferred to the memory area supplied by the operating system whenever a get, set, or get and set subfunction is requested

If unsuccessful

AH	80h, internal error in EMS software
	81h, malfunction in EMS hardware
	84h, undefined function
	8Fh, subfunction parameter invalid
	A4h, operating system denied access to this function

Comments: This function is for use by only the operating system and can be disabled by the operating system at any time by means of Function 5Dh, OS/E Functions. Details of its operation are extremely complex, and implementors should refer to the official LIM 4 specification.

Int 67h	**Function 5Bh**	**Subfunction 03h**	**LIM Spec V4.0**

Allocate Alternate Map Register Set

Operating-system-only function to control use of EMS hardware; allocates alternate map register set

Calling registers:	AH	5Bh
	AL	03h

Return registers:	If successful	
	AH	00h
	BL	Alternate map register set number; if no set available, it is 0
	If unsuccessful	
	AH	80h, internal error in EMS software
		81h, malfunction in EMS hardware
		84h, undefined function
		8Fh, subfunction parameter invalid
		9Bh, all alternate map register sets already allocated
		A4h, operating system denied access to this function

Comments: This function is for use by only the operating system and can be disabled by the operating system at any time by means of Function 5Dh, OS/E Functions. Details of its operation are extremely complex, and implementors should refer to the official LIM 4 specification.

Int 67h	**Function 5Bh**	**Subfunction 04h**	**LIM Spec V4.0**

De-allocate Alternate Map Register Set

Operating-system-only function to control use of EMS hardware; de-allocates alternate map register set

Calling registers: AH   5Bh

AL   04h

BL   Number of alternate map register set to de-allocate; cannot be zero

Return registers: If successful

AH   00h

If unsuccessful

AH   80h, internal error in EMS software

81h, malfunction in EMS hardware

84h, undefined function

8Fh, subfunction parameter invalid

9Ch, no alternate register sets are supported

9Dh, requested register set either undefined or unallocated

A4h, operating system denied access to this function

Comments: This function is for use by only the operating system and can be disabled by the operating system at any time by means of Function 5Dh, OS/E Functions. Details of its operation are extremely complex, and implementors should refer to the official LIM 4 specification.

Int 67h   **Function 5Bh**   **Subfunction 05h**   **LIM Spec V4.0**

Allocate DMA Register Set

Operating-system-only function to control use of EMS hardware; allocates DMA register set

Calling registers: AH   5Bh

AL   05h

Return registers: If successful

AH   00h

BL   Number of DMA register set that was allocated. Zero if no set available

If unsuccessful

AH   80h, internal error in EMS software

81h, malfunction in EMS hardware

84h, undefined function

8Fh, subfunction parameter invalid

9Bh, all DMA register sets already allocated

A4h, operating system denied access to this function

Comments: This function is for use by only the operating system and can be disabled by the operating system at any time by means of Function 5Dh, OS/E Functions. Details of its operation are extremely complex, and implementors should refer to the official LIM 4 specification.

Int 67h	Function 5Bh	Subfunction 06h	LIM Spec V4.0

Enable DMA Register Set

Operating-system-only function to control use of EMS hardware; enables DMA on alternate set

Calling registers: AH   5Bh
AL   06h
BL   DMA register set number to be enabled; if zero,
no special action is taken for DMA on specified
channel
DL   DMA channel number to associate with specified set

Return registers: If successful
AH   00h
If unsuccessful
AH   80h, internal error in EMS software
81h, malfunction in EMS hardware
84h, undefined function
8Fh, subfunction parameter invalid
9Ah, specified alternate DMA register set is not
supported
9Ch, no alternate DMA register sets are supported,
and BL was nonzero
9Dh, requested DMA register set either undefined or
unallocated
9Eh, dedicated DMA channels not supported
9Fh, specified DMA channel not supported
A4h, operating system denied access to this function

Comments: This function is for use by only the operating system and can be disabled by the operating system at any time by means of Function 5Dh, OS/E Functions. Details of its operation are extremely complex, and implementors should refer to the official LIM 4 specification.

Int 67h	Function 5Bh	Subfunction 07h	LIM Spec V4.0

Disable DMA Register Set

Operating-system-only function to control use of EMS hardware; disables DMA on alternate set

Calling registers: AH   5Bh

AL   07h

BL   DMA register set number to disable; if zero, no action is taken

Return registers: If successful

AH   00h

If unsuccessful

AH   80h, internal error in EMS software

81h, malfunction in EMS hardware

84h, undefined function

8Fh, subfunction parameter invalid

9Ah, specified alternate DMA register set is not supported

9Ch, no alternate DMA register sets are supported, and BL was nonzero

9Dh, requested DMA register set either undefined or unallocated

9Eh, dedicated DMA channels not supported

9Fh, specified DMA channel not supported

A4h, operating system denied access to this function

Comments: This function is for use by only the operating system and can be disabled by the operating system at any time by means of Function 5Dh, OS/E Functions. Details of its operation are extremely complex, and implementors should refer to the official LIM 4 specification.

Int 67h	Function 5Bh	Subfunction 08h	LIM Spec V4.0

De-allocate DMA Register Set

Operating-system-only function to control use of EMS hardware; de-allocates DMA register set

Calling registers: AH   5Bh

AL   08h

BL   Number of DMA register set that is to be de-allocated; if zero, no action is taken

Return registers: If successful

AH   00h

If unsuccessful

AH   80h, internal error in EMS software

81h, malfunction in EMS hardware

84h, undefined function

8Fh, subfunction parameter invalid

9Ch, no DMA register sets are supported, and BL was nonzero

9Dh, requested DMA register set either undefined or unallocated

A4h, operating system denied access to this function

Comments: This function is for use by only the operating system and can be disabled by the operating system at any time by means of Function 5Dh, OS/E Functions. Details of its operation are extremely complex, and implementors should refer to the official LIM 4 specification.

Int 67h	Function 5Ch	LIM Spec V4.0

Prepare Hardware for Warm Boot

Prepares EMS system for warm boot operation

Calling register: AH   5Ch

Return registers: If successful
AH   00h
If unsuccessful
AH   80h, internal error in EMS software
81h, malfunction in EMS hardware
84h, undefined function

Comments: This function prepares the EMS hardware for an impending warm boot operation. The current mapping context, the alternate register set in use, and any other EMS information requiring initialization generally are affected. Any application that maps memory below 640K must trap all possible conditions that would result in a warm boot and call this function before performing the boot.

Int 67h	Function 5Dh	Subfunction 00h	LIM Spec V4.0

Enable OS/E Functions

Operating-system-only function that enables access to operating system functions

Calling registers: AH   5Dh
AL   00h
BX/CX   32-bit access key (except on first use of function)

Return registers: If successful
AH   00h
BX/CX   32-bit access key (only first use of function)

If unsuccessful

AH	80h, internal error in EMS software
	81h, malfunction in EMS hardware
	84h, undefined function
	8Fh, subfunction parameter invalid
	A4h, operating system denied access to this function

Comments: This function is for use by only the operating system and can be disabled at any time. Subfunction 00h enables the use of Functions 59h, 5Bh, and 5Dh.

Int 67h	Function 5Dh	Subfunction 01h	LIM Spec V4.0
	Disable OS/E Functions		

Operating-system-only function that disables access to operating-system functions

Calling registers:

AH	5Dh
AL	01h
BX/CX	32-bit access key (except on first use of function)

Return registers: If successful

AH	00h
BX/CX	32-bit access key (only first use of function)

If unsuccessful

AH	80h, internal error in EMS software
	81h, malfunction in EMS hardware
	84h, undefined function
	8Fh, subfunction parameter invalid
	A4h, operating system denied access to this function

Comments: This function is for use by only the operating system and can be disabled at any time. Subfunction 01h disables the use of Functions 59h, 5Bh, and 5Dh. Access to them can be regained by use of Subfunction 02h.

Int 67h	Function 5Dh	Subfunction 02h	LIM Spec V4.0
	OS/E Access Key Code to EMS		

Operating-system-only function that controls access to other operating-system functions

Calling registers:

AH	5Dh
AL	02h
BX/CX	32-bit access key

859

Return registers: If successful
AH   00h
If unsuccessful
AH   80h, internal in EMS software
                        81h, malfunction in EMS hardware
                        84h, undefined function
                        8Fh, subfunction parameter invalid
                        A4h, operating system denied access to this function

Comments: This function is for use by only the operating system and can be disabled at any time. Subfunction 02h returns the access key code to the EMS and places the system back in its initial state; the OS/E functions then are enabled (if they had been disabled), and the next call to any of the subfunctions of this function return a new access key code.

XMS Reference

The XMS functions operate through an installed device driver, in much the same way as the mouse and EMS functions. They provide access to the upper memory blocks (UMBs), which consist of the memory between the standard 640K and 1M, the high memory area (HMA), and extended memory.

You can test for the presence of the XMS functions by using Int 2Fh, Function 4300h. If they are installed, AL contains 80h on return; if not, AL is unchanged.

After you have determined that an XMS driver is installed, you access it by using Int 2Fh, Function 4310h to determine the XMS driver entry point. The entry point address returned in ES:BX then should be saved and used for all future access to the XMS driver functions. You do this by loading AH with the XMS function you want and then calling the entry point address.

If you have any question about how the functions in this section are presented, refer to the "Reference Overview" section of this book.

Function 00h   XMS Spec V2.0

Get XMS Version Number

Determines which version of XMS is used and returns information about whether the HMA exists

Calling register:	AH	00h
Return registers:	AX	XMS version number
	BX	XMS driver revision number
	DX	HMA existence flag
		00000h, HMA does not exist
		00001h, HMA exists

Comments: The version number returned is a 16-bit BCD value. A value in AX of 01234h, therefore, means that the driver implements XMS version 12.34. The driver revision number is of value primarily for debugging. The existence of the HMA does not imply its availability.

Function 01h   XMS Spec V2.0

Request High Memory Area

Assigns the 65,520-byte HMA to the caller

Calling registers:	AH	01h
	DX	Space requested in bytes
Return registers:	AX	Status
		00000h, failure
	BL	Error code
		080h, function not implemented
		081h, VDISK device detected
		090h, HMA does not exist
		091h, HMA already in use
		092h, number of bytes requested is less than the /HMAMIN= parameter

Comments: The value placed in DX should be 0FFFFh if the caller is an applications program; otherwise, as in the case of device drivers or TSRs, the value should reflect the number of bytes needed. Assignment of the HMA is an all-or-nothing proposition, and the XMS driver can be told, through the /HMAMIN= parameter, how large a request must be before the driver can hand over the HMA to the caller.

Function 02h   XMS Spec V2.0

Release High Memory Area

Releases the HMA

Calling register: AH   02h

Return registers: AX   Status
                                     00000h, failure
                                     00001h, success
                         BL   Error code
                                     080h, function not implemented
                                     081h, VDISK device detected
                                     090h, HMA does not exist
                                     093h, HMA was not allocated

Comments: Programs that allocate the HMA must release it before exiting. Code or data stored in it becomes invalid and should not be accessed.

Function 03h   XMS Spec V2.0

Global Enable A20

Enables the A20 line

Calling register: AH   03h

Return registers: AX   Status
                                     00000h, failure
                                     00001h, success
                         BL   Error code
                                     080h, function not implemented
                                     081h, VDISK device detected
                                     082h, A20 error occurred

Comments: This call should be made only by programs with control of the HMA. Before exiting, Function 04h should be called. On many machines, toggling the A20 line is a relatively slow operation.

Function 04h   XMS Spec V2.0

Global Disable A20

Disables the A20 line

Calling register: AH   04h

Return registers: AX   Status
00000h, failure
00001h, success

BL   Error code
080h, function not implemented
081h, VDISK device detected
082h, A20 error occurred
094h, A20 line still enabled

Comments: This call should be made only by programs with control of the HMA. On many machines, toggling the A20 line is a relatively slow operation.

Function 05h   XMS Spec V2.0

Local Enable A20

Enables the A20 line

Calling register: AH   05h

Return registers: AX   Status
00000h, failure
00001h, success

BL   Error code
080h, function not implemented
081h, VDISK device detected
082h, A20 error occurred

Comments: This call should be made only by programs that need direct access to extended memory. Before exiting, Function 06h should be called. On many machines, toggling the A20 line is a relatively slow operation.

Function 06h   XMS Spec V2.0

Local Disable A20

Disables the A20 line

Calling register: AH   06h

Return registers: AX   Status
00000h, failure
00001h, success
BL   Error code
080h, function not implemented
081h, VDISK device detected
082h, A20 error occurred
094h, A20 line still enabled

Comments: This call should be made only by programs that need direct access to extended memory. On many machines, toggling the A20 line is a relatively slow operation.

Function 07h   XMS Spec V2.0

Query A20

Checks the status of the A20 line

Calling register: AH   07h

Return registers: AX   Status
00000h, failure
00001h, success
BL   Error code
000h, no error
080h, function not implemented
081h, VDISK device detected

Comments: As implemented by the Microsoft HIMEM.SYS driver, this function is performed in a hardware-independent manner by checking for memory wrap.

Function 08h   XMS Spec V2.0

Query Free Extended Memory

Checks the availability of extended memory

Calling register: AH   08h

Return registers: AX   Size of the largest free extended memory block in kilo
              bytes

          DX   Total amount of free extended memory in kilobytes
          BL   Error code
              080h, function not implemented
              081h, VDISK device detected
              0A0h, all extended memory is allocated

Comments: The HMA is not included in the returned values even if it is unassigned.

Function 09h   XMS Spec V2.0

Allocate Extended Memory Block

Allocates a block of the specified size from the pool of free extended memory

Calling registers: AH   09h
              DX   Size of memory block in kilobytes

Return registers: AX   Status
              00000h, failure
              00001h, success

          DX   Handle of allocated block
          BL   Error code
              080h, function not implemented
              081h, VDISK device detected
              0A0h, all extended memory is allocated
              0A1h, all extended memory handles are in use

Comments: The handle returned in DX should be used in all subsequent extended memory
calls. If no memory is allocated, the handle returned is null. The memory allocated should be
freed with a call to Function 0Ah before exiting.

Function 0Ah   XMS Spec V2.0

Free Extended Memory Block

De-allocates a block of extended memory

Calling registers: AH   0Ah
              DX   Handle of block to be freed

Return registers: AX   Status
              00000h, failure
              00001h, success

BL   Error code
080h, function not implemented
081h, VDISK device detected
0A2h, handle is invalid
0ABh, handle is locked

Comments: When a block is freed, its handle and all data stored in it become invalid and should not be accessed.

Function 0Bh   XMS Spec V2.0

Move Extended Memory Block

Transfers a block of data from one memory location to another

Calling registers: AH   0Bh
DS:SI   Pointer to extended memory move structure (see Table XMS.1)

Return registers: AX   Status
00000h, failure
00001h, success
BL   Error code
080h, function not implemented
081h, VDISK device detected
082h, A20 error occurred
0A3h, invalid source handle
0A4h, invalid source offset
0A5h, invalid destination handle
0A6h, invalid destination offset
0A7h, length is invalid
0A8h, move has invalid overlap
0A9h, parity error occurred

Comments: Although this function is intended to move blocks of data between conventional DOS memory and extended memory, it can move blocks of data also in conventional DOS memory and in extended memory.

Neither source nor destination handles have to be locked.

The length must be even. Performance is improved if the blocks are word-aligned, or double word-aligned on 80386 and 80486 machines. If the blocks overlap, only a forward move (the source base is less than the destination base) is guaranteed to work correctly.

The caller should not attempt to manipulate the A20 line before calling this function. The state of the A20 line is preserved by this function.

A reasonable number of interrupt windows are guaranteed during long transfers.

Table XMS.1 Layout of Extended Memory Block Structure

Offset	Meaning
000h–003h	32-bit number of bytes to be transferred
004h–005h	Source block handle
006h–009h	32-bit source offset
00Ah–00Bh	Destination block handle
00Ch–00Fh	32-bit destination offset

Function 0Ch   XMS Spec V2.0

Lock Extended Memory Block

Prevents a memory block from being moved and returns its physical address

Calling registers:	AH	0Ch
	DX	Handle of block to be locked
Return registers:	AX	Status
		00000h, failure
		00001h, success
	DX:BX	32-bit linear address of block
	BL	Error code
		080h, function not implemented
		081h, VDISK device detected
		0A2h, handle is invalid
		0ACh, block's lock count overflowed
		0ADh, lock failed

Comments: The pointer returned is valid only while the block is locked. A locked block should be unlocked as soon as possible. A lock count is maintained for extended memory blocks.

Function 0Dh   XMS Spec V2.0

Unlock Extended Memory Block

Unlocks a memory block

Calling registers:	AH	0Dh
	DX	Handle of block to be unlocked

Return registers: AX   Status

00000h, failure

00001h, success

BL   Error code

080h, function not implemented

081h, VDISK device detected

0A2h, handle is invalid

0AAh, block is not locked

Comments: Any 32-bit pointers used to access the block are no longer valid after unlocking the memory block.

This function decrements the block's lock count. To unlock a block, you must make the same number of unlock calls as lock calls.

Function 0Eh   XMS Spec V2.0

Get EMB Handle Information

Gets additional information about an extended memory block

Calling registers: AH   0Eh

DX   Handle of block

Return registers: AX   Status

00000h, failure

00001h, success

BH   Block's lock count

BL   Number of free EMB handles in the system if successful

DX   Block size (if AX=0)(kilobytes)

Error code if unsuccessful

080h, function not implemented

081h, VDISK device detected

0A2h, handle is invalid

Comments: To get the block's base address, use Function 0Ch.

Function 0Fh   XMS Spec V2.0

Re-allocate Extended Memory Block

Changes the size of an extended memory block

Calling registers: AH   0Fh

BX   New size in kilobytes

DX   Handle of block to be resized

Return registers: AX   Status

	00000h, failure
	00001h, success
BL	Error code
	080h, function not implemented
	081h, VDISK device detected
	0A0h, all extended memory is allocated
	0A1h, all available extended memory handles in use
	0A2h, handle is invalid
	0ABh, block is locked

Comments: If the new size is smaller than the old block's size, all data at the upper end of the old block is lost.

Function 10h   XMS Spec V2.0

Request Upper Memory Block

Allocates an upper memory block

Calling registers:	AH	10h
	DX	Size of block in paragraphs
Return registers:	AX	Status
		00000h, failure
		00001h, success
	BX	Segment number of UMB if successful
	BL	Error code only if AX=0000
		080h, function not implemented
		0B0h, a smaller UMB is available
		0B1h, no UMBs are available
	DX	Actual size of allocated block in paragraphs if successful; size of largest available UMB in paragraphs if not successful

Comments: Upper memory blocks (UMBs) are below the 1M address boundary, which makes manipulation of the A20 line unnecessary. UMBs are always paragraph-aligned. To determine the largest available UMB, attempt to allocate one with a size of 0FFFFh.

Function 11h   XMS Spec V2.0

Release Upper Memory Block

Releases an upper memory block

Calling registers:	AH	11h
	DX	Segment number of the UMB

Return registers: AX   Status

                                  00000h, failure

                                  00001h, success

           BL   Error code

                                  080h, function not implemented

                                  0B2h, UMB segment number is invalid

Comments: When an upper memory block (UMB) is released, the code or data stored in it becomes invalid and should not be accessed.

If a block is in extended memory, the block handle is a valid handle obtained from a call to Function 09h. If the block is in conventional memory, the block handle is set to zero and the offset is a standard segment:offset pair.

DPMI Reference

As Intel created more and more powerful microprocessors and as these microprocessors found their way into DOS systems, the constraints of running with only 1M of memory and 16-bit code became more and more chafing. The marketplace has produced a number of systems designed to get around these constraints. These systems take advantage of the 80286, 80386, and 80486 architectures to provide access to memory above 1M (EMS and XMS memory managers), multitasking environments (Windows, OS/2, DESQview), and environments called DOS extenders to run protected mode programs.

DOS extenders provide a protected mode with the capability to access 16-bit DOS functions and BIOS functions. They also typically allow access to more than 1M of memory. One popular DOS extender is the DOS protected mode interface (DPMI).

DPMI is a DOS extended specification developed by Borland International, Ergo Computer Inc., Intelligent Graphics Corporation, IBM Corporation, Intel Corporation, Locus, Lotus Development Corporation, Microsoft Corporation, Phar Lap Software, Inc., Phoenix Technologies Ltd., Quarterdeck Office Systems, and Rational Systems, Inc. DPMI can be implemented on any CPU that supports 80286 protected mode execution. Full utilization of DPMI, however, requires an 80386 or 80486.

DPMI Version 0.9 is part of the support structure of Windows 3.0. Version 1.0 adds enhancements to better support multitasking.

Under DPMI, a *DPMI client* is created when a real mode program calls the DPMI interface to request the initial switch to protected mode. A DOS environment and the one or more protected mode DPMI clients launched from it are referred to collectively as a *DPMI virtual machine*. A multitasking host can run several DPMI virtual machines concurrently. It is crucial, therefore, that a DPMI client not assume that it owns the resources of the entire machine. DPMI implementations on an 80386 or 80486 may choose to use hardware protection to virtualize I/O and interrupts and to enforce the supervisor-user privilege model; the DPMI client cannot make any assumptions, therefore, about its privilege level.

If you have any questions about how the functions in this section are presented, refer to the "Reference Overview" section of this book.

Int 2Fh	Function 1680h	DPMI Version 1.0

Release Current Virtual Machine's Time Slice

Enables the operating system to switch control to another client or to take power-conserving measures on laptop and notebook computers

Calling register:	AX	1680h
Return register:	AL	00h if supported by host
		80h if not supported by host

Comments: This call should be made whenever the program is idle, such as while waiting for keyboard input. As it regains control at intervals, it should continue to make this call as long as it is idle.

Int 2Fh	Function 1686h	DPMI Version 0.9

Get CPU Mode

Returns information about the current CPU mode

Calling register:	AX	1686h
Return register:	AX	00h if in protected mode
		Nonzero if in real mode or virtual 86 mode

Comments: Some environments support programs or libraries that can execute in either real or protected mode (*bimodal code*). This call allows such programs to determine at run time which CPU mode they are running under and to make use of system facilities accordingly. Programs and libraries that execute only in protected mode do not need to call this function.

This call should be made only after determining that a DPMI host is present; otherwise, the results may not be valid.

Int 2Fh **Function 1687h** **DPMI Version 0.9**

Obtain Real-to-Protected Mode Switch Entry Point

Tests for the presence of a DPMI host and obtains the address of a mode switch routine that can be called to begin execution in protected mode; call can be made only in real mode

Calling register:	AX	1687h
Return registers:	AX	Status
		00, success
		Nonzero, failure
	If successful	
	BX	Flags
		Bit 0 If set, 32-bit programs are supported; otherwise, 32-bit programs are not supported
		Bits 1–15 Unused
	CL	Processor type
		02h, 80286
		03h, 80386
		04h, 80486
		05h–FFh, reserved for future Intel processors
	DH	DPMI major version as a decimal number (in binary)
	DL	DPMI minor version as a decimal number (in binary)
	SI	Number of paragraphs required for DPMI host private data (may be 0)
	ES:DI	Segment:offset of procedure to call to enter protected mode

Comments: This call is made before entering protected mode for the first time. To enter protected mode, the caller must allocate the private memory required (the size in paragraphs is returned in SI), and a far call must be made to ES:DI with AX containing a flag that indicates whether the application is 16 bits (bit 0 is 0) or 32 bits (bit 0 is 1) and with ES containing the real mode segment that contains the DPMI private data (if SI was zero, ES is ignored).

If the carry flag is set on return, the mode switch failed, the client is still in real mode, and AX contains either 8011h (descriptor unavailable; could not allocate descriptors for CS, DS, ES, SS, the PSP, and the environment pointer) or 8021h (a 32-bit program was specified but is not supported).

If the carry flag is clear on return, the switch was successful. CS, DS, and SS are 16-bit selectors with bases of the real mode CS, DS, and SS, and 64K limits. ES is a selector with a base of the program's PSP and a limit of 100h. FS and GS are null selectors if they exist. The environment pointer in the program's PSP also is converted into a selector; if the client wants to free the

875

environment space, it must do so before entering protected mode and must clear the word at PSP:2Ch (the environment segment address). The program can free or modify the CS, DS, or SS descriptors; the program can change the environment pointer in the PSP after entering protected mode, but should restore it before exiting. The program should not modify or free the PSP or environment descriptors at any time.

Int 2Fh	Function 168Ah	DPMI Version 1.0
	Get Vendor-Specific API Entry Point	

Returns an address that can be called to access host-specific extensions to DPMI

Calling registers: | AX | 168Ah
| DS:(E)SI | Selector:offset of ASCIIZ string that identifies the DPMI host vendor

Return registers: | AL | 00h if successful
| | 8Ah if unsuccessful
| ES:(E)DI | Extended API entry point

Comments: This call can be made only in protected mode. It supersedes the equivalent function of calling Int 31h, Function 0A00h. DPMI 1.0 clients should use this function. It works also under Version 0.9, although it is not documented as such.

Clients must use a far call to the entry point. The string passed is case-sensitive.

Int 31h	Function 0000h	DPMI Version 0.9
	Allocate LDT Descriptors	

Allocates one or more descriptors in the task's local descriptor table (LDT)

Calling registers: | AX | 0000h
| CX | Number of descriptors to allocate

Return registers: | If successful
| Carry flag clear
| AX | Base selector
| If unsuccessful
| Carry flag set
| AX | 8011h, descriptor unavailable

Comments: The descriptors allocated are initialized to "data" with the present bit set and a base and limit of zero. The privilege level matches the caller's code segment privilege level.

876

If multiple selectors were allocated, AX references the first of a contiguous array of descriptors. The selector values for subsequent descriptors in the array can be calculated by adding the value returned by Int 31h Function 0003h.

Int 31h Function 0001h DPMI Version 0.9

Free LDT Descriptor

Frees an LDT descriptor

Calling registers:	AX	0001h
	BX	Selector for the descriptor to be freed
Return registers:	If successful	
	Carry flag clear	
	If unsuccessful	
	Carry flag set	
	AX	8022h, invalid selector

Comments: Each descriptor allocated by Int 31h, Function 0000h must be freed individually even if it was allocated as part of a contiguous array of descriptors.

Under Version 1.0, any segment registers containing the selector being freed are zeroed by this function.

Int 31h Function 0002h DPMI Version 0.9

Segment to Descriptor

Converts a real mode segment address into an LDT descriptor that can be used by a protected mode program to access the same memory

Calling registers:	AX	0002h
	BX	Real mode segment address
Return registers:	If successful	
	Carry flag clear	
	AX	Selector for real mode segment
	If unsuccessful	
	Carry flag set	
	AX	8011h, descriptor unavailable

Comments: This function provides easy access to commonly used real mode segments such as the BIOS data area at segment 0040h and the video memory at segments A000h, B000h, or B800h. The descriptors created by calls to this function cannot be modified or freed. If a client needs to access various real mode addresses by using the same selector, a descriptor should be allocated by a call to Int 31h, Function 0000h, and the base address changed by calls to Int 31h, Function 0007h.

The descriptor limit is set to 64K. Multiple calls to this function with the same segment address return the same selector.

Int 31h	Function 0003h	DPMI Version 0.9
	Get Selector Increment Value	

Returns the selector increment value used for accessing successive elements of a contiguous array of descriptors, such as that allocated by a call to Int 31h, Function 0000h or Int 31h, Function 0100h

Calling register: AX   0003h

Return registers: Carry flag clear
                       AX   Selector increment value

Comments: The value returned is always a power of two.

Int 31h	Function 0006h	DPMI Version 0.9
	Get Segment Base Address	

Returns the 32-bit linear base address from the LDT descriptor for the specified segment

Calling registers: AX   0006h

                        BX   Selector

Return registers: If successful
                        Carry flag clear
                        CX:DX   32-bit linear base address of segment
                        If unsuccessful
                        Carry flag set
                        AX   8022h, invalid selector

Comments: Client programs must use the LSL instruction to query the limit of the descriptor. On 80386 or 80486 machines, this must be the 32-bit form if the segment size is greater than 64K.

878

Int 31h   Function 0007h   DPMI Version 0.9

Set Segment Base Address

Sets the 32-bit linear base address field in the LDT descriptor for the specified segment

Calling registers:	AX	0007h
	BX	Selector
	CS:DX	32-bit linear base address of segment

Return registers:	If successful	
	Carry flag clear	
	If unsuccessful	
	Carry flag set	
	AX	Error code
		8022h, invalid selector
		8025h, invalid linear address

Comments: DPMI 1.0 automatically reloads any segment register that contains the selector specified in the BX register. DPMI 0.9 hosts may or may not do this.

Int 31h   Function 0008h   DPMI Version 0.9

Set Segment Limit

Sets the limit field in the LDT descriptor for the specified segment

Calling registers:	AX	0008h
	BX	Selector
	CX:DX	32-bit segment limit

Return registers:	If successful	
	Carry flag clear	
	If unsuccessful	
	Carry flag set	
	AX	Error code
		8021h, invalid value
		8022h, invalid selector
		8025h, invalid linear address

Comments: The value in CX:DX must be the byte length of the segment minus 1. If the limit is greater than or equal to 1M, it must be page-aligned (the least significant 12 bits must be set).

879

The DPMI host sets or clears the descriptor's granularity bit as required.

DPMI 1.0 reloads any segment registers loaded with the selector in the BX register.

Int 31h	**Function 0009h**	**DPMI Version 0.9**
	Set Descriptor Access Rights	

Modifies the access rights and type fields in the LDT descriptor for the specified segment

Calling registers:

	AX	0009h
	BX	Selector
	CL	Access rights type byte
	CH	80386 extended access rights type byte

Return registers:

If successful
Carry flag clear
If unsuccessful
Carry flag set

	AX	Error code
		8021h, invalid value
		8022h, invalid selector
		8025h, invalid linear address

Comments: The access rights type byte in the CL register has the following format:

Bit	Meaning
0	0 = not accessed, 1 = accessed
1	Data: 0 = read, 1 = read/write
	Code: must be 1 (readable)
2	Data: 0 = expand-up, 1 = expand-down
	Code: must be 0 (nonconforming)
3	0 = data, 1 = code
4	Must be 1
5–6	Must equal caller's CPL
7	0 = absent, 1 = present

The extended access rights type byte in the CH register has the following format:

Bit	Meaning
0–3	Ignored
4	Can be 0 or 1
5	Must be 0
6	0 = 16-bit, 1 = 32-bit
7	0 = byte granular, 1 = page granular

Client programs should use the LAR instruction to examine the descriptor's access rights.

DPMI 1.0 reloads any segment registers that reference the affected descriptor.

Int 31h	**Function 000Ah**	**DPMI Version 0.9**
	Create Alias Descriptor	

Creates a new LDT descriptor with the same base and limit as the specified descriptor

Calling registers: AX   000Ah
                          BX   Selector

Return registers: If successful
                          Carry flag clear
                          AX   Data selector (alias)
                          If unsuccessful
                          Carry flag set
                          AX   Error code
                                     8011h, descriptor unavailable
                                     8022h, invalid selector

Comments: The selector can be a data or code selector. The published DPMI 0.9 specification states that an error is generated if the selector is a data selector; this statement is untrue.

The descriptor alias that is returned does not track changes made to the original descriptor. If the base or limit of the original segment, therefore, is modified after creating an alias, the segment and its alias no longer map the same memory.

Int 31h   Function 000Bh   DPMI Version 0.9

Get Descriptor

Copies the LDT entry for the specified selector into an 8-byte buffer

Calling registers: AX   000Bh
                        BX   Selector
                        ES:(E)DI   Selector:offset of 8-byte buffer

Return registers: If successful
                        Carry flag clear
                        Buffer pointed to by ES:(E)DI contains descriptor
                        If unsuccessful
                        Carry flag set
                        AX   8022h, invalid selector

Comments: Sixteen-bit code should use ES:DI; 32-bit programs should use ES:EDI.

Int 31h   Function 000Ch   DPMI Version 0.9

Set Descriptor

Copies the contents of an 8-byte buffer into the LDT descriptor for the specified selector

Calling registers: AX   000Ch
                        BX   Selector
                        ES:(E)DI   Selector:offset of 8-byte buffer containing descriptor

Return registers: If successful
                        Carry flag clear
                        If unsuccessful
                        Carry flag set
                        AX   Error code
                                    8021h, invalid value
                                    8022h, invalid selector
                                    8025h, invalid linear address

Comments: Thirty-two-bit programs must use ES:EDI; 16-bit programs should use ES:DI.
DPMI 1.0 reloads segments that contain the specified selector.

Int 31h   **Function 000Dh**   **DPMI Version 0.9**

Allocate Specific LDT Descriptor

Allocates a specific LDT descriptor

Calling registers: AX   000Dh

         BX   Selector

Return registers: If successful

         Carry flag clear

         If unsuccessful

         Carry flag set

         AX   Error code

                8011h, descriptor unavailable

                8022h, invalid selector

Comments: The first 16 descriptors (values 04h–7Ch) are reserved for this function. Under DPMI 0.9, another application may have already been loaded and have allocated some of these descriptors, making them unavailable. Under DPMI 1.0, every client has its own LDT and has access to all 16 descriptors.

Resident service providers (protected mode TSRs) should not use this function.

Int 31h   **Function 000Eh**   **DPMI Version 1.0**

Get Multiple Descriptors

Copies one or more LDT entries into a client buffer

Calling registers: AX   000Eh

         CX   Number of descriptors to copy

         ES:(E)DI Selector:offset of a buffer in the following format:

Offset	Length	Contents
0000h	2	Selector #1 (set by client)
0002h	8	Descriptor #1 (returned by host)
000Ah	2	Selector #2 (set by client)
000Ch	8	Descriptor #2 (returned by host)

.

.

.

Return registers: If successful
Carry flag clear
Buffer contains copies of the descriptors for the specified selectors
If unsuccessful
Carry flag set

AX	8022h, invalid selector
CX	Number of descriptors successfully copied

Comments: If an invalid selector or descriptor is detected, all descriptor copies before the one that failed are valid.

Thirty-two-bit programs must use ES:EDI; 16-bit programs should use ES:DI.

Int 31h	Function 000Fh	DPMI Version 1.0
	Set Multiple Descriptors	

Copies one or more descriptors from a client buffer into the LDT

Calling registers:

AX	000Fh
CX	Number of descriptors to copy
ES:(E)DI	Selector:offset of a buffer in the following format:

Offset	Length	Contents
0000h	2	Selector #1
0002h	8	Descriptor #1
000Ah	2	Selector #2
000Ch	8	Descriptor #2
.		
.		
.		

Return registers: If successful
Carry flag clear

If unsuccessful
Carry flag set

AX	Error code
	8021h, invalid value
	8022h, invalid selector
	8025h, invalid linear address
CX	Number of descriptors successfully copied

Comments: If an error occurs because of an invalid selector or descriptor, the number of successfully copied descriptors is returned in CX. All descriptors copied up to the one that failed are valid. The remaining descriptors are not updated.

Thirty-two-bit programs must use ES:EDI; 16-bit programs should use ES:DI.

Any segment register containing a selector specified in the data structure is reloaded.

Int 31h	Function 0100h	DPMI Version 0.9
	Allocate DOS Memory Block	

Allocates a block of memory from the memory below the 1M boundary

Calling registers:	AX	0100h
	BX	Number of paragraphs desired
Return registers:	If successful	
	Carry flag clear	
	AX	Real mode segment base address of allocated block
	DX	Selector for allocated block
	If unsuccessful	
	Carry flag set	
	AX	Error code
		0007h, memory control blocks damaged
		0008h, insufficient memory
		8011h, descriptor unavailable
	BX	Size of largest block in paragraphs

Comments: If the size of the block is greater than 64K and the client is a 16-bit program, contiguous descriptors are allocated and the base selector is returned. Consecutive selectors can be calculated using the value returned from Int 31h, Function 0003h. The descriptors have limits of 64K, except the last one, which has a limit of block size MOD 64K. The first descriptor has a limit on the size of the entire block if the host is 32 bits; the limit of the first descriptor is 64K if the host is 16 bits, even if it is running on an 80386.

If the client is 32 bits, only one descriptor is allocated.

Client programs must never modify or free any descriptors allocated by this function. The descriptors are deallocated by a call to Int 31h, Function 0101h.

The DOS allocation function (Int 21h, Function 48h) is used to allocate the DOS memory.

Int 31h	Function 0101h	DPMI Version 0.9
	Free DOS Memory Block	

Frees a memory block previously allocated by Int 31h, Function 0100h

Calling registers: AX   0101h
DX   Selector of block to be freed

Return registers: If successful
Carry flag clear
If unsuccessful
Carry flag set
AX   Error code
0007h, memory control blocks damaged
0009h, incorrect memory segment specified
8022h, invalid selector

Comments: All descriptors allocated for the memory block are automatically freed and are no longer valid.

Under DPMI 1.0, any segment registers containing a selector being freed are zeroed.

Int 31h	Function 0102h	DPMI Version 0.9
	Resize DOS Memory Block	

Changes the size of a memory block previously allocated by Int 31h, Function 0100

Calling registers: AX   0102h
BX   New block size in paragraphs
DX   Selector of block to modify

Return registers: If successful
Carry flag clear
If unsuccessful
Carry flag set

AX	Error code
	0007h, memory control blocks damaged
	0008h, insufficient memory
	0009h, incorrect memory segment specified
	8011h, descriptor unavailable
	8022h, invalid selector
BX	Maximum possible block size

Comments: A request to increase size may fail if DOS memory is fragmented, if there is insufficient DOS memory, or if the block grows past a 64K boundary and the next descriptor in the LDT is unavailable.

A request to decrease size may free some descriptors and decrease the limit of the new last descriptor.

Under DPMI 1.0, any segment registers containing a selector being modified are reloaded, and any segment register containing a selector being freed will be zeroed.

Client programs should never modify or free any descriptors allocated by this function. Int 31h, Function 0101h deallocates them automatically.

Int 31h	Function 0200h	DPMI Version 0.9

Get Real Mode Interrupt Vector

Returns the contents of the current virtual machine's real mode interrupt vector

Calling registers: AX   0200h
                           BL   Interrupt number

Return registers: Carry flag clear
                           CX:DX   Segment:offset of real mode interrupt handler

Comments: The value returned in CX is a real mode segment address, not a selector. Attempts to place this value in a segment register may cause a general-protection fault.

Int 31h	Function 0201h	DPMI Version 0.9

Set Real Mode Interrupt Vector

Sets the current virtual machine's real mode interrupt vector for the specified interrupt

Calling registers: AX   0201h
                           BL   Interrupt number
                           CX:DX   Segment:offset of real mode interrupt handler

Return register: Carry flag clear

Comments: The address passed in CX must be a real mode segment address, not a selector. The handler must reside in DOS memory or the client must allocate a real mode callback address.

If the interrupt being hooked is a hardware interrupt, the memory used by the handler must be locked.

Int 31h   Function 0202h   DPMI Version 0.9

Get Processor Exception Handler Vector

Returns the address of the current client's protected mode exception handler for the specified exception number

Calling registers: AX   0202h
                          BL   Exception number (00h–1Fh)

Return registers: If successful
                          Carry flag clear
                          CX:(E)DX   Selector:offset of exception handler
                          If unsuccessful
                          Carry flag set
                          AX   8021h, invalid value

Comments: This function is supported under DPMI 1.0 for backward compatibility; DPMI 1.0 clients should use Int 31h, Functions 0210h and 0211h. The value in CX is a selector, not a segment address. A 32-bit offset in EDX is returned for 32-bit clients.

Int 31h   Function 0203h   DPMI Version 0.9

Set Processor Exception Handler Vector

Sets the address of a handler for a CPU exception or fault

Calling registers: AX   0203h
                          BL   Exception number (00h–1Fh)
                          CX:(E)DX   Selector:offset of exception handler

Return registers: If successful
                          Carry flag clear

If unsuccessful
Carry flag set
AX   Error code
               8021h, invalid value
               8022h, invalid selector

Comments: The value in CX should be a valid protected mode code selector, not a segment address. Thirty-two-bit clients must supply a 32-bit offset in EDX.

DPMI 1.0 clients should avoid this function, which is provided for backward compatibility, and use Int 31h, Functions 0212h and 0213h instead.

Int 31h	Function 0204h	DPMI Version 0.9
	Get Protected Mode Interrupt Vector	

Returns the address of the current protected mode interrupt handler for the specified interrupt

Calling registers: AX   02024h
                          BL   Interrupt number

Return registers: Carry flag clear
                          CX:(E)DX   Selector:offset of interrupt handler

Comments: The value in CX is a valid protected mode selector, not a real mode segment. A 32-bit offset in EDX is returned for 32-bit clients.

Int 31h	Function 0205h	DPMI Version 0.9
	Set Protected Mode Interrupt Vector	

Sets the address of a protected mode interrupt handler for the specified interrupt to the specified address

Calling registers: AX   0205h
                          BL   Interrupt number
                          CX:(E)DX   Selector:offset of interrupt handler

Return registers: If successful
                          Carry flag clear
                          If unsuccessful
                          Carry flag set
                          AX   8022h, invalid selector

Comments: The value passed in CX must be a valid protected mode selector, not a real mode segment address. Thirty-two-bit clients must pass a valid 32-bit offset in EDX.

Int 31h   **Function 0210h**   **DPMI Version 1.0**

Get Extended Processor Exception Handler Vector (Protected Mode)

Returns the address of the client's protected mode handler for the specified protected mode exception

Calling registers: AX   0210h
                         BL   Exception number (00h–1Fh)

Return registers: If successful
                         Carry flag clear
                         CX:(E)DX   Selector:offset of exception handler
                         If unsuccessful
                         Carry flag set
                         AX   8021h, invalid value

Comments: DPMI 1.0 clients should use this function instead of Int 31h, Function 0202h.

Int 31h   **Function 0211h**   **DPMI Version 1.0**

Get Extended Processor Exception Handler Vector (Real Mode)

Returns the address of the client's protected mode handler for the specified real mode exception

Calling registers: AX   0211h
                         BL   Exception number (00h–1Fh)

Return registers: If successful
                         Carry flag clear
                         CX:(E)DX   Selector:offset of exception handler
                         If unsuccessful
                         Carry flag set
                         AX   8021h, invalid value

Comments: CX:(E)DX is a selector:offset pair, not a segment:offset pair. The address returned is the address of the function that will receive control in protected mode after the real mode handler performs the mode switch into protected mode.

Int 31h   Function 0212h   DPMI Version 1.0

Set Extended Processor Exception Handler Vector (Protected Mode)

Sets the address of the client's protected mode handler for the specified protected mode exception

Calling registers: AX   0212h
                         BL   Exception number (00h–1Fh)
                         CS:(E)DX   Selector:offset of exception handler

Return registers: If successful
                         Carry flag clear
                         If unsuccessful
                         Carry flag set
                         AX   Error code
                                     8021h, invalid value
                                     8022h, invalid selector

Comments: DPMI 1.0 clients should use this function instead of Int 31h, Function 0203h.

Int 31h   Function 0213h   DPMI Version 1.0

Set Extended Processor Exception Handler Vector (Real Mode)

Sets the address of the client's protected mode handler for the specified real mode exception

Calling registers: AX   0213h
                         BL   Exception number (00h–1Fh)
                         CS:(E)DX   Selector:offset of exception handler

Return registers: If successful
                         Carry flag clear
                         If unsuccessful
                         Carry flag set
                         AX   Error code
                                     8021h, invalid value
                                     8022h, invalid selector

Comments: The address specified is the address of the protected mode handler to which control is passed by the real mode exception handler after performing a mode switch.

Int 31h   **Function 0300h**   **DPMI Version 0.9**

Simulate Real Mode Interrupt

Simulates an interrupt in real mode

Calling registers:	AX	0300h
	BL	Interrupt number
	BH	Flags (all zero)
	CX	Number of words to copy from the protected mode stack to the real mode stack
	ES:(E)DI	Selector:offset of real mode register data structure

Return registers:	If successful	
	Carry flag clear	
	ES:(E)DI	Selector:offset of modified real mode register data structure
	If unsuccessful	
	Carry flag set	
	AX	Error code
		8012h, linear memory unavailable
		8013h, physical memory unavailable
		8014h, backing store unavailable
		8021h, invalid value

Comments: This function transfers control to the real mode interrupt handler specified by the real mode interrupt vector. The CS:IP values are ignored. The SS:SP values are used by the real mode handler unless set to zero; in that case, the DPMI host supplies a real mode stack. The flags specified are pushed onto the real mode interrupt handler's IRET frame; the interrupt and trace flags are cleared. The segment register values must be real mode segment addresses, not selectors. Sixteen-bit hosts are not required to pass the high word of 32-bit registers or the FS and GS registers, even if running on an 80386 machine. On return from the interrupt handler, the data structure contains the values returned by the real mode interrupt handler.

The real mode register structure is set up as follows:

Offset	Contents
0000h	(E)DI
0004h	(E)SI
0008h	(E)BP

Offset	Contents
000Ch	Reserved; should be zero
0010h	(E)BX
0014h	(E)DX
0018h	(E)CX
001Ch	(E)AX
0020h	CPU flags
0022h	ES
0024h	DS
0026h	FS
0028h	GS
002Ah	IP (ignored)
002Ch	CS (ignored)
002Eh	SP
0030h	SS

Int 31h   **Function 0301h**   **DPMI Version 0.9**

Call Real Mode Procedure with Far Return Frame

Simulates a far call to a real mode procedure

Calling registers: AX   0301h
                        BH   Flags (should be zero)
                        CX   Number of words to copy from the protected mode stack
                                    to the real mode stack
                        ES:(E)DI   Selector:offset of the real mode register data structure

Return registers: If successful
                        Carry flag clear
                        ES:(E)DI   Selector:offset of modified real mode register data
                                    structure

893

If unsuccessful
Carry flag set
AX   Error code
                  8012h, linear memory unavailable
                  8013h, physical memory unavailable
                  8014h, backing store unavailable
                  8021h, invalid value

Comments: This function transfers control to the real mode procedure specified by the CS:IP values. The SS:SP values are used by the real mode handler unless set to zero; in that case, the DPMI host supplies a real mode stack. The segment register values must be real mode segment addresses, not selectors. sixteen-bit hosts are not required to pass the high word of 32-bit registers or the FS and GS registers, even if running on an 80386 machine. On return from the procedure, the data structure contains the values returned by the real mode procedure.

The real mode register structure is set up as follows:

Offset	Contents
0000h	(E)DI
0004h	(E)SI
0008h	(E)BP
000Ch	Reserved; should be zero
0010h	(E)BX
0014h	(E)DX
0018h	(E)CX
001Ch	(E)AX
0020h	CPU flags
0022h	ES
0024h	DS
0026h	FS
0028h	GS
002Ah	IP
002Ch	CS
002Eh	SP
0030h	SS

The procedure must return by executing the RETF (far return) instruction.

Int 31h	Function 0302h	DPMI Version 0.9
	Call Real Mode Procedure with IRET Frame	

Simulates a far call with flags pushed on the stack to a real mode procedure

Calling registers:
AX   0302h
BH   Flags (should be zero)
CX   Number of words to copy from the protected mode stack to the real mode stack
ES:(E)DI   Selector:offset of the real mode register data structure

Return registers:
If successful
Carry flag clear
ES:(E)DI   Selector:offset of modified real mode register data structure
If unsuccessful
Carry flag set
AX   Error code
           8012h, linear memory unavailable
           8013h, physical memory unavailable
           8014h, backing store unavailable
           8021h, invalid value

Comments: This function transfers control to the real mode procedure specified by the CS:IP values. The SS:SP values are used by the real mode handler unless set to zero; in that case, the DPMI host supplies a real mode stack. The flags value is pushed onto the real mode stack's IRET frame with interrupt and trace flags clear. The segment register values must be real mode segment addresses, not selectors. Sixteen-bit hosts are not required to pass the high word of 32-bit registers or the FS and GS registers, even if running on an 80386 machine. On return from the procedure, the data structure contains the values returned by the real mode procedure.

The real mode register structure is set up as follows:

Offset	Contents
0000h	(E)DI
0004h	(E)SI
0008h	(E)BP
000Ch	Reserved; should be zero

continues

Offset	Contents
0010h	(E)BX
0014h	(E)DX
0018h	(E)CX
001Ch	(E)AX
0020h	CPU flags
0022h	ES
0024h	DS
0026h	FS
0028h	GS
002Ah	IP
002Ch	CS
002Eh	SP
0030h	SS

The procedure must return by executing the IRET or RETF(2) instruction.

Int 31h	Function 0303h	DPMI Version 0.9
	Allocate Real Mode Callback Address	

Returns a unique real mode segment:offset known as a *real mode callback* that will transfer control from real mode to a protected mode procedure

Calling registers: AX   0303h
DS:(E)SI   Selector:offset of protected mode procedure to call
ES:(E)DI   Selector:offset of 32h-byte buffer for real mode register
data structure used when calling callback routine

Return registers: If successful
Carry flag clear
CX:DX   Segment:offset of real mode callback
If unsuccessful
Carry flag set
AX   8015h, callback unavailable

Comments: DPMI hosts are required to provide a minimum of 16 callback addresses per client. Callback addresses are limited resources, however, and should be freed when no longer necessary.

The data structure contains no valid data until the time of the actual callback.

Int 31h	Function 0304h	DPMI Version 0.9
	Free Real Mode Callback Address	

Releases a callback address previously allocated by Int 31h, Function 0303h

Calling registers: AX   0304h
                        CX:DX   Real mode callback address to be freed

Return registers: If successful
                        Carry flag clear
                        If unsuccessful
                        Carry flag set
                        AX   8024h, invalid callback address

Comments: Real mode callbacks are a limited system resource. Clients should release callbacks when no longer necessary.

Int 31h	Function 0305h	DPMI Version 0.9
	Get State Save/Restore Addresses	

Returns the addresses of two routines used to save the current task's registers

Calling register: AX   0305h

Return registers: Carry flag clear
                        AX   Size of buffer in bytes
                        BX:CX   Real mode address of save/restore function
                        SI:(E)DI   Protected mode address of save/restore function

Comments: The real mode address is the address of a routine, called *from real mode only,* that will save or restore the state of the protected mode registers. The protected mode address is the address of a routine, called *from protected mode only,* that will save or restore the state of the real mode registers.

These routines do not need to be called unless the client is using the raw switch services. Functions 0300h, 0301h, and 0302h do not require these routines.

The routines are called by setting AL to 0 to save the state or to 1 to restore the state, by setting ES:(E)DI to the address of a state save buffer, and by making a FAR CALL to the appropriate routine. The buffer must be at least as large as the value returned in AX. A DPMI host may not require that registers be saved; in that case, this function may return a size of zero. A call to the save/restore routine will still be safe, but will do nothing.

Int 31h	Function 0306h	DPMI Version 0.9
	Get Raw Mode Switch Addresses	

Returns the address of routines that can be called to perform low-level mode switching

Calling register: 0306h

Return registers: Carry flag clear
 BX:CX   Address of real-to-protected mode switch routine
 SI:(E)DI   Address of protected-to-real mode
     switch routine

Comments: The real-to-protected mode switch routine must be called only from real mode, and the protected-to-real mode switch routine must be called only from protected mode. The mode switch routines are entered by a FAR JUMP with the following parameters:

AX	New DS value
CX	New ES value
DX	New SS value
(E)BX	New (E)SP value
SI	New CS value
(E)DI	New (E)IP value

The values of (E)AX, (E)BX, E(CX), E(DX), (E)DI, and (E)SI are undefined after the mode switch. (E)BP is preserved across the mode switch. In 80386 and 80486 CPUs, FS and GS are set to zero. If interrupts are disabled when the mode switch is invoked, they are not reenabled by the DPMI host; the client must do this after the mode switch.

If the specified selector values are invalid when switching to protected mode, an exception will occur.

If the register state must be preserved, the functions accessible through Function 0305h must be used.

Int 31h   Function 0400h   DPMI Version 0.9

Get Version

Returns the version number of the DPMI specification supported by the host and additional information about the host's capabilities

Calling register: AX   0400h

Return registers: Carry flag clear

AH	DPMI major version (binary)
AL	DPMI minor version (binary)
BX	Flags
Bit 0	0 = 16-bit implementation
	1 = 32-bit implementation
Bit 1	0 = CPU returned to virtual 86 mode for reflected interrupts
	1 = CPU returned to real mode for reflected interrupts
Bit 2	0 = Virtual memory not supported
	1 = Virtual memory supported
Bits 3–15	Reserved
CL	Processor type
	02h, 80286
	03h, 80386
	04h, 80486
DH	Current value of virtual master PIC base interrupt
DL	Current value of virtual slave PIC base interrupt

Comments: Version 0.9 shows AH = 0, AL = 5A (90 decimal); Version 1.0 shows AH = 1, AL = 0.

Int 31h   Function 0401h   DPMI Version 1.0

Get DPMI Capabilities

Returns information about the DPMI host

Calling register: AX   0401h

Return registers: If successful

Carry flag clear

AX	Capabilities flag
Bit 0	0 = Page accessed/dirty not supported
	1 = Page accessed/dirty supported
Bit 1	0 = Exception restartability not supported
	1 = Exception restartability supported

Bit 2	0 = Device mapping not supported
	1 = Device mapping supported
Bit 3	0 = Conventional memory mapping not supported
	1 = Conventional memory mapping supported
Bit 4	0 = Demand zero-fill not supported
	1 = Demand zero-fill supported
Bit 5	0 = Write-protect client not supported
	1 = Write-protect client supported
Bit 6	0 = Write-protect host not supported
	1 = Write-protect host supported
CX	0
DX	0
ES:(E)DI	Selector:offset of 128-byte host information buffer
If unsuccessful	
Carry flag set	

Comments: This function always fails under Version 0.9.

Page accessed/dirty is the capability of the host to maintain page accessed and page dirty bits that can be read with Function 0506h and written with Function 0507h. If the DPMI host does not provide demand-paged virtual memory, this functionality must be supported. Otherwise, it is optional and, if present, gives the client the capability to read from and write to the virtual-page-accessed and page-dirty bits maintained by the host.

Exception restartability is the capability of restarting a faulting instruction inside the host kernel if the client's exception handler corrects the reason for the exception and returns.

Device mapping indicates whether Function 0508h is supported.

Conventional memory mapping indicates whether Function 0509h is supported.

Demand zero-fill, if supported, means that all committed pages are initialized to zero when created. If unsupported, the page contents are undefined.

Write-protect client is the capability to protect pages from the client's writes and to generate a page fault.

Write-protect host is the capability to protect pages from the host's writes and to generate page faults.

The host information buffer is defined as follows:

Offset	Length	Contents
0	Byte	Host major version number
1	Byte	Host minor version number
2	126 bytes	Null-terminated string identifying the host

The host major and minor version numbers are OEM-specific and are not the DPMI version.

Int 31h	Function 0500h	DPMI Version 0.9
	Get Free Memory Information	

Returns information about the amount of memory available

Calling registers: AX   0500h
                              ES:(E)DI Selector:offset of 48-byte buffer

Return register: Carry flag clear

Comments: This function is superseded by Function 050Bh for Version 1.0.

The buffer is defined as follows:

Offset	Length	Contents
00h	Dword	Largest available free block in bytes (largest block of contiguous linear memory that could be allocated if the memory were to be allocated and left unlocked).
04h	Dword	Maximum unlocked page allocation in bytes. This is the value of offset 0 divided by the page size. If unsupported, this is FFFFFFFFh.
08h	Dword	Maximum locked page allocation in pages (the largest block that could be allocated and locked). If unsupported, this is FFFFFFFFh.
0Ch	Dword	Linear address space size in bytes, including linear space already allocated. If unsupported, this is FFFFFFFFh.
10h	Dword	Total number of unlocked pages. These pages can be paged out and can include any free pages. If unsupported, this is FFFFFFFFh.
14h	Dword	Total number of free pages (number of physical pages not currently in use). If unsupported, this is FFFFFFFFh.
18h	Dword	Total number of physical pages. This includes free, locked, and unlocked pages. If unsupported, this is FFFFFFFFh.
1Ch	Dword	Free linear address space in pages. If unsupported, this is FFFFFFFFh.

continues

901

Offset	Length	Contents
20h	Dword	Size of paging/file partition in pages. If unsupported, this is FFFFFFFFh.
24h	12 bytes	Reserved; all bytes set to FFh.

The page size can be obtained from Function 0604h.

Int 31h	**Function 0501h**	**DPMI Version 0.9**
	Allocate Memory Block	

Allocates a block of linear memory

Calling registers:

	AX	0501h
	BX:CX	Size of block in bytes; must be nonzero

Return registers:

If successful
Carry flag clear

	BX:CX	Linear address of allocated memory block
	SI:DI	Memory block handle

If unsuccessful
Carry flag set

	AX	Error code
		8012h, linear memory unavailable
		8013h, physical memory unavailable
		8014h, backing store unavailable
		8016h, handle unavailable
		8021h, invalid value

Comments: The block is guaranteed to be at least paragraph-aligned. Pages created are committed; if virtual memory is supported, the pages are unlocked. Unlocked pages can be locked with Function 0600h. No descriptors are allocated; it is the client's responsibility to allocate and initialize descriptors needed to access the block.

Under many DPMI hosts, allocations are page granular; if the request is for n pages plus 1 byte, $n+1$ pages are allocated. Therefore, it is often best to allocate memory in units of granularity. Function 0604h can be called to get the unit of granularity; if it fails, a value of 4K is recommended.

Int 31h   Function 0502h   DPMI Version 0.9

Free Memory Block

Frees a memory block allocated by a call to Function 0501h or 0504h

Calling registers:	AX	0502h
	SI:DI	Memory block handle
Return registers:	If successful	
	Carry flag clear	
	If unsuccessful	
	Carry flag set	
	AX	8023h, invalid handle

Comments: This function correctly frees committed pages, uncommitted pages, and mapped pages. It does not free descriptors mapped to the block. Descriptors should be free before linear memory blocks.

Int 31h   Function 0503h   DPMI Version 0.9

Resize Memory Block

Changes the size of a block allocated by Function 0501h or 0504h

Calling registers:	AX	0503h
	BX:CX	New size of block, in bytes (must be nonzero)
	SI:DI	Memory block handle
Return registers:	If successful	
	Carry flag clear	
	BX:CX	New linear address of block
	SI:DI	New memory block handle
	If unsuccessful	
	Carry flag set	
	AX	Error code
		8012h, linear memory unavailable
		8013h, physical memory unavailable
		8014h, backing store unavailable
		8016h, handle unavailable
		8021h, invalid value
		8023h, invalid handle

Comments: This function invalidates the old handle; the old handle should not be used. When increasing a block size, the pages created are committed. When decreasing the size, unused pages are correctly freed. It is the client's responsibility to update descriptors that map the memory block.

Int 31h	Function 0504h	DPMI Version 1.0
	Allocate Linear Memory Block	

Allocates a block of page-aligned linear address space

Calling registers:	AX	0504h
	EBX	Desired page-aligned linear address or zero if the calling program does not care
	ECX	Size of block, in bytes (must be nonzero)
	EDX	Flags
	Bit 0	0, create uncommitted pages
		1, create committed pages
	Bits 1–31	Reserved

Return registers:	If successful	
	Carry flag clear	
	EBX	Linear address of memory block
	ESI	Handle of memory block
	If unsuccessful	
	Carry flag set	
	AX	Error code
		8011h, unsupported function
		8012h, linear memory unavailable
		8013h, physical memory unavailable
		8014h, backing store unavailable
		8016h, handle unavailable
		8021h, invalid size
		8025h, linear address not page-aligned

Comments: A 16-bit host will not support this function. A 16-bit client of a 32-bit host, however, can use this function.

Function 0501h, which also can allocate linear memory, does not guarantee page alignment, create uncommitted pages, or allocate a block at a specific linear address.

Int 31h   **Function 0505h**   **DPMI Version 1.0**

Resize Linear Memory Block

Changes the size of a block of memory previously allocated with Function 0504h

Calling registers:	AX	0505h
	ESI	Memory block handle
	ECX	New block size, in bytes (must be nonzero)
	EDX	Flags
	Bit 0	0, create uncommitted pages
		1, create committed pages
	Bit 1	0, do not update segment descriptors
		1, update segment descriptors
	Bits 2–31	Reserved
		If bit 1 of EDX is set
	ES:EBX	Selector:offset of buffer containing an array of selectors, 1 word (16 bits) per selector
	EDI	Count of selectors in the array

Return registers:	If successful	
	Carry flag clear	
	EBX	New linear address of memory block
	ESI	New handle for memory block
	If unsuccessful	
	Carry flag set	
	AX	Error code
		8001h, unsupported function
		8012h, linear memory unavailable
		8013h, physical memory unavailable
		8014h, backing store unavailable
		8016h, handle unavailable
		8021h, invalid size
		8023h, invalid handle

Comments: A 16-bit implementation will not support this function. A 16-bit client of a 32-bit host, however, can use it. On return, the old handle is no longer valid and should not be used.

On failure, the block's size and base address are unchanged.

If the block increases in size, the base address may change. If the size of the block decreases, pages at the end of the block are freed; the base address does not change.

If the block's base address is changed, and if bit 1 of EDX was set, the descriptors of selectors in the update list are modified when the segments fall within the memory block. Expand-up segments fall within the block if the base address is within the block; expand-down segments fall within the block if (base address + limit − 1) is within the block. If the block must be moved, no hardware interrupts will be delivered to the client during the move.

Function 0503h, which can be used also to resize linear memory blocks, does not necessarily page-align blocks, create uncommitted pages, or update descriptors.

Int 31h	**Function 0506h**	**DPMI Version 1.0**

Get Page Attributes

Returns the attributes of one or more pages of linear memory allocated by Function 0504h

Calling registers: AX   0506h
ESI   Memory block handle
EBX   Base offset in the page's memory block or in the first page
           of multiple pages
ECX   Number of pages
ES:EDX   Selector:offset of a buffer in which
           to receive page attributes

Return registers: If successful
Carry flag clear
Buffer updated
If unsuccessful
Carry flag set
AX   Error code
           8001h, unsupported function
           8023h, invalid handle
           8025h, offset is not within specified block

Comments: A 16-bit host will not support this function. A 16-bit client of a 32-bit host, however, can use it.

If EBX is not page-aligned, it will be rounded down to the next lower page boundary.

The page attribute buffer is an array of words, one per page, formatted as follows:

Bits 0–2   Page type

                   0 = Uncommitted page

                   1 = Committed page

                   2 = Mapped page

Bit 3

    0 = Page is read-only

    1 = Page is read/write

Bits 4–6

    0 = Page accessed/page dirty bits not available

    1 = Page has not been accessed, page is not dirty

    3 = Page has been accessed, page is not dirty

    5 = Page has not been accessed, page is dirty

    7 = Page has been accessed, page is dirty

Bits 7–15   Reserved

Int 31h	Function 0507h	DPMI Version 1.0
	Set Page Attributes	

Sets the attributes of one or more pages in a linear memory block allocated with Function 0504h

Calling registers: AX   0507h

                         ESI   Memory block handle

                         EBX   Offset in memory block of page or pages whose attributes are to be changed

                         ECX   Number of pages

                         ES:EDX Selector:offset of a buffer containing page attributes

Return registers: If successful

                         Carry flag clear

                         If unsuccessful

                         Carry flag set

                         AX   Error code

                                        8001h, unsupported function

                                        8002h, page is in wrong state

                                        8013h, physical memory unavailable

                                        8014h, backing store unavailable

                                        8021h, illegal value in bits 0–2 of one or more page attribute words

                                        8023h, invalid handle

                                        8025h, linear address not in memory block

Comments: A 16-bit host will not support this function. A 16-bit client on a 32-bit host, however, can use this function.

An uncommitted page can be created from a committed page or a mapped page. A committed page can be created from an uncommitted page or a mapped page.

The attribute word has the following format:

Bits 0–2   Page type

0 = Change page type to uncommitted

1 = Change page type to committed

2 = Invalid

3 = Modify attributes without changing page type

4–7, Invalid

Bit 3

0 = Make page read-only

1 = Make page read-write

Bits 4–6

0 = Do not modify page accessed/page dirty bits

1 = Mark page as not accessed, not dirty

3 = Mark page as accessed, not dirty

5 = Mark page as not accessed, dirty

7 = Mark page as accessed, dirty

Bits 7–15   Reserved; should be zero

The page accessed/page dirty bits are modified only if the host supports Page Accessed/Dirty.

Int 31h	Function 0508h	DPMI Version 1.0
	Map Device in Memory Block	

Maps the physical address assigned to a device onto the linear addresses of a memory block allocated by Function 0504h

Calling registers: AX   0508h
                             ESI   Memory block handle

	EBX	Offset within memory block of page or pages to be mapped (must be page-aligned)
	ECX	Number of pages to map
	EDX	Physical address of device (must be page-aligned)
Return registers:	If successful	
	Carry flag clear	
	If unsuccessful	
	Carry flag set	
	AX	Error code
		8001h, unsupported function
		8003h, invalid device address
		8023h, invalid handle
		8025h, linear address not in memory block or not page-aligned

Comments: Sixteen-bit hosts will not support this function; 16-bit clients running under 32-bit hosts, however, can use it.

This function is optional; applications programs or DOS extenders that require this function are *not* DPMI compliant.

Committed or mapped pages will be uncommitted or unmapped by the host.

Unlike Function 0800h, this function supports mapping a physical device within an existing memory block (which gives 32-bit programs the capability to access the device with near pointers) and can map addresses below 1M, such as display adapter refresh buffers.

Int 31h	**Function 0509h**	**DPMI Version 1.0**
	Map Conventional Memory in Memory Block	

Maps physical addresses below 1M to the linear addresses of a memory block allocated by Function 0504h

Calling registers:	AX	0509h
	ESI	Memory block handle
	EBX	Offset within memory block of page or pages to be mapped (must be page-aligned)
	ECX	Number of pages to map
	EDX	Linear address of conventional memory (must be page-aligned)
Return registers:	If successful	
	Carry flag clear	

If unsuccessful
Carry flag set

AX   Error code
                      8001h, unsupported function
                      8003h, invalid conventional memory address
                      8023h, invalid handle
                      8025h, linear address not in memory block or not
                         page-aligned

Comments: Sixteen-bit hosts will not support this function; 16-bit clients running under 32-bit hosts, however, can use it.

This function is optional; applications programs or DOS extenders that require this function are *not* DPMI compliant.

Committed or mapped pages will be uncommitted or unmapped by the host.

A client may map only conventional memory it already owns, either with a call to Function 0100h or with a call to DOS's Int 21h, Function 48h through the translation services.

Int 31h	Function 050Ah	DPMI Version 1.0
	Get Memory Block Size and Base	

Returns the size of a memory block that was allocated by Function 0501h or 0504h

Calling registers: AX   050Ah
                         SI:DI   Memory block handle

Return registers: If successful
                         Carry flag clear
                         SI:DI   Size of memory block in bytes
                         BX:CX   Base address of memory block
                         If unsuccessful
                         Carry flag set
                         AX   8023h, invalid handle

Comments: This function will fail in DPMI Version 0.9.

Int 31h	Function 050Bh	DPMI Version 1.0
	Get Memory Information	

Returns information about available physical and virtual memory

Calling registers: AX   050Bh
                         ES:(E)DI   Selector:offset of 128-byte buffer

Return registers: If successful
Carry flag clear
Buffer updated
If unsuccessful
Carry flag set

Comments: This function will fail in DPMI 0.9.

The buffer is formatted as follows:

Offset	Length	Contents
00h	Dword	Total allocated bytes of physical memory controlled by the host
04h	Dword	Total allocated bytes of virtual memory controlled by the host
08h	Dword	Total available bytes of virtual memory controlled by the host
0Ch	Dword	Total allocated bytes of virtual memory for this virtual machine
10h	Dword	Total available bytes of virtual memory for this virtual machine
14h	Dword	Total allocated bytes of virtual memory for this client
18h	Dword	Total available bytes of virtual memory for this client
1Ch	Dword	Total locked bytes of memory for this client
20h	Dword	Maximum locked bytes of memory for this client
24h	Dword	Highest linear address available to this client
28h	Dword	Size in bytes of largest available free memory block
2Ch	Dword	Size of minimum allocation unit in bytes
30h	Dword	Size of allocation alignment unit in bytes
34h	76 bytes	Reserved

Int 31h   **Function 0600h**   **DPMI Version 0.9**

Lock Linear Region

Locks the specified linear address range

Calling registers: AX   0600h
                          BX:CX   Starting linear address
                          SI:DI   Size of region in bytes

Return registers: If successful
                          Carry flag clear
                          If unsuccessful
                          Carry flag set
                          AX   Error code
                                      8013h, physical memory unavailable
                                      8017h, lock count exceeded
                                      8025h, invalid linear address

Comments: If the function returns unsuccessfully, none of the region is locked.

If the region overlaps part of a page at either end, the page or pages will be locked.

This function may be called more than once; a lock count is maintained.

Int 31h   **Function 0601h**   **DPMI Version 0.9**

Unlock Linear Region

Unlocks a region that was locked by Function 0600h

Calling registers: AX   0601h
                          BX:CX   Starting address of region
                          SI:DI   Size of region

Return registers: If successful
                          Carry flag clear
                          If unsuccessful
                          Carry flag set
                          AX   Error code
                                      8002h, page not locked
                                      8025h, invalid address

Comments: If the function returns an error, none of the memory was unlocked. The region is not unlocked until the lock count is zero; that is, there must be the same number of calls to this function as to Function 0600h.

Int 31h	Function 0602h	DPMI Version 0.9
	Mark Real Mode Region as Pageable	

Marks a region of memory below 1M as pageable to disk

Calling registers:
AX	0602h
BX:CX	Starting address
SI:DI	Size of region in bytes

Return registers:
If successful
Carry flag clear
If unsuccessful
Carry flag set
AX	Error code
	8002h, region already marked pageable
	8025h, address is above 1M boundary

Comments: If an error occurs, none of the memory is marked pageable. Unlike the lock state, if the region overlaps a page at either end, the overlapped pages will not be marked pageable and multiple calls to this function have no effect.

On termination, the client program should relock the memory with a call to Function 0603. DPMI 1.0 hosts will do so automatically on client termination, but DPMI 0.9 won't. Failure to do so could result in fatal page faults when another program executes in the same space.

The client should mark only the space it owns (that it acquired through calls to Function 0100h or by a direct call to the DOS memory allocation service). In particular, areas owned by DOS or the DPMI host should not be marked as pageable; to do so could result in a fatal page fault.

Int 31h	Function 0603h	DPMI Version 0.9
	Relock Real Mode Region	

Relocks a memory region previously marked pageable by Function 0602h

Calling registers:
AX	0603h
BX:CX	Starting address of memory to relock
SI:DI	Size of region in bytes

913

Return registers: If successful
Carry flag clear
If unsuccessful
Carry flag set
AX Error code
8002h, region not marked pageable
8013h, physical memory not available
8025h, region is above 1M boundary

Comments: If an error occurs, none of the region is relocked. Pages that overlap either end of the region are not relocked.

Int 31h **Function 0604h** **DPMI Version 0.9**

Get Page Size

Returns the size of a single memory page in bytes

Calling register: AX 0604h

Return registers: If successful
Carry flag clear
BX:CX Page size in bytes
If unsuccessful
Carry flag set
AX 8001h, unsupported function

Comments: This function returns the basic memory-allocation block size.

Int 31h **Function 0702h** **DPMI Version 0.9**

Mark Page as Demand Paging Candidate

Marks a page or set of pages to be placed at the head of the pageout candidacy list

Calling registers: AX 0702h
BX:CX Starting linear address
SI:DI Size of region in bytes

Return registers: If successful
Carry flag clear
If unsuccessful
Carry flag set
AX 8025h, range unallocated

Comments: This function does not force the indicated pages out of memory, and may be treated by the host as advisory. Partial pages will not be marked.

This function is useful if a client knows that the contents of the region will not be accessed for a long time and that the memory it occupies can be better utilized.

Int 31h   **Function 0703h**   **DPMI Version 0.9**

Discard Page Contents

Discards the contents of a specified linear address range so that it is not paged to disk unnecessarily

Calling registers: AX   0703h
                        BX:CX   Starting linear address
                        SI:DI   Size of region to discard in bytes

Return registers: If successful
                        Carry flag clear
                        If unsuccessful
                        Carry flag set
                        AX   8025h, range unallocated

Comments: Partial pages and locked pages will not be discarded. The contents of the discarded pages are not defined.

Int 31h   **Function 0800h**   **DPMI Version 0.9**

Physical Address Mapping

Converts a physical address into a linear address

Calling registers: AX   0800h
                        BX:CX   Physical address
                        SI:DI   Size of region in bytes

Return registers: If successful
                        Carry flag clear
                        BX:CX   Linear address
                        If unsuccessful
                        Carry flag set
                        AX   Error code
                                  8003h, address is in DPMI host memory region
                                  8021h, address is below 1M boundary

915

Comments: This function should be used only by clients that require direct access to a memory-mapped device above the 1M boundary.

The client is responsible for allocating and initializing a descriptor to access the region.

Int 31h   Function 0801h   DPMI Version 0.9

Free Physical Address Mapping

Releases a mapping of physical addresses to linear addresses previously obtained with Function 0800h

| **Calling registers:** | AX | 0801h |
| | BX:CX | Linear address to be released |

Return registers:	If successful	
	Carry flag clear	
	If unsuccessful	
	Carry flag set	
	AX	8025h, invalid address

Comments: The client should use this function when it is finished using the device mapped with Function 0800h.

Int 31h   Function 0900h   DPMI Version 0.9

Get and Disable Virtual Interrupt State

Disables the virtual interrupt flag and returns the previous state of the flag

| **Calling register:** | AX | 0900h |

Return registers:	Carry flag clear	
	AL	Previous status
		0, virtual interrupts previously disabled
		1, virtual interrupts previously enabled

Comments: AH is not modified by this function call; a client can restore the previous state without knowing what it was by simply calling Int 31h again.

The user can use CLI also to disable interrupts; the DPMI host will probably trap the instruction, however. The client must assume that CLI will execute very slowly.

916

Int 31h   Function 0901h   DPMI Version 0.9

Get and Enable Virtual Interrupt State

Enables the virtual interrupt flag and returns the previous state of the flag

Calling register: AX   0901h

Return registers: Carry flag clear
                         AL   Previous status
                                     0, virtual interrupts previously disabled
                                     1, virtual interrupts previously enabled

Comments: AH is not modified by this function call; a client can restore the previous state without knowing what it was by simply calling Int 31h again.

The user can use STI also to disable interrupts; the DPMI host will probably trap the instruction, however. The client must assume that CLI will execute very slowly.

Int 31h   Function 0902h   DPMI Version 0.9

Get Virtual Interrupt State

Returns the current state of the virtual interrupt flag

Calling register: AX   0902h

Return registers: Carry flag clear
                         AL   Virtual interrupt state
                                     0, virtual interrupts are disabled
                                     1, virtual interrupts are enabled

Comments: This function should be used instead of the PUSHF instruction because PUSHF returns the physical interrupt flag instead of the virtualized, per-client, interrupt flag.

Int 31h   Function 0A00h   DPMI Version 0.9

Get Vendor-Specific API Entry Point

Returns the address of a routine that can be called to access host-specific extensions to DPMI

Calling registers: AX   0A00h
                          DS:(E)SI   Selector:offset of null-terminated string identifying the
                                      DPMI host vendor

Return registers: If successful
                         Carry flag clear
                         ES:(E)DI   Selector:offset of extended API entry point
                         Other registers may be modified also
                         If unsuccessful
                         Carry flag set
                         AX   8001h, extension not found

Comments: The address returned should be accessed by a far call. Additional requirements are specified by the vendor. The string comparison is case-sensitive.

DPMI 1.0 clients should use Int 2Fh, Function 168Ah instead of this function.

Int 31h	Function 0B00h	DPMI Version 0.9
	Set Debug Watchpoint	

Sets a debug watchpoint at the specified address

Calling registers: AX   0B00h
                          BX:CX   Linear address
                          DL   Size of watchpoint (1, 2, or 4 bytes)
                          DH   Type of watchpoint
                                    0, execute
                                    1, write
                                    2, read/write

Return registers: If successful
                          Carry flag clear
                          BX   Watchpoint handle
                          If unsuccessful
                          Carry flag set
                          AX   Error code
                                    8016h, too many watchpoints
                                    8021h, invalid size or type of watchpoint
                                    8025h, linear address not mapped or alignment error

Comments: The handle returned is in the range 0–14 under DPMI 1.0; the range is unrestricted under DPMI 0.9.

Int 31h   Function 0B01h   DPMI Version 0.9

Clear Debug Watchpoint

Clears a watchpoint previously set with Function 0B00h and releases the handle

Calling registers: AX   0B01h
                        BX   Watchpoint handle

Return registers: If successful
                        Carry flag clear
                        If unsuccessful
                        Carry flag set
                        AX   8023h, invalid handle

Comments: This function should be called before terminating.

Int 31h   Function 0B02h   DPMI Version 0.9

Get State of Debug Watchpoint

Returns the state of a watchpoint previously set with Function 0B00h

Calling registers: AX   0B02h
                        BX   Watchpoint handle

Return registers: If successful
                        Carry flag clear
                        AX   Status
                        Bit 0   0, watchpoint not encountered
                                        1, watchpoint encountered
                        Bits 1–15   Reserved
                        If unsuccessful
                        Carry flag set
                        AX   8023h, invalid handle

Comments: Use Function 0B03h to clear the watchpoint's status without releasing the watchpoint.

Int 31h   **Function 0B03h**   **DPMI Version 0.9**

Reset Debug Watchpoint

Resets the state of the watchpoint so that a subsequent call to Function 0B02h will show no encounter

Calling registers: AX   0B03h
                          BX   Watchpoint handle

Return registers: If successful
                          Carry flag clear
                          If unsuccessful
                          Carry flag set
                          AX   8023h, invalid handle

Comments: This function should be called after a watchpoint is encountered.

Int 31h   **Function 0C00h**   **DPMI Version 1.0**

Install Resident Service Provider Callback

Used by resident service providers to request notification from the host whenever another DPMI client in the same virtual machine is loaded or terminated

Calling registers: AX   0C00h
                          ES:(E)DI   Selector:offset of 40-byte buffer, structured as follows:

Offset	Length	Contents
00h	8 bytes	Descriptor for a 16-bit data segment
08h	8 bytes	Descriptor for a 16-bit code segment
10h	2 bytes	Offset of a 16-bit callback procedure
12h	2 bytes	Reserved
14h	8 bytes	Descriptor for a 32-bit data segment
1Ch	8 bytes	Descriptor for a 32-bit code segment
24h	4 bytes	Offset of a 32-bit callback procedure

Return registers: If successful

Carry flag clear

If unsuccessful

Carry flag set

AX   Error code

8015h, callback unavailable

8021h, invalid access rights or type bytes; offset outside segment limits

8025h, descriptor references an illegal linear address range

Comments: Only a DPMI client that intends to provide resident protected mode services should call this function; the client must subsequently terminate and stay resident using Function 0C01h. DPMI clients that intend to provide only resident real mode services should not use this function.

The buffer is easily initialized by using Function 000Bh to get copies of its code and data descriptors. If only one mode, 16 or 32 bits, is to be provided, the code descriptor for the unsupported mode should be set to zero.

Int 31h	Function 0C01h	DPMI Version 1.0
	Terminate and Stay Resident	

Terminates the DPMI client's execution while leaving its protected mode and memory, and possibly some real mode memory, allocated

Calling registers: AX   0C01h

BL   Return code

DX   Number of paragraphs of DOS memory to reserve

Return registers: None; does not return

Comments: This function should be used only by DPMI clients providing resident services to other DPMI protected mode clients. A client that wants to provide resident services to only real mode programs should use Function 0300h to invoke DOS's Int 21h, Function 31h directly.

The value in DX is the number of DOS memory paragraphs; the DPMI host automatically leaves allocated all protected mode memory. The value in DX must be either 0 or a minimum of 6. If DX is 0, the DOS Int 21h, Function 4Ch function is called instead of Function 31h.

If the client has not called Function 0C00h beforehand, the client is simply terminated.

Int 31h   **Function 0D00h**   **DPMI Version 1.0**

Allocate Shared Memory

Allocates a block of memory that may be shared by DPMI clients

Calling registers: AX   0D00h

ES:(E)DI   Selector:offset of shared memory-allocation request
              structure, formatted as follows:

Offset	Length	Contents
00h	4 bytes	Length of memory block (set by client) may be zero
04h	4 bytes	Length actually allocated (set by host)
08h	4 bytes	Handle (set by host)
0Ch	4 bytes	Linear address of block (set by host)
10h	6 bytes	32-bit offset:selector of null-terminated ASCII name of block (set by client)
16h	2 bytes	Reserved
18h	4 bytes	Reserved; must be zero

Return registers: If successful
                          Carry flag clear
                          Fields at offsets 04h, 08h, and 0Ch updated
                          If unsuccessful
                          Carry flag set
                          AX   Error code
                                        8012h, linear memory unavailable
                                        8013h, physical memory unavailable
                                        8014h, backing store unavailable
                                        8016h, handle unavailable
                                        8021h, name too long

Comments: Sixteen-bit clients must set the high word of the 32-bit offset to zero. The maximum name length is 128 bytes, including the terminating null.

The linear address provided is guaranteed to be the same for all clients in the same virtual machine using the shared memory block. The client must establish addressability by allocating and initializing a descriptor itself.

No assumptions should be made about handle values; successive allocations of the same block by the same client may return different values.

The first client to allocate a shared memory block determines its size. Other clients may allocate the same block with a different size, but the size allocated will be the same as that reported to the first client.

A size of 0 is legal; the handle returned can be used with the serialization Functions 0D02h and 0D03h. The linear address is undefined, and referencing it may result in a page fault.

The first 16 bytes of the block will be set to zero on the first allocation. Clients can use this as an "area initialized" indicator.

Int 31h   **Function 0D01h**   **DPMI Version 1.0**

                     Free Shared Memory

Frees a block of shared memory allocated by Function 0D00h

Calling registers: AX   0D01h
                         SI:DI   Handle of block

Return registers: If successful
                         Carry flag clear
                         If unsuccessful
                         Carry flag set
                         AX   8023h, invalid handle

Comments: The handle is invalidated by a successful call.

It is the client's responsibility to free any descriptors used to map the block.

Two counts are maintained by the host: a virtual machine use count, which is the count of successful allocation calls for the block within the virtual machine, and a global use count, which is a count of virtual machines with access to the block. When the virtual machine count is zero, clients in that virtual machine no longer can address the block. When the global use count is zero, the block is destroyed by the host.

Int 31h   **Function 0D02h**   **DPMI Version 1.0**

                     Serialize on Shared Memory

Requests serialization of a shared memory block

Calling registers:

	AX	0D02h
	SI:DI	Handle of block
	DX	Flags
	Bit 0	0, suspend client until serialization available
		1, return immediately with error if serialization unavailable
	Bit 1	0, exclusive serialization request
		1, shared serialization request
	Bits 2–15	Reserved; must be zero

Return registers:

If successful
Carry flag clear
If unsuccessful
Carry flag set

	AX	Error code
		8004h, host detected deadlock
		8005h, request canceled by Function 0D03h
		8017h, lock count exceeded
		8018h, exclusive serialization owned by another client
		8019h, shared serialization owned by another client
		8023h, invalid handle

Comments: Successful serialization equates to ownership and right of access to the block. This system is used by DPMI clients to synchronize inspection and modification of the block.

Exclusive serialization is equivalent to ownership for writing; shared serialization is equivalent to read-only access. A successful request for exclusive serialization will block other requests, both exclusive and shared. A successful request for shared serialization will block requests for exclusive serialization.

Clients that poll a block by setting bit 0 of DX should yield the CPU with calls to Int 2F, Function 1680h when appropriate.

Clients blocked by waiting for the block can still service interrupts. A suspended serialization call may return when a client interrupt service routine calls Function 0D03h, freeing serialization. Error code 8005 is returned in this case.

The host is not required to detect deadlock.

Int 31h	Function 0D03h	DPMI Version 1.0
	Free Serialization on Shared Memory	

Releases a shared memory serialization previously obtained by a successful call to Function 0D02h

Calling registers: AX   0D03h
                            SI:DI   Handle
                            DX   Flags
                            Bit 0   0, release exclusive serialization
                                      1, release shared serialization
                            Bit 1   0, do not free pending serialization
                                      1, free pending serialization
                            Bits 2–15 Reserved; must be zero

Return registers: If successful
                            Carry flag clear
                            If unsuccessful
                            Carry flag set
                            AX   Error code
                                      8002h, client does not own the specified type of
                                            serialization
                                      8023h, invalid handle

Comments: This function should be called when the caller has finished using the shared memory.

Int 31h   **Function 0E00h**   **DPMI Version 1.0**

                     Get Coprocessor Status

Returns status about the existence of a coprocessor, the type of coprocessor, and whether the host supports coprocessor emulation

Calling register: AX   0E00h

Return registers: If successful
                            Carry flag clear
                            AX   Coprocessor status
                            Bit 0   0, numeric coprocessor disabled for this client
                                      1, numeric coprocessor enabled for this client
                            Bit 1   0, client is not emulating coprocessor instructions
                                      1, client is emulating coprocessor instructions
                            Bit 2   0, numeric coprocessor is not present
                                      1, numeric coprocessor is present
                            Bit 3   0, host is not emulating coprocessor instructions
                                      1, host is emulating coprocessor instructions

Bits 4–7 Coprocessor type
00h, no coprocessor
02h, 80287
03h, 80387
04h, 80486 with numeric coprocessor
Bits 8–15 Reserved

If unsuccessful (DPMI version 0.9)
Carry flag set

Comments: If bit 2 and bits 4–7 are in conflict, ignore bit 2.

Int 31h	**Function 0E01h**	**DPMI Version 1.0**
	Set Processor Emulation	

Enables or disables the numeric processor for the virtual machine and the reflection of coprocessor exceptions to the client

Calling registers: AX 0E01h
BX Flags
Bit 0 0, disable numeric coprocessor for this client
1, enable numeric coprocessor for this client
Bit 1 0, client will not supply coprocessor emulation
1, client will supply coprocessor emulation
Bits 2–15 Reserved

Return registers: If successful
Carry flag clear
If unsuccessful
Carry flag set
AX 8026h, invalid request

Comments: The client should register an exception handler for coprocessor-not-present faults before setting bit 1.

926

Task-Switching Reference

Task switching is a feature introduced with DOS 5. Provided by DOS 5.0's shell, it enables the user to suspend one program and start another, and then resume the suspended program where it left off. It is not a true multitasking system; the suspended program is removed from memory, its image is saved to disk, and the new program is loaded. The suspended program does no work, therefore, and the newly loaded program works alone.

The environment of task switching has two classes of programs: *task switchers*, which manage the task sessions, and *client programs*, which are the user programs that run under the management of a task switcher. Microsoft has documented three classes of functions required for task switching: notification services, service functions, and task switcher services. *Notification services* are provided by the client programs and used by the task switcher to notify the client programs of task switches and session events. *Service functions* are provided by the task switcher for client programs to control switching, to get information about the task switcher, and to get information about other client programs. *Task-switcher services* are functions provided by task switchers for other task switchers.

Data Structures

Several data structures are used in task switching. The functions invariably involve pointers to one or more of these structures. This section describes these structures in both C and assembler format.

SWAPIINFO

The SWAPIINFO structure describes the level of support a client program provides for a particular type of asynchronous API. This structure is provided for the use of network managers operating under a task switcher.

```
SWAPIINFO struc
    aisLength      dw   10
    aisAPI         dw   ?
    aisMajor       dw   ?
    aisMinor       dw   ?
    aisSupport     dw   ?
SWAPIINFO ends

struct SWAPIINFO
    {
    unsigned int   aisLength;
    unsigned int   aisAPI;
    unsigned int   aisMajor;
    unsigned int   aisMinor;
    unsigned int   aisSupport;
    };
```

aisLength is the length of the structure, in bytes. It should be 10.

aisAPI identifies the interface supported by the client program. Valid values and their meanings are shown in the following table:

Value	Meaning
0001h	NETBIOS interface
0002h	802.2 interface
0003h	TCP/IP interface
0004h	LAN Manager Named Pipes interface
0005h	NetWare IPX interface

All other values are reserved.

aisMajor identifies the highest major version of the application for which the client program provides the support described in the aisSupport field.

aisMinor identifies the highest minor version of the application for which the client program provides the support described in the aisSupport field.

aisSupport identifies the level of support provided by the client program for the interface described by the aisAPI, aisMajor, and aisMinor fields. Valid values and their meanings are shown in the following table:

Value	Meaning
0001h	Minimal support. The client program prevents a session switch after an application has called a function supported by the API, even after the request has been completed.
0002h	API-level support. The client program tracks asynchronous requests, prevents task switches when requests are outstanding, and allows task switches when all requests have been completed.
0003h	Switcher compatibility. The API provider allows switches to occur even when asynchronous requests are outstanding. This may be limited by resource limitations; some requests may fail.
0004h	Seamless compatibility. The API provider always allows session switches to occur.

SWCALLBACKINFO

The SWCALLBACKINFO structure contains information about the client program:

```
SWCALLBACKINFO struc
      scbiNext       dd   ?
      scbiEntryPoint dd   ?
      scbiReserved   dd   ?
      scbiAPI        dd   ?
SWCALLBACKINFO ends

struct SWCALLBACKINFO
      {
      struct SWCALLBACKINFO far     *scbiNext;
      void far                      *scbiEntryPoint;
      long                           scbiReserved;
      struct SWAPIINFO far          *scbiAPI;
      };
```

scbiNext is a 32-bit pointer (segment:offset) to the next SWCALLBACKINFO structure in the notification chain.

scbiEntryPoint is a 32-bit pointer (segment:offset) to the client's notification function handler. The task switcher uses this address to call the client program's notification functions.

scbiReserved is a reserved area; do not use it.

scbiAPI is a 32-bit pointer (segment:offset) of a zero-terminated list of SWAPIINFO structures that specify the type of support the client program provides for various asynchronous APIs.

SWINSTANCEITEM

The SWINSTANCEITEM structure contains information about a block of instance data. It is uncertain what such a block is; it is free-form enough to contain just about anything:

```
SWINSTANCEITEM struc
    iisPtr    dd   ?
    iisSize   dw   ?
SWINSTANCEITEM ends

struct SWINSTANCEITEM
    {
    void far        *iisPtr;
    unsigned int    iisSize;
    };
```

iisPtr is a 32-bit pointer (*segment:offset*) of a block of instance data.

iisSize is the size of the block of instance data in bytes.

SWSTARTUPINFO

The SWSTARTUPINFO structure contains information about a client program's instance data:

```
SWSTARTUPINFO struc
    sisVersion        dw   ?
    sisNextDev        dd   ?
    sisVirtDevFile    dd   0
    sisReferenceData  dd   ?
    sisInstanceData   dd   ?
SWSTARTUPINFO ends

struct SWSTARTUPINFO
    {
    int                        sisVersion;
    struct SWSTARTUPINFO far   *sisNextDev;
    long                       sisVirtDevFile;
    long                       sisReferenceData;
    struct SWINSTANCEITEM far  *sisInstanceData;
    };
```

sisVersion is not used.

sisNextDev is a 32-bit pointer (segment:offset) to the next SWSTARTUPINFO structure in the notification chain.

sisVirtDevFile is not used.

sisReferenceData is not used.

sisInstaceData is a 32-bit pointer (segment:offset) to a zero-terminated list of SWINSTANCEITEM structures.

SWVERSION

The SWVERSION structure contains information about the task switcher:

```
SWVERSION struc
    svsAPIMajor         dw    ?
    svsAPIMinor         dw    ?
    svsProductMajor     dw    ?
    svsProductMinor     dw    ?
    svsSwitcherID       dw    ?
    svsFlags            dw    ?
    svsName             dd    ?
    svsPrevSwitcher     dd    ?
SWVERSION ends

struct SWVERSION
    {
    unsigned int    svsAPIMajor;
    unsigned int    svsAPIMinor;
    unsigned int    svsProductMajor;
    unsigned int    svsProductMinor;
    unsigned int    svsSwitcherID;
    unsigned int    svsFlags;
    char far        *svsName;
    void far        *svsPrevSwitcher;
    };
```

svsAPIMajor is the highest major version of the task-switching protocol supported by the task switcher.

svsAPIMinor is the highest minor version of the task-switching protocol supported by the task switcher.

svsProductMajor is the major version of the task switcher.

svsProductMinor is the minor version of the task switcher.

svsSwitcherID is the switcher identifier. Each switcher has a unique 4-bit identifier; the identifier is the low-order four bits of this field.

svsFlags is the task switcher's operation flags. Currently, only bit 0 is defined; the others are reserved and must be zero. If bit 0 is set, the switcher is currently disabled; if bit 0 is zero, the switcher is enabled.

svsName is the 32-bit pointer (segment:offset) to the zero-terminated ASCII string containing the task switcher's name.

svsPrevSwitcher is the 32-bit pointer (segment:offset) to the previously loaded task switcher. This address can be used to call the previously loaded task switcher's service-function handler.

931

Notification Functions

This section describes the notification functions in a manner similar to the way interrupt functions are described elsewhere in this book.

The client program's notification function handler address is provided to the task switcher and the program that invokes and controls the task switcher by Interrupt 2F, Function 4B, Subfunction 01 (Build Notification Chain). The task switcher, or the program that controls and invokes it, calls the notification handlers with AX containing the function number, and with other registers in use also.

Notification Function 0000h   V5

Init Switcher

Notifies client programs that a new task switcher is being initialized

Calling registers:	AX	0000h
	ES:DI	Service function handler
Return register:	AX	Status
		0000h, task switcher can be loaded safely
		Nonzero, task switcher cannot be loaded safely

Comments: Task switchers or their controlling programs or both must call this function when they are initialized. The task switcher's service function handler, if present, must support Service Function 0000h (Get Version). The service function handler can be a NULL pointer, however, especially if the task switcher's control program is calling the notification function.

If any client program responds negatively (sets AX to nonzero on return), the task switcher should disable itself. The task switcher may make Notification Handler 0007 (Switcher Exit) calls to the other client programs. Client programs should ignore this call if it occurs without a preceding Init Switcher call.

Interrupts are enabled before the notification function is called. The client program may call any MS-DOS system function while servicing the notification call. The client program is allowed to modify the AX register, but must preserve the other registers.

Notification Function 0001h   V5

Query Suspend

Notifies the client programs that the task switcher is preparing to perform a session switch

Calling registers:	AX	0001h
	BX	Current session identifier
	ES:DI	Service function handler

Return registers: AX   Status

                                          0000, switch is allowed

                                          0001, switch is not allowed

                     All other values are reserved

Comments: Client programs in global memory can tell by the session identifier which session is about to be suspended when the switch occurs.

By calling Service Function 0001h (Test Memory Region), client programs can tell whether specific code or data in memory will be affected by the switch and whether the switch should be allowed.

Before blocking a session switch because of the state of an asynchronous API, the client should call Service Function 0006 (Query API Support) to make sure that another client program is not handling the API.

If any client program sends a nonzero response, the task switcher may make a Notification Handler 0002 (Session Active) call to all client programs. Client programs should ignore the Session Active call without a preceding call to Query Suspend or Suspend Session.

Interrupts are enabled before the notification function is called. The client program may call any MS-DOS system function while servicing the notification call. The client program is allowed to modify the AX register, but must preserve the other registers.

Notification Function 0002h   V5

Suspend Session

Notifies client programs that a session switch is about to take place

Calling registers: AX   0002h

                            BX   Session ID

                            ES:DI   Service function handler

Return register: Status

                                           0000h, switch is allowed

                                           0001h, switch is not allowed

                     All other values are reserved

Comments: If all client programs return 0000h to Notification Function 0001 (Query Suspend), the task switcher disables interrupts and calls Suspend Session. This is the client programs' last chance to prevent the session switch. Client programs must not issue software interrupts or make any calls that might enable interrupts.

If all client programs return 0000h, the task switcher replaces the current interrupt table with a saved copy before enabling interrupts; this ensures that no local interrupt handlers are called between the time that Suspend Session is called and Active Session is called.

Client programs in global memory can receive interrupts, but must not use nonglobal memory.

Before blocking a session switch because of the state of an asynchronous API, the client should call Service Function 0006 (Query API Support) to make sure that another client program is not handling the API.

If any client program sends a nonzero response, the task switcher may make a Notification Handler 0002 (Session Active) call to all client programs. Client programs should ignore the Session Active call without a preceding call to Query Suspend or Suspend Session.

Interrupts are disabled before the notification function is called. The client program may not call any MS-DOS system functions while servicing the notification call. The client program is allowed to modify the AX register, but must preserve the other registers.

Notification Function 0003h   V5

Activate Session

Notifies client programs that a session is about to become active

Calling registers:	AX	0003h
	BX	Session ID
	CX	Session status flags
		Bit 0
		1, session is being activated for the first time
		0, session was suspended and is now being resumed
	All other bits are reserved and must be zero	
	ES:DI	Service function handler
Return register:	AX	0000h

Comments: If a suspended session is being resumed, local memory has been reloaded, including the vector table.

If the session is being activated for the first time, it is preceded by a Create Session call.

Interrupts are disabled before the notification function is called. The client program may not call any MS-DOS system functions while servicing the notification call. The client program must clear the AX register and preserve the other registers.

Notification Function 0004h   V5

Session Active

Notifies client programs that a session has become active

Calling registers: AX   0004h
BX   Session ID
CX   Session status flags
Bit 0
1, session is active for the first time
0, session was suspended and has now resumed
All other bits are reserved and must be zero
ES:DI   Service function handler

Return register: AX   0000h

Comments: If any client fails a Query Suspend or Suspend Session call, the task switcher may call all client programs with a Session Active call, whether or not they had received a Query Suspend or Suspend Session call. Client programs should ignore the call.

Interrupts are enabled by the task switcher, and the client program may make any MS-DOS system function calls. The client must clear the AX registers and must preserve the other registers.

Notification Function 0005h   V5

Create Session

Notifies client programs that the task switcher is about to create a new session

Calling registers: AX   0005h
BX   Session ID for the new session
ES:DI   Service function handler

Return register: AX   Status
0000h, new session can be created safely
0001h, new session cannot be created safely
All other values are reserved

Comments: This call is made to allow client programs to block creation of a new session.

If any client program responds with 0001, the task switcher may make a Destroy Session call to all client programs. Client programs that receive a Destroy Session without a preceding Create Session should ignore that call.

Interrupts are enabled by the task switcher, and the client program can make any MS-DOS system function calls. The client must modify the AX register and must preserve the other registers.

Notification Function 0006h   V5

Destroy Session

Notifies client programs that the task switcher is about to destroy a session

Calling registers:	AX	0006h
	BX	Session ID for session to be destroyed
	ES:DI	Service function handler
Return register:	AX	0000h

Comments: The task switcher typically makes this call when the program in the current session terminates. It may be made, however, at the behest of the session manager, and may apply to the current session while the program is running or to a suspended session.

This call may be made without a preceding Create Session for the session if another client program has failed a Create Session call. Client programs should take no action in this case.

Interrupts are enabled by the task switcher, and the client program may make any MS-DOS system function calls. The client program must clear the AX register and preserve all other registers.

Notification Function 0007h   V5

Switcher Exit

Notifies client programs that the task switcher is no longer active

Calling registers:	AX	0007h
	BX	Flags
		Bit 0
		1, the task switcher is the only one present
		0, at least one other task switcher is active
	All other bits are reserved and must be zero	
	ES:DI	Service function handler
Return register:	AX	0000h

Comments: To coexist with the task switcher, global client programs should stop any additional processing they are running.

This function may be called by the program controlling the task switcher rather than by the task switcher. The service function pointer, therefore, may be different from the pointer passed to other notification handle functions, and it may be a NULL pointer.

Interrupts are enabled, and the client program may make any MS-DOS system function calls. The client program must clear the AX register and preserve all other registers.

Service Functions

This section describes the service functions in a manner similar to the way interrupt functions are described elsewhere in this book.

When the task switcher makes notification calls or task switcher service calls, it provides the client program with access to the service function handler. Because these calls may be made by different task switchers or by programs controlling the task switcher, the client program must not assume that the service function handler pointer is reusable. As far as the client program is concerned, that pointer is valid only while it is processing the call from the switcher. The client program calls the service function handlers with AX containing the function number, and with other registers in use also.

Service Function 0000h   V5

Get Version

Returns the address of the current task switcher's SWVERSION structure

Calling register: AX   0000h

Return registers: Carry flag clear if successful
                         AX   0000h
                         ES:BX   Pointer to SWVERSION structure
                         Carry flag set if not supported by task switcher

Comments: The task switcher may enable interrupts and call any MS-DOS system functions. It must preserve all registers except the AX, ES, and BX registers.

Service Function 0001h   V5

Test Memory Region

Determines whether a given block of memory is global or local to the current session; local blocks are swapped out when a session switch occurs

Calling registers: AX   0001h
                         CX   Size of buffer in bytes
                         ES:DI   Address of buffer

Return register: Carry flag clear if successful
                         AX   Memory status
                                         0000h, buffer is in global memory
                                         0001h, buffer is in both global and local memory
                                         0002h, buffer is in local memory
                         All other values are reserved
                         Carry flag set if function not supported

937

Comments: A client program should make this call whenever it receives a Query Suspend or a Session Active call to determine whether its memory is deemed global or local by the task switcher. Client programs such as network managers that provide services to other programs should identify those programs as either global or local.

The task switcher must not enable interrupts or make any MS-DOS system function calls while servicing this call. While the task switcher modifies the AX register, it must preserve all other registers.

Service Function 0002h   V5

Suspend Switcher

Notifies the task switcher that it should suspend operations

Calling register: AX   0002h
                       ES:DI   Pointer to new task switcher's service function handler

Return register: Carry flag clear if successful
                       AX   Status
                                   0000h, current task switcher has suspended operations
                                   0001h, current task switcher has not suspended opera-
                                       tions; the new task switcher must not start
                                   0002h, current task switcher has not suspended opera-
                                       tions, but the new task switcher may start anyway
                       All other values are reserved
                       Carry flag set if not supported

Comments: This function should be called only by another task switcher. Client programs should respond negatively to a Query Suspend call in order to stop a task switcher from switching sessions.

When a task switcher receives this call, it should continue to service functions, but it should not respond to keyboard interrupts or attempt to switch sessions until it receives a Resume Switcher call.

Suspend Switcher calls may be nested, and normal operations should stay suspended until an equal number of calls to Resume Switcher have been received. An exception to this is when a child program running another task switcher suspends its session manager's task switcher and fails to resume it before returning control to the session manager. In that case, the session manager can safely reactivate its task switcher.

Interrupts can be enabled by the task switcher and MS-DOS system function calls can be made while servicing this call.

The new task switcher acquires the previous task switcher's service function handler pointer by a call to Detect Switcher (Interrupt 2Fh, Function 4B02h).

Service Function 0003h

V5

Resume Switcher

Notifies a suspended task switcher that it can resume operations

Calling registers: AX   0003h
                         ES:DI   Caller's service function handler

Return register: Carry flag clear if successful
                         AX   0000h
                         Carry flag set if not supported

Comments: A task switcher that has suspended another task switcher by a Suspend Switcher call should make this call to reactivate the task switcher. The task switcher should use the same service function handle address it used to make the Suspend Switcher call.

Interrupts can be enabled by the task switcher and MS-DOS system function calls can be made while servicing this call.

Service Function 0004h

V5

Hook Notification Chain

Directs the task switcher to add a SWCALLBACKINFO structure to its notification chain

Calling registers: AX   0004h
                         ES:DI   Pointer to SWCALLBACKINFO structure

Return register: Carry flag clear if successful
                         AX   0000h
                         Carry flag set if not supported

Comments: Client programs can use the Detect Switcher (Interrupt 2Fh, Function 4B02h) call to detect a task switcher and get its service function handler's address. If a task switcher is present, the client program should then call this function. The client program must fill the SWCALLBACKINFO structure before making the call.

Some task switchers may choose to call Build Notification Chain (Interrupt 2Fh, Function 4B01h) before each session switch. In this case, the task switcher may simply return from this call with no action.

If the task switcher does not make the Build Notification Chain calls, it must modify its notification chain through client programs making this call.

Before terminating, a client program must unhook itself from the notification chain by calling Unhook Notification Chain (Service Function 0005h).

Interrupts can be enabled by the task switcher and MS-DOS system function calls can be made while servicing this call.

Service Function 0005h   V5

Unhook Notification Chain

Directs the task switcher to remove a SWCALLBACKINFO structure from its notification chain

Calling registers: AX   0005h

                     ES:DI   Pointer to SWCALLBACKINFO structure

Return register: Carry flag clear if successful

                     AX   0000h

                     Carry flag set if not supported

Comments: The client program must make this call before terminating, regardless of whether its notification handler is added to the list by a Hook Notification Chain or a Build Notification Chain call.

A task switcher that rebuilds it notification chain by calling Build Notification Chain before each session switch may return from this call with no action.

Interrupts can be enabled by the task switcher and MS-DOS system function calls can be made while servicing this call.

Service Function 0006h   V5

Query API Support

Returns the address of the SWAPIINFO structure of the client program that provides the highest level of support for the specified asynchronous API

Calling registers: AX   0006h

                     BX   API ID

                                 0001h, NETBIOS interface

                                 0002h, 802.2 interface

                                 0003h, TCP/IP interface

                                 0004h, LAN Manager Named Pipes interface

                                 0005h, NetWare IPX interface

                     All other values are reserved

Return registers: Carry flag clear if successful

                     AX   0000h

                     ES:BX   Pointer to SWAPIINFO structure

                     Carry flag set if unsuccessful

Comments: Before making any decisions regarding session switching, client programs that provide API support should make this call to determine whether another client program is providing a higher level of support for the same API. If a pointer to its own SWAPIINFO structure is returned, it must decide whether to suspend a session switch. If the pointer is to another client program's SWAPIINFO structure, that client program should make the decision.

If interrupts are disabled, the task switcher must not reenable interrupts or make any MS-DOS system function calls.

DoubleSpace Reference

One of the new features introduced with DOS 6 is referred to as *DoubleSpace*. In this technique, information is stored on the disk in compressed format. It is compressed before writing to disk, and decompressed after it is read. DoubleSpace uses a programmer's API that enables you to access functions stored within DBLSPACE.BIN. These functions are of interest only if you are writing disk utility programs; the existence and performance of DoubleSpace is transparent to most application programs.

The CVF Structure

DoubleSpace utilizes what is called a compressed volume file, or CVF, to track information stored on a compressed drive. This structure implements an expanded FAT and enables better management of drive space. It is the CVF that allows DoubleSpace to allocate file space on a sector-by-sector basis, as opposed to a traditional FAT approach in which space must be allocated a cluster at a time. The CVF is composed of the following, in the order indicated:

- A BPB, based on the DOS 4.0 BIOS parameter block. This is one sector long.

- A bit-oriented FAT. In this series of bits, each bit represents the allocation status of a sector in the sector heap (another part of the CVF). If the bit is set, the sector has been allocated. The size of this part of the CVF varies.

- A reserved sector.

- An expanded FAT. This series of 4-byte entries is used to map clusters to sectors in the sector heap (another part of the CVF).

- A reserved block of 31 sectors.

- The boot sector for the DoubleSpace drive, based on a DOS 5 boot sector.

- A reserved block of unknown length.

- A normal FAT. This is a standard DOS FAT; the length can vary.

- The root directory for the compressed drive.

- A reserved block of 2 sectors.

- The sector heap. A 60-sector structure used to store data about sectors and clusters in use on the compressed drive.

API Functions

This section describes the DoubleSpace API functions in a manner similar to the way interrupt functions are described elsewhere in this book. All DoubleSpace functions are handled through the multiplex interrupt, 2Fh. They use Interrupt 2Fh, Function 4Ah, Subfunction 11h. The actual API function desired is loaded in the BX register. Other registers are used as necessary for the particular function.

DoubleSpace	**Function 0000h**	**V6**
	Get Version Number	

Returns the DoubleSpace version number and other miscellaneous information

Calling registers:	AX	4A11h
	BX	0000h
Return registers:	AX	0000h (if successful)
	BX	444Dh
	CL	First drive letter used (0=A, 1=B, and so on)
	CH	Number of drive letters used
	DX	DBLSPACE.BIN version number

Comments: For programmers, the item of most interest from this function is the value returned in CX. CL contains the first drive letter used by DoubleSpace, and CH indicates the number of drives used by the system.

DoubleSpace   Function 0001h   V6

Get Drive Mapping

Returns information about whether a specific drive uses DoubleSpace

Calling registers: AX   4A11h
                          BX   0001h
                          DL   Drive number to check (0=A, 1=B, and so on)

Return registers: AX   0000h (if successful)
                          BL   Drive information
                          BH   Drive sequence number

Comments: Returns DoubleSpace mapping information about the specified drive letter. On return, check the high bit of BL. If it is set, the drive is a DoubleSpace drive. If it is not set, the drive does not use DoubleSpace. If it is a DoubleSpace drive, the low-order seven bits of BL indicate the host (physical) drive on which the data is located. BH contains the drive sequence number used by the CVF (compressed volume file).

On return, AX is nonzero if the function was unsuccessful.

DoubleSpace   Function 0002h   V6

Swap Drive

Swaps the drive letter of a compressed drive with a host drive

Calling registers: AX   4A11h
                          BX   0002h
                          DL   DoubleSpace drive to swap (0=A, 1=B, and so on)

Return register: AX   Status (0 if successful, error code otherwise)

Comments: Used to exchange the drive letters used by DOS to refer to drives. Effectively swaps logical drives. One drive must be a DoubleSpace drive, and the other is the host (physical) drive on which the DoubleSpace data resides. Returns with an error if, when calling, DL is not a DoubleSpace drive.

DoubleSpace   Function 0005h   V6

Mount a Drive

Creates a CVF (compressed volume file) for a specific drive

945

Calling registers: AX   4A11h
                                 BX   0005h
                                 DL   Drive number to use (0=A, 1=B, and so on)
                                 ES:SI   Activation_record pointer

Return register: ES:SI   Activation_record pointer

Comments: The code necessary to use this function properly is very complicated, and Microsoft suggests that it is easier to EXEC a copy of COMMAND.COM and use the DBLSPACE.EXE /MOUNT command to create a CVF.

When you are calling this function, DL should be set to the drive number you want assigned to the drive, and ES:SI should point to the activation_record structure. On return, check the byte at offset 3 of this structure to see whether there was an error. (The reason that the error code is not returned in AX is beyond reason.) The value at that offset is 0 if there was no error; otherwise, it contains the error code.

DoubleSpace   Function 0006h   V6

Unmount a Drive

Used to deactivate a DoubleSpace drive

Calling registers: AX   4A11h
                                 BX   0006h
                                 DL   Drive number (0=A, 1=B, and so on)

Return register: AX   Status (0 if successful, error code otherwise)

Comments: This function is the opposite of Function 0005h. It is used to unmount a compressed drive. After returning successfully, the drive is no longer available.

DoubleSpace   Function 0007h   V6

Get Drive Space

Returns the number of total and free sectors on a specified drive

Calling registers: AX   4A11h
                                 BX   0007h
                                 DL   Drive to check (0=A, 1=B, and so on)

Return registers: AX   0000h (if successful)
                                 DS:SI record pointer

Comments: Call this function with DL set to the drive number of a compressed drive. On return, DS:SI points to an 8-byte record that indicates the space use information for the drive. The structure of this record is as follows:

Offset	Length	Meaning
0000	DWORD	Total sectors on drive
0004	DWORD	Free sectors on drive

DoubleSpace   Function 0008h   V6

Get File Fragment Space

Returns the capacity of the file fragment heap for a specified drive

Calling registers: AX   4A11h
                                BX   0008h
                                DL   Drive number (0=A, 1=B, and so on)

Return registers: AX   0000h (if successful)
                                BX   Maximum entries in file fragment heap
                                CX   Number of free entries

Comments: When calling this function, DL must refer to a compressed drive. The file fragment heap is used to manage allocation of space to individual files on a compressed drive. The information returned in BX indicates the maximum size of the heap, and CX indicates how many are still available. The difference between the two is the number used.

DoubleSpace   Function 0009h   V6

Get Extra Information

Returns the number of disk structures allocated by DBLSPACE.BIN

Calling registers: AX   4A11h
                                BX   0009h
                                DL   Drive number (0=A, 1=B, and so on)

Return registers: AX   0000h (if successful)
                                  CL   Number of structures

Comments: When calling this function, DL must refer to a compressed drive. The value returned in CL is the number of disk units that can be allocated by DBLSPACE.BIN. It is the same number set in DBLSPACE.INI by the `MaxRemovableDrives` setting.

947

The ASCII Character Set

Dec X_{10}	Hex X_{16}	Binary X_2	ASCII Character	Ctrl	Key
000	00	0000 0000	null	NUL	^@
001	01	0000 0001	☺	SOH	^A
002	02	0000 0010	●	STX	^B
003	03	0000 0011	♥	ETX	^C
004	04	0000 0100	◆	EOT	^D
005	05	0000 0101	♣	ENQ	^E
006	06	0000 0110	♠	ACK	^F
007	07	0000 0111	●	BEL	^G
008	08	0000 1000	■	BS	^H
009	09	0000 1001	○	HT	^I
010	0A	0000 1010	■	LF	^J
011	0B	0000 1011	♂	VT	^K
012	0C	0000 1100	♀	FF	^L
013	0D	0000 1101	♪	CR	^M
014	0E	0000 1110	♪♪	SO	^N
015	0F	0000 1111	☼	SI	^O
016	10	0001 0000	►	DLE	^P
017	11	0001 0001	◄	DC1	^Q
018	12	0001 0010	↕	DC2	^R

Dec X_{10}	Hex X_{16}	Binary X_2	ASCII Character	Ctrl	Key
019	13	0001 0011	‼	DC3	^S
020	14	0001 0100	¶	DC4	^T
021	15	0001 0101	§	NAK	^U
022	16	0001 0110	–	SYN	^V
023	17	0001 0111	↕	ETB	^W
024	18	0001 1000	↑	CAN	^X
025	19	0001 1001	↓	EM	^Y
026	1A	0001 1010	→	SUB	^Z
027	1B	0001 1011	←	ESC	^[
028	1C	0001 1100	FS	FS	^\
029	1D	0001 1101	GS	GS	^]
030	1E	0001 1110	RS	RS	^^
031	1F	0001 1111	US	US	^_
032	20	0010 0000	SP		
033	21	0010 0001	!		
034	22	0010 0010	"		
035	23	0010 0011	#		
036	24	0010 0100	$		
037	25	0010 0101	%		
038	26	0010 0110	&		
039	27	0010 0111	'		
040	28	0010 1000	(		
041	29	0010 1001	)		
042	2A	0010 1010	*		
043	2B	0010 1011	+		
044	2C	0010 1100	,		
045	2D	0010 1101	-		
046	2E	0010 1110	.		
047	2F	0010 1111	/		
048	30	0011 0000	0		
049	31	0011 0001	1		
050	32	0011 0010	2		
051	33	0011 0011	3		

Dec X_{10}	Hex X_{16}	Binary X_2	ASCII Character	Ctrl	Key
052	34	0011 0100	4		
053	35	0011 0101	5		
054	36	0011 0110	6		
055	37	0011 0111	7		
056	38	0011 1000	8		
057	39	0011 1001	9		
058	3A	0011 1010	:		
059	3B	0011 1011	;		
060	3C	0011 1100	<		
061	3D	0011 1101	=		
062	3E	0011 1110	>		
063	3F	0011 1111	?		
064	40	0100 0000	@		
065	41	0100 0001	A		
066	42	0100 0010	B		
067	43	0100 0011	C		
068	44	0100 0100	D		
069	45	0100 0101	E		
070	46	0100 0110	F		
071	47	0100 0111	G		
072	48	0100 1000	H		
073	49	0100 1001	I		
074	4A	0100 1010	J		
075	4B	0100 1011	K		
076	4C	0100 1100	L		
077	4D	0100 1101	M		
078	4E	0100 1110	N		
079	4F	0100 1111	O		
080	50	0101 0000	P		
081	51	0101 0001	Q		
082	52	0101 0010	R		
083	53	0101 0011	S		
084	54	0101 0100	T		

951

Dec X_{10}	Hex X_{16}	Binary X_2	ASCII Character	Ctrl	Key
085	55	0101 0101	U		
086	56	0101 0110	V		
087	57	0101 0111	W		
088	58	0101 1000	X		
089	59	0101 1001	Y		
090	5A	0101 1010	Z		
091	5B	0101 1011	[		
092	5C	0101 1100	\		
093	5D	0101 1101	]		
094	5E	0101 1110	^		
095	5F	0101 1111	–		
096	60	0110 0000	`		
097	61	0110 0001	a		
098	62	0110 0010	b		
099	63	0110 0011	c		
100	64	0110 0100	d		
101	65	0110 0101	e		
102	66	0110 0110	f		
103	67	0110 0111	g		
104	68	0110 1000	h		
105	69	0110 1001	i		
106	6A	0110 1010	j		
107	6B	0110 1011	k		
108	6C	0110 1100	l		
109	6D	0110 1101	m		
110	6E	0110 1110	n		
111	6F	0110 1111	o		
112	70	0111 0000	p		
113	71	0111 0001	q		
114	72	0111 0010	r		
115	73	0111 0011	s		
116	74	0111 0100	t		
117	75	0111 0101	u		
118	76	0111 0110	v		
119	77	0111 0111	w		

Dec X_{10}	Hex X_{16}	Binary X_2	ASCII Character	Ctrl	Key
120	78	0111 1000	x		
121	79	0111 1001	y		
122	7A	0111 1010	z		
123	7B	0111 1011	{		
124	7C	0111 1100	¦		
125	7D	0111 1101	}		
126	7E	0111 1110	~		
127	7F	0111 1111	DEL		
128	80	1000 0000	Ç		
129	81	1000 0001	ü		
130	82	1000 0010	é		
131	83	1000 0011	â		
132	84	1000 0100	ä		
133	85	1000 0101	à		
134	86	1000 0110	å		
135	87	1000 0111	ç		
136	88	1000 1000	ê		
137	89	1000 1001	ë		
138	8A	1000 1010	è		
139	8B	1000 1011	ï		
140	8C	1000 1100	î		
141	8D	1000 1101	ì		
142	8E	1000 1110	Ä		
143	8F	1000 1111	Å		
144	90	1001 0000	É		
145	91	1001 0001	æ		
146	92	1001 0010	Æ		
147	93	1001 0011	ô		
148	94	1001 0100	ö		
149	95	1001 0101	ò		
150	96	1001 0110	û		
151	97	1001 0111	ù		
152	98	1001 1000	ÿ		
153	99	1001 1001	Ö		

953

Dec X_{10}	Hex X_{16}	Binary X_2	ASCII Character	Ctrl	Key
154	9A	1001 1010	Ü		
155	9B	1001 1011	¢		
156	9C	1001 1100	£		
157	9D	1001 1101	¥		
158	9E	1001 1110	Pt		
159	9F	1001 1111	ƒ		
160	A0	1010 0000	á		
161	A1	1010 0001	í		
162	A2	1010 0010	ó		
163	A3	1010 0011	ú		
164	A4	1010 0100	ñ		
165	A5	1010 0101	Ñ		
166	A6	1010 0110	ª		
167	A7	1010 0111	º		
168	A8	1010 1000	¿		
169	A9	1010 1001	⌐		
170	AA	1010 1010	¬		
171	AB	1010 1011	½		
172	AC	1010 1100	¼		
173	AD	1010 1101	¡		
174	AE	1010 1110	«		
175	AF	1010 1111	»		
176	B0	1011 0000	░		
177	B1	1011 0001	▒		
178	B2	1011 0010	▓		
179	B3	1011 0011	│		
180	B4	1011 0100	┤		
181	B5	1011 0101	╡		
182	B6	1011 0110	╢		
183	B7	1011 0111	╖		
184	B8	1011 1000	╕		
185	B9	1011 1001	╣		
186	BA	1011 1010	║		
187	BB	1011 1011	╗		
188	BC	1011 1100	╝		

Dec X_{10}	Hex X_{16}	Binary X_2	ASCII Character	Ctrl	Key
189	BD	1011 1101	╜		
190	BE	1011 1110	╛		
191	BF	1011 1111	┐		
192	C0	1100 0000	└		
193	C1	1100 0001	┴		
194	C2	1100 0010	┬		
195	C3	1100 0011	├		
196	C4	1100 0100	─		
197	C5	1100 0101	┼		
198	C6	1100 0110	╞		
199	C7	1100 0111	╟		
200	C8	1100 1000	╚		
201	C9	1100 1001	╔		
202	CA	1100 1010	╩		
203	CB	1100 1011	╦		
204	CC	1100 1100	╠		
205	CD	1100 1101	═		
206	CE	1100 1110	╬		
207	CF	1100 1111	╧		
208	D0	1101 0000	╨		
209	D1	1101 0001	╤		
210	D2	1101 0010	╥		
211	D3	1101 0011	╙		
212	D4	1101 0100	╘		
213	D5	1101 0101	╒		
214	D6	1101 0110	╓		
215	D7	1101 0111	╫		
216	D8	1101 1000	╪		
217	D9	1101 1001	┘		
218	DA	1101 1010	┌		
219	DB	1101 1011	█		
220	DC	1101 1100	▄		
221	DD	1101 1101	▌		
222	DE	1101 1110	▐		
223	DF	1101 1111	▀		

Dec X_{10}	Hex X_{16}	Binary X_2	ASCII Character	Ctrl	Key
224	E0	1110 0000	α		
225	E1	1110 0001	β		
226	E2	1110 0010	Γ		
227	E3	1110 0011	π		
228	E4	1110 0100	Σ		
229	E5	1110 0101	σ		
230	E6	1110 0110	μ		
231	E7	1110 0111	τ		
232	E8	1110 1000	Φ		
233	E9	1110 1001	θ		
234	EA	1110 1010	Ω		
235	EB	1110 1011	δ		
236	EC	1110 1100	∞		
237	ED	1110 1101	ø		
238	EE	1110 1110	∈		
239	EF	1110 1111	∩		
240	F0	1111 0000	≡		
241	F1	1111 0001	±		
242	F2	1111 0010	≥		
243	F3	1111 0011	≤		
244	F4	1111 0100	⌠		
245	F5	1111 0101	⌡		
246	F6	1111 0110	÷		
247	F7	1111 0111	≈		
248	F8	1111 1000	°		
249	F9	1111 1001	•		
250	FA	1111 1010	·		
251	FB	1111 1011	√		
252	FC	1111 1100	η		
253	FD	1111 1101	^{2}		
254	FE	1111 1110	■		
255	FF	1111 1111			

Selected Memory Locations

This table of selected memory locations is provided to help you understand the way the system functions. Direct access to any of these memory locations makes a program extremely nonportable and should be avoided unless there is no other way to provide the features or response you want.

Knowing the locations of this information in memory can help you, at best, get information. Changing the information in the BIOS and DOS data areas, however, can be extremely damaging (but a lot of fun if you don't mind crashing your system).

The Interrupt Table

The absolute address range from 00000 to 003FF is the interrupt address table. This table is composed of interrupt addresses for interrupts 00 through FFh, with each address occupying four bytes. To find the address in the table for a specific interrupt, therefore, you multiply the interrupt number by 4. The absolute address for interrupt C3h, for example, is 0030Ch. In Table B.1, the numbers in the first two columns are in hexadecimal notation.

Table B.1 Interrupt addresses for interrupts 00 through FFh.

Interrupt	Address	Meaning
Int 00	00000	Hardware divide by zero
Int 01	00004	Hardware single-step trap
Int 02	00008	Non-Maskable
Int 03	0000C	Debugger breakpoint set

continues

Table B.1 Continued

Interrupt	Address	Meaning
Int 04	00010	Arithmetic overflow
Int 05	00014	BIOS print screen
Int 06	00018	Invalid opcode
Int 08	00020	IRQ0—Clock tick
Int 09	00024	IRQ1—Keyboard action
Int 0A	00028	IRQ2
Int 0B	0002C	IRQ3—COM2
Int 0C	00030	IRQ4—COM1
Int 0D	00034	IRQ5—PC/XT Hard Disk
Int 0D		IRQ5—PC AT LPT2
Int 0E	00038	IRQ6—Diskette
Int 0F	0003C	IRQ7—LPT1
Int 10	00040	BIOS video services
Int 11	00044	BIOS equipment list services
Int 12	00048	BIOS memory size services
Int 13	0004C	BIOS disk/diskette services
Int 14	00050	BIOS communications services
Int 15	00054	BIOS system services
Int 16	00058	BIOS keyboard services
Int 17	0005C	BIOS printer services
Int 18	00060	Executes ROM BASIC
Int 19	00064	Reboots system
Int 1A	00068	BIOS time-of-day services
Int 1B	0006C	Ctrl-Break handler address
Int 1C	00070	Called by Int 08 handler
Int 1D	00074	Video-initialization parameter table
Int 1E	00078	Disk-initialization parameter table
Int 1F	0007C	Graphics character table
Int 20	00080	DOS program terminate
Int 21	00084	DOS function services
Int 22	00088	Program terminate address
Int 23	0008C	DOS Ctrl-Break

Table B.1 Continued

Interrupt	Address	Meaning
Int 24	00090	Critical-error handler
Int 25	00094	DOS absolute disk read
Int 26	00098	DOS absolute disk write
Int 27	0009C	DOS TSR
Int 28	000A0	DOS idle interrupt
Int 29	000A4	DOS fast putchar
Int 2A	000A8	MS-Net access
Int 2E	000B8	DOS primary shell program loader
Int 2F	000BC	DOS multiplex interrupt
Int 33	000CC	Mouse interrupt
Int 3F	000FC	Overlay manager
Int 40	00100	Diskette interrupt vector if hard disk is installed
Int 41	00104	Fixed disk 2 parameter table
Int 42	00108	EGA BIOS uses this to redirect the vide interrupt
Int 43	0010C	EGA-initialization parameter table
Int 44	00110	EGA character table
Int 44		Novell NetWare API
Int 46	00118	Fixed disk 2 parameter table
Int 4A	00128	PC AT: Int 70 alarm
Int 5A	00168	Cluster
Int 5B	0016C	Used by cluster program
Int 5C	00170	NetBIOS interface
Int 67	0019C	Expanded memory manager services
Int 70	001C0	IRQ8—PC AT real-time clock
Int 71	001C4	IRQ9—PC AT redirect to Int 0A
Int 72	001C8	IRQ10
Int 73	001CC	IRQ11
Int 74	001D0	IRQ12—Mouse interrupt
Int 75	001D4	IRQ13—PC AT math coprocessor
Int 76	001D8	IRQ14—Fixed disk event
Int 77	001DC	IRQ15
Int 7A	001E8	Novell NetWare API

The BIOS Data Area

The absolute address range from 00400 to 004FF is the data area for the ROM BIOS. This area is a hodge-podge of data structures, tables, addresses, and flags. In the following table, the first column provides the absolute address for the data, and the second column provides the offset from the beginning of the BIOS data area—the offset from a segment address of 0040. Both columns are provided so that you can use whichever one better fits your programming style. (The numbers in the first two columns are in hexadecimal notation.) The other two columns are self-explanatory.

Notice the flag included at address 00500. Although this flag is technically outside the BIOS data area, because it is used by the Print Screen routine, it is included with this data block.

Table B.2   BIOS Data Area

Address	Offset	Length	Meaning
00400	00	Word	COM1 address (zero if unused)
00402	02	Word	COM2 address (zero if unused)
00404	04	Word	COM3 address (zero if unused)
00406	06	Word	COM4 address (zero if unused)
00408	08	Word	LPT1 address (zero if unused)
0040A	0A	Word	LPT2 address (zero if unused)
0040C	0C	Word	LPT3 address (zero if unused)
0040E	0E	Word	LPT4 address (zero if unused)
00410	10	Word	Equipment flag
00412	12	Byte	Initialization flag
00413	13	Word	Base memory size in kilobytes
00415	15	Byte	Amount of memory in I/O channel
00416	16	Byte	Unused
00417	17	Word	Keyboard status flags
00419	19	Word	Alt-key keypad storage space
0041A	1A	Word	Keyboard typeahead buffer head
0041C	1C	Word	Keyboard typeahead buffer tail
0041E	1E	16 words	Keyboard typeahead buffer
0043E	3E	Byte	Diskette data
0043F	3F	Byte	Diskette motor status
00440	40	Byte	Diskette motor time-out count
00441	41	Byte	Status of last diskette operation

Address	Offset	Length	Meaning
00442	42	7 bytes	Disk command work area
00449	49	Byte	Current display mode
0044A	4A	Word	Number of screen columns
0044C	4C	Word	Size in bytes of display memory page
0044E	4E	Word	Offset to current display page
00450	50	Word	Cursor position for display page 0
00452	52	Word	Cursor position for display page 1
00454	54	Word	Cursor position for display page 2
00456	56	Word	Cursor position for display page 3
00458	58	Word	Cursor position for display page 4
0045A	5A	Word	Cursor position for display page 5
0045C	5C	Word	Cursor position for display page 6
0045E	5E	Word	Cursor position for display page 7
00460	60	Word	Current cursor mode
00462	62	Byte	Current video page number
00463	63	Word	Port address of active display card
00465	65	Byte	Video hardware mode select register value
00466	66	Byte	Color palette setting
00467	67	Double word	Cassette data
0046B	6B	Byte	Interrupt occurred flag
0046C	6C	Double word	Timer ticks since midnight
00470	70	Byte	Midnight flag (set if midnight passed since last read)
00471	71	Byte	Break flag
00472	72	Word	Reset flag
00474	74	Byte	Status of last fixed disk operation
00475	75	Byte	Number of fixed disk drives
00476	76	Byte	Fixed disk control byte
00477	77	Byte	Fixed disk I/O port offset
00478	78	Byte	LPT1 time-out counter
00479	79	Byte	LPT2 time-out counter

continues

Address	Offset	Length	Meaning
0047A	7A	Byte	LPT3 time-out counter
0047B	7B	Byte	LPT4 time-out counter
0047C	7C	Byte	COM1 time-out counter
0047D	7D	Byte	COM2 time-out counter
0047E	7E	Byte	COM3 time-out counter
0047F	7F	Byte	COM4 time-out counter
00480	80	Word	Offset to start of keyboard buffer
00482	82	Word	Offset to end of keyboard buffer
00484	84	Byte	Rows on EGA/MCGA/VGA screen (zero-based)
00485	85	Word	Character height on EGA/MCGA/VGA screen
00487	87	Word	EGA/VGA control flags
00489	89	Byte	MCGA/VGA control flag
0048A	8A	Byte	MCGA/VGA data offset pointer
0048B	8B	Byte	Diskette media control flag
0048C	8C	Byte	Fixed disk controller status
0048D	8D	Byte	Fixed disk controller error flag
0048E	8E	Byte	Fixed disk interrupt control flag
0048F	8F	Byte	Diskette controller information
00490	90	Byte	Diskette drive 0 current media state
00491	91	Byte	Diskette drive 1 current media state
00492	92	Byte	Diskette drive 0 starting media state
00493	93	Byte	Diskette drive 1 starting media state
00494	94	Byte	Diskette drive 0 track number
00495	95	Byte	Diskette drive 1 track number
00496	96	Byte	Keyboard state
00497	97	Byte	Keyboard LED control
00498	98	Double word	User wait routine flag pointer
0049C	9C	Double word	User wait counter
004A0	A0	Byte	User wait active flag
004A8	A8	Double word	EGA/MCGA/VGA video save table pointer
00500	100	Byte	Print Screen status flag

A Standard TSR-Identification Technique

An ongoing problem with using several TSR programs at the same time is the lack of standards for managing conflicts between such programs.

In early 1986, a group of TSR developers organized a team to establish such a standard. A majority of the leading independent TSR developers participated.

After first attempting to produce a full applications program interface (API) for use by both independent and commercial programs (an effort that could not get strong enough support from commercial TSR publishing houses), followed by a period during which many of the original team moved on to other activities, the team developed and published an interface that permits developers to communicate with their own (and other) TSRs. In addition to the interface, a prewritten library of routines for Microsoft and Turbo C, Turbo Pascal versions 4 and 5, and assembler programs, known as TesSeRact, is available as shareware from team headquarters.

The TesSeRact Standard specifies a group of functions that chain into DOS's multiplex interrupt (2Fh). Because DOS uses this interrupt to communicate with its own TSRs (such as ASSIGN, PRINT, and SHARE), the TesSeRact Development Team felt that it was appropriate to use the same interface to service independently developed TSR programs. These functions are accessed by generating an Interrupt 2Fh, with a special code (5453h, or TS in ASCII) in the AX register.

This usage is *not* in accordance with the standard documented usage of Int 2Fh: DOS specifies that the identification code should be in the AH register (and in the 80h–FFh range), with AL=0 used for the "Installed?" function.

The team developed its standard before the official usage was documented, and preliminary copies were too widely distributed to permit a change in such a basic aspect. The inconsistency should pose no problems because no known function currently uses the 54h code. (Even if one did, the chances of it also having a 53h function code are vanishingly small.)

It is also noteworthy that DOS did not follow its own rules when APPEND was introduced in V3.3; it uses the B7h code, which is officially reserved for non-DOS applications.

In keeping with the original goal of reducing conflict between TSRs from different sources, the team encourages all developers to support the TesSeRact Standard in their own code. This is done by developing a handler for Int 2Fh that can support the User Parameters block and the two functions described in this appendix, through the special TS identification code.

The User Parameters Block

One requirement for TesSeRact compatibility is to support the UserParms data area. The area is described in the following (this area must be at the start of the TSR's handler for Int 2Fh):

```
New_2F:     jmp  OverParms        ;Int 2F vector points here
UserParms db 8 dup (' ')          ;8-byte program ID string
IdNum       dw   0                ;TSR identification number
FuncFlag  dd   0ffffffffh         ;supported function bit map
HotKey      db   0                ;scan code of hot key to use
ShiftSt     db   0                ;shift state to use for popup
HotFlag     db   0                ;which hot key is in use
ExtCnt      db   0                ;number of extra hot keys
ExtHot      dd   0                ;pointer to extra hot keys
Status      dw   0                ;TSR status flags
OurPSP      dw   0                ;our PSP segment
OurDTA      dd   0                ;our DTA region
DSeg        dw   0                ;user's default data Segment
```

Note: This is only a partial listing of the structure; the elements not shown here are used and maintained only by the TesSeRact library.

FuncFlag is a bit-mapped, 4-byte variable that shows all Multiplex functions this TSR supports. In every case, the function number must be passed to the handler in BX rather than in the standard AL, as already explained. This variable is mapped as follows:

Bit 0   Function 00h (check install—required)

Bit 1   Function 01h (return userparms—required)

Bit 2   Function 02h (check hot key)

Bit 3   Function 03h (replace INT 24h)

Bit 4   Function 04h (return data pointer)

Bit 5	Function 05h (set extra hot keys)
Bits 6–7	Undefined—reserved for future use
Bit 8	Function 10h (enable TSR)
Bit 9	Function 11h (disable TSR)
Bit 10	Function 12h (release TSR from RAM)
Bit 11	Function 13h (restart TSR)
Bit 12	Function 14h (get current status)
Bit 13	Function 15h (set TSR status)
Bit 14	Function 16h (get pop-up type)
Bit 15	Undefined—reserved for future use
Bit 16	Function 20h (call user procedure)
Bit 17	Function 21h (stuff keyboard)
Bits 18–31	Undefined—reserved for future use

If the TSR supports the function, the bit should be set (1); otherwise, it should be 0. A program that uses the TesSeRact Library returns with `FuncFlag` set to FFFFFFFFh. Other TSRs should set the undefined variables to 0 to differentiate themselves.

Function 00h (Check Install)

Check Install (Function 00h) determines whether the program has been loaded before. It is called in the following manner:

```
mov     ax,5453h         ; TS code
mov     si,offset IDStr  ; see below
mov     ds,seg IDStr
xor     cx,cx            ; handle counter
xor     bx,bx           ; function 0000
int     2Fh
```

`IDStr` is an 8-byte data area that contains a unique TSR identification string. The Int 2Fh routine should compare the string passed (as shown in the next example) with its own 8-byte string. If the two strings match, the TSR should return with the CX register set to its own TSR handle and the AX register set to 0FFFFh.

If the identification strings do not match, restore all the registers, increment the CX register, and pass the interrupt down the chain. If every TesSeRact-compatible TSR in a system increments the CX register before chaining to the next with this function, when the interrupt

965

procedure eventually returns to the caller, the CX register will contain either the handle of the TSR being sought or the next available handle if no match can be found for IDStr.

If no match can be found, AL is *not* equal to FFh on return; the TSR installation program can then use the content of CX as the handle by which it identifies itself and store it in the IdNum word of the parameter block.

The following code, based on the TesSeRact Library's Int 2Fh handler but edited for clarity, shows what the handler must do to confirm program identity:

```
overparms:
        cmp     ax,5453h              ;ax=5453h for TesSeRact
        jne     not_our_2F            ;some other multiplex function
        push    ds                    ;save for next handler
        push    cs
        pop     ds                    ;set DS while here
        push    ax
        push    bx
        or      bx,bx                 ;do check for install first,
        jnz     test_for_1            ;try other function test
; following is the CHECK INSTALL code
;DS:SI points to ID string
;CX is current number in chain
        push    cx
        push    si                    ;save SI for next one
        lea     di,UserParms          ;the program copy of IDStr
        push    cs
        pop     es
        mov     cx,8                  ;test for match
        rep     cmpsb
        pop     si
        pop     cx
        jnz     next_one              ;no match, not us
        pop     bx                    ;matched, empty stack
        pop     ax
        mov     cx,es:[di]            ;return IdNum in CX
        xor     ax,ax
        dec     ax                    ;AX=-1 means already here
        jmp     short done_2F

next_one                              ;try next higher ID code:
        inc     cx
        pop     bx                    ;restore for next to use
        pop     ax
        pop     ds
not_our_2F:                           ;chain to next 2F handler
        jmp     dword ptr [oldint2F]  ;via saved pointer to it

done_2F:                              ;return to caller
        pop     ds
        iret
```

Function 01h (Return User Parameter Pointer)

The other function necessary for minimal support of the TesSeRact standard is Function 01h, which must return a far pointer to the User Parameters Block area. This function is called as follows:

```
mov     ax,5453h
mov     bx,01h              ;function number
mov     cx,TsrIdNum         ;identification number
int     2Fh
```

If the identification number in CX matches the TSR's ID number (which was returned by Function 00h), the function should return with ES:BX pointing to the UserParms area and AX equal to zero. The following code fragment shows one way to do this:

```
test_for_1:                 ;if not Function 00h
  cmp   cx,IdNum            ;the program copy
  jne   not_our_2F
  push  cs                  ;got it, set up for return
  pop   es
  lea   bx,UserParms
  xor   ax,ax              ;success status code
  pop   ds
  jmp   done_2F
```

Other TesSeRact Functions

The other TesSeRact functions are described in detail in the full TesSeRact documentation, which can be obtained from the development team or by downloading from a BBS or on-line service that distributes the library. If you want a copy of the source code for TesSeRact's Int 2Fh handler, send a self-addressed, stamped envelope to the following address:

TesSeRact Development Team
1657 The Fairways, Suite 101
Jenkintown, PA 19046

For more information, you can contact the TesSeRact Development Team at this address, at CompuServe 70731,20, or at MCIMAIL 315-5415 (TESSERACT).

967

The Reserved DOS Functions

The "DOS Reference" section of this book has attempted to describe virtually *all* the functions to which Int 21h responds; the functions include those officially labeled as "reserved" and not documented in most reference manuals. Some of the other reference sections also have interrupts or functions labeled as reserved or undocumented. Because of the active and ever-vigilant programming community, however, it is impossible to guarantee that every known function and interrupt is covered.

Nevertheless, the descriptions that are provided for the reserved functions in this book are derived from wholly unofficial sources. These descriptions in many cases are the result of disassembling portions of DOS code and analyzing what it might be accomplishing. Because of this, the descriptions might not be completely accurate, although every attempt has been made to provide the best information available.

These functions fall into four general groups, which are described in this appendix. After examining all four groups, a pair of programs is presented that use one of the most interesting reserved functions to provide otherwise unobtainable information.

One of the primary reasons these functions are "reserved" is to make it possible for designers to change them, between versions, in any way required. This happened to one degree or another with every new version of DOS. This type of occurrence is not only possible but also likely when these undocumented functions are used; it is one of the major risks you take when you design a program around them. One small comfort is that, as these undocumented functions are used more and more, they become entrenched in the marketplace, and Microsoft is more likely to formalize their purpose and use.

Types of Undocumented DOS Functions

The four types of undocumented DOS functions are shown in this list:

- The useful ones, which include such things as SetPID and GetDPB

- The ones not used, which simply return after doing nothing

- Hooks for "future" features, which may or may not ever be implemented

- Those whose true nature has not yet been determined

Every version of DOS has had its share of undocumented functions. DOS V1, for example, had only 1 undocumented function. By DOS V2, this list had grown to at least 9, and by the time DOS V4 rolled around, the list had exploded to more than 50. The category a function fits in depends largely on who is programming.

What Is Covered

A multitude of books on the market cover, in great detail, the undocumented functions of DOS. If you are a programmer serious about accessing DOS functions, you will want to add these types of books to your shelf. (See Appendix E for some suggestions.)

DOS Programmer's Reference, 4th Edition discusses a number of undocumented DOS functions. These functions are discussed in various places in the main part of the book and in the "DOS Reference" section. Table D.1 shows the undocumented functions that are covered. Not all these functions are discussed in this appendix. Rather, it focuses on one or two you may find particularly useful.

Table D.1   Undocumented Functions Covered in *DOS Programmer's Reference*

Int	Func	Sub	Name	Version
21	37	00h	Get Switchchar	V2 or later
21	37	01h	Set Switchchar	V2 or later
21	37	02h	Read Device Availability	V2 and 4.0 only
21	37	03h	Sets Device Availability	V2 only
21	52		Get Disk List	V2 or later
21	53		Translate BPB to DPB	V2 or later
21	55		Create PSP	V2 or later
21	5D	00h	Copy Data to DOS Save Area	V3 or later
21	5D	06h	Get Critical-Error Flag Address	V3 or later

Int	Func	Sub	Name	Version
21	5E	01h	Set Machine Name	V3.1 or later
21	60		Expand Path Name String	V3 or later
21	64		Set Current Country Byte	V3 or later
21	6A		Allocate Memory	V4 or later
29			Fast Putchar	V2 or later
2A			Microsoft Networks Interface	V3 or later
2E			Primary Shell Program Loader	V3 or later
2F	05		Get Outboard Critical-Error Handler Installation Status	V3 or later
2F	08		Get DRIVER.SYS Installation Status	V3 or later
2F	12	00h	Get DOS Installation Status	V3 or later
2F	12	01h	Flush File	V3 or later
2F	12	02h	Get Interrupt Vector Address	V3 or later
2F	12	03h	Get DOS Data Segment	V3 or later
2F	12	04h	Normalize Path Separator	V3 or later
2F	12	05h	Output a Character	V3 or later
2F	12	06h	Invoke Critical Error	V3 or later
2F	12	07h	Move Disk Buffer	V3 only
2F	12	08h	Decrement User Count	V3 or later
2F	12	0Ch	IOCTL Open Used by DOS	V3 or later
2F	12	0Dh	Get Date and Time for File Closing	V3 or later
2F	12	0Eh	Search Buffer Chain	V3 only
2F	12	10h	Find Modified Buffer	V3 only
2F	12	10h	Time Delay	V4 or later
2F	12	11h	Normalize ASCIIZ File Name	V3 or later
2F	12	12h	Find ASCIIZ String Length	V3 or later
2F	12	13h	Case and Country Conversion	V3 or later
2F	12	14h	Compare 32-bit Numbers	V3 or later
2F	12	16h	Get DCB Address	V3 or later
2F	12	17h	Get LDT Address	V3 or later

continues

Table D.1   Continued

Int	Func	Sub	Name	Version
2F	12	18h	Get User Stack Address	V3 or later
2F	12	19h	Set LDT Pointers	V3 or later
2F	12	1Ah	Get Drive Code from Path Name	V3 or later
2F	12	1Bh	Adjust for Leap Year	V3 or later
2F	12	1Ch	Calculate Days since Start-of-Month	V3 or later
2F	12	1Dh	Calculate Date	V3 or later
2F	12	1Eh	Compare Strings	V3 or later
2F	12	1Fh	Initialize LDT	V3 or later
2F	12	20h	Get DCB Number	V3 or later
2F	12	21h	Expand ASCIIZ Path Name	V3 or later
2F	12	22h	Translate Extended Error Codes	V3 or later
2F	12	24h	Execute Delay	V3 or later
2F	12	25h	Get ASCIIZ String Length	V3 or later
2F	12	26h	Open File	V4 or later
2F	12	27h	Close File	V4 or later
2F	12	28h	Position File Pointer	V4 or later
2F	12	29h	Read File	V4 or later
2F	12	2Bh	IOCTL Interface	V4 or later
2F	12	2Dh	Get Extended Error Code	V4 or later
2F	12	2Fh	Store DX	V4 or later
2F	15		CD-ROM Interface	V3 or later

Using Function 52h: The List of Lists

Starting with V3 and the introduction of network support, DOS found it necessary to standardize system-configuration information so that all the add-in optional programs required for network operation could obtain the information they needed. The result was what Dr. Edwin Floyd (one of the first people outside Microsoft and IBM to discover its existence and purpose) dubbed the *configuration variable table* (CVT), and what has subsequently come to be known as the *list of lists*. Much of the table was already there in V2, but it was significantly expanded in V3, and its location in RAM was also moved slightly.

The list of lists is located near the front of the MSDOS.SYS program. The table contains pointers to the memory control block (MCB) chain and other essential control information, and the number of drives present or permitted.

Content and Layout

In DOS V2, the CVT is only 25 bytes long. In both V3 and V4, it occupies 42 bytes. In all three versions, the CVT immediately precedes the NUL device driver, which is always the first driver in the chain. (Installable drivers are fitted between the NUL driver and the remaining drivers, which are part of the IO.SYS file.)

To locate the CVT, undocumented Function 52h of Int 21h is used. When this function is called with no parameters, it returns in ES:BX a pointer to the address of the first drive parameter block maintained by DOS. In V2, this item is the second one in the CVT (the segment address of the beginning of the memory control block chain, a 2-byte value, precedes it). In V3 or V4, this address is the eighth byte of the CVT because the 32-bit far pointer to the current buffer control block and the 16-bit offset value for the current buffer location were added in front of the MCB segment word.

In V2, therefore, you must subtract 2 from BX after returning from the function, and in V3 and V4 you must subtract 8, to be at the front of the CVT.

Now that you have learned how to access the CVT, let's see what it contains.

The Version 2 CVT

The following layout of the configuration variable table shows how it first appeared in DOS V2. The asterisk indicates the address returned by undocumented Function 52h of Interrupt 21h, and all byte offsets listed are relative to that address.

Offset Byte	Field Length	Meaning
–02h	Word	Segment of first memory control block
*00h	Double word	Pointer to first drive parameter block
04h	Double word	Pointer to first DCB (system file table device control block)
08h	Double word	Pointer to CLOCK$ device driver
0Ch	Double word	Pointer to CON device driver
10h	Byte	Number of logical drives

continues

Offset Byte	Field Length	Meaning
11h	Word	Maximum bytes per sector on any block device
13h	Double word	Pointer to start of disk buffer chain
17h		Beginning of NUL device driver; first device in device-driver chain

The format of the memory control blocks pointed to by the word at offset –02 is simple:

Offset Byte	Field Length	Meaning
00h	Byte	MCB identifier; M for every MCB except the last one, and Z for the last block. Always at offset 0000h within the segment.
01h	Word	PSP address of process that owns this MCB, or 0000h to indicate that memory in this block is unassigned.
03h	Word	Size of following memory block in paragraphs, not including this 16-byte MCB area.
05h	11 bytes	Remainder of paragraph unused.

The drive parameter block, pointed to by the double word at offset 00h in the CVT, is the structure described in the reference section of this book in connection with undocumented Function 53h of Interrupt 21h. It remained unchanged between DOS V2 and V3. Because the drive parameter block is described fully in the reference section, it is not repeated here. Every physical drive in the system (including drive B in a single-floppy system) has its own DPB; the next-block pointer of the last DPB contains FFFF:FFFFh to flag the end of the chain.

The number of DCBs in a system is established by the FILES= line in CONFIG.SYS. The default number is 5, if no FILES= value is specified. The DCBs are grouped in "links," and every link is preceded by a 3-word link header:

Offset Byte	Field Length	Meaning
00h	Double word	Far pointer to next link header, or FFFF:FFFFh to indicate that this is final link in chain
04h	Word	Number of blocks in this link

974

The double word at offset 04h in the CVT points to the header of the link containing the first device control block in the DCB chain. In DOS V2, the 40-byte DCB layout was a slightly modified version of the documented FCB structure:

Offset Byte	Field Length	Meaning
00h	Byte	Number of current users for this DCB
01h	Byte	Access mode in which DCB was opened
02h	Byte	Attribute byte from directory entry, or 00h for device
03h	Byte	Drive code (1 = A, and so on)
04h	8 bytes	File or device name
0Ch	3 bytes	File extension, or blanks
0Fh	13 bytes	Not deciphered; may be same as FCB for a file
1Ch	Double word	Far pointer to device driver for device; not deciphered for file
20h	8 bytes	Not deciphered

The word at offset 11h indicates the maximum sector size on any block device. It is set during power-up initialization as the block device drivers are installed, and it establishes the size of the buffers created during configuration. This process ensures that every buffer is large enough to hold the largest sector present in the system, but no larger than necessary to do so.

The disk buffer chain pointed to by the double word at offset 13h of the CVT was laid out as follows (very little of the buffer organization for Version 2 was deciphered):

Offset Byte	Field Length	Meaning
00h	Double word	Far pointer to next buffer, or FFFF:FFFFh to indicate end of chain
04h	4 words	Control information not fully decoded, including flag bytes, logical sector number, and drive code
0Ch	Double word	Far pointer to DPB associated with this buffer
10h	varies	The buffer itself, usually 512 bytes, but the actual size is set by the value stored at offset 11h in CVT

The Version 3 CVT

The configuration variable table in DOS V3 grew at both ends, as listed here. As in the V2 listing, the asterisk indicates the address returned by undocumented Function 52h of Interrupt 21h, and all byte offsets listed are relative to that address.

Offset Byte	Field Length	Meaning
–08h	Double word	Current buffer in BUFFERS= chain
–04h	Word	Offset within current buffer
–02h	Word	Segment of first memory control block
*00h	Double word	Pointer to first drive parameter block
04h	Double word	Pointer to first DCB (system file table device control block)
08h	Double word	Pointer to CLOCK$ device driver
0Ch	Double word	Pointer to CON device driver
10h	Word	Maximum bytes per sector on any block device
12h	Double word	Pointer to start of disk buffer chain
16h	Double word	Pointer to logical drive table
1Ah	Double word	Pointer to start of DOS's FCB chain
1Eh	Word	Number of FCBs to keep when swapping
20h	Byte	Number of block devices
21h	Byte	Number of logical drives, set by value of LASTDRIVE in CONFIG.SYS (defaults to 5 if not specified)
22h		Beginning of NUL device driver; first device in the device-driver chain

The double word at offset –08 points to the current buffer in the disk buffer chain; the layout of the buffer control blocks is described later. The word at offset –04 is the byte offset within the current buffer, relative to the buffer's first byte; a value of 0000h indicates that the last byte in the buffer has been used and the next buffer in the chain should be accessed.

As in V2, the word at offset –02 is the segment address of the first memory control block in the MCB chain. The layout of the actual memory control blocks are the same as in V2. The DPB chain, whose first entry is pointed to by the double word at offset 00h, is the same as in V2.

The drive control blocks for V3 underwent extensive changes from V2 to accommodate the addition of networking and multiple processes sharing the use of the same files or devices. As in V2, however, the drive control blocks still were collected into links with link headers, and the link header layout was not changed. The new structure layout for each DCB was as follows:

Offset Byte	Field Length	Meaning
00h	Word	Number of users for this DCB
02h	Word	Access mode per open
04h	Word	Disk attribute byte
05h	Byte	Device attributes
06h	Byte	Second device attribute byte
07h	Double word	Far pointer to driver
0Bh	Word	First cluster number
0Dh	Word	File time word
0Fh	Word	File date word
11h	Double word	Total file size
15h	Double word	Current byte position
19h	Word	Total cluster count
1Bh	Word	Current cluster number
1Dh	Word	Directory sector
1Fh	Byte	Directory entry index (within sector)
20h	8 bytes	Device or file name
28h	3 bytes	File extension or blanks
2Bh	Word	Unknown
2Dh	Word	Unknown
2Fh	Word	Unknown
31h	Word	PSP segment address of owner
33h	Word	Unknown

The word at offset 10h indicates the maximum sector size on any block device. The size is set during power-up initialization as the block device drivers are installed. It is used to establish the size of the buffers created during configuration, to ensure that every buffer is large enough to hold the largest sector present in the system, but no larger than necessary to do so.

The double word at offset 12h points to the beginning of the disk buffer chain. Every buffer in the chain is as large as specified by the word at 10h (usually 512 bytes), plus a 16-byte header that precedes the data area. The layout follows:

Offset Byte	Field Length	Meaning
00h	Double word	Far pointer to next buffer, or FFFF:FFFFh to indicate end of chain
04h	Byte	Logical drive code
05h	Byte	Action code
06h	Word	Logical sector number
08h	Byte	Number of FATs, or 01
09h	Byte	Sectors per FAT, or 00
0Ah	Double word	Far pointer to DPB associated with this buffer
0Eh	Word	Unknown
10h	varies	The buffer itself, usually 512 bytes, but the actual size set by the value stored at offset 10h in CVT

The "current directory" area that was part of the DPB in V2 became a separate table, the logical drive table, beginning with V3. The double word at offset 16h of the CVT points to the LDT, which contains one entry for every system logical drive, up to the value set in LASTDRIVE of the CONFIG.SYS file. The minimum number of entries defaults to five (A: through E:) beginning with drive A. The tables, each of which is 81 bytes long in V3, follow one another in memory. Each one is laid out as follows:

Offset Byte	Field Length	Meaning
00h	2 bytes	Actual drive designator and :
02h	65 bytes	Current path for this drive as an ASCIIZ string (includes root directory slash and room for terminating 00h byte)
43h	Word	Current status of drive (bit map):
		8000h = unknown, may indicate remote network drive
		4000h = ready for use
		2000h = unknown
		1000h = SUBSTed unit
45h	Double word	Pointer to DPB for drive
49h	Word	Current directory first cluster
4Bh	Word	Unknown

Offset Byte	Field Length	Meaning
4Dh	Word	Unknown
4Fh	Word	Number of bytes to skip over when reporting directory; 0002 for normal drive, more if SUBSTed unit

The double word at offset 1Ah and the word that follows it are related to the FCBS= line in CONFIG.SYS. They are, respectively, a far pointer to the chain of system FCBs, and the number of FCBs to protect against swapping if swaps are required. Though FCBs are intended primarily for network use, they are used at times by programs in a single-user environment also. The system FCBs follow the same layout as the DCBs and, like the DCBs, are organized into links, each of which contains multiple blocks.

The final two items in the V3 CVT, at offsets 20h and 21h, are the number of block devices and the number of logical drives. The first is established by the total number of units encountered while installing block devices, and the other by the LASTDRIVE= line in CONFIG.SYS.

The Version 4 CVT

The changes made to the CVT and its tables between DOS V3 and V4 were minor in comparison to what happened between V2 and V3. The addition of EMS support, however, did have some effect in the CVT area, as did the change from 16-bit to 32-bit logical sector numbers. And, the rewrite of the buffering algorithms had a major impact on the buffer structures. Here's the CVT as used in V4; the only significant change is that the old buffer-chain-head pointer at offset 12h became a pointer to a new EMS link record.

Offset Byte	Field Length	Meaning
–08h	Double word	Current buffer in BUFFERS= chain
–04h	Word	Offset within current buffer
–02h	Word	Segment of first memory control block
*00h	Double word	Pointer to first drive parameter block
04h	Double word	Pointer to first DCB (system file table device control block)
08h	Double word	Pointer to CLOCK$ device driver
0Ch	Double word	Pointer to CON device driver
10h	Word	Maximum bytes per sector on any block device

continues

Offset Byte	Field Length	Meaning
12h	Double word	Pointer to EMS link record that leads to DOS buffer chain (only change between V3 and V4)
16h	Double word	Pointer to logical drive table (see the discussion following this table for layout, which did change slightly)
1Ah	Double word	Pointer to start of DOS's FCB chain
1Eh	Word	Number of FCBs to keep when swapping
20h	Byte	Number of block devices
21h	Byte	Number of logical drives, set by value of LASTDRIVE in CONFIG.SYS (defaults to 5 if not specified)
22h		Beginning of NUL device driver; first device in the device-driver chain

Everything located at addresses below the address returned by Function 52h of Interrupt 21h remained unchanged in V4, but the buffer control block pointed to from the double word at offset –08 underwent drastic change. Previously, every buffer had its own unique segment address, and the buffers were linked by a chain of far pointers in only a forward direction. In V4, all buffers reached by way of a single EMS linkage block (described in this section) are in the same segment, and they are doubly linked (both forward and backward) by means of near pointers in an endless chain.

To accommodate the new buffering algorithms, the buffer control block size was extended from 16 to 20 bytes. Its structure in V4 is as follows:

Offset Byte	Field Length	Meaning
00h	Word	Offset of previous buffer in chain, within segment or EMS physical page
02h	Word	Offset of next buffer in chain, within segment or EMS physical page
04h	Byte	Logical drive code (same as V3)
05h	Byte	Action code (same as V3?)
06h	Double word	Logical sector number, expanded from V3
0Ah	Byte	Number of FATs, or 01; full meaning not known
0Bh	Word	Sectors per FAT if FAT in buffer; else meaning not known

Offset Byte	Field Length	Meaning
0Dh	Double word	Far pointer to DPB for physical drive associated with this buffer
11h	Word	Meaning not known
13h	Word	Meaning not known
14h	512 bytes	The buffer itself; as in V3, size is set by word in CVT, but 512 bytes is normal

To speed up the buffer searching, a brand-new linkage record was added to the buffering algorithm at V4. This 11-byte record holds a hash value and points to the associated BCB. Not all its details are fully understood, but the structure is as follows:

Offset Byte	Field Length	Meaning
00h	Word	Hash value
02h	Double word	Far pointer to associated BCB
06h	Byte	Usage counter
07h	Double word	Meaning not known

A second new record was added to accommodate the new capability to store the buffers in EMS rather than in conventional memory. This record associates an EMM handle and physical page with a linkage record. Because of compatibility problems between the system software and non-IBM EMS hardware, it was not possible to test in detail exactly how this record is used when EMS is active; the description that follows applies in a non-EMS environment:

Offset Byte	Field Length	Meaning
00h	Double word	Far pointer to linkage record described earlier
04h	Word	Number of pages controlled by this record
06h	Double word	Meaning not known
0Ah	Word	Meaning not known
0Ch	Byte	Flag; value is FF if EMS not being used
0Dh	Word	EMS handle value
0Eh	Byte	EMS physical page number

The next area to undergo change was the DPB structure, reached from the pointer at offset 00h of the CVT. The only change to the drive parameter blocks was that the "sectors per FAT" value changed from 8 bits to 16, increasing by one byte the offset for all subsequent entries.

Everything above the DPB pointer, to offset 12h, remained the same. The far pointer at offset 12h, though, became a pointer to the EMS record for the disk buffering, already described in connection with the BCB changes.

The LDT, reached by way of the far pointer at offset 16h in the CVT, was extended by seven bytes. The purpose of these seven bytes could not be determined. The new structure is shown in this table:

Offset Byte	Field Length	Meaning
00h	2 bytes	Actual drive designator and :
02h	65 bytes	Current path for this drive as an ASCIIZ string (includes root directory slash and room for terminating 00h byte)
43h	Word	Current status of drive (bit map):
		8000h = unknown
		4000h = ready for use
		2000h = unknown
		1000h = SUBSTed unit
45h	Double word	Pointer to DPB for drive
49h	Word	Current directory first cluster
4Bh	Word	Unknown
4Dh	Word	Unknown
4Fh	Word	Number of bytes to skip over when reporting directory; 0002 for normal drive, more if SUBSTed unit
51h	Byte	Unknown
52h	Word	Unknown
54h	Word	Unknown
56h	Word	Unknown

The remainder of the CVT escaped change from what it was in V3, as far as can be determined by disassembly and testing.

CVT3.PAS: A Program for V3

The accompanying program, CVT3.PAS, provides both an example of a practical use for undocumented Function 52h of Interrupt 21h and a tool for exploring just how the CVT is laid out in your own system running under DOS V3. This program is presented in Listing D.1.

Listing D.1

```
{ cvt3.pas - Turbo Pascal V5.0 version for DOS 3.x
 *      Copyright 1987, 1988, 1989 Jim Kyle - All Rights Reserved
 *
 *      The program, and the information it contains, may be freely
 *      distributed and used as long as this entire comment section
 *      is not altered.
 }
PROGRAM CVT3;
{$A-,B-,D+,E-,F-,I+,L+,N+,O-,R-,S+,V-}
{$M 8192,0,0 }
USES DOS;

TYPE

    bcb = RECORD                  { Buffer Control Block format      }
            nxcb   : pointer;          { +00 next one in chain  }
            ldrv   : byte;             { +04 logical drive code }
            action : byte;             { +05 action code        }
            lsect  : word;             { +06 logical sector #   }
            nf     : byte;             { +08 nbr FATs or 01     }
            secf   : byte;             { +09 sectors/FAT or 00  }
            pdrv   : pointer;          { +0A phys drv tbl ptr   }
            fill   : integer;          { +0E unknown            }
            buf    : array[0..511] of byte; { +10 the buffer itself  }
            END;
    bcbptr = ^bcb;

    mcb = RECORD                  { Mem Alloc Block header format    }
            flag  : char;              { +00 must be M or Z     }
            owner : word;              { +01 PSP seg or 0000    }
            siz   : word;              { +03 Number paragraphs  }
            END;
    mcbptr = ^mcb;

    dpb = RECORD                  { Drive Parameter Block format     }
            drvc   : byte;             { +00 drive code         }
            dunit  : byte;             { +01 unit number        }
            bps    : integer;          { +02 bytes per sector   }
            spc    : byte;             { +04 sec per cluster -1 }
            pwr2   : byte;             { +05 power of 2         }
            rsrvs  : integer;          { +06 reserved sectors   }
            nfats  : byte;             { +08 number of FATs     }
            dirsiz : word;             { +09 root dir size      }
            fus    : word;             { +0B first usable sectr }
            tcc    : word;             { +0D total clstr ct +1  }
```

continues

Listing D.1 Continued

```
            spf     : byte;                { +0F sec per FAT        }
            fds     : word;                { +10 first dir sector   }
            drvr    : pointer;             { +12 driver pointer     }
            mcode   : byte;                { +16 media code         }
            accflg  : byte;                { +17 access flag        }
            nxt     : pointer;             { +18 next table ptr     }
            lastused : word;               { +1C last used cluster  }
            filler : word;                 { +1E usually FFFF       }
        END;
    dpbptr = ^dpb;

    chn = RECORD               { Chain links for DCB, FCB chains  }
            nxtlnk : pointer;             { +00 next link or FFFF  }
            nmbr   : integer;             { +04 number blocks here }
        END;
    chnptr = ^chn;

    dcb = RECORD               { Device Control Block format       }
            nusers : integer;            { +00 users for this DCB }
            mode   : integer;            { +02 0,1,2 per OPEN     }
            datrb  : byte;               { +04 disk attrib byte   }
            dvatr  : byte;               { +05 device attrib (hi) }
            atrb2  : byte;               { +06 2nd device attrib  }
            pdrvr  : pointer;            { +07 points to driver   }
            frstc  : word;               { +0B first cluster nbr  }
            modtm  : word;               { +0D file time word     }
            moddt  : word;               { +0F file date word     }
            totsiz : longint;            { +11 total file size    }
            curpos : longint;            { +15 current byte pos   }
            clsctr : word;               { +19 total cluster ctr  }
            curcls : word;               { +1B current cluster    }
            dirsec : word;               { +1D directory sector   }
            dirndx : byte;               { +1F dir entry index 0..}
            name   : array[0..7] of char; { +20 dev/file name     }
            ext    : array[0..3] of char; { +28 file extension    }
            fill2  : word;               { +2B unknown            }
            fill3  : word;               { +2D unknown            }
            fill4  : word;               { +2F unknown            }
            owner  : word;               { +31 PSP of owner proc  }
            fill5  : word;               { +33 unknown            }
        END;
     dcbptr = ^dcb;

    ldt = RECORD                  { Logical Drive Table format   }
            name   : array[0..67] of char;{ +00 drive and path    }
            code   : byte;               { +44 drive in use code  }
            mydpb  : dpbptr;             { +45 DPB for this drive }
            dirclu : word;               { +49 directory cluster  }
            filler2: word;               { +4B FFFF               }
            filler3: word;               { +4D FFFF               }
            patlen : word;               { +4F SUBST path length  }
        END;
    ldtptr = ^ldt;

    cvt = RECORD                  { Configuration Variable Table  }
```

```
            curbfr : bcbptr;                  { current buffer pointer }
            memchn : mcbptr;                  { start of MCB chain      }
            pdrvs  : dpbptr;                  { Fn $52 points to here   }
            dcbchn : dcbptr;                  { set up by FILES=        }
            clkdev : pointer;                 { set by DEVICE= (clock$)}
            condev : pointer;                 { set by DEVICE= (con)    }
            secsiz : integer;                 { maximum block size      }
            bfrchn : bcbptr;                  { set up by BUFFERS=      }
            ldrvs  : ldtptr;                  { set up by LASTDRIVE=    }
            fcbchn : chnptr;                  { set up by FCBS=         }
            filler : integer;                 { number of FCBs to keep }
            npdrvs : byte;                    { set by driver list      }
            nldrvs : byte;                    { set by LASTDRIVE=       }
          END;
      cvtptr = ^cvt;

      dtstr = string[8];                      { date-time strings       }
      pstrg = string[9];                      { pointer-conversion fmt }
      memst = string[12];                     { memory usage string     }

  VAR
    cvtbase : cvtptr;
    curbuf  : bcbptr;
    curmcb  : mcbptr;
    curdpb  : dpbptr;
    curchn  : chnptr;
    curdcb,
    curfcb  : dcbptr;
    curldt  : ldtptr;
    bcbctr,
    dcbctr  : integer ;                { counters                       }
    b       : Registers;
    PawsFlag: Boolean;                 { controls screen-full pausing }
    lctr    : integer;                 { counts lines displayed         }

function hexn(b:byte) : char;          { converts nibble to char        }
  begin
    b := b and 15;                     { force to only 4 bits           }
    if b > 9 then inc(b,7);            { adjust for hex digits          }
    hexn := chr(b+48);                 { convert to character           }
  end;

function hexb(b:byte) : string;
  begin
    hexb := hexn(b shr 4) + hexn(b);   { assemble the nibbles    }
  end;

function hexw(w:word) : string;
  begin
    hexw := hexb(w shr 8) + hexb(w);   { assemble the bytes      }
  end;

function hexl(l:longint) : string;
  begin
    hexl := hexw(l shr 16) + hexw(l);  { assemble the words      }
  end;
```

continues

985

Listing D.1   Continued

```
PROCEDURE holdup;                        { count lines and wait if full }
  BEGIN
    IF PawsFlag THEN
      BEGIN
        inc(lctr);
        if lctr > 23 then
          BEGIN
            lctr := 0;
            readln;
          END
      END
  END;

FUNCTION xp( p : pointer ) : pstrg;    { displays pointer P }
  BEGIN
    xp := hexw(seg(p^)) + ':' + hexw(ofs(p^));
  END;

PROCEDURE  dmp(f : pointer);        { display hex dump of data to CRT }
  VAR
    x : ^byte;
    i : integer;
    c : char;
  BEGIN
    x := f;
    write( xp(f), '> ');
    FOR i:=0 to 15 DO
      BEGIN
        write( hexb(x^) );
        if i=7 then write('-')
               else write(' ');
        x := pointer(longint(x) + 1);
      END;
    write('  ');
    x := f;
    FOR i:=0 to 15 DO
      BEGIN
        c := char($7f AND x^);
        if c<' ' then c := '.';
        write( c );
        if i=7 then write(' ');
        x := pointer(longint(x) + 1);
      END;
    writeln;
    holdup;
  END;

PROCEDURE dpbtrc(a: pointer);      { trace and report DPB data }
  VAR
    ofsv : word;

  PROCEDURE dpbrpt;                      { reports each DPB's content }
    BEGIN
      writeln;
      holdup;
```

```
                  write('Drive ', char (curdpb^.drvc+ord('A')) );
                  write(': (unit ', curdpb^.dunit, ' of driver at ', xp(curdpb^.drvr) );
                  writeln(') media code = ', hexb(curdpb^.mcode) );
                  holdup;
                  write(' ', curdpb^.bps:3, ' bytes per sector,');
                  write(' ', curdpb^.spc+1:2, ' sectors per cluster,');
                  writeln(' ', curdpb^.tcc-1:4, ' total cluster count');
                  holdup;
                  write(' Res sectors: ', curdpb^.rsrvs, ' ');
                  write(' ', curdpb^.nfats, ' FAT''s, ', curdpb^.spf:2, ' sec ea ');
                  write(' FAT entry: ');
                  IF (curdpb^.tcc) > $0FFC
                    THEN  write( 16 )
                    ELSE  write( 12 );
                  writeln(' bits  Root: ', curdpb^.dirsiz:3, ' entries');
                  holdup;
                  write(' First root sector: ', curdpb^.fds:3  );
                  write(' First data sector: ', curdpb^.fus:3  );
                  writeln(' Last cluster used: ', hexw(curdpb^.lastused));
                  holdup;
                END;          { of dpbrpt proc }

            BEGIN
              curdpb := a;
              ofsv := 0;
              writeln;
              holdup;
              writeln('DRIVE PARAMETER BLOCK (DPB) DATA--');
              holdup;
              WHILE (ofsv <> $FFFF) DO
                BEGIN
                  ofsv := word(longint( curdpb^.nxt ));
                  dpbrpt ;
                  curdpb := dpbptr(curdpb^.nxt);
                END;
              write(#12);
            END; { of dpbtrc proc }

        PROCEDURE bcbtrc(a : pointer);
          VAR
            ofsv : word;

          PROCEDURE  bcbrpt(a : bcbptr);
            VAR
              i : integer;
              x : pointer;
            BEGIN
              writeln;
              holdup;
              inc(bcbctr);
              writeln('Buffer Control Block ', bcbctr:2, ' at ', xp(a));
              holdup;
              write('     Logical ''', char(ord('A')+a^.ldrv));
              write(':'',     Sector ', hexw(a^.lsect));
              writeln('     Action code: ', hexb(a^.action));
              holdup;
```

continues

987

Listing D.1 Continued

```
        write('    NFATS: ', hexb( a^.nf));
        write('   SPF: ', hexb(a^.secf));
        write('   DPB: ', xp(a^.pdrv));
        writeln('   FILL: ', hexw(a^.fill));
        holdup;
        x := addr(bcbptr(a)^.buf[0]);
        FOR i:=0 to 31 DO
          dmp(pointer(longint(x)+(i SHL 4)));
      END;        { of bcbrpt proc }

  BEGIN           { bcbtrc routine }
    bcbctr := 0;
    ofsv := 0;
    WHILE (ofsv <> $FFFF) DO
      BEGIN
        ofsv := word(longint( bcbptr(a)^.nxcb ));
        bcbrpt (a);
        a := bcbptr(a)^.nxcb;
      END;
    write(#12);
  END;            { bcbtrc routine }

PROCEDURE dcbtrc(t : dtstr; a : pointer);
  VAR
    ofsv : word;

  FUNCTION f_tm(n : word) : dtstr;
    VAR
      buf : dtstr;
      b   : byte;
    BEGIN
      b := ((n SHR 11) AND 31);
      buf[1] :=char((b DIV 10) + 48);
      buf[2] :=char((b MOD 10) + 48);
      buf[3] := ':';
      b := ((n SHR  5) AND 63);
      buf[4] :=char((b DIV 10) + 48);
      buf[5] :=char((b MOD 10) + 48);
      buf[6] := ':';
      b := ((n SHL  1) AND 63);
      buf[7] :=char((b DIV 10) + 48);
      buf[8] :=char((b MOD 10) + 48);
      f_tm := buf;
    END;

  FUNCTION f_dt(n : word) : dtstr;
    VAR
      buf : dtstr;
      b   : byte;
    BEGIN
      b :=((n SHR  5) AND 15);
      buf[1] :=char((b DIV 10) + 48);
      buf[2] :=char((b MOD 10) + 48);
      buf[3] := '/';
      b := ( n        AND 31);
```

```
      buf[4] :=char((b DIV 10) + 48);
      buf[5] :=char((b MOD 10) + 48);
      buf[6] := '/';
      b := ((n SHR  9) AND 15) + 80;
      buf[7] :=char((b DIV 10) + 48);
      buf[8] :=char((b MOD 10) + 48);
     f_dt := buf;
  END;

PROCEDURE dcbrpt( var t : dtstr; n : integer );
   type
     acctyp = array[0..3] of string[7];
   const
     actyp : acctyp = ('READ', 'WRITE', 'R/W', 'unknown');
   var
     isdvc : Boolean;
   BEGIN
     WHILE (n > 0) DO
     BEGIN
      INC (dcbctr);
      writeln;
      holdup;
      write  (t, ' ', dcbctr:2 );
      IF (curdcb^.name[0] = #0)  THEN
      BEGIN
        writeln(' at ', xp(curdcb), ' not used since bootup');
        holdup;
      END
      else
      BEGIN
        isdvc := (curdcb^.dvatr and 128) <> 0;
        write(' for ');
        IF isdvc
          THEN write( 'device ' )
          ELSE write( 'file ' );
        write(curdcb^.name[0], curdcb^.name[1], curdcb^.name[2]);
        write(curdcb^.name[3], curdcb^.name[4], curdcb^.name[5]);
        write(curdcb^.name[6], curdcb^.name[7]);
        IF (NOT isdvc) THEN  { block driver }
          write('.', curdcb^.ext[0], curdcb^.ext[1], curdcb^.ext[2]);
        write(' at ', xp( curdcb ) );
        write(' shows ', curdcb^.nusers);
        writeln(' OPENs');
        holdup;
        write('  Opened for ', actyp[3 AND (curdcb^.mode)]);
        write(' access' );
        IF ($FFFC AND (curdcb^.mode))<>0 THEN
          write(' (', hexw(curdcb^.mode), ')');
        writeln(' by process ', hexw(curdcb^.owner));
        holdup;
        IF( isdvc ) THEN                { Device        }
          BEGIN
            write('  Device driver at ', xp(curdcb^.pdrvr) );
            write(' is in ');
            if ((curdcb^.dvatr) AND 32)<>0 THEN write('Raw')
                                        ELSE write( 'Cooked' );
```

continues

989

Listing D.1 Continued

```
                   write(' mode and is ');
                   if ((curdcb^.dvatr) AND 64)=0 THEN  write('not ');
                   writeln('ready');
                   holdup;
                END
             else                           { File        }
                BEGIN
                   write('  File is on drive ', char(ord('A')+((curdcb^.dvatr) AND 31)));
                   write(': (driver at ', xp(curdcb^.pdrvr));
                   write(') and has ');
                   if ((curdcb^.dvatr) AND 64)<>0 THEN  write('not ');
                   writeln('been written to.');
                   holdup;
                   writeln('  File''s attribute byte = ', hexb(curdcb^.datrb));
                   holdup;
                END;
             write  ('  Mod Time/date: ');
             write  (f_tm(curdcb^.modtm), ', ');
             writeln(f_dt(curdcb^.moddt));
             holdup;
             write  ('        Dir Sector:  ', hexw(curdcb^.dirsec), ' ');
             writeln('        Dir Index:  ', curdcb^.dirndx:4, ' ');
             holdup;
             write  ('    First Cluster:  ', hexw(curdcb^.frstc), ' ');
             write  ('    Prev Clusters:  ', curdcb^.clsctr:4, ' ');
             writeln('  Current Cluster:  ', hexw(curdcb^.curcls), ' ');
             holdup;
             write  ('   Directory size:',   curdcb^.totsiz:6, ' ');
             writeln('  Curr byte count:',   curdcb^.curpos:6       );
             holdup;
             write  (' Fill2=', hexw(curdcb^.fill2), ' ');
             write  (' Fill3=', hexw(curdcb^.fill3), ' ');
             write  (' Fill4=', hexw(curdcb^.fill4), ' ');
             writeln(' Fill5=', hexw(curdcb^.fill5)     );
             holdup;
          END;
          curdcb := pointer(longint(curdcb) + sizeof(dcb) - 1);
          DEC( n );
       END;        { n >= 0 loop    }
    END;           { of dcbrpt      }

BEGIN
   curchn := chnptr(a);
   dcbctr := 0;
   ofsv := 0;
   WHILE (ofsv <> $FFFF) DO
      BEGIN
         ofsv := word(longint(curchn^.nxtlnk));
         curdcb := dcbptr(longint(curchn)+sizeof(chn));
         writeln;
         holdup;
         write  ( 'Link at ', xp(curchn), ' contains ');
         writeln( curchn^.nmbr, ' ', t, 's--');
         holdup;
         dcbrpt (t, curchn^.nmbr);
```

```
              curchn := chnptr(curchn^.nxtlnk);
          END;
        write(#12);
    END;

PROCEDURE memtrc(a : pointer);
  VAR
    z : longint;

  PROCEDURE memrpt(s,o,a : word);

    FUNCTION memu(a : word) : memst;      { determine memory use }
      var
        x : char;
      BEGIN
      x := char( mem[a:0] );
      CASE x OF
        #$CD:
          memu := 'Program';
        'A'..'Z':
          memu := 'Environment';
        else
          memu := 'Data';
        End;
    END;

  BEGIN
    z := longint(s) SHL 4;
    write( z:6, ' bytes ' );
    IF (o<>0) THEN
      writeln('USED by proc ', hexw(o), ', at ', hexw( a ), ':0000, for ', memu(a))
    else
      writeln('FREE at ', hexw( a ), ':0000' );
    holdup;
  END;  { of memrpt      }

BEGIN
  curmcb := mcbptr(a);
  writeln;
  holdup;
  writeln('MEMORY ALLOCATION CHAIN');
  holdup;
  WHILE (curmcb^.flag = 'M') DO
    BEGIN
      memrpt( curmcb^.siz, curmcb^.owner, SEG(curmcb^)+1);
      curmcb := ptr( seg(curmcb^) + (curmcb^.siz + 1), 0 );
    END;
  IF (curmcb^.flag <> 'Z') THEN
    BEGIN
      writeln(#13, #10, 'MEMORY ALLOCATION ERROR at ', xp(curmcb) );
      halt(255);
    END;
  memrpt( curmcb^.siz, curmcb^.owner, SEG(curmcb^)+1);
  write(#12);
END;    { of memtrc }

PROCEDURE ldttrc( a: ldtptr; n: byte );
```

continues

991

Listing D.1 Continued

```
PROCEDURE ldtrpt( l: ldtptr; d: byte );
  VAR
    ldrive : char;
    i      : integer;
  BEGIN
    ldrive := chr( $41 + d );
    if (l^.code AND byte($40))=0 then
      writeln( 'Logical Drive ', ldrive, ' not yet defined' )
    else
      begin
        write  ( 'Logical Drive ', ldrive );
        writeln( ' = Physical drive ', l^.name[0] );
        holdup;
        write  ( 'The current (full) pathspec is: ' );
        i := 0;
        repeat
          write  ( l^.name[i] );
          inc( i );
        until (l^.name[i] = #0);
        writeln;
      end;
    holdup;
    if(l^.code = $50) then
      writeln( 'Code = 0x50 -- result of SUBST command')
    else if(l^.code = $40) then
      writeln( 'Code = 0x40 -- physical (or aliased) device')
    else
      writeln( 'Code = 0x', hexb(l^.code), ' -- unknown');
    holdup;
    writeln( 'Directory Cluster = ', hexw( l^.dirclu ));
    holdup;
    writeln( 'Path Length to ignore = ', hexw( l^.patlen ));
    holdup;
    writeln;
    holdup;
  END; { of ldtrpt }

VAR
  o  : byte;

BEGIN
  curldt := a;
  writeln;
  holdup;
  writeln('LOGICAL DRIVE TABLES (set by LASTDRIVE=, SUBST, etc.):');
  holdup;
  dec( n );                    { convert for zero-based reference  }
  for o := 0 to n do           { loop through contiguous tables     }
    begin
      ldtrpt(curldt, o);
      curldt := ptr(seg(curldt^), ( ofs(curldt^) + sizeof(ldt)));
    end;
  write(#12);
END; { of ldttrc }
```

```
{ main  }
BEGIN
  b.ah := $30;                      { Check for correct DOS version      }
  MsDos(b);
  if b.al <> 3 then                 { If not version 3.x, get right out  }
    begin
      writeln( 'Wrong DOS version: ', b.al, '.', b.ah );
      halt(255);                    { return ErrorLevel=255              }
    end;
  PawsFlag := ParamCount = 0;   { else set up for paging output          }
  lctr := 0;
  writeln( 'Configuration Variables, DOS version ', b.al, '.', b.ah );
  holdup;
  b.ah := $52;                      { Get CVT pointer set up             }
  msdos(b);                         {   (using undocumented function)    }
  cvtbase := ptr(b.es, b.bx-8); { hold pointer to CVT                    }

  writeln;
  holdup;
  writeln('CVT is located at ', xp(cvtbase));
  holdup;
  write  ('No. of Phys Drives (at ', xp(@cvtbase^.npdrvs));
  writeln('): ', cvtbase^.npdrvs);
  holdup;
  write  ('No. of Log. Drives (at ', xp(@cvtbase^.nldrvs));
  writeln('): ', cvtbase^.nldrvs);
  holdup;
  write  ('  Clock Device (ptr at ', xp(@cvtbase^.clkdev));
  writeln('): ', xp(cvtbase^.clkdev));
  holdup;
  write  ('    CON Device (ptr at ', xp(@cvtbase^.condev));
  writeln('): ', xp(cvtbase^.condev));
  holdup;
  write  ('    Sector Size(?) (at ', xp(@cvtbase^.secsiz));
  writeln('):      ',hexw(cvtbase^.secsiz));
  holdup;
  write  ('     FCBs to keep (at ', xp(@cvtbase^.filler));
  writeln('):      ',hexw(cvtbase^.filler));
  holdup;
  write  ('1.    Memory Chain (ptr at ', xp(@cvtbase^.memchn));
  writeln('): ', xp(cvtbase^.memchn));
  holdup;
  write  ('2.       DCB Chain (ptr at ', xp(@cvtbase^.dcbchn));
  writeln('): ', xp(cvtbase^.dcbchn));
  holdup;
  write  ('3.       DPB Chain (ptr at ', xp(@cvtbase^.pdrvs));
  writeln('): ', xp(cvtbase^.pdrvs));
  holdup;
  write  ('4.       FCB Chain (ptr at ', xp(@cvtbase^.fcbchn));
  writeln('): ', xp(cvtbase^.fcbchn));
  holdup;
  write  ('5.       LDT Chain (ptr at ', xp(@cvtbase^.ldrvs));
  writeln('): ', xp(cvtbase^.ldrvs));
  holdup;
  write  ('6.  Current Buffer (ptr at ', xp(@cvtbase^.curbfr));
  writeln('): ', xp(cvtbase^.curbfr));
  holdup;
```

continues

993

Listing D.1 Continued

```
        write  ('7.    Buffer Chain (ptr at ', xp(@cvtbase^.bfrchn));
        writeln('): ', xp(cvtbase^.bfrchn));
        holdup;

        writeln;
        holdup;
        writeln('TRACING      MCB Chain===');
        holdup;
        memtrc(cvtbase^.memchn);

        writeln;
        holdup;
        writeln('TRACING      DCB Chain===');
        holdup;
        dcbtrc('DCB', cvtbase^.dcbchn);

        writeln;
        holdup;
        writeln('TRACING      DPB Chain===');
        holdup;
        dpbtrc(cvtbase^.pdrvs);

        writeln;
        holdup;
        writeln('TRACING      FCB Chain===');
        holdup;
        dcbtrc('FCB', cvtbase^.fcbchn);

        writeln;
        holdup;
        writeln('TRACING      LDT Chain===');
        holdup;
        ldttrc(cvtbase^.ldrvs, cvtbase^.nldrvs);

        writeln;
        holdup;
        writeln('TRACING Current Buffer===');
        holdup;
        bcbtrc(cvtbase^.curbfr);

        writeln;
        holdup;
        writeln('TRACING    Buffer Chain===');
        holdup;
        bcbtrc(cvtbase^.bfrchn);
    END.
```

CVT3 is written in Turbo Pascal. It has been tested and compiles properly with any version of Turbo Pascal beginning with version 5.0 (including version 7.0). Although the listing for CVT3.PAS may look formidable at first glance, do not be dismayed. The listing is a collection of relatively simple procedures. The first few pages of the listing simply define all the CVT structures so that they can be referenced by the program. Following the declarations, a number of utility functions to assist in displaying output are defined. Then the individual tracing functions for each major structure are built, and finally it is all pulled together into the main program. Let's go through it in detail, a little at a time.

The Data Structures

The CVT3 program begins by declaring a number of special data types, one for each CVT structure and another as a pointer to that structure. Thus, bcb defines the format of the buffer control block as a *record* (the Pascal equivalent of the C *struct*), and bcbptr defines a pointer to such a record.

Similarly, mcb and mcbptr define the memory control block format; dpb and dpbptr define the drive parameter block format; chn and chnptr define the link header used in the DCB and FCB chains; dcb and dcbptr define the format of the device control block (also used by system FCBs); ldt and ldtptr define the logical drive table; and cvt defines the CVT.

The remaining special types defined are dtstr (the size of the string used for date and time reporting), pstrg (the size used when reporting pointer values), and memst (the size used in reporting memory use). These types are defined because Turbo Pascal considers two different string[8] definitions as being two unique types; defining special types permits the compiler's type checking to work properly and also documents the use of the shorter strings.

With all the special types defined, they in turn are used to declare the global working variables the rest of the program uses: cvtbase is the pointer that will be returned as the base of the CVT; curbuf, curmcb, curdpb, curchn, curdcb, curfcb, and curldt are the current pointers to the various records being traced; and the remaining variables are used by the report-generating process.

Utility Functions

With the types and variables declared, the program next defines a number of utility functions. hexn is passed a single byte and converts its low four bits to a hex digit returned as an ASCII character. hexb, in turn, uses hexn twice (shifting by four bits on the first call) to convert a full byte to a 2-character string; hexw uses hexb in the same way to convert a 16-bit word to a string of hex digits, and hexl does it again with hexw to convert 32-bit values. When something is simple and it works, keep using it!

The procedure holdup, which is called after each line of output is generated during the tracing procedures, does nothing if the global PawsFlag is false. This permits continuous output if you are redirecting the report to the printer or to a file. If PawsFlag is true, however, holdup increments the line counter lctr and, if its value is greater than 23 (a full screen for comfortable viewing), resets lctr and waits for you to press Enter before returning.

Function xp is a special function that converts pointer values into the conventional ASCII representation *ssss:oooo*, by using hexw to do the binary-to-hex conversion of the pointer.

The final utility procedure, dmp, is a general building block you can use anywhere to generate a DEBUG-like listing of any 16 consecutive bytes in both hex and ASCII format. It accepts a far pointer as input and then writes to the screen the pointer value, the 16 bytes in hex format, and the same 16 bytes converted to ASCII (with the high bit stripped off and control characters converted to '.' to prevent confusion). Most of the procedures described earlier are used by dmp, either directly or indirectly. The reporting procedures use dmp to display the content of memory areas such as buffers.

Tracing the DPBs

Procedure dpbtrc performs both the tracing and the reporting of drive parameter block content. It defines a local procedure, dpbrpt, which does the reporting. This procedure can be called only from within dpbtrc and is not available to other routines; the capability of using such a "local" procedure is one of the most significant differences between Pascal and C.

The dpbrpt procedure depends on the pointer curdpb being set properly and simply converts data from the DPB, which is pointed to, into a more descriptive format for display by translating drive codes to letters and so forth. Some of its display is presented in hex format, and some values are output in decimal, all to increase the readability of the report. This might be considered a bare-bones "expert system" procedure that translates the knowledge of the DPB format into relatively plain language that is easier to understand.

Following the definition of dpbrpt, the dpbtrc procedure begins by setting global pointer curdpb to the value of the pointer passed in (from the CVT). Next, local variable ofsv is set to zero; this saves the offset of the next DPB pointer inside each record; when its value becomes FFFFh, the trace loop terminates.

With variables set up, the procedure prints a title line and goes into the tracing loop controlled by ofsv. On every pass through the loop, the value of ofsv is changed, dpbrpt is called to report everything contained in the current DPB, and curdpb is set to the value found in the next DPB pointer. Until ofsv becomes FFFFh, the loop continues so that all valid DPBs are reported. Every time the screen fills during this process, holdup introduces a wait, which gives you time to read the screen.

After the last DPB report is displayed, dpbtrc sends a form-feed character to its output with "write(#12)". This line simply displays a graphics character on the CRT; if output is sent to the printer, however, it forces the next trace function's output to appear on a fresh page. Most of the tracing procedures do this immediately before returning to the main calling routine.

Tracing the BCBs

The procedure bcbtrc traces and reports the buffer control blocks. This procedure, like dpbtrc, includes a local reporting function appropriately called bcbrpt.

Like dpbrpt, bcbrpt translates the information from the buffer headers into a more comprehensible format and displays the information on the screen. It then uses dmp to display the complete contents of the buffer, before returning to bcbtrc.

996

Like `dpbtrc`, the `bcbtrc` routine is essentially a shell that first initializes its associated variables and then loops through calls to `bcbrpt` until it reaches the end of the buffer chain. When the end of the chain is reached, the procedure outputs a form-feed and returns to its caller.

Unlike `dpbtrc`, however, `bcbtrc` cannot use a global variable to hold its pointer for `bcbrpt` because `bcbtrc` is called for two different chains. Instead, the pointer is passed as the sole argument to each of these procedures.

Tracing the DCBs

The procedure that traces and reports both the device control blocks and the system FCBs (which share the same structure) is a little more complex. In addition to its local reporting routine, `dcbrpt`, it also defines a pair of functions: `f_tm`, which translates the time value kept in the DCB into conventional display format, and `f_dt`, which does the same for the date value.

Both `f_tm` and `f_dt` are straightforward examples of what is often called *brute force* programming. In `f_tm`, for example, the input time variable—packed tightly in the DOS-prescribed file-directory format—is shifted and masked as required to extract the hour as a single byte, and then this byte is converted to a 2-digit decimal by a sequence of DIV and MOD operations (the value 48 added here is the binary value of an ASCII 0 character). The same is done for the minutes and for the seconds.

When the packed value therefore has been expanded to a string of type `dtstr`, that string is returned as the function's value. The `f_dt` function works in the same way for month, day, and year values.

Because the DCB can hold information about either a file or a device, and the descriptions of that information differ depending on which one is present, `dcbrpt` is a little more complex too. It includes code to determine whether each DCB refers to a file or to a device, and decision structures to change the report accordingly.

Another complicating factor is the way in which DCBs are grouped sequentially into links, with the links chained by pointers. To track this, `dcbrpt` receives a count (n) telling it how many DCBs to report on before returning to `dcbtrc`; the `dcbtrc` routine takes care of the linkage between chains. Because `dcbrpt` can refer to either DCBs or FCBs, the appropriate string is passed to it as `t`, an argument of type `dtstr`.

When you finally reach the beginning of `dcbtrc`, where the global and local variables are initialized, it is almost an anticlimax. As in the previous tracing routines, it is just a loop that cycles through the chains until it reaches the end of the chain, indicated by an offset value of FFFFh in the `nxtlnk` pointer. When the loop is finished, a form-feed character is written to the output and `dcbtrc` returns.

Tracing the MCB Chain

The MCB tracer procedure, `memtrc`, repeats the now familiar pattern: A local reporting procedure, `memrpt`, contains a local function, `memu`. These are significantly shorter, however, than the ones you have seen.

997

The memu function interprets the first character of the memory block controlled by each MCB, to make an educated guess of the use of that block. Because all programs begin with a PSP, which in turn begins with the two bytes CDh and 20h (the opcode for Int 20h), if memu finds CDh as the first byte, it assumes that a *program* is there. If not, if the first byte is an uppercase alphabetic character in ASCII, it is assumed to be an *environment* block; otherwise, it is reported as containing *data*. One of these three description strings is returned by memu as its value.

The memrpt procedure is given three arguments: s, o, and a. They are, respectively, the size, owner process, and address of the first byte. If the owner is 0000, the memory block is free; otherwise, it is the process ID of the process for which the block is reserved.

The memtrc routine initializes the curmcb global pointer from the value passed to it by the main program, displays a title banner for the report, and then enters a loop. This loop calls memrpt for the current MCB, calculates the next MCB segment value from the size of the current one, and sets curmcb to that address. The loop continues as long as the MCB identifier byte, M, is found in the first byte of each MCB. When the loop fails, a z in the first byte identifies the valid last-MCB block; any other value indicates that the MCB chain has been corrupted. All this checking is done by memtrc in only a few statements.

LDT Tracing

The final tracer routine is ldttrc, which displays the area used to keep the current directory information for every logical drive in the system and is used also to record SUBSTed and ASSIGNed drive information.

The local reporting routine, ldtrpt, gets a pointer to the first LDT when called and also a drive code numeric value in the range zero through the number of logical drives (minus one because this drive code is zero-based). It converts the drive code to a letter value for reporting use and then checks the status byte in the LDT to determine whether the drive has in fact been defined.

If the drive has been defined, the physical drive and current directory information stored in the LDT are printed along with the logical drive letter, and the status byte (and other LDT entries whose meanings have been decoded) is translated and displayed.

The ldttrc procedure first sets curldt and displays a title. Next, it decrements the logical drive count that was passed to it in order to adjust for the zero-based drive-code usage. It then loops through the LDT for every possible logical drive, calls ldtrpt for each one and then sets curldt to point to the next, and calculates the address from the size of each entry.

The Main Routine

Now that each tracing module has been examined, they can be put together in the main calling sequence. It begins by verifying that the program is running under DOS V3.x, by using Function 30h of Interrupt 21h (invoked through the Turbo Pascal library procedure MsDos). If the program is not running under DOS V3.x, the program displays an error message and terminates with an errorlevel code of 255.

998

If the DOS version is correct, operation continues and the global variable PawsFlag is set to true if an argument accompanied the program name on the DOS command line, or to false if only the name was given. This capability lets you control the full-screen pause feature by furnishing or omitting an argument; no other use is made of any argument you supply.

The program then initializes the lctr global variable that holdup uses, in case full-screen pauses are needed, and displays a banner line. Next, it uses undocumented Function 52h of Interrupt 21h to obtain the address of the CVT from DOS, subtracts eight from the returned offset, and stores the result in the global pointer cvtbase.

The CVT address is used to obtain a number of system statistics that are then displayed to the screen—not necessarily in the sequence in which the CVT holds them but, rather, in a sequence that may be more informative.

Following the display of these items, each trace/report routine is called. The holdup routine ensures that you have ample time to read every screenful of information supplied. This step completes the CVT3 program.

You can easily adapt any part of the program to deal with only one area. By changing the memtrc routines to search but not display data, for instance, you can create a program by using only the routines that can access the master DOS environment, no matter how deeply its running shell is nested.

CVT4.PAS: Updating the Program to V4

The changes made to the undocumented DOS structures at the introduction of V4 rendered CVT3.PAS unusable with the new version. This illustrates perfectly one of the major drawbacks in using undocumented functions—anything in them can change from one version of DOS to another. This caution was already mentioned at the beginning of this appendix.

Because of the way in which the data structures were defined in CVT3.PAS, it was not practical to make the program capable of running under either version. Instead, the required changes were put in a new program, CVT4.PAS. In the discussion following CVT4.PAS (in Listing D.2), only changes are described; the remainder of the program is identical to what is presented in CVT3.PAS. CVT4.PAS also compiles with Turbo Pascal versions 5.0 through 7.0.

Listing D.2

```
{ cvt4.pas - Turbo Pascal V5.0 version for DOS 4.x
 *       Copyright 1987, 1988, 1989 Jim Kyle - All Rights Reserved
 *
 *       The program, and the information it contains, may be freely
 *       distributed and used so long as this entire comment section
 *       is not altered.
}
PROGRAM CVT4;
```

continues

999

Listing D.2 Continued

```
{$A-,B-,D+,E-,F-,I+,L+,N+,O-,R-,S+,V-}
{$M 8192,0,0 }
USES DOS;

TYPE

  bcb = RECORD                  { Buffer Control Block format, V4   }
          prcb   : word;                { +00 prev one in chain }
          nxcb   : word;                { +02 next one in chain }
          ldrv   : byte;                { +04 logical drive code }
          action : byte;                { +05 action code         }
          lsect  : longint;             { +06 logical sector #    }
          nf     : byte;                { +0A nbr FATs or 01      }
          secf   : word;                { +0B sectors/FAT or 00   }
          pdrv   : pointer;             { +0D phys drv tbl ptr    }
          fill2  : word;                { +11 unknown             }
          fill3  : byte;                { +13 unknown             }
          buf    : array[0..511] of byte; { +14 the buffer itself }
        END;
  bcbptr = ^bcb;

  bcblnk = RECORD               { BCB link record, new in V4       }
            bxval : word;               { +00, unknown            }
            pagebase : bcbptr;          { +02, points to a BCB    }
            usrs    : byte;             { +06, count of usage     }
            fill    : longint;          { +07, unknown            }
           END;
  bcblkp = ^bcblnk;

  bufctl = RECORD               { EMS control for buffers, new in V4 }
            lnkptr  : bcblkp;           { +00, point to pagebase  }
            pgs     : word;             { +04, number of pages    }
            fill1   : longint;          { +06, unknown            }
            fill2   : word;             { +0A, unknown            }
            emsflg  : byte;             { +0C, FF if no EMS used  }
            emshdl  : word;             { +0D, EMS handle         }
            emsppg  : byte;             { +0F, EMS physical page  }
           END;
  bcptr = ^bufctl;

  nam8 = array[1..8] of char;

  mcb = RECORD                  { Mem Alloc Block header format     }
          flag  : char;                 { +00 must be M or Z      }
          owner : word;                 { +01 PSP seg or 0000     }
          siz   : word;                 { +03 Number paragraphs   }
          junk  : array[5..7] of byte;  { +05-+07 not used        }
          name  : nam8;                 { +08 Name of owner       }
        END;
  mcbptr = ^mcb;

  dpb = RECORD                  { Physical Drive Table format       }
          drvc  : byte;                 { +00 drive code          }
          dunit : byte;                 { +01 unit number         }
          bps   : integer;              { +02 bytes per sector    }
```

```
            spc    : byte;                  { +04 sec per cluster -1 }
            pwr2   : byte;                  { +05 power of 2         }
            rsrvs  : integer;              { +06 reserved sectors   }
            nfats  : byte;                  { +08 number of FATs     }
            dirsiz : word;                  { +09 root dir size      }
            fus    : word;                  { +0B first usable sectr }
            tcc    : word;                  { +0D total clstr ct +1  }
            spf    : word;                  { +0F sec per FAT **CHG**}
            fds    : word;                  { +11 first dir sector   }
            drvr   : pointer;              { +13 driver pointer     }
            mcode  : byte;                  { +17 media code         }
            accflg : byte;                  { +18 access flag        }
            nxt    : pointer;              { +19 next table ptr     }
            lastused : word;                { +1D last used cluster  }
            filler : word;                  { +1F usually FFFF       }
         END;
   dpbptr = ^dpb;


   chn = RECORD                   { Chain links for DCB, FCB chains   }
            nxtlnk : pointer;              { +00 next link or FFFF  }
            nmbr   : integer;              { +04 number blocks here }
         END;
   chnptr = ^chn;


   dcb = RECORD                   { Device Control Block format       }
            nusers : integer;              { +00 users for this DCB }
            mode   : integer;              { +02 0,1,2 per OPEN     }
            datrb  : byte;                  { +04 disk attrib byte   }
            dvatr  : byte;                  { +05 device attrib (hi) }
            atrb2  : byte;                  { +06 2nd device attrib  }
            pdrvr  : pointer;              { +07 points to driver   }
            frstc  : word;                  { +0B first cluster nbr  }
            modtm  : word;                  { +0D file time word     }
            moddt  : word;                  { +0F file date word     }
            totsiz : longint;              { +11 total file size    }
            curpos : longint;              { +15 current byte pos   }
            clsctr : word;                  { +19 total cluster ctr  }
            curcls : word;                  { +1B current cluster    }
            dirsec : word;                  { +1D directory sector   }
            dirndx : byte;                  { +1F dir entry index 0..}
            name   : array[0..7] of char;  { +20 dev/file name      }
            ext    : array[0..3] of char;  { +28 file extension     }
            fill2  : word;                  { +2B unknown            }
            fill3  : word;                  { +2D unknown            }
            fill4  : word;                  { +2F unknown            }
            owner  : word;                  { +31 PSP of owner proc  }
            fill5  : word;                  { +33 unknown            }
            fill6  : word;                  { +35 unknown            }
            fill7  : word;                  { +37 unknown            }
            fill8  : word;                  { +39 unknown            }
         END;
    dcbptr = ^dcb;


   ldt = RECORD                       { Logical Drive Table format  }
            name   : array[0..67] of char;{ +00 drive and path      }
            code   : byte;                  { +44 drive in use code   }
```

continues

Listing D.2 Continued

```
            mydpb  : dpbptr;            { +45 DPB for this drive }
            dirclu : word;             { +49 directory cluster  }
            filler2: word;             { +4B unknown            }
            filler3: word;             { +4D unknown            }
            patlen : word;             { +4F SUBST path length  }
            filler4: byte;             { +51 unknown            }
            filler5: word;             { +52 unknown            }
            filler6: word;             { +54 unknown            }
            filler7: word;             { +56 unknown            }
        END;
    ldtptr = ^ldt;

    cvt = RECORD               { Configuration Variable Table }
            curbfr : bcbptr;           { current pos in chain   }
            memchn : mcbptr;           { start of MCB chain      }
            pdrvs  : dpbptr;           { Fn $52 points to here   }
            dcbchn : dcbptr;           { set up by FILES=        }
            clkdev : pointer;          { set by DEVICE= (clock$)}
            condev : pointer;          { set by DEVICE= (con)    }
            secsiz : integer;          { maximum block size      }
            bfrchn : bcblkp;           { set up by BUFFERS=      }
            ldrvs  : ldtptr;           { set up by LASTDRIVE=    }
            fcbchn : chnptr;           { set up by FCBS=         }
            filler : integer;          { number of FCBs to keep }
            npdrvs : byte;             { set by driver list      }
            nldrvs : byte;             { set by LASTDRIVE=       }
        END;
    cvtptr = ^cvt;

    dtstr = string[8];                 { date-time strings       }
    pstrg = string[9];                 { pointer-conversion fmt }
    memst = string[12];                { memory usage string     }

VAR
    cvtbase : cvtptr;
    curbuf  : bcbptr;
    curmcb  : mcbptr;
    curdpb  : dpbptr;
    curchn  : chnptr;
    curdcb,
    curfcb  : dcbptr;
    curldt  : ldtptr;
    bcbctr,
    dcbctr  : integer ;                { counters                }
    b       : Registers;
    PawsFlag: Boolean;                 { controls screen-full pausing }
    lctr    : integer;                 { counts lines displayed  }

function hexn(b:byte) : char;          { converts nibble to char }
  begin
    b := b and 15;                     { force to only 4 bits    }
    if b > 9 then inc(b,7);            { adjust for hex digits   }
    hexn := chr(b+48);                 { convert to character    }
  end;
```

```
function hexb(b:byte) : string;
  begin
    hexb := hexn(b shr 4) + hexn(b);   { assemble the nibbles   }
  end;

function hexw(w:word) : string;
  begin
    hexw := hexb(w shr 8) + hexb(w);   { assemble the bytes     }
  end;

function hexl(l:longint) : string;
  begin
    hexl := hexw(l shr 16) + hexw(l);  { assemble the words     }
  end;

procedure outcstr( var s : nam8);  { output ASCIIZ string       }
  VAR
    i : integer;
  BEGIN
    i := 1;
    while (s[i] <> #0) and (i < 9) do
      begin
        write(s[i]);
        inc(i);
      end;
  END;

PROCEDURE holdup;                      { count lines and wait if full }
  BEGIN
    IF PawsFlag THEN
      BEGIN
        inc(lctr);
        if lctr > 23 then
          BEGIN
            lctr := 0;
            readln;
          END
      END
  END;

FUNCTION xp( p : pointer ) : pstrg;    { displays pointer P }
  BEGIN
    xp := hexw(seg(p^)) + ':' + hexw(ofs(p^));
  END;

PROCEDURE  dmp(f : pointer);       { display hex dump of data to CRT }
  VAR
    x : ^byte;
    i : integer;
    c : char;
  BEGIN
    x := f;
    write( xp(f), '> ');
    FOR i:=0 to 15 DO
      BEGIN
        write( hexb(x^) );
        if i=7 then write('-')
```

continues

Listing D.2 Continued

```
              else write(' ');
        x := pointer(longint(x) + 1);
      END;
    write('  ');
    x := f;
    FOR i:=0 to 15 DO
      BEGIN
        c := char($7f AND x^);
        if c<' ' then c := '.';
        write( c );
        if i=7 then write(' ');
        x := pointer(longint(x) + 1);
      END;
    writeln;
    holdup;
  END;

PROCEDURE dpbtrc(a: pointer);       { trace and report DPB data }
  VAR
    ofsv : word;

  PROCEDURE dpbrpt;                  { reports each DPB's content }
    BEGIN
      writeln;
      holdup;
      write('Drive ', char (curdpb^.drvc+ord('A')) );
      write(': (unit ', curdpb^.dunit, ' of driver at ', xp(curdpb^.drvr) );
      writeln(') media code = ', hexb(curdpb^.mcode) );
      holdup;
      write(' ', curdpb^.bps:3, ' bytes per sector,');
      write(' ', curdpb^.spc+1:2, ' sectors per cluster,');
      writeln(' ', curdpb^.tcc-1:4, ' total cluster count');
      holdup;
      write(' Res sectors: ', curdpb^.rsrvs, ' ');
      write(' ', curdpb^.nfats, ' FAT''s, ', curdpb^.spf:2, ' sec ea ');
      write(' FAT entry: ');
      IF (curdpb^.tcc) > $0FFC
        THEN  write( 16 )
        ELSE  write( 12 );
      writeln(' bits  Root: ', curdpb^.dirsiz:3, ' entries');
      holdup;
      write(' First root sector: ', hexw(curdpb^.fds)  );
      write(' First data sector: ', hexw(curdpb^.fus)  );
      writeln(' Last cluster used: ', hexw(curdpb^.lastused));
      holdup;
    END;          { of dpbrpt proc }

  BEGIN
    curdpb := a;
    ofsv := 0;
    writeln;
    holdup;
    writeln('DRIVE PARAMETER BLOCK (DPB) DATA--');
    holdup;
    WHILE (ofsv <> $FFFF) DO
```

```
        BEGIN
          ofsv := word(longint( curdpb^.nxt ));
          dpbrpt ;
          curdpb := dpbptr(curdpb^.nxt);
        END;
      write(#12);
  END;  { of dpbtrc proc }

PROCEDURE bcbtrc2(a : pointer);
  VAR
    ofsv : word;
    ofst : word;

  PROCEDURE  bcbrpt(a : bcbptr);
    VAR
      i : integer;
      x : pointer;
    BEGIN
      writeln;
      holdup;
      inc(bcbctr);
      write('Buffer Control Block ', bcbctr:2, ' at ', xp(a));
      write('     Prev: ', hexw(a^.prcb));
      writeln('        Next: ', hexw(a^.nxcb));
      holdup;
      write('     Logical ''', char(ord('A')+a^.ldrv));
      write(':'',    Sector ', hexl(a^.lsect));
      writeln('    Action code: ', hexb(a^.action));
      holdup;
      write('     NFATS: ', hexb( a^.nf));
      write('        SPF: ', hexw(a^.secf));
      writeln('       DPB address: ', xp(a^.pdrv));
      holdup;
      write('     FILL2: ', hexw(a^.fill2));
      writeln('        FILL3: ', hexb(a^.fill3));
      holdup;
      x := addr(bcbptr(a)^.buf[0]);
      FOR i:=0 to 31 DO
        dmp(pointer(longint(x)+(i SHL 4)));
    END;          { of bcbrpt proc }

  BEGIN           { bcbtrc2 routine }
    bcbctr := 0;
    ofsv := 0;
    ofst := ofs(a^);
    WHILE (ofsv <> ofst) DO
      BEGIN
        ofsv := bcbptr(a)^.nxcb;
        bcbrpt (a);
        a := ptr(seg(a^),ofsv);
      END;
    write(#12);
  END;            { bcbtrc2 routine }

PROCEDURE bcbtrc1(a:pointer);
```

continues

1005

Listing D.2 Continued

```
        PROCEDURE bcbtrl(a:bcblkp);
          BEGIN
            writeln;
            holdup;
            writeln( 'Page base is at ', xp(a^.pagebase));
            holdup;
            write  ( 'BX Val = ', hexw(a^.bxval) );
            write  ('    Users = ', hexb(a^.usrs) );
            writeln( '    Fill = ', hexl(a^.fill) );
            holdup;
            bcbtrc2(a^.pagebase);
          END;

      BEGIN
        writeln( 'Link table is at ', xp(bcptr(a)^.lnkptr));
        holdup;
        write  ( 'Page count = ', bcptr(a)^.pgs:4 );
        write  ('    Fill1 = ', hexl(bcptr(a)^.fill1) );
        writeln( '    Fill2 = ', hexw(bcptr(a)^.fill2) );
        holdup;
        write  ( 'EMS Flag = ', hexb(bcptr(a)^.emsflg) );
        write  ('        Handle = ', hexw(bcptr(a)^.emshdl) );
        writeln( '    PhysPg = ', hexb(bcptr(a)^.emsppg) );
        holdup;
        bcbtrl( bcptr(a)^.lnkptr );
      END;

    PROCEDURE dcbtrc(t : dtstr; a : pointer);
      VAR
        ofsv : word;

      FUNCTION f_tm(n : word) : dtstr;
        VAR
          buf : dtstr;
          b   : byte;
        BEGIN
          b := ((n SHR 11) AND 31);
          buf[1] :=char((b DIV 10) + 48);
          buf[2] :=char((b MOD 10) + 48);
          buf[3] := ':';
          b := ((n SHR  5) AND 63);
          buf[4] :=char((b DIV 10) + 48);
          buf[5] :=char((b MOD 10) + 48);
          buf[6] := ':';
          b := ((n SHL  1) AND 63);
          buf[7] :=char((b DIV 10) + 48);
          buf[8] :=char((b MOD 10) + 48);
          f_tm := buf;
        END;

      FUNCTION f_dt(n : word) : dtstr;
        VAR
          buf : dtstr;
          b   : byte;
        BEGIN
```

```
            b :=((n SHR  5) AND 15);
            buf[1] :=char((b DIV 10) + 48);
            buf[2] :=char((b MOD 10) + 48);
            buf[3] := '/';
            b := ( n         AND 31);
            buf[4] :=char((b DIV 10) + 48);
            buf[5] :=char((b MOD 10) + 48);
            buf[6] := '/';
            b := ((n SHR  9) AND 15) + 80;
            buf[7] :=char((b DIV 10) + 48);
            buf[8] :=char((b MOD 10) + 48);
            f_dt := buf;
          END;

       PROCEDURE dcbrpt( var t : dtstr; n : integer );
         type
           acctyp = array[0..3] of string[7];
         const
           actyp : acctyp = ('READ', 'WRITE', 'R/W', 'unknown');
         var
           isdvc : Boolean;
         BEGIN
           WHILE (n > 0) DO
           BEGIN
             INC (dcbctr);
             writeln;
             holdup;
             write  (t, ' ', dcbctr:2 );
             IF (curdcb^.name[0] = #0)  THEN
             BEGIN
               writeln(' at ', xp(curdcb), ' not used since bootup');
               holdup;
             END
             else
             BEGIN
               isdvc := (curdcb^.dvatr and 128) <> 0;
               write(' for ');
               IF isdvc
                 THEN write( 'device ' )
                 ELSE write( 'file ' );
               write(curdcb^.name[0], curdcb^.name[1], curdcb^.name[2]);
               write(curdcb^.name[3], curdcb^.name[4], curdcb^.name[5]);
               write(curdcb^.name[6], curdcb^.name[7]);
               IF (NOT isdvc) THEN  { block driver }
                 write('.', curdcb^.ext[0], curdcb^.ext[1], curdcb^.ext[2]);
               write(' at ', xp( curdcb ) );
               write(' shows ', curdcb^.nusers);
               writeln(' OPENs');
               holdup;
               write('  Opened for ', actyp[3 AND (curdcb^.mode)]);
               write(' access' );
               IF ($FFFC AND (curdcb^.mode))<>0 THEN
                 write(' (', hexw(curdcb^.mode), ')');
               writeln(' by process ', hexw(curdcb^.owner));
               holdup;
```

continues

1007

Listing D.2 Continued

```
                 IF( isdvc ) THEN              { Device       }
                    BEGIN
                      write('  Device driver at ', xp(curdcb^.pdrvr) );
                      write(' is in ');
                      if ((curdcb^.dvatr) AND 32)<>0 THEN write('Raw')
                                                  ELSE write( 'Cooked' );
                      write(' mode and is ');
                      if ((curdcb^.dvatr) AND 64)=0 THEN  write('not ');
                      writeln('ready');
                      holdup;
                    END
                 else                           { File         }
                    BEGIN
                      write(' File is on drive ', char(ord('A')+((curdcb^.dvatr) AND 31)));
                      write(': (driver at ', xp(curdcb^.pdrvr));
                      write(') and has ');
                      if ((curdcb^.dvatr) AND 64)<>0 THEN  write('not ');
                      writeln('been written to.');
                      holdup;
                      writeln(' File''s attribute byte = ', hexb(curdcb^.datrb));
                      holdup;
                    END;
                 write  ('  Mod Time/date: ');
                 write  (f_tm(curdcb^.modtm), ', ');
                 writeln(f_dt(curdcb^.moddt));
                 holdup;
                 write  ('        Dir Sector:  ', hexw(curdcb^.dirsec), ' ');
                 writeln('         Dir Index:  ', curdcb^.dirndx:4, ' ');
                 holdup;
                 write  ('    First Cluster:  ', hexw(curdcb^.frstc), ' ');
                 write  ('    Prev Clusters:  ', curdcb^.clsctr:4, ' ');
                 writeln('  Current Cluster:  ', hexw(curdcb^.curcls), ' ');
                 holdup;
                 write  ('   Directory size:',  curdcb^.totsiz:6, ' ');
                 writeln('  Curr byte count:',  curdcb^.curpos:6    );
                 holdup;
                 write  (' Fill2=', hexw(curdcb^.fill2), ' ');
                 write  (' Fill3=', hexw(curdcb^.fill3), ' ');
                 write  (' Fill4=', hexw(curdcb^.fill4), ' ');
                 writeln(' Fill5=', hexw(curdcb^.fill5)    );
                 holdup;
                 write  (' Fill6=', hexw(curdcb^.fill6), ' ');
                 write  (' Fill7=', hexw(curdcb^.fill7), ' ');
                 writeln(' Fill8=', hexw(curdcb^.fill8)    );
                 holdup;
               END;
               curdcb := pointer(longint(curdcb) + sizeof(dcb) - 1);
               DEC( n );
          END;          { n >= 0 loop    }
        END;            { of dcbrpt      }

   BEGIN
     curchn := chnptr(a);
     dcbctr := 0;
     ofsv := 0;
     WHILE (ofsv <> $FFFF) DO
```

```
      BEGIN
        ofsv := word(longint(curchn^.nxtlnk));
        curdcb := dcbptr(longint(curchn)+sizeof(chn));
        writeln;
        holdup;
        write  ( 'Link at ', xp(curchn), ' contains ');
        writeln( curchn^.nmbr, ' ', t, 's--');
        holdup;
        dcbrpt (t, curchn^.nmbr);
        curchn := chnptr(curchn^.nxtlnk);
      END;
    write(#12);
  END;

PROCEDURE memtrc(a : pointer);
  VAR
    z : longint;

  PROCEDURE memrpt(s,o,a : word; var n : nam8);

    FUNCTION memu(a : word) : memst;     { determine memory use }
      var
        x : char;
    BEGIN
      x := char( mem[a:0] );
      CASE x OF
        #$CD:
          memu := 'Program';
        'A'..'Z':
          memu := 'Environment';
        else
          memu := 'Data';
        End;
    END;

  BEGIN
    z := longint(s) SHL 4;
    write( z:6, ' bytes ' );
    IF (o<>0) THEN
      begin
        write  ('USED by proc ', hexw(o));
        write  (', at ', hexw( a ), ':0000, for ', memu(a));
        if n[1] in ['A'..'Z'] then
          begin
            write('. Pgm name: ' );
            outcstr( n );
            writeln;
          end
        else
          writeln('. No program name');
      end
    else
      writeln('FREE at ', hexw( a ), ':0000' );
    holdup;
  END;  { of memrpt      }
```

continues

Listing D.2 Continued

```
BEGIN
  curmcb := mcbptr(a);
  writeln;
  holdup;
  writeln('MEMORY ALLOCATION CHAIN');
  holdup;
  WHILE (curmcb^.flag = 'M') DO
    BEGIN
      memrpt( curmcb^.siz, curmcb^.owner, SEG(curmcb^)+1, curmcb^.name);
      curmcb := ptr( seg(curmcb^) + (curmcb^.siz + 1), 0 );
    END;
  IF (curmcb^.flag <> 'Z') THEN
    BEGIN
      writeln(#13, #10, 'MEMORY ALLOCATION ERROR at ', xp(curmcb) );
      halt(255);
    END;
  memrpt( curmcb^.siz, curmcb^.owner, SEG(curmcb^)+1, curmcb^.name);
  write(#12);
END;    { of memtrc }

PROCEDURE ldttrc( a: ldtptr; n: byte );

  PROCEDURE ldtrpt( l: ldtptr; d: byte );
    VAR
      ldrive : char;
      i      : integer;
    BEGIN
      ldrive := chr( $41 + d );
      if (l^.code AND byte($40))=0 then
        writeln( 'Logical Drive ', ldrive, ' not yet defined' )
      else
        begin
          write ( 'Logical Drive ', ldrive );
          writeln( ' = Physical drive ', l^.name[0] );
          holdup;
          write ( 'The current (full) pathspec is: ' );
          i := 0;
          repeat
            write ( l^.name[i] );
            inc( i );
          until (l^.name[i] = #0);
          writeln;
        end;
      holdup;
      if(l^.code = $50) then
        writeln( 'Code = 0x50 -- result of SUBST command')
      else if(l^.code = $40) then
        writeln( 'Code = 0x40 -- physical (or aliased) device')
      else
        writeln( 'Code = 0x', hexb(l^.code), ' -- unknown');
      holdup;
      writeln( 'Directory Cluster = ', hexw( l^.dirclu ));
      holdup;
      writeln( 'Path Length to ignore = ', hexw( l^.patlen ));
      holdup;
```

```
        write  ( 'Filler2 = ', hexw(l^.filler2), '  ');
        write  ( 'Filler3 = ', hexw(l^.filler3), '  ');
        writeln( 'Filler4 = ', hexb(l^.filler4)      );
        holdup;
        write  ( 'Filler5 = ', hexw(l^.filler5), '  ');
        write  ( 'Filler6 = ', hexw(l^.filler6), '  ');
        writeln( 'Filler7 = ', hexw(l^.filler7)      );
        holdup;
        writeln;
        holdup;
      END; { of ldtrpt }

    VAR
      o  : byte;

    BEGIN
      curldt := a;
      writeln;
      holdup;
      writeln('LOGICAL DRIVE TABLES (set by LASTDRIVE=, SUBST, etc.):');
      holdup;
      dec( n );                     { convert for zero-based reference  }
      for o := 0 to n do            { loop through contiguous tables     }
        begin
          ldtrpt(curldt, o);
          curldt := ptr(seg(curldt^), ( ofs(curldt^) + sizeof(ldt)));
        end;
      write(#12);
    END; { of ldttrc }

{ main  }
BEGIN
  b.ah := $30;                  { Check for correct DOS version     }
  MsDos(b);
  if b.al < 4 then              { If not V4.x or higher, get out     }
    begin
      writeln( 'Wrong DOS version: ', b.al, '.', b.ah );
      halt(255);                { return ErrorLevel=255               }
    end;
  PawsFlag := ParamCount = 0;   { else set up for paging output      }
  lctr := 0;
  writeln( 'Configuration Variables, DOS version ', b.al, '.', b.ah );
  holdup;
  b.ah := $52;                  { Get CVT pointer set up             }
  msdos(b);                     {    (using undocumented function)    }
  cvtbase := ptr(b.es, b.bx-8); { hold pointer to CVT                }

  writeln;
  holdup;
  writeln('CVT is located at ', xp(cvtbase));
  holdup;
  write ('No. of Phys Drives (at ', xp(@cvtbase^.npdrvs));
  writeln('): ', cvtbase^.npdrvs);
  holdup;
  write ('No. of Log. Drives (at ', xp(@cvtbase^.nldrvs));
  writeln('): ', cvtbase^.nldrvs);
```

continues

1011

Listing D.2 Continued

```
holdup;
write  ('  Clock Device (ptr at ', xp(@cvtbase^.clkdev));
writeln('): ', xp(cvtbase^.clkdev));
holdup;
write  ('   CON Device (ptr at ', xp(@cvtbase^.condev));
writeln('): ', xp(cvtbase^.condev));
holdup;
write  ('    Sector Size(?) (at ', xp(@cvtbase^.secsiz));
writeln('):      ',hexw(cvtbase^.secsiz));
holdup;
write  ('     FCBs to keep (at ', xp(@cvtbase^.filler));
writeln('):      ',hexw(cvtbase^.filler));
holdup;
write  ('1.   Memory Chain (ptr at ', xp(@cvtbase^.memchn));
writeln('): ', xp(cvtbase^.memchn));
holdup;
write  ('2.      DCB Chain (ptr at ', xp(@cvtbase^.dcbchn));
writeln('): ', xp(cvtbase^.dcbchn));
holdup;
write  ('3.      DPB Chain (ptr at ', xp(@cvtbase^.pdrvs));
writeln('): ', xp(cvtbase^.pdrvs));
holdup;
write  ('4.      FCB Chain (ptr at ', xp(@cvtbase^.fcbchn));
writeln('): ', xp(cvtbase^.fcbchn));
holdup;
write  ('5.      LDT Chain (ptr at ', xp(@cvtbase^.ldrvs));
writeln('): ', xp(cvtbase^.ldrvs));
holdup;
write  ('6.  Current Buffer (ptr at ', xp(@cvtbase^.curbfr));
writeln('): ', xp(cvtbase^.curbfr));
holdup;
write  ('7.  Buffer Chain (link at ', xp(@cvtbase^.bfrchn));
writeln('): ', xp(cvtbase^.bfrchn));
holdup;

writeln;
holdup;
writeln('TRACING     MCB Chain===');
holdup;
memtrc(cvtbase^.memchn);

writeln;
holdup;
writeln('TRACING     DCB Chain===');
holdup;
dcbtrc('DCB', cvtbase^.dcbchn);

writeln;
holdup;
writeln('TRACING     DPB Chain===');
holdup;
dpbtrc(cvtbase^.pdrvs);

writeln;
holdup;
```

```
writeln('TRACING     FCB Chain===');
holdup;
dcbtrc('FCB', cvtbase^.fcbchn);

writeln;
holdup;
writeln('TRACING     LDT Chain===');
holdup;
ldttrc(cvtbase^.ldrvs, cvtbase^.nldrvs);

writeln;
holdup;
writeln('TRACING Buffer Chain from current buffer===');
holdup;
bcbtrc2(cvtbase^.curbfr);

writeln;
holdup;
writeln('TRACING   Buffer Chain thru EMS link record===');
holdup;
bcbtrc1(cvtbase^.bfrchn);
END.
```

Buffer Control Block and EMS Links

The first major change in CVT4, as compared with CVT3, is in the definition of the bcb record. The old 4-byte far pointer to the next buffer (nxcb) changes to a pair of 2-byte near pointers to the previous buffer (prcb) and the next one (nxcb). The remaining functions in the control block are the same, except that the lsect element (logical sector number) changes from a 16-bit value to 32 bits and the secf element (sectors per FAT) expands from a single byte to a 16-bit word. These changes increase the size of the BCB from 16 to 20 bytes.

To accommodate DOS's use of expanded memory, introduced in V4, two new structures were added. They are defined in CVT4 as bcblnk, a link record that contains a hash word (bxval) and points to the corresponding BCB (pagebase), and bufctl, a record that associates the EMM handle with a bcblnk record and also maintains other data used by the EMS software. Not all the fields in either record have been fully decoded as of this writing. The corresponding pointer types defined are bcblkp (to a bcblnk record) and bcptr (to a bufctl record).

Because of the extensive changes in buffer handling, the bcbtrc and bcbrpt procedures were almost completely rewritten, and retained as much of the original modularity as possible. The changes in bcbrpt reflect the added information in the V4 BCB. The bcbtrc routine was replaced by two new procedures (bcbtrc1 and bcbtrc2) that deal with the changed method of accessing the buffers and accommodate the new EMS link structures. An additional new procedure, bcbtrl, was added in bcbtrc1.

The loop that calls bcbrpt, which was originally in bcbtrc, now is located in bcbtrc2. The bcbtrl procedure reports page base data from the bcblnk record and then calls bcbtrc2; bcbtrc1 passes a bcblnk pointer to bcbtrl after reporting data from the bufctl record. The apparent simplicity of these changes, which are required in order to handle a major change to the input data, is a strong testimonial to the power of the modular design used for these programs.

The Memory Control Block

One minor change was made to the MCB in V4; an MCB used for program loading now includes the program's name (the name, minus the extension, of the file from which it was loaded). CVT4 handles this change by defining a new type, nam8 (which is an array of char rather than a string because the MCB contains neither a Pascal length byte nor a C end-of-string byte), and extends the definition of the mcb record to include the nam8 field.

The addition of the program name required a modification to the memrpt procedure so that the nam8 field would be reported if a program name is present. No other change was made, however.

The Drive Parameter Block

The only change to the DPB between V3 and V4 was that the sectors-per-FAT field changed in size from a byte to a word. The definition of the dpb record was modified to accommodate the change. This change was conceptually minor, but it was one of the major reasons that CVT3 cannot trace a DOS V4 system; the change in size for the spf element in the dpb record changes the position of the nxt pointer used to trace through the DPB chain, and the program goes wild.

The Device Control Block

In DOS V4, the size of the DCB was extended by six bytes. Three words (of unknown meaning) were added to the definition of the dcb record to account for this change.

The dcbrpt procedure was changed to report the added words, but no other change to the tracing or reporting of DCBs and FCBs was required.

The Logical Drive Table

The LDT size also was extended in DOS V4, by seven bytes. The program adds one byte and three words, all of unknown meaning, to the definition of the ldt record to keep things synchronized.

Because of the added data, the ldtrpt procedure was modified slightly to report the content of the new fields.

The CVT Definition Itself

Only one change was made in the definition of the cvt record, and it was so small that it is easy to overlook: The type for the pointer bfrchn changed from bcbptr (in V3) to bcblkp (in V4). The effect of this change, however, is significant.

1014

Utility Routines

One utility routine, `outcstr`, was added to CVT4 to provide output capability for the new `nam8` data type used by the modified MCB. This routine is passed the address of a `nam8` variable and outputs its characters until either all eight have been processed or a 00h byte is encountered. It is used by only the `memrpt` routine.

The Main Routine

The first change in the main calling sequence is that CVT4 tests for operation with DOS V4 rather than V3 and terminates if the version is not 4.

The wording of the summary statistics report changed slightly, reflecting the changed meaning of the `curbfr` field in the `cvt` record. Similarly, the heading for the buffer tracing changed somewhat because the entire EMS link page (or all buffers if no EMS is in use) is reported at the same point that CVT3 reported only the current buffer.

The changes between programs, however, generally are far less complex than were the actual changes between DOS versions.

Summary

This appendix has presented one method for using the undocumented DOS functions to explore the internal workings of DOS, with an example you can modify to make use of the information available to you as DOS runs.

Keep in mind, however, that making use of such features will cause you headaches whenever a major version change occurs in DOS. The use of undocumented features, therefore, should be held to an absolute minimum in any program that will be distributed widely, either commercially or by way of the public domain.

A Resource List

Hardware

Hogan, Thom. *The Programmer's PC Sourcebook*. Microsoft Press, Redmond, Washington, 1991.

Intel Corporation. *80286 and 80287 Programmer's Reference Manual*. Intel Corporation, Santa Clara, California, 1987.

Intel Corporation. *80386 Programmer's Reference Manual*. Intel Corporation, Santa Clara, California, 1986.

Intel Corporation. *80387 Programmer's Reference Manual*. Intel Corporation, Santa Clara, California, 1987.

Intel Corporation. *i486 Microprocessor Programmer's Reference Manual*. Intel Corporation, Santa Clara, California, 1989.

Intel Corporation. *iAPX 86/88, 186/188 User's Manual*. Intel Corporation, Santa Clara, California, 1987.

International Business Machines Corporation. *Mouse Technical Reference*. IBM, Boca Raton, Florida, 1987.

International Business Machines Corporation. *Personal Computer Technical Reference*. IBM, Boca Raton, Florida, 1984.

International Business Machines Corporation. *Personal System/2 and Personal Computer BIOS Technical Reference*. IBM, Boca Raton, Florida, 1987.

Morse, Stephen P. *The 8086/8088 Primer*, 2nd Edition. Hayden Book Company, Rochelle Park, New Jersey, 1982.

Woram, John. *The PC Configuration Handbook*. Bantam Books, New York, New York, 1987.

MS-DOS and BIOS Programming

Brown, Ralf, and Kyle, Jim. *PC Interrupts*. Addison-Wesley, Reading, Massachusetts, 1991.

Campbell, Joe. *C Programmer's Guide to Serial Communications*. Howard W. Sams and Company, Indianapolis, Indiana, 1987.

Chesley, Harry R. and Mitchell Waite. *Supercharging C with Assembly Language*. Addison-Wesley, Reading, Massachusetts, 1987.

Duncan, Ray. *Advanced MSDOS Programming*, Second Edition. Microsoft Press, Redmond, Washington, 1988.

Hyman, Michael. *Memory Resident Utilities, Interrupts, and Disk Management with MS and PC DOS*. MIS Press, Portland, Oregon, 1986.

Jamsa, Kris. *DOS Programming: The Complete Reference*. Osborne/McGraw-Hill, Berkeley, California, 1991.

Jourdain, Robert, and Norton, Peter. *Programmer's Problem Solver*, 2nd Edition. Brady Books, New York, New York, 1986.

Kyle, Jim. *DOS Developer's Guide*, New Edition. Sams Publishing, Carmel, Indiana, 1993.

Lai, Robert S. *Writing MS-DOS Device Drivers*. Addison-Wesley, Reading, Massachusetts, 1987.

Phoenix Technologies Ltd. *System BIOS for IBM PCs, Compatibles, and EISA Computers*, 2nd Edition. Addison-Wesley, Reading, Massachusetts, 1991.

Porter, Kent. *Stretching Turbo Pascal*. Brady Books, New York, New York, 1987.

Schulman, Andrew. *Undocumented DOS*. Addison-Wesley, Reading, Massachusetts, 1990.

Wadlow, Thomas A. *Memory Resident Programming on the IBM PC*. Addison-Wesley, Reading, Massachusetts, 1987.

Williams, Al. *DOS 5: A Developer's Guide*. M&T Books, Redwood City, California, 1991.

Wilton, Richard. *Programmer's Guide to PC and PS/2 Video Systems*. Microsoft Press, Redmond, Washington, 1987.

Programming Languages

Abel, Peter. *Assembler for the IBM PC and PC-XT*. Reston Publishing, Reston, Virginia, 1984.

Feldman, Phil and Tom Rugg. *Using QuickBASIC 4*. Que Corporation, Carmel, Indiana, 1988.

Harbison, Samuel P. and Guy L. Steele, Jr. *C: A Reference Manual*. Prentice Hall, Englewood Cliffs, New Jersey, 1987.

Holzner, Steve, and Peter Norton Computing, Inc. *Advanced Assembly Language*. Brady Books, New York, New York, 1991.

Johnson, Marcus. *Assembly Language for Real Programmers ONLY!* Sams Publishing, Carmel, Indiana, 1993.

Lafore, Robert. *Microsoft C Programming for the PC*, 2nd Edition. Howard W. Sams and Company, Indianapolis, Indiana, 1990.

Scanlon, Leo. *IBM PC and XT Assembly Language*. Brady Books, Bowie, Maryland, 1983.

Socha, John, and Norton, Peter. *Peter Norton's Assembly Language Book for the IBM PC*. Brady Books, New York, New York, 1986.

Wyatt, Allen. *Advanced Assembly Language*. Que Corporation, Carmel, Indiana, 1992.

Wyatt, Allen. *Using Assembly Language*, 3rd Edition. Que Corporation, Carmel, Indiana, 1992.

Yester, Michael. *Using Turbo Pascal 6*, 2nd Edition. Que Corporation, Carmel, Indiana, 1991.

General Programming

Birrell, N.D. and M.A. Ould. *A Practical Handbook for Software Development*. Cambridge University Press, Cambridge, England, 1986.

Ledgard, Henry. *Software Engineering Concepts*. Addison-Wesley, Reading, Massachusetts, 1987.

Liffick, Blaise W. *The Software Developer's Handbook*. Addison-Wesley, Reading, Massachusetts, 1985.

Yourdon, Edward. *Techniques of Program Structure and Design*. Prentice Hall, Englewood Cliffs, New Jersey, 1975.

Index

1035

M

Q

X-Z